GUIDE TO THE GREAT SIBERIAN RAILWAY (1900)

Guide to the Great Siberian Railway (1900)

Edited By

A. I. DMITRIEV-MÁMONOV and A. F. ZDZIÁRSKI

Translated By

MISS L. KÚKOL-YASNOPÓLSKY

Revised By

JOHN MARSHALL

DAVID & CHARLES REPRINTS

ISBN 0 7153 5401 9

First published in 1900
This reprint published in 1971

Reproduced and Printed in Great Britain by
Redwood Press Limited, Trowbridge & London
for David & Charles (Publishers) Limited
Newton Abbot Devon

HIS IMPERIAL MAJESTY

NICHOLAS ALEXANDROVICH,

Autocrat of All the Russias.

MOST AUGUST PRESIDENT OF THE COMMITTEE OF THE SIBERIAN RAILWAY.

Print with the aut. of the Minist. of the Court Imperial. „Art. Printing Society“. St. Petersburg. Prosp. Engl., № 28.

GUIDE

TO

The Great Siberian Railway.

Published by the Ministry of Ways of Communcation,

EDITED BY

A. I. Dmítriev-Mámonov

and

A. F. Zdziárski, Railway Engineer.

English Translation by ***Miss L. Kúkol-Yasnopólsky,***

REVISED BY

John Marshall.

With 2 phototypes, 360 photo-gravures, 4 maps of Siberia and 3 plans of towns.

ST. PETERSBURG.

Typography of the Artistic Printing Society, English Prospect, 28.

1900.

Printed with the autority of the Ministry of Ways and Communication.

The Artistic

Printing-Society.

Typography, Litography,

PHOTOTYPY,

Printing of notes, Photo-lithography,

Chromo-phototypy.

St.-Petersbourg,

English Prospect, № 28.

Geographical and Historical Review of Siberia.

First acquaintance of Russians and foreigners with Siberia.—Superficial area and extension, administrative division.—Relief, orography and geological structure of the continent.—Mineral wealth.—Hydrography and climate.—Vegetation.—Fauna.—Gradual occupation by the Russians of the whole of Siberia.—Exploration by sea and land.—Colonisation and exile.—Population according to the census of 1897.—Siberian native tribes.—Results of the civilising policy of the Russian Government in the East.

THE first acquaintance with the northern inhabitants of the Asiatic continent was due to the enterprising citizens of Nóvgorod who, already in the XI century, were in commercial relations with them. All the tribes dwelling in the neighbourhood of the northern Urál and along the shores of the Arctic Ocean were known under the name of Yúgry. The geographical knowledge of foreigners as regards the lands lying beyond the Urál Range begins only with the XIII century, or with the time of the travels of Ascelin, Rubrukwiss, Plano Carpini and Marco Polo.

The work of the famous Venetian contains some precious particulars about the Pamír, Eastern Turkestán, Mongolia, China and even Japan, but Siberia remained unknown to him.

The towns of Bukhará and Samarkánd are marked on a map compiled in 1375, but the north of Asia is represented as a desert. Later on, the Dzhagatái, Altái and other mountains are to be found on the globe constructed by Fra Mauro in 1457, but the country, comprising the present territory of Siberia, was designated by him as a narrow strip of unknown land stretching between the Altái and the Arctic Ocean. More precise geographical notions relative to the Transurál countries were first given in 1544 by the Cosmography of Sebastian Münster published in Basle and, two years later, by the famous work of Baron Herberstein entitled: „Rerum Moskoviticarum commentarii". Münster's map contains the river Ob in the extreme East, the lands of the Vogúls, Kalmyks, Kirgíz-Kaisáks and the town of Sybír. The map of Herberstein, although somewhat more detailed than Münster's, still gives but a slight idea of the Transurál countries. For example, the Ob is supposed to flow from the extensive „lake of Cathay" (Kithay lacus); the Urál ridge bears the name of „the girdle of the earth" (Montes dicti cingulus terrae), the town Sybír is not shown at all; to the north, between the Urál and the Ob, a place is set apart for heathen temples (Aurea anus, Slata baba).

Among the oldest maps, there is one made for the Tsarévich Feódor Borísovich Godunóv, completed in 1624 by Gessel Gerard for the Tsar Mikhaíl Feódorovich, which includes Siberia comprising a region containing the towns of Tiumén and Tobólsk.

At the present time, Siberia is the collective name for all the Asiatic dominions of the Russian Empire, exclusive of Transcaucasia, Transcaspia and Turkestán; the Urál and Turgái steppe territories, stretching beyond the river Urál and far into the interior of Central Asia do not belong to Siberia, their administrative centres being situated in European Russia. There have been frequent discussions among philologists as to the meaning of the word „Siberia": some suppose that it is a local word of the Zyriáns and Ostiáks, but common to all the Urál races and adopted by the Nogáis. In connexion with some archaeological researches among the remains of prehistoric civilisation, students of the East of Asia suppose that the word Siberia may be identified with the name of the Huns or Savirs.

Plate 1. Monument to Yermák, the Conqueror of Siberia.

At present Siberia proper includes the following regions:

1) Western Siberia comprising the governments of Tobólsk and Tomsk in the basin of the Ob, subject to the general system of administration adopted in the governments of European Russia.

	sq. miles.	sq. versts.
Tobólsk gov	26,749.9	1,295,758.0
Tomsk gov . . . . , ...	15,572.5	749,819.3
Total	42,322.4	2,045,577.3

2) Eastern Siberia, comprising the governments of Yeniséisk and Irkútsk in the basin of the Yeniśéi, and the territory of Yakútsk in the basin of the Léna, Yána, Indigírka and Kolymá, under a governor-general resident at Irkútsk.

	sq. miles.	sq. versts.
Yeniséisk gov	46,699.8	2,259,562.3
Irkútsk gov	14,542.8	703,650.3
Yakútsk ter	71,358.3	3,452,655.3
	132,600.9	6,415,867.9

3) The north-western part of the Asiatic steppes, comprising two territories under the authority of the governor-general of the Steppe country.

	sq. miles.	sq. versts.
Akmolínsk ter.	9,903.0	479,200.2
Semipalátinsk ter.	8,856.7	428,527.8
	18,759.7	907,728.0

Pl. 2. Cone of Og-Dzhetnés on the shore of Lake Borovói, Kokchetávsk district. Akmolínsk terr. (phot. by Krékov).

4) The Amúr Littoral region comprising three territories and the Island of Sakhalín, united under the governor-general of the Amúr region, including the Russian part of the Amur basin and the Littoral belonging to the basin of the Pacific Ocean, together with the peninsula of Kamchátka and the Island of Sakhalín.

	sq. miles.	sq. versts.
Transbaikál	11,325.2	547,965.6
Amúr ter.	8,128.1	393,366.6
Littoral ter.	32,125.0	1,562,662.0
Sakhalín	1,379.0	66,762.0
	52,957.3	2,570,756.2

Thus, Siberia embraces an immense superficial area of 246,640.3 square geographical miles, within 45° and 77° of N. latitude and 60° and 190° E. longitude.

Bounded on the north by the Arctic, and on the east by the Pacific Ocean, Siberia extends towards the south to the Chinese Empire, and is bounded on the west by the Urál range.

Pl. 3. The Altái, Bom Ity-Kaïa on the river Chulyshmán (phot. by prof. Sapózhnikov).

In size, the area of Siberia represents the 1/13 part of the continental surface of the globe, and is about 1½ times as large as Europe, 2⅓ times as large as the surface of European Russia, and 25 times as large as Germany.

Covering so vast an area, Siberia must necessarily possess a very diversified relief and geological structure, and a most varied climate, flora and fauna.

Beyond the Urál, the traveller comes to the limitless plain of Western Siberia, having but a slight altitude above the level of the Arctic Ocean, extending over 1,500 versts to the east, and sloping from south to north. Its surface is occasionally broken by low ridges and hills with an altitude of scarcely 500 feet. The Kirgíz steppe gradually emerging on the southwest from this lowland, comes up to the Caspian and Arál Sea, which at a remote time formed one wide sea, whose bed including the three basins of the Balkásh, the Arál, and the Caspian, is known by the collective name of Aralo-Caspian depression.

The region of the Kirgız steppes is not absolutely level; their wide surface is sometimes broken by low, but very distinct ridges and dome-like hills of crystalline rock, mostly granite, diorite, diabase and other minerals including ores of copper, argentiferous lead and, at some points, auriferous gravels (pl. 2).

This treeless country with characteristic vegetation, salt marshes, brackish lakes and scanty steppe rivers, imperceptibly passing into the desert plains of Central Asia, reaches the plateau of Turán, and is only visited by

Pl. 4. Altái, the Yedygém torrent (phot. by prof. Sapózhnikov).

nomads. Extending towards the west, these steppe lands once served as an outlet for different tribes leaving Central Asia, during the great migrations of nations which, beginning with the movement of the Huns, continued till the great Mongolian invasion of the XIII century. At a remote date, centres of civilisation belonging to different Arian and Turanian races were created at the points where the steppes are traversed by the river basins of the Amú, Syr-Dariá and Ilí.

The character of the country, having a general inclination towards the Arctic Ocean, changes upon reaching the tributaries of the Ob-Irtysh basin, which represents one of the largest basins on the earth's surface, and can only be compared in respect of its volume to some of the Siberian watersystems, and to that of the Yellow and Blue Rivers, the Nile, the Mississippi and the Amazon.

The steppe, containing a great number of large and small lakes, presents a more varied flora and a more abundant tree vegetation. The Ishím, Barabá, and Kulundín steppes included in the middle zone of Siberia, although bearing the name of steppes, contain extensive areas of

Pl. 5. Altái, the Belúkha and the Katún glacier (phot. by prof. Sapózhnikov).

fertile and arable „chernoziom“ or black earth. This region comprises the most prosperous districts of the Tobólsk and Tomsk governments (Kurgán, Ishím, Yalutoróvsk, Tára, Tiukalínsk, Kaínsk, Barnaúl and Bíisk), which constitute the granary of Siberia.

The agricultural zone of Western Siberia covers a space of 8,600 sq. geogr. miles, and including throughout areas of forest land, is essentially fit for the development of agriculture by a settled population.

As stated by Brehm, the chernoziom or black earth is the real treasure

Pl. 6. The river Katún (phot. by Sazónov).

of Siberia, upon which depends the future prosperity of the country. The land stretching towards the north with an increased fall, becomes more swampy within the intricate system of the Ob and Irtysh tributaries, and in the Vasiugánsk steppe, bounded by these rivers, presents a low plain covered by dense forests of lofty trees.

This forest zone alternating with tracts of cultivable land, comprises the northern parts of the Turínsk, Tobólsk and Tára districts, the southern portion of the Surgút and Beriózov districts, within the Tobólsk government, and the extensive Narym country in the Tomsk government.

The forest zone or „taigá“ which divides Siberia into well marked sections has a total area of 17,000 sq. geogr. miles. The gloomy and thick firwoods offer more varied species of trees upon reaching the high land preceding the Kuznétsk Alatáu and the Altái. Extending towards the north, these continuous forests separate into scattered groves, with a thinner and diminishing vegetation, which gradually passes into dwarf bushes. This section characterised as „túndra“, with an almost perpetually frozen soil and a marshy surface, covered with moss and lichens, is entirely unfit for civilised settled colonisation.

This polar zone, lying beyond 64° of N. latitude and comprising an area of 7,000 sq. geogr. miles, includes parts of the Beriózov and Surgút districts of the Tobólsk government. The frozen subsoil of this region in summer thaws only to a depth of half an arshin, and consists of alternate layers of frozen earth, clay and ice, which serve as a basis to the túndra formations.

The West-Siberian lowland possesses an alluvial soil which contains no stones over its whole extent.

It is only the south-eastern part of Western Siberia that rises to a considerable altitude above the sea level, gradually passing into the grand Altái highland, bounded on the west by the extensive Sayán mountain range (pl. 3, 4, 7, 9, 10, 11).

This alpine plateau, embracing a superficial area of about 7,800 sq. geogr. miles, is ten times as large as Switzerland. Its surface is covered with numerous mountain ridges, divided by parallel, and at some points perpendicular valleys.

These hills run from east to west, their respective ranges representing a half opened fan. The Narym mountain ridge, which on the south is bounded by the valley of Bukhtarmá, pursues an almost parallel course, while the

Pl. 7. Altái, the Talmén lake (phot. by prof. Sapózhnikov).

Kuznétsк Alatáu, leaving the eastern border of the Altái highland, stretches to the north-west in a perpendicular line, and the Salaír range takes a diagonal direction between the two above mentioned mountain ridges. The high summits of the Altái bear the name of „belkí“, which means „alps“, reaching above the zone of eternal snow. The Katúnskie Stolby are the highest among them, the Belúkha, which is its most elevated and picturesque point, having an altitude of 11,500 f. (pl. 5).

Many other mountain ridges are perpetually snow-clad, some of their peaks exceeding the height of 9,000 feet.

The „belki" of the Altái are formed principally of crystalline rocks, containing granite, syenite, diorite and porphyry.

The sedimentary rocks raised by crystalline strata belong to the palaeozoic age, divided into the upper silurian, the devonian and the carboniferous systems. The jurassic formation occurs only on the northern slope of the Altái. Deposits of silver-lead and copper ores are found between crystalline and sedimentary rocks. The considerable glaciers of the Belúkha are the feeding-ground of the Katún (pl. 6) which together with the Bíya forms the river Ob. The picturesque and large Lake Telétsk which in its beauty is not inferior to the Lake of the Four Cantons (Vierwaldstätter), has an outflow through the Bíya.

Pl. 8. Altái, the Razsypnói cataract (phot. by prof. Sapózhnikov).

The shores of this alpine lake, situated at an elevation of 473 feet above the level of the sea, have a wild and imposing beauty.

The surface of the blue waters, framed in verdant and hilly shores, narrows gradually, pressing its gushing and silver-lined waves over reefs into the steep and rocky bed of the Bíya.

Both rivers meet at the foot of the Altái and, joining their waters, form the majestic Ob. The Anúi, Charysh, and Aléi which, upon the left, are the upper tributaries of the Ob, take their rise on the Altái plateau. The Chumysh, Tom, and Chulym, rising among the Kuznétsk Alatáu, fall into the Ob on the right. The upper branches of the Irtysh, flowing into the Zaisán lake, also take their rise on the northern slope of the Altái plateau within the confines of the Chinese Empire. After leaving the lake, the Irtysh receives from the right the Bukhturmá, Ubá and Ulbá, rising among the belkí of the Siberian Altái. The valleys of these rivers, the north-western slope of the Altái, the Salaír ridge and the Kuznétsk Alatáu are well provided with silver-lead and copper ores, with iron-ore, quarries of varied-coloured stones, and gold in veins and gravel.

The remains of the ancient Chud mines found at many places, and the name of the mountains „Altái", which means „gold mountains", are a testimony to the mineral wealth of the country, which already in prehistoric times was known to its inhabitants. The Altái mountains contain beautiful porphyries and jaspers of different colours, occurring particularly on the Korgón ridge, on the banks of the Charysh and Aléi, and in the environs of the Rídersk mines.

Rich beds of coal, included chiefly in the Kuznétsk coal-basin lying in the eastern part of the Altái mining district between the ridges of Salaír and Alatáu, represent the greatest treasure of the Altái.

The greater portion of the Altái plateau is almost uninhabitable on account of its elevated position and its rocky and stone-scattered soil; the well-watered plains, stretching at the foot of the mountains and interrup-

Pl. 9. Altái. The Great Akbóm on the Chúisk road (phot. by Sazónov).

ted by hills and valleys, are however well adapted for colonisation, agriculture, trade and industry.

The Tarbagatái mountain ridge stretches from the 47° parallel of N. latitude, south-west of the Altái group. It has an altitude of 10,000 feet at its highest point, and runs parallel to the gigantic Thian-Shan. The mountain ranges separate appreciably, forming a wide passage between the Siberian steppes and Central Asia, through which passed the prehistoric nations coming from the heights of Turán and Central Asia.

The relief of Eastern Siberia is of a quite different nature. From the borders of the Maríinsk and Achínsk districts, the country grows more hilly and is clad with forest. The Sayán mountain ridge leaving the chain of Tannu-olá runs in a solid mass through the Yeniséisk and the western part of the Irkútsk government, divided further into many branches which stretch far northwards beyond 60°, and give a mountainous character to the whole country.

After leaving the Sayán, the Yeniséi breaks through its chain and flows among mountains and passes, winding its way among fine cliffs. The highest ridge of the Sayán, stretching from the southern part of the Irkútsk government to the Chinese border, culminates there in the Munkú-Sardyk, rising to an

Pl. 10. Altái, Valley of the Upper Ilgumén (phot. by Sazónov).

altitude of 11,430 feet above the level of the sea. The Tunkínsk mountain range, which is the most important among the foremost ridges, runs somewhat north of the Sayán in a parallel line to this group, and lies nearest to Irkútsk.

The Baikál mountains, which continue the range of the Sayán in a north-eastern direction, have an elevation of about 6,000 feet above the level of the sea, and skirt lake Baikál which, lying at a height of 1,561 feet above the level of the sea, is one of the largest lakes in the world, covering an area of 30,034 sq. versts. It receives the waters of the Upper Angará, the Bargusín and the Selengá, and is the source of the mighty branch of the Yeniséi, the Angará, which pushing aside the barrier of mountains, rushes past cliffs to the north, meeting frequent impediments in its course.

The Stanovói or Yáblonovy mountain ridge stretching up to Kamchátka, north-east from the Baikál, for a distance of above 3,000 versts, forms the watershed of the rivers flowing along its north-western side to the Arctic

Ocean, and of those which along its south-eastern slope drain into the Pacific Ocean.

This mountain chain is not particularly high, rising at some points barely to 2,500 feet above the level of the sea, while its most elevated peaks or „goltsy" are only about 7,000 feet in height.

Besides the Olékma and the Aldán which are both tributaries of the Léna, these mountains give rise to the affluents of the Yána, the Indigírka and Kolymá. The waters of the gigantic Léna take their source among the Baikál mountains. Crystalline rocks containing granite, syenite, diabase, diorite, porphyry and crystalline slate, form the principal ridges of the Sayán and its branches, and also those of the Yáblonovy chain. Basalt, dolerite, and real lavas coming from extinct volcanoes with volcanic tuffs, obsidian and pumice of volcanic origin, occur on the eastern side of the Sayán, as well as on the low ridges running across the East-Siberian plain between the Angará and the Podkámennaya Tungúzka. Some of these volcanic formations are also detected in the Yakútsk territory, on the Aldán mountain ridge. On the side of the Sayán mountains and along the branches and slopes of the Yáblonovy chain, as well as on many other mountains in the territory of Yakútsk, the sedimentary rocks are chiefly represented by sandstone, slate and lime-

Pl. 11. Bom on the river Ursúl (phot. by Sapózhnikov).

stone of the palaeozoic age consisting of the upper silurian, the silurian and the carboniferous systems. The jurassic formations, which sometimes are found on the southern Sayán, occur more frequently ou the north. All the mountain ridges running in every direction over the vast East-Siberian territory contain great mineral wealth.

Silver-lead and copper ores are met with on the northern slope of the Sayán, within the confines of the Yeniséisk government, while, at the same time, rich beds of coal and iron-ore, of excellent quality, lie at the foot of the mountains. The branches of the Sayán include also rich graphite deposits.

The Yáblonovy chain is particularly well provided in the Yakútsk territory with silver-lead, iron and coal deposits. But the essential resource of Eastern Siberia consists in its gold deposits, scattered all over the range of

Pl. 12. Four-barrel gold-washing apparatus.

mountains and at many elevated places. The basins of the rivers Vitím and Olékma, and some of the other tributaries of the Léna, most particularly abound in gold (pl. 12).

The greater portion of the East Siberian territory, containing numerous mountain ridges and elevated plateaus, has a considerable altitude, especially as compared with the steppe land of West Siberia. A well marked fall towards the sea is noticed at the 60° N. lat., on the north of the Yeniséisk government, and at 68° N. lat., in the Yakútsk territory, where the country passes into the plain through which the Yeniséi and Léna roll their majestic waves.

Eastern Siberia is just as abundantly watered as its western part. The Yeniséi (pl. 13) which is not inferior to the Ob and, like the latter, is formed by the junction of two streams, the Yeniséi proper and the Angará, flows towards the north through the Yeniséisk and Irkútsk governments. The basin of the Léna also formed by two branches, the Léna and the Aldán, waters the vast Yakútsk territory and pours its waves into the Arctic Ocean by means of a delta of islands extending far into the sea (pl. 14).

Stretching from the Chinese boundary, from south to north, East and West Siberia comprise many regions of varied nature and climate.

The cultivable zone of Eastern Siberia covering a superficial area of 10,000 sq. geogr. miles, includes the Minusínsk, Achínsk, Krasnoyársk and Kansk districts of the Yeniséi government, and the entire Irkútsk government, exclusive of the Kirénsk district.

The southern valley of the Yeniséi has a most convenient position, and has long since been in great favour with the peaceful labourer and the half wild nomad.

Monuments dating from ancient times are scattered throughout the south of the Yeniséi government. Ruins of old buildings, earthen bulwarks, remains of towns, stones covered with inscriptions, rocks with designs and

Pl. 13. Ice-drift on the Yeniséi (phot. by Akselrod).

writing, abandoned pits and mines testify to former inhabitants and to a former independent culture (pl. 17).

Pl. 14. The river Léna (phot. by Gavrílov).

The forest zone, where forestry and agriculture are alternately practised, extends to the north, and comprises an immense area of about 65,000 sq. geogr. miles covered with forests and swamps which only on the south, at a few points near the rivers, give place to oases of land more adapted for cultivation.

Pl. 15. The Léna near the town of Yakútsk.

The Kirénsk district of the Irkútsk government, part of the Yeniséisk government reaching the 66° N., and the greater portion of the Yakútsk, Olékminsk and the southern part of the Vilúisk district, are included in this zone.

Pl. 16. Post-boat on the Léna (phot. by Arnold).

The forest vegetation of Eastern Siberia is practically similar to that found in its western part, represented by the same gloomy „taigá“ and inaccessible „urmán“ with its poor covering of thin grass passing into moss and lichens.

The polar tundra zone embracing all the northern part of Eastern Siberia, comprises an area of 56,000 sq. geogr. miles and includes one of the poles of greatest cold in the northern hemisphere. Near Verkhoyánsk, under 67° 34′ of N. latitude, which has the most continental climate of the old world, the mean annual temperature is—17° C., the mean winter temperature is—47°. At Ustiánsk, 70° 53′ of N. latitude, three and a half degrees nearer north, the average annual temperature (—16° C.) is a degree higher than at Verkhoyánsk; in the winter (—37° C.) there is a difference of ten degrees between the mean temperature of these two points. The climate, the conditions of the soil, which remains perpetually frozen and melts only under the hottest sun's rays to a depth of 3/4 arshin, and the short period of vegetation, exclude the possibility of agriculture in

Pl. 17. Tombstones in the Minusinsk steppes.

Pl. 18. On the Baikál, village of Kultúk.

this region. This vast polar zone is only exploited by the northern reindeer tribes and by native and foreign hunters and fishermen.

After having crossed the stormy Baikál (pl. 18), to its eastern shore, the traveller reaches the wide spreading Amúr-Littoral province which, forming the eastern limit of the Siberian continent, is divided by its physical conditions into four well marked regions: Transbaikália, Amúr, Ussúri-Littoral and Okhótsk-Kamchátka, united for purposes of internal administration under one governor-general of the Amúr province.

Pl. 19. The Transbaikál, mouth of the river Nerchá.

Transbaikália characterised by the Transbaikál and Daurian plateaus, is a mountainous country, with the exception of the steppe lands comprising its south-eastern part, and coming up to the Chinese frontier, between the rivers Argún and Onón which by their joint course form the Amúr.

Pl. 20. Landing place for steamers near Strétensk.

The Yáblonovy chain, which in a diagonal line presses to the eastern part of the plateau, runs from south-west to north-east, and represents the central axis of the mountains.

The Baikál mountain group, with its dominant ridge Khamár-Dabán, stretches to the west, while the Nerchínsk chain extends to the east. The dominant axis of the Yáblonovy mountains forms the watershed of the rivers flowing from its north-western side into the Baikál, and into the Vitím the right tributary of the Léna, and of those which, from its south-eastern slope, fall into the Shílka river included in the Amúr basin.

Among the mountains of the Transbaikál, the Chokóndo without reaching the snow-line, rises to an altitude of 8,000 feet above the level of the sea. All the others are of an inferior height, some of their summits attaining barely 3,400 feet. Here the Great Siberian railway reaches its most elevated point crossing the Yáblonovy chain at an altitude of 3,416 feet above the sea level.

Almost all the mountain ridges of this plateau contain granite, gneiss and mica-slate obtruding through crystalline strata and, at some places, trachyte and basalt of volcanic origin. The sedimentary rocks lifted up by the crystalline strata include chiefly silurian and carboniferous formations of

Pl. 21. Mole on the Amúr at Blagovéshchensk.

the palaeozoic age, as well as formations of the secondary (jurassic) and tertiary systems.

This great variety of geological structure testifies to the untold wealth of the Transbaikál region, which abounds in gold ores and auriferous gravels, in silver-lead, copper and iron ores, in tin and mercury, and includes quarries of varied—coloured stones of fine quality, and extensive coal measures.

The extraordinary geological structure of this country, in connexion with a well regulated irrigation, and a fairly favourable climate, promises a prosperous future to this region, and opens a wide range to the development of mining industry. The line of the Great Siberian Railway, connected by the basin of the Amúr with the section of the Ussúri Railway, traverses the south-eastern part of Siberia, and is now interrupted within the confines of the Transbaikál, near Strétensk (pl. 20) situated on the left bank of the Shílka. The route resumes its course at Strétensk and reaches the eastern border of the Transbaikál region where the waters of the Shílka and Argún are collected into the Amúr basin, proceeding along the Shílka to the Cossack village of Ust-Strélochny.

The Amúr country commencing at the same place as the Amúr basin has quite different physical conditions from the adjacent Transbaikál and the other regions comprising the Siberian continent. Its relief is represented by an elevated plain inclining from the west to the Pacific Ocean, bounded on the north, by the Yáblonovy chain, and on the south and south-west, by the Khingán stretching far over Chinese territory. The average height of the mountains which surround and cover the country with their branches, varies

Pl. 22. The river Amúr. Monument to Count N. N. Muraviòv-Amúrsky in Khabárovsk.

from 3,000 to 7,000 feet above the level of the sea, and at some points rises only to about 2,000 feet.

The geological structure of these ridges, which are in close connexion

Pl. 23. Landing place at Nikoláevsk.

with the mountain masses of the Transbaikál, is chiefly characterised by the same crystalline and sedimentary rocks including rich and varied minerals.

Gold mines, with an ever increasing output, are worked in this region, where coal-beds, silver-lead and silver ores, as well as copper and iron ores occur plentifully.

The Amúr territory, which in the places bordered by the principal ridges is mountainous, has in respect of its geological formation some connexion with the Transbaikál and the northern portions of Siberia included within the range of the Yàblonovy mountains. It contains a series of flat elevations which gradually decline into pasture steppes, stretching far over the valleys of the Amúr and its tributaries the Zéya and Buréya, covered by a rich vegetation recalling the prairies of North America.

The peculiar nature of this region characterised by a rich vegetation and a varied fauna, is due to its orographic and climatic conditions.

Pl. 24. The Ussùri province, Suifùn pass (phot. by Matskévich).

The waters of the Amúr rise more than 49 feet above their ordinary level at the time when, twice a year, the river overflows an immense extent of country. Although causing considerable damage, it for a long time furnishes the neighbouring land with moisture. Frequent and heavy rainfalls, caused by the quantity of moisture brought from the Pacific Ocean by the south-western winds, also exert a decided influence upon the structure of the surface and its vegetation.

The land that stretches at the foot of the mountains and along their branches is covered with thick grass. The slopes of the mountains are clothed by dense forests of various species; by retaining the moisture, they transform the entire surface into a continuous swamp out of which rise bare hills scattered with stones.

Although this region occupies a southerly position, yet the Russian colonist has to cope with superabundant moisture and a severe climate, fighting for each foot of cultivable land; this hard contest with nature is the cause of the unsufficient population of the Amúr country up to the present time.

The imposing river Amúr which, from west to east, traverses the entire Amúr country and serves throughout its whole course as a navigable waterway, is the frontier between the Russian Empire and China, constituting at the same time the most important river system of Siberia, yeilding the most convenient access to the coast of the Pacific Ocean.

After having reached the eastern limit of the Amúr territory, the travel ler comes to the town of Khabárovsk, the administrative centre of the country, standing on the right bank of the Amúr at its junction with the full-flowing Ussúri, and enters the Amúr territory comprising, from south to north, the Russian coast of the Pacific Ocean, stretching for a distance of 28 degrees, within the 42° and 70° of N. lat.

The Amúr river divides this region into two portions, north and south, which shew a well marked difference in respect of climate, soil and conditions of life: the Okhótsk-Kamchátka territory, situated on the left side of the Amur and bounded by the Yáblonovy Chain, the Arctic Ocean and the Okhótsk and Bering Seas; and the Ussúri-Littoral territory, situated on the right side of the Amúr, and bounded by the Ussúri and the Sea of Japan.

The Okhótsk-Kamchátka territory which includes the narrow and hilly coast of the Okhótsk Sea, the land of the Chukch and the peninsula of Kamchátka, is scarcely fit for a settled agricultural colonisation, on account of its geographical position, and severe climate; and can only be effectively exploited after a hard struggle with nature. According to explorations effected on the south-western coast of the Okhótsk Sea, there are mineral deposits obtruding through crystalline and sedimentary rocks.

Pl. 25. Railway pass over the Niurtsé ridge (phot. by Matskévich).

The northern portions, in particular the peninsula of Kamchátka, have up till now only been subjected to scientific explorations directed to the investigation of the action of volcanoes.

The Middle Kamchátka Chain running up through the peninsula, and all parallel ridges, contain a series of active and extinct volcanoes, among which the Kliuchevskáya Sópka still active, rises higher than Mont Blanc, and is not inferior in size to Kazbék with its altitude of 16,000 feet above the sea level This peninsula includes a total of 12 active and 30 extinct volcanoes.

All the islands of the Siberian seabord offer but a slight commercial interest, on account of the inadequate exploitation of their resources. Wrangel's land is quite ignored and only visited by whale-fishers, as also the group of the New Siberian Islands which, having once afforded shelter to a now extinct organic life thriving at a remote date under the 75° and 76° N. lat., is now resorted to only by Siberian traders in search of the mammoth ivory abounding there.

Better known are the Commander Islands and Sakhalín. The former lie in the Bering sea, near Kamchátka, and are somewhat high, partly consisting of volcanic rocks. Seals are caught on their shores. The latter possesses a penal settlement.

On these islands the climate is very severe, and they are scarcely adapted for permanent colonisation, although endowed with rich coal mines already partly developed; these and the naphtha springs, which have been discovered of late on Sakhalín, will give some commercial importance to this inhospitable island.

The Ussúri Littoral territory (pl. 25), although lying near the ocean, presents a more elevated relief than the Amúr region, and affords geographical and climatic conditions, which are more favourable to the development of cultivation.

The climate is modified by the forest clothed Sikhoté-Alín Chain stretching parallel to the coast of the Japan Sea, which retains the excess of moisture in the narrow strip of land bounded by the sea. This mountain ridge which, at its highest point, is 3,600 feet in height, descends westwards, with a gradual fall to the interior, and gives the Ussúri region a mountainous character with here and there rich mineral deposits among crystalline and sedimentary rocks. Gold mines are worked at many points, chiefly in the south, and on Askóld Island near Vladivostók, where the bottom of the sea consists of gold-bearing strata producing auriferous sands.

Silver-lead mines which evidently were worked in former times, have been discovered in the vicinity of St. Olga and Transfiguration Bays; rich deposits of iron-ore occur in the same littoral regions, and coal of excellent quality is also to be found in thick seams in many parts of this rich country.

Among all the regions of Siberia, the Ussúri-Littoral territory is particularly well adapted for cultivation and colonisation; abundantly watered by the Ussúri and with a favourable climate, it possesses a fertile black-earth soil, a rich vegetation and a varied fauna which, together with abundant mineral deposits and its nearness to the ocean, opens a wide prospect for the development of trade and industry.

Leaving the town of Khabárovsk, the traveller reaches Vladivostók by the Ussúri railway, and comes to the coast of the Pacific Ocean, finding there the wide gulf of Peter the Great with its bay of the Golden Horn. This inlet situated on the north-western coast of the Japan Sea is accessible during all seasons with the exception of winter, which however, as in Odessa, does not last over two months (pl. 26).

The climate of Siberia is, on account of its vast area, very varied, but in general it is very severe, especially as compared with that of the corresponding latitudes of Europe and America; from its more continental character it has an inferior mean annual temperature.

This peculiar climate is due to the structure of the surface, which is left unprotected from the keen northern winds blowing on the coast of Siberia, bounded by the Arctic Ocean. Being separated from Central Asia by a barrier of snow-clad mountains, this region is entirely shut off by them from the mild influence of the south (pl. 27).

The highest mean annual temperature on the Siberian continent occurs at Vladivostók and in the bay of St. Olga (+4.5° C). as also in the southern

Pl. 26. View of Vladivostók.

portion of the Kirgíz steppe including Akmolínsk and Semipalátinsk (from +2 to 2.5°). As a rule, the mean annual temperature throughout Siberia does not rise above zero, exclusive of the following places in West and East Siberia, where the mean temperature is somewhat higher: Turínsk, +1.5°, Tiumén +1.4°, Kurgán +1.2°, Barnaúl +0.14°, Krasnoyársk +1.0°, Minusínsk +0.7°, and Khabárovsk +0.6°. According to the mean annual temperatures and to the average temperature in the winter months, the greatest cold is experienced on the north-east of the Asiatic continent; at the same time, it has been noticed that the mean annual temperature rises from north to south, and falls from west to east. As an example Tobólsk and Tomsk lying much further north than Nikoláevsk on the Amúr, and the Nerchínsk works, situated eastwards of both, have annual temperatures of —0.12° and—0.79°, while the latter have —2.7° and —3.7°. This difference increasing towards the east, is still more evident when the temperature of Vladivostók is compared with that of Vladikavkáz standing under the same latitude, or with that of Florence and Nice which are only three-quarters of a degree further north.

January is the coldest month in Siberia, June and July are the hottest; soon after the latter the temperature becomes colder.

The transitions from winter to summer are extreme, almost excluding spring, the most welcome season of the year. The differences of greatest cold and heat in Siberia, as shewn by the following figures, are of a wider range han anywhere in Europe:

	January.	July.	Difference of temperature in the hottest & coldest months.
Verkhoyánsk	— 48.9	+ 15.4	63.3
Yakútsk	41.8	17.3	59.1
Nerchínsk works	29.4	18.4	47.8
Blagovéshchensk	25.5	20.7	46.2

In general, the temperature in the cultivable zone of Siberia, which in Western Siberia is +13·5°, in the Eastern part +14°, in the Transbaikàl +13.5°, in the Amúr Territory, +12° in its northern part and +16° on the south,

Pl. 27. Winter road in the northern taigá.

+15° and +17° in the Ussúri-Littoral Territory, is almost the same as that of the corresponding latitudes of European Russia, during the five months period of vegetation, from May to October.

Accordingly, the cultivable zone of Siberia is better adapted for agriculture than the regions of European Russia situated between the same 55° and 58° N. lat., being provided with a better soil of blackearth, with more fertile and extensive pastures, with abundant rivers, and a sufficient quantity of forest land.

Pl. 28. Harnessed reindeer.

The population of Siberia is not excessively affected by the sharp winters, owing to the prevailing stillness of the air, the absence of strong winds, and to a generally clear and cloudless sky which, taken together, temper the effect of the extreme cold.

As stated by Réclus, there are few places which can boast of a healthier climate than cold Eastern Siberia, characterised as it is by an exceedingly calm, dry and clear atmosphere. Cases of consumption are unknown in Chitá, situated in the heart of the Transbaikál, where mercury freezes in the thermometer and remains thus during several weeks. These favourable conditions vanish towards the north, as appears from the difference in the flora and fauna; however, the traveller can testify that the aborigenes of the

Pl. 29. Horse of the Yakút breed (phot. by Gavrílov).

Yakútsk Territory notwithstanding the frightful cold, enjoy perfect health and are endowed with a good humour and lively character which many might envy.

The amount of the annual rainfall in particular is evidence of the more continental climate of Siberia as compared with the corresponding regions of European Russia; this difference is still more striking as regards the cultivable zone.

The rainfall in Western Siberia amounts to 380, in Eastern Siberia to 360 mm. and in the Transbaikál to 290 mm.: in the corresponding countries of European Russia, the rainfall rises to 500 millimetres. These figures are exceeded in the Altái plateau, in the Amúr territory and in that of the Ussúri-Littoral, where they reach 500 and 600 mm.

Pl. 30. „Skopéts" or „castrated" ploughman of the Viliúisk distr. in the Yakút terr. (phot. by Gavrílov).

The distribution of the rainfall according to the season is also characteristic in Siberia. In the period of vegetation and especially in summer, there is but a slight difference in this respect between Siberia and European Russia; in winter this difference increases considerably, the amount of moisture falling in Siberia being little more than half that of the corresponding European zones.

This distribution accounts for the sufficient quantity of moisture received during the period of vegetation, and the snowless winters prevailing over the entire agricultural area of Siberia.

Pl. 31. Calf bred by Skoptsy. Viliúisk distr. Yakút terr. (phot. by Gavrílov).

The forest zone is characterised by a far more abundant rainfall, and in this respect stands almost on a line with the corresponding European countries. A considerable decrease in the rainfall is to be noted further north, nearer to the polar tundra, so for example at Obdórsk with only 218 mm.

The climate of this country is more strikingly illustrated by the vegetation. The herbaceous flora covering the whole of Western Siberia but slightly differs from that of the corresponding European zones.

After crossing the Urál, the traveller traverses Siberia by a railway of 2,000 versts and reaches the Yeniséi without noticing any difference in the herbaceous flora, which throughout retains the same character except for a greater succulence and freshness, and more gaily coloured flowers than in European Russia.

Pl. 32. Skopéts farm. Viliúisk district (phot. by Gavrílov).

Beyond the Yeniséi, the vegetation changes, not only under the influence of the climate, but also on account of the hilly surface intersected by the spurs of the Sayán mountains. A mountain flora characteristic of the Altái-Sayán system now predominates, presenting the typical pecularities of alpine and subalpine pastures and hill-sides, with luxuriant and brilliantly coloured flowers.

Beautiful anemones (Anemone umbrosa, fischeriana, pulsatilla), peculiar varieties of buttercups (Ranunculus altaicus, R. pulchellus, R. natans and others), Altái species of cruciferae, various kinds of violets (Viola altaica, V. macrocarpa, V. acuminata and others), peculiar species of pinks and starworts (Dianthaceae and Alsineae), the Altái flax (Linum violaceum), many species of astragalus, alpine roses, peculiar saxifrages, among which „chagír tea“ (Saxifrage crassifolia), whose big leaves are employed as a surrogate for ordinary tea, represent the characteristic flora of the Altái and Sayán mountains.

The chief ornament of these mountains are its spring flowers, yellow and blue hyacinths, irises and other bulbs.

The arboreal vegetation of the Siberian continent is very poor. Oak, hazel, elm, every species of maple, ash and apple disappear altogether just beyond the Ural, which is thickly clothed with a varied and rich forest growth. The forests of the Siberian plains, subject to periodical extinction, are very monotonous and contain but few species, represented by birch (Betula alba), aspen (Populus tremula), alder (Alnus glutinosa, incana), poplar (Populus alba), common hagberry (Prunus padus), and mountain ash (Sorbus aucuparia tomentosa).

Pl. 33. Church in a leper colony. Yakútsk terr. (phot. by Gavrílov).

The desert and gloomy „taigás“ or „urmáns“ consist mainly of species of fir-trees which usually characterise the north-eastern portions of European Russia, with the exception of the „cedar“ (Pinus cembra) which occurs throughout Siberia to the Bering sea, and passes over into North America.

The lofty tree flora of the Altái, although divided into many zones on the elevated mountain chains, does not differ, as far as the Yáblonovy range, from that of Western and Eastern Siberia; among the shrubs there are some varieties of acacias, wild roses, honeysuckles, and burning-bushes; dwarf rhododendrons and azaleas are only found on the southern slopes. The flora visibly changes on the eastern slope of the Yáblonovy mountain chain. Within the confines of the Transbaikál, the tree flora is much more varied, receiving an admixture of oak (Quercus mongolica), elm (Ulmus campestris), nut (Corylus heterophylla), and wild apple (Pyrus baccata). The shrubs present more characteristic forms and the herbaceous vegetation is of a quite peculiar nature, forming the transition between the floras of Siberia and Mongolia, viz. the so-called Daurian flora.

Pl. 34. Drove of horses in the steppe.

The flora of the Amúr territory and the Ussúri-Littoral region is still richer and more peculiar. Within these regions the species of trees are quite different from those of Siberia, and even the Transbaikál.

The Manchurian cedar (Pinus mandshurica), the ajanen fir (Picea ajanensis), the yew, native to the Caucasian mountains, mingle here with the

Pt. 35. Kirgíz removing their camp. (phot. by von Kinits).

ordinary Siberian fir-trees. Foliage trees and shrubs are particularly well represented.

The lime tree assumes two different shapes: Tilia cordata and Tilia mandshurica, while the maple, unknown in western Siberia, has here four repre-

Pl. 36. Kirgiz girls on horseback. (phot. by von Kinits).

sentatives. The apple-tree, which in the Transbaikál bears very small fruits, develops here into new and beautiful specimens of Pyrus ussuriensis. Two different forms of walnut (Juglans mandshurica and J. stenocarpa) are the chief ornaments of the Amúr forests. Shrubs of still more peculiar forms are represented by 24 kinds which are quite new to Siberia and the Transbaikál.

The herbaceous flora includes about 110 species only found in the Amúr country, others occur as well in the Transbaikál, China, Japan, Kamchátka, and even America.

The fauna like the flora is distributed throughout Siberia in accordance with climate and surface.

The West-Siberian plain, together with the Kirgíz Steppe border-land and Eastern Siberia provided with rich pastures and leafy groves, giving a wide scope to the breeding of live-stock, support a greater number of cattle than the countries of America corresponding to this portion of the Asiatic mainland.

Pl. 37. Kirgíz cart.

Siberia can also rival America with respect to the quantity of fur animals finding shelter in the thick undergrowth of the taigá and urmán of the forest zone. The animal life is but poorly represented in the polar tundra, which is scarcely at all exploited by man.

Among the mammals, the white bear (Ursus maritimus) is the most northern inhabitant of Siberia; then comes the arctic fox (Canis lagopus), and the small striped „Ob leming" (Myodes torquatus, M. obensis). The polar hare (Lepus variabilis) and the reindeer (Cervus tarandus), both characteristic of the tundra, are to be found on the hilly uplands of Siberia (pl. 27—28).

Pl. 38. Flock of sheep in the steppe.

All the other mammals of the Siberian plain are almost the same as in the northern and central regions of European Russia.

The alpine wolf (Canis alpinus), two kinds of large cats (Felis irbis, F. manul), a kind of deer. the „marál" (Cervus elaphus), pl. 39, the mountain ram (Aegoceras montanus), the „arkhár" (Ovis Argali), the musk-deer (Moschus moschiferus), are the mammals most characterislic of the Altái - Sayán plateau.

The vertebrate animals are abundantly represented in Siberia by birds and fishes.

Siberia is particularly well provided with aquatic birds, gathered in immense troops on the coast of the Arctic Ocean, and along lake and river banks. In spring the river-floods coincide in time with the migration of the birds, and offer a beautiful sight, with their wide expanses of shining water, thickly dotted with birds of every hue moving rapidly in all directions.

The number of birds which find a shelter in some of the river systems is so great that, for example on the Baikál, the surrounding cliffs and rocks disappear under a thick layer of guano, which will long suffice as a source of manure.

All the immense river basins of Western and Eastern Siberia draining in one direction to the Arctic Ocean, as well as the abundant and extensive lakes, offer a great scope for the development of animal life.

These waters contain most varied kinds of fine and coarse fish represented by perch, pike, lote, sturgeon and sterlet. The Siberian rivers abound in particular in different species of gwiniad including nélma (Salmo nelma or Corregonus leucichthys) „ómul" a kind of salmon (Salmo or Corregonus omul), muksún (Salmo or corregonus muksun) and others.

The fauna of the Amur Littoral region changes essentially on the eastern side of the Yáblonovy chain, towards the Amur basin. Besides all the species prevailing in the cultivated and forest zone of Siberia, here are to be found species common to the Altái-Sayán mountains, and to the Mongòlian and Manchùrian steppes. Specially characteristic are: the musk-deer (Moschus

Pl. 39. Marál stud in the Altái (phot. by prof. Sapózhnikov).

moschiferus, the roe-buck (Cervus capreolus), the rat-hare (Lagomys alpinus), the korsák (Canis korsac), the steppe cat (Felis manul), the tiger (Felis tigris), the irbis (Felis irbis), two kinds of antilopes (Antilope gutturosa, A. crispa), the kulán (Equus hemionus), the Amúr raccoon (Canis procyonoides), the marál (Cervus elaphus), the boar (Sus scrofa), the mountain wolf (Canis alpinus), the Tibet bear (Ursus tibetanus) and others.

The bird fauna comprises northern and southern species, the latter being represented by prairie chickens (Syrrhaptes paradoxus), black cranes (Grus monachus), blue mag-pies (Pica cyana) and others. A peculiarly rich and varied bird fauna is to be found on the last southern bends of the Amúr, breaking the mountain chain of the Little Khingán, and also at the junction of the Ussúri and Sungarí basins with the Amúr.

The ichthyological fauna of the Amúr and its tributaries is particularly noteworthy; there is the „kalúga" among the sturgeon family, which sometimes weighs about 50 puds, and the sturgeon itself 10 puds. The predominating salmonoid species are an article of commerce, and are employed for food by the inhabitants of the lower reaches of the Amúr. Remarkable among them are the Salmo proteus or „gorbúsha", so called from the hump appearing during the spawing season, and the „ketá" (Salmo lagocephalus).

Further typical forms are the Amúr fish (Pristidion Semenovii) the Daurian silurus (Silurus asotus), a roach (Plagiognathus Selskii) the „white fish" (Culter abramoides) and a peculiar kind of pike attaining a huge size (Esox Reicherti).

The fauna of the Arctic Ocean, although unsufficiently investigated, is known to be very rich, but not being easily accessible yields scarcely any profit. The Okhótsk and Bering Seas afford better conditions, but are also very insufficiently explored; hardly anything is known regarding their ichthyological fauna, although some species, as the „ketá" (Salmo lagocephalus) and the „malmá" (S. callaris) occur here most plentifully. Every year, an enormous quantity of herring, cod and gwiniad appear in shoals on the coasts of the Bering Sea. These waters give shelter to the following large mammals: seals (Phoca barbata groenlandica, leporina and others) dolphins (Phocaena orca, Delphinus leucas), whales (Balaenoptera longimana); the Bering sea contains sea-lions (Eumetopias Stelleri), occurring very rarely, the Kamchátka or sea beaver (Enhydris lutris), which is very like a walrus; the sea-bear (Otaria ursina) is abundantly represented on the islands of the Bering Sea, where from 10,000 to 50,000 of them are taken annually.

The annexation of Siberia to Russia was gradually effected within the space of three centuries, commencing from the XVI century; it was achieved without any particular bloodshed, chiefly by means of „Free Cossack" colonisation, which afterwards was utilised and regulated by the Government.

The Free Cossacks who gave the lead to the Russian emigration movement towards the lower reaches of the Don and Dnepr, very soon took possession of the Transurál countries, thus becoming the pioneers and founders of Russian colonisation in Asia. The vast empire of Chingiz-Khan, which fell to pieces in the XV century, was divided into the following kingdoms: Kazán, Astrakhán, Siberia, Khíva, Bukhará, and into the separate Nogái and Kirgíz-Kaisák hordes.

The Kazán and Astrakhán kingdoms, included in the Vólga basin, were of no long duration; in the XVI century, they were already conquered by the ever-growing state of Moscow, thus leaving an open road to the mineral wealth of thə Urál and the fur animals of the Transurál forests.

The fall of these two mighty Tatar kingdoms and the constant dissensions in the Chingiz empire of Central Asia obliged the Siberian Tatar prince Yedigér to declare himself vassal of the Tsar Iván IV; however the Khan Kuchúm, who succeeded Yedigér, soon put an end to this peaceful submission to the Muscovite power and began hostile operations against his western neighbours.

The Muscovite government, being at the time engrossed in a war with Livonia, entrusted the defence of its Urál dominions to the Stróganovs, who became promoters of Russian trade and industry in the North-East, and to the Free Cossack bands of Yermák. In the year 1580, Yermák reached the banks of the Turá and, having defeated the Tatar prince Yepanchá, took by assault the Ostiák Tatar town of Chingí-Turá, which was situated on the spot where the town of Tiumén now stands.

According to a popular belief, which has a curious likeness to the legend connected with the conquest of Mexico by Cortez, two animals emerging from the Irtysh and the Toból were seen to fight on a sandy island in the Irtysh opposite its junction with the Toból. One was said to be white and shaggy and like a wolf, the other small, black and resembling a hound. The smaller animal killed the bigger one and disappeared under the water, but the latter rose in a few minutes, and also sought refuge in the river. Wizzards and soothsayers gave the following explanation of the portent to Kuchúm saddened by his reverses: his kingdom, represented by the big animal, was to be conquered by a Russian warrior, represented by the smaller one.

Pl. 40. Cape Chuvásh near Tobólsk (phot. by Usakóvsky).

Pushing on further, Yermák reached the Toból on the 23-rd October 1581, and completely defeated the hordes of Kuchúm near the Chuvásh Hill (pl. 40), and thus secured the Russian dominion beyond the Urál. He entered Iskér or Sibír, the capital of the Siberian kingdom, and hoisted there the Russian flag on the 26-th of October, the day of St. Demetrius of Solun (pl. 41). As Kazán was the key to the possession of the Vólga-Káma region, so was Iskér to that of Siberia. After its conquest, the entire country became open for Russian colonisation, Yermák's exploit determining the virtual annexation of Siberia to Russia. Yermák informed the Stróganovs of his success and despatched to Moscow the ataman Koltsó, his faithful companion, with a quantity of rich Siberian sables and a petition to the Tsar Iván Vasílievich to accept the new kingdom of Siberia.

The ambassadors were graciously received by the Tsar who duly rewarded them, and sent Yermák a pelisse he had worn himself (a special distinction), a gilded silver cup, two cuirasses and a hundred rubles. Yermák however did not long rule over Siberia; in 1584, lured by the wary Tatars, he met his death on the 6-th August in the waters of the Irtysh. „Thus perished“, writes an historian, „the Russian Cortez and Pizarro, this brave and wise ataman, who from being a bold robber, thanks to circumstances and his great gifts, became a hero, whose name will never be forgotten by the Russian people“. After having annexed Siberia to its dominions, the Muscovite government took good care to tighten the bond, between the old and new country, by sending at different times voyevodas or captains with Cossack, and Streléts troops for the establishment of administrative centres with a view to future colonisation. Tiumén, Tobólsk, Verkhotúrie, Pelym, Beriózov, Surgút, Obdórsk, Narym, and Tára were selected already in the XVI century as such centres for the Transurál.

The first attempts at colonisation made by the State, the establishment of the exile system, dates from the end of the same century. Thirty families of husbandmen from Solvychegódsk were sent as first settlers to Siberia, by order of the Tsar on the 3-rd May 1590. The first exiles were inhabitants of the town of Uglich, who served as witnesses in the case of the murder of the Tsarévich Dimítri, and were banished to the town of Pelym in 1593. In the same year, the Uglich bell, weighing 19 puds and 20 pounds, by way of punishment, was brought to Toból for having given the alarm at the time of the Tsarévich's murder.

Pl. 41. Iskér, former capital of Kuchúm (phot. by Ussakóvskaya).

The establishment of strongholds was continued in the XVII century, contributing largely to the rapid extension of Russian power in the East. The following stockaded posts: Tomsk, Turínsk, Yeniséisk, Kansk, Krasnoyársk, Yakútsk, Achínsk, Olékminsk, Barguzínsk, Irkútsk, Balagánsk, Nerchínsk, Kirénsk arose one after the other, and became later on prosperous towns. Thus the Russian dominion, rapidly reaching the Amúr, embraced the three immense water-systems of Siberia constituted by the rivers Ob, Yeniséi and Léna. After having established the needful centres, extended and regulated the frontiers, the government was anxious about the organisation of the Siberian province; for this purpose it fostered the development of agriculture and established a settled population by the addition of exiled husbandmen, post-drivers, women destined as wives to the Cossacks, and granted various immunities and exemptions in regard to taxation

In 1621, a diocese was established at Tobólsk for missionary purposes and for the satisfaction of the spiritual wants of the growing population. Besides the colonisation organised by the State, there was a free emigration of much greater proportions, consisting of husbandmen escaping from the bonds of serfdom, who gradually occupied and settled the country, building numerous villages. As a result of this movement, the number of the population at the beginning of the XVIII century amounted to 230,000.

Pl. 42. At a medical and feeding station for emigrants.

From the beginning of the XVIII century, a line of fortresses: Omsk, Bíisk, Semipalátinsk, Ust-Kamenogórsk, was built along the southern border of Siberia in order to protect the young colonies from invasion by the plundering Kirgíz-Kaisák and Kalmyk tribes.

The first relations of the Muscovite government with Siberia were, to a large extent, promoted by the trade and industrial enterprises of the Strógano vs, which had a great influence on the movement of the Russians to the East. In the XVIII century the miner Demídov, who in 1723 discovered the first mineral deposits on the Altái and established there copper and silver works, by his example rendered a similar service to the government.

At the same time, the Russians began to understand the necessity of exploring and studying the new country. The genius of Peter the Great took the initiative in this matter, by establishing communication between the Okhótsk Sea and Kamchátka, employing exiled Swedes to build the ships. In 1719, the scientific exploration of Siberia was entrusted to Dr. Messerschmidt. Bering's expedition, for the purpose of ascertaining the existence of a passage between the Asiatic and American continents through the Arctic Ocean, was organised in 1725.

The great Siberian scientific expedition, furnished with an extensive programme, continued its activity during ten years (1733—1743) and was the most important step taken in the XVIII century towards a nearer acquaintance with Russia's dominions in the East. Captains Chérikov, Spanberg, the naval officers and topographers Chelyúskin, Mínin, Ovtsyn, Pronchíshchev the two Láptevs, the astronomer Delille, the naturalist Gmélin, the historians Miller and Fischer, Steller, the student of the Academy of Science, Krashéninnikov and the geodesic surveyors Krasílnikov and Popóv were members of Bering's expedition. Its scientific results were the first detailed description of Kamchátka written by Steller and Krashéninnikov, the description of the Siberian flora by Gmélin, and a historical review of Siberia by Miller. Its practical result was manifested in the gradual Russian occupation of the north-western portion of America and of the Aleutian Islands.

The expedition of the academicians Pallas and Lepékhin, which took place in 1770—1774, was also of great import on account of its geographical results.

The discovery of the group of the New Siberian Islands by the merchant Liákhov between 1760—1770, coincides with the same epoch, as well as that of an island on the Bering Sea by the merchant Pribylov, which received his name, and soon became the centre of the seal trade.

At the same time as the Russians pushed their dominions further to the north and the nort-east, they moved their boundaries into the interior of Asia.

This extension began in 1731 by the subjection of the Little Kirgíz tribe to Russia, which was followed towards the end of the XVIII century by the subjection of the Middle tribe. During the XVIII century, colonisation was connected with the exile system which, at first adopted in extraordinary cases, soon became generally applied by the Government in order to increase the number of colonists. Compùlsory settlements were established for the

Pl. 43. Movable school at an emigration station.

same purpose; this organisation however, in many instances, proved unsuccessful from the lack of the necessary provision for the welfare of the emigrants. The greatest contingent of colonists was represented by free settlers who squatted on the land without any authorisation.

According to the census made by the sixth revision towards the end of the XVIII century, Siberia contained about 770,200 tax paying males, and a total of 1,500,000 inhabitants.

The most important territorial annexations strengthening the Russian power in the East, were made in the XIX century. All these occupations were effected according to the Russian custom without any bloodshed, by means of peaceful agreements and treaties. The nomads of the Kirgíz-Kaisák steppes, having confidence in the force of the Russian arms, often sought shelter against the invasions of the hostile Asiatic Tatar tribes, and applied to the Russian authorities for the settlement of family dissensions.

Russia was thus encouraged to push her foreposts into the interior of the steppe, beyond the Siberian and Irtysh boundaries. In this way the Cossack settlement of Kokchetávsk was founded in 1824; that of Bayán-Aúl in 1826, and Akmolínsk in 1827.

An exploration of the steppes undertaken by the Russian naturalists and geologists Karélin, Schrenk, and Vlangáli, was carried on simultaneously with their colonisation.

Pl. 44. Settler's hut in winter.

The Russian government and men of science spared neither money nor labour for a scientific and geographical investigation of the north of Siberia; the first scientific exploration of the New Siberian Islands was organised in 1809—1810 under Hedenstrom. During the period from 1815 to 1820, an expedition of famous Russian navigators: Kotzebu, count Litke, baron Wrangel and Anjou surveyed the Arctic Ocean and the Bering Sea.

The Russian government was still more anxious about the exploration of the southern portions in view of future colonisation.

In 1826, the expedition of Ledebur, Meier and Bunge had for object the study of the peculiar Altái flora; while the expedition of Humboldt, Rose and Erenberg formed by the Emperor Nicholas I, was entrusted with the investigation of the geological structure of the Altái plateau. Two important scientific journeys to Siberia were made within the years 1842—1845: one by Chikhachóv, directed to the south-eastern part of the Altái; the other, by Middendorf to the Taimyr peninsula and to the coasts of the Okhótsk Sea.

Pl. 45. Settler's earthen huts in the steppe.

The discovery, in 1840, of the estuary of the Amúr, by the transport „Baikál" under command of Capt. Nevélsky, and of the mouth itself, by Lieut. Kazakévich on a sloop of the same vessel, gave a fresh start to Russian colonisation in the Amúr region.

The occupation of the Amúr mouth was effected without resistance from any side, the Chinese government having made no claim either to the lower reaches of the Amúr or to the land lying between the Ussúri and the Eastern Ocean. The important achievement of the annexation of the entire Amúr province to Russia was due to the energy of count Muravióv-Amursky, then Governor-General of Eastern Siberia. The organisation of settlements, on the lower waters of the Amúr, together with the opening of water communication with the Transbaikál, and the movement of Cossacks and peasants to the desert valleys of that river and its tributaries, led to the Pekin treaty of the 2 November 1860, concluded by Count N. P. Ignátiev, according to which the Chinese government, acknowledging the force of the Aigún treaty and the Tian-Tsin agreement, surrendered the possession of the Amúr river and of the entire Ussúri province to Russia. At the same time, the rich highland of Zailísk was annexed to the south-western part of Asiatic Russia.

Pl. 46. Group of emigrants from the Poltáva government on the shore of the Baikál (phot. by Drizhénko).

After these two regions were occupied, they were subjected to scientific exploration, and soon afterwards colonised.

Tha astronomer Schwartz, the naturalist Radde, the geologist Schmidt the zoologist Schrenk and the botanists Maksimóvich and Maak, who were despatched to Eastern Siberia in 1855, rendered an immense service to the new country by their scientific investigations. This portion of Siberia was also carefully explored by such eminent men as Semiónov, Sévertsov, Veniukóv, Fedchénko, Mushkétov, Potánin, Przewálski, Pevtsóv, Yádrintsev, Bogdanóvich and others, who all played an important part in the history of this country.

More lately, special attention was paid to the southern fertile zone of Siberia which is by nature itself particularly well fitted for colonisation; the economic conditions of peasant life in the already colonised districts, and the customs of the natives, have been subjected to special investigation in connexion with the geological exploration of the country traversed by the Great Siberian Railway.

In accordance with the programs which were drawn up for this purpose in 1881 by the Ministry of Agriculture and State Domains, in Western Siberia, and by the former Governor-General of Irkútsk, Count A. P. Ignátiev, in

Pl. 47. Settlement of Novo-Nikoláevsk.

Eastern Siberia, the condition of the village population was made the object of a special study, with the best ethnographical and economical results. At the same time, the geological researches of the mining parties, sent by the Ministry of Agriculture and State Domains, have ascertained the nature of the soil, and indicated the points where building-stone, fuel and other useful minerals are to be found throughout the entire course of the Great Siberian Railway, thus opening a wide prospect to the development of mining and industrial enterprise.

The attempts at establishing a sea-route for trade to the coasts of Northern Siberia, which from the end of the XVI and the beginning of the XVII centuries had been abandoned for a period of 250 years, have again been taken up in the present century by some Russian, and even Scandinavian, English and American, navigators. The success obtained in this direction by Wiggins in 1874 and by Nordenskjöld in 1875, modified the opinion hitherto held as to the inaccessibility of the Kára Sea; the expedition of Nordenskjöld organised in 1878—1879 with the assistance of Sibiriakóv reached the Siberian northern coast and the Pacific Ocean through the Bering Strait, and thus proved that the Arctic Ocean, in direct water communication with the sources of the Ob and Yeniséi, offers a most suitable route for navigation and trade.

About 20 expeditions, undertaken since 1887, all succeeded in reaching the coasts of Siberia, and thus served to establish the feasibility ot this route now further facilitated by the use of icebreakers, insuring a free passage through the Kára Sea.

During the whole of the last century, Russian colonisation in Siberia was ever on the increase. At first, the number of exiles was about two thousand a year; from 1830, rising gradually, their number reached ten times this figure, amounting to 20,000. This great contingent of exile settlers ought to have considerably influenced colonisation and the increase of the population; neither phenomenon was however observed.

The importance of the exile system, as a means of colonisation, was diminished by the unsuitable choice of localities; the exiles were not settled on unoccupied lands, but merely attached to settlements and villages of the older inhabitants in a proportion not exceeding $^1/_5$ of the original population.

Want of economic organisation, poverty, absence of domestic habits, immorality produced by prison life and long wanderings from one étape to another, all these causes together produced a great mortality. The age of the convicts, which generally varies from 36 to 50 years, is not suitable for marriage and for a fresh start in family life. This too was an impediment to a sound economic organisation of convict life. On the whole, in the majority of cases the presence of exiles weighed heavily both materially and morally on the original population.

The greater part of the increase in the population, during the XIX century and the precedent period, was due to the settlement of peasants by the State, and to free emigration. Each time the State gave permission to settle certain localities indicated by it, all parts of Russia profited by this permission and joined in the movement.

Such periods of emigration occurred in the twenties, and again from 1847 to 1855. This movement was encouraged by the State. Part of the settlers, registered in the Siberian Cossack class, founded new settlements in the steppe borderland, and helped to colonise the western governments of Siberia. Emigration reached its greatest extent prior to the Crimean war, followed by a lull in 1855; it began again after the war, being evoked by the proposition of the government to settle on the banks of the Amúr.

Previous to 1862, which was the year of the abolition of serfdom, the stream again decreased, rising considerably soon afterwards, under the influence of the propagation of the emigration movement started in many governments of Russia.

Besides the legal emigration, which was attended with many difficulties, the movement beyond the Urál frequently took place naturally without any formal permission, according to the custom of former years, taking its course by different routes and spreading in all directions over the wide area bounded by the Irbít-Tiumén highway and the southern borders of the Orenburg government. Regulation of the emigration movement and registration of the bodies of settlers, bound for Siberia through the Vólga and Ob basins, was instituted at some central points in 1881.

The law of the 13 July, 1889, with regard to the free emigration of the village and town population to state lands, providing the new settlers with arable land, gave a more effectual regulation to this movement. According to this law, which at first comprised the government of Western Siberia, Tobólsk and Tomsk, and the Steppe countries, and in 1892 included the eastern governments of Yeniséisk and Irkútsk, the emigrants who had quitted their former abodes upon fulfilment of all the necessary conditions, received a grant of 15 desiatins of agricultural land a head with the right to enjoy the same for three years free of taxes. During the following three years, the tax is reduced to half, and is imposed in the full amount of R. 2. 71 k., or $18^1/_{18}$ k. per desiatin, only after the lapse of 6 years.

According to this same law, all lawful emigrants are permitted to postpone heir military service for three years.

The poorest settlers who are in need of help, in some cases receive additional grant of wood for the construction of their houses, and a loan of seed-corn, an alimentation allowance and farm inventary. This loan advance may be returned within a period of ten years reckoned after the first three years use of the land.

Since the time of the formation of the Committee for the construction of the Siberian Railway, which took charge of the emigrants on their way to Siberia, and organised their settlement within the range of the railway line, and since the opening ot the traffic on the West-Siberian section, the greater part of the emigrants, whose numbers increased considerably, proceded to Siberia by the Samára-Zlatoúst line, by way of Cheliábinsk (pl. 42—48).

Pl. 48. Type of church in emigration settlements and at railway stations.

The increase of this movement, partly occasioned by the various economical considerations which generally cause a popular emigration, may further be explained by the facilitation in the methods ot conveyance, which to a great extent reduced the expenditure and shortened the time formerly required for emigration. Provided with railway facilities and receiving assistance at the sanitary stations organised by the Committee of the Siberian Railway, where tree medical help and cheap or free food is offered them, the settlers arrive at their new abodes without loss of strength and energy, which enables them to apply all their faculties and activity to the hard work connected with the establishment of a new husbandry. Only an eyewitness can judge of the great force of resistance and endurance of hard work, which the settlers bring with them and which increases as they approach the chosen and desired land, in prevision of the battles they will have to fight with a harsh and unknown nature, before settling down and organising their households. Their only support is the hope of a better future and their strong religious faith

State Secretary Kulomzín, who visited the colonised regions, situated along the Siberian Railway and is well acquainted with peasant life and the conditions of emigration, declares that the leading element of the present emigration is represented by men who morally seem to be related to those enterprising Russians who in the XVI and XVII centuries wandered to the limits of the Muscovite state, to the Steppes, the Don, to the Yaík and to Siberia, and settled there as Free Cossacks, strengthening Russian power and planting Russian civilisation. The difference between the present emigrants and the hero colonists of former days consists in the absence among the former of the warlike spirit.

Our emigrants of to-day are more peaceful, more inclined to satisfy the homely tastes which have survived amidst the untoward conditions of their former life; at the same time, they are energetic and enterprising, capable of standing up for themselves and of fighting against misfortune, and also restless, dissatisfied with the existing order, neither fit nor willing to submit to the legal forms and ever increasing authority of the law prevailing in European Russia: all these traits give them a likeness to those ancient conquerors who developed and expanded Russian power.

As a result of natural increase and of emigration from without, comprising therein both exiles and settlers, the population of the four governments of Tobólsk, Tomsk, Yeniséisk and Irkútsk, and the six territories of Akmolínsk, Semipalátinsk, Yakútsk, the Transbaikál, the Amúr and the Littoral, including the island of Sakhalín, reached the figure of 7,091,244 at the census of the 28 January, 1897.

Within a space of 39 years, the total population of Siberia, comprising the same territories (exclusive of the Amúr, the Ussúri provinces and the island of Sakhalín, which at that time were almost uninhabited) increased by 100 per cent. (with a predomination of males over females) as compared with the data of the X-th revision of 1858—1859.

The following figures given by the X-th revision and those of the last census, illustrate the growth of the population in each separate territory:

GOVERNMENTS AND TERRITORIES.	POPULATION IN 1858.		
	Males.	Female .	TOTAL.
Tobólsk	504,105	517,161	1,021,266
Tomsk	354,580	340,071	694,651
Yeniséisk	160,676	142,580	303,256
Irkútsk	115,110	107,423	222,533
Akmolínsk	149,131	128,320	277,451
Semipalátinsk	118,040	99,411	217,451
Transbaikál	179,765	172,769	352,534
Amúr	—	—	—
Littoral	12,666	9,194	21,860
Total	1,763,099	1,667,839	3,430,930

GOVERNMENTS AND TERRITORIES.	POPULATION ON THE 28 JANUARY 1897.			
	Area in sq. versts.	Males.	Females.	TOTAL.
Tobólsk	1,295,758.3	711,982	726,502	1,438,484
Tomsk	749,819.3	970,780	958,312	1,929,092
Yeniséisk	2,259,592.3	291,555	268,347	559,902
Irkútsk	703,650.3	267,520	238,997	506,517
Yakútsk	3,452,655.3	136,061	125,670	261,731
Akmolínsk	479,200.2	354,839	324,587	678,957

GOVERNMENTS AND TERRITORIES.	POPULATION ON THE 28 JANUARY 1897.			
	Area in sq. versts.	Males.	Females.	TOTAL.
Semipalátinsk	428,527.8	364,832	320,358	685,197
Transbaikál	547,965.6	338,722	325,349	644,071
Amúr	393,366.6	66,595	51,975	220,557
Littoral	1,629,424.0	150,826	69,731	220,557
Sakhalín	66,762.0	20,518	7,648	28,166
Total ...	12,006,691.4	3,673,768	3,417,476	7,091,244

	Inhab. per sq. versts.	Proport. of women to 100 men.
Tobólsk	1.2	102.0
Tomsk	2.6	98.7
Yeniséisk	0.3	91.0
Irkútsk	0.8	68.1
Yakútsk...............	0.1	94.5
Akmolínsk	1.3	92.5
Semipalátinsk.........	1.7	87.8
Transbaikál...........	1.3	96.2
Amúr	1.3	75.6
Littoral	0.1	45.5
Sakhalín..............	0.4	37.3
All Siberia.....	0.58	93.3

Largest towns, according to the last census.

TOWNS.	POPULATION.			
	Males.	Females.	TOTAL.	Prop. of women to 100 men.
Tomsk....................	27,140	25,290	52,430	93.2
Irkútsk	26,567	24,917	51,484	93.2
Omsk.	20,106	17,364	37,470	86.4
Blagovéshchensk	19,665	12,941	32,606	65.3
Tiumén	14,988	14,600	29,588	97.4
Barnaúl	15,122	14,286	29,408	94.4
Vladivostók...............	24,361	4,535	28,986	15.6
Krasnoyársk..............	14,573	12,027	26,653	88.2
Semipalátinsk.............	14,153	12,200	26,953	82.5
Khabárovsk...............	11,673	3,259	14,972	27.9
Chitá......................	6,429	4,603	11,032	71.6
Yakútsk	3,506	2,691	36,197	76.8

The proportion of the town population, forming not above 8 per cent. of the total, is much inferior to that of European Russia, a result of the insufficient development of manufactures, trade and industry.

The Russian orthodox element takes the most important place among the ethnographical divisions of the whole population.

The traveller on his way from the Urál to the coast of the Pacific Ocean by the Great Siberian Railway running through the agricultural zone, traverses a broad stretch of land narrowing to the East, inhabited by Russians. To the south and north, the Russian population is surrounded by natives among whom it is also scattered in groups.

The native population of Siberia is divided with regard to its origin into the following tribes: 1) Turks, 2) Finns and 3) Mongols.

Among the aborigenes of the country, the Kirgíz, Tatárs, Bukhárians and Yakúts belong to the Turk race.

The Kirgíz, forming the fundamental population of the Akmolínsk and Semi-

Pl. 49. Kirgiz removing their camp. (phot. by von Kinits).

palátinsk steppe regions, represented by above one million souls, speak a Turkish dialect, profess Mohammedanism and are nomadic cattle-breeders (pl. 49, 50, 51).

The Tatárs and Bukhárians, who have received an admixture of Finnish and Mongolian blood, are met within all the districts of the Tobólsk and

Pl. 50. Types of Kirgíz women and girls (phot by von Kinits).

Tomsk governments; they also speak a Turkish dialect, profess Mohammedanism, and subsist by agriculture and trade.

A number of Tatárs (pl. 52), inhabiting the Altái district, retain their nomadic habits and their ancient shamanistic faith. Many of them are related to the Tatárs of Kazán and inhabit tho towns in the steppe region, occupying themselves chiefly with trade. Various localities in Eastern Siberia are inhabited by Tatárs. Thus for example, in the Yeniséisk government, at the foot of the Sayán, there are are about forty thousand russified, mainly orthodox, Tatárs engaged in agriculture. Approximately the total number of Tatárs and Bukhárians in Siberia is about 250,000. The Yakúts dwell in the Yakútsk territory; their number is given as 230,000. They speak a Turkish dialect, containing an element of Mongolian words; their religion is Shamanism and their occupation hunting and cattle-raising. The ethnographical character of this tribe is distinctly evidenced by their existing type, general appearance, manners, customs and dress (pl. 55—58).

The Vogúls and Ostiáks are descended from the Finnish race. The Vogúls belong to the ancient Ugro-Finnish tribes, and are closely related to the

Pl. 51. Chiefs and Bis of a Kirgíz village (phot. by Kessler).

historical Chud and Ugor; the Hungarians are a branch from the same stem, and the Bashkírs or Paskotírs also come of this stock. They occupy the northern part of the Tobólsk government being settled along the rivers Tavodá, Kondá and Sosvá. They number about 7,000 and inhabit forests and swamps. Hunting, fishing, gathering cedar-nuts, and other similar pursuits engage them in a nomadic existence for half the year. They stand at a very low stage of culture and their religion is mainly shamanistic, although they were nominally converted to orthodoxy by Filophéi Leshchínsky in 1714 and 1722. They are baptised, but have a preference for paganism, the faith of their forefathers.

The Ostiáks, scattered throughout the north of Siberia between 57° and 73° of N. latitude, dwell partly on the coast of the Arctic Ocean, in the Northern Urál, and partly within the area lying between the Irtysh and Ob, comprising the swampy and wooded wastes of the Vasiugánsk tundra (pl. 60, 63). It has not yet been ascertained what part they played in history, but it has been proved that they came from the south of Siberia. This tribe possesses a beautiful epos bearing some analogy to the Scandinavian sagas. They number approximately 30,000. Tha greater part of the Ostiáks, inhabiting the forest zone, get their livelihood by hunting, fishing and collecting cedar-nuts. Like the Vogúls, they only nominally belong to the orthodox religion, being virtually Shamanists. A number of them, dwelling in the polar tundra zone, pass their lives in tending their reindeer, and have become very much assimilated to the Samoyéds. Some of the Ostiáks in close connexion with the permanent Russian population of Northern Siberia, are thoroughly russified and profess the orthodox religion.

Pl. 52. Altáyans on the river Katún (phot by prof. Sapózhnikov).

The Mongolian stock is represented by the Teleút and Telengút, the Buriát, Samoyéd, Manchúrian, Tungús and Giliák tribes.

The Teleúts inhabit the Altái plateau in the Tomsk, Kuznétsk and Bíisk districts: they number about 20,000 (pl. 53, 54), and are nomads devoted to cattle-breeding and hunting. They have a Mongolian type and belong to the Buddhist religion.

The Telengúts, wandering along the valleys of the Altái rivers, the Chúya, Chulishmán and others, are also known as Uriankháets and Kalmyks, and are split into many different insignificant tribes under such names as Akshishtym, Eliút, Oirát etc.

Pl. 53. Teleúts on the Altái.

The Buriáts, whose number is about 290,000, form the main population of the Transbaikál and Irkútsk government (pl. 64). They are engaged partly in agriculture, but principally in cattle-breeding, and are either Buddhists or Lamaists.

The Manchurians, belonging to the permanent native population of the Amùr territory, practise agriculture. With regard to their habits and religion, they have a great likeness to the Chinese, although they seem to be less civilised than their Korean neighbours. Their number is given as about 3,000. The Samoyéd inhabit the extreme north of Siberia; their camps are scattered throughout the coasts of the Arctic Ocean, within the borders of the governments of Tobólsk and Yeniséisk. Their number amounts to 6,000. They lead a nomadic life spent in hunting, fishing, and searching for mammoth ivory, which they sell. Reindeer are their chief resource, the more wealthy Samoyéds owning several thousand head. They possess in perfection the art of preparing furs and tanning hides. All the Samoyéds are pagans. The Yuráks wandering over the Tazóvsk tundra are related to them, as are also some of the small tribes of the Sayán now fast becoming extinct.

Pl. 54. Teleút dwellings

Pl. 55. Yakút of the Olékminsk district (phot. by Gavrílov).

The Tungús together with the allied Mongol tribes, account for the greater portion of the native population of Eastern Siberia (pl. 65, 66). Their nomadic life leads them from the Yeniséi to the Pacific Ocean, and southwards to the Chinese frontier.

Their herds of reindeer, hunting and fishing constitute their chief resources. The majority of the Tungús belong to the orthodox religion, but as they are ignorant of the Russian language, and their churches are few and at a great distance apart, the zeal of the missionaries meets with but little success.

The Lamút, Yukagírs, Chúkch and Chuvánets, Koriáks and other tribes inhabiting the arctic and polar regions belong to the Tungús stock, but have not passed the lowest stage of civilisation. The Manégr, Orochén, Gold, Olch and Mangún tribes, no more civilised than their northern brethren, come of the Tungús-Manchú race, and are located on the Amúr and in the Littoral territory. The proximity of China has had a marked influence upon them, as appears from their dress, the architecture of their dwellings, their wearing pig-tails etc. The women of the Gold tribe have the peculiar fashion of wearing a ring in the partition of the nose, while those of the Orochén, insert it through the right nostril. Most characteristic are the fish-skin dresses worn in summer by the Golds and Orochéns; for which reason they have been nicknamed by the Chinese „fish-skinned". All these natives, amounting to about 50,000, profess Shamanism (pl. 67—68).

Pl. 56. Yakút boy from Olékma (phot. by Gavrílov).

The Giliáks, dwelling on the lower reaches of the Amùr, and on the coast of the Okhótsk Sea, represent the most numerous aboriginal tribe of the Far East; they live by hunting and fishing. The dog is an animal which holds an important place in the life of this people; in winter they are employed in drawing sledges,and when they are too old for this, they are eaten and their skins used for making clothes. All the Giliáks, about 15,000 in number, are Shamanists.

All the Siberian native tribes are certainly derived from the interior of Asia.

Archaeological researches, begun in the XVIII century, have shewn that the ancient tombs, tumuli and ruins of towns, starting from Central Asia, all follow the direction of the Siberian river basins, the natural ways of communication for the Asiatic aborigenes in their march to Europe. The discovery of stone figures, so-called „baba's", scattered over the steppes of Central Asia and Novorossía, has further confirmed the view of prehistoric migrations from Asia into Europe.

Pl. 57. Yakút types (phot. by Arnold).

The past history of these little known tribes forms part of the general history of mankind. If Siberia is the land of the future, it may be affirmed with certainty that it contains a mass of future discoveries for history and archaeology.

The past century including many historical events consolidating the Russian power on the Asiatic continent, closed with the triumph of the civilising mission of the Russian government in the East, pointing out a new course for civilisation and opening new prospects for the universal and historical development of the nations.

By the provisional rules, which in the beginning of the XIX century were drawn up during the reign of the Emperor Alexander I, and comprised a complete system of public instruction for the Empire, a university was to be founded in Siberia. The project, after being abandoned for half a century, was recalled to life by the Emperor Alexander II, who on the 25 April 1875, gave the following order to Adjutant-General Kaznakóv, former Governor-General of Western Siberia:

Pl. 58. Yakút tents (yúrtas) in Olékma (phot. by Arnold).

„By raising the level of public instruction, the population of Siberia will be able to produce a number of educated and well informed men, sufficient to satisfy the local demand. After a thorough discussion of the subject, let a project for founding a university in Siberia be pre-

Pl. 59. Lepers in the Yakútsk territory.

sented for the Imperial Consideration by the Ministry of Public Instruction.

The Tomsk university, which was to be the intellectual centre and promoter of culture in Asia, was inaugurated on the 22 July 1888, on the name-day of the Empress Mária Feódorovna, during the reign of the deceased Monarch-Pacificator Alexander III.

Pl. 60. Ostiák types (phot. by Poliakóv).

The recognition that the rich Siberian territory with its many needs was worthy of special attention, and that numerous important questions, not only regarding this country, but the whole Russian population, demanded to be solved, in a great measure determined the construction of a railway line which was to traverse Siberia from end to end.

The first step towards the realisation of this grand enterprise was taken by the laying of the first stone at Vladivostók on the 19 May 1891 by His Imperial Majesty the Emperor Nicholas II, then His Imperial Highness the Tsesarévich. In His rescript of the 17 March 1891, He decided the question regarding the construction of the Great Railway, manifesting to the whole world, by the active part He took in the achievement of this essentially national work, His desire to facilitate the intercourse of Siberia with other lands and to secure peace and prosperity to His beloved country.

Pl. 61. Ostiák girls (phot. by Poliakóv).

The official acts dated August 26-th and December 4-th 1896, relative to the concession given to the Russo-Chinese Bank for the construction and exploitation of the East-Chinese Railway, and to the stipulation in the statutes of this railway, determining the mode of construction of the eastern section of the main Siberian Railway, are the result of the peaceful and civilising policy of the Russian Government.

Pl. 62. Ostiák man and woman (phot. by Poliakóv).

As a consequence of the construction of the Siberian Railway connecting the Transbaikál with the Ussúri territory through Manchúria, this north - eastern portion of the Chinese Empire, although remaining politically under the Chinese dominion, economically, i. e. as far as trade and industry are concerned, enters into the sphere of the continuous line of railway.

The special agreement of the 15 March 1898, come to in Pekin by the delegates of Russia and China, according to which Port-Arthúr and Talienván on the Liaodún peninsula, with their respective territories and waters, were assigned to Russia, together with the permission to construct a branch line, connecting these ports with the Main Siberian Railway, is a fact of great political significance to which the work of the Siberian line was the prelude. The opening of the port of Talienván to the merchant fleets of all nations, leading to the creation of new centres for trade and industrial enterprise in the Pacific Ocean, connected by the great Railway with the civilised trade centres of Europe, is surely a most important event, which finds a fit expression in the official communication of the 17 March 1898:

Pl. 63. Ostiák Prince Taishín of Obdórsk (phot. by Poliakóv).

Pl. 64. Buriát types (phot. by Máslov).

„It must be gladly welcomed by those who value the welfare of the world, based on the mutual intercourse of nations".

Until now, the life of Asia followed a separate course, being only out-

Pl. 65. Tungús types of the Yakút territory (phot. by Máinov).

wardly connected with European culture and civilisation, and serving as an object for European exploitation.

Pl. 66. Tungús (phot. by Drizhénko).

The civilising policy of Russia in the East, which may be regarded as an exception to that of other countries, was guided by other principles and, as mentioned in the above quoted communication, was directed to the mutual welfare of nations by the maintenance of peace throughout the immense extent of her dominions. The honour of having planted the flag of Christianity and civilisation in Asia, is due to Russia. The near future will show the

Pl. 67. Orochéns in the Transbaikál.

results of the activity of our Government and of our civilising enterprises, which will add to the glory and power of Russia and her Sovereign Chief.

Pl. 68. Golds[1] (phot. by Mazkévich).

The official communication published on the 6-th May 1899, removed from Siberia the shameful stain attached to it as a place of exile, by putting it on the same footing with all other countries of the Empire, as regards social life and the struggle for civilisation.

The deliverance of Siberia from the sad lot of affording a refuge to the worthless elements of the Empire, was the logical result of that work of civilisation which, giving social capacity and competency to that country, thereby

Pl. 69. Monumen to N. M. Przewálski on the shore of lake Issyk-Kul in Semiréchie.

strengthened its position as mediator in the great mission of Russia in the East for the introduction of the principles of Christian civilisation into Asiatic life.

THE LATE

EMPEROR ALEXANDER III,

TSAR PACIFICATOR.

MOST AUGUST FOUNDER OF THE GREAT SIBERIAN RAILWAY.

Print. with the aut. of the Minist. of the Court Imperial. „Art. Printing Society", St. Petersburg, Prosp. Engl., № 28.

MAP O

composed in 1614 by Hessel Guérard from a sketch of Tz

RUSSIA

n Feodor Borisovitch Godunof for the Tzar Michail Feodorovitch.

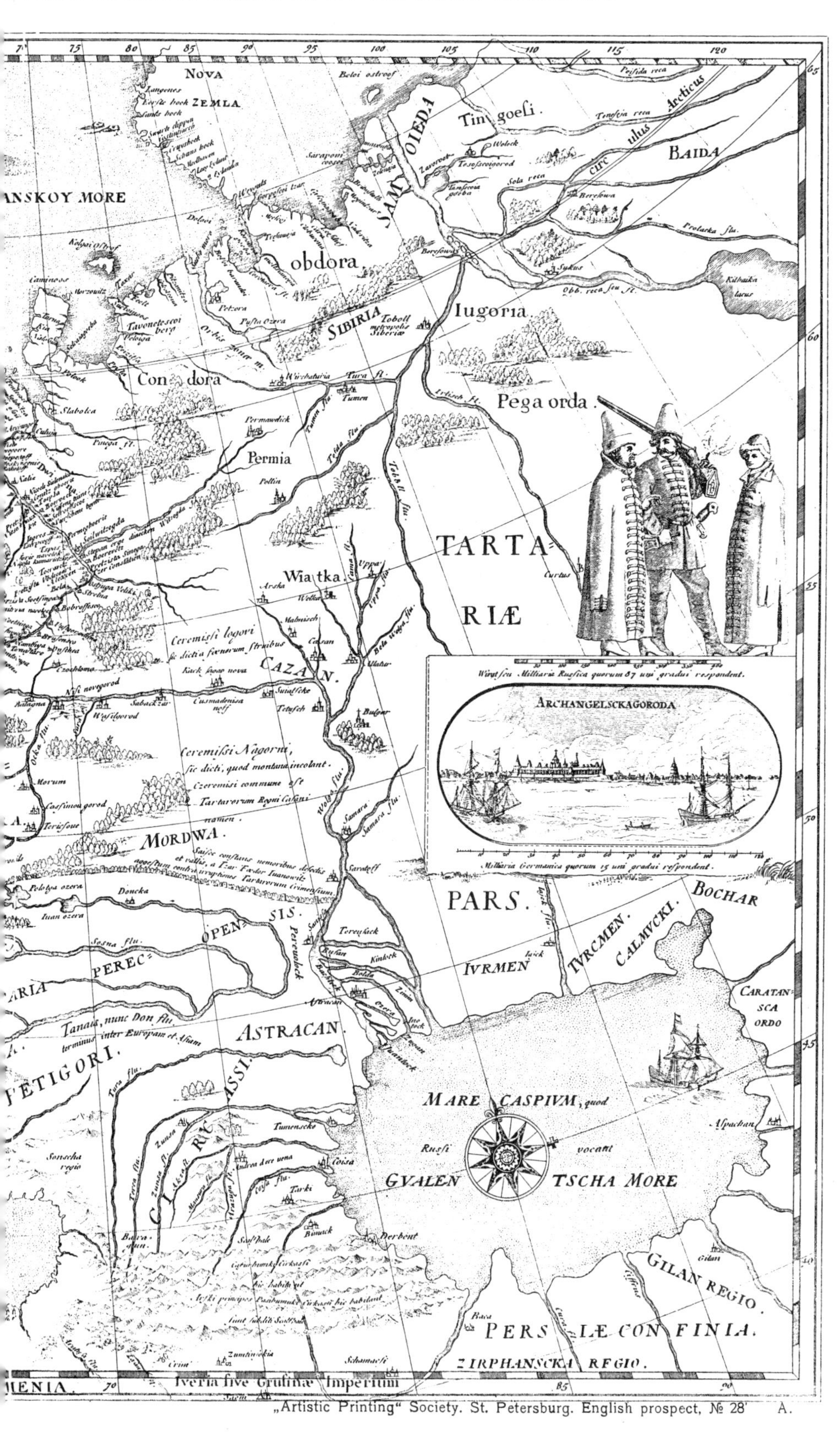

„Artistic Printing" Society. St. Petersburg. English prospect, № 28' A.

The construction of the Great Siberian Railway.

Historical review of the plan for the construction of the Siberian Railway.— Inauguration of the work at Vladivostok.—Organisation of the Committee for the construction of the Siberian Railway.—Topographical and technical conditions of the Great Siberian Railway.—Cost of construction.—Subsidiary enterprises.—The importance of the Great Railway in connexion with civilisation and trade.

The annexation of the vast Amúr, Littoral and Ussúri provinces to the Siberian territory by the treaty of Pekin was effected at the time when the internal renovation of the Empire by the reforms of the Tsar Liberator excited the interest of the Russian Government, society and foreigners,who clearly foresaw the future which lay in store for this new acquisition of Russia in the East.

The construction of new ways of communication in Siberia, and the connexion by rail of its different centres of population in view of strategical and commercial considerations, together with the building of a main railway line from Moscow or the Vólga to the Pacific Ocean, were projected at that time.

All these schemes were based solely on conjectures without any preliminary surveys or calculations as to the needs and trading possibilities of the districts affected and remained without any practical result. In was at the end of the sixties that three routes for the Siberian Railway, suggested by private individuals and supported by the petitions of Russian and Siberian merchants, seemed feasible.

These projected lines, which were frequently the subject of discussion in scientific societies and in the press, were as follows:

1) The northern project of Messrs. Rashét, Kókorev and Co. from Perm, through Nízhni-Tagíl and Ekaterinbúrg to Tiumén, with a branch line to Irbít.

2) The central project of Mr. Liubímov, from Perm, through Kungúr, Ekaterinbúrg, Shadrínsk to the village of Belozérsk on the river Toból, 49 versts north of Kurgán.

3) The southern project of Mr. Bogdanóvich, from the village of Ershóv (Sarapúl district), through Ekaterinbúrg to Tiumén.

Upon further deliberation, the special commission organised in the Urál, and entrusted with the selection of the most suitable direction for the route, in order to satisfy the requirements of the Urál mining industry and the Siberian transport trade, came to the conclusion that these two interests were incompatible.

The preference afterwards given to the Urál scheme for some time put the idea of the Siberian Railway in the background. The Government surveys conducted during 1872—1874 followed three directions:

1) Kineshmá, Viátka, Perm, Ekaterinbúrg, Tiumén.

2) Nízhni-Nóvgorod, Kazán, Krasnoufímsk, Ekaterinbúrg, Tiumén.

3) Alatyr, Ufá, Cheliábinsk.

The first direction was based on the northern project of Mr. Rashét more extensively developed; the second was taken from the southern project of Mr. Bogdanóvich, while the third, which was quite new and more to the south, leaving out the greater portion of the Urál, aimed at satisfying the requirements of Siberian and Central Asiatic trade.

Upon further deliberation, the Committee of Ministers deemed that of these three routes two only were worthy of consideration, while giving preference to the southern direction, as uniting existing railways with the Urál for further continuation to Siberia, and on account of its coincidence with the general direction adopted by the transport trade for many years past.

On the 19-th December 1875, the route selected by the Committee of Ministers was sanctioned by the Emperor; the execution of this project was, however, postponed by political complications and by the war in the East during 1877—1878.

Meanwhile the direction of the Siberian main road was still under discussion, the railways within European Russia were receiving a considerable extension, connecting the future commercial centres of Siberia with the metropolis. The railway line reached Orenbúrg in 1877, and in 1878 the mining railway, uniting Perm and Ekaterinbúrg, was open to traffic. The construction of the great bridge of the Emperor Alexander II over the Vólga, was completed in 1880 and thus an uninterrupted line of railway connected the general railway system of European Russia with Orenbúrg, constituting the entrance to her Central Asiatic dominions.

The opening of the traffic on the Urál mining line from Perm to Ekaterinbúrg formed the motive for the humble petition of the Nízhni-Nóvgorod merchants laid before His Imperial Majesty in 1880, praying for the construction of a railway branch of 300 versts from Ekaterinbúrg to Tiumén to connect the basins of the Ob and Vólga.

The petition was handed by order of the Emperor Alexander II to the Committee of Ministers in order to find the necessary means for the construction of this branch.

According to the resolution of the Committee of Ministers of the 23 September 1880, the immediate construction of the Ekaterinbúrg-Tiumén line was to be effected at the cost of the Government.

The execution of this project, together with the further extension of Russian railways towards the East, as also the results of additional surveys, shewed the advisability of changing the direction chosen in 1875 for the Siberian main line.

Actual Privy Councillor N. K. Bunge, ex-President of the Committee of Ministers, and first Vice-President of the Committee for the Siberian Railway.

In 1882, after the project of 1875 had been reexamined, the Minister of Ways of Communication, by order of His Imperial Majesty, was directed to present a new scheme to the Committee of Ministers as regards the route of the Siberian Railway.

This was accordingly done in the year 1884 by Adjutant-General Possiét. According to this plan and the technical and economic considerations upon which it was based, the southern route was to give place to the following lines:

1) Nízhni-Nóvgorod, Kazán, the Nikólo-Beriózov wharf, Ekaterinbúrg, Tiumén.

2) Samára, Ufá, Krasnoufímsk, Ekaterinbúrg, Tiumén.

3) Samára, Ufá, Zlatoúst, Cheliábinsk.

In accordance with the order of the Committee of Ministers, sanctioned by the Emperor on the 6 January 1885, the selection of the route through Siberia was deemed premature on account of the want of the necessary data; at the same time, the construction of a line beginning at the point where the Orenbúrg railway crosses the river Kinél, and thence passing through Ufá and Zlatoúst along the eastern slope of the Urál, to meet at some point the Ekaterinbúrg-Tiumén line then in process of construction, was decided upon as a first step. The continuation of this line to Cheliábinsk would have once for all determined the direction of the future route through Siberia.

After a final investigation of the Samára-Zlatoúst line, the work of construction, begun in the spring of 1886, was brought to a conclusion and the line opened to passenger and goods traffic in 1888. The total cost of this line, 453.19 versts long, was R. 24,122,252, or R. 53,227.3 per verst.

The final surveys for the Ufá-Zlatoúst line were made during 1886—1887; the construction was begun in the spring of 1888, and the line was opened to regular traffic in 1890. The total cost of construction of the 298.68 versts, was R. 20,439,481, or R. 68,432 per verst.

Meanwhile, the projects regarding the direction of the Siberian main line in connexion with the future economical progress of the country, were discussed in the highest administrative spheres. The Siberian Governors-General, Baron Korf and Count Ignátiev, tried to prove the necessity of providing for the needs of Russia's eastern possessions.

On a report drawn up in 1885—1886 by Count Ignátiev, then Vice Governor-General, the late Tsar-Pacificator, who was always anxious to further Siberian interests, traced with his ewn hand the following resolution, which so greatly influenced the decision of the question:

„I have read many reports of the Governors-General of Siberia and must own with grief and shame that until now the Government has done scarcely anything towards satisfying the needs of this rich, but neglected country! It is time, high time!“

The petitions of Count Ignátiev and Baron Korf presented at the end of 1886, for the construction of a railway-line from Tomsk to Irkútsk, and from the Baikál to Srétensk, uniting by means of the Amúr the West and East Siberian navigation systems, together with the plan for connecting by rail Vladivostók and the post of Bussé, were submited by Imperial command to a special Conference of Ministers under the presidentship of Actual Privy Councillor Abazá.

As a result of this Conference, a Special Commission was directed to make surveys along the Mid-Siberian, Transbaikál and South-Ussúri lines. His Imperial Majesty wrote the following decision on the report of the Minister of Ways of Communication presented to him on the 12 June 1887, in consequence of the data obtained by the Conference and from the surveys made:

„Quite right. I hope the Ministry will practically prove the possibility of the quick and cheap construction of the line“.

This note of the Emperor's was made known by the Minister of Ways of Communication to the Board of Government Railways and to the Survey Commissions.

The Emperor shewed a special interest in the execution of the surveys, which were carried on most successfully. Frequent reports as to their pro-

Actual Privy Councillor I. N. Durnovó, President of the Committee of Ministers.

gress were presented to His Majesty by the Minister of Ways of Communication.

In the mean time, the events which occurred in the countries adjoining the Far East: the opening of the Canadian Railway, the subsidies given by the English Government to the Canada-China steamers, the introduction of the telegraph in China and the building of Chinese steamers for the navigation of the rivers Sungarí and Amúr, together with other preparations of the Chinese Government in connexion with the organisation of its military forces, excited the special attention of the Amúr Governor-General, Baron Korf, causing him to maintain the opinion, expressed by him in 1887, at the time of the beginning of the surveys, of the necessity of quickly establishing railway connexion between Vladivostók and the Ussúri in view of strategical considerations.

The necessity of uniting Vladivostók and the Amúr basin by rail was made evident in 1875 by a Commission presided over by His Imperial Highness the Grand Duke Alexis Alexándrovich. Without such facilities, our most important port in the Pacific Ocean remained cut off from the interior of the country and lost much of its significance. By resolution of the Committee of Ministers, sanctioned by the Emperor on the 29 November 1887, the Minister of Ways of Communication was desired to make arrangements for carrying out immediately the necessary financial and technical investigations, and to proceed to the construction of the above mentioned line, excepting it from the general plan of the projected Siberian railways.

Various requirements of the Government engrossing the attention of the administration, for some time delayed the realisation of the projected railway in Siberia.

The proposal of State Secretary von Hubbenet, Minister of Ways of Communication, relative to the construction of the Ussúri line founded on Baron Korf's peition, and by Adjutant-General Vannóvsky, Minister of War, was laid before the Committee of Ministers on the 8 May 1890, but as the necessary sums for its execution were not assigned, the Committee, in accordance with the Imperial command of the 2 June 1890, decided to continue only the Ufá-Zlatoúst line to Miás. The Board of Government Railways was entrusted with the execution of this project.

In consequence of a report presented to the Emperor by the Acting Minister of Ways of Communication on the 12-th July 1890, based on fresh information received from Baron Korf, demonstrating the urgent necessity for the construction of the Ussúri line, His Imperial Majesty made the following inscription:

„Necessary to proceed at once to the construction of this line“.

As the result of this decision and in accordance with the Imperial desire made known on the 16-th August, the plan of the Ussúri line was added to the general plan and submitted to the consideration of a special council, and thence to the Committee of Ministers. The means and conditions for the construction of the Siberian Railway, and the detailed note presented on the 15-th November 1890 by State Secretary von Hubbenet as to the points of junction of the Siberian line with the lines of European Russia, and the course of construction of the Siberian Railway, were made the subject of a special conference held under the presidentship of Actual Privy Councillor Abazá.

Taking the extension of Russian railways towards the East into consideration, with their termini, Tiumén on the Urál line, Orenbúrg on the Orenbúrg line and Miás on the Zlatoúst-Miás, State Secretary von Hubbenet demonstrated the economic importance of continuing the communication from these points into the interior of Siberia, and presented the specifications for their construction.

The considerations set forth in the report of State Secretary Hubbenet had a decisive effect upon the choice of the direction for the great Siberian Railway, and therfore merit a place in the history of the question. They were,

1) Beginning at Tiumén, the line was planned through Yalutoróvsk: Tiukalínsk, Kaínsk, avoiding Tomsk to Maríinsk, and thence to Achínsk, Krasnoyársk, Kansk and Nizhneúdinsk, with a total length of 2,474 versts from Tiumén to Nizhneúdinsk.

Actual Privy Councillor State Secretary S. I. Witte, Minister of Finance.

In order to preserve the commercial importance of this line, it would be necessary to construct an expensive railway, connecting Perm and Nízhni-Nóvgorod, 1000 versts in length, running parallel to the existing water-way.

A railway line of 3,474 versts reaching Nizhneúdinsk would have been necessary for the same object, leaving Moscow at a distance of 4,656 versts.

2) From Orenbúrg the line was to pass by way of Orsk, Atbasár, Akmolínsk, Pavlodár, Bíisk, Minusínsk, and Nizhneúdinsk, in its eastern portion crossing the Altái mountains; this route would be very expensive and have a length of 3,400 versts, running a total distance of 4,820 versts from Moscow to Nizneúdinsk.

3) Starting at Miás, 2,683 versts from Nizhneúdinsk, the road traversed the most populated localities of Western Siberia, following the fertile black-earth zone and having a total length pf 4,551 versts from Moscow to Nizhneúdinsk. Thus the line beginning at Miás was 791 versts shorter than that from Tiumén; beginning at Orenbúrg it was reduced by 717 versts, while from Moscow to Miás works, it was to be 105 versts shorter than the northern route, and 269 versts less than the southern line.

According to the estimates, the cost of the Miás line would be less than the others; thus it became evident that the continuation of the Samára-Zlatoúst line passing through Cheliábinsk, Kurgán and further east was the most advantageous.

As regards the course of the work, State Secretary von Hubbenet referred to the note of the Minister of Finance, which was laid before the Council, where Privy Councillor Vyshnegrádsky, comparing the respective importance of the diferent sections of the Siberian Railway, gave his view of the commercial importance and the future progress of Siberia.

According to the plan of Privy Councillor Vyshnegrádsky, the construction of the Siberian Railway was not to aim solely at the opening of new Siberian markets for the products of European Russia, but also to assure the regular economic development of Siberia, thus placing this vast and rich, but hitherto inaccessible country, on a level with European Russia.

Siberia's growth and prosperity depended solely on a close economic intercourse with European Russia which in its return would find there new sources of progress and wealth.

The Minister of Finance was further of opinion that it would not be expedient to commence the Siberian Railway by the construction of the Ussúri line. According to his view, this line did not possess any great economic or strategic importance, but merely established communication between Vladivostók and the Ussúri river. To begin operations from the west would be much more to the purpose. Traversing a more densely populated country, the new line would yield a certain revenue and at the same time increase economic intercourse with European Russia, and secure the more rapid conveyance of reserve troops to Eastern Siberia, serving at the same time the interests of the Russian population of Siberia settled between the Urál and the Baikál.

Although holding the same opinion as to the economic importance of the Siberian main line, State Secretary von Hubbenet, referring to its political and strategical significance, urged by the Ministers of War and Foreign Affairs, attached great importance to the Ussúri line and insisted on the necessity of its construction, as previously decided by the Committee of Ministers and sanctioned by the Emperor on the 29-th November 1887.

The special conference, leaving the decision as to the construction of new railways to the Committee of Ministers, only discussed the sum which, according to the estimate for the extraordinary expenditure of 1891, could be assigned for commencing the construction of the new railways.

Having received the Imperial authorisation to carry into effect the resolution of the special conference, State Secretary von Hubbenet, on the 4-th

Actual Privy Councillor Prince M. I. Khilkóv, Minister of Ways of Communication.

February 1891, proposed to the Committee of Ministers to commence the construction of the Siberian Railway by the Miás-Cheliábinsk line, a distance of 94 versts, and the Ussúri line running from Vladivostók to Gráfskaya, a distance of 293 versts, in connexion with the surveys conducted from Cheliábinsk to a point on the Mid-Siberian section, and from the Gráfskaya station to Khabárovsk.

The Committee of Ministers, having taken the project of the Minister of Ways of Communication into consideration, issued the following order sanctioned by the Emperor on the 15 and 21 February 1891: 1) To approve the direction of the Ussúri line from Vladivostók to Gráfskaya station; 2) To commence the construction of the Miás-Cheliábinsk line in 1891; 3) To conduct surveys in the same year, from Cheliábinsk to Tomsk or some other point of the Mid-Siberian section, and from the terminus of the first section of the Ussúri line to Khabárovsk; 4) To carry out these works under the direction of the State; 5) The Minister of Ways of Communication to receive the sanction of the State Council for the necessary expenditure.

The Imperial Rescript addressed to His Imperial Highness the Grand Duke Tsesarévich on the 17-th Marsh 1891, finally and irrevocably decided the question of the construction of the Great Siberian Railroad.

This memorable document was made known by His Imperial Highness upon his again treading Russian soil at Vladivostók, on the 14-th May 1891, on his way back from the Far East.

Your Imperial Highness!

„Having given the order to build a continuous line of railway across Siberia, which is to unite the rich Siberian provinces with the railway system of the Interior, I entrust to you to declare My will, upon your entering the Russian dominions after your inspection of the foreign countries of the East. At the same time, I desire you to lay the first stone at Vladivostók for the construction of the Ussúri line, forming part of the Siberian Railway, which is to be carried out at the cost of the State and under direction of the Government. Your participation in the achievement of this work will be a testimony to My ardent desire to facilitate the communications between Siberia and the other countries of the Empire, and to manifest My extreme anxiety to secure the peaceful prosperity of this Country“.

I remain your sincerely loving

ALEXANDER.

The question of the construction of the Great Siberian Railway, which for a third of a century had occupied the attention of the Government and

General view of the Siberian train by the saloon.

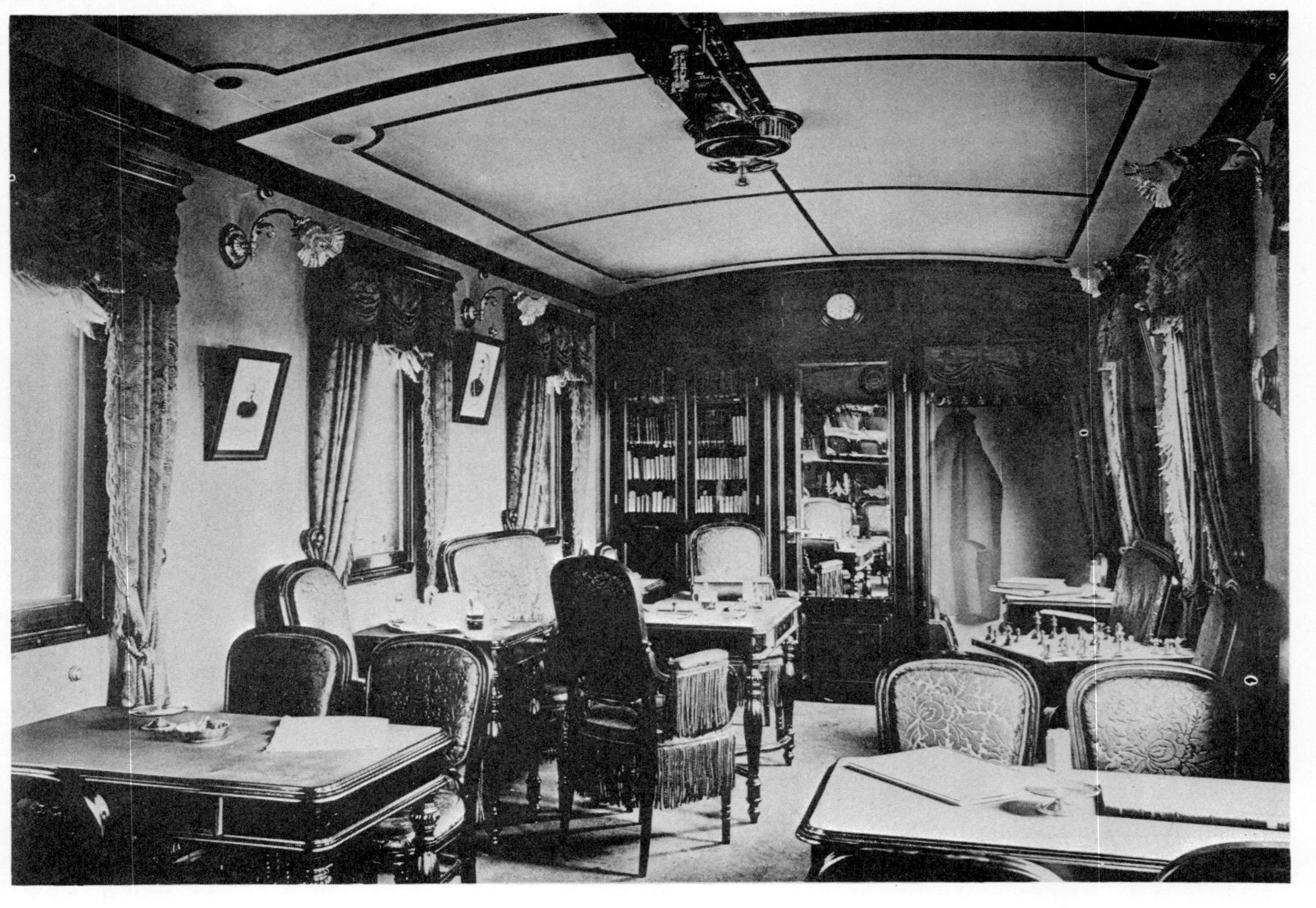

Dining saloon (view of the library).

society, was now settled, representing the most important event of the century, not only in our country, but in the whole world.

On the 19-th May, at Vladivostók, His Imperial Highness the Grand Duke Tsesarévich, with his own hands filled a wheelbarrow with earth and emptied it on the embankment of the future Ussúri line, and then laid the first stone for the construction of the Great Siberian Railway.

Actual Privy Councillor State Secretary Kulomzín, Secretary to the Committee of Ministers and to the Siberian Railway Committee.

In the same year, surveys were carried out from west and east, the results of which made it possible to establish the course to be pursued in the Great Work, which were the subject of preliminary discussion by the special conference on the 21 November 1892. The following points, included in a note by State Secretary Witte, the Minister of Finance, were submitted to this conference:

1) Determination of the order of construction.

2) Means for the construction of the Siberian line.

3) Successive construction of sections in connexion with subsidiary enterprises.

4) Organisation of the Committee for the Siberian Railway.

The resolution of the Committee, based on the opinion of State Secretary Witte, and sanctioned by the Emperor at Gátchino on the 10 December 1892, included the following points:

I) The division of the work into three parts; the first comprising the construction of the West-Siberian line, from Cheliábinsk to the river Ob, a distance of 1328 versts; the Mid-Siberian line, from the river Ob to Irkútsk, 1754 versts, and the termination of the Vladivostók-Gráfskaya line, as well as the construction of the branch line (uniting the Urál mining line and the Siberian Railway), the necessity of the last being urged by the Minister of Agriculture and Imperial Domains.

The second part included the construction of the Gráfskaya-Khabárovsk line, 347 versts, and that of Mysováya along the shore of the Baikál to Srétensk, 1009 versts. The third comprised the line running round the Baikál, 292 versts, and the section from Srétensk to Khabárovsk of about 2000 versts.

The following dates were fixed for the termination of the works: the sections from Cheliábinsk to the Ob, and from thence to Krasnoyársk, 2059 versts, were to be finished in 1896; the Krasnoyársk—Irkútsk section of 1023 versts, in 1900; the branch line to Ekaterinbúrg, in 1894; the section from Vladivostók to Gráfskaya, in 1894—95. At the same time it was proposed to develope subsidiary enterprises, such as the colonisation of the fertile West-Siberian districts in connexion with the progress of peasant emigration, the extension of water communications, and the growth of some branches of mining industry.

II) The Acting Minister of Ways of Communication was requested to present without delay to the Committee of Ministers and to the State Council for their confirmation, the direction and estimates of the lines to be first constructed.

III) A sum of R. 150,000,000 was appropriated for the construction of the Siberian Railway, including from R. 14,000,000 to R. 22,000,000 for subsidiary objects.

IV) It was decided to organise a special Committee, to be styled the Siberian Railway Committee under the presidentship of a person appointed by the Emperor.

On the 14-th January 1893, His Imperial Highness the Grand Duke Tsesarévich, the present Emperor Nicholas II, by a rescript of His Imperial Father was appointed President of the Committee. On the 15-th January 1893, Actual Privy Councillor Bunge was named Vice-President; the management of the business of the Committee was entrusted to the Secretary of the Committee of Ministers and the expedition of business was concentrated in the Chancery of that Committee.

At its first meeting on the 10-th February 1893, His Imperial Highness the Grand Duke Tsesarévich addressed the following words to the members of the Committee:

„In opening the first meeting of the Committee for the construction of the Siberian Railway, I contemplate with emotion the grandeur of the task before us. But love of my country and an ardent desire to contribute to its welfare, have induced me to accept the commission from my beloved Father. I am convinced that you are animated by the same feelings, and that our joint efforts will bring us to the desired end".

The composition of the Committee was decided at this meeting, as follows: the President and the Vice-President appointed by the Emperor, the Ministers of the Interior, Finance, War, Agriculture and State Domains, Ways of Communication and the State Comptroller".

The Committee was entrusted with the direction of the construction of the Siberian line and with the ancillary works connected therewith, while the executive power was left to the Ministers. Matters of legislation laid before the Emperor, were subject to the juridiction of the joint Session of the Members of the Committee and of the Department of the State Council. This resolution was sanctioned by Imperial ukaz given to the Senate on the 24 th February 1893.

The execution of the construction of the Siberian Railway was at first entrusted to the Board of State Railways but, upon the further development of operations, a special board for the construction of this Railway was organised, according to the Imperial command of the 5-th June 1893, in the Central Administration of the Ministry of Ways of Communication in which, under the chief direction of the Minister, was concentrated the executive power for the construction of the Siberian Railway.

The Central Administration of the Ministry of Ways of Communication was reorganised on the 1 July 1899, and the special Board for the construction of the Siberian Railway included in the general Administration for the construction of all the Russians Railways in the Emqire.

Since the institution of this Committee, all the affairs regarding the construction of the Siberian Railway and the organisation of the auxiliary works, were submitted to the consideration of the Committee, whose resolutions together with those of the Department of State Economy of the State Council, required the direct sanction of the Emperor.

After the decease of his Imperial Father, the present Emperor Nicholas Alexándrovich retained the post of President of the Committee of the Siberian Railway.

At the meeting held on the 30-th November 1894, which was the first after his ascension to the throne, His Imperial Majesty addressed the following memorable words to the members of the Committee and of the Department of State Economy:

„Gentlemen! To have begun the construction of the railway line across Siberia is one of the greatest achievements of the glorious reign of my never to be forgotten Father. The fulfilment of this essentially peaceful work, entrusted to me by my beloved Father, is my sacred duty and my sincere desire. With your assistance, I hope to complete the construction of the Siberian line, and to have it done cheaply and, most important of all, quickly and solidly."

After having heard the gracious words of His Imperial Majesty, the Vice-President of the Committee, Actual Privy Councillor Bunge expressed as follows the loyal feelings of all the members:

„We are most happy that in accordance with Your Imperial Majesty's desire, the work of construction of the Siberian Railway will remain under Your Majesty's immediate direction. At the time of Your visit to distant lands, Your Majesty took the first step at Vladivostók towards the execution of the Siberian Railway. Upon Your Majesty's return, You were appointed President of the Committee for the construction of the Siberian line by the late Emperor, Who thus assured the fulfilment of the task entrusted to the Committee, which always was the object of Your constant endeavour. At present, Your Majesty having desired to retain the direction of this vast enterprise, which is to connect European Russia with the shore of the Pacific Ocean, we are convinced that this grand work bequeathed to Your Majesty by Your Imperial Father, will be brought to a successful end and constitute the glory of the late and present reigns".

Strictly following the plan set by the Emperor Pacificator, the Committee always endeavoured to satisfy as far as possible the various requirements attached to the execution of the grand work in Asia.

The activity of the Committee, directed towards the moral and material renewal and quickening of the productive forces of Siberia and towards the extension of the influence of the Great Siberian Railway over the culture and the economic life of the East, comprised:

1) The construction of the Siberian main line and of other routes in accordance with the interests of the East and with the development of commercial intercourse.

2) The arrangements for the general economic welfare of Siberia and for the revival of its commercial intercourse with the Asiatic Continent.

3) The settlement of the country within the range of the Siberian line, and the regulation of the emigration movement to the East.

The Siberian main line, from Cheliábinsk to Strétensk, has a total length of 4865 versts, and is divided into the following sections: the West-Siberian, 1329 versts, the Mid-Siberian, 1715.5 versts, the Irkútsk-Baikál, 64 versts, the Transbaikál 1035.5 versts, and the Ussúri, 721 versts.

The total length of the railways, connected with the Siberian line and under the control of the Committee, is about 6445⅓ versts, including besides the main line the branch-lines to the landing places of the Siberian rivers, traversed by the main trunk, with a length of 19 versts, the branch-line to Tomsk, 89 versts, and the Ekaterinbúrg-Cheliábinsk line, 226 versts.

The branch-line of the Manchúrian railway, from Kaidálovo to the Chinese frontier, comprises 3241.3 versts; that from Nikólsk to the Chinese frontier, 110 versts; and that from Perm to Kotlás, 812 versts.

The total cost of these railway works under the control of the Committee is R. 355,377,911.

In accordance with the desire of the Monarch Pacificator, this costly Siberian line was constructed exclusively by Russian engineers and with Russian materials.

During the achievement of this work, the principal attention was paid to the speedy and solid construction of the permanent way; the building of stations was to be effected gradually, with a view to economy, and to avoid the risk of useless expenditure, which might result from a false estimate as to the future traffic. The buildings for the accomodation of passengers and goods were to be constructed in proportion as they were called for by the actual requirements. Considerable modifications and technical simplifications were admitted in the construction of the Siberian Railway, with a view to a more speedy execution of the work and a reduction of the expenditure.

Privy Councillor K. Y. Mikhailóvsky, Engineer, Constructor of the West-Siberian Railway.

Thus for example, the gauge of the Siberian line is 2.35 instead of 2.6 sazhéns, the standard usually adopted on European Russian railways; the grades on straight runs are 0.0074 on level, and about 0.0174 on hilly sections; the curves have a radius of 250 and 150 sazhéns, and the depth of the ballasting of the roadbed is reduced; all the engineering works and station buildings are simplified and the rails employed throughout the whole extent of the Siberian Railway are 18 pounds to the foot.

The construction of a branch line to Tomsk, one of the most important intellectual and economic centres of Siberia, was considered necessary by the Committee alike for the development of the existing commercial activity of this city, and to avoid the displacement of other points traversed by the Siberian trunk line

The addition of a branch line connecting the Trans-Siberian with the Manchúrian railway, was also approved after the Russo-Chinese bank, founded in 1896, had received the concession from China for the construction and exploitation of a line within the limits of Manchúria. A joint stock company for the East-Chinese Railway was organised for this purpose.

The plan of this last great work quite abolished the necessity for continuing the Siberian line to the Amúr, attended as this would be by considerable technical difficulties, and put a stop to the construction of the Transbaikál line from Strétensk further East.

Branch lines, running from the Transbaikál and Ussúri railways to the Chinese frontier for a length of 434¹/₃ versts, were to be constructed in place of the abandoned scheme, thus reducing by about 500 versts the distance to be traversed from one terminus of the Siberian Railway to the other.

The branch-line uniting the Trans-Siberian and the Urál railways, was laid down at the end of 1895, with a view to providing for the needs of the Urál mining industry, and for those of Siberia which, although possessing great mineral treasures, had hitherto suffered from a dearth of metal goods and the high prices produced by the insufficient development of mining industry.

For this purpose, the districts including the greatest number of works were selected by the Committee for the route of the line which, commencing at Cheliábinsk, without neglecting the interests of Siberian traffic, was made to join the Urál line at Ekaterinbúrg, the chief mining centre of the Urál.

The project of the line from Perm to Kotlás, situated on the northern Dviná, was laid before the Committee by special Imperial command.

The Committee paid special attention to the establishment of railway communication between Siberia and the port of Archángel by the Urál line and the branch from Ekaterinbúrg to Cheliábinsk. This line would make Archángel an important trading port for Siberia, and greatly contribute to the reanimation of the North, and to the development of our commercial fleet.

The opening of the White Sea route, representing the nearest and most independent outlet for the export abroad of Siberian goods, consisting chiefly of grain, would coincide with the interests of agriculture in Siberia, and save the central districts of Russia from the excessive fall of prices produced by the flow of cheap grain to the interior markets of the Empire and to the Baltic ports.

In the opinion of the Committee, the construction of the Perm-Kotlás line was also necessary for satisfying the local requirements of the North of Russia, and chiefly for securing the food supply of that region. The establishment of a close commercial intercourse between the Siberian governments and the energetic and purely Russian population of the Archangel government, would also favourably influence the development of private enterprise in Siberia.

Endeavouring to develop trade and the exploitation of Siberia, the Committee instituted geological explorations which were carried on along the Railway line in order to ascertain the existence of useful minerals which, like coal, anthracite, iron ores etc., used in the mining industry, were necessary for the exploitation of the railway line.

By order of the Committee, mining parties explored the country from Cheliábinsk to Irkútsk, the Kirgíz steppe and the regions along the Angará river, round Lake Baikál, along the Ussúri line, and along the rivers of the Amúr basin. As a result of these investigations, many useful minerals were discovered near the Siberian main line, and also in more distant spots, which however are easily accessible by branch lines.

Actual State Councillor N. P. Mezhéninov, Engineer Constructor of the Mid-Siberian Railway.

Deposits of fuel were found at many points throughout the course of the Siberian Railway, from the Kirgíz steppe to the coasts of the Pacific Ocean, and the Island of Sakhalín. The untold wealth of Siberia in brown ore and magnetite, the best varieties of iron ore, was once more confirmed by geological parties, which discovered many hitherto unknown deposits.

The few iron works and foundries actually existing in Siberia, although situated in the proximity of rich mineral deposits and well supplied with fuel, do not suffice for the local demand for iron goods. Thanks to the very limited iron industry, the prices are high in Siberia. A few merchants hold a monopoly and charge what they like.

The increasing demand for iron required for household, agricultural and industrial purposes, makes the construction of new iron works absolutely necessary on the Siberian Railway, and especially in the Mid-Siberian and Transbaikál sections where a great number of rich iron mines have been found of late.

Among other useful metals, silver, lead and copper have deen discovered by mining parties at many points near the Railway. The annual output of lead iu the Empire is not much more than 100,000 puds, while an import of 2,000,000 puds only just suffices for its needs; this fact clearly demonstrates the necessity for increasing the exploitation of the mineral wealth of Siberia. Copper smelting is practised on a very limited scale in Siberia, and exists only in ihe Altái mining district, within the confines of His Majesty's Cabinet lands, and in the Kirgíz steppe where it is obtained, either by smelting copper ores or in refining silver. The annual output of copper amounts to about 20,000 puds.

The development of the goldmining industry, which is of first rate importance for the Government and for the economic welfare of Siberia, was also the object of the special solicitude of the Committee.

In view of the wide prospect opened for this industry in Siberia, the Committee recognised the immediate necessity for its technical and statistical economic study, in order to establish the extent of its requirements, and also the value of explorations to ascertain the extension of the gold bearing regions.

At the present time, the gold-mining industry of Siberia, yielding gold to the value of R. 20,000,000, comprises a vast area. Gold is obtained in the Ob, Yeniséi, Léna and Amúr basins, and throughout all the governments of this enormously rich country. All the goldbearing regions on the Ob, Yeniséi and Léna, are situated in the basins of rivers flowing from the east, viz, from the western slopes, falling gradually to the North Siberian plain, of the mountain ridges bounding the basin of the Arctic Ocean on the south.

The strata containing auriferous gravels have a thickness which varies from 2 feet to 3 sazhéns, and are covered by an alluvial soil or turf. They are from 1 to 50 versts in length, and include sometimes uninterrupted beds of auriferous sand fit for exploitation. The proportion of gold is not the same in all the mines: the top of the mine generally contains an accumulation of coarse grained gold, with an admixture of quartz, magnetic iron ore and pyrites; in the middle of the mine, the gold grains are smaller and its richness inferior, while at the bottom the mines contain only gold dust.

The thickness and the width of the gold strata vary greatly. In Siberia auriferous quartz is found in the Yeniséisk government, on the Altái, in connexion with silver in the Zyriánov and Ríddersk mines, and in the Transbaikál region. Several beds of gold ore have been discovered more lately in the Maríinsk district of the Tomsk government.

The first step towards a more complete study of the mining industry of Siberia was made in 1895 by the organisation of a special commission attached to the mining department, comprising representatives of different departments entrusted with the collection and elaboration of all the particulars of the gold mining industry, and with the establishment of a programme for the exploration of the auriferous regions.

One of the problems of the commission was to shew clearly and in a popular form the actual extent of gold mining in the Empire, others consisted in the collection of materials and the making of calculations, which were to serve as a basis for the more accurate elaboration of the general plan and programme for future geological, technical and statistical-economic investigations.

According to the data obtained, it appears that, with few exceptions, gold is at present obtained in Siberia by washing machines of very primitive construction, the goldbearing regions are but imperfectly exploited, and the mines unsufficiently worked, while two thirds of them are entirely undeveloped for want of capital and workmen. Some technical improvements in the working of gold mines are being adopted now at a few places; thus for example, in the Lensk district, gold is washed in winter with warm water; in the Amúr territory, dredging machines are employed, and the work time is extended by washing the ore in the night by electric light. The resolution of the Committee of Ministers sanctioned by the Emperor in 1898, permitting during 10 years (till the 1 January 1909) the free import of foreign machinery and appliances required for the mining industry in Siberia and the Urál, will surely, in the near future, contribute to the development of a more regular exploitation and of a greater production of gold by enlarging the districts worked, and getting a greater quantity of gold from the existing fields.

The greater part of Siberia's mineral wealth is as yet lying waste, and is even scarcely known; the results of the extensive and varied investigations carried out within the range of the Great Siberian Railway, will undoubtedly attract promoters who, on the basis of the existing information, will find application for their capital and labour, and duly develop many branches of the mining industry, for which Siberia offers the most advantageous conditions.

The progress of economic life in Siberia produced by the Great Railway, marked by the increase of freights over the water systems of Siberia, raised the question of improving the navigation on the Siberian rivers, which represent the chief natural branches and feeding lines of the main railway. With this in view, the Committee selected the water-ways of the Ob basin. Accordingly a department of ways of communication was organised at Tomsk in 1895. Further, the channels of the rivers Turá, Toból, Irtysh, Ob and Tom were put in order, and water-gauges and meteorological stations established. The exploration of the Shílka, Ussúri and Amúr rivers has been undertaken with a view to facilitating navigation of the Amúr system; their fair-ways have been straightened and cleared, and a special dapartment for the management of the water-ways belonging to this basin has been organised for the same purpose. Considerable expenditure was required for the improvement of the navigation on the Angará and for a provisional steamboat service established for the shipment of railway materials and especially for the conveyance of the heavy and bulky parts of the icebreaker for the Baikál.

The Committee gave special attention to the regulation of the navigation on the Baikál, closely connected with the interests of the railway traffic, for which this lake is one of the most important natural factors. The Committee is further anxious to insure the regular navigation of the Baikál, in order to develop the economic growth of the localities situated on its shores, endowed with fisheries and mineral deposits.

A special commission was entrusted with the detailed study of the Baikál, and with the collection and registration of topographical, meteorological and astronomical observations in its basin. Its principal object was to secure safe navigation by making a map, placing pilot marks and buoys.

In order to establish regular water communication with Siberia and encourage the industry of the North, the Committee organised special expeditions for the hydrographic exploration of the sea route to the mouths of the Ob and Yeniséi, and for the description of the straits of the Yúgorsky Shar and Kára Sea, and the islands Bély and Vilkítsky.

After having selected the town of Vladivostók on the coast of the Pacific Ocean as the commercial port of the terminus of the Siberian Railway, the Committee occupied itself with the organisation in the bay of the Golden Horn of the necessary facilities for foreign trade and for our navy.

An icebreaker purchased in Denmark was put to work in the port of Vladivostók in order to maintain navigation uninterrupted in winter, which is of great importance for our commerce and for our Pacific squadron.

The Russo-Chinese Bank, founded on the 27-th August 1896, for the commercial transactions of Eastern Asia, contributed to a great extent to the promotion of Russian trade with China and Japan in the Far East, brought nearer by the Great Siberian Railway to the centres of trade and consumption in Europe. The East-China Railway Company, entrusted by the Bank with the construction and the working of a railway line within the confines of China, began operations by building a line from Port-Arthúr to the town of Nikólsk situated at the junction of the Littoral and Manchúrian Railways, which was to serve as a link to the Great Siberian line.

The Imperial founder of the Great Siberian Railroad attached special importance to the settlement of the regions traversed by it, regarding emigration as a factor which in Russian history had always tended to secure Russian dominion and Russian culture, and would serve as a stronghold of orthodoxy and Russian law in Siberia.

According to the plan of the late Emperor, His Imperial Majesty Nicholas II expressed the desire to give a more conscious and regular character to the emigration movement, and to prevent such emigration from injuriously affecting the economic condition of the settlers. For this purpose the Committee made all sorts of arrangements to harmonise with the former life of the peasants at home, meeting their needs on the road and facilitating their settlement in the new locality.

To ascertain the prospects offered by emigration to Siberia, and to avoid false information, villagers who intend to emigrate have the right to previously send a pioneer to examine the places of future settlement. These men travelling at a reduced fare and subsidised with grants of money, are allowed the right to choose land for the families left behind, as being better able than any else to form exact notions as regards colonisation in Siberia. Short but exact descriptions of Siberia, including the general regulations for peasant emigration were spread among the population with the same object. Special land surveying parties, sent by the Ministry of Agriculture and State Domains to assist the settlers, are entrusted with the exploration of the cultivable areas fit for colonisation, traversed by the Great Siberian Railway, and with the surveying of the lands allotted to the emigrants.

With the continued growth of the movement and its expansion over wider regions, in 1896 was begun the settlement of the taigá or urmán districts adjacent to the railway line, a measure of much importance for colonisation in general, as it greatly extends the limits of the cultivable area.

The settlement of the steppe lands, which are well suited for agriculture, has been carried into effect at the same time.

Engineer A. N. Púshechnikov, Constructor of the Transbaikál Railway.

The interests of the indigenous nomad population, the Kirgíz, have been taken into consideration during the colonisation of the steppe regions; detailed investigations of the natural history and statistics of the Akmolínsk, Semipalátinsk and partly of the Turgái steppes, have been made with a view to determining the extent of the districts occupied by the nomads, and of the free lands which might be allotted to emigrants, without damage to the aborigenes. In arranging the allotments for settlers, care was taken that they might include land suitable for cultivation and be sufficiently provided with water. Since the first organisation of these survey and allotment parties, including the work done in 1898, 5,744,000 desiatins have been assigned for accomodation of settlers along the Siberian Railway, of which 4,308,000 are already occupied.

The land statistics give about 5,000,000 surplus desiatíns of Kirgíz land in the Akmolínsk territory, which are partly to be colonised. The unfavourable hydrographic conditions of the Ishím and Barabá steppes traversed by the Railway, within the confines of the Akmolínsk territory and the Tobólsk and Tomsk governments, necessitate the organisation of an irrigation system for these localities.

The hydrotechnical parties sent by the Ministry of Agriculture and State Domains have undertaken the regulation of the irrigation of the scantily watered emigrant lands in the Ishím steppe, and the drainage of the swampy Barabá steppe.

Putting a free land-fund at the disposal of the settlers, the Committee at the same time has taken measures to provide them with the due authorisation and to supply them with grants of money for travelling expenses. It has further organised medical and feeding stations along the road. Every emigrant suffering from an infectious disease is detained at Cheliábinsk, the starting point of the Siberian railroad. The medical and feeding stations are organised at the points of the railway where the emigrants leave the train and continue their journey with horses. At these stations, they get gratuitous medical assistance and hot food at very low rates. Loans of money for the installation of the household, seed-corn, and timber for housebuilding are also allotted to settlers. Special stores of necessary household furniture and of timber, obtainable by the settlers at low prices or instead of money loans, are organised at places where forests are scarce and the supply of wood attended with difficulty.

The Committee is not only solicitous for the material welfare of the settlers in their new dwelling places, but also provides for their spiritual wants by the building of churches and primary schools in the new settlements.

The topographical conditions of the cultivable zone of Siberia require a considerable distance between the settlements, which places the Russian colonist in a very isolated position. The few parish churches, which very of ten are situated at some distance from the villages, are hardly accessible to the whole of the population. In this respect, the emigrants settling amidst nomad Mohammedans in the steppes are in a still worse condition.

Dwelling sometimes at a distance of 150 to 200 versts from the orthodox churches of the Cossack villages, they are visited for the performance of the rites of the church by the clergy of these temporary parishes not more than twice a year.

The number of national schools in Siberia is also very small.

The Siberian Railway plays a part of the first importance in the creation of churches and schools. The stations, although situated at a considerable distance from existing churches, become fresh centres of population. Further, at stations distinguished by a large traffic, are concentrated considerable numbers of railway officials, while some stations have become centres of the emigration movement, whence emigrants start for the inspection or definite settlement of the localities indicated for the purpose.

The first step towards the building of churches and schools was taken by the Emperor-Pacificator, followed in 1894 by an appeal to public benefi-

Actual Privy Councillor Engineer O. P. Viázemsky, Constructor of the Ussúri Railway.

cence, and by the establishment of a fund for the construction of churches and schools in Siberia, sanctioned by the present Emperor and entitled the Fund of the late Emperor Alexander III. This has afforded the means for the building of a number of churches and schools to meet the requirements of the numerous population.

The sum of R. 21,800,000, or R. 4,000 per verst, have been assigned at various times in addition to the total expenditure for the construction of the Siberian Railway, with a view to organising auxiliary works, settling the localities contiguous to the railway line, and developing trade and industry in Siberia.

In making the vast outlay of several hundred million rubls for the construction of the great Siberian Railway, the Government did not expect in the near future to get a strictly commercial return. Its profit was based on numerous elements of increase in the national economy, conjectural and incapable of arithmetical calculation, connected with the commercial and industrial development of the country.

Church-car.

The Railway exercised however such a mighty influence on the growth of economic life in Siberia that its commercial success far exceeds the most extravagant expectations.

Upon the opening of provisional traffic on the West Siberian Railway in 1895, and of regular traffic in October 1896, the means at its disposal were far from sufficing for the transport and conveyance of the passengers and goods which presented themselves. In order to obviate this difficulty, thirty one sidings were added in 1896—1898 to facilitate the traffic, while the rolling stock was increased by thirty locomotives and 600 carriages. However during the winter af 1899, 7,000 waggons carrying over 5,000,000 puds of goods blocked the line.

The following figures illustrate the increase of passenger and goods traffic:

The West Siberian Railway conveyed in 1896: 160,000 passengers, 169,000 emigrants, and 10,500,000 puds of various goods; in 1897—236,000 passengers, 78,000 emigrants, and 21,190,000 puds of goods; in 1898—379,000 passengers, 195,000 emigrants and 30,000,000 puds of goods.

The Mid-Siberian Railway conveyed in 1897—177,000 passengers and 5,393,000 puds of goods; in 1898—476,000 passengers and 11,000,000 puds of goods.

On the West Siberian Railway, which was first opened, the passenger traffic increased by 50 percent and the goods traffic by still more.

Further progress in the development oi the traffic of the Great Siberian

Interior of the Church-car.

Railway is certain, especially upon the junction of the main line with the port on the Pacific Ocean, when there will be continuous railway communication between Europe and the East of Asia, and there will be created the safest, quickest, cheapest and most convenient route. Brought into connexion with the network of European railways and running through the Russian Empire for a distance of about 10,000 versts, the Siberian Railway mostly traverses cultivated and productive countries, uniting their commercial centres and offering new outlets and prospects for Russian and international intercourse and trade. It must be mentioned that China, Japan and Korea, comprising a total population of about 460,000,000 souls, and having a foreign trade to the amount of R. 500,000,000 gold, are yet far from having fully developed their commerce with Europe. Upon the completion of the Manchurian railway, they will be able to take a greater share in the international market, thanks to the Great Siberian Railway, constituting a most important factor in the further development of trade.

At the present time, Europe communicates with Asia via the Suez Canal by means of four great steamship companies: the Peninsular and Oriental, the Messageries Maritimes, and the German and Austrian Lloyds and the lesser companies: the Russian Steamship and Trading C° and the Volunteer Fleet. They all work well, but do not suffice to meet the demand for transport, so that it is necessary to apply in good time in the case of both passengers and goods.

Considering Moscow as the centre of Russia, and London and Shanghai as the termini for foreign trade, it appears that the voyage from Moscow, via Odéssa to Vladivostók, requires not less than forty days, and costs R. 600 for first class cabin passengers, and R. 450 for second class passengers while the passage from London to Shanghai requires from 34 to 36 days, and costs from R. 650 to R. 900.

The journey from Moscow to Vladivostók or Port-Arthur, comprising a distance of about 8,000 versts, at the rate of 30 versts an hour and with the existing tariff, will take ten days, and cost R. 114 first class, by fast train, inclusive of Government tax and sleeping accomodation; R. 74 second class, and R. 51 third class, by post train. Without sleeping car, the fares are R. 89, R. 56, and R. 36.

According to this calculation, the journey from London to Shanghai includes: three days from London to Moscow, cost R. 125, ten days from Moscow to Vladivostók, cost R. 114, three days from Vladivostók to Shanghai, cost R. 80, or a total of 16 days and R. 319. The journey second class costs R. 200, third class-about R. 130.

The conveyance by the Siberian Railway will be over twice as quick as and 2½ times cheaper than that now existing. By increasing the speed up to that adopted in Europe, the journey from London to Shanghai will be reduced to ten days.

There can be no doubt that, besides the international mails of Europe and Eastern Asia, the greater part of the more vaulable goods, as well as such as are liable to spoil or require to be conveyed rapidly, will go by the Great Siberian Main Line.

All these considerations relative to the actual progress and to the future importance of the Siberian Railway, led to the organisation of a commission in 1898, for establishing the necessary facilities for the increase of the through traffic and means of transport on the Siberian Railway. Its result shewed that the Siberian line, uniting as it does the European and Asiatic markets, and running a distance of 10,000 versts through countries promising a great development of industry, will soon acquire an immense importance for local traffic and for international transit, with a view to which, it must be made equal to the future wants of the home and foreign passenger and goods traffic.

Arrangements for a more extensive organisation were deemed most necessary by the Committee to meet the interests of the public and, in view of the unexpected commercial success of the Siberian Railway which, as is estimated, upon its completion, will have an annual revenue of about R. 8,000,000. Even this amount will in time be exceeded, and R. 16,000,000 will not be too high a figure, if we include all the indirect benefits which may be expected by the Government.

The estimated cost of these additional facilities, required for the Siberian Railway, from Cheliábinsk to the station Kaidalóvo (united by a branch line with the Manchurian railway) is R. 91,316,791 inclusive of the expenditure for the increase of the capacity for through traffic and conveyance, the introduction of a higher speed, the replacement of the light by heavy rails, and the improvement of the roadway.

The rapid increase in the profits of the Great Siberian Railway, connected with the general economic growth of Siberia, strikingly illustrates the effect produced upon civilisation and commerce by this great work, which will serve as a monument to the reign of the Tsar Pacificator and to the Russian Slavonic nation, which is destined to propagate Christianity and civilisation in the East of Asia.

Sections of the Great Siberian Line already built and in course of construction.

COMMENCEMENT.		SECTION.	Length in versts.	Cost of line in rubls.	Cost of rolling stock in rubls.	Working capital in rubls.	Opening of regular traffic.
1892	7 July.	West-Siberian.......	1329	37,571,940	9,552,758	1,200,000	1 Oct. 1896.
1894	Summer.	Ekaterinbúrg Cheliábinsk branch	226	6,2026,40	—	—	10 Oct. 1896.
1893	May.	Mid-Siberian I Section.	711	31,541,481	4,715,690	624,000	1 Jan. 1898.
1894	Summer.	II section	1004 1/2	65,133,379	6,646,085	888,000	— 1898.
1896	Summer.	Tomsk Branch	89	2,494,198	—	79,000	1 Jan. 1898.
		Irkútsk-Baikál Branch.	64	3,626,336	—	—	— 1899.
1895	11 April.	Transbaikál	1035 1/2	54,992,381	3,258,000	1,000,000	In course of construction.

COMMENCEMENT.		SECTION.	Length in versts.	Cost of line in rubls.	Cost of rolling stock in rubls.	Working capital in rubls.	Opening of regular traffic.
1897	—	Kaidalóvo Chinese frontier	324 1/3	25,281,278	2,727,600	314,280	In course of construction.
1894	3 July.	North-Ussúri	339	20,365,033	2,093,846	579,200	1 Nov. 1897.
1891	19 May.	South-Ussúri	382	19,117,229	1,466,250	681,000	1 Febr. 1896.
1897	—	Nikólsk Chinese frontier	110	8,046,867	811,120	176,000	In course of construction.
		Total . . .	5614 1/3	274,372,762	20,271,379	5,571,480	

The Samara-Zlatoust Railway.

Importance of the line as connecting the Russian European railways with the Siberian trunk.—Its divisions and the time of construction.—Topography.—The economic and commercial conditions of the localities traversed by the Railway.—Guide from Batrakí to Cheliábinsk.—Description of the stations and environs.—Effect of the railway.—Batrakí.—Samára.—Kinél.—Krotóvka.—Cherkásskaya.—Buguruslán.—Abdúlino.—Belebéi - Aksákovo.—Davlekánovo.—Yumátovo.—Ufá.—Miniár.—Tímskoe.—Kropachévo.—Ust-Katáv.—Viazováya.—Suleyá.—Zlatoúst.—Urzhúmka.—Syrostán (Asiatic frontier).—Miás.—Cheliábinsk.—Emigration medical and food station.—Importance of the Cheliábinsk station as the junction of three railways.—The Cheliábinsk-Ekaterinbúrg and Perm-Tiumén line.—Chief points along the railways.—Description of the towns of Ekaterinbúrg and Tiumén.—Commercial operations of the Perm-Tiumén railway.—Bibliography.

The Samára-Zlatoúst line represents the principal link between the network of railways in European Russia and the main Siberian line. Commencing at the station of Batrakí, the terminus of the Syzràn-Viázma railway, situated on the western or right bank of the Vólga, the line runs eastwards a distance of 1,057 versts and terminates at Cheliábinsk, which is the junction of three railways: the Samára-Zlatoúst, West-Siberian and Perm-Tiumén lines. The construction of the Samára-Zlatoúst line was divided into the following sections: 1) Batrakí-Kinél, 155 versts, belonging to the Orenbúrg railway, constructed in 1875—1876, including a bridge over the Vólga, and opened to traffic in 1880; 2) Kinél-Ufá, 452 versts, open to traffic in 1888; 3) Ufá-Zlatoúst, 299 versts, completed in 1890; 4) Zlatoúst-Cheliábinsk, 151 versts, open to traffic in 1892.

The sections of this line have been successively constructed by the engineer Mikhailóvsky under the direction of the Government, with the exception of the first section, which was constructed by a joint stock company, and passed under the management of the Government in 1893 together with the Orenburg line. Commencing at the eastern border of the Simbírsk govern ment, the railway line, throughout its extensive course, runs from west to east through the central parts of the Samára and Ufá governments, and terminates at Cheliábinsk, situated on the northern frontier of the Orenbúrg government.

The topography of this line is very varied. In its extreme western section, from Batrakí station to Kinél, it runs through a level and almost steppe country, only interrupted by hills near the river Pádovka at the 138-th verst. At this point, the conditions for the construction of the line are more favourable: its maximum grades are 0.010 (both ways) and the maximum radius 250 sazhens, it has 50.63% of horizontal sections, and 82.275% of straight runs throughout its course. In the Kinél-Ufá section, the line passes mainly through a level country, where straight sections and horizontal planes predominate. Its ruling grades are .008 in the direction from Ufá to Kinél, where a greater goods traffic is expected, and .010 in the reverse direction; the maximum radius for curves is 200 sazhens; 39.82% of its total length is taken up by horizontal planes, and 71.24% by straight sections. The Ufá-Zlatoúst section is essentially mountainous, the line has a most irrigular profile and a great number of curves. There is a maximum grade of .0085 in the direction of the expected greatest goods traffic, while the maximum radius of curves is reduced to 150 sazhens; horizontal planes form 26.66%, and straight sections 54.53% of the total length.

The extreme eastern section, Zlatoúst-Cheliábinsk, is mostly hilly, as far as the station Cherbakúl, whence it changes into level country towards Cheliábinsk. The line crosses the highest point of the Urál chain between the stations Zlatoúst and Urzhúmka, a section which has also numerous grades and curves. The maximum rate of both is the same as on the Ufá-Zlatoúst line, but the horizontal planes form only 21.30%, and the straight sections 55.66% of the total length. This section is characterised by a zigzag of four versts between the stations of Zlatoúst and Urzhúmka, by which the line ascends to the principal ridge of the Urál, having in a direct line only 400 sazh. from end to end.

The section, comprising a distance of 286 versts, from the station of Ashá to Cherbakúl, intersected by the Urál chain, is mainly hilly. The line proceeds along rocky ravines, winding its course on the banks of sinuous mountain streams, crossing cliffs through cuttings and passing alternately from one side to the other of the rivers it meets. This district is peculiarly picturesque and' with its various constructions answering to local conditions, presents also great technical interest.

The Samàra-Zlatoúst line may be divided into the following four sections in regard to its economic position, industry and technical conditions:

From Batrakí to Ufà, running a distance of 607 versts, the line passes through a country where manufacturing industry is but little developed, and where the inhabitants are mainly engaged in agriculture and cattle raising. Beyond the Ufà, the line traverses a wooded district, where besides agriculture and cattle-breeding, forestry holds an important position. From Miniàr to Miàs, the line runs a distance of 244 versts, through a country with a predominating mining and metallurgic industry.

Beyond Miäs, near Cheliábinsk, the country is level, and tge population is engaged in agriculture and cattle-breeding and, within tge confines of the eastern Uràl, in gold-mining.

Along the course of the railway, the Samàra government (pop. 2,763,478: 1,365,215 m., 1.398.263 f.) has tho most extensive trade, especially in grain, which is despatched from all the stations of the agricultural zone, principally from Samára, Cherkásskaya, Buguruslán and Abdúlino.

The total freights sent and received by the stations situated within this government amount to 40,000,000—50,000,000 puds, exclusive of freights in transit. The goods traffic on the railway traversing the Ufá government (pop. 2,277,158; 1,116,541 m., 1,160,617 f.) increases every year, in connexion with the expansion of the region under cultivation and with the progress of mining industry. At present the quantity of goods conveyed to and from the stations of the Ufá government exceeds 20,000,000 puds. The stations of Belebéi-Aksákovo and Devlekánovo may be held to take the first place as regards grain export.

The following iron-works situated along the railway line also yield a considerable quantity of metal goods for conveyance by rail: the Simsk works

Railway line near the station of Miniár (phot. by Arséntiev.)

(Miniár, Simsk and Nikoláev) belonging to Mr. Balashóv; the Katávsk works (Ust-Katávsk, Katáv-Ivánov) of Prince Belosélsky-Belozérsky; the Yuruzánsk works of Mr. Sukhozanét, and the Government works of the Zlatoúst district (Sátkin, Kúsinsk and Zlatoúst). All these works produce pig-iron, iron rails and fastenings; the Government works produce in addition shells and side-arms.

The Samára-Zlatoúst railway comprises a total of 56 stations:

1) **Batrakí**. Buffet. (53°9′ of N. lat., 18°23′ E. long., 1500 v. from St. Petersburg, 896 v. from Moscow, 1057 v. from Cheliábinsk). The station is situated near

the village of Batrakí on the right bank of the Vólga, in the Syzrán district of the Simbírsk government, and has a convenient wharf for steamers and other craft. The village contains a population of 2,500, a church and a school. Many of the peasants occupy themselves with gardening and have fine orchards.

The naphtha masters Nóbel, Dochár and Bóberman, have constructed large reservoirs near the station for the storage of naphtha and petroleum, 10,000,000 puds of which are brought here by barges, whence they are forwarded by the Syzrán-Viázma railway in special tanks to the interior governments. A smaller quantity is conveyed further east by the Samára-Zlatoúst railway. Deposits of asphalt occur along the Vólga banks, which is converted into mastic at the factory established by a company near the village of Batrakí.

From the station, the line runs east along the right bank of the Vólga, crossing the river at the 8-th verst by the Alexander bridge, so named in honour of the Emperor Alexander II. This bridge is worthy of consideration on account of its dimensions and the technical details of its construction. It has 13 spans of 50 sazhens each, a total length of 650 sazhens and a distance of 674.125 sazhens between abutments. It is built on the double girder system with parallel chords, and road-way upon the lower chord; the rails are laid on metal beams; the piers and abutments are made of stone, and the ice-breakers are covered with granite brought from Finland. All the piers are laid on caissons, the right abutment rests on the rock, while the left is supported on piles.

Beyond the bridge, the line after reaching the left bank of the Vólga passes through the Samàra government along the Vólga valley, only quitting the river in order to avoid spring floods and the engineering work involved.

2) **Obshárovka** (17 v.), 3) **Mylnaya** (32 v.), 4) **Bezenchúk** (56 v.); 5) **Tomylovo** (79 v.), 6) **Lipiági** (101 v.), 7) **Kriazh** (109 v.). All these stations are situated in the Vólga valley. The line here traverses a mountainous country, affording however favourable conditions of construction

Between the stations Bezenchúk and Tomylovo, it crosses the river Mócha on a bridge 40 sazhens in length. The stations of Obshárovka and Kriazh have some importance, being the points whence cattle and animal products are forwarded from the Samára and Orenbúrg steppes.

There are several mills near the station of Obshárovka, producing annually about one million puds. Two steam flour-mills belonging to Bashkírov with a daily output of 3,000 puds, stand near the station Bezenchúk. Close to the station of Kriazh is the mill of Shikobálov grinding about a million puds of grain a year, and a shambles where about 200,000 sheep are killed yearly. Upon approaching Samára, the line runs closer to the Vólga, and crosses its right tributary, the river Samára, on a bridge 120 sazhens in length with three spans of 40 sazhens each.

8) **Samára.** Buffet (116 v.). The railway station is situated near the government town of Samára on the left bank of the Vólga, at its junction with the river Samára (pop. 91,654; 53° 11' N. lat.; 19° 46.5' E. long.).

The Samára government contains an area of 132,724 square versts divided into seven districts: Samára, Stavropól, Bugulmínsk, Buguruslán, Buzulúk, Nikoláev, Novouzénsk. Its surface offers scarcely any variety, although there is a noticeable difference between its northern and southern portions, delimited by the river Samára, flowing through the government in a north-western direction. The northern portion, including the Bugulmínsk, Buguruslán. Stavropól and part of the Samára and Buzulúk districts, is mountainous; the suthern part, comprising the remainder of the Samára and Buzulúk districts, and those of Nikoláev and Novouzénsk, presents a steppe. In the north of the government, the soil consists of clayey blackearth or sand. The subsoil is formed of different kinds of clay and, at some points, of sandstone and limestone. On the south, in the eastern portion of the government, the soil consists of sedimentary rocks, while on the west, the steppe

Alexander Bridge on the Vólga.

is chiefly characterised by tertiary and more recent formations. In the first instance, it is represented by a thin layer of argilaceous blackearth which, diminishing in thickness towards the south, further on disappears altogether. The banks of the Vólga have a sandy and blackearth soil, while in this part of the government the subsoil contains clay, limestone and different kinds of slate.

The climate of the Samára government is continental, the highest mean temperature in July being 21.4°, and the lowest in January,—16.2°. In its southern portion, the heat and cold are greater. Near Samára, the Vólga is free of ice from the 16-th April to the 13-th December; thus, the winter lasts four months. The settlement of the Samára government, whose past history is closely connected with that of the Vólga river. the chief water-way of Russia, dates from the end of the XVI century. Its colonisation progressed rapidly after 1764, when the Empress Catherine II permitted the settlement of foreigners and dissenters, granting them considerable immunities. The whole population may be ethnographically divided into the following groups: 1) the Russian Slavonic village and town population forming 68%; 2) the natives belonging to the Finnish race, and represented by Mordvá, Chuvásh, Votiák, and Cheremís (14%), inhabiting the north of the government; 3) the natives of the Mongolian race, the Tatars (2%); 4) those of the Vogúl race, the Bashkírs (8%), and 5) German colonists, forming about (8%) of the total population.

Agriculture is the most important industry in this government, which on account of its physical conditions is one of the most fertile in Russia.

Cattle-raising is practised in its southern portion, which abounds in pastures and salt-marshes. Manufactures are limited to the conversion of the local raw materials, serving as an aid to agriculture. Steam flour-mills and sugar refineries occupy the first place among the local factories.

The town of Samára stretches along the eastern bank of the Vólga, and being situated at the spot where the river causes the most extensive spring floods, is justly considered one of the finest of the Vólga towns. Here the river has a breadth of 600—700 sazhens and turns westwards, forming the long and narrow peninsula called Samárskaya Luká 200 v. in length. The famous Zhíguli hills commence at this point, and run along the right bank, while the Sókol hills stand opposite between the rivers Sok and Samára.

The ridges which are intersected by the bed of the Vólga, gradually fall towards the river, changing into limestone cliffs which have an altitude of 400 to 700 feet. Above Samára, the hills are wooded while, below the town, they are treeless, and contain some asphalt seams. The mouth of the Samára river forms a deep and extensive bay which together with the port can accomodate about 50 vessels. None of the Vólga towns afford more convenient wharves than Samára, situated as it is close to the river, which at this point has a considerable depth. The landing places for passengers and light cargoes lie on the Vólga, while those for grain, furnished with a branch line, are situated on the Samára river, the grain being shipped direct from the warehouses. During high water, vessels are enabled to come almost right up to the storehouses, which greatly facilitates their loading.

The first colonisation of this spot dates from the end of the XVI century (1586), when a stockaded post with earthen bulwarks and ditches was established here on the confines of the Russian domains, for strategical considerations, with a view to restraining the Nogái and Kirgíz-Kaisák tribes and the Free Cossacks. According to an existing legend, the Moscow Metropolitan St. Alexis, on his way to the Golden Horde in 1357, visited the site of the present town, and finding there a pious hermit, gave him his blessing and foretold the founding of a great town. A stone chapel has been built on the banks of the Vólga in commemoration of this event. In 1688, the military post was transformed into a town, which for a long time belonged to the Simbírsk government. The Samára government was created in 1850. The rapidly growing town contains two cathedrals called respectively Voznesénie and Kazán, 22 orthodox churches, the monastery of St. Nicholas, the nunnery of Our Lady of Iberia, a dissenting chapel, four sectarian prayer-houses and a Mohammedan mosque. The number of houses exceeds six thousand, 1362 of which are of stone.

There is a stone theatre, and over 40 schools. Among the latter are two gymnasiums for boys and girls, the professional school of the Emperor Alexander the Blessed, a technical railway school, a seminary, a clergy school, a diocesan school for girls, a school for the education of village women teachers, a local school for assistant surgeons and midwives, and several elementary parish and urban schools. Among the charitable institutions and societies, the most important are: a humane society, the local administration and the ladies' committee of the Red Cross Society, the Society for the Relief of the Poor, and the Mary Soldiers' Children's Home; the Alexis Children's Home, the Nicholas Orphanage, a foundling hospital, a night refuge, a workhouse, a committee of Orthodox missionaries, and three poorhouses. There is a local hospital with 250 beds, with a lying-in room, and a bacteriological station, a lunatic asylum within 10 versts of the town, and a railway hospital.

A bronze monument to the Emperor Alexander II, after the design of the Academician Sherwood, stands in the Alexis square; the pedestal is of Finnish granite. Symbolic figures stand at the feet of the Tsar-Liberator, representing the four most important events of his reign: the liberation of the serfs, the subjugation of the Caucasus, the liberation of the Slavonic tribes, and the conquest of Central Asia.

Banks: branches of the State Bank, of the Nobles' Land Bank, of the Peasants' Land Bank, and of the Vólga-Káma Commercial Bank, and the Samára Town Bank. Private credit institutions of Samára and its environs: the Samára Mutual Credit Co., the Samára District Branch Board of the Mutual Land Credit Co. and the Vólga Bankers and Commissioners Associations Office; the banks of Serbulóv, Níkonov, Kalachóv and the village banks in the Samára, Nikoláev, and Novouzénsk districts.

Periodicals: 1) non-official: Samára Gazette (daily), Samára Messenger, Samara Advertiser. 2) Official: Government Gazette, Diocesan Gazette.

The Alexander Public Library, the reading room of the Emperor Alexander II and the Samára Museum are open every day (on working days from 9 to 1 and from 4 to 9 in the evening, on holidays from 9 to 12). A society for the encouragement of education exists in Samara since 1873. The Society of Doctors and that of Musical and Dramatic Amateurs date from 1882.

Hotels: European, Central, Theatrical. Clubs: Nobles' Assembly, Merchants' Assembly.

There is a kumys sanatorium near the town.

The history of the town is marked by the following events:

1) The visit of the Emperor Alexander the Blessed on the 8—9 September in 1824. He arrived on a steamer by the Vólga, attended by a brilliant suite, on His way to Orenbúrg.

2) The solemn opening of the first government zémstvo meeting by N. P. Mansúrov, governor of Samára, on the 28 February 1865.

3) The arrival of the Tsar Liberator, the Emperor Alexander Nikoláevich with the Grand Duke Tsesarévich, the future Tsar Pacificator and the Grand Duke Vladímir Alexándrovich on the 29 August 1871.

The construction of a railway to Orenbúrg and Zlatoúst transformed Samára into one of the most important grain, cattle and tallow markets of the Empire. The opening of the traffic on the great Siberian Railway still further increased the importance of this town, which became a centre for freights coming from the Far East and Central Asia. The market of Samára attracts a great quantity of grain, which is brought by rail, by water along the Vólga and Samára, and by road from the adjacent villages of the Samára, Buguruslán, Nikoláevsk and Novouzénsk districts. The total yearly dealings in grain in Samára amount to about 18,000,000 puds, including about 12,000,000 puds of wheat. There are private granaries in the town containing about 12,000,000 puds, and others, situated on the Samára river, near the branch line, containing about 7,000,000 puds. Upon the opening of navigation, the grain accumulated in Samára is loaded on barges and forwarded to the towns of Kazán, Nízhni-Nóvgorod, Rybinsk and other commercial centres. Thus Samára is a grain depot, but is not a centre for its conveyance by rail.

The grain of the Samára market is purchased not only by local merchants, but also by strangers. Among the latter the most important are: the St. Petersburg Export Trade Company of Brandt and Co., Messrs Polezháev, who in 1897 puchased about 1,000,000 puds of grain; the Bashkírovs of Nízhni-Nóvgorod; Blinóv (purchaser of 1,800,000 puds), the Rostóvskys of the Russian Company of Export Trade; Vagliano (purchaser of 910,000 puds); Dreifus and Co. of Paris (puchaser of 590,000 puds).

Samára drawing its grain supplies from all the Samára-Zlatoúst line and the Orenbúrg branch line, is at the same time the centre of the wheat flour trade on the Vólga; besides imported flour, its mills situated in the environs of the town produce an average of 10,000,000 puds of flour yearly. These mills belong to the following firms: Shikobálov, Bashkírov, Romashóv, Krásikov, Shadrín. The sale of the flour and grain is mainly effected in summer to the Vólga towns, whither they are conveyed in steamers in considerable quantities.

An elevator on the bin system holding 300,000 puds of grain, supplied with machinery for loading, is situated near the railway station.

From Samára station, the line proceeds along the river of the same name.

9) **Smyshliáevka.** (136 versts). Having crossed the river Pádovka on a bridge 10 sazhens in length, the line ascends the hills and having reached the siding Pádovka, situated at their highest point, descends from this altitude and crosses the river Great Kinél, a tributary of the Samára, by a bridge 60 sazhens in length.

10) **Kinél.** Buffet (155 v.). From here a branch line runs south-west for a distance of 353 versts towards the town of Orenbúrg. This branch commences its course on the right bank of the Samára, and traverses the elevation between the rivers Samára and Kulutúk, the latter being a tributary of the Kinél. Further on, it crosses to the left bank of the Samára by a bridge of 100 sazhens long near the town of Buzulúk, and reaches the source of this river near the station Perevolótskaya, situated on the watershed of the Samára and Urál. Here the line commences its ascent and reaches the Orenbúrg government along the slope of the Obshchi Syrt. Coming to its highest point at the 304 verst, the line descends toward Orenbúrg.

The greater portion of this branch line is included within the confines of the Samára government, and terminates in the north-western corner of the Orenbúrg government, within a distance of 63 versts from the frontier of Samára. Throughout its entire course, the line runs through a steppe country, where the population is mainly engaged in agriculture and cattle breeding. The following stations are the most important on the line as regards the quantity of forwarded freights:

1) **Bórskaya** station (74 v. from Kinél), situated near the trading village of Bórskoye with a population of 4,000, belonging to the Buguruslán district (grain).

2) **Buzulúk** (129 v. from Kinél), within 2 versts of the town of the same name with a population of 14,000 (grain, flour and meat).

3) **Sarochínskaya** (194 v. from Kinél) near the great trading village of the same name with a population of 6,000, in the Buzulúk district (grain, flour, buckwheat meal, millet).

4) **Orenbúrg** (51°45′ N. lat. and 24°46.5′ E. long.; pop. 72,740), (grain, flour, millet, tallow, leather, wool, cotton.).

Orenbúrg, which formerly played an important part in the history of Russia's occupation of Central Asia, lost its importance as a strategical base after the conquest of Tashként and Turkestán, and since 1865, which is the date of the organisation of the Orenbúrg government, became an ordinary government town.

The line connecting it with the other railways of the Empire somewhat contributed to the development of its trade and industry. However, the opening of traffic on the Transcaspian line soon diminished the commercial importance of this town; cotton and other Central-Asiatic goods are now mostly conveyed by this line, and Orenbúrg no longer acts as a medium between the interior and the Central Asiatic markets.

The execution of the proposed plan to connect by rail the town of Orenbúrg with Tashként, will again raise the commercial importance of Orenbúrg, and call to life the productive forces of the Steppe region, lying in the northern part of the Aralo-Caspian plain.

From the station of Kinél, the Samára-Zlatoúst line proceeding further east follows the valley of the river Great Kinél till its junction with the river Kísla near the station, of Zaglādino (306 v.)

11) **Turgénevka.** (169 v.) Approaching the next station, the line crosses the river Kutulúk, a tributary of the Kinél, by a bridge 25 sazhens in length.

12) **Krótovka.** Buffet (190 v.) The Timashóv refinery of the State Domains is situated within 8 versts of the station. This refinery produces brown and loaf sugar (about 600,000 puds) from beetroot of local growth and from brown sugar imported in considerable quantity from the neighbouring governments The refinery is united by a branch line to the Krótovka station.

Naphtha received from Samára is employed as fuel in the production of sugar. Another sugar refinery is situated 30 versts from the first, near the station Bogátoye, on the Kinél Orenbúrg line, belonging to the Bogátovsk Sugar Refining Company, The operations of this refinery, owning 2,000 desiatins of beetroot, are being still further developed.

The Krótovka-Sérgievksk narrow-gauge railway branch runs a distance of 80 v. from the station of Krótovka to the supernumerary town of Sérgievsk (pop. 4,000) of the Bugurauslán district, situated in the vicinity of the Sérgievsk mineral springs (pop. 1500).

Among the Russian waters, the Sérgievsk springs are remarkable as containing a great percentage of sulphuretted hydrogen and for their strong effects. The temperature of the mineral water is 6 1/2°; it produces the same results as the springs of the Caucasus, and has like properties to those of Aix-la-Chapelle and Neudorf. Several doctors reside there during the season, which is from the 15-th May to the 15-th August. A bath costs 50 kop., a shower bath—25 k., a mud bath—75 k., a slime bath R. 1. There are rooms at the rate of from R. 10 to R. 20 a month, and family lodgings of R. 20 and upwards, with furniture and attendance.

On its way to the next station, the line crosses the river Kurtamák, a tributary of the Kinél, by a bridge 10 sazhens long.

13) **Mukhánovo.** (204 v.)

14) **Cherkásskaya.** Buffet. (220 v.) The large commercial village of Cherkásskaya in the Buguruslán district, with a population of 8,000 lies 2 versts from the station. It is the centre of the local grain, mainly rye trade, whence the grain is forwarded to Samára. There is a special granary near the station, holding 90,000 puds.

Proceeding from the station eastwards, the line crosses the river Little Kinél by a bridge 30 sazhens long.

15) **Kliuchí.** (244 v.)

16) **Pókhvisnevo.** Buffet (266 v.)

17) **Bugouruslán.** Buffet (285 v.)

The district town of Bugouruslàn, belonging to the Samára government, is situated at a distance of 3 versts from the station, (53°39' N. lat., 22°27' E. long.; pop. 20,000) It stands on a flat elevation, surrounded by mountains on three sides, on the right side of the Kinél, at its junction with the Tarkhánka.

The large village of Bugouruslán was founded in 1748, and created a town in 1797. It contains two churches, two hospitals, a clergy school, and urban school with three classes, a preparatory gymnasium for girls, and two parish schools; the Pokróv nunnery with three churches, founded in 1874. Grain is the principal article of trade; it is brought to the town, not only from the neighbourhood, but also from the contiguous Bugulmín and Buzulúk districts. Some of the local traders are in direct relations with the ports of St. Petersburg, Libáva and Révél. Great quantities of, in the main, rye flour amounting to as much as 300,000 puds, are ground by Shuválov's water mill. About 400,000 puds of unhulled buckwheat meal are annually forwarded from this point. A granary holding 90,000 puds of grain is situated near the station.

18) **Zagládino.** (306 v.). After passing over the river Kinél by a bridge 30 sazhens long, the line proceeds along the valley of the Kísla, and gradually ascends to the watershed of the Vólga and Káma.

19) **Alexéyevo.** (316 v.).

20) **Elán (Filíppovka).** (335 v.).

21) **Sarái-Gir.** (353 v.). Reaching here the highest point of the watershed, the line descends to the next station.

22) **Abdúlino.** Buffet (374 v.). Previous to the construction of the Samára-Zlatoúst line, an insignificant Bashkír village, taking no part in trade, was situated on the spot where the station stands at present. Its geographical position in a fertile and cultivated region, at some distance from commercial centres (Bugouruslán 90 v., Belebéi 54 v. the village of Sorochínskoye 150 v. to the south) soon transformed the small Bashkír village into an important corn market, where mainly agricultural products are offered for sale. At the present time the population of the village of Abdúlino exceeds 2,000; grain is brought to this point, especially in the winter time, from the Bugulmínsk, Belebéi and Buzulúk districts. Besides the local merchants, corn-traders from St. Petersburg, Révél and Riga come to this village. Agents of different manufacturing firms are to be met here, and the Russian Trading Bank is starting operations by advancing money on duplicates of way-bills. The greater portion of the grain exported is rye, which forms 70% of the whole, and is forwarded direct to the ports. A considerable quantity of rye flour is also exported. Four water-mills with a grinding capacity of about 1,200,000 puds of rye per annum, are situated near the station. They belong to the merchants Márkov, Svirídov, Rogóv, Zhídkov and others. Great freights of buckwheat, grown within the range of the Samára-Zlatoúst line, are annually forwarded from this station. A steam wheat-flour mill producing about 600 puds a day, and buckwheat shelling mills, belonging to Rogóv, Svirídov and others, are also situated close to the station. The export of buckwheat is effected in very large quantities; good harvests yield occasionally about

750,000 puds of this grain. Two granaries holding 30,000 puds each, are situated near the station.

From the station of Abdúlino, the line resumes its ascent to the watershed of the rivers Káma and Bélaya, and crossing the river Ik on a bridge 15 sazhens long, enters the confines of the Ufá government.

23) **Taldy-Bulák.** (392 v.).

24) **Priútovo.** (408 v.).

25) **Belebéi-Aksákovo.** Buffet (427 v.).

The district town of Belebéi (54° 7′ N. lat., 23° 52½′ E. long; pop. 5,161) of the Ufá government, is situated on the left bank of the Belebéika river, within ten versts of the station. This place was first settled in 1745. The district town of Belebéi was founded in 1781; it was superseded in 1797, and reestablished in 1802. The town contains 671 houses, only six of which are of stone, 5 churches (four of stone, 1 of wood), one Mohammedan mosque, one parish school, two schools belonging to the church, and a hospital.

Bridge over the river Bélaya (phot. by Arséntiev).

The town revenue is R. 24,596. Its inhabitants are mainly engaged in agriculture or small trade. Manufactures do not exist, and the town has scarcely any commercial importance. The station is in a more favourable condition, surrounded as it is by cultivable land, whose products go to feed the railway, and exports a considerable quantity of grain. The corn is chiefly purchased by local merchants, among them the firm of Rogóv carries on trade with the ports, sending the grain direct to its destination. A considerable quantity of rye flour is exported from this point, after having been ground in small water mills of most primitive construction. It is bought up straight from the village carts.

26) **Glukhovskáya.** (444 v.).

Here the line reaches the highest point of the watershed of the rivers Káma and Bélaya, and commences its descent to the Bélaya.

27) **Aksénovo.** (464 v.). From this station to Ufá, the line for a distance of 143 v. follows the valley of the river Déma, the left tributary of the Bélaya. The river is scantily supplied with water and not navigable. Its picturesque and steep banks consist of friable schistous sandstone, containing copper ores, those of Karakalínsk being the most important. Remains of Chud mines occur along the banks. The picturesque banks of the Déma with their oak and linden groves were sung by S. T. Aksákov.

28) **Shafránovo.** (479 v.). On its course to the next station, the line crosses a tributary of the Déma, the river Kyly by a bridge 25 sazhens in length.

29) **Ráevka.** Buffet (499 v.). Between this and the next station the line passes over a bridge of 20 sazhens spanning the river Tiulén, a tributary of the Déma.

30) **Davlekánovo.** (517 v.). The station is situated near a small Bashkír settlement, Itkúlovo which, previous to the opening of the railway traffic, had no commerce of its own; at the present time Itkúlovo is transformed into a corn market. Trade is carried on exclusively in winter. A special granary holding 30,000 puds of grain stands near the station. A number of estates with considerable areas under cultivation lie in the neighbourhood of the station.

Approaching the next station, the line traverses the river Urdiák, a tributary of the Déma, by a bridge 25 sazhens long.

31) **Shingák-Kul.** Buffet (539 v.). Pursuing its course to the next station, the line crosses the river Balyshly, tributary of the Déma, by a bridge of 10 sazhens.

32) **Chishmá.** (563 v.). Further on, it passes over the tributaries of the Déma, the rivers Kolomysh and Uzá spanned by bridges of 20 sazhens each.

A peculiar geological phenomenon called „funnels" is observed throughout the whole course of the line Chishmá-Yumátovo-Ufá-Urákovo. These funnels are produced by the sudden sinking of the surface, forming pits of considerable dimensions. An immense funnel having a diameter of 15 sazhens and a depth of 10 sazhens is to be seen 6 versts from Ufa on the way to Urákovo.

New funnels appear every year in spring and summer, and are a usual occurrence at the time of the spring floods. It has been observed that the strata of the Permian system, generally containing a great number of caves, are liable to sink. The limestone mountains rising above the Bélaya abound in natural caves among which those of Baislán and Shulliugín consist of a number of superposed hollows united by passages.

33) **Yumátovo** (586 v.) Approaching the next station Ufá, the line crosses the river Bélaya spanned by a bridge of 300 sazhens, having six spans of 50 sazhens each of the semi-parabolic system, with the track upon the lower chord; the piers and abutments are laid on caissons lowered to a depth of 8.14 sazhens below the ordinary water level.

The course of the river Bélaya, called Ak-Isyl by the Bashkírs, flowing on the left into the Káma, is about 1,000 versts long. The country along its upper reaches, between the branches of the Urál and Bugulchán, is mountainous; the cliffs on the banks consist mainly of chlorite and mica slate, gneiss and partly of limestone of the silurian system. Picturesque and wooded mountains abounding in caves surround the basin of this river; copper and iron works are established on its tributaries. Limestone of the carboniferous system occurs plentifully between Bugulchán and Sterlitomák; on its lower reaches, especially nearer to Ufá, gypsum, marl and sandstone of the permian system are the predominating rocks. The left bank is low, the right has a higher level. The river has a very sinuous course and near Ufá a breadth of 80 sazhens, which further on widens to 175 and 250 sazhens. Its waters are navigable from the Belorétsk works, within 70 versts of its mouth; there is regular navigation for passengers and freights throughout the summer from Ufá. On the average, the ice on the river breaks up by the 11 April and freezes again by the 4 November.

34) **Ufá.** Buffet (607).

The railway station is picturesquely situated near the government town of Ufá, on the right elevated bank of the Bélaya at its junction with the Ufá (54°43′ N. lat., 25°37.5′ E. long.; pop. 50,576.).

The vast territory embracing the Ufá government (107,217 sq. v.) and part of the contiguous Orenbúrg, Samára, Perm and Viátka governments, included in the Russian dominions towards the end of the XVI-th century, is known under the name of Bashkíria, derived from the name of the Bashkírs, who have inhabited this region since a remote date. The land of the Bashkírs became known to the Russians since the Mongol conquest. However, their nearer acquaintance with this country dates from the time when the Moscovite government was struggling for the possession of the Horde of Kazán. Wearied by internal and family dissensions, persecuted by the Kirgíz-Kaisáks, and seeing the growing power of Moscow, the Bashkírs voluntarily submitted to Russian dominion, and paid in 1557 their first tribute in furs, called „yasák". Ufá was the first Russian town founded in Bashkíria for collecting yasak. Iván Nagói was the founder of this town. The date of its foundation is not positively known; however it is supposed that it was between 1573 and 1586. According to an ancient tradition, an old Tatar town with the same name of Ufá was situated on the site of the present town; remains of earthworks, now called the Devil's mound, testify to its former existence. With the foundation of Ufá, the Russians were securely established in Bashkíria and then began the colonisation of this country. The

Types of Bashkírs.

frequent revolts of the Bashkírs, joined in by almost the whole of the native population, especially in 1662, during the Seit rebellion, and in 1708, assumed considerable proportions, and led to the institution of military Cossack settlements, which were organised in the reign of the Empress Anna by Nepliúev, a statesman of Peter's school.

Private mining industry was established in the Urál Bashkíria on the initiative of Nepliúev, which greatly contributed to the colonisation of the country. In 1760, 28 factories, including 15 copper and 13 iron works were in full operation, with a Russian population of 20,000 men. Although the Bashkírs joined in the Pugachóv revolt and in other mutinies of the Vólga inhabitants, still they were pacified towards the end of the XVIII century, and employed in 1798 as irregular troops, specially formed for maintaining military cordons along the Orenbúrg frontier.

Types of Mordvá women.

This army of natives, as well as the irregular Cossack cavalry, became famous during the campaign of 1812—1813; the French called them the Cupids of the North on account of the effectiveness of their arrow shots. Since 1863, the Bashkírs have been put on the same footing with the rest of the country population and, after the disbanding of the Bashkír troops in 1874, they have all become subject to obligatory military service.

The origin of the Bashkírs is not yet scientifically ascertained. Some suppose that they descend from the Ugro-Finnish race and only in course of time acquired the Mongol type, others believe that they are Vogúls, who represent one of the Ugor tribes, or form part of the great Altái family, to whom belong also the Magyars. The present Bashkírs have two marked types. One is the more common Kalmyk or Mongól type characteristic of the steppe Bashkírs, recognised by a large and flat face, by a broad and straight nose or by one bent in at the root; they have a protruding chin, a large head, and are of middle size. The other, which is more like the Caucasian type, and common to many Central-Asiatic nations, is characterised by a hooked nose, a marked profile and high stature; these are the forest Bashkírs, inhabiting such mountainous and wooded regions as are situated at the source of the Bélaya.

All the Bashhírs are Mohammedans. The majority of them read and write Tatar, thanks to the efforts of the clergy attached to a great number of mosques scattered all over Bashkíria. They are provided with a certain quantity of land, and pursuing agriculture and cattle-breeding are settled in groups, forming small villages. In spring, they leave their crowded and smoky huts and live in felt „kibitkas", which they pitch in fields and pastures, forming their common property. The poorest among them have summer dwellings made of lime bast. They usually wear the same costume as the Tatars. The Ufá government contains a total of about one million Bashkírs. The minority of the native population of Ufá is represented by Teptiárs and Meshcheriáks, who mostly live in the north of the government. Their mode of life differs but little from that of the Bashkírs, but they are at a much lower stage of civilisation, and are heathens. The whole of the population, comprising 2,277,158 souls, is distributed among the six following districts: Ufá, Belebéi, Birsk, Zlatoúst, Menzeínsk and Sterlitomák. Of these, 105,667 represent the town population; there are 967,757 Russian peasants and 1,059,126 Bashkírs, Teptiárs and Meshcheriáks. The remainder includes smaller ethnographical groups. The greater portion of the inhabitants are Mohammedans, namely 1,151,198; there are 994,508 orthodox; 106,029 heathens, 4,812 dissenters, 1,312 catholics, 766 lutherans and 722 jews. The Ufá government occupies the south-eastern part of European Russia, and is one of the central Vólga governments belonging to the fertile zone. According to the last local statistics, the land is divided as follows:

DISTRICTS.	Fields and pasture in desiatins.	Forests.	Uncultivable land.	TOTAL.
Ufá	644,696.4	1,090,327.1	68,138.4	1,803,161.9
Birsk	862,550.5	1,278,329.9	95,989.2	2,286,869.6
Menzelínsk	707,436.4	388,580.5	69,557.2	1,165,574.1
Belebéi	1,390,683.2	547,497.4	123,401.4	2,061,582.0
Sterlitomák	976,338.	864,248.2	71,834.7	1,917,470.9
Zlatoúst	419,074.7	1,167,951.1	62,660.3	1,679,686.1
TOTAL	5,090,779.2	5,341,984.2	521,581.3	10,864,344.6

The soil and climate of the Ufá government are mostly well adapted for agriculture, which is extensively practised by its inhabitants everywhere, with the exception of the mining district. Within the last few years, the area sown comprised:

Winter corn	630,049	desiatins.
Spring corn	819,561	„
Potatoes	29,830	„
Total	1,479,440	desiatins.

Mining is the principal industrial feature in the Ufá government. According to the last data, the production of all the works, 130 in number, was represented by R. 8,029,637. The State mining works of the Zlatoúst district and the private concerns of the Simsk and Katáv districts have an annual production of R. 5,480,000.

The pretty town of Ufá is the capital of Bashkíria. It contains 4,726 houses (165 of stone, 4,561 of wood), 23 churches (7 house chapels, 12 of stone, 4 of wood), 2 monasteries, one Roman catholic wooden church, 2 Mohammedan mosques. There are 24 schools, inclusive of two gymnasiums for boys and girls, a geodetic school, a seminary, two clergy schools for boys and girls, a commercial school, a district school, several primary and parish schools. The charitable institutions are: 2 homes for orphans and waifs, under the managemeut of Her Imperial Majesty's Chancery for the Institutions of the Empress Mary, and a poor-house established by the local administration. The following institutions are kept up at the cost of the Ufá patronage committee of the Imperial Philanthropic Society: 1) a free day-hospital, 2) free lodgings for the poor, 3) an old women's asylum, 4) the Alexander poor-house for women, 5) asylum for aged Mohammedans, 6) a free workhouse, 7) a free information office for providing work. There are also a school with two classes for blind boys, under the management of the local committee, night refuges with cheap dinners, a work-house, a division of the Red Cross Society, a branch of the Imperial Humane Society, a society for agricultural colonies and artisans asylums' a diocesan committee for helping the poor clergy.

Scientific and other societies are represented by: a branch of the Agronomic Society of Moscow, a society of physicians, a committee for public readings, a society for amateur singing, music and dramatic art, a racing society. Further there are a town library and museum, the latter founded in

Bridge over the Ufá (phot. by Arséntiev).

1864 by the local statistical committee. The museum occupies a separate building on the Trade Square, and includes ten divisions: agriculture, forestry mining industry, mineralogy, archaeology, palaeontology, entomology, zoology, numismatics and history.

Agricultural tools made at the Vótkin State Works are offered for sale at the museum. The periodicals are: the Diocesan Gazette, twice a month, the Government Gazette, and the Ufá Advertiser, the two latter dailies.

The 29 factories working in the town yield a revenue of R. 467,349; a wax candle manufactory (R. 63,000) a beer and mead brewery (R. 89,000), a sweatmeat manufactory (R. 30,000), a rope walk (R. 30,000), and a saw mill (R. 90,000), are the most important among them. There are the following banks: a branch of the State Bank, a branch of the Peasant Land Bank and the Town Bank.

The town has an annual revenue of R. 175,000.

The town of Ufá, representing the administrative centre of a vast government, used to be an important commercial centre for the entire Urál, where local and imported goods were bought and sold. Formerly, also, this town served as a depot for a great quantity of Siberian wares. However, since the opening of the Samára-Zlatoúst line, Ufá has lost much of its importance, and its commercial operations are greatly reduced.

The Ufá station has some significance as the point to which considerable quantities of grain are brought for further conveyance by the river Bélaya. and on account of the imports of other grain products consisting principally of wheaten flour for local supply. It has no importance for the corn traffic by rail. Shitóv and Stakhéev have built naphtha reservoirs near the station, to supply the localities situated in the direction of Cheliábinsk.

Ufá might recover its former prosperity by the construction of the projected railway uniting Orenbúrg and Perm, connecting the commercial centres of the Perm government with the plains of Orenbúrg. If this line were run further into Central Asia and reached Tashként, it would certainly exert a most beneficial effect upon the town of Ufá.

From the station of Ufá, the line ascends again and reaches the watershed of the rivers Bélaya and Ufá, crossing the latter by a bridge 150 sazhens in length.

35) **Urákovo.** (628 v.). A great tallow melting manufactory belonging to Krestóvnikovs is situated near the station; the Samára-Zlatoúst railway supplies this manufactory with over 350,000 puds of tallow, bought chiefly at the Ishím fair in the Tobólsk government. From Urákovo, the tallow is forwarded to the candle and soap manufactory of the Krestóvnikovs in Kazán, by the rivers Ufá, Bélaya and Káma.

Sale of onions and boiling water at a railway station.

The line follows the left or eastern bank of the Ufá, and gradually ascends the watershed of the rivers Ufá and Síma. On its way to the next station, the line passes over a bridge of 10 sazhens spanning the river Tauzh.

36) **Iglino.** (640 v.). Two steam saw-mills belonging to Bolshakóv and Bazilévsky are situated close to the station.

37) **Tavtimánovo.** (658 v.). Leaving this station, the line reaches the highest point of the watershed between the rivers Ufá and Síma, and descending towards the Síma traverses the river Ulú-Teliák by a bridge of 10 sazhens.

38) Approaching the next station, the line crosses the river Ashá by a bridge of 15 sazhens in length.

39) **Ashá-Balashóv.** Buffet (704 v.). New blast furnace works are being constructed by Messrs Balashóv close to the station.

The Miniár ronworks (phot. by Arséntiev).

From here the line winds its course amidst ridges, and is intersected by the Síma.

The famous Kazarmén rock, consisting of limestone, lies within a few versts from the station and falls in a plumb line to the water's edge. The line is built on a recess separating the Kazarmén rock from the river. The Vorobéi mountains stretch further to the left of the railway, the Andzhigordák stands on the right.

40) **Miniár.** (723 v.). The Miniár works of Messrs Balashóv, founded in 1784 by Tvérdyshev and Miasnikóv, is situated within two versts of the station. Its annual output exceeds 800,000 puds of iron and 200,000 puds of steel. The foundry has no blast furnace, and for this reason does not produce any pig-iron; the latter is brought from the Síma works situated 18 versts from Miniár. Rolled iron is the most important item of this works, wrought iron plates being the chief article of sale. The roof-iron of Messrs Balashóv enjoys a considerable reputation. The Miniár works and its environs stretching along the Síma, which flows into the Bélaya, offer one of the most picturesque sites on the western side of the Urál. The works support about four and a half thousand inhabitants, and employ about 900 men. Upon reaching the valley of the river Síma, the line follows along it and, on its way to the next station, crosses the same river four times by bridges 40, 25 and 25 sazhens in length; the latter has three spans of 5, 25 and 5 sazhens, and a height of 7.72 sazhens above low water mark.

41) **Símskaya.** (736 v.). Is picturesquely situated at the foot of a mountain ridge. The Síma works of Messrs Balashóv, within 8 versts of the station, are connected with it by a tramway. These works were founded in 1759 by Miasnikóv. They contain two blast furnaces, and produce mainly cast-iron (about 1,300,000 puds per annum). For this purpose, iron-ore is brought from the station of Viazováya, whither it is forwarded from the Bakál mine. The Shíshka, which is a conical mountain standing half a verst from the works, emerging on its western side from a small lake, contains a large cave at a height of 100 sazhens. At a small distance up the Síma, is the mountain called Yamazé-Tau, which has another cave of still larger dimensions, where Pallas found bones of man and animals. In general, caves occur very frequently in the southern Urál.

The Síma works have about 5,000 inhabitants, and employ about 300 men regularly, and about 800 occasionally. The valley is surrounded with high tree-clad mountains. There is a hospital, a school, a very good theatre, and

Cutting through the Dergách mountain (phot. by Arséntiev).

tea and reading rooms open to the public. A telephone connects the works with other manufactories in the district.

Here begins again the ascent toward the watershed of the rivers Síma and Yuriuzán. At its highest point is the station.

42) **Kropachévo.** (758 v.). The Nicholas iron works of Messrs Balashóv, founded in 1866 by Count Strógonov, are situated at a distance of 23 versts from the station. There is also a blast furnace with an output of about 500,000 puds per annum, which is principally forwarded direct to the station of Púshchino and the New Port. The ore is obtained from the same mine which supplies the Síma iron works. The number of workmen is from 50 to 60, wbile 600 others are employed about the works. From this station, the line descends to the valley of the Yuriuzán, traversing it by a bridge with spans of 10, 46 and 10 sazhens, and a height of 12.02 sazhens above the low water mark. This is one of the most picturesque spots on the whole line.

43) **Ust-Katáv.** (774 v.). Lies amidst cliffs and rocks. The Ust-Katáv iron works of Prince Belosélsky-Belozérsky, founded in 1759, are situated within four versts of the station, in a deep mountain pass at the junction of the rivers Katáv and Yuriuzán. The works have above 5,000 inhabitants and 300 workmen, the number of men employed about the works exceeding 1,000. There is no blast furnace and the pig-iron for the production of assorted iron is brought by road from the Katáv-Ivánovsk and Yuriuzán works. After the construction of the railway, these iron works lost much of their importance, and are now specially occupied with the manufacture of rail spikes and fastenings.

Puddling, welding, finery and cast-steel production are carried on there. It has lately been proposed to establish a railway-carriage works. Remarkable caves are to be found in the mountains within a few versts of the iron works. They contain numerous and spacious chambers united by narrow passages.

The caves in the Ignatius mountain are celebrated as having given shelter to the lay-brother Ignatius who is regarded by the people as a saint and is buried there. This cave is one of the most extensive in the southern Urál. The saint's image is placed over the grave, where an oil lamp is perpetually kept burning. A crowd of people from the neighbouring works and villages stream to this cave on the ninth Friday after Easter. According to popular belief, it was the refuge of many other hermits, called „workers" in the Urál.

From the station of Ust-Katáv, the line follows continuously the right bank of the Yuriuzán. Rocks, at times quite bare, at others clad with moss and trees, rise perpendicularly on either side of the way.

44) **Viazováya.** Buffet (791 v.). This is one of the important and well organised stations on the Samára-Zlatoúst line. Its situation is picturesque. Around it are hills and fir forests, which are like a park. The river Yuriuzán with its fine banks and islands is in close proximity to it. A small wooden church was built at the station in 1898. M-r Sukhozanét's Yuriuzán works, founded in 1798 by Tvérdyshev and Miasnikóv, are situated at a distance of nine versts. The works have 7,896 inhabitants of both sexes. At the present time, they are leased by Prince Belosélsky-Belozérsky and, within recent years, have considerably extended their operations. The works are provided with three blast furnaces, twelve welding furnaces and eight rolling lathes. The ore for the production of pig-iron is conveyed by carts from the Bakál mine, situated 35 versts from the works. As much as 1,000,000 puds of pig-iron and iron are turned out yearly. The chief products are rolled merchant iron and rail fastenings and bridges, besides a certain quantity of wrought iron plates and hoop iron. About 800 men are occupied in the works and as many as 2,400 are employed outside. Yuriuzán has long since been a centre of various sects

which are represented by 1,400 adherents of the chapel sect, 190 of the maritime sect, 10 of the Austrian sect, and 21 dissidents. The surrounding hills serve as an asylum for hermits, who there occupy themselves with gardening and beekeeping.

The Katáv-Ivánov rail-rolling and iron works of Prince Belosélsky-Belozérsky founded in 1755 by Tvérdyshev and Miasnikóv, are situated 27 versts from the Viazováya station. They may be ranked among the first Urál mining enterprises for their output. The population of the works is 10,000. There are now four blast furnaces, a rail-rolling mill, puddling, welding and machinery works, a locksmith's shop, a forge and a saw-mill. The works and the adjacent grounds are provided with electric light and a telephone uniting all the works in the district. The iron ore is conveyed by carts from the Bakál mines. Rails are the chief article of produce, exceeding a million puds per annum. Warehouses and sheds for the storage of the metal

The Sátka ironworks (phot. by Arséntiev.).

goods of the Katáv-Ivánov and Yuriuzán works, have been built near the station, and connected with it by a branch line. The goods are brought to these warehouses in winter, and gradually forwarded further. The Katáv works, having extended their operations, adopted mineral fuel in 1890, and naphtha since 1893.

The Viazováya station also receives the metal goods from the Belorétsk iron works, situated in the Verkhneurálsk district of the Orenbúrg government, belonging to the Belorétsk works of Vogau and Co. The Tirliand works, which is one of them, is 110 versts from the station. The output is about one million puds of pig-iron and iron; 200,000 puds are transported by the Samára-Zlatoúst line from Viazováya to Ufá. The remainder is floated in barges down the river Bélaya. The greatest quantity of metal goods for the whole line are conveyed from the Viazováya station.

From here the line runs through cuttings and mountain passes; further on the country is more open, with far-stretching fields and meadows surrounded by high mountains.

45) **Mursalímkino.** (813 v.). The Bashkír village Mursalímkino with its half ruined buildings is situated near the station. From here the railway proceeds almost in a straight line, without encountering any mountains, but only occasional ridges, covered with a rich vegetation, and intersected by pretty valleys.

Leaving the station, the line traverses the rivers Uluír and Sikiáz spanned by bridges of 10 sazhens each. Near the next station, it crosses the river Ishelgá by a bridge 10 sazhens long.

46) **Suleyá.** (837 v.). The Sátka iron foundry, belonging to the State and founded by Mosólov in 1757, is situated 18 versts from the station. It contains about 10,000 inhabitants of both sexes, including a great many sectarians. The number of workmen emplyed is 1800. The works contain two blast furnaces, a puddling furnace, a rolling mill, a foundry,—the latter is mainly

The station of Zlatoúst from Mt. Kosutúr (phot. by Arséntiev).

used for producing shells,—there is also a forge and a locksmith's shop. The machinery and casting shops are united by 135 sazhens of rail on the Decoville system. Iron, amounting to about 1,800,000 puds per annum, is brought from the Bakál and Yelník mines. Pig-iron is the chief article of produce, amounting to above a million puds per annum; about 250,000 puds of pig-iron are employed in the manufacture of iron and shells. The rest of the pig-iron,

Station of Zlatoúst.

amounting to about 800,000 puds, is forwarded, for the use of the Navy and Artillery Department to the Izhórsk, Obúkhov, Perm, Vótkin, Zlatoúst and Ártinsk works.

Wood and charcoal obtained from the adjacent forests are employed as fuel in the Sátka iron works. A telephone unites the works with the Zlatoúst and Bakál mines. In 1824, the iron works were visited by the Emperor Alexander I. The famous Bakál mine, which contains one of the most extensive iron beds in the Russian Empire, is situated 21 versts from the works, on the Bulandíkha mountain. The quantity of ore is estimated at 400,000,000 puds. Its chemical composition is: 81.44% of oxide of iron, 6.78% of silica, 5.46% of alumina, 57.36% of metallic iron. The Síma and Katáv iron works obtain iron from mines belonging to the same group. A bed of tripoli, employed for the polishing of metals and for roof slates, is situated within five versts of the station.

Up to the river Sátka, the line runs through a hilly country, and crosses this river by a bridge having three spans of 64, 30 and 6 sazhens, and an elevation of 8.46 sazhens above the low-water mark. Further on, it runs through a more level country.

47) **Berdiaúsh.** (859 v.). A wide gauge railway branch twenty versts in length connects the Sátka iron works with the station.

The iron from the Bakál mine, supplying the Zlatoúst works, has been forwarded to the station since 1893.

48) **Tundúsh.** (878 v.) Proceeding further east, the line descends to the valley of the river Ai, crossing the latter at the 881 verst by a bridge 30 sazhens long, and then mounts again towards Zlatoúst. The line winds its course along the bank of the Ai, among fir-clad mountain ridges.

The **Kusínsk** platform. The State iron foundry, founded by Lugínin in 1778, stands at a distance of 14 verts from this place. It contains about 4,500 inhabitants, and has two blast furnaces producing about 300,000 puds of pig-iron per annum; the output of iron is from 70,000 to 100,000 puds; cast-iron and founded wares represent 70,000 to 100,000 puds. Special attention is given to neat and artistic work; in this respect, the works rival the famous Kaslínsk works. The number of workmen employed amounts to 500. Iron is supplied by the Akhténsk mine, from a distance of 25 versts; it represents a kind of bog-ore with 73% of oxide of iron, and above 50% of metal. Pig-iron is forwarded from the Kusínsk works to the works of Vótkin and Artinsk, while the iron is sent partly to Kólpino near St. Petersburg, for the Izhóra works, and partly to Nízhni-Nóvgorod, where it is stored in the Government iron works. Wood and charcoal are employed as fuel. The works are connected by a telephone with Zlatoúst and the Kusínsk platform.

The line runs through extensive cuttings in which chalk is noticeable At the 902 verst, near the station of Zlatoúst, there is a parabolic tube which is the first of this system on Russian railways.

49) **Zlatoúst.** Buffet (907 v.). Is picturesquely situated at the foot of fir-clad mountains. A whole settlement, containing a telephone, a school, and a small theatre, has been founded quite close to the railway on a piece of land belonging to the town. The town of Zlatoúst is at a distance of two versts from the station. It belongs to the Ufá government, and spreads over the valleys of the rivers Ai, Gramotúkha, Tesmá, Kámenka, Chuváshka and Tatárka (55°10' N. lat. and 29°21'E. long.; population 23,676 souls). The Ai, held up by a dam, forms a large pond which supplies the iron works with water.

The Túla mechant Mosólóv established an iron foundry in 1754 on a piece of land purchased from the Bashkírs, and from a church erected in honour of the three saints: Basil the Great, Gregory the Theologian, and John Chrysostom, it received its name. In 1811, the foundry became the property of the State. At the time of the organisation of the Ufà government, in 1865, Zlatoúst was ranked as a district town. It contains 2.916 buildings (2,617 of wood, 299 of stone), 4 Russian orthodox churches (2 of stone, 2 of wood), 8 chapels (3 of stone, 5 of wood), a stone dissenting chapel, a Roman catholic and a protestant church, both of stone.

The schools are: a town school with three classes, two schools with one class for boys and girls at the iron works, 4 town primary schools. There is also a hospital and dispensary built by the local administration. The Government iron foundry has also a dispensary and hospital. The town library contains a reading room. There are a private typography, three book shops and two clubs. Within the town are the following factories: a soap works producing goods of an annual value of R. 11,200, a beer and mead brewery (R. 15,300), a pig-iron and iron foundry (R. 941,264) seven polishing works (R. 16,740), a cloth factory (R. 3,000), a gingerbread manufactory (R. 2,300) and a cracknel manufactory (R. 1,700). The town revenue amounts to R. 22,684. A monument to the Emperor Alexander II stands in the middle of the square in front of the arsenal buildings and the cathedral. The pedestal is made of marble, the iron statue representing the Emperor at full length, was cast at the Kusínsk works belonging to the Government. Samples of all the articles produced at the side-arms factory since the time it opened operations, are kept in the arsenal, which can be seen from 9 to 12 in the morning and from 3 to 5 in the evening.

The Emperor Alexander I visited the foundry in 1824, and a nail forged with his own hands is preserved in the local museum. The Emperor Alexan-

View of the town of Zlatoúst (phot. by Arséntiev).

der II, then heir apparent to the throne, visited Zlatoúst in 1857; a stone chapel was built on one of the hills in commemoration of this event.

The Zlatoúst works produce pig-iron, Marten steel in three furnaces, cast steel in two furnaces of the Siemens system, puddled and rolled iron; blades are worked in the forge division. There is also a machinery tool and a railway fastenings works. The number of workmen is about 1,000. Many of them occupy themselves with the manufacture of hand-made metal goods, exemplified by the famous Zlatoúst knives and forks. Since 1895, the workmen have organised associations with a store for their hand-made wares. They receive orders for different articles in steel and iron, excepting side-arms, the manufacture of which is forbidden. About 3,000 men are occupied in working knives and forks with a business of R. 200,000 to 300,000.

The metal goods produced here are distributed in the following manner: the iron is forwarded to Nízhni-Nóvgorod, the side-arms to Moscow, the shells to Kóvno, Osovéts, Kíev, Dvinsk and other towns; the fastenings are sent to Cheliábinsk for the use of the Siberian Railway. The works being insufficiently provided with fuel, cannot further develop their operations; in order to obviate this difficulty, petroleum is employed in many maufactories to the amount of about 300,000 puds per annum. Coke and anthracite from the Donéts basin are also used for the same purpose.

In 1897, the average output of the Zlatoúst works was: 415,000 puds of half-rolled iron, about 200,000 puds of different kinds of iron, 180,000 puds of pig and cast steel, and 41,000 puds of assorted steel.

Leaving the station of Zlatoúst, the line descends to the river Tesmá crossing it by a bridge having three spans of 4, 15 and 4 sazhens, and an elevation of 6.35 sazhens above the low-water mark, and ascending the Uràl mountain ridge, reaches the highest point on its entire course.

Bridge oner the Tesmá (phot by Arséntiev).

50) **Urzhúmka.** (925 v.) The station stands in a place remote from all habitation, where the Urál ridge forms a cavity among the wide and lofty rocks of the principal central chain.

The frontiers of the Tróitsk and Zlatoúst districts, viz of the Ufá and Orenbúrg governments meet near the station. A stone pyramid with the inscription „Europe" on one side, and „Asia" on the other, is placed within half a verst of the station. Here the line passes its summit on the Urál and begins its descent by a zigzag four versts in length crossing the river Great Syrostán, tributary to the Miás of the Ob basin, by a bridge of three spans of 4, 10 and 4 sazhens, and a height of 6.50 sazhens above low-water level. Thence the line continues its descent along the right bank of the Great Syrostán. The summit of the Alexander cone, having an elevation of 3,500 feet 'above sea-level, remains in view all the time. The top of this mountain consists of bare stone ridges. It was visited by the Emperors Alexander I, Nicholas I and Alexander II.

51) **Syrostán** (947 v.) surrounded by mountains, has received its name from the village lying beyond them at a distance of one verst. Continuing its descent, the line enters the Cheliábinsk district, which represents the Asiatic portion of the Orenbúrg government, and taking a north-eastern direction, towards the Little Syrostán, twice crosses this river, effecting a circuit of 2½ versts. The descent towards the eastern slope of the Urál terminates at the second passage over the Little Syrostán. Further on, at the 953 verst, the line traverses the river Atlián, spanned by a bridge of 15 sazhens, and passing the watershed of the rivers Atlián and Miás, crosses the latter by a bridge with an opening of 25 sazhens. It then approaches the station of Miás.

The vast area of the Orenbúrg government (50°49' and 55°52'N. lat. and 23°7' and 34°5'E: long. Area 167,989 squ. versts. Pop. 1,609,388, males 802,936, females 806,452.) is divided by the Urál chain and the river Urál into a western and eastern portion. The former lies in Europe and comprises 70,736 sq. versts, the latter is in Asia, and covers an area of 97,253 sq. versts. The natural frontier between these two quarters of the globe runs along the meridian. The Ilmen mountains, stretching to the east from the central Urál cháin, culminate in the Ishkúl mountain, 2,245 feet in height. They are at first covered by a rich vegetation of trees, but gradually lose it and pass into the steppes of the Cheliábinsk and Tróitsk districts, representing the Transurál portion ot the Orenbúrg government. At first the steppes are varied by hills and dotted by sopkas of granite and porphyry. Further east, they become more level, abounding in lakes and covered with leafy groves. The eastern slopes of the Urál are richly provided with gold, copper and iron ores, giving scope to a considerable development of mining industry. Auriferous gravel is found partly on lands belonging to the State, and partly on that of the Bashkírs and Orenbúrg Cossacks. Deserving of mention are the Kachkár mines, containing gold in veins, situated 50 versts west from the town of Tróitsk.

The mining industries of the Orenbúrg Transurál are comprised in the Cheliábinsk, Tróitsk and Verkhneurálsk districts, which from their geographical, topographical and economic conditions, are in close connexion with the Samára-Zlatoúst line; their management is entrusted to the Orenbúrg Mining Office located in the Miás iron works. Besides the Miás goldmining association, leasing the State mines of Miás and washing over 70 puds of gold annually, the following mines should be mentioned on account of their output: the Vladímir goldmining Company in the Cheliábinsk district, yielding from 6 to 7 puds, Podvintsév and Co, belonging at present to a newly organised association (over 50 puds), the mines of Tarásov and Co, Sokolóv and others (over 20 puds), of Símonov (10 puds); the Karatybáno-Baratynsky Association (from 8 to 10 puds), the trading firm of Paklévsky-Kózell (about 4 puds); the Russian goldmining Company established in the Transural in the Tróitsk district since 1895 (about 6 puds), Pribylov (about 5 puds), Ratkóv-Rozhnóv in the Verkhneurálsk district (the same quantity). The gold production of the Urál mining region reaches from 550 to 580 puds, of which 40%, or 10% of the total gold production in the Empire, are obtained in the Transurál from the Orenbúrg government. The granites of the Ilmen mountains abound in precious stones.

The steppe portion of the Cheliábinsk and Tróitsk districts bounded by the Toból and Miás rivers is characterised by a great number of lakes; about 1150 of them are scattered throughout this region, where fresh water lakes occur in close proximity with brackish or bitter lakes. Without mingling their waters, they are even sometimes connected by a channel. The steppe lakes are either entirely covered with reeds, or girt by red flowers called salt-wort (Salsola kali, Salicornia herbaria). The quantity of salt contained in the lakes, and their chemical properties are not always the same. The salt lakes, where salt has been obtained since the middle of the XVIII century, are now granted on lease to private individuals. The bitter lakes, containing much Glauber's salt, are not worked at all.

The water in some of the lakes has medicinal properties. The climate of the Transurál is continental, with extreme transitions. The highest mean temperature is +28.6°, the lowest on the average is —38.8°, with a total range of 67.4°. The annual rainfall is more abundant in the north of the Transurál, than in its southern part. The climate is healthy, particularly in the mountainous regions; only a few places in the Cheliábinsk district must be excluded as containing lakes with unhealthy exhalations. In the mountainous part of the country, the forests contain various species, such as fir, pine, spruce, larch, birch, linden and oak; in the steppe, the small groves and tree clumps shew a predomination of birch. The oak does not occur beyond the Urál, and appears again only in the region of the Amúr. The fauna does not differ from that of the contiguous governments of Enropean Russia. Woody Bashkíria gives shelter to a great number of bears. The soil mainly consists of sand and clay; blackearth occurs only in river valleys, and in localities lying at the foot of the mountains; further away, the blackearth seam diminishes in thickness. For this reason, the vegetation of the steppes grows richer as they approach nearer the mountains. However, the harvests are very uncertain, being sometimes very poor on account of the drought. The mountain valleys and the steppes abound in pastures and are well adapted for cattle-breeding.

The conditions of soil and ciimate in this region are favourable to the growth of good qualities of wheat, other kinds of corn and oil producing plants. Agriculture is principally based on the fallow-land system. The extensive pastures are well suited for the development of cattle-breeding, which is practised on a large scale by the Bashkírs. Grain and animal products are exported into the interior governments of Russia and abroad.

The construction of a railway from the Samára-Zlatoúst line towards the south, to the town Tróitsk and further to Turkestán, intended to meet the economic interests of the country, has frequently been proposed, the project being supported by the extraordinary fertility of the southern part of the Transural.

52) **Miás.** Buffet (967 v.) Is situated at the foot of the Ilmen mountains on the shore of the lake Ilmen. The environs are extremely beautiful. The Miás works, founded in 1777 by Lugínin, stand 6 versts from the station, in a deep valley surrounded by the Cháshkov mountains. Formerly, the works smelted copper; this industry is abandoned at present and replaced by the machine shop of the gold mining company. Externally the works resemble a town; there are many stone houses, stores and shops, a club and two libraries. The number of inhabitants exceeds 14,000. At the present time, the works forms the centre of an extensive corn trade. The valley of the Miás is well known on account of its gold-bearing strata. The famous Tsar Alexander mine, in which the Emperor Alexander I worked in 1824, lies within two versts of the iron works. The tools employed by His Imperial Majesty are kept in the museum of the works. In these mines, gold is found in veins

and gravel. The number of workmen employed is about 3,000 men. The Ilmen mines, which are quite close to the station, are connected with the goldwashing works by a narrow-gauge line, provided with diminutive trucks and engines.

The gold-bearing strata contain clayey sand with a considerable admixture of pebbles and gravel. In it occur fragments of quartz, gneiss and flinty slate. Its depth is about 7 metres, the thicknesss of the surface or turf varies from 2 to 4 metres. One hundred puds of auriferous gravel contain from 25 to 55 dolias of gold. Miás is a station which, on account of its position, receives freights of metals, grain and animal products. In 1897, 301,658 puds of grain were forwarded from this point to the ports and abroad. The quantity of animal products despatched from the town of Tróitsk, in the Turgái

View of the town of Cheliábinsk.

territory, and from Kustanái, exceeds 100,000 puds. Leaving the Miás station, the line mounts to the branches of the Ilmen ridge, which precede the Urál chain and, descending again, passes through the narrow and uneven isthmus between the Chebarkúl and Yelóvy lakes.

53) **Chebarkúl.** (990 v.). The village of Chebarkúl is situated near the station on the lake of the same name. A fortress, which was included in the line of the Uisk fortifications, stood here at the end of the XVII century. After having served, at the time of the revolt of Pugachóv, as a rallying point for the Siberian troops employed in opposing that popular leader, itwas burned by Pugachóv when he was pursued by the brave Colonel Míchelsohn.

54) **Bishkíl.** (1,009 v.). Proceeding eastwards from the station, the line crosses the river Bishkíl spanned by a bridge of 20 sazhens. Mines of vein and gravel gold are to be found in the environs.

55) **Poletáevo.** (1.033 v.). In the direction of Cheliábinsk, the line passes over the river Birgildá by a bridge 10 sazhens long, and ascends to the elevation where are situated the gold mines of Krasheninnikov.

56) **Cheliábinsk.** Buffet (1.057 v.). The railway station is at a distance of four versts from the district town of Cheliábinsk, included in the Orenbúrg government, and situated on both sides of the Miás (55° 10'N. lat., 72° 2' E. long; 2,451 versts from St. Petersburg, 7,112 versts from Vladivostók. Pop. 18,454). This town, which is the oldest in the government, was founded in 1658. It arose, like many other Russian towns, out of a small wooden fortress which, in the north-eastern part of Bashkíria, served to protect the villages and the works established by Russian colonists, on the picturesque and fertile banks of the rivers Isét and Miás. It is thought that the town was called after the name of the Bashkír Cheliába, the fortress having been built on his land. Constant revolts and disturbances occurring among the Bashkírs and Meshcheriáks, gave this fortress some importance as an administrative centre. In 1743, the famous historian V. N. Tatíshchev, who at that time was director-general of the iron works in Siberia and Perm, established there the headquarters of the voyevóda of the newly organised province of Isét, comprising the left side of the river Yaík, now called the Urál. In the years 1773 and 1774, from the beginning to the end of Pugachóv's revolt which spread all over Bashkíria, Cheliábinsk was frequently attacked by the rebels, and was the rallying point of the Siberian troops commanded by Lieutenant General Clappier de Colongue, who became famous for the suppression of the revolt and the defence of the Isét province, the works of Ekaterinbùrg and the Siberian territory.

Cheliábinsk, the Odigidri nunnery.

At the time of the Pugachóv revolt, Cheliábinsk had a male population of 736, inclusive of 243 soldiers, 189 town Cossacks, with a chancery, an ecclesiastic department and a town-hall.

In 1781, Cheliábinsk was registered among the district towns of the Ufá province; in 1796, upon the abolition of the latter, it was included in the Orenbúrg government.

The Emperor Alexander I visited the town in 1824.

It is situated on the river Miás which, picturesque higher up, loses its mountainous character in the Cheliábinsk district and falls into the river Isét, left tributary to the Toból, beyond the confines of the Orenbúrg government. Notwithstanding its extensive course of about 500 versts, rafting by the Miás is possible only in spring; for this reason, the river has but slight economic importance.

The Cathedral erected in honour of the Nativity of our Lord, the chapel built in memory of the Tsar-Liberator Alexander II, and the Odigidri nunnery, are the chief ornaments of the town. There are 6 stone orthodox churches, a chapel for old-believers, a mosque and a jewish prayer-house. The schools are: a clergy school for boys, a preparatory gymnasium for girls, a school with four classes for boys, a parish and three municipal schools. There are also an orphanage, three hospitals organised by the municipality, the local and the prison administrations. A library with a free reading-room was opened in memory of the 14 November 1894, the day of the marriage of Their Imperial Majesties, the Emperor Nicholas II and the Empress Alexándra Feódorovna.

The town consists mainly of wooden buildings, and is without a pavement, although situated in proximity to rich quarries of gray sandstone. Of

View of the town of Cheliábinsk.

the 1,308 houses, only 30 are of stone; about 40 shops are built of the same material, the rest being of wood. Cheliábinsk takes the first place in the northern part of the Transurál on account of its corn (mainly wheat) trade. Horses, cattle, sheep and various animal products are sold for several hundred thousand rubls at the St. Nicholas and St. John fairs, held in the town in May and October. The market is open every day with the exception of sundays and holidays.

There is a private warehouse capable of holding over half a million puds of grain. A considerable quantity of grain is ground in the surrounding mills. The steam flour-mill of Messrs Stepánov, situated within 10 versts of the town, is specially remarkable on account of its working capacity, the daily output amounting to about 2,400 puds. Among other factories etc., may be mentioned: the distillery of Messrs Pokróvsky producing 500,000 vedros of spirit, a slaughter-house, where about 80,000 head, mostly sheep, are killed annually, tanneries with an annual production of about 50,000 skins, and tallow-boileries producing 100,000 puds per annum. The town has a revenue of about R. 50,000.

A branch of the State Bank has been established here since 1893, and a town pawnshop since 1896. Other financial institutions are represented by branches of the Commercial Bank of St. Petersburg and of the Yarosláv-Kostromá Bank.

The hotels are very bad (the Siberian Rooms, the Commercial Hotel and others). Hackney coaches without springs ply according to tariff. Carriages (linéikas) run several times a day between the railway station and the town (5 kopeks a seat).

Cheliábinsk contains the Department for the Exploitation of the West-Siberian Railway, the Railway Control Department, and a first-class custom house for goods. The station Cheliábinsk possesses special importance as the junction of the European railways with the Siberian main line.

The connexion with the Perm-Tiumén line, carried right on to Kotlás, by causing an increase of goods traffic to the northern water-systems of European Russia, will undoubtedly still further enlarge the operations of this central station.

Occupying an important position in regard to the transit goods traffic, the station of Cheliábinsk in also distinguished by a considerable export of goods from the surrounding localities. Great supplies of wheat are forwarded from this station. The local merchants buy up annually about 500,000 to 700,000 puds; a considerable quantity of this grain is also purchased by representatives of firms at Révél, Libáva and Rostóv on the Don.

The increasing importance of the station attracted a numerous new population, which, in 1896 founded the Nikólsk settlement in close proximity to the railway line. At present, the number of its inhabitants exceeds 3,000 souls. A wooden church capable of holding 750 has been built near the station, at the cost of the Emperor Alexander III fund, in order to satisfy the spiritual needs of the railway and country population. The first stone of this church was laid in presence of State Secretary Kulomzín on the 5 June 1897, and it was inaugurated on the 30 January 1898, in honour of the Blessed Virgin.

A school with two classes under the direction of the Ministry of Public Instruction was established in 1898 near the station in a special wooden building constructed for this purpose; it is supported by the West-Siberian Railway, and by the fees of the scholars. A parish school for girls is being built near the church in honour of Father John Sérgiev.

A station for emigrants has been erected near by, with a branch line to the barracks for parties of emigrants bound for Siberia. This branch line is provided with sidings, platforms, lodgings for railway and telegraph agents. The wooden barracks can accomodate 1,500 emigrants; in summer the number rises to 2,500. The hospital barracks contain 70 beds, 50 of them for infectious diseases. There is a pharmacy, a dining-room supplying the emigrants with 1,500 rations of food in winter and with 2,000 in summer, which during the latter season are boiled in pots in the open air. A bath, with two divisions for women and men, is arranged for 50 persons, and there is also a laundry. This fully organised emigration station resembles a small town, including 25 separate, clean and sanitarily planned cottages. It is also the residence of the official entrusted with the regulation of the emigration movement.

Since 1893, when the West-Siberian line was opened to traffic, over 600,000 emigrants of both sexes have been registered at the emigration station of Cheliábinsk.

The Smolínsk lake, which in the Transurál is famous for its salutary properties, lies within 9 versts of the town. It contains a considerable quantity of chloride and iodide of potassium. In the summer, many people re-

Church near the station of Cheliábinsk.

siding in the environs and other patients visit the lake for bathing. The latter, whose number increases every year, live in the cottages of the Smolínsk Cossack settlement on the shore of the lake.

The Cheliábinsk-Ekaterinbúrg Branch.

This branch, connecting the Great Siberian Railway with the Perm-Tiumén line, leaves the West Siberian section at the Cheliábinsk station, and runs in a north-western direction a distance of 226.5 versts.

Within four versts of Cheliábinsk, the branch line crosses the river Miàs, spanned by a bridge of 40 sazhens, and ascends towards the watershed of the rivers Ufá and Miás. Leaving the latter, it traverses the river Ziuzélka and reaches the first station.

1) **Esaúlskaya.** (24 v. from Cheliábinsk). From here the line runs through the steppes adjoining the Urál dotted by lakes of various sizes for the most part picturesquely situated.

2) **Argayásh.** (53 v.). Is situated near the lake of the same name. Beyond it, the line leaves the Orenbúrg government, and enters into the confines of the Perm government (Ekaterinbúrg district) where commences the forest-clad region passed through before reaching the Urál.

3) **Kyshtym.** Buffet (84 v.). Lies at a height of 200 sazhens above the level of the sea, and is one of the prettiest spots on the Ekaterinbúrg branch. The Nízhni-Kyshtym works is at a distance of one verst. The Vérkhni-Kyshtym, founded by Nikíta Demídov in 1757, is within two versts of the station. The works belongs to the successors of the Baroness K. A. Meller-Zako-

The Shíshka cliff (104 v.).

mélsky, the widow of General-Major Druzhínin, and the successors of the hereditary citizen A. A. Zótov. The Vérkhni-Kyshtym works is one of the largest in the Transurál, having a population of about 18,000 souls of both sexes, while the Nízhni-Kyshtym contains only 2,000. A marble monument, erected in memory of the liberation of the serfs, stands on an elevated spot in the centre of the works. The existing museum contains articles manufactured at the Káslin cast-iron foundry, well known for its artistic work, as well as mineralogical and geological collections. The works produces pig, Marten and fagotted iron and different kinds of machinery. About 500,000 to 600,000 puds of pig-iron, and about 1,000,000 puds of iron are turned out annually.

All the Kyshtym district contiguous to the works, where the Ilmen mountains stretch northwards, is richly provided with mines and mineral deposits and contains, besides gold, copper, iron and chrome-iron ores, many other minerals. From here, the line mounts to the station Maúk, crossing numerous dales, ravines and streams, and ascends along a steep and broken slope towards the watershed of the rivers Maúk and Ufaléika to a height of 286.90 sazhens above sea-level.

4) **Maúk.** (106 v.). 240 sazhens above the level of the sea. The Káslin works contains a population of 15,000 and, founded in 1747, is situated 18 versts

from the station. The works produces above 400,000 puds of pig-iron and has some reputation on account of its fine and artistic castings.

After having crossed the great swamp called Constantine Dale, the line enters into a country with a broken surface.

5) **Ufaléi.** Buffet (133 v.). 250 sazhens above the sea level. The Ufaléi works with a population of 6,000 founded in 1761 by Mr. Mosólov, stands within half a verst of the station. The works now belongs to the Sérginsk Ufaléi Mining Company. It has an annual output of about 400,000 puds of pig iron, 220,000 puds of raw iron, and 150,000 puds of common iron.

The Nízhni-Ufaléi works (4,500 inh.) belonging to the same joint-stock company, is situated 15 versts from the station. The annual output amounts to 400,000 puds of pig iron, 350,000 of raw iron, and 300,000 puds of common iron. From here the line runs north, and twice crossing the river Korkadín ascends to the watershed of the rivers Ufá and Chusováya. Leaving the latter it proceeds along the Poldnévnaya river.

6) **Poldnévnaya.** (162 v.). Stands in a desert and wooded country, 244 sazhens above the level of the sea. The village of Poldnévnaya, containing 200 inhabitants, lies close by. The famous chrysolite mines, almost unique in the Transurál, are situated on the right bank of the Chusováya river, on land belonging to the Polévsk works. Proceeding further through a level

The Ará-Kul sopka (114 v.).

country, the line twice crosses the upper reaches of the Chusováya, on bridges of 10 and 15 sazhens each, and enters the district containing the Sysert mining works.

7) **Mrámor.** (191 v.). Is situated in a wooded district at an elevation of 262 sazhens above the sea level. Close by is the Mrámor works with a population of 1,000 souls; it is well known for the marble goods it produces. Large articles, such as marble monuments, baths, washstands, window sills, tables etc. are manufactured here, besides smaller objects made of selenite,

serpentine and ophite. The blue and white Polévsk marble is considered the best. The marble quarries are situated four versts from the village. Although living in a salubrious climate, a great percentage of the population is affected by consumption, owing to the bad organisation of the workshops.

A monument to the Emperor Alexander II stands in the centre of the village, in commemoration of the liberation of the serfs. There is a warehouse for the productions of the Sysért district at the station.

The Sysért works is situated 20 versts to the south-east; there are further the Vérkhni-Sysért and Ilyínsk works, which together with the Sysért and Polévsk works are the property of D. P. Solotírsky and of the successors of A. A. and P. M. Turchanínov. The Sysért works contains 10,000 inhabitants and above 50 different branches of iron and copper manufacture, among which are axes, horse-shoes, trivets, hooks and eyes, door locks, pails, fire-proof doors, candle-sticks, tea-urns, saucepans and other copper articles. There are blast furnaces, puddling and welding works. Over 700,000 puds of pig-iron, and 350,000 puds of iron are produced. The number of workmen employed is 600; besides 1500 occupied about the works. The works is connected by telephone with Ekaterinbúrg and other works in the district. The grounds and works are provided with electric light. The Vérkhni-Sysért works containing puddling and welding furnaces, stand within 9 versts south-west of those of Sy-

View taken near the Ufaléi station.

sért. It numbers a population of 1000 souls; there are 300 workmen, while 400 men are employed about the works. The annual output of iron amounts to 400,000 puds. The Ilyínsk works, manufacturing only sheet-iron, is situated on the river Sysért six versts from the Sysért works. It contains 500 inhabitants, employs 150 workmen, and 100 about the works.

The Séversk works (pop. 4,000, with 500 workmen, and over 1000 supplementary hands) lies south-west of the railway within 12 versts of the Mrámor works. It contains two blast, furnaces, one puddling, furnade, two Marten furnaces, a fagotted iron furnace etc. and machinery shops. The annual pro-

View of the town of Ekaterinbúrg (phot. by Ravénsky).

duction of pig-iron exceeds 900,000 puds, while that of iron amounts to 100,000 puds. The Polévsk works lies 6 versts from the latter with a population of 7,000 souls. The number of workmen employed is 300, with about 600 supplementary hands. Puddled, fagotted and rolled iron are manufactured at the works. The Séversk works supplies the pig-iron required.

Archaeölogical discoveries were made at the end of the XVIII century near the works in the Chumashév mines. The objects date from a prehistoric age and belong to a nation which in ancient times occupied itself with mining.

After leaving the station of Mrámor, the line runs along the watershed of the rivers Chusováya and Isét, through a level country which further north grows more and more monotonous.

8) **Uktús.** (221 v.). Lies in a treeless plain, 182 sazhens above the level of the sea. The village of Uktús is situated at a distance of two versts. Its inhabitants occupy themselves with agriculture and domestic industries, mainly that of pottery, carried on in about 30 shops. The wares are of a good quality and find a ready sale.

The Nízhni-Isét Government works founded in 1797 (pop. 3,500) is situated within 5 versts of the station. The annual production amounts to 200,000 puds of iron, 12,000 puds of cast-iron, and about 15,000 puds of sheet-iron. The works employs 350 workmen and contains about 30 shops for hand-made metal wares. A monument to the Emperor Alexander II stands on an open place in the works. There is telephone communication with Ekaterinbúrg. From here, the line runs along a plain covered with dwarf bushes and, after having crossed the river Isét by a bridge of 15 sazhens, joins the Perm-Tiumén Railway line.

9) **Ekaterinbúrg** 2 (226 1/2 v.). The Tiumén, Cheliábinsk and Ekaterinbúrg lines meet at this station, the latter runs on further to Perm. On its course to the station Ekaterinbúrg 1, the line sweeps round the town following its outskirts for a distance of 4 versts. Ekaterinbúrg is a district town of the Perm government (56°49′ N. lat; 30° 16 1/2′ E. long.) stands on the river Isét and, being one of the best district towns of European Russia, may be called the capital of the Urál. The census of 1897 shewed a population of 43,052 inhabitants; the town was founded by Tatíshchev in 1721, and received its name in honour of the Empress Catherine II. A mint, striking special copper and other coins called „platas", was established here in 1735. Ekaterinbúrg contains above 5,500, mostly wooden, houses; the Novotíkhvinsk nunnery; 15 orthodox churches, besides those of the monasteries and inclu-

Cathedral in Ekaterinbúrg (phot by Ravénsky).

sive of six house chapels; one church and two dissenting chapels; an evangelical Lutheran and a Roman catholic chapel; a Mohammedan mosque and a jewish prayer-house. Ekaterinbúrg is also the residence of the bishop of the Ekaterinbúrg-Irbít diocese, and is the seat of a consistory. The fraternity of St. Simon the miracle-worker of Verkhotúrie is established in the diocese. The schools are: a clergy school, a diocesan school for girls, a classical gymnasium, the Alexis modern school, a gymnasium for girls, the Urál mining school, town schools of four and three classes; eight primary schools, three parish schools and a number of private schools .The town contains also: the Urál mining department, the Imperial stone-cutting works, the Urál chemical laboratory with a gold-melting department, which receives all the slich gold from the Urál mines, a meteorological and magnetic observatory, the council of the congress of mine-masters. Charitable institutions are represented by a children's home in the nunnery, a lodging for children, night shelters, the Alexander poor-house, a work-house, the Núrov children's home. The medical institutions are: the town hospital, a local day-hospital for the poor, a lying-in hospital, the hospital of doctor Onúfriev. Besides these, there are charitable and other societies: the society of orthodox missioners, the local Red Cross commitee, a charitable society, the committee for the classification and care of beggars, the miners' children's home, a humane society, an amateur society of art, the sporting society, a racing society and a society for natural science with a museum founded in 1870, and considerably enlarged since the Siberia and Urál Science and Trade Exhibition, organised by the society in 1887. The museum includes sections for palaeontology, mineralogy, geology, zoology, botany, ethnography, archaeology and numismatics. The town numbers four libraries and contemplates opening one in honour of V. G. Belínsky. There are two clubs, one for the public, the other for the nobles. A wooden theatre of considerable dimensions belongs to the town. There are two summer gardens, one belonging to Kharitónov, the other to the public club; two boulevards from the Moscow barrier to Uspénsk street, and along the Voznesénsk prospect; a square, containing busts of Peter the Great and Catherine II. The pedestal for the projected monument to the Tsar Liberator stands in front of the cathedral. The periodicals of Ekaterinbúrg comprise: the Diocesan Journal, and three private papers: the Ekaterinbúrg Week, with a literary tendency; the Urál founded in 1896, discussing politics, public life and literature; the Business Correspondent, containing mainly trade and industrial information. Memoirs in Russian and French are periodically issued by the Ural Society for Natural Sciences under the patronage of His Imperial Highness the Grand Duke Michael Nikoláevich.

The Annual revenue of the town amounts to R. 200,000. For the development of trade and industry, there exist an office of the State Bank, a Branch of the Vólga-Káma Commercial Bank, the Siberian Trade Bank, the Town and Public Banks. Bankers: Y. P. Andréev, with a loan bank, Pelénkin and Co., a branch of the St. Petersburg Lombard.

Factories and works: 1) the steam mill of the merchant Símonov, which is an immense six-storeyed building, standing near a pond almost in the centre of the town, surrounded by a beautiful garden with hot-houses; 2) the match manufactory of the joint stock company of Vorontsóv and Lóginov, turning out annually about 60,000 boxes of phosphorus and safety matches, and employing 250 workmen; 3) the cloth factory of the Brothers Zlokázov on the river Isét, weaving daily over 600 arshins of different kinds of cloth, made of Kirgíz wool, mainly for Siberia; 4) the machinery works of the Brothers Korobéinikov and Yates, constructing steam-engines, boilers of different systems etc. 5) the paper-mill of Vorontsóv and Co. manufactoring over 10,000 puds of common writing-paper; 6) the pottery of Davydov producing fire-bricks, tiles etc.; and a number of soap-boileries, tallow-factories, oil manufactories, and beer and mead breweries. The total production amounts to over R. 4,000,000.

The town contains the following hotels and rooms: the American Hotel of Khólkin is the best, rooms from R. 1 to R. 4 a day; Atamánov's furnished rooms from 1 r. 25 k. to 2 r. 50 k., Wunder and Plótnikov, 75 k. to 2 r. The hackney coaches are driven by one horse and are hired by the tariff: 25 k. an hour or 15 k. the drive; the rate for a drive out of town is fixed by mutual agreement; the drive from the railway-station costs 35—50 k. in the daytime according to the distance, and 50—80 k. at night. In autumn and spring, 5 k.

are added to the usual rate. At Easter. Christmas and during the Butter Week, the tariff is not adhered to. Within the last ten years, the town has greatly improved. Electric light was introduced three years ago. The chief defect is the absence of water-pipes, which makes it necessary to bring water from springs in the neighbourhood. The most important events in the

Ekaterinbúrg. Quay, court of justice (phot. by Ravénsky).

history of the town are: the visit of the Emperor Alexander I in 1824; the institution of the Court of Justice; the publication of the first private newspaper in 1878; the opening of the Urál mining railway from Perm to Ekaterinbúrg; the Siberia and Urál Exhibition in 1887; the completion of the branch line between the Siberian and Urál railways in 1895.

The Vérkhni-Isét works, belonging to the Countess Stenbock-Fermor is situated at a distance of one verst from the town; it includes blast, fining, Marten and puddling furnaces, rolling mills and machinery works (pop. 10,000) About 350,000 puds of iron and 250,000 puds of assorted iron are produced annually. Roof iron is supplied in considerable quantity.

The number of workmen employed is 1500. The pond belonging to the works is 10 versts long and 3 versts wide, and is an ornament to the country.

The Ekaterinbúrg-Tiumén line.

This line, which is comprised in the Perm-Tiumén railway, goes by the name of the Tiumén section and is formed by the main line and the Kámensk branch. The main line which has a total length of 308.88 versts connects the district towns of Ekaterinbúrg and Kamyshlov in the Perm government, and terminates at the station Túra close to the town of Tiumén. The Kámensk branch, 37.31 versts in length, unites the Bogdanóvich station, on the main line, and the Ostróvskaya station, situated near the Kámensk Government cast iron foundry.

From the Ekaterinbúrg station, lying at an elevation of 121.73 sazhens above the level of the sea, the line rnns through a level country in a north-eastern direction.

1) **Istók.** (15 v.). The line reaches its highest point at the 24 v. lying 128.95 sazhens above sea-level.

2) **Kosúlino.** (33 v.).

3) **Bazhénovo.** Buffet (53 v.). Emerald mines are situated 35 v. from the station in the forests belonging to the Ekaterinbúrg mint, along the river Great Réfta falling into the Pyshma. These are the only emerald mines in Russia. They are leased for 24 years to Mr. Necháev, who with a view to extending the enterprise formed an agreement with the New Emeralds Company in Paris, working emerald mines in Columbia. Asbestos mines belonging to Baron Girade, successor to the trading firm of Poklévsky-Kózell and Korévo, are at some distance from the first.

4) **Griaznóvskaya.** (75 v.).

5) **Bogdanóvich.** Buffet (94 v.). The Kurínsk mineral springs are situated 15 versts from the station in the Kamyshlov district of the Perm government. They are efficacious for rheumatism, paralysis, scrofula and anaemia Furnished houses and an hotel with good rooms are situated near the baths there is a garden and a promenade with band; theatricals and concerts take place in the casino. The Government cast-iron foundry, producing annually about 400,000 puds of cast-iron, with a population of 10,000, is situated at a distance of 37 versts from the station of Ostróvskaya.

6) **Pyshmínskaya.** (113 v.). Approaching the town of Kamyshlov, the line traverses the Pyshma by a bridge 30 sazhens long.

7) **Kamyshlov.** Buffet (134 v.). The district town of the same name in the Perm government, with a population of 7,000, is situated near the station. It contains 5 orthodox churches and the following schools and institutions: a preparatory gymnasium for girls, a district and clergy school, a municipal poorhouse and a children's home. There are also a distillery, a tannery and a tallow-candle manufactory. The local trade in grain is rather considerable. The Mutual Credit Company have a bank in the town.

The Obúkhov brackish, sulphurous and chalybeate mineral springs are situated within six versts of the station. There are furnished houses with rooms and buffet for the patients. There are further a library and a band of music. A drive from the station Kamyshlov to the Obúkhov springs costs 50 k. The town of Irbít famous for its fair, lies 110 versts from Kamyshlov.

8) **Arsárikha.** (151 v.).

9) **Oshchénkovo.** (171 v.).

10) **Poklévskaya.** Buffet (201 v.). The Tálitsk factories, belonging to the successors of Poklévsky-Kózell, are four versts from the station. They comprise a spirit distillery, a yeast manufactory, a rectifying works and a brewery. Their production is: 450,000 vedros of spirit of wine, 100,000 vedros of the same, about 15,000 puds of yeast, and 450,000 and 160,000 vedros of spirits. The population is 4,000, and the number of workmen 350. There is a stud producing a thorough-bred stock founded by Poklévsky-Kózell.

The successor of this gentleman established a glass works near the village of Ertársk, 30 versts from the station. The annual output is 1,500 boxes of sheet glass, and about 600,000 spirit bottles.

11) **Yushála.** (232 v.).

12) **Tugulym.** (248 v.).

13) **Karmák.** (266 v.). Close by is the Uspénsk paper-mill founded by Shcherbakóv and producing yearly about 100,000 puds of different kinds of paper. The mill employs 300 workmen.

14) **Pereválovo.** (285 v).

Tiumén. (304 v). Buffet (304 v.). Leaving the station, the line skirts the town and descends to the landing place on the Turá which is the terminus oı the East-Siberian section of the Perm-Tiumén line (308 v., 26.15 sazh. above the level of the sea).

Tiumén, which is a district town of the Tobólsk government, is situated 57° 10' N. lat., 35° 12' E. long., and is one of the oldest towns of Siberia. It was built on the site of the former Tatar town of Chingí Turá, which is believed to have been fonded in the XIV century by the Tatar Khan Taibúga. The voyevódas Vasíli Súkin, Iván Miasnói and Iván Chulkóv, sent to Siberia by the Tsar Feódor Ivánovich in 1581, after the death of Yermák, founded the first Russian town on the bank of the Turá, giving it the name of Tiumén in remembrance of the Tiumén Khan to whom this place formerly

View of the town of Tiumén.

belonged. These voyevódas erected also in the new town the first Russian church in honour of the Nativity of the Blessed Virgin. Fragments of a rampart and a moat exist to the present day in the part designated by the name of Tsar town, and are clear evidence of the former Tatar dominion.

The commercial importance of Tiumén was established long ago. Previous to the construction of the Great Siberian Railway, this town represented the connecting point of Siberia and European Russia, a consequence of its water communication and proximity to Ekaterinbúrg and Perm. After its foundation in 1782, Tiumén was under the command of voyevódas; among them may be mentioned Voéikov, Prince Bariátinsky, Godunóv, Volynsky, who all contributed to the power and progress of the town. In 1782, Tiumén was included in the Tobólsk government.

At present, this town comprises over 3,500 houses and a population of 29,588, according to the census of 1897. It is built on uneven ground broken by ravines, and contains 15 churches, inclusive of three house chapels (in the prison, modern school and orphans' home). The church of Our Saviour, that of the Holy Trinity in the ancient monastery, and the church of the Annunciation, are noteworthy on account of their architecture. The Tiumén monastery was founded in 1616; the Metropolitan of Tobólsk, Filoféi Leshchínsky became a hermit in this monastery in 1711, receiving the name of Feódor. This famous missioner and ascetic was buried at the gate of the church erected in the monastery during his life time, in honoûr of the Holy Trinity. An iron-roofed monument, representing this zealous servant of God, stands on his grave. A wooden altar-cross, covered with silver, and containing relics, was sent by the Tsar Alexis Mikháilovich in 1664, and is now kept in the church of the Annunciation. The church of the Blessed Apparition contains a miraculous image of rude design dating from 1624, representing the Apparition of the Virgin Mary. This image has been held in particular veneration since the time when the cholera ravaged Tiumén in 1848. Schools are represented by the Alexander modern school, the preparatory gymnasium for girls, four municipal schools, one district school. The former town-bailiff of Tiumén, P. I. Podarúev, built a modern school at his own cost, while its director I. Y. Slovtsév arranged a most remarkable museum, including many branches of natural history, opened in 1879. Since 1896, professional lectures have been added to the school.

The charitable institutions are: the Vladímir orphans' home, founded by the citizen Trúsov in commemoration of the Grand Duke Vladímir Alexándrovich's visit to Tiumén; a poor-house maintained out of the fund given by the merchants Maxímov and Vóinov: the Alexander lying-in hospital, instituted by the merchant Vóinov in commemoration of the happy escape of the Emperor Alexander II, and a night shelter. The town with a considerable population, has but one hospital, for men and women, with 30 beds. Outpatients are received only thrice a week. Among the charitable and other institutions may be mentioned: a temperance society (tea-rooms and a library for the lower classes), a society for the relief of the poor, one for the pupils of district and primary schools with a public library and Sunday school, a volunteer fire-brigade, a racing society, a society for the protection of animals with a hospital, a cooperative supply society, a society for the relief of poor emigrants on their way from European Russia to Siberia.

Before the construction of the Great Siberian Railroad, the greater number of emigrants passed through Tiumén, which was the centre of different medical and other organisations for the help of the settlers. A total of about 500,000 emigrants moved through Tiumén in a space of 16 years, from 1883 to 1900. The society for the assistance of poor emigrants, since the time of its organisation on the 4 July 1892, has constantly endeavoured to collect means for the help of the emigrants, and on account of its unwearying activity merits an honourable mention in the history of the emigration movement.

A. I. Efímov and P. P. Arkhípov were the leaders and initiators of this society, whose activity has now somewhat fallen off.

The exile office of Tiumén, registering and regulating the exiles and their distribution throughout Siberia, is an important and active institution. From 1823 to 1898, a period of 75 years, 908,266 peasons have been registered

The museum of the Tiumén modern school.

and forwarded by this office. The town has neither gardens nor boulevards; a small wood out of town is little frequented, being too far off. There are two clubs, one for public assemblies, the other for clerks; the latter has at its disposal scenery for amateur theatricals, belonging to A. I. Tekútiev. The circus of Borovskói, built of wood, is situated on the market place of the town.

The Siberian Trade Gazette with an extensive literary and industrial programme, has been published in Tiumén since 1897. There is also a branch office for the Urál Gazette issued in Ekaterinbúrg.

Although the town revenue amounts to R. 175,000 per annum, it is badly kept: only the Tsar street and those leading to the landing places have been paved. Petroleum is used for lighting, and the telephone has only recently been adopted. Tiumén as the centre of an active trade is provided with numerous financial institutions represented by a branch of the State Bank, a branch of the Siberian Bank, a town loan-bank, two State savings banks and Andréev's private loan-bank.

A first class custom-house was established here at the end of 1899. Hotels: Central Hotel, on Tsar street, North Hotel, near the theatre, the Warsaw on the Sadóvaia street. Rooms for travellers are kept by Zalévsky.

The hackney coaches are very bad, without springs and are hired by tariff. A fair is held annually from the 20 June to the 20 July, the goods sold exceeding in value R. 2,000,000. The town line includes many factories: tanneries (Kolmagórov is the most important firm) soap boileries, candle works and pelisse manufactories, a bell foundry, belonging to Gilév and supplying the churches constructed along the main Siberian line with bells; the machinery works of Gullet, the shipbuilding wharf of Ignátiev and Kurbátov, and the wheat-flour mills of Tekútiev. Their total production is above R. 3,000,000.

The inhabitants of the town are mainly engaged in house industries, of which carpet weaving, introduced from Bukhará and employing women, occupies the first place. The carpets are offered for sale at the fairs of Irbít and Nízhni Nóvgorod.

The town of Tiumén has several times been visited by Imperial personages, as by the Emperor Alexander II, when heir apparent to the throne, on the 31 May 1837. On the 1 July, the Imperial Guest crossed the Turá and arrived at Tobólsk. For this purpose, the inhabitants of Tiumén built a fine boat with a crew of 11 oarsmen, taken from the most honoured citizens of the town.

The Grand Duke Vladímir Alexándrovich was conveyed in the same boat in the year 1868, and the Grand Duke Alexéi Alexándrovich in 1873. The first exhibition of articles manufactured in the Tobólsk government took place during the stay of the Grand Duke Vladímir Alexándrovich.

The banks of the river Turá have been so strengthened that railway carriages may be brought right up to the steamers, which considerably facilitates loading and unloading. Landing places belonging to the Ship and Trade Company (Kurbátov and Ignátov), to Kornílov, Trapéznikov, Plótnikov, Morózov and to the Bogoslóv mining district, are situated on the quay. They are lighted by electricity and connected by telephones.

Landing-places for steamers in Tiumén.

Previous to the construction of the Great Siberian Railway, the Ekaterinbúrg-Tiumén line, which belongs to the Perm-Tiumén Railway, was the sole means of communication between the basins of the rivers Ob and Vólga, the most important water systems of Asia and Europe. The Siberian main line, connecting the southern sections of these basins, brought new life to a vast, but scarcely civilised country and, although somewhat lessening the importance of the northern route, secured the commercial development of the latter, by promoting the industry of Siberia.

The data concerning the Perm-Tiumén line, covering the period it was under the management of the Government, from 1888 to 1898, clearly illustrate the growth of its operations. In 1888, the gross receipts were R. 5,119,605, with an expenditure of R. 3,228,167, and a revenue of R. 1,908,438; the total number of versts run by engines was 2,545,915, the total run by trains 1,941,540; the number of passengers carried was 480,212; and the number of puds of goods conveyed 42,816,771. In 1897, the gross receipts were R. 7,969,740, expenditure R. 5,096,784, revenue R. 2,902,955, the total versts run by engines 4,733,810, the total run by trains 3,511,655, the number of passengers carried 1,034,389, and the number of puds of goods conveyed 77,046,083. In 1898, the total revenue amounted to R. 8,538,778.

BIBLIOGRAPHY:

Review of the Samára government. Supplements to official reports. The centres of population of the Russian Empire, published by the Centr. Statist. Com. of the Minist. of the Int. Bashkíria and the Bashkírs by Florínsky. European Messenger, 1874, № 12. Anthropological review of the Bashkírs by Máliev. Kazán. 1876. The Samára-Zlatoúst line, Orenbúrg branch, publ. by the Min. of Ways of Com. Samára. 1896. The Perm-Tiumén railway, publ. by the Min. of Ways of Com. Perm. 1898. Concise review of the operations of the Samára-Zlatoúst Railway in 1897. publ. by the Min. of Ways of Com. 1898. Mining industry and metallurgy at the Nóvgorod exhibition, by Baklévsky, Nésterovsky, Troyán, Afrosímov and others. Guide to the Urál. Ekaterinbúrg. 1899.

САМАРО—ЗЛАТОУСТОВСКАЯ Ж.

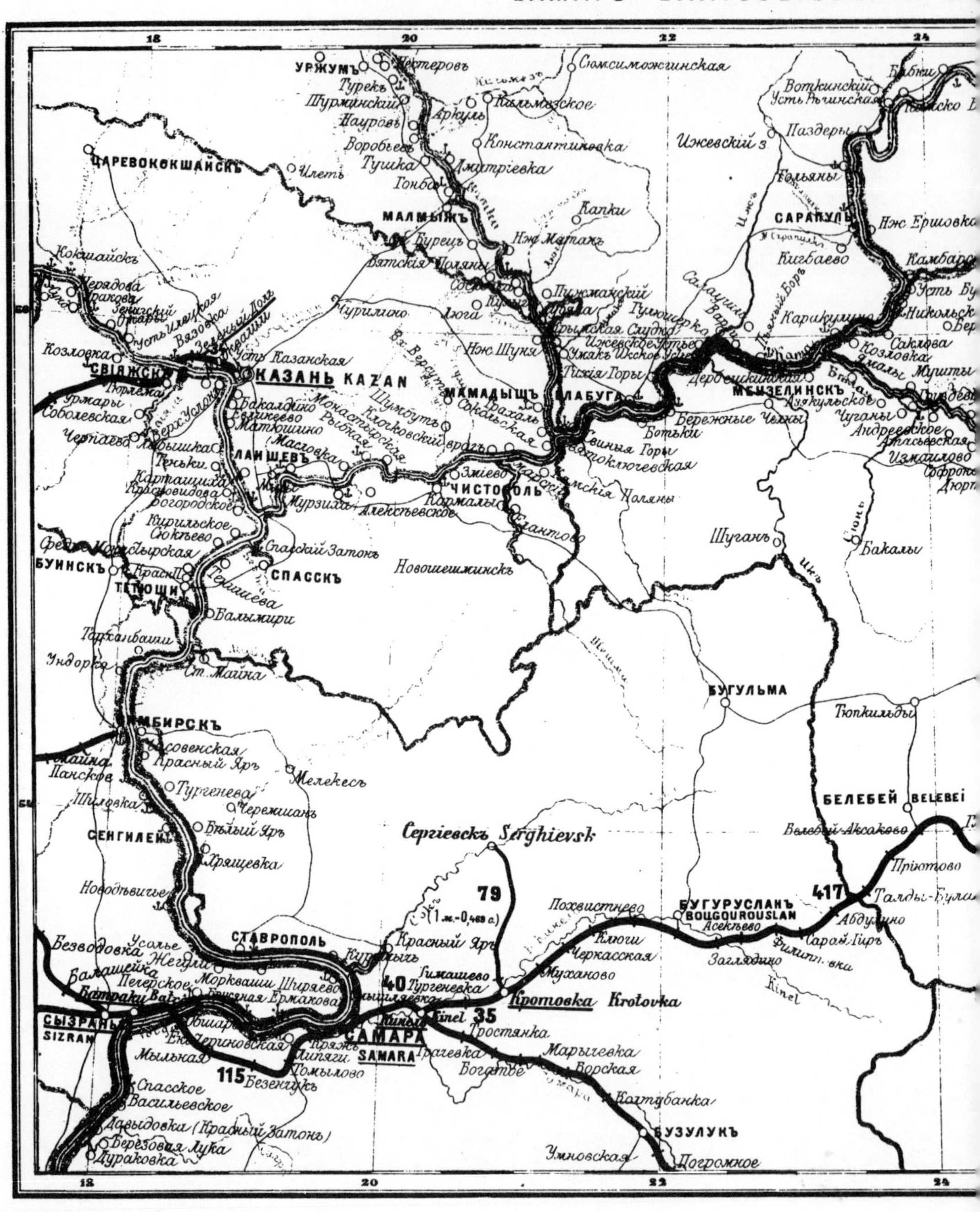

Chemin de fer SAMARA–ZLATOOUST.

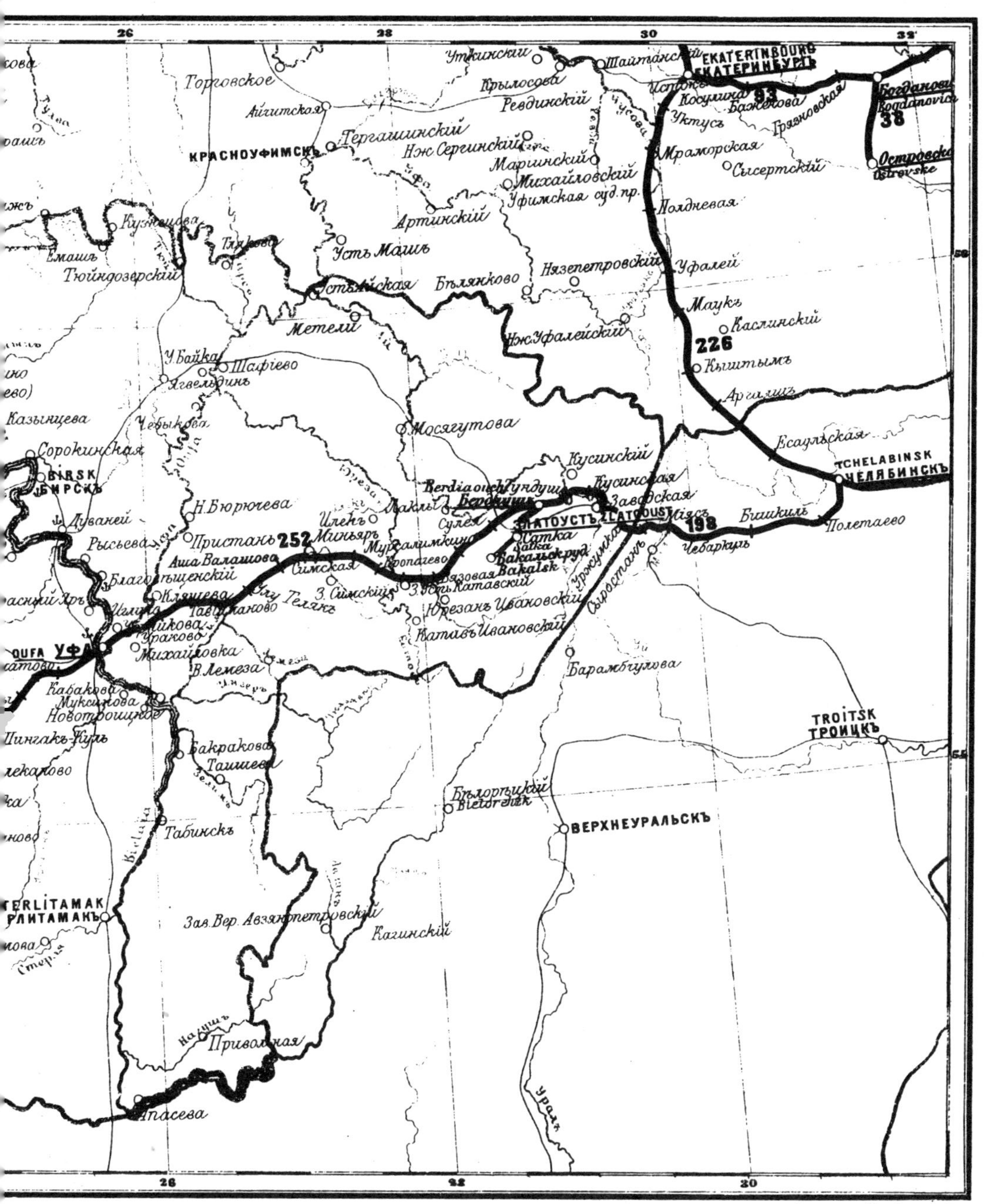

Картогр. зав. А Ильина СПБ

The West Siberian plain and the Kirgíz Steppe Borderland within the Range of the Great Siberian Railway.

Tobólsk Government. — Geographical position and extent. — Superficial structure and orography within the range of the Great Siberian Railway.—Climate.—Flora and forests of the Southern zone.—Fauna.—Population.—Settlers and colonisation.—Historical review of the exile system and of exile settlement. — Land tenure. — Soil and subsoil of the Ishím steppe.—Agriculture and cattle breeding.—Butter manufacture.—Export of grain and animal products. — Manufactures, industry and village industry within the range of the Great Siberian Railway.—Trade.—The Kirgíz Steppe Borderland.—Review of the territories of Akmolínsk and Semipalátinsk.—Mineral wealth of the Kirgíz steppe.—Climate.—Flora. — Fauna. — Population.—Aborigenal Kirgíz.—Siberian Cossack troops and their organisation. — Colonisation of the Kirgíz steppe by peasants. — Agriculture and cattle breeding.—Manufactures and industry.—Trade and export of animal products.—Intercourse with West China and Mongolia. — The Barabá country.—Urmans and the river and lake region. — The Tatars of Barabá.—Drainage.—The future of the country.—Bibliography.

THE western section of the Great Siberian Railroad commences at Cheliábinsk in the Orenbúrg government, in the Transurál belonging to the Asiatic continent. The portion of the Orenbúrg government traversed by the Siberian main line from Cheliábinsk to the border of the Tobólsk government forms a plain where agriculture and cattle-raising are extensively developed. This area retains the same nature as characterises the country stretching east from Miás, crossed by the eastern section of the Samára-Zlatoúst line. The sphere of influence of the Orenbúrg Transurál section, running a length of 200 v. from west to east, besides the Cheliábinsk, Tróitsk-Verkhneurálsk districts of the Orenbúrg government, comprises also the Shádrinsk district of the Perm government.

The effect produced by the railway upon trade is well illustrated by the quantity of goods, consisting mainly of grain, brought to the railway stations from the fertile districts for further transmission. After having crossed the administrative frontier of Siberia, within 200 versts of Cheliábinsk, the great Siberian line enters the confines of the Tobólsk government, comprising the western border of the Siberian continent included in the Russian Empire 300 years ago. The superficial area of the Tobólsk government amounts to 25,156.61 squ. geogr. miles and, lying between 72° 54′ N. lat. and 54° 59′ N. lat., comprises 18° lat. from north to south, or a distance of about 1100 versts. Among the governments of European Russia, not one attains such an extent, which however is surpassed by the Asiatic governments of Yeniséisk, Yakútsk, and the Littoral. The Tobólsk government is equal to about 2/5 of European Russia, and is four times as large as Germany. On the north it is bounded by the Arctic Ocean, on the west by the governments of Arkhángelsk, Vólogda, Perm, Orenbúrg; the Kirgíz steppes stretching to the south and east are limited by the Tomsk and Yeniséisk governments. The whole area of the government is divided into ten unequal districts.

	squ. versts.	squ. miles.
Beriózov .... Surgút	838,341.2	17,116.9
Tobólsk	109,361	2,259.84
Tára	71,542	1,478.86
Turín	67,691	1,398.76
Tiumén	16,127	333.25
Kurgán	20,367	420.79
Yalutoróvsk	19,044	392.52
Ishím	30,088	787.05
Tiukalín	46,853	968.18
	1,217,411.2	25,156.61

The surface of the Tobólsk government presenting a vast plain, with a general inclination from south to north towards the Arctic Ocean, is varied in its north-western part by the ridges of the Urál branches.

The Great Siberian Railway, twice crossing the Tobólsk government, at its south-western corner and at the south-eastern extremity, extends its influence over the districts of Kurgán, Ishím, Tiukalínsk, and part of the Yalutoróvsk, the three first of which comprise the steppe region known under the collective name of the Ishím steppe, very fertile and suitable for agriculture and cattle-breeding, whereas the Yalutoróvsk district forms a transition from the northern forest zone to the steppes. The greater part of the government on the north feels the influence of the Perm-Tiumén Railway.

The broken surface of the Ishím steppe, intersected by ridges, contains numerous fresh-water brackish, alkaline, and sulphurous lakes. Forests consisting chiefly of birch, aspen, and willow are met within the northern part, whereas the south is dotted with groves and covered with young wood. Salt marshes occur more and more frequently further south, towards the limit of the Kirgíz steppe, where at some points the soil also contains salt. The soil and subsoil of the vast Tobólsk government, devoid of hard rocks raised by volcanic action, excepting the branches of the Urál, consists of friable sediments of more recent formation; this is the reason why this government is but poorly provided with minerals.

As a result of this scarcity, stone for building has to be brought from the Orenbúrg and Perm governments, and lime from the Semipalátinsk territory. The southern more populous and fertile part of the government is surrounded by the tributaries of the navigable Irtysh which flows on the left into the Ob. The Ishím and Toból are the most important tributaries of the Irtysh. The Ishím entering the confines of the Tobólsk government beyond the town of Petropávlovsk, flows for a distance of 500 versts across the Ishím and Tára districts; its course through the Ishím district is 300 versts long. Rafting is practised on this river, although it might be adapted for regular navigation. The river-bed consists of sand and lime; its banks are bordered by wide stretching meadows which in spring are flooded by the swollen waters.

The usual width of the river bed is about 60 sazhens. The Toból traverses the Kurgán and part of the Yalutoróvsk district, and after flowing

Town of Tobólsk.

through the Tiumén and Tobólsk districts falls into the Irtysh near the town of Tobólsk. The total length of its course through the government being 723 versts, it flows through the Kurgán district for a distance of 275 versts, through the Yalutoróvsk district a distance of 200 versts, and through that of Tiumén, 155 versts. The breadth of the river bed varies from 20 to 60 sazhens, with a depth of about one sazhen and a half. Pursuing its course through the Tobólsk government for a distance of 93 versts, the river widens to about 110 sazhens, with a depth of about two sazhens. From its mouth to the town of Yalutoróvsk, small steamers ply on the river; above Yalutoróvsk to Kurgán navigation is possible only in spring.

The abundance of swamps and lakes is to be explained by the orographical character of the country, its inclination towards the north and the absence of elevations. The swamps covering immense areas in the north of the government, still further pass into tundra stretching far over the northern deserts.

Swamps also occur frequently in the southern part of the government in the Yalutoróvsk, Ishím and Tiukalínsk districts but, without attaining such an extent, they here give place to lakes. The Tobólsk government, with the exception of its northern border, contains more than 1,600 lakes:

478 lie in the Kurgán district, 329 in the Yalutoróvsk, 204 in the Tiumén, 200 in the Tiukalínsk, 152 in the Tobólsk, 124 in the Ishím and 112 in the Tára districts. The rise and fall of the water-level observed in many swamps and lakes, is a characteristic and as yet unsufficiently explained phenomenon Water systems sometimes disappear altogether, and again fill with water and fish after the lapse of many years. As a result of this strange fact, many cultivated spots meadows and arable land lose their fertility for certain periods, and afterwards recover it. The majority of the fresh-water lakes situated in the southern steppes of the government have sloping reed-covered shores and an oozy and limy bottom; the water is yellow and seems to be covered with slime, which comes partly from the mud at the bottom, partly from the stagnancy of the water heated by the sun, and also from the guano of the birds, building their nests on the shores of the lakes.

Museum in the town of Tobólsk.

The brackish and bitter lakes have no outlet and are scattered very irregularly over the Tobólsk steppes, alternating with fresh-water lakes. Among the first, the most important are: Lake Akhtabál in the Kurgán district, the Great and Small Medvézhie in the Ishím district, and the Glubókoe and Kolmagórovskoe in the Tiukalínsk district; they all contaln salt which is hardly worked at all.

The climate of the Tobólsk government is very severe, with a mean temperature inferior to that of the corresponding zones in European Russia. The winters are colder and the difference between summer and winter temperature is more extreme than in the countries lying west of the Urál chain. The continental nature of the climate of the Tobólsk government is more strikingly marked than in European Russia. January, February and

December are the coldest months. The number of cold days, with a temperature of —20° is 26 in Kurgán, 27 in Ishím. The following are the highest and lowest temperatures of these localities;

	Cold.	Heat.	Difference.
Kurgán	—35°	+33°	68°
Ishím	—42°	+29°	71°

Early frosts in autumn, and the morning frosts in spring have a most disastrous effect upon agriculture. In the Kurgán district the temperature falls sometimes below zero in the beginning of September; while in the Ishím district, the same thing occurs at the end of August, whereas the morning frosts last to the beginning of June in both districts. Thus July is the only warm month. In consequence of the continental climate of the government, the amount of moisture is insignificant, and the rainfall in the Kurgán and Ishím districts ist wice less than that in the corresponding latitudes of European Russia. The greatest rainfall occurs in July. The absence of snow in winter severely affects agriculture. The prevailing winds blow from the west and south-west.

The Abaláksk monastery near Tobólsk.

Although the severe conditions of climate exert a certain effect on the flora, the existing vegetation of the Ishím steppe but slightly differs from that of the corresponding zones in European Russia.

The few species unknown there and occurring on the eastern sides ot the Urál within the confines of the Tobólsk government, are represented by varieties of anemone (A. reflexa, altaica, pensylvanica), by a form of peony (Paeonia anomala), some cruciferae (Dentaria tenuifolia, Chorispara sibirica, Hesperis aprica), a kind of violet (Viola uniflora), the Lychia sibirica of the genus of pinks, some varieties of wormwood (Artemisia desertorum, A. Turczanowiana, macranta, latifolia), some forms of gentian (G. auriculata, aquatica, Halenia sibirica).

The tree vegetation has quite an other character beyond the Urál: both species of oak (Quercus sessiliflora, Q. pedunculata) here disappear altogether, and nut-tree (Corylus avellana), elm (Ulmus campestris, U. pedunculata), all kinds of maple (Acer), ash (Fraximus excelsior), apple tree (Pyrus malus), linden (Tilia parviolia), which thickly clothe the country along the rivers Távda and Turá, within the Tiumén and Turínsk districts, are absent from the steppe regions of the Tobólsk government. Almost the sole form of arboreal vegetation in the steppe is the birch, with a slight admixture of aspen and willow near rivers and moist places. The forests grow only beyond the region of birch, on the left bank of the Toból, and on the right side of the Irtysh.

The forests, lying in the southern part of the Tobólsk government, are divided for purposes of administration as follows:

1) Yalutoróvsk, comprising the north and the river Toból, with rich fir forests belonging to the former brandy distilleries of the State.

2) Boravliánsk, along .the Isét, west of the first, contains fir and foliage woods. Both these divisions, which raft timber to the north, have but small importance in the economy of the southern Ishím steppe.

3) The Kurgán division, stretching along the Toból, in the neighbourhood of the town of Kurgán, in the western part of the government, contains 85,000 desiatins of forest, with 18,000 of arable land. The forests consist mainly of fir-trees, with a slight admixture of other species. These forests supply the Siberian railway with wood, ties and telegraph poles, and are considerably exhausted by it.

4) The Kurgán steppe division contains small groves of birch and other foliage trees, and is entirely devoid of fir-trees. These plantations date from a rather recent period, and occur in parts of the steppe which formerly were occupied by lakes, they may not be exploited, and are carefully preserved: only dry and fallen trees are removed.

5) The Ishím division comprises about 110,000 desiatins of scanty birch woods.

6) The steppe division of Ishím bordered by the Kirgíz steppe includes birch forests, scattered in copses and groves among meadows.

7) The Tiukalínsk division consists of about 100,000 desiatins clothed with foliage trees and marsh firs. In this section much land is allotted to emigrant settlements.

8) The steppe division of Tiukalínsk contains only young birch wood. The rapid extermination of forests in Siberia may be illustrated by the fact that some 60 or 70 years ago the Tiukalínsk district was thickly covered with wood; now this same locality is converted into steppe. The chief reason for this extraordinary disappearance of forests lies in the total absence until lately of any system regulating their use. It is only since 1860 that the Government put a restraint on the disastrous exploitation of the forests, and in 1884 established a forest department as in Russia.

Miraculous image of the Holy Virgin of Abalák.

The frequent fires, spreading sometimes over a thousands quare versts, cause terrible havoc in the forests. Their cause is commonly to be traced to the existing custom of burning hay fields practised by peasants and natives with a view to destroying weeds and improving the grass.

The systematic extermination of forests in Siberia, particularly in the regions traversed by the Great Siberian Railway, where they yield fuel and material for its construction, was brought before a special committee of members of the Central Forestry Department, delegated to Siberia by Imperial command. The fauna of the Tobólsk government is rich and varied only in the north, within the forest zone and in the Ob basin united to the Arctic Ocean, whereas the southern steppes contain a fauna which but slightly differs from that of European Russia.

Ikonostasis in the monastery of Abalák.

The following animals occur in this part of the territory and in the existing forests: the brown bear, the elk, the glutton, the lynx, the ermine, many kinds of rodents, the common and striped squirrel, the badger, the wolf, the fox, the polecat (Mustela foetorius sibiricus), the bat, the shrewmouse, the mole, the Siberian marmot, the harvest mouse, the water rat, the white hare.

Among birds are: the black - cock (Tetrao tetrax), the capercailzie (T. urogallus), the white partridge (Lagopus albus), the grey partridge (Perdrix cinerea), the starna, the wood hen (Pterocle), the quail (Coturnix communis), the bustard (Otis tarda), the field-duck (O. tetrax), the tirwit (Vanellus cristatus), the river plover (Charadrius hiaticulus) the grey crane (Grus cinerea), the bittern (A. stellaris), a kind of snipe (Numenius aryatus), the Limosa aegocephala, the sand piper (Machetas pugnans), the snipe (Scolopax rustilica), two species of snipes (S. gallinago, S. gallinula), the Totanus glottis, the crake (Crex pratensis), the coot (Fulica atra), the singing swan (Cygnus musicus), the grey goose (Anser cinereus), different kinds of ducks (Anas).

Birds of prey: the eagle (Aquila clanga), the kestrel (Falco tinnunculus), the hawk (F. vesperinus), (Astur palumbarius), the wood owl (Strix otus), (S. aluco), (S. passerina), the woodpecker (Picus major), the cuckoo (Cuculus canorus), the hoopoo (Upupa epops), the blackbird (Turdus pilaris), the gold-hammer (Oriolus galbula). (Lanius excubitor), the rook (Corvus frugilegus), the jack-daw (C. monedula), the grey crow (C. cornix), the mag-pie (C. pica), the nut-hatch (Nucifraga cariocatactes), the jay (Garrulus glandarius), the common starling (Sturnus vulgaris), the cross-bill (Loxia curvirostria), the turtle dove (Columba turtur).

The reptiles are: the common and the steppe lizard (Lacerta vipera and L. muralis), the viper (Vipera berus).

Among the fish there are: the sterlet (Accipenser ruthenus), the nelma (Salmo nelma), the lote (Gadus lota), the pike, the perch, the crucian carp, the common gremille, the bream, the sandre, the sea-eel.

The insects are almost the same as in European Russia. The thrips (Culex reptans), a torture to both man and beast, occurs in multitudes. The cicada (Gomphocerus, Pezotettix, Stethophyma and others) appears at intervals in great numbers in the agricultural zone, as well as the prúsik (Caloptenus italicus) which devastates fields and meadows.

According to the census of 1897, the population of the government amounted to 1,438,484 (711,982 m. and 726,502 f.) shewing an increase of 125,084 when compared with the statistics of 1890 (1,313,400). The population is distributed among the districts in the following manner:

DISTRICTS.	Total population. Males.	Females.	Both sexes.	To a square verst in 1897.	To a square verst in 1890.
Ishím	133,844	136,614	270,463	7.1	6.5
Kurgán	127,135	134,937	262,072	12.8	11.1
Tiukalínsk	106,265	101,451	207,716	4.4	2.9
Yalutoróvsk	91,350	98,736	190,096	10.0	9.5
Tára	79,643	79,929	159,572	2.2	2.2
Tobólsk	64,058	63,410	127,965	1.1	1.2
Tiumén	60,154	61,677	121,831	7.5	5.7
Turin	34,715	35,655	70,370	1.0	1.0
Beriózov	10,788	9,856	20,644	0.03	0.05
Surgút	4,020	3,732	7,752		
				1.18	1.08

The population is very irregularly distributed in the government, which includes immense and completely desert areas in the north, whereas the

Types of Samoyéds (phot. by Tulénkov).

south is thickly populated. The steppe region, within the range of the main Siberian line contains the greatest number of inhabitants; 70 per cent of the total population amounting to 930,347, is concentrated in the steppe districts of Kurgán, Ishím, Yalutoróvsk and Tiukalínsk. The inhabitants of the government are ethnographically divided into three groups: the Russians constitute 93 per cent, the natives (Tatárs, Bukhárians, Kirgíz, Ostiáks, Samoyéds, Vogúls) 4 percent; other tribes, comprising Finns, Germans, Poles, Jews, Gypsies, 3 per cent.

The Ostiák Prince Arténziev (phot. by Poliakóv).

Among the natives, only Tatárs, Bukhárians and Kirgíz are met within the southern districts, included in the Ishím steppe region. The Tatárs and Bukhárians concentrated in a few settlements in the Ishím and Yalutoróvsk districts, occupy themselves with agriculture, fishing and trade, and profess the Mohammedan religion. The Kirgíz are met with in the Ishím and Tiukalínsk districts without any permanent abodes; they are obliged to be furnished with passports. They are nomadic cattle breeders and Mohammedans. Finns and Germans hold the first place among other nationalities as regards their number; then come Poles, Jews and Gypsies. The first predominate in the Tiukalínsk district where the volost of Yelán, situated near the stations of Shádrinsk and Tatárskaya of the West-Siberian Railway contains the Lutheran colonies of Helsingfors, Nárva, Ríga and Rével, numbering a population of 5,000 souls. Thousands of rebellious Poles were settled throughout the Tobólsk government. The majority retured to their own country while the rest were distributed over the Siberian territory. Their descendants are now met with in the Ishím and Tiukalínsk districts. The Jews mostly inhabit Tiukalínsk. The Gypsies came to the Tobólsk government at the beginning of the XIX century and are now scattered throughout the government excepting its northern part. They were admitted to the peasant communities and received grants of land; they, however, do not occupy themselves with agriculture, but lead the life of nomads. The Russians are the predominating element of the population, being either the descendants of the first settlers of Siberia who arrived there at the beginning of the XVI century, or recent emigrants and exiles from different parts of Russia. The Sibiriáks or descendants of the first settlers are of average height, square built, with brown hair; the women are smaller, vigorous and ugly. The Sibiriaks are not communicative, their dialect is mixed with many provincial words. The peasants of Siberia hardly knew serfdom; on the day of the liberation of the serfs, the 19 February 1861, the Tobólsk government contained it is true 3,002 serfs belonging to 23 landowners, but they were only nominally so and even in most cases were not liable to any tax.

Voluntary emigration from European Russia to Siberia lasted during three centuries, directing its course through the Urál, bordering upon the Tobólsk government. After the year 1870, the water communications of

Western Siberia received a further development, and the emigration movement kept mostly to the way through Perm and Tiumén. The station for emigrants organised in 1883 in the town of Tiumén to regulate the movement and to afford medical assistance, became the chief centre whence the voluntary settlers were dircted to the localities to be colonised in the vast Siberian territory. They were forwarded from Nízhni-Nóvgorod on barges which towed by steamers brought them to Perm, thence they were sent on to Tiumén, since the opening of traffic on the Perm-Tiumén, line in 1885. Their further movement depended upon the spot destined for their final settlement. The colonists who intended to stay in the Tobólsk government were conveyed by cart from Tiumén to the place of their destination, after having received the necessary information from the official entrusted with the regulation of the emigration movement. Those bound for the Tomsk government and thence for Eastern Siberia, were also conveyed to Tomsk by barges towed by steamers. However since the opening of traffic on the West-Siberian section from Cheliábinsk to Kurgán, the Perm-Tiumén line has lost its prior importance, and the majority of settlers proceed by the Samára-Zlatoúst line through Cheliábinsk, and further by the Great Siberian Railway.

According to the data of the Tiumén registration office under the management of Mr. Arkhípov, who for a period of 17 years has been occupied with the regulation of the movement, about 500,000 voluntary settlers have passed through Tiumén. Above 80 percent of the total number settled in the territory of Western Siberia, for the most part in the Tomsk government. Upon the opening of traffic to the town of Kurgán in 1894, the movement took another route, and Kurgán became for some time the terminus of the emigration movement on the Siberian Railway. During the summer of 1894, the number of emigrants received and forwarded from Kurgán exceeded 7,000. At that time Cheliábinsk, which is now the first emigration station, was not yet fully organised. At the end of the spring of 1895, when the railway line was opened as far as Omsk, and continued further to the junction with the river Ob, above 91,000 emigrants were conveyed by it in the course of a year.

The Ostiák Prince and Princess Artenziev (phot. by Poliakóv).

In 1896, when parties of emigrants could be sent direct from Cheliábinsk to Omsk, the movement still further increased and during this year rose to 192,000 souls, 28,000 of whom however including pioneers, returned to their former homes. At the same time, medical and feeding stations were organised at the station of Petukhóvo, Petropávlosk, Omsk and Tatárskaya, to assist the settlers colonising the free lands of the Ishím steppe, within the range of the Siberian main-line. The emigration station at Cheliábinsk was considerably extended by the spring of 1897, with a view to meet the further development of the movement; warm wooden barracks were made ready for the accomodation of 1,500 emigrants, and a hospital barrack to hold 70 beds. The kettles for the preparation of food have been increased and the baths and laundries rebuilt. A special branch line coming straight up to the barracks was constructed from Cheliábinsk to the emigration station. In 1897 the movement was somewhat restrained by certain measures taken by the Government; the numbers hardly exceeded 80,000. In 1898 it increased again and during this year rose to 205,645, inclusive of about 50,000 pioneers. Since the opening of traffic on the Great Siberian main line, about 600.000 people have passed through Chelíabinsk within a period of five years.

The emigrants arriving in the Tobólsk government either settled on the lands in the district officially allotted for colonisation, and founded new settlements, or were added to the original peasant population after obtaining the consent of the community.

Since the opening of traffic on the Great Siberian main line and the consequent increase in the emigration movement, 2,100 people settled in the Tobólsk government in 1894; 21,386 in the year 1895, and 6,889 families representing 41,791 persons in 1896; ninety four new settlements have been created in the country. The rush for the Tobólsk government markedly decreased during the following years in consequence of the overflowing of the steppe districts. The inhabitants of the Chernígov government hold the first place among the contingent of settlers in the Tobólsk government, then follow in order those of the Orlóv, Poltáva, Vítebsk, Gródno, Smolénsk, Kursk, Khárkov, Khersón and Túla governments. The immense human flood moving along the Siberian line soon filled the steppe districts of the Tobólsk government, allotted for colonisation, so as to leave free only the wooded sections called „urmans“ comprised in the Tára district, along the tributaries of the Irtysh, the rivers Uya, Shíshka and Túya. The following constructions were undertaken at the cost of the Emperor Alexander's III fund to satisfy the spiritual needs of the settlers and of the population of the Tobólsk government comprised within the range of the Great Siberian Railway. A church and a parish school were built near the station of Makúshino; 10 churches and 25 schools were erected in different emigration settlements; 18 churches and 12 schools are still in process of construction.

Type of an old Ostiák woman (phot. by Poliakóv).

The exiles form 8 to 9 percent of the total population. The exile system which was introduced after the occupation of Siberia in the XVI century at first served as a mitigation of the death sentence pronounced over persons of high rank, of whom the Government wished to get rid. In course of time the lower classes were also banished to Siberia. A regular exile system was established only at the beginning of the XIX century. The „Bell of Uglich“, which sounded the alarm at the time of the murder of the Tsarévich Dmítry on the 15-th May 1591, was one of the first exiles to the Tobólsk government.

The two brothers Románov, Iván and Vasíli Nikítovich, the Yúrievs, Zakhárins, were banished in 1601 by Borís Godunóv to the town of Pelym, which is now a village in the Turínsk district of the Tobólsk government. Prince P. I. Prónsky, Prince M. Belosélsky, Prince A. V. Lobánov-Rostóvsky, Prince I. N. Khovánsky, R. R. Vsévolozhsky, Prince D. V. Romadánovsky, the Hetman Samoilóvich, were among the statesmen banished to Siberia in the XVII century.

A great number of exiles of mark were sent to the Tobólsk government in the XVIII century, among them being prince Ménshikov with his son and daughter Mary, the affianced bride of the Emperor Peter II; the Dolgorúkovs with Natália Borísovna, daughter of Count Sheremétev, married to Prince Ivan Alexéievich Dolgorúkov, and the Princess Catherine, the affianced bride of the Emperor Peter II; Count A. I. Osterman with his wife, Biron with his wife, and Mínikh. At the beginning of the XIX century, the Tobólsk government was a place of exile for Polish rebels, also for Russians sentenced to exile for the mutiny of the fourteenth December 1825. In the XVII century, the exile system was regulated by the Strélets Court, and the Detective Court in the next.

Till the year 1807, the control and registration of exiles was effected in Verkhotúrie, at the frontier of Siberia. A general council for the regulation of exile was established in Tiumén in the same year, and entrusted with the registration and distribution of the exiles troughout the governments of Siberia. This however was not done with sufficient care, and as in many cases there were no documents affording evidence as to the number of exiles, no statistics could be collected till 1823 when a special Exile Office was established at Tobólsk. The existing documents of this office which are now kept in Tiumén, the starting point for exiles forwarded along the water ways of Siberia, shew within a period of 75 years, from 1823 to 1898, a total of 691,866 exiles followed by 216,360 voluntary companions, or in all 908,266. Within the last five years (1893—1897) 50,632 exiles were forwarded to Sibe ria with the addition of 30,061 voluntary followers, which shews an average of 10,000 exiles and 6,000 voluntary companions per annum.

Types of Ostiáks (phot. by Poliakóv).

During the same period of 75 years, 186,867 criminals of both sexes and 106,778 voluntary companions, or a total of 293,645 exiles, were banished to the Tobólsk government and added to its population. During the five years (1893 — 1897) an average of 3,000 exiles of this class with 2,700 voluntary followers, were deported to the same government (total 15,231 exiles, 13,594, voluntary followers). Within the space of 75 years one third of the total number of exiles was settled in the Tobólsk government. The exiles who were forwarded of late to the Tobólsk government comprise the following divisions:

1) Those condemned for a short period, brought to the prison of Tobólsk, and after a stage of hard labour, forwarded as settlers to Eastern Siberia.

2) Those belonging to the upper class sentenced to loss of all privileges and civil rights, and to exile for life.

3) Those of the lower class banished to Siberia by order of the commune or by court, after having been in prison or in correctional penal servitude.

The last category comprising all those designated by the collective name of administrative exiles or those banished without trial, is predominant in the Tobólsk government; all the exiles belonging to this class are sent to the Tobólsk and Tomsk governments and settled in towns and chiefly near villages on free lands allotted for their use by the Department of State Domains.

The population of the Ishím steppe contains the largest percent of exiles in the Tiukalín and Ishím districts.

It must be mentioned in regard to land ownership in the Tobólsk government, that the greater portion of this territory, as the rest of all Siberia, belongs to the State. The vast Asiatic dominions upon their annexation to Russia, became the property of the State, and were included in the number of its real estates. Safeguarding its own interest, the Government made liberal grants of free lands for temporary use, retaining the right of property over them. According to this arrangement all the lands comprised in the vast Siberian territory lying free or occupied by Russian settlers, aborigenes, and native nomad tribes, are the property of the State, with the exception of a few estates which the Government bestowed or sold to some private individuals, to monasteries or town communities. Such lands form but a very small percentage in comparison with the total area of the government. The greater portion of private lands which now belong mostly to merchants, lie in the Kurgán and in the southern part of the Tiukalínsk district bordered by the Omsk district belonging to the Akmolínsk region.

Ostiák woman (phot. by Poliakóv).

By the existing order of land tenure in Siberia, the majority of the peasants in the Tobólsk government received a grant of 18 desiatins to every man, with an addition of three desiatins for the settlement of exiles, as shewn by the revision of 1859. The extent of the grant is such as to form a whole volost or village. In the south of the Ishím steppe it comprises whole groups of villages.

According to the land law regarding the peasants, introduced into the Tobólsk, Tomsk, Yeniséisk and Irkútsk governments in 1896, the extent of the grant is 15 desiatins to every man. The subsoil of the Ishím steppe consists mainly of yellow and red clay, and of heavy brownish clay, whereas its soil is brown sand or black earth mixed with sand at some elevated points or ridges, and brown-grey clay at others. Fine mould, with a subsoil of saline clay occurs in level places in the south of the steppe. Patches of land covered with dwarf cherry bushes (Prunus chamaecerasus) and having a most fertile soil, occur throughout the south western part of the Ishím steppe and in the Kurgán district. This kind of cherry disappears entirely in the south—east of the Ishím and in the Tiukalínsk districts. The inhabitants of the Tobólsk government have different modes of livelihood: hunting and fishing are practised in the north, whereas agriculture and cattle-raising predominate in the south.

Agriculture is the principal resource; it is carried on as far as 57¼° N. lat. and after feeding the population yields a surplus of grain for sale. Further north agriculture is practised on a much smaller scale, and only at certain points. The characteristic and customary method of husbandry is the fallow land system, which consists in sowing the fields not every year, but at intervals, during which they lie waste; after a certain period the land is cultivated again in the same order. The fields which are ploughed for the first time, or had been lying fallow, are sown with the best kind of corn: wheat, rye and spring corn; when the soil is somewhat exhausted, sowing is interrupted more frequently, and before being entirely abandoned, the fields are left waste after every harvest. The alternation of crops varies according to the conditions of soil and climate.

In more populous centres, where the quantity of fallow land is necessarily reduced, this system of husbandry will soon give place to a more rational one. In some localities this is an accomplished fact and the manuring of the fields has been already introduced. The following systems of husbandry are practised in the districts lying within the range of the Great Siberian Railway: sowing without manure in the Kurgán, in the south of the Ishím and in part of the Ishím district the fallow-land system is replaced by the manuring of fields, whereas in the Tiukalínsk district fields are sown according to the former system. In the north the predominating grain is rye; in the south it is spring wheat.

The Resurrection Cathedral in the town of Beriózov with the grave of Prince Alexander Danílovich Ménshikov who died in 1729 (phot. by Gólubev).

Seed of a better quality is now sown in the southern region of the Tobólsk government, where a kind of oats yielding good seed and growing very thick, imported from the Tomsk government, is spreading fast. A spring wheat called „kubánka“ and „belotúrka“ is cultivated in this region, while the kind of wheat predominating in the Tiukalínsk district is known under the name of „lediánka“. Various kinds of grain are cultivated in the Kurgán district. As may be seen from the statistics of the Ministry of Agriculture and State Domains presented after the inspection of Siberia in 1895, agriculture has made considerable progress aud assumed numerous and varied forms. The Siberian peasant easily conforms himself to local conditions, and if necessary willingly reforms his system of husbandry. Depots of agricultural machinery supply iron ploughs, which are now replacing the wooden plough, drawn by three horses. Threshing and winnowing machines are frequently employed throughout the fertile Ishím steppe. A great number of these machines are made by the local inhabitants.

Flax and hemp are also extensively cultivated in the Kurgán, Yalutoróvsk and Ishím districts. The Yalutoróvsk and Kurgán districts contain potato fields which besides supplying the inhabitants are used in the manufacture of molasses.

The following figures drawn from the Government statistics for 1894—1896 shew the extent of the area sown with grain and the quantity of crops raised in the respective districts:

DISTRICTS.	Number of Chétverts sown.			Number of Chétverts raised.		
	1894.	1895.	1896.	1894.	1895.	1896.
Kurgán.........	244,723	281,492	345,461	1,838,886	651,814	2,159,456
Yalutoróvsk	266,690	234,172	214,692	807,861	698,251	533,688
Ishím...........	223,876	234,978	264,467	2,691,891	3,063,741	2,553,094
Tiukalínsk......	174,198	155,644	283,706	1,465,952	1,076,397	1,737,764
Tára	122,104	117,041	165,172	880,218	606,305	875,386
Tiumén	88,133	90,898	97,068	630,891	753,804	451,314
Turín	61,946	67,534	71,107	306,078	305,631	360,081
Tobólsk	56,660	49,741	69,978	302,928	274,489	400,028
Total....	1,238,320	1,231,500	1,511,651	8,924,735	7,430,432	9,070,811

The total amount of grain raised in 1894 shewed a seven-fold crop, in 1895 and 1896 sixfold. The richest crop namely thirteen-fold was obtained in the Ishím district in 1895, while that in the Kurgán district was only 2,3 fold in the same year. The extent of the land under cultivation and the crops were the same in the following years 1897 and 1899.

The quantity of grain obtained in the government, principally in the districts of Kurgán, Yalutoróvsk, Ishím, Tiukalínsk, comprised within the range of the Great Siberian line, clearly testifies to the welfare oı the population of this fertile region able to export annually about a million puds of grain to the interior markets of the Empire and abroad.

Cattle breeding is also an important feature in the southern steppe districts, but is inferior to agriculture which holds the first place throughout the Ishím steppes, where cattlebreeding is only considered as an auxiliary resource. Farm stock is raised for sale only in the south of the Tiukalínsk district, the number of cattle varies greatly in the respective localities and in every homestead. The peasants of the Tiukalínsk districts own the greatest number of cattle, namely an average of 5 horses, 3 cows and about 12 sheep to every household. According to these data, 2—3 horses, 2—3 cows and 5—6 sheep may be taken as the average for every household throughout the more fertile region of the government. The Siberian horse is small, not particular about food, and capable of enduring both heat and cold; he goes well, but is no- strong and can draw a load of only 25 puds on a level road.

Within the last ten years, with the flow of emigrants from the interior governments of Russia, bringing their own horses, the stock of the Ishím steppe has much improved. The cattle comes from the common Russian breed, which with good care and fodder yields a fair quantity of milk. Upon the whole, the home bred cattle under proper selection produces now better specimens, as may be noticed in the new settlements, where the emigrants have introduced more rational methods of husbandry and stockraising. The local Siberian sheep, which are kept by the peasants solely for their own use, come from a bad and poor stock with inferior wool. The fat-tailed sheep predominate in the south of the Ishím steppe; the sale of their fat yields a considerable profit. Sheep with long tails and thick wool of the Vorónezh breed are raised in the colonists' settlements.

The great quantity of cattle in the Ishím steppe region, now traversed by the Great Siberian main line, has led to the organisation of shambles in both town and villages. From 100,000 to 125,000 head of horned and 250,000 of sheep etc. are killed annually in the Kurgán, Yalutoróvsk, Ishím and Tiukalínsk districts. The greater part of the meat is sent to the works in the Perm government, or exported to the central markets of European Russia since the opening of traffic on the Siberian Railway.

Butter is the principal food product representing the chief resource of the southern steppes of the Tobólsk government.

Previous to the construction of the railway, about 300,000 to 350,000 puds of melted butter, of the value of R. 2,000,000 were forwarded from the Ishím steppe to Tiumén and Kurgán, and sold by the peasants at local fairs to small purchasers and to the agents of large firms. It was also sold in European Russia at the fair of Nízhni Nóvgorod, at Moscow and in the south of Russia, at Rostóv on the Don, whence it was forwarded partly to Germany and partly to Turkey. The larger firms purchased the butter and melted it themselves. A model butter-boilery exists in Kurgán belonging to the merchant Smólin, where about 50,000 puds of butter are melted annually. The Oshúrkovs and Krestóvnikovs of Ekaterinbúrg are also important firms, who annually buy about 150,000 puds of butter. In the Yalutoróvsk district the butter-boileries belong to the Bótovs, Kalmykóvs and, in the Tára district, to Piátkov.

The Siberian Railway greatly promoted the development of this lucrative branch of industry and also improved the processes employed. At the present time the inhabitants living within the range of the railway have abandoned the former primitive systems, and manufacture cream butter with the help of separators and churners, which is exported to the European markets in specially fitted refrigerators. Besides private firms, butter manufactories now exist in many villages in the south of the Tobólsk government, organised for the benefit of the peasants by the Ministry of Agriculture and State Domains and by the local administration, and provided with the necessary apparatus according to Mr. Vereshchágin's system. At present there is scarcely a village in the Ishím steppe in proximity to the railway which is without a cream-butter manufactory with a separator of the newest system.

Manufactures and industry are very limited in the Tobólsk government, which is but poorly provided with minerals, and chiefly subsists by the production of raw materials. Flour-milling is the principal industry in the southern steppe region, followed by the animal produce industries: butter, leather-tanning, preparation of sheep-skins, tallow-boiling and felt-boot manufacture. The total value of the produce is known only approximately. According to certain data it amounts to R. 4,000,000 or R. 5,000,000 in the southern part of the government.

Village industries have received a wider development in the Tobólsk government which, of all the governments of Siberia, offers the greatest number and variety of goods manufactured in this way. The articles however, for want of technical knowledge, are still of a very primitive character.

The following industries are practised in the Kurgán district: pottery, manufacture of agricultural tools, coopery (specially barrels for tallow and butter), turnery, painted wooden cups, plates, spoons and other articles, trunks and saddles, tannery, sheepskins, shoemaking, felt-boots, ginger-bread, tallow-boiling and butter.

The Yalutoróvsk district contains the greatest number of persons engaged in village industries, such as: potters, blacksmiths coopers, weavers, tanners, shoemakers, saddlers. Many occupy themselves with preparing sheepskins and pelisses, which in the Shátrov volost represent every year a capital of R. 1,500,000; others make felt-boots, are employed in fulling cloth, beating wool, boiling tallow, making butter and ginger-bread.

The following industries are pursued in the Ishím district: digging lime and grey clay, manufacture of agricultural machinery. mainly threshers, spinning and weaving, rope-making, tanning, tallow-boiling, and butter manufacture.

The blacksmith's trade, tanning, shoemaking, fur-dressing, tallow-boiling, and butter manufacture are chiefly practised in the Tiukalínsk district.

Since the Great Siberian Railway has united Sibéria with Asiatic markets, the Government would do well to encourage and develop these kinds of industry with a view to both the public interest and to political considerations, and thus to compete with foreign manufactures in the Far East and in the markets of Central Asia.

For the development of village industries in the Tobólsk government, it would be necessary to attach trade classes to the village schools, to settle Russian workmen in the government, and to organise an association supported by State credit.

Grave of Count Andrew Ivánovich Osterman in the town of Beriózov (died in 1747) (phot. by Gólubev).

The unsufficient development of local manufactures and industry has caused Siberia to depend on other countries, and so far influenced its economic life as to condemn its population to the exclusive use of imported goods. Trade in Siberia has consisted strictly in the exchange of raw materials for all sorts of necessary articles manufactured in European Russia. Till of late Siberia had no local manufactures; iron was imported from the Urál, cloth from Moscow and Lodz, printed calico from Ivánov Voznesénsk, crockery wares were purchased at the fairs of Nízhni Nóvgorod and Irbít, but as the Siberian merchants did not pay ready money, they received old goods. The bad quality of the Irbít goods became proverbial: articles regarded as good for nothing in other countries were considered good enough for Siberia.

The local trade of the Tobólsk government is chiefly concentrated in the towns of Tiumén, Kurgán, Tobólsk and Ishím, and is in the hands of but a few merchants; the absence of competition caused by the difficulties of transport, permit them to sell their goods at very high prices. The Siberian peasant is very fond of cotton and cloth goods, and the merchants well know how to profit by this taste. Printed calico, boots, cloth, cotton and woollen drugget etc. are in special favour with them. There is no steady trade; it greatly depends upon the topographcal condition of the country, which at certain periods is animated by fairs and markets. This occurs principally in the autumn when the peasants have finished work in the fields, and bring for sale raw materials, which are bought up by large and small merchants, who in return supply the peasants with bad manufactured goods and grocery.

About 409 fairs and markets take place in the southern steppe region of the Tobólsk government during the year: 121 in the Kurgán district, 122 in the Ishím, 99 in the Ỳalutoróvsk, 67 in the Tiukalínsk district. The most important is the Nikólskaya fair, held in Ishím from the 1 to the 25 December with a turnover of R. 5,000,000, where the prices for tallow and butter are established. The financial operations of the fairs held within the range of the Siberian Railway amount to R. 4,500,000. While bringing a new life into this distant country, the Great Siberian line has not as yet brought any change into the ancient mode of sale and purchase, but by opening the way to large Russian and foreign traders, will cause the decay of the Siberian fairs, and introduce regular commercial institutions.

BIBLIOGRAPHY:

1) Centres of population (X) Tobólsk government. Published by the Centr. Statist. Commit. of the Ministr. of the Inter. St.-Petersb. 1871.

2) Statistics of the Russian Empire XXIX volosts and centres of population. 1893. Tobólsk govern. Publ. by the Centr. Statist. Commit. M. of the Inter. 1894.

3) Materials for the study of the economic life of the State peasants and natives of Western Siberia. Publ. by the Minist. of State Dom. St.-Petersb. 89—98.

4) Memorandum for the Tobólsk govern. 1884 recommended by the scientific Commit. of the Minist. of Publ. Instr. for schools and public libraries of the Empire by Dmítriev-Màmonov and Golódnikov. Tobólsk. 1884.

5) Piecturesque spots in Russia, edited by P. P. Semiónov. Western Siberia. St.-Petersb. 1884.

6) The land tenure and husbandry of the peasants in the Tomsk govern. Publ. by the Depart. of Gnr. Aff. M. of State Dom. St.-Petersb. 1894.

7) Supplement to the report of the Minister of Agriculture and State Domains presented to the Emperor after his visit to Siberia in 1895 and 1898 St.-Petersb. 1899.

8) Report by State Secretary Kulomzín on his visit to Siberia to investigate the emigration question. St.-Peterb. 1896.

9) Siberian calendar for trade and industry 1897—1898. Publ. by the M. of Finance. St.-Petersb. 1896.

The Kirgíz Steppe borderland.

The Kirgíz Steppe borderland is administered by the Governor-General of the Steppe territories and comprises the Akmolínsk and Semipalátinsk territories occupying the southern portions of the Irtysh and Ishím basins. The commercial interests of this borderland were always attracted towards the north, to the localities bounded by the West Siberian government of Tomsk and Tobólsk, on the borders of which the Central-Asiatic nomads Dzhangúrs, Kalmyks and Kirgíz-Kaisáks, since the beginning of the XVIII century, carried on barter with Russian merchants. Barter courts and customs barriers were established with this object. The Great Siberian Railway in its course from Petropávlovsk to Omsk (280 versts) runs along the ancient frontier, which is connected by the steppe highways and caravan routes with the centres of the steppe region and comprises the whole area of the vast steppe borderland, lying within the sphere of its mighty influence. The Akmolínsk territory occupying the northern part of the steppe region, between 44° and 55° N. lat. and 34° and 45° E. long., for purposes of internal administration, is divided into five districts-Petropávlovsk, Omsk, Kokchetávsk, Atbasár, and Akmolínsk, and covers a superficial area of 9,902 square geographical miles. It is bounded on the north by the Tobólsk government, and the east by the Semipalátinsk territory, on the south by that of Syr-Dária, and on the west by the Turgái territory and the Orenbúrg government.

The Semipalátinsk territory lies between 44° and 54° N. lat. and. 40° and 58° E. long. and is divided into five districts: Semipalátinsk, Pavlodár, Karkalínsk, Ust-Kamenogórsk, Zaisán, with a superficial area of 9,138 square geographical miles, bounded on the north-east by the Tomsk government, on the west by the Akmolínsk territory, on the south by the Semiréchensk territory, while the eastern and part of its southern border are bounded by the Chinese Empire.

The Akmolínsk territory is chiefly level, and orographically divided into two sections: one lying north-west belonging to the Ishím river system, the other south east to the Arálo-Caspian basin with a higher surface. The central steppes are traversed by a watershed represented by detached mountain groups or elevations, running from east to west, and terminating in the Kokchetávsk, Imantáv, Airtáv mountains and the Ulu-Tan or Western group culminating in the Ulieák-Mechét 3,730 feet in height. The southern portion bounded by the Tobólsk government and that lying east and west of the Kokchetávsk mountains represent a uniform plain broken by hillocks. The eastern side of this plain, extending towards the Irtysh, has a clayey and saline soil, is treeless and contains a great number of brackish lakes. Its western part is the continuation of the fertile Tobólo-Ishím plain which, being scattered with birch groves and clumps, abounds in fine pastures extending chiefly along the Ishím. The south of the territory comprises the desert called the Hunger Steppe lying within 45° and 48° of N. lat. consisting of shifting sands. This steppe presents an elevated plateau with a clayey and limy soil, and thanks to the absence of water, is utterly uninhabitable. The investigations of I. A. Schmidt proved that the area stretching south of the central watershed towards the river Chu and comprising about 176,000 square versts is totally unfit for permanent settlement. The surface of the Semipalátinsk district is much more varied, mountains and steppe occurring alternately. Its eastern portion, broken by ridges of the Altái mountains with an altitude of 7,000 to 8,000 feet,

Lake Chebáchie, Kokchetávsk district, Akmolínsk territory.

and its southern part, separated from China by the Tarbagatái chain, bear an essentially alpine character. These mountains run along the frontier of China having summits of 9,700 feet, and send out the ridge of Chingíz-Tan.

The central area of the territory is also mountainous, containing the Kizyl-Tásh mountain group, separating into numerous ridges—Karkalín, Ku, Edréi, Dzhigelík and others. Its western side falls gradually towards lake Balkásh and passes into a vast steppe. The Irtysh region and the north of the territory present also a level plain.

The Cossack village of Bayán-aúl, Semipalátinsk territory.

The soil of the steppes varies greatly and consists either of a fertile blackearth of unequal thickness, or of sands, clay, gypsum, marl and sterile saltmarshes. The level surface of the steppe is utterly unprotected from the winds, which sometimes raise immense columns of sand The Semipalátinsk mountains, consisting of rocks denuded by atmospheric influence, are on the contrary very well suited for agriculture and settlement on account of their soil, climate and vegetation.

The mountain groups of the Akmolínsk, and the alpine ridges of the Semipalátinsk territory are mainly formed of crystalline rocks; the first con-

Goldwashing machine.

tains granite, the others shew a predominance of lime and talc slates, limestone, quartz and sandstone. The level areas, having a soil and subsoil including rocks of recent formation and forming part of the Arálo-Caspien basin, were formerly under water, as evidenced by the great number of shells found among the pebbles.

The mountain ridges of the Kirgíz border include an untold mineral wealth which is as yet scarcely at all exploited; the country lying at their foot is provided with abundant coal deposits. Auriferous strata occur in the Akmolínsk territory near the Kokchetávsk mountains, and in that of Semipalátinsk, in the Ust-Kamenogórsk district, on the Kolbén mountains, and in the northern part of the Zaisán district. There are about 400 auriferous areas, but only one-third of them is being worked.

Within recent years the gold-mining industry has fallen off considerably in the Akmolínsk territory, under the influence of the present economic con-

Types from the Steppe borderland, Kirgiz deputation from the Akmolínsk territory (phot. by Kessler).

ditions, and chiefly on account of the rise in wages produced by the construction of the Siberian railway giving employment to many workmen. The quantity of gold obtained in the Semipalátinsk territory is constantly increasing thus, 16 puds 34 pounds were raised in 1891, whereas in 1897 the output amounted to 32 puds 12 pounds. Silver—lead mines occur frequently in the Akmolínsk and the Atbasár districts in the Akmolínsk territory, but remain entirely unexploited. Rich deposits of these ores containing much silver are to be found in the Karkalínsk, Pavlodár and Zaisán districts. Their exploitation is conducted by the gold miners Popóv in the Karkalínsk and Pavlodár districts. Copper mines are to be found in the Kokchetávsk and Atbasár districts, and principally in that of Akmolínsk, where they were worked after the year 1860 at the Spas copper works of Messrs Riazánov. This copper tested in the Urál chemical laboratory proved to be equal to the best copper obtained in the Urál works. In the Semipalátinsk territory copper mines occur in the Pavlodár, Karkalínsk and Zaisán districts, but are very inadequately worked in proportion to their wealth.

The Kirgíz steppe abounds in iron deposits which are especially rich near the town of Karkarálov; the different kinds of iron contain on the average 59.18 of iron, 1.12 of sulphur, 0.31 per cent of lead. There is no local iron industry notwithstanding the increasing demand and the high price of the Urál iron. Manganese beds were discovered in 1895 near the town of Semipalátinsk, on the Arkalyk mountains. According to prospectings, this deposit covers a considerable area and is very rich. When explorations were made in 1896, the quantity of 5,000 puds of manganese was obtained by 15 workmen.

Seams of coal, in various formations, covered by an alluvial soil of clavey sand, occur frequently in the Kirgíz Steppe. In the Akmolínsk territory it is found in the Kokchetáv district on the river Burlúk, a tributary of the Ishím, and in the districts of Atbasár and Akmolínsk. Specially noteworthy is the Karagandín coal pit, situated in the Akmolínsk district, within 30 versts of the Spas copper works of Messrs Riazánov, and on the sections called Bosách and Ak-Tiube, discovered by Mr. Dérov.

In the Semipalátinsk territory the principal coal deposits are distributed throughout the Semipalátinsk, Pavlodár, Karkalínsk and Zaisán districts. The most important are:

1) Those situated in the Semipalátinsk district on the left bank of the Irtysh, at the places called: Tyn-Kudúk, Tagdy-Kudúk, Ķum-Kúl (belonging to the Irtysh company), Dzhungulék-sor, 20 versts from the station Grachévka, Uzún-sor, 8 versts from the latter. The coal is bright and compact, yielding a good quality of coke.

2) Those of the Pavlodár district, situated on the left bank of the Irtysh at Dzhamán-Tuz (belonging to the goldminer Popóv), 150 versts south of Pavlodár. The deposits contain a series of seams, attaining a thickness of about 5 sazhens. The coal has been frequently tested and contains a considerable percenting of ash, although compact and black. The deposits of Kun-Chekú (belonging to the Voskresénsk gold-mining company) 300 versts from the Irtysh and 480 versts from Tomsk, must be mentioned on account of the quality of the coal, its abundance and the thickness of the seam, attaining 6 sazhens.

LOCALITY.	Chemical composition.			
	Water.	Volatile matter.	Pure Coke.	Ash.
Dzhamán-Tuz	1.51	6.61	6.020	3.245
Oinák-Sor	1.07	1.914	6.457	1.492
Tyn-Kudúk	3.38	2.592	5.850	1.220
Kum-Kúl	2.68	2.422	4.730	2.580
Kun-Chekú	0.80	1.870	5.870	2.180

The Ekibás-Tuz, belonging to the Voskresénsk mining company, situated 123 verst from Pavlodár, was carefully investigated in 1896 by Engineer Meister. It contains dry and fat coal. On analysis it gave the following results: the coal of the Artémy bed—3.22% water, 34.47% volatile matter, 65.53% coke (58.90% pure coke); that of the Vladímir bed—11.50% water, 32.78% volatile matter, 47.22% coke (38.44% pure coke) 8.78% ash. According to the approximative data of the Engineer Meister, the explored strata contain 6,448,680,000 puds of coal.

3) In the Karkalínsk district, at Ak-Chekí, within 150 versts of the town of Karkarálov, a coal deposit 10 sazhens deep, is imbedded between masses of carbonic slates. Almost all the coal is of the same formation, compact, bright and burning with a clear flame. The beds of Ekibás-Tuz are provided with the best quality of coal throughout the Kirgíz steppe. They belong to the Voskresénsk gold-mining company, and are connected by a broad gauge branch line 100 versts long with the water system of the Irtysh. Coal is to be conveyed by it to the town of Omsk to supply the demand of the Siberian main line. A wider exploitation of the Ekibás-Tuz coal-pits must contribute to the development of mining industry in the Kirgíz Steppe, richly provided with minerals, and to the creation of new manufactories which are in need of cheap mineral fuel.

Precious stones occur in the rocky ridges of the Kirgíz steppe broder land, e. g. ashirite, a rare kind of emerald; it is found in the locality of Al-

Types from the Steppe borderland, Kirgíz deputation from the Semipalátinsk territory (phot. by Kessler).

tyn-sú within 200 versts north-west of Karkalínsk. The locality is characterised by considerable outcrops of limestone, in which are found fine crystals of this mineral. In the Semipalátinsk district, granite is obtained at many points along the left bank of the Irtysh, near the town of Semipalátinsk and the Cossack villages of Semiár and Dolón. In 1895, granite was brought from here to Omsk for the construction of a railway bridge over the Irtysh.

Alabaster is obtained in the Semipalátinsk district, near the settlements of Podpusknóe and Lebiázhie, 6 versts from Semipalátinsk, and also at the places called Krásny-Yár and Chístoe, whence it is forwarded by the Irtysh. Mill-stones are found in the Semipalátinsk and Pavlodár districts along the banks of the Irtysh. Fire-proof clay occurs in different qualities in the Steppe region, but is scarcely worked.

The Akmolínsk territory is but poorly provided with running water. Its north-eastern part is watered by the Irtysh, flowing for a distance of 200 versts along the border of the Omsk district; the north-west is traversed by the Ishím, watering the most fertile area of the territory, stretching over parts of the Akmolínsk and Atbasár districts, the whole of the Kokchetáv and over a portion of the Petropávlovsk districts. Three rivers belonging to the basins of the steppe lakes Sary-sú, Núra and Chu, flow from the interior watershed, in the south of the territory. They have a great importance for the regulation of the nomad life of the Kirgíz. This territory is much more abundantly provided with lakes, especially in its northern part.

These lakes, above 500 in number, contain different kinds of water, and being scattered all over the steppe, brackish, freshwater and bitter lakes

Types from the Steppe region: Dungán deputation (phot. by Kessler).

occur in proximity to each other. All the lake basins bear the same character, with sloping and reed-covered banks and a muddy and slimy bottom. In many of these lakes the water level is inconstant; the same is noticed in the lakes of the Ishím steppe in the West-Siberian plain, where they sometimes disappear completely, and then again appear after a period of several years.

The Semipalátinsk territory is better provided with lakes and rivers than that of Akmolínsk. The Irtysh taking its rise in the Chinese Empire, flows through the territory for a distance of 1,150 versts; it receives several tributaries and is navigable throughout its entire course. Among the lakes, the most important is the Balkhásh, the southern part of the territory is bounded by its northern shore. It lies 560 feet above the level of the sea and covers an area of 16,196 square versts. The maximum depth is ten sazhens; the water is clear, blackish, unfit for drinking, and contains only small fish.

Lake Márka-Kul, in the Zaisán district, covers a superficial area of 302 square versts, and lies in a mountain pass, surrounded by high ridges, at a height of 5,700 feet.

Lake Zaisán-Nor is situated in an open and elevated plain, between the Altái mountains and the Tarbagatái chain; it has an area of 1,608 square versts and a height of about 1,800 feet above sea level, with a maximum depth of 5 sazhens; this lake abounds in fish.

The Irtysh plain contains the greatest number of lakes, which in the steppe region give a wide scope to the development of the salt-industry, especially in the Semipalátinsk district. All these lakes, in this respect, are divided into two categories comprising those which are exploited by the State, and those which are worked as private concerns for the supply of the local demand. The best salt is obtained in the Semipalátinsk territory from lake Koriákov, whose annual output exceeds 700,000 puds.

The climate of the Kirgíz steppe border, although more continental, is much warmer than in the neighbouring cultivated zone of Western Siberia. The mean annual temperature of Akmolínsk and Semipalátinsk, lying in 51° and 50.5° N. lat., is from + 2° to 2.5° C., two degrees higher than in Siberia

Farther south, the mean annual temperature in the Steppe regions is + 5° and 6°. The winter temperature is—16°, and—18,5° during the coldest month, corresponding to that of the agricultural zone in West Siberia; the mean temperature in summer rises to+20° and to + 22° in the warmest month, while in West Siberia summer is not so warm. The difference between the winter and summer temperature is 36°, and the difference between the coldest and warmest month 40°. In Akmolínsk the rainfall amounts to 229 mm., and in Semipalátinsk to 186 mm., whereas in the Hunger Steppe (Bed-Pak-Dalá) on the south of the Akmolínsk territory, there is no rain at all in the summer.

Kirgíz type from the Akmolínsk territory. The Sultan Valikhánov (phot. by Delazari).

These climatic conditions together with the want of irrigation serve as an impediment to the development of agriculture; the early morning frosts have especially a very bad effect upon the fields. Under the influence of the heat prevailing at the end of May and thanks to the absence of rain, the grass is soon withered and the steppe assumes a desolate greyish hue. In summer, the wind often blows a storm driving up masses of sand; in winter, the same winds produce blizzards.

The flora of the Kirgíz steppe border, with the exception of a few places at the foot of the mountains, is of the same nature as that of the Arálo-Caspian lowland, and is influenced by a climate characterised by hot summers, cold winters and an absence of moisture. In the Akmolínsk territory, fir forests occur only in the Kokchetávsk district, where the mountain cones, formed of granite gradually denuded by the atmosphere, are thickly clad with a verdant vegetation of trees.

The Semipalátinsk territory is more hilly and contains fir forests; the greater portion of the northern slopes of the Altái are covered with foliage trees, whereas forests of fir stretch on the right of the Irtysh, in the Pavlodár and Semipalátinsk forest sections. A great number of mountain firs occur also in the Karkalínsk district, on the slopes of the Karkalínsk and Bayán-Aúl mountains.

Birch, aspen and alder are the predominating foliage trees, scattered in innumerable groves all over the northern portion of the Akmolínsk and Semipalátinsk territories. Black poplar, poplar and ash occur sometimes in the plains, while the Halixylon ammondendron, the „dzhída" and „taráng", grow in the south.

The steppe flora is especially characterised by dwarf bushes, which are sometimes thorny and covered with a grey or silvery foliage and particularly

A Kírgíz village (phot. by Krékov).

gnarled, such as the hard-hack, cytisus, dwarf-almond, wild-cherry, hawthorn and, in the south, by „bayalyk", „kokpek", „teraskep" and others. The bush species which in the south may be mentioned among the herbaceous vegetation, are very important in distributing the rainfall, retaining the snow, and consolidating the sand, which contributes to the formation of a cultivable soil. The bayalyk and saksaúl answer specially this purpose, and at the same time serve as fuel.

The herbaceous vegetation of the steppe is abundantly provided with characteristic species. Karélin, Schrenk, Semiónov, Sévertsov, baron Osten-Saken, Slovtsóv, Siazóv, who all explored the flora of the Kirgíz Steppe border-land, discovered a great variety of typical species. The soil in the steppes is particularly favourable to the growth of herbs, such as wormwood, willow-herb, feather-grass, Sasiagrostis splendens, Ceratocarpus splendens reeds, which can be employed as fodder for the cattle. Fibre plants are represented by flax and madder; medicinal plants, by rhubarb and liquorice root.

The fauna of the invertebrate animals prevailing over the southern parts of the steppe regions is of the same type as that found in the deserts and steppes of the Arálo-Caspian plain.

The ornithological fauna of the northern Kirgíz Steppes, which does not differ from that of the West-Siberian steppe regions in the south alone, along the river systems and in warm valleys, receives an addition of varied birds, some of which come for the winter from the far north, while the others are common to the Central Asiatic uplands.

The mammals are more abundantly and variously represented than in Western Siberia. The tiger (Felis tigris) „dzhulbárs" in Kirgíz, and the Felis Irbis or „ilpis" in Kirgíz, lurk among the reeds of the Lake Balkhásh; the lynx (Felis lynx) dwells in the Aktáv and Ortáv mountains; wild boar are met with in the southern steppes, on the borders of rivers Sary-Su, Chu, and near large lakes; the Ovis Argali (a kind of wild sheep) is to be found in the alpine zone of the Altái and Tarbagatái, on the south of the Semipalátinsk, and also in the Karkaralínsk and Akmolínsk districts, together with the two-humped camel, a kind of deer, the „maral" (Cervus elaphus), the roebuck (capreolus vulgaris), the gazelle, some varieties of the antilope (antilope subguttorosa), the „kulón" (Equus hemionus), the wolf, the bear, the fox, the marmot, the badger, the jumping hare, the ermine, the hare and others. The sturgeon, the sterlet, the nelma, the salmo thymallus, the roach, the lote, the pike, the carp, the sudak and others are the fishes which particularly abound in the Irtysh and in lake Zaisán-Nor.

The population of the steppe border-land is given as 1,364,154 by the census of 1897 (719,209 males, 644,945 females).

The Akmolínsk territory contains 678,957 inhabitants (354,370 males, 324,587 females); in that of Semipalátinsk their number is 685,197 (364,838 males, 320,358 females). In the first there is a proportion of 92.4 women to every 100 men. In the Akmolínsk territory the population is represented by 1.3 inhabitant to every square verst, in Semipalátinsk by 1.7. The population consists of Kirgíz natives, Cossacks of the Siberian Cossack troops and of peasant settlers.

Interior of a Kirgíz yúrta; entertaining guests with kumys (phot. by Delazari).

The Kirgíz or Kirgíz-Kaisáks are the last representatives of the Túrko-Mongol hordes, who used to invade the more civilised countries of Asia and Eastern Europe. They form over 80 per cent. of the total population in the Steppe borderland, speak a Turkish dialect, are Mohammedans, with a religious belief manifested only in external performance of rites with an admixture of Shamanism.

They are nomads and, from the first spring days till late in autumn, live in the open steppe sheltered by light movable tents or „yúrtas", and wander with their herds in a direction determined by ancient custom. The „yúrta" represents the movable property of the Kirgíz; it can be folded up and transported together with other articles, following the movements of the nomads. In the northern steppes, only the poorest Kirgíz live in yúrtas in winter whereas, further south, where timber is more scarce and the climate more favourable, they are used both in summer and winter. A great number of yúrtas are always pitched among the reeds near Lake Balkhásh and the river Chu. They are made of wood, plaited, woven and felt materials. The door of the yúrta usually looks N. E. in an opposite direction to the land to which the Mohammedan Kirgíz addresses his prayers (Mecca and Medina). This is also done with a view to avoid the south and south-western winds prevailing in the steppe. The yúrtas are characterised by two different shapes: one is conic, the other has the form of a cupola. The possession of a great number of yúrtas of various shapes constitutes the pride of the Kirgíz. An ordinary grey felt yúrta costs from R. 50 to R. 40, a better one made of ornamented felt costs R. 150 and even more. The whole life of the Kirgíz is centred in the yúrta. It gives a shelter to his childhood and youth, and is witness of his private and public life. His ideas of the outer world coloured by a scanty poetry take their rise in the life of the yúrta. The life of the Kirgíz with their scanty joys and sorrows passes in the yúrta; he reluctantly seeks another refuge for the winter, under the pressure of cold and wind. With the sun's first rays, the Kirgíz is happy to quit his cramped and close winter shelter and to return again to his beloved steppe.

Kirgíz winterquarters (phot. by Delazari).

The Kirgíz pitch their winter-camps at the foot of the mountains, in river valleys, on a forest border, on reed-covered lake shores, and in places protected from cold and snow drifts.

They inhabit small wooden huts without chimney and with open hearth covered by a ceiling but without roof. The winter huts of the rich recall common peasant cottages. The Kirgíz attach a special importance to these winter quarters as forming the centre of their land tenure; as soon as these winter settlements become permanent they will lead to a gradual passage from nomad to settled life, and to a more

A sótnia (hundred) of Siberian Cossacks.

fiixed use of the land. The Kirgíz in this territory belong to the Central Horde, including numerous families, marked by different characteristic traits. For purposes of administration, they are grouped in volosts and villages. All the land of the Kirgíz Steppe borderland belongs to the State, and is only granted to the perpetual use of the nomads; the frontiers between the possessions of the wanderers are fiixed in accordance with former occupation or hereditary custom.

The Cossacks forming the Siberian troops were the first colonists of the Kirgíz steppe; representing about ten per cent. of the total population of the Steppe territories, the Siberian Cossack troops are located in the Akmolínsk and Semipalátinsk territories, and the Bíisk district of the Tomsk government. Most of the Siberian Cossack settlements stretch in a line, commencing at the boundary of the region occupied by the Orenburg Cossack troops, following the northern border of the Kirgíz steppe and the south of the Tobólsk government, through the town of Petropávlovsk and eastwards to Omsk, which bears the name of Presnogórkovskaya or Górkaya line. This line is traversed by the Great Siberian Railway, between the towns of Omsk and Petropávlovsk. The Presnogórkovskaya or Górkaya line comprises an area of a million and a half desiatins, and is occupied by the right flank of the troops. From Omsk, this line takes a south-eastern direction, and continues along the right bank of the Irtysh by way of the towns of Pavlodár, Semipalátinsk, Ust-Kamenogórsk, thence turning north-east into the valley of the Bukhtarmá river. This portion of the territory occupied by the troops is called the Irtysh line, forming the left flank, wlth a length of 1,247 versts and a breadth varying between 10 and 30 versts. The Bíisk line, running through the Tomsk government, occupies the slopes of the Altái. Many of the Cossack settlements are scattered all other the steppe.

Siberian Cossack in marching outfit (phot. Col. Katanáev).

The territory occupied by the troops has an area of 5,174,949 desiatins, with a population of 131,344 of both sexes.

The troops are under the chief administration and command of the Governor-General of the Steppe Territory and of the commandant of the Siberian military department, bearing the title of Chief Atamán of the Siberian Cossack troops. The Board of Home Miltary Affairs is under his direct control, the management of the troops being entrusted to three subordinate Atamáns.

The chief element of the military population is represented by Great Russians, only a small number being Little Russians, Mordvas or members of some other tribe. Orthodoxy is the prevalent religion among the troops, those professing any other creed forming but a small percentage of the whole contingent. The greater number of Cossacks professing Mohammedanism (about 1,700) are concentrated in the Kokchetávsk and Petropávlovsk districts of the Akmolínsk territory. The number of dissenters amounts to 1,200, divided into two sects: one recognising the clergy, the other disowningt; they are settled in the Kokchetávsk, Petropávlovsk and the Ust-Kamenogórsk districts. The principal sources of the economic welfare of the troops are agriculture, cattle-breeding and fishing. According to the existing organisation, the contingent of the Siberian Cossack troops is divided into the following classes: the preparatory class, comprising Cossack boys, registered from the age of eighteen for a period of three years; the class comprising Cossacks in the ranks enrolled from the age of 21 for a period of 12 years; and the reserve class, including for five years the Cossacks who have passed the second stage. At the age of 38 they are discharged. On the first January 1897 the number of registered Cossacks aged from 18 to 38, was 16,752 troopers and 192 officers. In time of war, the Siberian Cossack troops must turn out nine cavalry regiments of six hundred men each, or fifty four cavalry sótnias, and three reserve sótnias.

Election to public offices in the Kirgíz steppe.

The peasant colonisation of the Kirgíz steppes followed the colonisation by the Cossacks, and was begun only at the end of the XIX century. At the time of the organisation of the Akmolínsk and Semipalátinsk territories in 1868, they did not possess one single peasant settlement, the permanent population of these territories was represented solely by town inhabitants and Cossacks. In 1875, the Governor General of West-Siberia, Adjutant-General Kaznakóv stated in his report to the Emperor, that Cossack colonisation little contributed to the civilisation of the half wild nomad population, and insisted upon the necessity of settling the steppes with Russian peasants, as a means of planting Russian civilisation among the natives and of connecting the interests of the local inhabitants with those of the Russian cultivator.

For this purpose, sections of land which were to be colonised by peasants from the interior governments of European Russia were chosen and surveyed in the centre of the Akmolínsk steppe.

Although many mistakes were made as regards the selection of the land, still the settlements of emigrants produced a most civilising effect not only on the nomad natives, who previous to their acquaintance with the emigrated peasants were ignorant of any mode of land cultivation, but also on the Cossacks of the Siberian troops, who profited by the farming experience of the new colonists. Since 1898, the movement to the Akmolínsk steppe was greatly increased by the permission granted to the peasants to voluntarily settle this region and to occupy the free State lands, principally in the Kokchetávsk distrist. Upon the opening of the West-Siberian Railway, the colonisation of the steppe took a more regular course, the localities which were to be settled being selected beforehand.

Kirgíz court of justice held in the steppe (phot. by Delazari).

According to an order of the Committee for the construction of the Siberian Railway, a special survey party was entrusted with the ascertainment of the free State lands, lying within the range of the railway (not above a distance of a hundred versts) in the Petropávlovsk and Omsk districts, best suited for present and future colonisation. From 1893 to 1895, seventy-three sections of land were selected in both districts, having a superficial area of 386,695 desiatins, with a reserve of nine sections, with an area of 43,736 desiatins in the Kokchetávsk district.

The progress of colonisation is strikingly illustrated by the following data:

Year.	Villages.	Population.
1879	18	1,749
1889	24	11,740
1892	38	28,584
1893	45	30,544
1894	54	39,705
1895	87	61,809
1896	132	99,399

During the year 1896, the settlement of lands lying near to the railway line, was carried on mainly in the Petropávlovsk and Omsk districts. Being almost devoid of running water, grants of land were made in proximity to lakes and wells. The emigration movement to the steppes of the Akmolínsk and Omsk districts somewhat diminished in 1897, but increased again in 1898—1899.

Considerable portions were detached from the Kirgíz lands for the colonisation of the steppes; this involved the investigation of the natural history and statistics of the Akmolínsk territory, with a view to ascertaining the economic condition of the nomad population, and to establishing the normal extent of land needed for the subsistence of a Kirgíz family; at the same time suitable districts for new settlements were to be selected without causing damage to the interests of the existing steppe population. The plan of exploration was furnished with the following programme:

1) The study and description of the region from a physical and mainly an agricultural point of view, together with the demarcation of the land needed for pastures, crops and hay;

2) The ascertainment of the lands and economical conditions of the wandering Kirgíz, with a view to determine the extent of the land needed for their use, and also to note all attempts made by the nomads towards permanent settlement;

3) The investigation of the mode of life of the settled Russian population with a view to ascertain the conditions upon which depend the results of colonisation.

These physical and statistical explorations carried into effect in the Kokchetávsk and Akmólinsk districts shewed 5,000,000 desiatins of free Kirgíz land, of which about 500,000 desiatins are already occupied by settlers, and 400,000 desiatins were assigned in 1899 for future colonis ation. With a view to consolidate the settlement of emigrants, the Committee for the Siberian Railway has undertaken the improvement of the land and started a series of hydrotechnical works for the watering of the steppe districts.

Types of Kirgíz women (phot. by Delazari).

The emigration movement to the Semipalátinsk territory goes on at a much inferior rate to that to Akmolínsk; up to the present time, new settlements in the Semipalátinsk territory have been established solely in the Semipalátinsk and Ust-Kamenogórsk districts, with a respective population of 5,940 (3,084 males, 2,856 females) and 3,029 souls (1,576 males, 1,455 females).

The following constructions have been carried out in the Akmolínsk territory at the cost or with the help of the fund of the Emperor Alexander III, in order to satisfy the spiritual wants of the settlers and of the whole orthodox population, comprised within the range of the Great Siberian Railway:

A wooden church near the station of Isyl-Kul, and two fully organised parish schools at the stations of Petropávlovsk and Isyl-Kul. Thirty churches have been erected at the stations of Petropávlovsk and Omsk, built in various settlements scattered all over the wide steppe area, and nine are in process of construction in the new settlements; ten schools have been erected and organised within the emigration settlements, nine are still in course of construction.

Agriculture and cattle-raising are the principal sources of the welfare of the population in the Kirgíz borderland. Upon the whole, the cultivation and particularly agriculture in this recently settled region is not as yet developed as might be expected from the favourable conditions of soil and climate. The plains on the west of the Akmolínsk territory, stretching along the Ishím, and the lands lying to the south of the town of Akmolínsk along the river Núra, are specially well adopted for agriculture and are in great favour with the settlers. The lands in the Semipalátinsk territory are a great deal less fit for cultivation. Its elevated surface accounts for the absence of moisture and for the continental climate which in many places excludes the possibility of cultivating land without artificial irrigation.

Kirgíz bride in wedding attire (phot. by Delazari).

The peasant settlers receive a grant of 15 desiatins to every man, and an extensive area of land belongs to the Cossacks or is in the use of the Kirgíz; this gives scope for the application of the fallow land system, which is the predominating form of husbandry in the fertile districts of the West Siberian lowlands. This system is essentially based on the exploitation of the natural productive force of the soil, which is restored to it after every harvest by leaving it unsown; after a period of 6—12 years in which 4—6 crops have been raised, the land is left waste for I0—12 years. The first crops raised on fallow land are very rich amounting to 200 puds per desiatin; the second time the fields are sown without any previous preparation.

The predominating grain is wheat. The Little Russian plough drawn by oxen is chiefly employed. Many among the peasant settlers have ploughs on the Ekkert and Sakk systems, and purchase agricultural tools manufactured in the State works of Vótkin, in the depots of the Department of State Domains.

The spring corn is sown in the following order from about the 10 April to the 10 of May: „yáritsa", wheat, oats, barley and millet. Winter corn is sown from the 6 August. With every year agriculture grows more familiar to the Siberian Cossacks, who a short time ago had no cultivated fields and were supplied with grain by the neighbouring governments of Western Siberia. At present they own extensive cultivated areas and offer their produce for sale. As regards the Kirgíz, the quantity of cultivated fields is small in proportion to the total number of the population. Employing as food milk and meat obtained from their numerous herds, the Kirgíz eat little bread, using mainly wheat meal, and prefer to get it by purchase or barter to obtaining it at the cost of the hard and unused labour attached to agriculture. Still the Kirgíz are adopting already some of the agronomic systems imported by peasant settlers who, leasing considerable portions of their land in return for part of the harvest, contribute to the development and expansion of the cultivated area. The gardens extensively cultivated by the Siberian Cossacks represent an important resource for their households. The Cossack population always suffered from the want of workmen diverted from household duties by military service and public duties; the cultivation of the gardens by the women was the characteristic feature of a Cossack homestead; in them the following vegetables are raised: water melons, melons, cucumbers, turnips, carrots, beet-root, cabbages and onions. The cultivation of tobacco is also practised throughout the Cossack settlements, and exclusively by the Cossacks; the Kirgíz and the peasants do not occupy themselves with it, and are the principal consumers of this product. The tobacco cultivated by the Cossacks, or properly speaking by the Cossack women, is of a very inferior quality and is mostly planted in the orchards. Seeds of a strong Russian tobacco, distributed every year to the Cossacks by their authorities for sowing, are obtaining an ever increasing favour. The cultivation of melons and water melons is also a great help to the peasants, principally in the southern steppe.

The vast pastures of the steppe region combined with favourable conditions of soil and climate give a wide scope to cattle-raising which, as the principal economic feature of the Kirgíz, meets every requirement of the nomads.

Their herds supply fully their simple needs, giving them as food horse-flesh, mutton and milk, products such as kumys and airán, one made of mare's milk, the other of cow's or sheep's milk, and a kind of cheese called kurt or eremchík, dress and dwelling (felt covers for the yúrtas), household utensils made of smoked skins, bags for kumys, water pails and fuel. They also choose for races among their droves of horses the swiftest runner, the pride and delight of the Kirgíz. The great love they have for animals manifests itsel in the greeting they give each other when they meet; before asking about the welfare of the family, they say: „mal-dzhisky-ma", which means, „Is the cattle thriving?" The stock raised by the Kirgíz is represented by sheep, horses, cattle, goats, and camels.

A Kirgíz bride being sent off to her bridegroom (phot. by Delazari).

The sheep possess a coarse wool and a fat tail, and represent the chief resource of the Kirgíz. They are characterised by their great size, hanging ears, hooked nose and fat tail, which in a well-fed sheep, weighs about 30 to 40 pounds, with 20 to 30 pounds of fat. The flesh is full of fat, which is the principal article of sale. This kind of sheep are very big and strong; they are covered with an abundant but rather coarse wool, which shorn twice a year, yields from 4 to 7 pounds every time. Further south, the sheep are of a better breed and fetch a higher price. The best sheep are found in the south of the Akmolínsk and Semipalátinsk territories, and cost twice as much as in the north. The skins are rated according to the time when the sheep was slaughtered and its age. The best skins come from the sheep killed in autumn and are employed for pelisses.

The Kirgíz horse is endowed with an unpromising exterior; but has inestimable qualities. The thorough-bred possesses the following characteristic marks: a middle height (about 2 arshins), a short back (12 vershoks), a well proportioned muscular and expressive head, with small standing ears, a hooked nose with broad nostrils, a well-formed chest, a low neck, a broad and strong croup, strong feet with flat hoofs and a very light and swift pace. Grazing the whole year round, the Kirgíz horse gets used to the inclemency of the weather and finds its own fodder. The winter lasting six months demands a great store of strength and force of endurance. As a rule the Kirgíz ride a distance of 100—150 versts on the same horse in 10—12 hours, with only short rests. According to the data of the Omsk Amateur Racing Society a Kirgíz horse, for a distance of 20 versts, runs at the rate of a verst in one minute and a half. Special attention has been paid to these horses by the managers of the Imperial Studs; stud stables are organised in the neighbouring Turgái territory, with a view to improve the exterior of the Kirgíz horse by a proper selection and crossing of the blood.

A Kirgíz musician (phot. by Delazari).

The cattle is of middle size, strong and well proportioned, furnishing good meat, good beasts of burden and a considerable quantity of milk. The export of these cattle, which are very easily fattened and are rated at a low price, has assumed large proportions. Some specimens of the local cattle yield about 15 puds of meat and 2 puds of fat. Eight puds of meat is obtained from a cow.

Goats are kept among the sheep for their hair or as leaders to the herds, which can more easily be managed when goats shew the way.

Two-humped camels are kept mainly in the southern steppes. Being employed for the transport of burdens, they also provide the Kirgíz with milk, meat, hair, and skins, and more recently have been used for agricultural purposes.

Cattle-breeding is carried on by the Kirgíz in a most primitive and careless way, according to the drove system which was established some hundred years ago. The Kirgíz herds, grazing all the year in the open steppe, are utterly uncared for and left to the mercy of snow, storm, frost, wolves and other wild beasts, which often cause great damage to the cattle-owners.

According to the information of the veterinary inspection of the steppe region in 1897, the number of cattle in the Akmolínsk territory was 3,402,134 head, and in the Semipalátinsk territory was 3,099,052 head.

	Akmolínsk territory.	Semipalátinsk territory.
Horses	858,673	800,048
Cattle	574,126	450,000
Camels	91,769	90,000
Sheep	1,794,014	1,709,404
Goats	72,810	49,600
Swine	10,742	—

In the Akmolínsk territory, the nomads dwelling in the Akmolínsk and Atbasár districts, and those of the Zaisán district in the Semipalátinsk territory, are well provided with cattle.

Hunting and fowling are much practised by the population. The Kirgíz are fond of these sports, which are the single pleasure they have in the steppes. Being remarkably long-sighted, the Kirgíz goes on horseback in search of wolves armed with a short stick (soil) or with a thick tightly twisted whip (nagáika).

As soon as the wolf is detected, the huntsman pursues him with loud shouts indicating the success of his efforts. Other hunters join him, and after a race of about 15 versts, the wolf is run down exhausted. The tired wolf sits on his hind legs with open jaw and hanging, swollen tongue. One hard stroke with stick or whip hitting the animals head or nose is sufficient to kill him. The Kirgíz seldom use poison or gun for destroying wolves, which moreover can hardly be approached within gunshot. The favourite sport of the Kirgíz is fox hunting with a falcon; the fox and the Vulpes corsac are also chased with hounds, which are a mixture of the Turkmén and Kirgíz steppe greyhounds. The Kirgíz shoot the badger and marmot in order to get their skin and fat, the latter being considered by them as a medicine and a good preservative against frost bites. The fat is also employed to grease the leather straps of their saddles. The aborigenes seldom use firearms to shoot birds, but take them chiefly in nets, traps etc. With a view to preserve game, the laws for regulating hunting were introduced into the region in 1893. The number of various hides sold at the central Constantine fair held at Akmolínsk illustrate the extent of the industry. The following figures shew the quantity sold there annually: 4,000 wolf, 2,500 fox, 18,000 corsac, 150,000 marmot, 10,000 badger, and 200,000 hare skins.

Kirgiz hunter with falcon (phot. by Delazari).

Beekeeping has been for some time an occupation of the Cossack population of the Ust-Kamenogórsk district, in the Semipalátinsk territory. Bees were brought to this country for the first time from the Kíev government at the end of the XVIII century. The rich flora of the Altái contributed to the successful development of this pursuit, which is now carried on thoughout the Altái. Some apiaries with hives of new systems yield about 3,000 puds of honey annually.

Fishing represents a most important resource for the Cossack population; Lakes Zaisán, Marká-Kul and many others of various dimensions as well as the Irtysh are contained within the confines of the land allotted to them. The Kirgíz get fish from the Balkhásh, the rivers Chu, Ishím, Núra and others. The Zaisán and the upper reaches of the Irtysh are abundantly provided with fish and, although the sale of this article has been carried on for a long time past, the Cossacks are entirely ignorant of the methods for preserving fish.

Hunting falcons of the Kirgiz steppe.

Factories and works in the Kirgíz steppe are mainly employed in the getting of animal products, such as fat, the skins of sheep and other animals, wool etc. which are abundantly supplied by the steppe herds. The goods manufactured in the existing works are few in kind and of an inferior quality, testifying to the insignificant industrial development of this country; the existing manufactories are very small and of a very primitive construction, without any modern machinery or the assistance of trained mechanics, they have the appearance of simple workshops. The abundance of raw materials and of common and Glauber's salt found in the steppe region, might be made the basis of an extensive and profitable leather, soap and soda trade.

The Kirgíz steppe borderland, containing a population of about a million and a half, possesses an industry the annual produce of which scarcely amounts to the value of R. 2,000,000. All the raw materials are exported from this region, where tallow boileries, tanneries, sheep-skin, wool-washing and gut-works, occupy an important place on acount of their yearly output. The tallow boileries are established near places called „salgány" where the cattle are slaughtered in autumn. They take the form of wooden sheds provided with iron kettles for tallow melting, fitted in hearths placed below the floor close to the wall of the building. Wooden boxes in which the tallow is poured to cool stand in the middle.

The tanning consists of a most primitive process producing a coarse material called „yúkhta". The sheepskins are left untanned in the factories, and are despatched to Russia for final preparation, which is done principally in the town of Shúya of the Vladímir government.

Wool is washed also in a very primitive way, in plain wooden boxes placed on the banks of rivers and lakes; the wool is put into the boxes, which are filled with water, and is trampled by the workmen; it is then spread on a net, washed over again and dried.

The guts are prepared merely in spacious cottages, without any special appliances. They only have tables for cleaning and salting the guts, which are put in a tub standing at hand. The guts cleaned with wooden knives, are wound in skeins which, after having been dipped in fine salt, are ranged in tubs where they lie for two to four days thus becoming hard. They are then stored in small barrels, closed up and made ready for export.

The domestic industries pursued by the peasants, but recently settled in the Kirgíz steppe border-land, have not as yet assumed any characteristic form; however, according to the statistical information given by the colonists, these kinds of industries would find very willing adherence among them, if they received some assistance and were helped to the organisation of associations. The condition of the Cossack troops shews that domestic industries have there the same extent as in the governments of Great Russia. The spread of reading and writing will certainly promote the development of industry among the Cossack population, endowed wíth a ready wit and a taste for occuptions which do not require too great an amount of physical labour; it is only necessary to find some means to encourage them in this line.

The trade and industry of the nomad population of the Kirgíz border are quite independent and original as to the articles produced and the means of their manufacture. Excepting some metal wares such as: kettles, tea-urns, teapots, trunks, axes etc. and trinkets, all the domestic and household articles employed by the Kirgíz, including the yúrta and the horse harness, are made by the members of the Kirgíz family, chiefly by the women or by the Kirgíz artisans specially engaged in some branch of industry.

The materials employed in the domestic industry of the Kirgíz are principally wool and hair, of which are made felt (koshmá), a woollen stuff (armiachína) sheep-wool ropes with an admixture of horse hair (arkán), a kind of braid of various breadth for the arrangement and ornament af the yúrtas (baskúr), woollen carpets with patterns (alachá). The felt is entirely made by the women. They assemble at the appointed time and beat the washed wool on dry horse or ox-skins, then it is spread on mats made of a grass called Lasiagrotis splendens. A big roll is made of the mat and the wool which previously was wetted with hot water. This roll is tied with a string and has rope rings on both ends. Two women pull the roll by these two rings and turn it, pushing it with their feet. The roll is dragged through the village and the steppe. This promenade is accompanied by laughter, chatter and joking and an unusual animation in the village, as often happens in Russia when work is being done by the whole commune.

Hot water is poured several times over the roll; the woman to whom it belongs thinks it also her duty to pour sour sheep milk over it, repeating the words: „alte kun ash bolsan, ata kadende ummutna", which means that it is better not to eat for six days than to forget the custom of one's forefathers. When the wool is sufficiently fulled, it is brought inside the yúrta and rolled up without the mat; the women then sit in a row and beat the roll with their elbows, pushing it to and fro on the mat. After it has been rolled in this way for some time, the felt is put aside to dry.

The surplus of home manufactured articles is bought up by purchasers wandering about the steppe, or bartered for manufactured goods. The Kirgíz have their dress made of home-spun woollen stuff „armiachína", while the coarser kind is employed for sacks for the storage and transport of grain and flour; horse-hair ropes are used for harness.

Tanning holds the second place among the industries of the Kirgíz, including the preparation of the skins of the domestic animals and particularly of leather for boots, dress and other household uses. The population is also engaged in making saddles and harness, in the trades of the blacksmith and the silversmith, the making of the wooden parts for the yúrtas, and other household necessaries.

The internal trade of the Kirgíz steppe borderland comprises three divisions according to the local and economic conditions of the population: a permanent trade centred in towns and some large villages, barter carried on with the Kirgíz, in which a ram one year old is the unit of exchange, and a periodical or market trade. The towns of Petropávlovsk, Omsk, and Akmolínsk are the chief centres of the permanent trade in the Akmolínsk Territory; Semipalátinsk, Pavlodát and Ust-Kamenogórsk—in the Semipalátinsk Territory. Besides these permanent centres of Russian and Kirgíz trade, commerce is carried on in the Cossack settlements and villages. Each settlement or village offers a market for Kirgíz goods. The barter trade now gradually diminishing was the basis of the first commercial relations with the Central Asiatic steppes. Now the market trade is the most important, and is carried on at centres chosen according to the season and the conditions of their nomad life, attracting the Kirgíz and their herds. The chief articles of sale are: cattle, animal produce and Kirgíz domestic wares, Asiatic goods from Turkestán such as long coats (khalát), blankets, stuffs of cotton and silk, dried fruit, rice, pistachio nuts, raisins etc.; the products of European industry, grocery, drugs, trinkets and other goods.

The fairs held in the steppe region comprise the two categories of summer and winter fairs. This is explained by the fact that in winter the cattle scarcely find enough fodder to maintain their existence, and are utterly exhausted; as soon as the new grass appears in spring, the cattle quickly regain their strength and are fit for slaughter. During this season, the Kirgíz are able to determine the number of cattle which can be sold; the Russian cattle buyers also avail themselves of the fresh pastures for driving the newly purchased cattle to the European markets. This is why the summer fairs are only important for the cattle trade. Further south, the fairs begin earlier. In the Semiréchensk Territory, they are held in april, in the Semipalátinsk Territory in the middle of may, in that of Akmolínsk in the middle of June, whereas the Tainchakúl fair which takes place in proximity to the West-Siberian railway line and to the highways leading to the towns of Petropávlovsk and Kurgán, is opened only in the beginning of July.

In autumn, the Kirgíz retire to their close and smoky huts, and settle down for the winter. As soon as the frost begins, they kill part of their cattle for the coming winter's store, and bring part of the animal products, wool and hair collected during the summer to the winter fairs, where animal products are chiefly offered for sale.

The winter fairs are in close dependence on the conditions of nomad life, and have only some significance for the Kirgíz inhabiting the northern steppe regions. Those wandering in the south, during the winter dwell at a great distance from the centres of population and consequently are obliged to purchase and sell their supplies only at the summer fairs.

The latter are distributed in the following way throughout the territories and districts: fifty-eight take place in the Akmolínsk territory (twenty in the Petropávlovsk, eight in the Omsk, twenty-seven in the Kokchetávsk, two in the Atbasár, one in the Akmolínsk districts). Eighteen are held in the Semipalátinsk Territory: five in the Semipalátinsk, seven in the Pavlodár, one in the Karkaralínsk and five in the Ust-Kamenogórsk districts.

The most important among them is the Bótovskaya or Kuyándy fair, with a turn-over amounting to R. 4,000,000, held from the 25 May to the 25 June in the Semipalátinsk Territory, in the Karkaralínsk district, near the military post of Kuyándy standing on the post road from Karkaralínsk to Pavlodár. The Constantine fair held in Akmolínsk from the 10 June to the 4 July, is visited after the close of the first. According to information given by the veterinary inspection, 11,825 head of horned cattle, 3,188 horses, 11,472 sheep, 2,933 goats, and 271 camels were brought to this fair in 1897, with the following number of skins: 5,469 neat skins, 17,729 horse skins, 2,033 camel skins, 191,670 sheep skins and 37,777 goat skins; the quantity of wool amounted to 25,727 puds sheep's, 11,773 puds camel's, and 423 goat's wool, besides 1,429 puds of horsehair. The turn-over is estimated at R. 4,000,000. The Petróvskaya fair takes place in the Cossack settlement of Atbasár, in the Ákmolínsk Territory from the 10 June to the 5 July. Its importance increases every year.

Formerly the Kirgíz inhabiting the southern part of the Atbasár district used to drive their best sheep to the town of Tróitsk in the Orenbúrg government; now they bring them to this fair. In 1897, the number of sheep was

Orthodox missionary in the Kirgíz steppe.

94,499 head. The transactions at the fair amounted to R. 1,000,000. The Tamchakúl fair, held nar the lake of the same name situated in the Petropávlovsk district of the Akmolínsk Territory, is held from the 15 June to the 15 July, and within recent years attracted an average of 17,000 head of cattle, 5,000 horses and 150,000 sheep. Its business amounted to R. 2,000,000.

The total business done at the fairs held throughout the Kirgíz steppe borderland exceeds R. 15,000,000 per annum.

The Kirgíz steppes possessing a great amount ot food and animal produce, supply not only the demand of the permanent population of the nearest mining region of the Transurál, but also of more distant Russian centres such as Kazán, Nízhni Nóvgorod and Moscow. The Akmolínsk Territory bounded by the most populous portions of the Tobólsk and Orenbúrg governments, since the time of its organisation, has occupied an important commercial position on account of its physical and orographical conditions, by selling animal products and serving as a medium for the transit of these goods between the Kirgíz steppe regions and the commercial centres of the Empire. The Great Siberian main line, running along the northern part of the Akmolínsk Territory in proximity to the frontier of the Tobólsk government and through the Irtysh basin, has still further increased the importance of the region, affording new facilities for the export of Kirgíz steppe productions. The following data based on the veterinary inspection of 1897 clearly illustrate the great prevalence of cattle-breeding in the Kirgíz steppes, and the extent of the trade in animal products exported to the interior and European markets.

The quantity of meat and of animal products, conveyed during 1897 through Siberia by rail and water, may be stated as follows: 337,569 puds of fresh meat, 99,180 puds of mutton and goat's meat, 753 puds of pork, 78,000 p. of fat, 565,042 puds of guts, 202 puds of feet, 8,211 p. of offal; further, untanned horse skins 239,942, cow skins—201,077, camel skins—13,077, sheep and goat skins—2,389,805; sheep's wool 121,339 puds, camel's hair 15,894 puds, goat's wool 841 puds, superior quality 5,525, besides horsehair 31,570 puds and horns 940 puds.

The greater part of the meat was conveyed by railway and distributed in the following way: to St. Petersburg 134,185 puds, to Moscow 62,674 puds and to the Perm government 78,750 puds. The fat was forwarded to Kazán (71,520 puds), guts were sent by rail to the Samára government (275,000 puds) and to Odéssa (153,525 puds), horse meat, to the Perm government (81,130) to Nízhni Nóvgorod (48,624), to Belostók (36,650) and to Libáva (23,246); neat skins were sent to the Perm government (64,275) to Nízhni-Nóvgorod 178,337, to Vladímir 345,792, to Revel 26,330, to Odéssa 10,700, to Warsaw 60,150 and to the New Port 14,000.

Tho quantity of sheep's wool forwarded to Riazán represented 36,398 puds, to Perm 22,062, to Tambóv 14,089, to Kazán 13,502; 9,769 puds of camel's hair and 403 puds of goat's wool were sent to Nízhni Nóvgorod, 17,142 puds of horsehair were conveyed to Révei, 4,800 puds to Nízhni Nóvgorod, and 3,276 puds to Moscow.

During the same period (1897), 173,072 animals were driven to the Tobólsk government and European Russia, comprising 10,455 horses, 28,868 cattle, 132,676 sheep and goats and 83 calves.

The Kirgíz steppe borderland is bounded on the east and partly on the south by Western China, and serves as a natural transit road between China and the Russian Empire carrying on trade along the extensive land frontier Passing the customs at Zaisán Alkabék and Koto-Karagái, trade is concentrated chiefly in Chuguchák, whence the Russian traders proceed to Urumchí. Shikhó Manás, Guchén, Karashár and Turfán. Unsufficient means of communication in the south of the Kirgíz steppe region, together with the absence of navigation by the Irtysh to Zaisán, and the want of enterprise hinder the further development of trade in this borderland. The navigation on the Irtysh now reaching lake Zaisán Norá and continuing further along the black Irtysh, established by Baron Amínov, will exercise a marked effect on the commercial relations of the Russian Empire with China, and bring new life into the Kirgíz steppe borderland. Possessing innumerable natural trea, sures, this region offers wide prospects for enterprise and capital. Means of communication leading south from the Great Siberian Railway and giving access to the richest mines of the world, coal deposits and fertile plains, are greatly wanted now that navigation already exists in the Irtysh basin, for the exploitation of the natural wealth of the region, for the development of trade with Western China and Mongolia and to promote the political influence of the Russian Empire in Central Asia.

BIBLIOGRAPHY.

1) Description of the Kirgíz-Cossack or Kirgíz-Kaisàk Hordes and steppes, by Lévshin. St. Pbg. 1832. 2) Geographical and statistical materials for Russia collected by officers of the General Staff. Siberian Kirgíz region, by Krasóvsky. St. Pbg. 1868. 3) Volosts and centres of population 1893. Akmolínsk Territory. Publ. centr. Stat. Comm. of the Min. of the Int. St. Pbg. 1893, Semipalàtinsk Territory. Publ. Cent. Stat. Comm. of the Min. of the Int. St. Pbg. 1895. 4) Review of the Akmolínsk Territory. Supplement to Reports on the Akmolínsk Territory presented to the Emperor from 1895—1898. 5) Review of the Semipalàtinsk Territory. Supplement to the Reports on the Semipalàtinsk Territory from 1895 to 1898. 6) Reports on the condition of the Cossack troops. 7) Memorandum of the West Siberian division of the Russian Geographical Society. 8) Report by State Secretary Kulomzín presented to the Emperor after his visit to Siberia to enquire into the emigration movement. St. Pbg. 1896. 9) Supplement to the reports of the Minister of Agriculture and State Domains presented to the Emperor after his visit to Siberia in 1899, St. Pbg. 1896, and in 1898, St. Pbg. 1899.

The Barabá Region.

The Barabá region, wrongly called Barabá Steppe, forms part of the extensive West Siberian plain and lies between the Irtysh and Ob basins.

Occupying part of the Tára and Tiukalínsk districts in the Tobólsk government, the greater portion of the Káinsk and part of the Tomsk and Barnaúl districts in the Tomsk government, the Barabá stretches from north to south between 57° and 53° N. lat.

The Great Siberian Railway runs almost through the centre of the Barabá a distance of 578 versts, between the rivers Irtysh and Ob. A monotonous, but original landscape accompanies the traveller on his way across the Barabá; greenish plains clad with coarse reeds and sedge grass, covering a miry and swampy ground, stretch indefinitely on both sides of the railway line. This grass-covered plain is marked by frequent copses formed by birch, aspen, and willow, growing on flat ridges rising above the level of the swamp. These copses seem to be ingeniously planted by nature herself, intersected by long vistas of the greenish plain, forming a background to the monotony of small lakes, glancing through reeds and sedge grass, or by level stretches of salt marsh with a peculiar vegetation and surrounded by large pieces of waste ground and peat bogs. This monotonous landscape scarcely gives an exact idea of this vast and most peculiar region, characterised by varied physical conditions. From north to south, the Barabá is divided into three parts, on account of its nature, its vegetation and its geological and hydrographic conditions: the northern or urmán section, the southern or steppe lake section. The northern or urmán section comprises the north-eastern parts of the Tára and Káinsk districts and is known under the collective name of urmán; its surface consists of swamps broken by elevated spots of land clad with a vegetation of mixed trees, and also sometimes by thick fir forests. Such hydrographic conditions render this region scarcely fit for agriculture and colonisation, although the soil is most fertile. On its southern border, the urmán is marked by isolated tree groves alternating with meadows covered with rich grass.

The Academician Middendorf who visited the urmán says that he never expected to find such a vegetation at 56° N. lat.: „the grass growing on the banks of the Om attains a height of 3 feet. At the bottom of steep ravines there is a thick overgrowth of spear-grass (Festuca), which may be taken for reeds. When after a low meadow you come to a space of steppe land, you are surrounded by a luxurious herbaceous vegetation of meadowsweet, hare lettuce etc. rising to a height of 2½ feet; wild peas and vetches hinder your advance. Above this thick and verdant cover, tower the deep red, pink and yellow heads of flowering herbs and nettles some of which have a height of 8½ feet".

The Russian settlements are established chiefly on the southern border of the urmán on ridges bounding the rivers; the density of the population diminishes towards the north, where occur but few inhabited points and solitary huts. Among the Russian population, are the settlements of the Barabá Tatars, who are the oldest inhabitants of the country.

The northern urmán, containing an immense quantity of moisture and gradually falling from the north-east to the south-west, gives rise to rivers feeding the Irtysh and flowing through the centre of the Barabá, chief among which are the Om and its tributaries, the Uya, Tára, Kargáta, Chulym. Besides swamps and a few streams, the urmán contains a considerable number of lakes scattered all over its surface.

The central birch or river and lake section covers an area of hundreds of versts, stretching across the Barabá from west to east. It comprises the most animated centres of this region. the town of Káinsk and the most populous peasant settlements, and is traversed by the famous Siberian highway and the Great Siberian main line. As compared with the urmán, this section is less wooded and has no fir trees, which here disappear altogether. The foliage trees are represented only by birch, aspen, and two kinds of willow. The level character of the surface may be seen by its relief; the railway line which near the station of Shádrinskaya (869 v. from Cheliábinsk) runs at an altitude of 122.1 sazhens near the station Duplénskaya (1,262 v. from Cheliábinsk) has an elevation of 146.8 sazhens. This ascent from west to east, 393 versts in length, shews a difference of only 24.7 sazhens, or an average grade of 3 vershóks to the verst.

The rivers in this region take their rise in the urmán and in the swamps on its southern border. The river Om is the most important in the country, and on its banks from the town of Káinsk downwards are concentrated the greater number of inhabitants throughout the Barabá. The rivers Kozhúrla, Karapús, Kargát, Chulym and others draining into the landlocked lakes of Sary-Kúl, Chány, Sartlán surrounded by low and muddy shores, slowly roll their yellow waves so characteristic of the swampy waters of the Barabá. They are included in small and large basins, the latter sometimes having an area of some hundred of square versts, as for example the lakes Chány, Ubínskoe, Sartlán, Kargát and others. None of the lakes in this region and throughout the Barabá, containing several hundred of them, are fed by underground springs or by tributary streams but, with the exception of the lakes Ubínskoe, Sartlán, Chány, Tándovo, they are all formed by the rainfall. The stagnant lakes can easily be recognised by their sloping shores, encircled by a broad band of reed and sedge grass, and with pieces of land at times under water. The depth of these lakes is not great, and but rarely attains two and a half sazhens (Ubínskoe, Sartlán).

For this reason many of them dry up in summer, and freeze to the bottom in winter. The same phenomenon, consisting in the periodical disappearance and reappearance of the lakes, observed in the Ishím steppe in the West Siberian plain, and in the Kirgíz steppes, is repeated here. The low shores are fringed with reeds and grass, which on withering fill up the shallow lake, and give a yellow colour to the water; the shores are also covered with the putrified remains of vegetation exhaling a heavy smell of sulphuretted hydrogen.

Among the largest lakes on this side of the Barabá may be mentioned: the lakes Chány, lying on the frontier of the Káinsk and the Barnaúl districts (2,876 square versts), Ubínskoe (578 square versts) and Sartlán (288 square versts). Besides the greater number of fresh water lakes, there are some containiug brackish, bitter and sour water.

The dried up lakes give place to saltmarshes which, in this region, are of the same nature as those of the Ishím and Irtysh steppes.

The soil of this part of the steppe has a great reputation, especially that which consists of black and dark earth, covering the ridges and mounds. Clay-marl is the predominating subsoil on hills and slopes.

The southern part of the Barabá extending southwards from 55° N. lat., loses its arboreal vegetation and gradually passes into the treeless Kulundínsk steppe, comprising the southern side of the Barnaúl district. The water system of this region is represented exclusively by lakes. Besides the large lake Chány, there are about 200 lakes which slowly but continually diminish in size. They contain either fresh or brackish water. This and the northern portion of the Barabá are higher than the central part.

The fauna here does not differ from that of the neighbouring districts of the Tobólsk government. The urmáns are inhabited by bear, glutton, wolf, fox, elk, and squirrel. Further south, there are striped squirrels, badgers, hares, ermines and fitchets. At times the lakes and basins are enlivened by a quantity of moor fowl.

The Barabá region is particularly famous for the innumerable clouds of gnats and mosquitos which so torture the inhabitants that in summer and spring they do not venture out of doors without covering the face with a net.

The colonisation of the Barabá by Russian peasants began only in the middle of the XVIII century; before this time, the last descendants of the dismembered Kuchúm Horde, split up into smaller tribes called Barabá, Tunúkh, Choi, Liubéi, wandered about this region. The Russians gave the name of Barabíntsy to the native half-nomad Tatars, deriving it from that of the Barabá tribe, from which the country also took its name.

It yet remains unknown who lived in the Barabá before it was occupied by the Tatars. That it was formerly inhabited by some tribes is evidenced by the tumuli still existing and the small Chud towns occurring in the Barabá, having now the appearance of grass and bush-covered mounds. At present the Tatar population of the Barabá amounts to 4,500; they belong to the Turkish race with an admixture of the Mongol. The Barabíntsy are of average size, have a healthy constitution and a tawny complexion; they lead a settled life apart from the Russian peasants.

Every volost has its chief. The villages which form a volost stand at a great distance from each other and contain only from 10—12 houses each. In former times, the Barabíntsy were shamanists but, towards the end of the

XVIII century, when they became subject to the Russian dominion, they gradually went over to Mohammedanism. The economic condition of the aborigenes who have been pushed into the northern urmáns by the Russians is not over brilliant; they may even be considered as poor.

The first settlers in the Barabá were post-drivers who in 1775 were transported by the Siberian governor Miátlev from the settlements of the Tobólsk government in order to promote the means of communication. Further, during the reign of Catherine II, a number of dissenters from Poland were settled in the Barabá. With a view to reinforce Russian colonisation, along the Siberian post road, which extended for a distance of 600 versts, Chichérin the former Governor of Siberia added convicts sentenced to imprisonment for different crimes and serfs exiled to Siberia by their masters for immorality or disobedience, to the contingent of drivers and peasants. This was the reason that in the last century, murder and robbery were here of every day occurrence, which obliged the governor Chichérin, who was the founder of this colony, to lay down a rule according to which the death of an exile settler was not imputed as a crime to the Tatars of Barabá. Since then, the population of the Barabá has been considerably increased, mainly by means of free colonisation by emigrants, attracted to this country by the fertility of the soil. According to the census of 1897, the population of the Barabá within the confines of the Káinsk district is given as 186,561, inclusive of the inhabitants of the town of Káinsk, amounting to 5,534.

As a consequence of the fertility of the soil, agriculture is the fundamental resource of the population in this country; the regulation grant of land is 15 desiatins to every man, and the fallow land system is generally adopted. Freshly ploughed fields with the best soil are sown 5—7 times with different kinds of grain; those which are endowed with less fertility may be sown 3 or 4 times; lands cultivated before yield the same number of crops or sometimes a little less. The fields with a very good soil lie waste for a period of 10—15 years; while the period for others varies from 20—25 years.

In wooded regions, winter rye is chiefly cultivated, whereas wheat is sown in the plains. The alternation of crops-wheat, yáritsa, barley, oats and winter rye-varies in accordance with local conditions. In the fertility of its soil, the Barabá recalls the Ishím steppe.

Rich pastures and hayfields present a wide prospect for the development of cattle breeding. As compared with the neighbouring districts of the West-Siberian plain, the peasants of the Barabá possess a greater number of cattle and sheep.

Horse breeding is not extensively practised in the Barabá country, but deserves to be mentioned on account of the first rate selection practised and the care bestowed on the horses. They are represented by the following stocks: the Barabínka, to which belongs the ordinary horse, the Kulundínka employed for labour, the Sargátka, from the village of Sargát, a strong working horse and the Smiátka a mixture of the two first bloods, with a slow pace and dearer than the others. The horses are sold at village fairs.

As a consequence of the construction of the Great Siberian Railway across the Barabá, the question of a more extensive colonisation by peasant settlers was raised, and a series of works for draining this vast but swampy country, which could be well adapted for cultivation and colonisation, was undertaken. According to some appoximate data, the total area which ought to be drained exceeds 4,000,000 desiatins. The drainage of the swamps was begun in the summer of 1895; the clearing of the river Kargát was undertaken in 1896. By 1899, drainage works had been instituted in 74 sections, comprising 320,000 desiatins and a population of 15,000; canals 412 versts in length have been dug, and 127 versts of them cleared. The sands bordering on the railway line, which were considered unfit for colonisation, are now being willingly occupied by settlers. The drainage conducted farther north, within the basins of the rivers Kargát and Om, will open new fields for colonisation. The supervision of the hydrotechnical works being made for the benefit of the peasants is entrusted to the local administration and to the population itself.

The drainage of the Barabá, which is being carried out according to the directions of the Committee for the Construction of the Siberian Railway, is done with a view to enlarge the cultivable area, to improve the growth of tree plantations, to render the country more healthy and even to modify the climate.

The Great Siberian Railway but recently opened to traffic, has already produced an enlivening effect upon the productive capacity of the Barabá country. Almost all the railway stations situated within its confines have become centres for the export of grain and other agricultural products to the interior markets of the Empire. The increase of population by colonisation and the improvement in the systems of agriculture will soon give to the Barabá the same reputation as the granary of Siberia, which has been hitherte enjoyed by the Ishím steppes of the West Siberian plain.

BIBLIOGRAPHY.

Supplement to vol. XIX of the Memoirs of the Academy of Science The Barabà. by A. T. Midenddorf. St. Pbg. 1871. Picturesque Russia edited by P. P. Semiónov. vol. XI Western Siberia. Barabà by G. N. Potànin. St. Pbg. 1884. Statistics of the Russian Empire XXXII. Vólosts and centres of population 1893. Tomsk government publ. by the Central Statistical Committee of the Min. of Int. St. Pbg. Peasant land tenure and husbandry in the Tobólsk and Tomsk governments. Publ. by the Min. of State Dom. St. Pbg. 1894. Geological and hydrographical explorations of the Barabà by G. O. Ossóvsky. Publ. by the Statist. Commit. of Tomsk. Tomsk 1895.

The West Siberian Railway.

Direction of the line.—Cost of construction. Description of the stations and countries traversed: Cherniàvskaya.—Chumliàk.—Shumíkha.—Míshkino.—Yurgamysh.—(Frontier of Siberia).—Zyriànka.—Town of Kurgán.—Toból basin.—Vargachí.—Lebiàzhya. — Makúshino.—Petukhóvo.—Mamliútka.—Town of Petropávlovsk.—Ishím basin.—Steppe highways, caravan routes.—Tokushí.—Medvézhie.—Isil-Kúl.—Kochubéevo.—Mariánovka.—The Omsk military post.—Town of Omsk.—Irtysh basin.—Navigation in West Siberia.—Korníloyka.—Kaláshinskaya.—Shádrinskaya.—Tatárskaya.—Karáchi.—Tebísskaya.—Town of Káinsk.—Kozhúrla.—Ubínskaya. — Kargát.— Chulym.—Duplénskaya.—Kochenévo.—Chik. — Krivoshchékovo.—Ob basin.—Navigation on the Ob.—The Ob-Yeniséi canal.—The northern searoute.

THE West Siberian Railway, which represents the first link of the Great Siberian main line, commences at the eastern terminus of the Samára-Zlatoúst Railway.

Running eastwards, it follows the parallel of 55° N. lat. almost throughout its entire course to the crossing of the Ob, swerving therefrom slightly only to approach towns, to find an easy passage across large rivers or to avoid obstacles, mainly lakes. The surveys for the line were conducted by Engineer K. I. Mikhailóvsky, manager of the works on the Zlatoúst-Cheliábinsk line; the whole of the West Siberian Railway was constructed by him.

The total length of the line, from the platform of the Cheliábinsk station to the extreme eastern pier of the bridge across the Ob, is 1,328.49 versts, with the addition of a branch line to the landing place on the Irtysh of 2.5 versts.

The total cost of the line was estimated at R. 47,369,824 or R. 35,832 per verst. In fact, the construction of the line came to R. 46,124,698 or R. 34,736.19 kop. per verst.

From the station of Cheliábinsk, the line runs parallel to the boundaries of the Shádrinsk (Perm government) and the Cheliábinsk districts (Orenbúrg government) for a distance of 200 versts, until it reaches the confines of Siberia in the Tobólsk government.

The total number of stations on the West Siberian Railway is 34.

1) **Cherniávskaya.** V class (41 v. from Cheliábinsk). The settlement Konashévskaia (pop. 360) is situated within one verst of the station, in a level and swampy district covered with young birch wood; the water is not good in this locality. The agricultural district connected with the station comprises a population of 5,000, and has an annual export of wheat amounting to 60,000 puds.

At the 76-th verst, the line crosses the river Chumliák by a bridge having an opening of 10 sazhens.

2) **Chumliák.** V class (82 v.). The village of Chumliák (pop. 2,000) stands 12 versts from the station. There are about 34 settlements within the range of the station with a population of 30,000. About 600,000 puds of goods are forwarded from here every year by freight trains; in 1898, 399,244 puds of grain were sent to the western ports of Russia. Running through the deep ravines of Tukmán, the line crosses the river Kámenka, at the 110-th verst, by a bridge of 15 sazhens.

3) **Shumíhka.** IV class. Buffet. (116 v.). Since the opening of the traffic, a settlement containing 40 houses has been established for trading purposes within a verst and a half of the station.

Station of Shumíkha.

At the station there is a school under the management of the Ministry of Public Education with a wooden building. It has one class for boys and girls. Water is obtained from wells, is brackish and contains an admixture of lime. Artesian wells are being dug. The large village of Ptíchie (pop. 3,000) is situated 14 versts from the station; there are about 55 settlements and villages within the range of the station, with a population of 40,000. The rich agricultural region bordering on the railway line exports annually over 2,000,000 puds of goods, mainly grain, to the western ports of Russia; while tallow (10,000 puds), meat and hemp are forwarded to the interior markets.

Private forwarders of goods have their own warehouses in the settlement near the station. Grain and other products amounting to 2,019,425 puds were conveyed from this station in 1898 (120,431 puds of rye, 1,830,930 puds of wheat, 42,673 puds of oats, 525 puds of peas, 3,830 puds of wheat meal and 2,257 puds of rye meal, 300 puds of bran, 18,497 puds of hempseed and linseed).

Míshkino. V class (155 v.). The country is level and dry, scattered with birch copses. Near the station are situated the settlement of Míshkino (pop. 1,000) and a small settlement established along the railway line since the opening of traffic.

The population is occupied with trade and industry. Fifteen settlements with a population of 20,000, and the district town of Shádrinsk with a population of 15,968 (Perm government) are situated within the sphere of action of the station There are also the steam flour mills of Bótov and Treúkhov, yielding annually about 1,000 waggons of grain. The quantity of grain transported annually from this station by freight trains direct to the western ports of Russia exceeds 2,500,000 puds. In 1898, the total transport of grain etc. amounted to 2,123,304 puds (53,664 puds of rye, 1,872,833 puds of wheat, 34,626 pnds of oats, 949 puds of peas, 180,244 puds of wheat flour, 12,514 puds of rye flour, 8,272 puds of bran, 49,943 puds of hempseed and linseed). This station also serves as a centre for the export of meat and other animal produce to the interior markets of the Empire. The goods received at this station supply mainly the town of Shádrinsk; the part coming from different points of Siberia is sent to the Irbít fair.

5) **Yurgamysh.** V class (188 v.). A settlement inhabited by corn merchants is being established near the station. The nearest village called Béloe is at a distance of 5 versts (pop. 1,000). There are eight settlements with a population of 7,000 within the range of the station, as well as the distillery of Shmurló and the steam mill of Ilín. Butter manufactories are established in the settlements of Kipely, Karasínskoe and Kisliánskoe producing about 2,000 puds of cream butter annually. From this point also 700,000 to 900,000 puds of wheat, are annually conveyed to the western markets of the Empire. The total amount of grain exported in 1898, was 888,255 puds.

The railway line, deviating slightly northwards, at the 200 verst enters the Kurgán district in the Tobólsk government, which is within the limit of Siberia.

6) **Zyriánka.** V class (205 v.). The settlement of the same name (pop. 100) and the village of Logoúshka, containing the molasses manufactories of Balákshin, lie at a distance of 6 versts from the station. Near at hand is a forest belonging to the State which supplies the railway with timber and fuel. Within the range of the station, are six settlements with a population of 4,000, exporting annually over 200,000 puds of grain to the west. In 1898, the quantity of grain despatched was 223,290 puds.

7) **Kurgán.** III class. Buffet (241 v.). Is situated within a verst and a half from the district town of Kurgán in the Tobólsk government.

Kurgán, which is the first Siberian town on the western end of the Great Siberian main line, stands on the right bank of the Toból (pop. 10,579, 5,303 males, 5,276 females), (55° 26′ N. lat., 35° 57½′ E. long.). On the site of the present town originally stood the village of Tsarévo Gorodíshche or Tsarév Kurgán, so called on account of its position near an earthen mound (kurgán), having a circumference of 80 sazhens and a height of nearly 4 sazhens, and surrounded by a ditch and rampart. The date of the creation of the town is unknown; some refer the event to 1663, others, as for example Hagemeister, to 1596. A legend attached to this place says that, at a remote date, a wealthy Tatar Khan lived here on the high bank of the Toból, and erected this earth-

Station of Kurgán.

en mound over the grave of his beautiful daughter. Hord-hunters frequently bored this barrow in search of the treasures which adorned the wealthy beauty, but the Khan's daughter unable to bear this desecration to her grave, one day fled on a silver-bound chariot drawn by white steeds, and disappeared in the waters of the neighbouring lake Chuklóm. Another tradition tells how the tumulus was the halting place of a Tatar Prince, vanquished by the Siberian Khan Kuchúm. The last version is confirmed by the fact that mounds of the same character surrounded by ditches and earthen walls, formerly representing a kind of entrenched camp, are found on the banks of many rivers in the Ob basin with some tale about Tatar encampments always attached to them. Many of these tumuli, stretching along the Irtysh, are distinguished by historical events of the time of Yermák. The question as to the origin of the fortified points, whether created under the influence of the Tatar dominion or found there by the Tatars as relics of another race, is interesting not only for history in general, as determining the part the East played in the great movement of nations from Asia to Europe, but it remains till now unsolved by science. In course of time, the village of Kurgán was transformed into a fortress, and furnished the base for opposing the Kalmyk and Kirgíz-Kaisák invasions. When the boundary line was traced more to the south, it lost its significance as a fortress, and became again a simple village. At the time of the Pugachóv revolt, 1773—1774, it joined the neighbouring villages, which now represent centres of population in the Kurgán, Yalutoróvsk and Ishím districts, in the mutiny of the Bashkírs and Yaítsk Cossacks, and in the invasion of Siberia. Since the organisation of the Tobólsk province in 1782, the village has been transformed into a district town.

The following Dekabrists, exiled to Siberia by Imperial manifest on the 13 July 1826, lived in Kurgán until the year 1845: Naryshkin, Lorér, Nazímov, Baron Rósen, Svistunóv, Kinchelbecker, Poválo-Shveikóvsky, Vogt, Prince Shchépin-Rostóvsky. Among them, Vogt who died in 1892 and Poválo-Shveikóvsky in 1845 are buried in Kurgán.

Siberia was first visited by an Imperial personage in the year 1837. The late Tsar-Liberator Alexander II, then Heir apparent to the throne, having visited the towns of Tiumén, Tobólsk, Yalutoróvsk, arrived at Kurgán in the beginning of July, attended bu Adjutant-General Kavélin, his preceptor, the famous poet Zhukóvsky, the statistician and geographer K. I. Arséniev, his personal adjutants Yuriévich and Nazímov, court-surgeon Yenókhin and ensigns Pátkul and Adlerberg.

An exhibition of agricultural and domestic industries organised in Kurgán in 1895, and visited by the Minister of State Domains Yermólov and the Minister of Ways of Communication Prince Khilkóv, was an event which is worth mentioning in the history of the town. During the exhibition, from the 1 August to the 1 October, a special gazette was published there by the Tobólsk agronomist Mr. Skalozúb.

The river Toból, on which the town is situated is navigable in its lower reaches; within the confines of the Kurgán district, it is navigable only at high water time for small vessels, on account of its sinuous bed and variable channel. For this reason the conveyance of goods is insignificant on the upper part of the Toból. This however will change as soon as the navi-

View of the town of Kurgán.

gation shall be improved and the channel cleared, as the river flows through the most fertile parts of the Yalutoróvsk and Kurgán districts, which stand in need of cheap transport for their products to the Siberian main line.

The town is not very populous. Stretching along the level and grassy bank of the Toból, it produces an agreable impression by its external appearance. It contains 5 stone orthodox churches, and among the town buildings (1,150 houses) there are many fine structures.

The educational institutions are: a district school, a preparatory gymnasium for girls, three municipal schools, a parish school, a third class elementary school for boys, supported out of the fund of the Relief Society for Scholars. The charitable institutions are: the Nicholas Children's Home, founded in commemoration of the Emperor Nicholas II's visit to Siberia as Heir Apparent to the throne; the Vladímir Poorhouse created in commemoration of the Grand Duke Vladímir Alexándrovich's visit to Siberia in 1868. Among the charitable Societies operating in Kurgán, there are: the Ladies Patronage Commitee, founded in 1892, and the Society for the Care of Schoolchildren in Kurgán, a nightshelter, the Town Hospital, the best in the government. Since June 1897, a branch of the West Siberian Society of Agriculture has been opened in Kurgán, publishing periodically its transactions regarding the agricultural conditions of the country. A depot of agricultural machinery has been added to it.

The town contains a public and a free library for the lower class. There is a store of agricultural tools, machinery etc. organised by the Ministry of Agriculture and State Domains. There are two private printing offices. Further, there are a public club and two hotels with rooms from R. 1 to R. 2 a day. Kurgán, on account of its industries, holds an important place not alone in the Tobólsk government but throughout Siberia. It is also the centre of an extensive trade in agricultural and animal products. The town factories and works yield an annual revenue of R. 1,800,000. The most important among them are: a distillery, a brewery, a tallow boilery, a wheat flour mill belonging to Smólin and Poklévsky-Kózell.

Trade is particulary lively during fair time, four fairs being held annually; the Alexis fair from 5 to 18 March, the Tíkhon fair from 10 to 17 June, the Demetrius fair from 18 to 24 October, the Christmas fair from 14 to 24 December. The commercial operations transacted at the fairs amount to R. 4,000,000 per annum. The chief articles of export are: corn as grain and flour, tallow, skins, butter, meat, potato molasses, game and fish. The local merchants purchase droves of cattle in the Kirgíz steppe, and after having fattened them on the extensive pastures situated in the environs of the town along the banks of the Toból, slaughter them in the autumn.

According to the estimates for 1899, the revenue of the town amounted to R. 61,445 17 k.

The Public Town Bank, opened in 1865, has an annual business of R. 3,000,000. Manufactures and industry are represented by the firms of Smolin—wheat-flour mill, distillery, brewery, molasses manufactory, tallow boilery; Ménshikov — glassworks; Bolshakóv and Co. — a starch manufactory; Brónnikov and Shvétov—wheat-flour mills; Bakúnin, Kaltashév, Veniukóv and Co., Márgenev have molasses manufactories; Kolpakov, a butter manufactory The transport offices are: The Russian Society, Kukhtárin and Sons, The Brothers Kaménsky, the Nadézhda Society.

Upon the opening of traffiic, a settlement was established near the station, which is gradually extending; it consists of houses belonging partly to railway employees and partly to merchants, The sphere of influence of the station, besides the town of Kurgán, comprises 132 settlements with a population of 68,000. This populous and fertile region yields annually about 5,000,000 puds of various goods — grain, tallow, butter, meat, game — which are despatched direct to the ports of Russia, and to the interior markets of the Empire. This explains the great importance of the station of Kurgán. In

1898, the quantity of grain bound west amounted to 4,007,667 puds, viz. 544.13 puds of rye, 2,553,669 puds of wheat, 708,473 puds of oats, 13 puds of millet, 3,695 puds of buckwheat, 15,464 puds of barley, 6,374 puds of peas, 55,367 puds of wheat meal, 22,530 puds of rye meal, 427 puds of buckwheat flour, 2,415 puds or buckwheat, 111 puds of milletmeal, 437 puds of different kinds of grain, 1,366 puds of bran, 91,212 puds of hempseed and linseed, and 945 puds of other oil seeds.

A medical and feeding station for the emigrants is established near the railway station, which is also the residence of an official employed for the regulation of the emigration movement. This point is particularly important for the emigrants bound for the north-west of the Akmolínsk territory.

The medical and feeding station for emigrants near the station of Kurgán.

The railway line skirting the town on its northern side, at the 247 verst crosses the river Toból by a bridge 247 sazhens in length with the roadway upon the lower chord. The bridge has four spans, two of 50 and two of 10 sazhens at each end. The height of the embankment is 4.73 sazhens on the west, and 4.47 sazhens on the east. The five piers are laid on caissons, while the abutments and the retaining walls are supported on piles; the girders are semiparabolic.

After having crossed the Toból, the line ascends to the watershed of the rivers Toból and Utiák. At the 266-th verst, it runs over the Utiák spanned by a bridge 10 sazhens long.

8) **Vargashí.** V class (276-v.) is situated 3 versts from the village of the same name (pop. 1,200). The country is level and covered with young birch woods. Water is supplied from wells.

About 100,000 puds of grain, furnished by the surrounding villages, are annually conveyed from here to the western markets. A distillery belonging to Ushakóv and a butter manufactory to Léster, are situated within 8 versts of the station. At the 282-th verst, the line reaches its highest point on the watershed of the Toból and Ishím.

9) **Lebiázhie.** V class (318 v.). The village of Lebiázhie (pop. 1,700) stands 6 versts from the station. The place is swampy, and provided with wells containing bad water. There are about 60 settlements and villages with a population of 38,000 within the range of the station, whence 500,000 puds of goods are forwarded by freight trains to the interior western markets of the Empire. The quantity of grain conveyed in 1898 was 404,287 puds. The surrounding settlements contain over 15 butter manufactories, producing annually about 20,000 puds of cream butter.

10) **Makúshino.** IV class. Buffet. (362 v.). The locality is low and swampy. It is supplied with water by a lake; in winter this freezes to the bottom and melted ice is then used. The village of Makúshino (pop. 1,266) is at a distance of one verst from the station; 40 settlements and villages with a population of 20,000 are scattered in the environs. The tallow-boilery of Ushakóv is situated near. The agricultural region surrounding the station

furnishes annually about a million and a half puds of different goods which are exported direct to the western markets of the Empire. In 1898, the quantity of grain etc. conveyed from this point amounted to 1,217,926 puds (10,296 puds of rye, 932,622 puds of wheat, 250,211 puds of oats, 15,976 puds of barley, 934 puds of bran, 6,457 puds of oil seeds).

A church holding 450 people has been erected near the station; it was inaugurated on the 21 March 1898 in honour of the Presentation of the Holy

Bridge over the Toból.

Virgin. There is also a parish school with one class for 30 boy and girl pupils, built in the name of the archpriest John Sérgiev.

At the 368 th verst, the line deviates considerably to the north avoiding the large lake Elánich. Near the station of Petukhóvo it enters into the limits of the Ishím district of the Tobólsk government.

11) **Petukhóvo.** V class (407 v.). The country is level and dry. Water is provided from a neighbouring lake. In winter, the water is not good. The village of Petukhóvo is situated within a distance of 6 versts. At the time of the construction of the line. the Voznesénie suburb was built, in 1893, near the station; it is inhabited by peasant settlers from the governments of Poltáva and Chernígov. The agricultural region around the station numbers 5 settlements and 10 villages containing a population of 8,000, and furnishing annually about 500,000 puds of various goods exported to the interior markets of the Empire. The quantity of grain transported from this station in 1898 amounted to 440,570 puds. In this district there is a butter manufactory belonging to Mr. Véntikh, and manufactories of the same kind belonging to the peasants organised on the cooperative principle in the settlements Kámenskoe and Utchánskoe, producing over 5,000 puds of cream butter annually.

A medical and feeding station with a barrack holding 50 people is established near the station. When the movement is at its maximum, the emigrants are accomodated in Kirgíz yúrtas.

This station is of essential importance to the emigrants settling the free lands of the Ishím district in the Tobólsk government and the northern part of the Petropávlovsk district in the Akmolínsk territory.

12) **Mamliútka.** V class. (448 v.). The country is level and swampy. The water is of an inferior quality. The village of Mamliútka is in close proximity to the station (pop. 400). There are about 10 settlements within the range of the station, exporting annually 100,000 puds of grain to the interior markets of the Empire. At the 465-th verst, the line enters the limits of the Petropávlovsk district in the Akmolínsk territory, and begins its descent along the Ishím valley. At the 482-th verst, it passes over the Ishím by a bridge with an opening of 100 sazhens.

The bridge has two spans of 50 sazhens and two of 10 sazhens on both sides. The height of the embankment at the west end is 5.12 sazhens, at the east—5.40 sazhens. Its three piers are laid on caissons. The abutments have a beton foundation. After having crossed the Ishím, the line ascending along the right slope of the valley reaches the station of Petropávlovsk.

13) **Petropávlovsk.** III class. Buffet. (490 v.). Is situated within two versts of the district town of the same name in the Akmolínsk territory.

The town of Petropávlovsk stands on the right bank of the Ishím (pop. 19,637—10,180 males, 9,457 females; 54°3' N. lat., 38°47' E. long).

The creation of a permanent centre of population on the site of the present town dates from 1752; it was founded with a view to protect the Russian settlements, extending to the south along the valleys of the rivers Ishím and Toból; a fortified boundary line was at the same time traced between the Siberian territory and the land occupied by the Kirgíz-Kaisák hordes.

Church near the station of Makúshino.

A fort in the name of S-t Peter and S-t Paul was built on the elevated bank of the Ishím, surrounded by wooden walls and stockades. The boundary line marked by a series of wooden fortresses (Pokróvskaya, Nikoláevskaya, Lebiázhia, Polúdennaya, Stánovskaya, Presnóvskaya, Kabánia, Presnogórkovskaya) began here stretching straight to the west, for a distance of 250 versts, to the ford over the Toból. This frontier was called the Bitter Line, on account of the great number of bitter lakes lying in this direction.

In consequence of its position at the junction of the caravan steppe routes and the highways suitable for cattle driving, the outskirts of the S-t Peter and Paul fort became the centre of a lively trade which, besides the Central Asiatic nomads and particularly the inhabitants of Bukhará and Tashként, embraced China whose outposts at that date, advancing far into the interior of the actual Steppe region, reached to Kokchetáv, situated at a distance of but 170 versts south of the Bitter Line.

A special barter court was established at this point where Russians and Asiatics exchanged goods, cattle and even men, the Kirgíz-Kaisáks having

Bridge over the Ishím.

received the permission, according to a law promulgated by the Russian Government in 1756, to sell and truck for goods Kalmyks and other prisoners of war belonging to some subject Asiatic race, to all Russians of the orthodox religion, irrespective of rank, in order to increase in Siberia the number of those possessing serfs. The sale of prisoners was forbidden by an ukáze given on the 8 October 1825.

At the end of the XVIII century (1782), the Sultan of the Middle Kirgíz Vali Horde, in the presence of Lieutenant General Yakóbi sent by the Empress Catherine II, solemnly swore allegiance to Russia in the fortress of Peter and Paul. In 1807, the fortress was transformed into the town of Petropávlovsk and included in the Tobólsk government; lying on the frontier and being the centre of an extensive trade with the Asiatic tribes, this town was chosen as the headquarters of a customs board, which was abolished about 1860. Since the organisation of the Akmolínsk territory, the town of Petropávlovsk has ranked among the district towns.

To the present time, the town of Petropávlosk is of the first importance in the local steppe Central Asiatic trade; in its population and outward appearance,it differs much from other Siberian towns, retaining a half Asiatic, half Mohammedan character. Its population contains 35 percent of Mohammedans, viz. Tatars, Bukhárians, Tashkéntians and a few Kirgíz chiefly engaged in the sale of animal products. The town contains 2,972 houses including 200 of stone. The shops and stone houses are all of stone. Special attention should be paid to the Barter Court, comprising 137 stone shops under one roof, occupying a rectangular area 245 sazhens long and 50 sazhens wide, employed as a depot for various raw materials, and for the sale of Asiatic goods. The shopfronts are inside the court. There are five stone orthodox churches, a wooden Jewish synagogue, and six stone Mohammedan mosques with high minarets of fine architecture. Educational institutions: school with five classes for boys, preparatory gymnasium with four classes for girls, two parish schools, parish school for girls, two Cossack schools, six Tatar schools (medreseh) attached to the mosques. Town hospital. A small stone theatre. Public club. A branch of the State Bank. Public Town Bank. Two hotels with rooms at 50 k. to R. 1 50 k. a day. The annual town revenue amounts to R. 60,000. There are two fairs: The Petróvskaya, held from the 25 June to 25 July, and the Ignátievskaya, lasting from the 18 December to the 1 January where principally agricultural and animal products are sold. The financial operations effected at these fairs are not considerable and do not contribute to the development of local trade. The town line and its environs include over 50 works using animal products (tallow boileries, sheepskin works, tanneries, wool-washeries, gut manufactories), and also a great number of „salgány", where from 250,000 to 400,000 head of cattle driven from different parts of the Steppe region are slaughtered annually. The salgán presents a quadrangular fence made of timber or more frequently of metal, with a superficial area of 1 to 3 desiatins. One part of it is covered with a shed, where the beasts are slaughtered and cut up, and the sheep guts cleaned; another side is occupied by closed store-houses serving for the hanging and storing of the carcases; on the third side there is a tallow-boilery, situated in a wooden building with a log floor. Large kettles of solid sheet iron are fitted in hearths placed under the floor near the wall; in the middle of the building are placed massive wooden boxes, into which the boiled tallow after standing is poured for cooling, and then is put straight into barrels.

Station of Petropávlovsk.

The annual commercial operations of the town of Petropávlosk closely depending on the general development of trade in the vast Kirgíz steppe, according to certain official data, referring to the last ten years, amounted to R. 5,000,000. However, since the opening of traffic on the Great Siberian main line, they have much increased and now exceed R. 12,000,000.

The most important firms are: Kazántsev—iron wares and cattle, Butórin—iron and leather goods, Zakhárin—iron and leather goods, Rakhmetbáev—Asiatic goods, Tiuménev—horsehair and down, Faizúlin—leather goods; manufactories of Cheremízinov, of the Brothers Ovsiánikov and of Ganshín and Sons, Kilb and Co, leather, hair, and lamb-skins. Musumbáev and Irkibáev—both Asiatic goods.

The river Ishím on which the town stands, called Isél or Esél by the Kirgíz, is the left tributary of the Irtysh. Taking its rise in the Yamán Kiáz mountains, it flows for a distance of 2,000 versts; half of its course is inclu-

Barter Court in Petropávlosk.

ded in the Kirgíz steppe, which in spring is widely flooded by its. waters. The valley of the Ishím has a sandy and clayey soil, abounds in pastures and is dotted with numerous lakes, which at a remote time were river beds. This vast valley, richly provided with pastures, was always the favourite resort of the nomads, within the confines of the Kirgíz steppe. From the Kokchetáv district, the river becomes suitable for rafting, but the great number of dams and pile bridges occurring principally on its lower reaches, present an impediment to the development of this mode of navigation,

On the 18 July, 1891, the town of Petropávlovsk was honoured by the visit of His Imperial Majesty the present Emperor Nicholas II, then Heir Apparent to the throne, on his way from the Far East. Having been conveyed by horses from Omsk to Petropávlovsk through the territory of the Cossack troops, His Imperial Majesty was greeted at the triumphal arch erected at the entrance to the town, by the military governor of the Akmolínsk territory

Major-General Sánnikov, by deputies from the public town board and from the citizens, by the Mohammedan clergy, by the Petropávlovsk Cossacks, and by the public board of Akmolínsk. After a visit to the cathedral, a municipal school with 5 classes was solemnly opened in the presence of His Imperial Majesty, and His name given to it.

Upon the opening of traffic on the Siberian main line, a settlement was established near the station consisting partly of houses belonging to railwaymen and merchants. At the cost of the Emperor Alexander III fund, a stone church capable of holding 450 persons is being erected near the station in order to satisfy the spiritual needs of the railway employees and of the population of the new settlement. It is dedicated to the patroness of the Empress María Feódorovna, Saint Mary Magdalen, with side aisles in honour of the image of the Mater Dolorosa, and of Saint Theodosius of Chernígov. A parish school for 80 boy and girl pupils is built near the station in the name of Privy Councillor Teréshchenko. A medical and feeding station with barracks accomodating 300 persons is established within a verst and a half from the station, principally for the use of the settlers bound for the Akmolínsk territory. As a result of the peculiar conditions of the steppe trade and of the life of the nomad population within the range of the Petropávlovsk station, its influence embraces an immense area, including not only part of the Akmolínsk territory, but also the adjacent steppe regions.

Parish school near the station of Petropávlovsk.

The quantity of goods forwarded from this station at the present time exceeds 3,000,000 puds; the greater portion is represented by animal products.

About 1,233,247 puds of grain were conveyed from here in 1898 (47,492 puds of rye, 765,895 puds of wheat, 354,772 puds of oats, 357 puds of barley, 12 puds

Quantity of raw products conveyed in 1897 from the station of Petropávlovsk.

Governments.	Fresh meat		Guts.	Offal.	Raw hides.				Wool.				Horsehair.	Horns and hoofs.
	Beef	Lamb.			Horse.	Cow.	Camel.	Sheep and goat.	Sheep's	Camel's.	Goat's.	Superior quality.		
	Puds.				Number.				Puds.					
St. Petersburg	127,063	1,210	—	3,060	—	—	—	—	—	—	—	—	—	—
Moscow	57,034	630	2,660	200	—	—	—	31,000	2,045	—	—	—	671	—
Tobólsk	200	7,300	—	—	4,168	8,180	1,403	24,890	4,642	—	—	—	—	—
Vladímir	25.540	450	—	81	—	—	—	345,792	—	—	—	—	—	—
Kazán	8	—	—	—	9,327	5,500	100	272,245	12,624	2,500	179	—	93	—
Orenbúrg	—	3,940	257,572	—	4,369	32,105	647	32,806	2,165	—	—	—	—	—
Nízhni Nóvgorod	12,200	—	—	—	4,400	18,065	—	131,572	6,576	9,769	353	4,235	4,612	—
Perm	6,391	26,887	—	202	1,588	3,336	160	70,821	2,784	—	—	—	—	—
Gródno	—	—	—	—	23,226	—	—	202,525	4,884	—	—	—	749	—
Samára	—	419	96,320	—	—	400	—	1,150	—	—	—	—	—	—
Túla	610	1,200	—	3,040	12,183	500	—	—	—	—	—	—	—	—
Khersòn	—	—	—	—	—	1,180	—	6,100	—	—	—	—	—	—
Estonia	—	—	—	—	—	—	—	10,000	—	—	—	—	1,686	—
Warsaw	—	—	—	—	—	—	—	60,150	—	—	—	—	—	—
Podólia	—	—	—	—	—	—	—	2,000	—	—	—	—	—	—
Simbírsk	—	—	—	—	—	—	—	2,600	3,188	1,260	—	—	—	300
Tambóv	—	—	—	—	—	—	—	5,650	14,084	—	—	—	—	40
Yarosláv	9,150	—	—	610	—	—	—	—	—	—	—	—	—	—
Towns.														
Sarátov	—	—	12,000	—	—	—	—	1,894	25	—	—	—	—	—
Astrakhan	—	—	—	—	—	—	—	2,000	—	—	—	—	—	—
Kostromá	1,220	—	—	—	—	—	—	—	—	—	—	—	—	—
Ufá	—	200	—	—	5,690	3,280	—	8,176	283	68	—	400	—	600
Riazán	—	—	—	—	—	—	—	38,680	—	—	—	—	—	—
Tomsk	—	—	—	—	—	—	—	700	500	—	—	—	—	—
Kóvno	—	—	—	—	—	—	—	28,000	14,084	—	—	—	—	—
Tver	2,440	—	—	—	—	—	—	5,650	—	—	—	—	—	—
Pénza	—	—	—	—	—	—	—	1,500	—	—	—	—	—	—
Kalúga	—	—	—	1,220	—	—	—	—	—	—	150	—	—	—
Omsk	—	—	5,000	—	868	567	—	23	—	—	—	—	—	—
Petróvsk (Dagestán)	—	—	—	—	—	—	—	—	—	—	—	—	—	—
Ríga	—	—	—	—	—	—	—	470	—	—	—	—	586	—
New Port	—	—	—	—	—	—	—	14,060	—	—	—	—	1,268	—
Total	235,857	37,236	373,352	8,413	119,656	73,113	2,310	1,295,354	53,801	13,597	682	4,635	9,661	940

of peas, 24,144 of wheat meal, 22,323 of rye meal, 124 puds of various grain, 12,078 puds of seeds of oil plants). The total export of steppe and animal products is clearly shewn in the data obtained by the veterinary survey of the Akmolínsk territory regarding the quantity of raw products conveyed during 1897 by the West-Siberian railway from the station of Petropávlovsk.

In reality, the raw products are neither consumed nor exploited in the given centres, which serve only as stages for the further transport of the goods, a great part of the animal products from the steppe being forwarded to the ports of Libáva and Rével, whence sheepskins are sent to Vienna and goatskins to Paris and Boston. From Odéssa, many products are conveyed to Turkey. Guts are transported through Samára to Berlin and Hamburg. The German subjects, the brothers Akkola, for several years past, have exported some thousands of guts from the town of Petropávlovsk. The choice of raw products for export testifies to the fact that the local traders do not know how to avail themselves of the advantages offered by the railway communication, but keep to the ancient customs, according to which tallow and butter, representing the products of the steppe cattle to the yearly amount of several hundred thousand puds, are even to the present time transported by nomads and traders by road to the fair of Irbít, where the prices for these products are fixed, this mode of conveyance being very cheap. The organisation of butter churners with separators, as in the Tobólsk government, has not here received a large development; many animal products left totally unexploited offer wide prospects for the application of capital and enterprise.

ROUTES

from Petropávlovsk to Akmolínsk Territory.

1) Orenbúrg post road: From the town of Petropávlovsk-Arkhángelskaya 20 v., Malovoznesénskaya 25 v., Stanováya 22 v., Senzhárskaya 30¾ v., Novorybinskaya 29¼ v., Presnóvskaya 16 v., Ekaterínenskaya 29 v., Kabánia 15½ v., Peschánaya 24¼ v. (260 versts to the frontier of the Orenbúrg government).

2) The Akmolínsk post-road: From the town of Petropávlovsk, Karatálskaya station 18 v., Karatomárskaya 20,6 v., Kamyshlòvskaya 28,6 v., Emantúzskaya 24¾ v., Mizgílskaya 23¼ v., Aksúiskaya 20 v., Azátskaya 18 v., town of Kokchetáv 28 v. (180 versts to the town of Kokchetáv), Priréchny picket 20 v., Zerendínskaya 18 v., Víktorovskaya 24¾ v., Sandyktávskaya 16 v., Mikháilovskaya 19 v., Pokróvskaya 19 v., town of Atbasár 19 v. (176¾ versts to the town of Atbasár), Baidchigítskaya 34½ v., Amantáiskaya 22¼ v., Koluntónskaya 24¼ v., Karabínskaya 27 v., Chanchárskaya 29 v., Dzhilandínskaya 22 v., Karamedínskaya 32 v., Barmátskaya 30 v., town of Akmolínsk 35 v. (255¼ versts from the town of Akmolínsk).

Caravan Routes.

From the town of Petropávlovsk two caravan routes lead to Turkestán:

1) Along the valley of the Ishím to Dzhargáin-achág (an ancient fort at the turn of the Ishím northwards), thence past the Ulutávsk mountains, by the valley of the Dzhida-Kengír to the Sarysú river, and further past the sands of Arys to Ak-mechét (fort of Peróvsky) to Bukhará. This is one of the most ancient routes. The present ways to Bukhará on leaving the town of Petropávlovsk, turn to the Tróitsk post-road before reaching Dzhargáin-achág, near the place called Bekchentái.

2) To the town of Akmolínsk. Commencing at the Barter Court of Petropávlovsk, it runs southwards by the picket road, turning south-east near the woods of Karatomársk, and crossing

the, small river Cháglinka (ford at Daúr-Kará) 20 versts above its junctiou with lake Bolshíe-Chagly. From Cháglinka, the road continues in the direction of lake Eserké-Dzhaltyr-Sor and runs further between lakes Bozorbói and Maldybói towards lake Bulat-Chalkár, thence proceeding south to the former Public Court of Uch-Bulák (near lake Dzhukéi), and then past lakes Kurtúl-Kul and Chagalák-Kul, over the small river Tatymbét to the lake Chuchkaly and further through Uch-Bulák, the picket Chubár Kul, the Kuchekú and lake Sasyk-Kul reaches Akmólinsk. From August till March, the caravans follow a more western route through the Cossack village of Shchúchenskaya. The total length of the route between Petropávlovsk and Akmolínsk is 430 v. The road is mainly sand and lime, rarely stone. The goods brought to Akmolínsk by cart, are here transferred to camels. The Akmolínsk market, furnisheng the needful supplies for the further journey to the south, the traders start with the caravans by the following roads, under the guidance of the caravan-bash.

a) From the town of Akmolínsk, the road fords the Ishím and runs southwards to the Nurínsk picket 117 versts, keeping mostly to the right bank of the Nurá which is provided with abundant pastures and very good water; everywhere are Kirgíz winterquarters.

b) From the Nurínsk picket to lake Bozgúl, a distance of 226 versts, the road deviates to the south-west; the population is thinner at some places water is supplied from wells, and reeds are employed as fuel.

c) The distance between lake Bozgúl and Agalák is 463 versts. At first the road is sandy, then hard and clayey with red clay and fine red pebbles. The eyes are hurt by looking at the ground and at the air which on the surface of the earth is of a crimson colour. Salt-marshes and soft sands occur beyond Bel-Kudúk, forming at some points large sand hills. The road is very hard for the caravans. The inhospitable steppe of Bekpak-Dalá stretches beyond the Taban-Kudúk, presenting a perfectly level plain for a distance of 60 versts. The soil of this dry steppe is clayey with fine gravel. Further on, the surface is more varied and water is to be found at the 85-th verst in Chulák-Espé; twenty-six versts from Espá is the sandy bed of the river Chu. After having crossed the river, the road is clayey as far as Agalák. The fodder on the way is very bad, especially in Begpak-dalá which, for a distance of 85 versts, is waterless. The saksaúl bush is employed as fuel.

d) The distance between Agalák and Turkestán is 100 versts. Till Ak-Tiubé, the road winds its way among mountain passes and ridges. Fuel is scanty. Rivulets run along the road.

From the station of Petropávlovsk, the railway line ascends the watershed of the rivers Ishím and Irtysh, and near the Tokushí station, at the 515 verst, reaches its highest point.

Hence the line proceeds along the northern slope of the Kamyshlov and Irtysh depression, which stretches eastwards to the Irtysh and contains a series of brackish lakes known under the name of the Kamyshlov lakes. This depression represents the valley of a former river with a whole system of rivulets and streams which are drying up and through which the brackish water of the lakes drains into the Irtysh. The lake system existing at the present time terminates near the Irtysh by the small river Kamyshlovskaya; almost all the lakes have bitter and brackish water; during the summer they are nearly dry and covered with reeds which in rotting produce unhealthy exhalations.

This depression is situated in the territory occupied by the Siberian Cossack troops, and contains a line of Cossack settlements and former fortresses and redoubts, which, between the town of Omsk and the frontier of the Orenbúrg government, represents the right flank of the Siberian Cossack troops and is called the Bitter Line.

Previous to the construction of the railway, the post road from Omsk to Orenbúrg followed the Kamyshlov depression.

14) **Tokushí.** V class (522 v.). The country is level, surrounded by swamps and lakes and dotted with birch groves. A lake lying near the station furnishes good water. The settlement of Tokushí is situated in proximity to the

station, having been established before the construction of the railway line. It contains a school for boys and girls, which is maintained by the community.

15) **Medvézhia.** V class (567 v.). The country is level, covered with birch groves. Water is taken from a swamp, lying a verst and a half from the station. The Medvézhy settlement (pop. 250) is situated within 4 versts.

Wooden church near the station of Isil-Kúl.

16) **Isil-Kúl.** IV class. Buffet (616 v.). Omsk district. The country is dry and level with copses of birch. Water is got from lake Isil-Kúl, lying two versts from the station. In winter the lake often freezes to the bottom. A wooden church holding 450 people erected at the cost of the Emperor Alexander III fund, stands near the station. The church was inaugurated on the 18 March in honour of the Moscow Saints Peter, Alexéi, Iván and Philip. There is also a wooden building containing an elementary parish school

with one class, founded in the name of the archpriest John Sérgiev. Gorodíshche (pop. 650) is the nearest settlement; it has been inhabited since 1895, principally by emigrants from the Pénza government. The range of influence of the station comprises 20 settlements with a total population of 10,500. Notwithstanding the recent organisation of many setlements, grain products are already transported from here to the west. In 1898, the quantity of exported grain amounted to 49,531 puds.

Ikonostasis in the church at the station of Isil-Kúl.

17) **Kochubáevo,** V class (657 v.). The country is level, clad with birch groves. Water of an inferior quality is supplied by wells. The Cossack settlement Vólchy (pop. 1,000) is at a distance of three vertsts.

18) **Mariánovka.** V class (699 v.). The country is level, the water bad. The Cossack settlement of Kurgán (pop. 100) is situated within 4 versts. At a former date tumuli (kurgáns) described in 1771 by the Academician Falk, stood near the settlement, whence the name Kurgán; at present there is no trace of them left. In 1898, about 22,423 puds of grain were exported from here to the west.

19) The **Omsk** military post (741 v.). A branch line, half a verst in length, runs hence to the Irtysh to meet the necessities of the railway. A saw mill and works for chemical preservation of ties are being built on the wood platform of the railway. A wheat-flour mill and another mill belonging to the merchant Reménnikov stand in close proximity.

The station is not open for commercial operations. At the 743 verst, the line crosses the Irtysh by a bridge of 300 sazhens. It has 6 spans of 50 sazhens. The height of the embankment on the west is 6.54 sazhens, on the east 9.72 sazhens. The breadth of the river bed is about 500 sazhens; dams projecting into the river have been constructed for the regulation of the current. The piers are laid on caissons. The abutments and piers are made of granite brought from Cheliábinsk and laid with cement. The girders of welded iron produced by the Vótkin works were made in the temporary shops of Enginer Berézin in Ufá. The construction of the bridge was carried out by the contractor, Engineer Berézin, under the supervision of the Engineers Zalússky and Olshévsky. After having crossed the Irtysh, the line approaches the town of Omsk.

20) **Omsk.** II class. Buffet (745 v.). Is situated within 3 versts of the town.

The town of Omsk belonging to the Akmolínsk territory stands on the right, at the junction of the rivers Om and Irtysh (54° 59′ N. lat., 43° 6′ E. long). The census of 1897 shewed a population of 37,470, 20,106 males, 17,364 females; according to the record of the local administration, the number of inhabitants in 1899 is given as 50,768 (27,029 males; 23,739 fem.). By order of the Great Reformer Peter I, a special expedition was organised in 1714 under Colonel Buchholz with a view to enlarge the commercial relations of Russia and Central Asia. Having been opposed by the Dzhungárs who occupied the greater part of the territory of the present Siberian steppe border land, Buchholz upon receiving the authorisation of Prince Gagárin, then the influential governor of all Siberia, founded in 1719 a small fortress on

Bridge over the Irtysh.

the left bank of the Om with a view to strengthen the Russian dominion among the nomads of the Asiatic steppes. Very soon the Omsk fortress obtained stategical importance, being the point of junction of the Orenbúrg and Tobólsk roads with the Kolyván-Kuznétsk border line. Lieutenant-General Springer, who in 1763 was appointed commander of all the border lines in Siberia, deeming that fortresses contributed to the pacification of the neighbouring Asiatic tribes, abandoned the existing fortifications on the left bank of the Om, and erected more solid ones on the right bank in the angle formed by the Om at its union with the Irtysh. The construction of the new fortress was begun in 1765, according to the Vauban system, forming a polygon with five bastions; the strengthening of the southern boundary of Siberia was undertaken at the same time. The Elisabeth light-house was placed opposite to the fortress on the left bank of the Irtysh, where a market for

Passenger station at Omsk.

the native nomads was opened. From 1782, when the Tobólsk province was organised, the Omsk fortress was included in its confines, and transformed into a town, which on account of its fortifications ranked till the beginning of the XIX century among the best and strongest bases of the Siberian boundary line. Upon the organisation in 1822 of a separate Omsk territory, comprising all the lands occupied by the conquered Kirgíz hordes, Omsk was made the centre of the local administration, and for administrative purposes, in 1839 became the residence of the Governor-General of Western Siberia; all the administrative institutions were also transferred here from Tobólsk.

The separate administration of Western Siberia was abolished in 1882, and subjected to the general control of the Ministries while the Akmolínsk and Semipalátinsk territories were formed into a special Steppe government under the command of a governor-general resident at Omsk. At the present time, this town represents the centre of the Akmolínsk and Steppe government civil administration. It contains also the diocesan department of the Steppe country and the Court of Justice of the Omsk juridical district. In it are concentrated the administration of the Siberian military district and of the Cossack troops. The entrance gate is the single archaeological monument left from the fortifications of the former fortress. For purposes of administration the town is divided into seven divisions: Kadyshev, Butyrkí, Mókrinsk, Lug, Slobodá, Ilyín and Cossack. The town stands on an even site, somewhat above the level of the rivers Irtysh and Om; the soil is sandy and dry and partly saline. The climate is unfavourable, being characterised by a very dry air, an unsteady temperature with extreme changes from cold to heat and continuous winds, which in winter produce blizzards and in summer raise clouds of dust. The maximum temperature in Omsk is +36.4°, the minimum —41.1°, the absolute moisture is 5.1°, the amount of rainfall 309.3.

The town is almost entirely of wood, containing small one-storeyed buildings. The total number of houses is 3,605; among them 81 are of stone, 46 of which belong to the State, 3 to the public, 32 to private individuals. Among the 342 shops only two belonging to private persons are of stone.

The monotonous architecture of the small wooden buildings, the unpaved streets with wooden side-walks, the absence of any vegetation, which perishes on the saline soil, give to Omsk the aspect of a large Cossack set-

View of Omsk (phot. by Krékov).

tlement. A few stone buildings housing State and public institutions stand out on this uniform background: the Cadet Corps, the Siberian Cossack troops Economical Department, the barracks of the local garrison, the residence of the Governor General and of the Commander of the troops, and the Engineer Department are situated within the space formerly occupied by the fortress; there are also a gymnasium for boys and girls, a central school for surgeons' assistants, a technical school and the Territorial Administration. The town includes two gardens, one on the banks of the Om, organised by the Society for the Promotion of Elementary Education. A birch wood, situated on the northern side of the town within a verst of it, is the object of walks by the inhabitants. On the southern side near the railway line and close to the camp of the local battalion, is another birch wood with a sanitary station, whither patients from the military hospital are brought in summer and where Kirgíz yúrtas are pitched for those who wish to drink kumys prepared under the supervision of the railway physicians.

Remains of the Omsk fortress.

The description of the Siberian penal settlements belongs to the historical recollections of the abolished fortress.

At the edge of the fortress near the ramparts on the Om, stood a wooden penal prison surrounded by high stockades which, from the middle of the XVII century, was a centre for convicts banished from Russia, and played an important part in the history of convict exile and in the organisation and settlement of the Siberian frontier lines. Towards the end of the XVIII century, in the time of Pugachóv, over 800 convicts were kept in the Omsk prison. In 1849, the great Russian writer and thinker F. M. Dostoévsky (1821—1881) was condemned to hard labour for a period of four years, and was banished to this prison, for having played a part in the political affair of Petrashévsky. Recollections of this imprisonment with a description of the convict prison were recorded with great talent by Dostoévsky in his „Memoirs from a Dead House" which have immortalised in history the Omsk fortress and its „Dead House". The poet Dúrov (1816—1869) was also condemned to hard labour, having participated in the same political affair, and passed four years in the Dead House together with Dostoévsky. This historical house has not existed for a long time, and the spot on which it formerly stood is occupied by new buildings. There are 13 orthodox churches in the town (4 parish churches, 2 without parishes, 7 house chapels) and a Mohammedan wooden mosque. The first stone in the construction of the cathedral in honour of Christ's Ascension was laid on the 16 July 1891, in the presence of His Imperial Majesty the present Emperor Nicholas II, then Heir Apparent to the throne, on his journey across the Steppe region. The successful erection of this vast cathedral, which is capable of holding 1600 people and was inaugurated the 9 September 1898, is entirely due to the efforts of the president of the building committee, Lieutenant-General N.I. Sánnikov, Military Governor of the Akmolínsk territory. The materials for the construction having been provided without recourse to contractors, the total cost amounted only to R. 141,316 47¾ k. This sum included R. 15,000 granted by the Holy Synod, R. 38,000 from the Voskresénsk church fund, the remainder being donations by private individuals and institutions. Among the most venerated antiquities of the orthodox church, the following are worthy of attention: a bible, a cross, a paten and an altar-cloth given by the Empress Catherine II in 1774, and kept in the cathedral of the Ascension. In the Nicholas Cossack troops church is kept the banner of Yermák, which by the pious offerings of the Cossacks of the Siberian troops has been attached to a valuable shaft. This banner was brought from the town of Berióžov and is 2 arshins and 6 vershoks long. On one side is represented the Archangel Michael on a red winged horse, striking the Devil with his spear and precipitating houses and towers into the water; on the other, is seen St. Demetrius on a dark green horse thrusting Kuchúm, mounted on a white horse, into an abyss. The holy spears from the miraculous image of the Blessed Virgin of Abalák are kept in the church of the Prophet Elias.

The Omsk cathedral of the Ascension.

The educational institutions are 29 in number: the Siberian Cadet Corps, a military preparatory boarding school, a school for boys, a school for girls, a preparatory gymnasium for girls, a seminary for masters, a preparatory school attached to the seminary, a lower mechanical and technical school in the name of the Emperor Alexander III, a central school for surgeons' assistants, a district school, 2 movable schools, an elementary industrial and reading school, an elementary handwork school maintained by the Society for the Promotion of Elementary Education, 2 Cossack schools, a boarding school for Kirgíz children, 3 parish schools, a lower school of forestry, and a Mohammedan school.

The first military school on the Siberian border line was opened in the middle of the XVIII century according to the statute concerning garrison schools, in the Bíisk fortress, by the commander of the dragoon regiment of Kolyván, Colonel de Harrig. Taking this school as a model, Lieutenant General Springer, Chief of the Siberian border lines created similar ones in the towns of Omsk and Petropávlovsk, which were the first official military educational establishments on the former West Siberian frontier. In 1789, an Asiatic school for training interpreters was founded in Omsk; further, a military school with three classes for the spread of reading and writing among the class destined for military service. In 1826, the Omsk military school was transformed into a school for the Siberian Cossack troops of the line, with a course of study of seven years; it existed to the year 1846, when the Cadet Corps was opened in Omsk according to the plan generally adopted for military educational establishments. At the present time, this corps is the single military school of this kind throughout Siberia and in the Russian dominions in Asia. The majority of the public educational institutions such as the classical gymnasium for boys, the school for teachers, the central school for assistant surgeons, the technical school, are due to the enlightened activity of Adjutant General N. G. Kaznakóv, Governor-General of Western Siberia from 1875 to 1880.

Charitable institutions: a town hospital, an orphanage, a baby's home, a refuge for poor children, cheap dinners, and public tea-rooms.

Missionary, charitable, scientific and other societies operating in accordance with the charters:

1) Diocesan Committee of the Orthodox Missionary Society. 2) Charitable Society under the patronage of the Empress. 3) Relief Society for destitute boy pupils of the Omsk gymnasium. 4) Relief Society for poor emigrants to the Steppe region. 5) Relief Society for destitute girl pupils of the Omsk gymnasium. 6) Omsk Society for the Promotion of Elementary Education. 7) Relief Society for teachers and pupils of the Akmolinsk territory. 8) The Omsk district Board of the charitable society of the Department of Justice. 9) The Omsk diocesan clergy Benevolent Society. 10) The Clerks' Mutual Society in Omsk. 11) Relief Society for lying-in women. 12) Town Society for mutual fire insurance. 13) Volunteer fire brigade. 14) Local Branch of the Red Cross Society. 15) Local Branch of the Humane Society. 16) Branch of the Russian Society for the protection of animals. 17) „Self Help“ Coperative Supply Society. 18) West-Siberian section of the Russian Geographical Society. 19) Omsk Medical Society. 20) Branch of the Imperial Russian Musical Society. 21) Dramatic Society. 22) Chess-players' Society. 23) Racing Society. 24) Legitimate Sport Society. 25) Public club. There is no theatre in the town, but private individuals on a plot of land leased in the centre of the town have built a theatre-circus, to which actors are occasionally invited. The military clubs are well arranged and housed in a Government building in the former fortress.

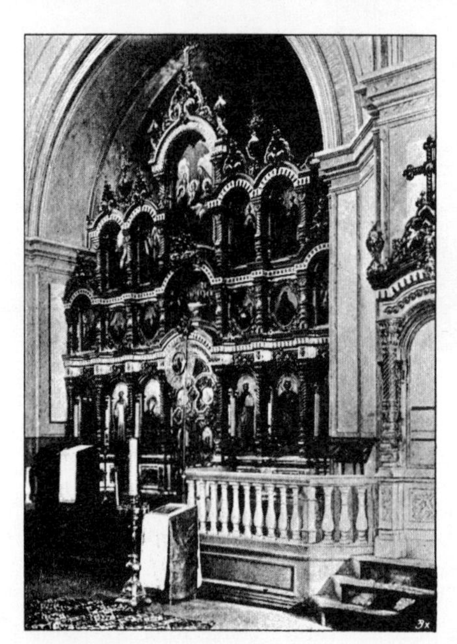
Ikonostasis in the Cathedral of the Ascension.

Among the charitable institutions must be mentioned the society under the patronage of the Empress, which has existed since 1861, comprising a children's home with an elementary trade and reading school and cheap dinners. The first material support for these charitable institutions was secured by E. I. Kaznakóv, wife of the former governor-general of Western Siberia, Adjutant-General Kaznakóv. Her name will always be closely connected with the further destiny of these institutions and of the Charitable Society. The children's home is also noteworthy on account of the good organisation and development of hand-work; it is the creation of E. A. Sánikov, wife of the governor of the Akmolínsk territory. Among the scientific institutions, the first place belongs to the West-Siberian Branch of the Imperial Russian Geographical Society, whose works relative to the exploration of Siberia and the neighbouring countries comprising observations in geography, natural history, archaeology, ethnography, and statistics, are published periodically in „Memoirs“ which have been issued since 1879.

The scientific activity of the society is connected with the names of the explorers of Siberia and Central Asia: Przeválski, Potánin, Pevtsóv, Yádrintsev, Adriánov, Klémenz, Slovtsóv, Katanáev, Schmidt and others. The Society possessess a house and a large museum with interesting collections relative to the ethnography of the native population of the steppe borderland, represented by Kirgíz, Dungán and Taranchís; there are also articles made by the peasants and Cossacks of the steppe regions, a collection of fossils from the steppe border and from the Tobólsk government. The ornithological collection is extremely rich, and the archaeological remains of prehistoric Asiatic races are very interesting. The Society owns also a small library and a meteorological station opened in 1886. It receives annually R. 2,000 from the Government for the organisation of scientific expeditions, the publication of its works etc.

Omsk contains the following libraries: 1) Town public library under the care of the Society for the Promotion of Elementary Education in Omsk. 2) Militrry library attached to the Siberian Cossack Economic Department. 3) Jewish library.

Booksellers: Orlóv, Alexándrov, Kessler.

Printing offices: Akmolínsk district department, Omsk military staff, Demídov, Mrs. Sungúrov.

Photographies: Kessler, Kórkin, Vasíliev.

Periodicals published in Omsk: Akmolínsk Territory Gazette, with suplement in Kirgíz and Russian; Diocesan Gazette; Memoirs of the West Siberian Branch of the Imperial Russian Geographical Society; Records of the Omsk Medical Society; Steppe Region.

Medical institutions: Town hospital with 25 beds; lunatic asylum maintained by local taxation; prison hospital; lying-in hospital; large military hospital for the troops. Two chemists' shops, bacteriological station and dispensary of the Omsk military district.

Every year, from the 15 November to the 1 December, a fair corresponding to the feast of the Presentation is held in the town; animal products are the chief articles of sale. Its operations are not considerable, for three years scarcely exceeding R. 120,000. Manufactures and industry remain as yet undeveloped in Omsk, although the Siberian main line is open to traffic. Ten years ago, in 1890, the town of Omsk contained 35 factories and works with an annual output of the value of R. 120,000; according to statistical data of 1899, their number was 34 and the annual production R. 191,689: fourteen brick-kilns (R. 56,600), four potteries (R. 1,356), a distillery (R. 19,920), two beer and mead breweries (R. 43,543), two yeast manufactories (R. 4,000), a tobacco manufactory (R. 28,870), three tallow boileries (R. 32,000), a tannery (R. 6,000), two sheepskin factories (R. 1,300).

The town revenue, according to the estimates for 1897—1899, amounts to R. 110,000 annually. For purposes of trade and industry the following banks operate in Omsk: a branch of the State Bank, the Omsk town and public Bank, the Siberian Trade Bank. The most important firms are:

Vólkov for manufactured articles and trinkets; Sobénnikov and Brothers Molchánov, tea and sugar; Serebriakóv, tobacco manufactory; Neidlinger, sewing machines; Bostanzhóglo, tobacco; Alexándrov, bookshop; Bebénin, druggist and apothecary; Borodín, timber; Yeroféev, wine; Záitsev, grocery wares and wine; Mérin, officers'outfitter; Poklévsky-Kózell, wine; Reménnikov, baker; Zhánin, haberdashers; Shróev, ditto; Chírikov, tea. Government stores of agricultural machinery.

Transport offices: St. Petersburg Nadézhda Society; Brothers Kaménsky; Russian Insurance and Goods Transport Society. The freights per pud without insurance are R. 2 to St. Petersburg, R. 1. 80 K. to Moscow, R. 2. 50 K. to Vílno, R. 2. 20 K. to Warsaw.

Hotels and furnished rooms: Shchepánov's rooms for travellers from R. 1 to u. 2 a day. Záitsev's rooms are the best; they are newly opened, provided with water and good dinners and cost from 75 K. to R. 3 a day. Next follow Veselóvsky's, Vodzínsky's, Samétnikov's. The price is from R. 1 to R. 1. 50 K. a day. Hackney coach tariff:

First class (open and closed carriages with two horses) 75 K. an hour, drive within the limit of the town costs 30 K. Second class (a kind of victoria and little carts with springs), in winter 20 K. an hour, in summer 25 K. Drive in a first class coach to the railway station of Omsk costs R. 1, second class carriage—75 K. and third class—50 K. Drive to military camp and to wood out of town costs there and back 50 K for first class coach, 30 K. for second class and 25 K. for third class.

The first visit of an Imperial personage to the military territory must be mentioned as an historical event in the life of the town and of the Siberian Cossack line. In 1868, His Imperial Highness the Grand Duke Vladímir Alexándrovich accompanied by Adjutant-General Count Peróvsky and the Academician Middendorf, from the 8 to the 22 June honoured with his visit the following centres of population in the Siberian Cossack troops territory: entering within its confines at the settlement of Peschánoe, His Highness proceeded along the Presnogórkovskaya, Górskaya, Irtysh and Bukhtarmín Cossack lines through Petropávlovsk, Omsk, Pavlodár, Semipalátinsk, Ust-Kamenogórsk, Bukhtarmínsk.

From the 14 to 16 July, in 1891, the town of Omsk was honoured by the visit of His Imperial Majesty the present Emperor Nicholas II, then Heir Apparent to the throne, on his way from the Far East. The Imperial traveller arrived in Omsk on the 14 July, coming from Tobólsk by the Irtysh on the steamer Nicholas. His Majesty was greeted at the landing place in an elegant pavilion by Baron Taube, Governor-General of the Steppe region, and by Dmítriev-Mamónov, Vice-Governor of the Akmolínsk territory, acting as governor, with town deputations of all classes and representatives of the societies.

On the first day, His Imperial Majesty visited the Omsk gymnasium for girls and the children's home, where the august guest was greeted by Baroness Taube, wife of the Steppe Governor-General, the president of the charitable society under the patronage of Her Majesty the Empress, and Mrs. Dmítriev-Mamónov, the patroness of the home, the members of the Society together with the lady patronesses. On the same day was held a review of three cavalry regiments of the Siberian Cossack troops, of the Omsk reserve battalion, and of three squads from the Siberian Cadet Corps.

On the 15 July, the Imperial Atamán of all the Cossack troops, after having attended divine service celebrated in the military cethedral on the namesday of His Imperial Highness the Grand Duke Vladímir Alexándrovich was present at the military nobles'club, members of the military administration and settlement atamans. After a gala lunch in the building of the Military Economic Department, to which were invited generals, staff and subaltern officers, officials of the military class, representatives from the settlements and honorary guests, the Imperial traveller made a trip on the Irtysh, landing on its left bank in order to inspect a Kirgíz winter camp, where a deputation from the Kirgíz Steppe region had the honour to offer to His Imperial Majesty, according to local custom, kumys instead of bread and salt. Here the high officials and honorary Kirgíz were presented to His Majesty. At 8 o'clock in the evening, races took place on the ground of the Racing Society, arranged with a view to acquaint the Imperial traveller with the steppe horses, which form one of the essential elements of the local wealth. At the entrance to the pavilion, His Imperial Majesty was greeted by Dmítriev-Mamónov, Vice-president of the Racing Society, and all the members. Upon the termination of the races, His Majesty personally distributed the prizes won by the horse owners, adding to the first prize a gold watch and chain. Having graciously accepted a copy of the records of the activity of the Racing Society for 1887—1891 with a description of the horse studs in the steppe region, His Majesty addres ed his thanks to Dmítriev-Mamónov, the Vice-president, for the entertainment, and praised the good order and arrangements of the races. After leaving the course. His Majesty visited the

Workshops at the Omsk station. General view.

camp of the Siberian Cadet Corps of the Omsk reserve battalion, and the summer club of the officers. At 11 o'clock, the Imperial party quitted the camp accompanied by prolonged and enthusiastic hurrahs, and drove along the illuminated streets to the house of the Governor-General. On the 16 July, at 10 o'clock in the morning, was laid the first stone for the cathedral in honour of Christ's Ascension, in presence of His Imperial Majesty, who, after the ceremony, left Omsk by the post-road, proceeding along the Presnogórkovskaya Siberian Cossack line, to the Orenbúrg government. The station of Omsk holds an important place in the West-Siberian railway line on account of its dimensions; besides the passengers' station, there are over 70 buildings for the requirements of the railway. Here are the chief workshops and stores for railway materials, an extensive engine house and a hospital. Fifty one houses afford accomodation for the railway employees. A large stone church in honour of the Holy Trinity, to hold 750 people, is being erected near the station at the cost of the Emperor Alexander III fund.

A donation of R. 10,000 has been made by the honorary citizen A. I. Deróv towards the expenses of the construction of this church.

A special wooden building contains a parish school with two classes for boys and girls (73 boys, 42 girls), under the control of the Ministry of Education; it is maintained at the cost of the railway. A parish school for girls has also been founded. Lectures are held on Sundays in the large rooms of the railway schools. Upon the opening of traffic on the West-Siberian railway in 1894, two settlements were established on the ground belonging to the station and on the adjacent land of the Siberian Cossack troops, for railway servants and Cossacks. The Tsar's settlement has grown rapidly; it stands on the Omsk Cossack land contiguous to the station and is inhabited by Cossacks from neighbouring settlements and from the town of Omsk. The population of the Omsk station inclusive of the adjacent settlements exceeds 8,000. A branch line of 3½ versts runs from the station to the town of Omsk, conveying passengers and workmen, and also goods brought by the Irtysh. Besides the main track. the station has several sidings to meet the necessities of its extensive operations: a passenger way 300.31 sazhens long, a goods way 959.47 sazhens long, a turnout way 3,166.64 sazhens long, a traction way 1,320.14 sazhens, a workshops way 3,953.24 sazhens, an emigrants way 130 sazhens long, a way for conveying materials 130 sazhens.

Workshops at the station of Omsk. Foundry and Forge.

A medical and feeding station, with barracks accomodating 1,500 people, is established near the station. When the movement is at its height, about 3,500 emigrants meet at this point, and Kirgíz yúrtas are then erected for them. This station, situated as it is at the junction of the railway line with the roads, serves as a stage for the settlers bound for the Omsk and Akmolínsk districts, for the south-eastern part of the Tobólsk government, the districts of Tiukalínsk and Tára and the Semiréchensk territory.

Being favourably situated at the junction of water communication and railways, the Omsk station represents an important transshipping and warehousing centre for the south-eastern portion of the Kirgíz steppe, and has the same signifacance in this region as is possessed by Petropávlovsk in the Western Steppe district.

The quantity of goods exported annually from this station exceeds a million puds. Half the total amount is represented by grain, the other consisting of animal products. In 1898, the export of grain conveyed from this station to the interior markets of the Empire was given at 496,373 puds. The export of animal products is exhibited by the following data obtained from the veterinary inspection of the Akmolínsk territory for 1897:

Governments.	Fresh meat.			Raw Hides.				Wool.						
	Beef.	Pork.	Guts.	Horse.	Cow.	Camel.	Sheep and goat.	Sheep's.	Camel's.	Goat's.	Scrapings.	Horsehair.	Bones.	Felt.
	Puds.							Puds.						
Orenbúrg	—	—	—	348	3,774	—	700	31,520	5	—	—	23	—	—
St. Petersburg ..	6,447	1,025	70,550	—	250	—	4,000	—	—	—	—	155	—	—
Pénza	—	—	—	420	910	—	5,700	—	—	62	—	—	—	—
Nízhni Nóvgorod	—	—	—	4,619	9,673	31	46,765	5,936	—	50	100	188	—	—
Perm	3,790	—	—	—	—	—	1,055	900	—	—	—	—	—	—
Moscow	11,970	200	2,500	—	1,300	—	—	—	—	—	—	2,065	—	180
Yeniséisk	329	—	—	—	—	—	—	—	—	—	—	—	—	—
Révél	—	—	—	—	—	—	16,330	—	—	—	—	282	—	—
Odéssa	—	—	153,525	263	7,205	—	4,600		—	—		—	—	—
Alexándrov	—	—	41,000	—	—	—	—	—	—	—	—	35	—	—
Vladímir	—	—	1,200	5,139	621	—	—	—	—	—	—	—	—	—
Siziúm	—	—	—	—	—	—	9,022	5,392	32	—	—	—	—	—
Leonídovka	—	—	—	—	—	—	3,128	—	—	—	—	—	—	—
Pachelmú	—	—	—	—	—	—	800	3,258	—	—	—	—	—	—
Taganróg	—	—	6,340	—	—	—	—	—	—	—	—	—	—	—
Libáva	—	—	75	20	20	—	8,006	—	—	—	—	116	—	—
Ríga	—	—	—	—	—	—	25,050	—	—	—	—	—	—	—
Belostók	—	—	—	36,650	3,042	—	—	—	—	—	—	—	—	—
Petropávlovsk ...	—	—	—	22,115	24,888	474	356,039	22,436	121	27	—	1,224	—	—
Berduyásh	—	—	—	459	1,500	—	—	—	—	—	—	—	—	—
Total	22,536	1,225	275,190	70,033	55,183	505	481,223	69 943	159	139	100	4,830	—	180

The cattle exported as fresh meat to the western markets are mainly slaughtered in Omsk; in 1898 there were 19,849 head. This figure remained the same in the following years. The animal produce is brought to the station from the distant parts of the Kirgíz steppe.

Workshops at the Omsk station. Turningshop.

The river Irtysh (in Mongol Irtsís) is the left and chief tributary of the Ob, taking its rise within the confines of China on the south-western slope of the southern Altái from two sources the Ak-Irtysh and Kun-Irtysh or Black Irtysh so called on account of its turbid and black water. Flowing from east to west a distance of 700 versts, the Black Irtysh falls into the lake Zaisán-Nor, lying between 47°60′ and 48°30′ N. lat. and 37°E. long. in an open, elevated and even plain amidst the Altái, the Kólbinsk and Tarbagatái mountain ridges, at an elevation of 1,800 feet above the sea, covering a superficial area of 1,608 square versts.

The Black Irtysh flows, within Russian territory, from the source of the Alkabék to its junction with the Zaisán for a distance of about 120 versts, while its upper reaches water the Chinese dominions. Throughout its entire course, there are no permanent settlements; the whole region is occupied solely by Kirgíz nomads, and only at a distance of about 25 versts from the river, at the Altái chain, where the river Kran falls into the Irtysh, stands the small Chinese town of Túlta. Along the sandy banks of the river grow poplar, willow, aud birch. The river is navigable for flat-bottomed steamers from lake Zaisán to the mouth of the Kran; further it is not practicable on account of the low water level, which in autumn falls considerably.

The Black Irtysh, within the Russian territorry, has two ferryboat passages, at the mouths of the rivers Kaldzhír and Alkabék, and three within the Chinese Empire, at those of the rivers Bilizék, Kába and Burgúm. The banks of all the right tributaries of the Irtysh, taking their rise in the Altái mountains, are clad with a rich coniferous vegetation of larch, cedar, fir and pine, which can afford a large quantity of timber for future exploitation by means of rafting. In the contiguous Saúr chain, occur deposits of black and brown coal, found on both sides of the Kendyrlyk. The quality of the coal has not yet been tested, and it has been very little worked, being only used to supply the town of Zaisán. The coal seams are close to the surface and are easily worked. The coal-pits belong to the inhabitants of Zaisán: Títov, Khokhlóv and the Kokpektínsk merchant Proskuriakóv. Near the picturesque lake Marka-Kúl, lying at an absolute altitude of 5,700 feet and giving rise to the Kaldzhír river, the right tributary of the Black Irtysh, are found gold mines now primitively worked by Kirgíz workmen. They belong to Moskvín, Diákov, Stepánov, Sizóv, Valítov and Menovshchikóv, and have an annual output of 3—4 puds of gold. Fishing is more extensively carried on in China than in the Russian dominions.

At its outflow from the north-western bay of the large lake, the river, there 150 sazhens wide, receives the name of Irtysh. Running northwards, it traverses first steppe plain which gradually passes into a broad steppe valley, bordered by the mountain ridges of the Altái. The river leaves the Zaisán, rolling its turbid and sluggish waves between low, reed-covered banks; at the 278 verst from the lake, it receives the tribute of the Bukhtarmá, and further on, meeting the mountain mass of the western branches of the Altái, breaks through them by a narrow and picturesque gorge. Before reaching the mouth of the Bukhtarmá, the mountains at a few points touch the river; 5 versts further, the Irtysh enters a desert defile which continues to Ust-Kamenogórsk. The steep and rocky cliffs falling to the water's edge consist mainly of clayey slates, but partly of granite, while in some places they are veined with diorite. The pass contains the cliffs known under the name of the Seven Brothers. Beyond the mouth of the small river Ognevka, one of the cliffs standing on the shore is called Petúkh (the Cock) and is very remarkable on account of its shape and the echo which it yields to every sound. Near Ust-Kamenogorsk, the Irtysh leaves the defile and enters an open plain accompanied to Semipalátinsk by the low ridges of the Ubéik and Ulbéik mountains. The right bank of the river is at some points high and steep, mainly consisting of slates. while the left bank is level and sandy. Between the mouth of the Shulbá and Semipalátinsk, lies the only wooded locality on the middle reaches of the Irtysh, called the Shulbínsk and Karagài forest. From Semipalátinsk, with the exception of the Semitán, which is seen at a considerable distance on the left bank of the Irtysh, its left bank is level, whereas the right is high and steep, rising to an elevation of 200 feet; it consists of horizontal strata of clay and sand containing fresh-water shells of the upper tertiary formation. The bottom of the river is sandy and in places muddy; it has a depth ot 8 to 12 sazhens and is from 500 to 700 sazhens wide. During the spring flood, the water rises from 4 to 6 sazhens above its ordinary level, and covers immense areas of land. Throughout its course, there are many islands and shifting bars. The Irtysh abounds in fish, and fishing is largely carried on between Tobólsk and the estuary of the river, and also between Omsk and the Lake Zaisán.

The principal fish are sterlet, sturgeon and nelma. The course of the Irtysh is tortuous: the greatest curve occurs below the mouth of the Vagái, and is called the Vagái Bend. The total length of the river exceeds 4,000 versts; its system comprises about 1,250 large and small streams. Among Siberian rivers, the Irtysh holds the fourth place and is the largest river in Western Siberia. Within the confines of the Russian dominions, the Irtysh waters the most fertile regions of the Semipalátinsk territory, part of that of Akmolínsk and all the Tobólsk government.

Among Siberian rivers, the Irtysh is very important on account of its favourable geographical position,a nd also the great number of tributaries draining into its lower stream and connecting its course with the Káma basin in the watershed of the Urál chain. Occupying a central position in Western Siberia, this river from the town of Tobólsk presents a most extensive water communication running in four directions: northwards to the Ocean, eastwards to Eastern Siberia, soutwards to the western border of China and to the Russian Central Asiatic dominions, and westwards to European Russia. Flowing through many longitudes with a N. N. W. direction from its source to Tobólsk, the Irtysh is bound or free of ice according to the latitudes it traverses. At Tomsk, the ice breaks between the 14 and 24 April and the water freezes again about the 20 October and the 15 November. In Semipalátinsk, the river is free from ice for 215 days, at Tára for 190 days, at Tobólsk for 189 days. The Irtysh is divided into two separate systems, with quite different imporatnce as to trade. The lower reaches of the river, from the town of Tobólsk to the settlement of Samárovo, with the rivers Turá, Toból and Ob, form an uninterrupted transit water-way between the towns of Bíisk, Barnaúl, Tomsk on the east, and Tiumén and Irbít on the west. One part of the river, south of Tobolsk, offers a separate water-way leading into the interior of the southern steppes and further to nothern Dzhungária. Steam navigation on the Irtysh began at the same time as navigation in Western Siberia, viz. in 1884. The Irtysh has no specially organised fleet; all the steamers and other craft plying within its basin belong to the fleet of the whole of the vast Ob basin. According to the data obtained from the Tomsk Department of Ways of Communication, during 1898—1899, the trading fleet of the Ob basin contained:

STEAMERS.

119	with total of	7750 H. P.
1	„ „ „	250 H. P.
1	„ „ „	180 H. P.
2	„ „ „	160 H. P.
3	„ „ „	150 H. P.
2	„ „ „	130 H. P.
1	„ „ „	125 H. P.
7	„ „ „	120 H. P.
12	„ „ „	100 H. P.
2	„ „ „	85 H. P.
18	„ „ „	80 H. P.
15	„ „ „	60 H. P.
1	„ „ „	55 H. P.
6	„ „ „	50 H. P.
3	„ „ „	45 H. P.
9	„ „ „	40 H. P.
6	„ „ „	30 H. P.
5	„ „ „	25 H. P.
4	„ „ „	20 H. P.
15	„ „ „	6 to 20 H. P.

OTHER VESSELS.

380 vessels, with a tonnage of about 17,000,000 puds.

8	barges:	100,000 to	110,000 puds.
32	„	80,000 „	110,000 „
62	„	60,000 „	80,000 „
44	„	50,000 „	90,000 „
60	„	40,000 „	50,000 „
42	„	30,000 „	40,000 „
62	„	20,000 „	30,000 „
15	„	15,000 „	20,000 „
20	„	10,000 „	15,000 „
24	„	below	10,000 „
4	„	for conveyance of recruits and convicts.	

The important shipowners are represented by the West-Siberian S. S. Company (formerly Kurbátov and Ignátov), Kornílov, the Bogoslóv works, the firm of Plótnikov, the Trapéznikov C°, the joint stock company Yermák.

The steamers for the Siberian rivers are built mainly at the Zhábinsk works, Tiumén, belonging to Kurbátov and Ignátov, at Hullet's works and also in the Perm works of Liubímov and Motovilkínsky. The steamers built to the west of the Urál are brought to Tiumén in pieces and are fitted there. Goods are conveyed along the rivers by tugs; this system is also adapted for the conveyance of passengers and quick freights. The construction of the vessels is very various; the predominating type is that of the Vólga wooden barge, somewhat altered and smaller. They are built in Tiumén, on the river Tavdá, in the town of Tára and on the upper part of the Ob, and mainly belong to the same steamer-owners. The navigation season betweeu Tiumén and Tomsk lasts during four months; under favourable conditions, the passage of a steamer in tow takes 18 to 22 days. Thus, the steamers of the Irtysh-Ob line make only about 3 trips during the season. The passenger steamers, with one or two barges in tow make the passage from Tiumén to Tomsk in 13 days, and return in 7 or 10 days.

The navigation from Tobólsk southwards by the Irtysh reaches only the town of Semipalátinsk. Further south, between Semipalátinsk and Lake Zaisán, and also on this lake and the Black Irtysh, there is no steam communication either for goods or passengers. On this part of the river, the navigation season is longer. In spring, the steamers reach Semipalátinsk, in midsummer they come only as far as the Cossack village of Chernoyársk, whence goods are brought from Semipalátinsk in small vessels.

The unsatisfactory organisation of the navigation on the rivers of the Ob basin, inadequate for the demands of the goods traffic, reacts unfavourably upon the export trade and the economic development of the country. The shippers are never sure of exporting the total supply of goods and of delivering them at the appointed time. This, together with the constant fluctuation of the freight rates, has also a pernicious influence upon local trade and industry. The time and the tariff for the transport of goods is fixed by the shipowners and entirely depend upon their discretion. However, they do not assume the responsibility for safe and due delivery. The freights in force during the time of navigation are not fixed beforehand; they depend mainly on the quantity of water in the rivers Turá and Toból, and vary according to the demand. On the Vólga, the transport of goods costs 3 or 4 times less than in Siberia.

The lower stream of the Irtysh, connected with the waterways of the Ob basin, plays an important part in the trade and industry of Siberia, being the chief waterway feeding the Perm-Tiumén railway connected with the Vólga basin and the Port of Archángel. Its upper part, flowing south of the Great Siberian main line, will also in the near future bring new life into the thinly populated and hardly civilised countries of Central Asia. Upon the opening of traffic on the Great Siberian Railway, the upper Irtysh acquires the importance of a cheap and convenient communication destined to enlarge the productive capacity of the southern Kirgíz steppe borderland and of the region at the foot of the Altái, and also to promote Russian trade with western China or Dzhungária, with western Mongolia the Tian-Shan region and the more distant Chinese provinces. The route across the Zaisán by the Black Irtysh to Mongolia was deemed worthy of attention even in 1863; expeditions for its exploration were organised in 1871 and 1879, but without any precise results. It is only recently, in 1896 that the engineer, Baron Amínov, manager of the Tomsk Department of Ways of Communication, having personally explored the route to the Zaisán during very low water on the Irtysh, acknowledged the possibilty of navigation as far as the headwaters of the Irtysh and throughout its entire course, within the confines of the Russian dominions, viz, to the mouth of the river Alkabék.

The trade of western China and Mongolia centres in the following towns: Chuguchák, Urumchí, Manás, Guchén and Kobdó. These points are reached by a post road, crossing the town of Sergiópol, the Cossack village of Udzhársk and Bakhtín fort. The town of Kobdó is connected by the Irtysh with the mouth of the Bukhtarmá, and further by a highway running over the summit of Ulón-Dabá and along the valley of the river Eríkh.

The establishment of a navigable way through the Zaisán-Nor, by the Black Irtysh, would greatly facilitate the trading relations which are at present maintained by a difficult caravan route. The chief articles of import to China are grain, vegetables, dry fruit, flax, seeds, hides, manufactured articles, iron, iron wares, lump sugar, honey, stearine and tallow candles. The exports are fruit, nuts, horsehair, tea, carpets, silk stuffs, china, wool and cattle.

The Zyriánov mining company, together with some steamship companies, contemplate the exploitation of the upper Irtysh, by building steamers on the Vólga system. They require little water and are provided with a large paddle-wheel. The success of this enterprise is much to be desired for the opening up and development of new markets in Mongolia.

Landing places on the Irtysh at the town of Omsk:

West-Siberian Steamship Company, Trapéznikov Company.

The river Om, which is a right tributary of the Irtysh, takes its rise in the swamps of Vasiugánsk, in the Tomsk government. The breadth of its bed is from 20 to 40 sazhens; here are numerous pools and holes in its bottom, and the current is very slow. The banks are steep, but in spring the river floods the surrounding meadows. Wood for building and fuel is floated down this river from the Káinsk district to the town of Omsk, as are also sometimes barges with grain. After some fortresses were built along the upper Irtysh, in the XVIII century, the Dzhungárs censidered Om as the frontier of Siberia. From the station of Omsk, the railway line runs along the Om.

21) **Kormílovka.** V class (790 v.). Tobólsk government, Tiukalínsk district. The settlement of Kormílovka (pop. 130) is situated 18 versts off. The emigrants have established a settlement near the station. Although the station is situated in proximity to Omsk, it is a centre of grain export. In 1898, 12,035 puds of wheat were forwarded from here to Révei and Libáva.

22) **Kaláchinskaya.** V class (819 v.). The settlement of Kaláchiki is situated at a distance of 2 versts (pop. 400). Within the range of influence of the station, are a number of settlements and villages with a population of 5,000. From here are forwarded annually about 100,000 puds of goods, mainly grain, to the western markets of the Empire. In 1898, were exported 81,162 puds of wheat and oats.

24) **Tatárskaya.** IV class. Buffet (903 v.). Káinsk district, Tomsk government. The country is swampy and infested with fever. The water is bad, supplied by a pond formed by spring and bog water. A wooden church has been erected near the station at the cost of the Emperor Alexander III fund, holding 200 people. It was inaugurated on the 27 May, 1897, in honour of the Archistrategus Michael. Near the church, there is a house made of brick for the accomodation of newly arrived parishioners, and a wooden house for the

clergy. The is also a parish elementary school with one class for boys and girls in the name of the archpriest John Sérgiev, a medical and feeding station with barracks holding 300 people, for the accomodation of the emigrants settling in the Káinsk district, and a depot of agricultural machinery.

Church near the station of Tatárskaya.

The settlement of Tatárskoe is one and a half versts from the station: within range of the station there are 15 settlements with a population of 10,000 situated in a locality which is favourable to agriculture and cattle-breeding. The region contains the butter manufactories of Mariúpolsky, Pádin, Soshóvsky, Pópel and Weiss producing annually about 15,000 puds of cream butter, which is conveyed by the railway to the interior markets of the Empire. From this station, about 300,000 puds of goods as well as poultry are forwarded annually to St. Petersburg and Moscow.

25) **Karachí.** V class (952 v.). The locality is swampy, girded by birch copses. Water is got from Lake Artugán, situated within a verst and half from the station, the water is clear and has a good taste. From 1896, the settlement of Nóvo-Pokróv (pop. 300) was established near the station by emigrants from the Oriól government.

The settlement of Karachí with a population of 2,000 is at a distance of 30 versts. The environs of the station comprise from 9 to 13 settlements with a total population of 25,000. Within range of the station are situated 12 butter manufactories, producing annually about 10,000 puds of cream butter. The Spassk and Pokróvsk settlements contain tanneries, forwarding their produce by rail; the Spassk settlement is provided with a water-mill, yielding annually about 50 waggon-loads. The thickly populated region contiguous to the station exports annually over 400,000 puds of goods to the ports and the interior markets of the Empire, such as grain, flour, meat, fish poultry and butter. In 1898, the quantity of goods forwarded from this station was 253,349 puds.

Within 45 versts to the southwest of the station, lies Lake Chány, the largest in the Tomsk government, occupying an area of 2,876 square versts. The sloping shores are covered with reeds. Formerly it was famous on account of its fish and contained big pike weighing about 30 pounds and carp of 10 pounds. Now this abundance is much reduced: some kinds of fish no longer exist, but perch and bream occur plentifully. This lake belongs to the State, but is given on lease to private individual for exploitation; it yields annually about 100,000 puds of fish, partly exported by the railway.

At a distance of 15 versts from the station, is situated Lake Karachí, possessing medicinal properties, which lies in an open and dry country. The lake is under the control of the Department of State Domains; the water is clear, of a brackish taste, and very unhealthy for drinking. The slime at the bottom has a strong sulphurous smell. In summer, the lake is resorted to by persons suffering from rheumatism, siphilitic and skin diseases. The lake is leased by a private individual, the sick are received in barracks with about 50 rooms. The Tatárs furnish very good kumys.

Ikonostasis in the church near the station of Tatárskaya.

26) **Tebísskaya.** V class (996 v.). The country round is swampy; in summer cases of fever occur frequently. The water of the lake is not good. Near the station, a settlement for emigrants is in process of organisation. The settlement of Tebísskoe (pop. 300) is four versts from the station. There are 4 settlements and 10 villages with a population of 9,000 within range of the station. The settlements of Pokróvskoe, Nóvaya Derévnia, Bulátova contain ten butter manufactories. Above 100,000 puds of various goods are exported from this region to the interior markets of the Empire.

27) **Káinsk.** III class. Buffet (1049 v.). The country is level and surrounded by birch copses and swamps. Water of a bad quality is obtained from Lake Kally, situated a verst from the station. There is a wooden church holding 450 people, erected at the cost of the Emperor Alexander III fund, and inaugurated on the 18 December 1897 in honour of Saint Andrew Stratelates

and St. Catherine the Martyr. A brick parish school with two classes for boys and girls has been built out of the same fund in the name of the archpriest John Sérgiev. On sundays, lectures illustrated by a magic lantern are held in the school. A medical and feeding station accomodate 60 emigrants bound for the Káinsk district. The town of Káinsk is situated within 12 versts of the station in the centre of the Barabá steppe, at the junction of the river Káinka with the Om. The town stands on the left bank of the latter (55°27′ N lat., and 47°58′ E. long.), on the Great Siberian highway, on low and even ground with an elevation of only 320 feet above sea-level.

In 1722, a field fortress was founded near the town, with a view to subdue the wandering Tatárs of Barabá, the Kirgíz and Kalmyks. This spot received the name of Káinsk Pas. A village founded near the fort, was transported in 1772 to the site of the present town, which in 1782 was transformed into a district town of the Tobólsk province. In 1804, Káinsk was included in the Tomsk government. At present the town of Káinsk contains a population of 5858 (3,292 males, 2,566 females) mainly consisting of exiled Jews and their descendants. The General Exile Board, in distributing exiles troughout Siberia, for many years added persons belonging to the Jewish religion to the population of Káinsk, with a view to concentrate Jewish exploitation in one place.

The town contains 525 houses mainly wooden, 2 orthodox churches, a cathedral, a wooden church and a Jewish synagogue.

Educational institutions: preparatory gymnasium for girls, district and two parish schools, church school. Model farm founded at the cost of the

Ecclesiastical-parish school at the station of Tatárskaya.

merchant Yeroféev, which received the name of Alexander farm. Meteorological station. Hospital of the Public Charities Board, with 55 beds and dispensary. Military hospital. Public club, library, society for elementary education.

The town has no great commercial importance, and its industry is but little developed, amounting in value to about R. 400,000 per annum.

The following industrial concerns are the most important: distillery, beer and mead brewery, tannery and soap boilery. Every year, two fairs are held in the town: that of St. Michael (from the 8 to the 17 January) and that of St. Peter and St. Paul (from the 29 June to the 8 July); the business done is small.

Church at the station of Káinsk.

The revenue of the town for 1899 was estimated at R. 15,049.44 k., the expenditure at 14,864.43 k.

There are no hotels, but inns only. Hackney coaches are hired by the tariff: a drive within the town costs 15 k.—30 k. the hour, to the railway station from 50 k. to R. 1. The road between the station and the town runs through a swampy country, and in spring and autumn is about 18 versts long.

The trading firms are: Vólkov—draper's goods and trinkets; Yeroféev—distillery, beer and mead brewery, and steam flour mill, draper's goods; Shkróev drapery, haberdashery; wine cellar, distillery; Moshchínsky, drapery and groceries, tallow boilery; Mitrókhin, tannery, tallow and soap, boileries.

Agents: Malygin, agent of the Rossia Company; Urniázh. of the Northern Insurance Society. Belózerov, of the Russian Company. The sphere of influence of the station, besides the town of Káinsk, comprises 17 settlements and villages with a population of 8,000 engaged in agriculture. About 500,000 puds of various goods are annnally forwarded from here to the ports and interior markets of the Empire In 1898, the quantity of grain exported from the station of Káinsk was 315,963 puds.

The articles of export to the East are: spirit, wine, beer; to the West: grain, meat, tallow, poultry and fish.

Twenty versts south-west of the station lies lake Ustiántsev, containing: alkali and Glauber's salt, possessing the same properties as the springs of Karlsbad, Franzensbad, Marienbad and Essentúki № 4. The water is good for catarrh of the stomach.

There is no bath accomodation, and the patients live in cottages in the village of Ustiántsevsk situated near the lake. Good kumys is supplied by the Tatárs and Kirgíz. The country is open and dry, the bridle path connecting the railway and the lake is good.

From the station of Káinsk, the line proceeds by the valley of the Káinka and further along the watershed of the Om and Lake Chány.

28) **Kuzhúrla.** V class (1089 v.) the country is swampy, the water from lake Márovo is of bad quality; in winter it is provided by wells. Two settlements, St. Alexándra and the Pescháný, were established near the station,

during the construction of the line, by peasant emigrants from the Túla, Mogilióv and Orióol governments. At the St. Alexándra settlement, a parish school is being built of stone. Within range of the station are 18 settlements (pop. 4,000) and tanneries belonging to Rosenfeld in Osínovy Kolkí and to Abramóvich in the village of Chumakóvo. The quantity of goods exported from the station of Kuzhúrla is inconsiderable. Leaving the watershed, the line crosses the river Kuzhúrla at the 1099 verst, and the Karapúz at the 1124 verst.

Earth-clearing with „New Era" machines.

29) **Ubínskaya.** V class (1,127 v.). The country is swampy. The supply of water of inferior quality is from a lake. The village of Ubá (pop. 500) is situated near the station. The range of the station comprises 12 settlements (pop. 3,500). To the northeast and in proximity to the station, lies lake Ubínskoe, covering a superficial area of 578 square versts. The shores of the lake are swampy and low. It abounds in fish which is forwarded frozen from this station, representing the chief article of export.

Station of Duplénskaya.

30) **Kargát.** V class (1,166 v.). The country is elevated. Water got from the river Kargát is particularly bad in winter, when it becomes musty and yellow. During this season, ice supplies the water. A medical and feeding station is established here with barracks accomodating 60 emigrants, bound for the Káinsk district.

The Kargát forepost (pop. 300) is situated 12 versts from the station. Within its range are only 5 settlements with a population of 1,200. In proximity to the station, on the banks of the Kargát, a new settlement is being established by local peasants from the neighbouring villages.

Grain, meat, butter, leather etc. are the goods exported from this station, to the amount of 50,000 puds per annum.

31) **Chulym.** IV class. Buffet (1,209 v.). The country is swampy and infested with fever, the water is bad for drinking and smells of mud. Since the time of the construction of the railway, a settlement with 20 inhabitants has been established near the station by small traders and workmen. A barrack, holding 30 people, was built here to meet the needs of the emigrants. The settlement of Chulym is 2 versts from the station (pop. 290). The environs comprise 5 settlements (pop. 1,200) whence about 90,000 puds of goods, mainly grain, are forwarded to the western markets of the Empire.

Bridge over the Chik.

32) **Duplénskaya.** V class (1,285 v.). Tomsk district. The country is swampy and wooded. Good water is supplied by wells. There are 4 settlements within range of the station (pop. 1,000). Export inconsiderable. At the 1,282 verst, the line crosses the river Kargát.

33) **Kóchenevo.** V class (1,285 v.). The country is level, dry and covered with young birch wood. Good water is provided by wells. The settlement of Kóchenevo is situated near the station. Within range are 7 settlements with a population of 3,000. Emigrants bound for the Barnaúl district stop here. The agricultural area of the station yields annually over 500,000 puds of various goods for export to the interior markets of the Empire. In 1898, 489,520 puds of grain was forwarded from this point.

Station of Krivoshchékovo.

Chik crossing (1,298 v.). The country is elevated and open, provided with good water from the river Chik. At this point the line crosses the river. The station is not open for transport operations. The goods conveyed from here towards Cheliábinsk are registered at the station of Krivoshchékovo, and those bound east, at the station Kóchenevo. At the 1,317 verst, the line crosses the river Krivodónka.

34) **Krivoshchékovo.** II class. Buffet (1,324 v.). The country is level and dry. Water is supplied by a pulsometer at the 1,327 v. and brought here in tanks. A private school for boys and girls is established near the station; it is maintained by the railway employees. At a distance of a verst, stands the settlement of Krivoshchékovo (pop. 200). Within range of the station are the town of Kolyván (pop. 11,703), the settlement of Bérskoe (pop. 4,000) and 15 other settlements (pop. 12,000).

Bridge over the Ob.

The quantity of goods transported from this station amounts to a million puds. In 1898, the grain export was represented by 847,724 puds (3,183 puds of rye, 692.555 puds of wheat, 110,208 puds of oats, 214 puds of peas and millet, 12,660 puds of wheat meal, 10,304 puds of rye meal, 4,898 puds of buckwheat; 210 puds of various other corn, 13,492 puds of oil seeds.), The goods are conveyed to Libáva, Révél, the New Port and St. Petersburg.

At the 1,328 verst, the line crosses the Ob by a bridge 372.50 sazhens long, having 7 spans, the I and VII openings are 46.325 sazhens, the II, IV and VI, 53.65 sazhens, and III and V, 53.15 sazhens. The upper girders of the bridge are on the Herber's system with four clear spans of 41 sazhens each, and with three balanced spans, 69½ sazhens in length. The stone abutments of the bridge are laid on granite rocks, the right pier N° 1 near the bank is not supported on a caisson, the other piers NN° 2, 3, 4, 5 and 6 are laid on caissons sunk to a depth of 1.81 to 3.40 sazhens below the lowest water level. The minimum elevation of the trusses above the low water mark is 8.23 sazhens, and 4.42 sazhens above its highest level; the height of the embankment on the left side is 7 sazhens, and 5 sazhens on the right. Both spans near the bank have an opeing of 10 sazhens between the piers and the retaining walls. The thin alluvial soil covering the rocky river bed and the insufficient quantity of water having been taken into consideration, some of the piers without caissons are laid on the bottom of the river by means of coffer-dams.

The fagoted iron for the upper structure was supplied by the Vótkin works; everything connected with the construction of the bridge was entrusted to the contractor Engineer Berézin. The river Ob (Tatar: Omár, Surgút-Ostiák: As, and Samoyéd: Kúia (soul) is the largest river of Western Siberia falling into the Ob Gulf of the Arctic Ocean; it is formed by the junction of two large streams the Bíya and Katún. The river Bíya (Biy means „prince" in Tatar) flows out of the picturesque Altái lake Telétsk, the Katún (woman of high rank, „queen" in Kalmyk) is fed by the glaciers of the Altái Montblanc, the Belúkha. Its chief affluents are the Tom, watering the fertile Kuznétsk district, navigable to the town of Kuznétsk and serving as a connecting link to the navigable ways, leading from the west to Eastern Siberia and back; the Chulym, by which steamers with some difficulty reach the town of Achinsk (1,000 v.); the Ket, which has a great importance, connecting the extensive Ob and Yeniséi basins through the Ob-Yeniséi canal; the Vakh, navigable for a distance of 500 versts; the Irtysh with its extensive system of navigable ways reaching the confines of Western China and the Urál. The Ob, from the junction of the Bíya with the Katún, 15 versts below the town of Bíisk, has a total length of 3,200 versts. The immense river is still

Bridge bend tested by the Frenkel apparatus.

more extensive, if the Irtysh be considered as the main branch flowing for a distance of 4,000 versts. The Ob from its junction with the Irtysh (over 1,000 versts) being added to that distance, the total course of the Ob-Irtysh exceeds 5,000 versts. The breadth of the river, within the confines of the Tomsk government, is from 350 to 850 sazhens; at places blocked by islands it amounts to 3 versts; in the Tobólsk government, the river has an average breadth of 1½ to 3 versts, but where here and there its branches are divided by islands, this reaches from 30 to 40 versts. Falling into the Ob Gulf, the river has a breadth varying from 5 to 20 versts. The depth of the Ob is from 2 to 20 sazhens. Its bottom is at first rocky, and further on consists of sand and sandy clay. Upon joining its right tributary, the Charysh, watering the Bíisk district, the river flows along a narrow valley between steep banks, covered on the right with thick wood. Beyond Barnaúl, the river pursues its tortuous course along abroad valley and making a wide sweep skirts the Salaír Chain; its right bank is elevated. Further on the Ob widens, being bordered by low, swampy and scantily wooded banks to the mouth of the Irtysh. Upon its junction with the latter, the river separates into numerous branches, which embrace an immense area. On the average, the Ob freezes at Barnaúl on the 30 October, it opens on the 15 April; thus the river remains free of ice for 146 days. In spring, at the end of April or the beginning of May, the Ob leaves its banks and overflows vast expanses of land. The Ob abounds in many kinds of fish: the muksun (Salmo muksun), the nelma (Salmo nelma), the salmo thymallus (Salmo fluviatilis), the sturgeon (Accipenser sturio), the sterlet (Accipenser rathenus) and others.

Throughout the entire course of the river, and especially on its lower reaches, fishing is pursued on a large scale by the inhabitants of the river banks. The railway has caused an increase of fish exports to Russia, and will contribute to a further development and improvement of this industry. The preparation of fish conserves in the town of Tobólsk, the establishment in the village of Samárovo of the first school for the preparation of fish products, together with the canning works, established by the firm of Plotnikov on the lower Ob, where cheap conserves are mainly manufactured, shew the beginning of more perfect systems of Siberian fish industry,

Representing the limit of Europe and Asia, the navigable Ob, with its wide stretching tributaries, comprising 15,000 versts, always served as the cheapest means of communication uniting the two vast continents. Previous to the construction of the Perm Tiumén railway, goods were mainly transported by the Káma, whence they were conveyed by carts over the Urál and further floated along the rivers of the Ob basin. From 1870 to 1884, the total quantity of goods trasported by the West-Siberian rivers did not exceed 2,500,000 puds. Since 1885, when the line was opened to traffic, uniting two extensive water basins, local trade was considerably enlivened, and the conveyance of goods on the water ways of the Ob basin much increased by a greater export of Siberian produce to the western markets of the Empire. In 1888, the number of steamers plying in the Ob basin was 56 with 3,486 H. P. while the total of goods transported amounted to 7,799,540 puds; in 1890 their number rose to 63, with 4,332 H. P., and goods transported to 8,371,800 puds. In 1894, at the time of the opening of traffic on the Omsk-Cheliábinsk line of the Great Siberian Railway, the fleet of the Ob basin comprised 103 steamers, with 7,235 H. P. which, during this year, transported 15,433,900 puds of various goods. The conveyance of private goods by the Perm-Tiumén railway, within this period, increased in the same proportion as that on the Ob basin. The quantity of private goods transported in 1888 was 42,816,771 puds; in 1894, it amounted to 59,809,479 puds.

The transport of goods by the chief water ways of the Ob basin, the Irtysh and the Ob proper, during the period preceding the construction of the Great Siberian line (which crosses the middle course of these water ways) maintained almost invariably the same proportion: 25 per cent were conveyed from the estuary of the Toból towards the upper Irtysh, and 75 per cent towards the Ob.

The traffic on the Siberian main line, having changed the direction of transport, at the same time so much enlarged the productive capacity of Siberia, that the progress of steam navigation on the Ob basin, and the increase of the goods traffic over the Perm-Tiumén line was not stopped by it. The Great Siberian Railway, in 1897, conveyed 24,000,000 puds of various goods from the region where it crosses the navigable basins of the Ob and Irtysh and from Western Siberia; whereas the fleet of the Ob basin transported above 16,000,000 puds of various goods. At the same time, as much as 77,046,083 puds of private goods were carried by the Perm-Tiumén line.

The navigation on the Ob commences at the town of Bíisk, viz. from the junction of the rivers Bíya and Katún, whence the goods are carried for a distance of 2,000 to 3,000 versts.

Notwithstanding the competition existing among the shipowners, the

The Ob-Yenisei Canal, sluice at the 15 verst.

rates of transport are much higher than on the Vólga; this partly depends upon the insufficient security of navigation, and partly upon the risk run by the steamers during their passage, from the want of auxiliary measures. The absence of any precise notions regarding the time of freezing and opening of rivers, of the telegraph or any means to obtain information, the scarcity of the population along the chief rivers, especially on the Ob, and the low water level of the Toból and Turá, canse many accidents, loss of goods and much injury to shipowners.

The measures which have been taken by the Government with a view to improve the water system of Western Siberia, feeding the Great Siberian main line and the Perm-Kotlás railway, will undoubtedly contribute to the further development of navigation and to the lowering of the rates of transport. The increase of navigation, provoked by the lively trade of Siberia with the European markets, clearly point to the future commercial importance of the Ob-Yeniséi Canal.

The Ob-Yeniséi Canal, sluice at the 103 verst.

The connexion of the rivers Ket (tributary to the Ob) and Kass (tributary to the Yeniséi) by a canal, was effected by the engineers, Baron Amínov and Zhbikóvsky. It presents now an immense water way 5,000 versts in length, uniting Tiumén and Irkútsk. The canal and the nearest rivers are now provided with nine sluices, which are necessary on account of the difference of level between the Ob and Yeniséi basins; to the present day steamers carrying 5,000 puds can pass through the canal only

The steamer „Nicholas" on which His Imperial Mayesty the present Emperor made his voyage in the Ob basin from the town of Tomsk to Omsk in 1891.

during somewhat more than a month, from the time of the opening of navigation to the beginning of June; after this season, the water falls rapidly and only barges with a cargo of 500 puds can use it. In order to adapt this waterway for the steam transport of goods, two sluices ought to be constructed on the river Kass, two of them on the side of the Ob must be widened, and a bar obstructing the Great Kass within a few versts of its mouth cleared.

We fully share the opinion of Jules Legras, professor of the Dijon university, who, having visited the canal, saw the significance of this enterprise which, together with the Siberian main line, is most important for the progress of the productive capacity of northern Siberia.

The development of navigation on the Ob greatly depends upon the establishment of a regular searoute through the Kára Sea which for a long period remains frost bound. The exploration of Nakhódka Bay in the Ob Gulf made by Captain Sergéev in 1897 with a view to find an anchorage for river steamers, and the attempts of Admiral Makárov to secure a free passage through the Kára Sea with the help of icebreakers, open the prospect of a regular and advantageous trade communication by the estuary of the Ob.

The passage between Tomsk and Tiumén is effected mainly by steamers of the Trade and Industry Company plying on the rivers of Western Siberia (formerly Ignátov and Kurbátov), of Trapéznikov and Co., of the Bogoslóv Mining district, of Kornílov, Plótnikov, Morózov and the Yermák Company. Steamers belonging to the last reach Krivoshchékovo, Barnaúl and Bíisk. Rapid steamers with a light barge of the Trade and Industry Company leave Tomsk for Tiumén once a week, all the others ply at irregular intervals. Between Tomsk and Barnaúl regular trips are made by the light steamers belonging to Mélnikov and Eldstein.

Tomsk government and Eastern Siberia within the range of the Great Siberian Railway.

Government of Tomsk.—Geographical position and extent.—Configuration of surface. — Altái and Alatau. — Geological structure and mineral wealth (gold, silver, lead and copper, iron ores, precious stones, coal beds, rock-salt, mineral waters). — Hydrography. — Climate. — Flora and fauna.—Altái natives.—Present population.—Ethnographical composition.—Exile.—Colonisation. Industries and occupations of inhabitants (agriculture, cattle-breeding, bee-keeping, fishing, trapping and hunting, cedar-nut gathering, domestic industries).—Factories and works. Trade.—Projected railway lines. — Eastern Siberia.—Review of the Yeniséisk and Irkútsk governments.—Surface configuration and mineral wealth (auriferous gravel, vein gold, silver and copper ores, iron ores and mining industry, green copperas, coal beds, graphite, naphtha, salt deposits, nephrite, precious stones, fire clay, mineral springs). — Hydrography.—Climate.—Vegetation.—Fauna.—Population (natives, exiles, emigration movement).—Land tenure —Industries and occupations of inhabitants.—Factories and works. — Yakútsk borderland and its gold mining wealth.—Bibliography.

THE middle link of the Great Siberian Railway, traversing the section from the river Ob to the Baikál, runs through the centre of the Tomsk government, and the south-eastern and most populous parts of the Yeniséisk and Irkútsk governments in Eastern Siberia, spreading its mighty influence all over the vast area of their territory. The Tomsk government, embracing the south-eastern portion of Eastern Siberia, has a superficial area of 15,797.50 sq. miles or 768,663.8 sq. versts, lying between 49° and 61° N. lat. and 45° and 61° E. long. Extending in the direction of the meridian, it is 1,400 versts from south to north, and about 900 versts from east to west, exceeding by 2½ times the dimensions of Great Britain's European dominions, and being 1½ times as large as France.

On the east and north-east it is bordered by the Tobólsk government and the Akmolínsk and Semipalátinsk territories, on the north-east and east by the Yeniséisk government, touching on the south upon Chinese territory.

For purposes of internal administration, this vast government is divided into 7 unequal districts:

Tomsk, inclusive of the Narym region,	246,325	sq. versts
Káinsk	66,061	„
Maríinsk	65,807	„
Barnaúl	114,512	„
Bíisk and Zmeinogórsk	169,943	„
Kuznétsk	87,171	„

The northern portion of the government, the districts of Káinsk, Maríinsk the Narym country and the greater part of the Tomsk district, a total of 402,543 sq. versts, belong to the crown lands and are under the management of the Ministry of Agriculture and State Domains. Its southern part, the Barnaúl, Bíisk, Zmeinogórsk, Kuznétsk and part of the Tomsk districts, form the property of His Imperial Majesty's Cabinet under the name of the Altái Mining District.

The surface of the Tomsk government is very varied: its southern and eastern parts are occupied by mountains of the Altái system and the Kuznétsk Alatáu, the western, north-western and northern portion by lowlands representing part of the extensive West Siberian plain. The whole area has a great fall to the north and north-west. The elevation of the Katún mountains, which on the south reaches 11,000 feet above sea-level, does not exceed 200—300 feet on the north. The northern direction of nearly all the rivers, belonging exclusively to the basin of the Arctic Ocean, is due to this inclination.

The Altái (Chinese „Cin-Shan" or gold mountains) representing an immense highland, coming up to the western boundaries of the Sayán mountain ridge, covers the southern portions of the Bíisk and Zmeinogórsk districts. Its superficial area is 630 versts long by 520 versts wide. The average height of these mountains above sea-level is 5,000 feet, and that of its highest summit, the Belúkha, 11,500 feet.

Several valleys traversing the Altái mountains divide the whole system into many parallel chains and ridges, known under the name of „belkí" (alps) „stolby" (columns) etc., running from north to south in the following order:

1) The Kolyván mountains, containing rich silver-lead and copper ores, with picturesque dome-shaped summits, are of no great elevation, rising barely to 4,500 feet at their highest point, the Seniúkha. They are situated between the headwaters of the Aléi and the middle reaches of the Charysh

2) The Tigeréts Belkí, whose summits have a height of 7,000 to 8,000 feet above sea-level, stand between the rivers Ubá and Charysh, and contain a great number of caves formed by weathering in the dolomite masses.

3) The Korgón mountains, lying between the rivers Koksúk and Charysh, rise to an altitude of about 7,000 feet above sea-level, and abound in beautiful jaspers, porphyries, agates, marbles and breccia.

4) The Terektín mountains are situated between the rivers Katún and Ursúl.

5) The Bashchalák, Aniúi and Ursúl Mountains consist of separate cliffs with an elevation of from 4,000 to 5,000 feet above sea-level; they are uninhabited and visited only by hunters.

6) The Ubá mountains which, like the Kolyván, abound in silver lead ores, are situated between the rivers Ubá and Ulbá, and attain an altitude of 5,400 feet above sea-level at their highest points.

7) The Ulbá mountains between the Great and Little Ulbá, rise to an elevation of 7,000 feet.

Altái. The Little Ak-bóm on the Chúya road (phot. by Sazónov).

8) The Turgusún mountains lie between the rivers Koksún and Ulbá.

10) The Kholsún mountains, situated between the upper stream of the Katún river and the Bukhtarmá, have peaks covered with perpetual snow of about 8,200 feet above sea-level.

11) The Katún Stolby represent the loftiest group of the Altái system, bound by the river Katún on the north-west and south, and by the rivers Argúta and Koksún on the east. Their highest point is the Belúkha with an elevation of 11,000 feet above sea-level; its glaciers, lying in deep ravines, feed the rivers Katún and Berél. The largest of the Katún glaciers is 11 versts long as measured by Professor Sapózhnikov. It accordingly ranks with the first-class glaciers of Switzerland.

12) The Saldzhár, Aigulík, Kurá and Chúya Belkí have summits called respectively Bózhia and Lysaya Gorá, which rise to a height of 10,000 feet above sea-level.

13) The Telétsk mountains, running parallel to the Kuznétsk Alatáu.

The Alatáu mountain ridge (Kirgiz „motley mountains") traverses the Kuznétsk district, its branches spreading over the southern part of the Barnaúl and Tomsk districts. These mountains extend for 600 versts in length and 100—150 versts in breadth and like the Altái consist of separate ridges with snow-clad summits. These snow peaks bear the local name of „Taskyl" or alps. The most southern extremities of the Altái, rising to an altitude of 15,000 feet above sea level, reach the Sayán mountains and stretch to the N. N. W. under the name of the Abakán, and further under that of Salaír mountains. Through nearly their entire course, they form the watershed of the vast Ob and Yeniséi river basins. Chains of inferior size, branching off from the main range, constitute the watersheds of the numerous large and small tributaries. The mountain ridges, falling gradually towards the north, disappear altogether only in the environs of Tomsk.

The Great Siberian main line, running through the Tomsk government, from the river Ob to the frontier of the Yeniséisk government, winds for a distance of 544 versts among the foothills of the spurs of the Alatáu, covered with vegetation and in some spots with impenetrable taigá or forest. All the Tomsk mountain region is bordered on the west, north-west and north by vast lowlands: the Kulundínsk Steppe, the Birch Barabá and the Vasiugánsk tundras forming part of the West Siberian plain. The Geological struc-

Altái, valley of the river Chúya (phot. by Sazónov).

ture of this government is characterised by the most marked contrast existing between the composition of the Altái-Alatáu highland and the lowlands surrounding it, scantily endowed with mineral wealth.

In its geological structure, the Altái and Alatáu upland is similar to all the great Central-Asiatic mountain ridges such as: Tarbagatái, Tian Shan, and others. The crystalline rocks are represented here by granite, syenite, crystalline slates, diorite, porphyry, serpentine and gabbro. Granite and syenite are mostly found in the western Altái. Diorite is scattered sporadically throughout the whole of the Altái, but is most extensively found along the

Altái. The Chúya road from the summit of the Chiki-Tamán pass. (phot. by Sazónov).

rivers Kondóma, Miás, Tom and in the gold-bearing districts themselves of the Alatáu on the headwaters of the Black Yus and the Yáya. Porphyry is found scattered in groups all over this region, serpentine and gabbro, along the river Chúya. The hard sedimentary rocks of the whole of the Altái-Alatáu consist of sandstone, slates, limestone and dolomite, belonging exclusively to the most ancient palaeozoic formations. The devonian and carboniferous systems predominate among the palaeozoic formations. The mining district of the Tomsk government holds one of the most important places in the whole Empire on account of its mineral wealth. This wealth was known already in remote times to nations dwelling in this region, as may be seen by the remains of mining works which still exist. In 1726, Akínfi Demídov appeared as the first promoter of Russian mining industry in the Altái, which dates its development from that time.

Gold is worked in the Tomsk government partly in the quartz veins of the Riddersk and Zyriánov mines and the Altái, and partly got in placers principally found in the Kuznétsk Alatáu in the Salaír mountains, and in the

Mariínsk, Kuznétsk, Bíisk and Barnaúl districts. According to the latest information, the Mariínsk taigá includes 71 mines with an output of 32 puds of gold; the other districts within the Altái region, lying along the rivers Miás, Kondóma, Balyksa, Kazás and Abakán contain 53 mines with a production of 85 puds of gold, belonging to the Cabinet lands of His Majesty. In the same space of time, 16 puds of gold were obtained from the mines of the Tomsk government at the cost of His Majesty's Cabinet exclusive of private exploitation. The proportion of gold contained in the gravel varies from 20 to 30 parts (dólias) of gold in 100 puds of gravel. In the Mariínsk taigá, the mines are in the hands of small owners and are worked in a rapacious and primitive way. The following considerable gold mining companies work the mines situated on the lands of His Majesty's Cabinet: tbe Altái gold mining Company, with from 16 to 18 puds per annum; the South Altái gold mining Company getting from 40 to 43 puds annually, Danílov and Company, from 7 to 8 puds, and Kuznetsóv and Company about 8 puds.

The Great Siberian Railway on its way through the mining districts comprising the river system of the Ob, the Mariinsk and the Altái mining districts, will undoubtedly exert an effect upon the development and the improvement of the gold-mining industry and attract capital and enterprise.

Silver, lead and copper are to be found at many points, 800 of them occurring in the Altái mining district. The ore deposits of the Altái country are divided into two separate groups in respect of their geographical situation: the first, under the name of the Zmeinogórsk country is situated in the southern part of the mining district within the range of the river systems

Two-storeyed barrel machine for the washing of gold gravel. Altái district, Danílov's mine.

of the Ob and the Irtysh; the second, the Salaír country, embraces the northeastern border of the mining district comprised within the system of the Tom.

The entire silver-lead exploitation was carried on from 1747 at the cost of His Majesty's Cabinet. However, since the year 1880, the Cabinet has obtained silver only at the Suzánsk works, this falling off being due to changes in the economical conditions of the country, and to the reduction in the productive capacity of the mines. The Zyriánov mine with its factory and the Zmeyévsk works, situated in the Zmeinogórsk country, are entrusted to the management of a private company. More careful explorations and some improvements in the mining industry will in the future open wide prospects

General view of the Kolyván polishing works in the Altái distr. (phot by Borísov).

for the mines of the Altái. Iron ores are to be found at many points of the Tomsk government, being specially frequent on the slopes of the Salaír mountain ridges and on the Kuznétsk Alatáu.

Precious stones, obtained in the Bíisk district from the quarries of the Altái mountains, are sent to the Kolyván polishing factory situated in tue Zmeinogórsk district, and thence are forwarded to the Imperial Court.

Rich deposits of coal are to be found within the territory of the Tomsk government. The Kuznétsk coal basin, 400 versts long and 100 versts wide, is particularly noteworthy on account of the thickness of the seam and the extent of the bed. Its southern boundary lies within 60 versts south of the town of Kuznétsk, this region being divided by the river Tom. The Kolchúgin coalpit, situated in the northern part of this section, is leased to the East-Siberian Metallurgic Company. Quite recently mining parties have discovered many coal-pits within the range of the Midsiberian railway which, having a most advantageous situation, offer a great practical interest. The coal bed near the Súdzhenka station is specially remarkable with respect to the thickness and quality of the coal. As may be seen from the analysis made, the coal obtained in this district is very similar to that found in the Donéts basin. In the year 1889, the Ministry of Ways of Communication concluded a contract with Mr. Michelson, who works the Súdzhenka mine, to supply the Siberian railway. At the same time, the Andzhársk coal-pit, near the Súdzhenka station, belonging to the government, is also to be exploited at the cost of the State and by means of the fund assigned for subsidiary enterprises in connexion with the Siberian railway, and the working capital of the line.

Rock salt is obtained from the Borovói and Burlínsk lakes, lying in the Barnaúl district. The annual production of salt from the Borovói lake is 600,000 puds, 1,250,000 puds being obtained from the Burlínsk lake, both constituting the principal salt producing centres of Western Siberia.

Glauber's salt is got from the Mormyshánsk and Saltpeter lakes in the Barnaúl district, and is chiefly used for the preparation of soda.

The mineral waters of the Tomsk government may be divided into two groups: 1) hot mineral springs, exclusively in the mountainous district, and 2) mineral lakes scattered over the steppe land The Rakhmánov and Belokúrikha springs are best known among the Altái mineral waters, and belong to the first division; the Solónovka, Karáchi and Ustiantsév lakes-to the second. The Rakhmánov spring is situated in the Bíisk district, almost on the frontier of Mongolia, lying in the picturesque valley of Arasán at an elevation of 2,034 metres above sea level. Arasán or Arshansá means warm spring. The temperature of the water is very high, and varies from 34° to 42°C., as stated by professor Sapózhnikov. It is colourless, very clear, has an agreeable taste and contains a considerable quantity of natural carbonic acid. It is reckoned among inert hot springs.

The Kolyván Factory.

The Belokúrikha spring lies within 63 versts south of the town of Bíisk near the village of Nóvaya Belokúrikha. Its temperature rises to 32°C. and, although it has a slight sulphuretted hydrogen smell, it has a good taste, is clear and soft, but totally inert, containing but a small quantity of mineral salts.

The water of the Solónovka lake, in the Barnaúl district, is strongly saturated with salt, and has a high specific gravity; being unfit for drinking on account of a predominating brackish and bitter taste and a slight smell of sulphuretted hydrogen, it is only employed for baths. The Karáchi lake situated in the Káinsk district, within 9 versts of the railway station of Karáchi, contains brackish and bitter water, having but a slight alkaline reaction A thick layer of greyish and greasy mire with a sulphuretted hydrogen smell covers the bottom of the lake, and is employed for mud baths. The Ustiántsev lake lies in the Káinsk district, within 25 versts of the town. Its water has an iridescent milky colour, a brackish and bitter taste, a smell of sulphuretted hydrogen and an alkaline reaction.

The rivers watering the Tomsk government belong to the basins of the Ob and the Yeniséi. The Ob basin comprises almost the whole territory of the government and, on account of its size may be separated into the Ob and the Irtysh river systems.

The Yeniséi river-basin extends only over the south-eastern part of the Kuznétsk district, traversed by its left tributary the Abakán.

The most important affluents of the Ob after its junction with the rivers Bíya and Katún are: the Chumysh, Berd, Yúya, Tom, Chulym, Ket, Tym on the right, and the Peschánaya, Aniú, Charysh, Aléi, Barnaúlka, Kosmálla, Vasiugán, on the left.

Altái. Lake Kolyván. (phot. by Borísov).

The Ulbá and Ubá crossing the southern part of the government and the Om and Tára flowing through the Káinsk district, within the limits of the West Siberian lowland, belong to the Irtysh river basin.

The government contains about 1,500 lakes. In its mountainous part, the following are specially noteworthy. Lake Telétsk (Altynka or Golden Lake) about 70 versts long, is picturesquely situated at an altitude of 1,702 feet. Lake Talménsk lies at an elevation of 5,000 feet above sealevel: according to Helmersen, one of the finest lakes in the world. It has a circumference of 12 versts and is surrounded by the peaks of the Katún alps. Lake Kolyván has a circuit of 7 versts and is situated at the foot of the Altái at an elevation of 1,180 feet in the midst of huge piles of boulders.

The northern section of the Tomsk and Maríinsk districts and the entire Narym region, occupying one-fifth of the whole territory of the government, present a continuous swamp cevered with forests, where dry and elevated points are most exceptional.

The climate of the Tomsk government is just as varied as its surface. In the northern portion of the government it is severe, changeable and damp, on the south-west, in the steppes and on the southern slopes of the Altái, it is warmer, and of an essentially continental character. At Tomsk, the average annual temperature is—0,74, at Káinsk—0,34, at Narym—1,98, at Barnaúl+0,34. At Narym, the winter is 3° colder than at Tomsk and Barnaúl. The average summer temperature is higher in the steppe region of the government. Southerly and south-westerly winds prevail. The greatest quantity of rainfall (383. 7 mm.) occurs in Tomsk, situated in a country abounding in forests and water. A lesser quantity (256.8 mm. in Barnaúl, 249.1 mm. in Káinsk) belongs to the south-western part of the gouvernment. Upon the whole, the climate is very severe, as may be seen from the long period during which the rivers remain frost-bound: from 165 to 218 days. On an average, the ice breaks up about the 13 April and sets again on the 19 October.

The flora of the Tomsk government, characterising the region of the plains, forming a continuation of the West-Siberian lowland, and also found on the southern and south-western sides of the Altái in the neighbourhood of the Kirgíz steppe borderland, is similar to the flora of the Tobólsk government and of the Aralo-Caspian depression. Most characteristic is the Altái mountain flora, found at a height of 2,000 feet above sealevel, and represented by some peculiar species of vegetation common to the whole of the elevated mountain region of the central Asiatic highland. The Tatar honeysuckle (Lonicera tatarica), the robinia (Caragana arborescens) and others, are to be found here. The greater part of the Altái vegetation corresponds to that of the middle European zone, which however boasts of a greater variety of species. This comparative scarcity is however compensated by the luxuriant development of the existing species. The arboreal forms of the Altái forests have, on an average, twice the size of those growing in the forests of tho Atlantic coast; and the flowering plants have remarkably large aud bright coloured blossoms; as for example the aconite, the larkspur and others, surprising the traveller, coming from the west, by their sturdy growth and deep blue flowers rising high above the bushes.

The rich vegetation of the Altái stretches to the utmost border of the forest zone, which covers the northern slopes of the Altái to a height of from 5,000 to 6,000 feet and reaches 6,000 feet on its southern side.

Altái. Station of Aiguläk on the Chúya road (phot. by Sazónov).

The zone of alpine herbs and bushes succeeds to the forest belt, the first including many kinds of plants which are also to be found in the European Alps. Among the wild plants, may be mentioned a nettle (Urtica cannabina) whose fibres in the Narym region are made into thread and yarn. The „cheremshá" or „kólba" (Allium ursinum) occurs in coniferous woods and is important as food. Different kinds of rhubarb grow on the Altái mountains.

The „kandyk" (Erythrotium dens canis) frequently found in the Kuznétsk district, is a very nutritive plant, employed by Tatars and Russians as a substitute for farinaceous food. Its perennial roots are gathered in May and are eaten raw or boiled in milk, when they are converted into a kind of sweet jelly.

Altái. Station of Kuréi on the Chúya road (phot. by Sazónov).

The Kondom natives use this plant for the preparation of an intoxicating beverage called „abyrtka". The root of the plant „karandys" (Inula helenum) is gathered in tho Altái, and exported as a medicine to Mongolia. The „kyrlyk", which is a kind of oat, grows on the slopes of the Altái, and is sometimes employed by the natives as food for themselves and as fodder for cattle and fowls.

Forests cover an immense area in the Tomsk government. They are particularly abundant in its northern part, the Narym country, and also in some parts of the neighbouring Tomsk, Maríinsk and Káinsk districts. The predominating trees are: pine, red fir, larch, fir and „cedar". The Kuznétsk, the southern part of the Tomsk, and the eastern side of the Bíisk districts are also thickly clothed with forests, which in the mountainous sections present a dense jungle and bear the name of „taigá". Fir and red fir predominate in the first, the second contains foliage trees, represented by birch and aspen slightly mixed with pine and red fir.

The fauna of the Tomsk government, within the limits of the West Siberian plain is very much like that of European Russia. Assuming a great variety of shapes, it is represented on the Altái by both Alpine and Mongolian species. The Altái is inhabited by the common bear and a kind of Syrian bear (Ursus sureanus var. lagomyarius Sévery), having long and curly hair of a lighter colour. Besides the lynx and the steppe cat, there are panthers, common and red or alpine wolves (Cyon alpinus. Pall.), common foxes and the „karagán" (Vulpes melanotus. Pall.) which is like the steppe fox, but easily known by its black ears, mountain and other skunks (Putorius alpinus

Altài. The station of Kuyaktonár on the Chúya road (phot. by Sazónov).

Gelb. Putorius altaicus. Pall). Putorius Eversmani. Among the hoofed animals, besides the common elk, the reindeer and the mountain sheep, there are the Altái black goat „tak-teke" (Aegoceros ibex. Pall. Capra Sibirica Mayer), Siberian roebuck, the marál (Cervus maral), muskdeer, pishchúkha (Lagomys alpinus L. minutus; Pall.) marmot (Arctomys bobac Schreb).

The bird species are represented by gigantic lammergeyers (Gypaetus barbatus L.) Altái mountain turkeys, alpine partridges, mountain capercailzies and partridges, alpine daws, hoopoos, cormorants and others. Among the reptiles, there are vipers and five-toed tritons (Ranodon Sibiricus) peculiar to Siberia.

The characteristic feature of the ichthyological fauna is that it contains only salmonoid species. Pike, gremille, carp and bream, which are frequent in other parts of the government, do not exist in the central Altái. The waters of this region abound mostly in grayling, taimén, uskúch (Brachymystax coregonoides. Pall.) There are few insects in the Altái, although many different forms of grasshoppers (Oedipoda) are to be found in the steppe regions. Some varieties of vertebrated animals are in particular abundantly represented in the Tomsk government.

As stated by Professor Káshchenko of the Tomsk university, the country is specially characterised by the following large mammals: elk, reindeer, marál, roebuck, bear, fox, lynx, glutton, otter, and others.

„Our country affords shelter to all" says Professor Káshchenko, „we are here living in a time which in Europe has long since passed away. Central

Europe, with respect to its fauna, held a similar position about 2,000 years ago, at the time of Julius Caesar, and the central zone of Russia, 800 years ago, at the time of Vladímir Monomákh. At present, however, evolution is more rapid, and the time is drawing nigh, when the primitive, but rich conditions of our country, which now seems to the stranger to belong to far distant days, will in fact exist no more. Special attention must be given to this rapid transition from past to present, which is now going on in order that it may not deprive us of the many advantageous of our wild nature, possessing a charm of her own. All her living creatures should be carefully preserved, not only because they are useful, but also because they adorn nature equally with ourselves".

Population. The Chud, belonging to the Finnish race, were the original inhabitants of the Tomsk government; numerous barrows, standing along the Altái and the fertile valleys of the Katún, Charysh and Alél rivers, testify to their presence there. In course of time, the Chud mingled with Turkish races; the first inhabited the northern and north-western slopes of the Altái

Altài. Pinewood on the way to the Zyriánov mines.

and Sayán mountain groups, the second settled on their southern side. Both occupied themselves with mining industry, employing the ore obtained for their own use, and for trade with the neighbouring people. In this way, the gold and silver of the Altái reached the Greeks and the Scythians, as confirmed by Herodotos and some of the Chinese chroniclers. The Mongols, who became famous from the XIII century A. D., united under their dominion the Turko-Finnish races of the Tomsk government, and contributed to dislodge the purely Finnish tribes from their original dwelling places towards the north-west, and to the mixture of their representatives, remaining in the Altái region, with the Turkish races. In the XV century, when the Golden Horde was already in its period of decline, the Turko-Finnish tribes, inhabiting at that time the south of the Tobólsk and the greater part of the Tomsk government, were already free and divided into several smaller states. Upon meeting with the intrepid Russian emigrants and the first Slavonic settlers of Siberia, they very soon submitted to the Russian power.

With respect to population, the Tomsk government holds the first place among all the other governments and territories of Siberia; the census of 1897 gives a population of 1,929,092 (970,780 males, 958,312 females) which,

Town of Barnaúl (phot. by Borísov).

when compared with the statistics of 1890 (1,299,729), shews an increase of 626,363.

Number of inhabitants in the respective districts:

DISTRICTS.	TOTAL POPULATION.			per sq. verst in 1897.	per sq verst in 1890.
	Male.	Female.	Total.		
1) Tomsk and Narym region..	139,912	135,577	275,489	1.0	0.7
2) Barnaúl	292,104	293,240	585,344	5.1	3.0
3) Bíisk	166,104	167,217	334,042	3.4	2.2
4) Zmeinogórsk	122,554	120,936	243,490	3.4	2.2
5) Káinsk	95,443	91,118	186,561	2.8	1.9
6) Maríinsk	72,023	67,843	139,866	2.1	1.5
				2.57	1.7

The greater number of inhabitants falls to the Barnaúl, Bíisk and Zmeinogórsk districts, containing tracts of very fertile arable land, belonging to the Imperial Cabinet of His Majesty. The ethnographical divisions of the population are very numerous in this government. The original inhabitants of the country belong to different tribes of the Urálo-Altáic races, representing $4^1/_2$ per cent of the total population; outlanders, chiefly of the Slavonic race, form $93^1/_2$ per cent, leaving $2^1/_2$ per cent to other nations of the Indo-European stock. The Urálo-Altáic race is divided into 4 different tribes: Finns, Turks, Mongols and Samoyéds.

The Finnish tribe is represented by the Ostiáks, who are the original natives of the land, and by the Mordvá, Zyrián, Chuvásh descendant of the former settlers. The Ostiáks of Tomsk are the last representatives of the Finnish stock in the east; they inhabit only the northern part of the govern-

Town of Bíisk (phot. by Borísov).

ment, and occupy themselves with hunting, fishing, and gathering cedar-nuts Their winter abode is a log-hut with a chuvál or hearth; in summer they dwell in conical huts made of stakes covered with birch bark. The total number of the Ostiáks in the government does not exceed 2,000.

The Chulym Barabá, Kuznétsk and Chernevy Tatars and the Bukharians belong to the Turkish tribe with an admixture of the Finnish and even the Mongolian stock. Most of these natives lead a settled life; many of them closely allied to the Russians have adopted the orthodox faith. Others, as for instance the Chernevy Tatars refuse to give up their nomad life. There are few Christians in the country, where Shamanism is the predominating religion. The total number of the representatives of this tribe throughout the vast territory of the government does not exceed 30,0000 or 35,000.

The Mongolian race is represented by the Teleúts or Telengúts inhabiting the Altái. The Telengúts wandering about the valleys of the river Chulyshmán, Bashkaús, Chúya and the headwaters of the rivers Anúi, and Charysh, are called Uriankháets.

Leading a nomad life, these tribes occupy themselves with cattle-breeding and hunting. They are Buddhists and belong to the Mongolian type. The Telengúts mostly live in movable tents called „kereché“ composed of latticed wooden frames covered with felt. On the northern slopes of the Altái, wooden and birch-bark huts (yúrta's) are met with. The total number of Telengúts is 40,000.

The Samoyéd tribe occupies the Narym region being settled along the Ob and its tributaries the Tym, Kétia, Parabél and the lower reaches of the Chulym. With respect to their mode of life, the Ob Samoyéds differ from their countrymen dwelling in other river regions. They have huts which are constructed like the Russian izbá, while those living on the tributaries of the Ob have yúrtas like the Ostiáks, with whom they follow a similar mode of life. The number of Samoyéds in the government is 6,500.

Among the other nationalities, Poles hold the first place, being followed by Jews, Finns and Germans. The increase of the population of the Tomsk government was effected by natural growth and by means of immigration of exiles and free settlers from European Russia. The Káinsk, Maríinsk and the northern portion of the Tomsk district are selected throughout the Tomk government for the settlement of exiles, who are not admitted to the Altái mining district containing land belonging to the Cabinet of His Majesty. The exiles distributed in the localities of the Tomsk government are of the same kind as those settled in the Tobólsk government Within the last ten years 17,659 exiles, inclusive of those who voluntarily accompanied them, have been settled within the confines of the three northern districts. The considerable

Bishop's house in the town of Bíisk (phot. by Ovchin).

increase of the population, which within the last five years has given, in this respect, a foremost importance to the Tomsk government, is due to the great influx of free settlers, principally colonising the Altái mining district

Up to the year 1865, settlers having received formal permission from the Government, occupied exlusively Crown lands in the northern parts of the Tomsk government; those who fixed their residence on the Altái lands, belonging to the Cabinet of His Majesty, did so at their own risk, without any licence from the Chief Office of the Altái district which strove carefully to protect the country from the intrusion at settlers. Since 1865, when the Altái district opened its confines to colonisation, the movement to this region has been ever on the increase. By the year 1889, 143,751 colonists had settled on the lands belonging to the Imperial Cabinet. The rush to the Cabinet lands of His Majesty was particularly remarkable within the last ten years of the past century. The number of settlers during this period exceeded 300,000. For the present, no new grants of land will be made in the Altái mining district until the former settlers are properly established. Until a new order, newcomers can only settle in already regulated communes, upon receiving permission from their representatives, without however obtaining any assistance or subsidy, such as are granted to peasants emigrating to Siberia with formal permission to

The town of Kuznétsk.

localities specially allotted them. The opening of traffic on the Great Siberian Railway effected a considerable increase in the voluntary colonisation of the Crown lands lying along the railway line in the Káinsk, Maríinsk and partly in the Tomsk districts, where the land along the railway was soon allotted. Hence arose the necessity for finding lots which, although lying at a greater distance from the railway, would yet be available for cultivation.

Besides the Barabá lands of the Káinsk district bordered by the west Siberian section of the main line, State Secretary Kúlomzin on his journey to Siberia in 1896, with the object of a thorough investigation of the emigration movement, has allotted to future settlers the land situated along the Mid Siberian railway in the Tomsk, Chulym and Chulym-Maríinsk taigás. Vast areas called „yelán“ once covered with ancient forest subsequently burned down, are now dotted with fine birch; these lands have been found fit for settlement, although requiring the application of stubborn and continuos labour on the part of energetic settlers. These wooded sections situated in the Tomsk and Maríinsk districts, contain Crown lands free to be colonised

Several medical and feeding stations, which are the places of residence of the emigration officials, are situated along the railway line at stations and towns (Tatárka station, Káinsk, Kargát station, in the Káinsk district, Ob stations, Tomsk, (Tomsk district), Maríinsk, Bogotól station (Maríinsk district). Here settlers are registered and directed to the unoccupied lands of the Tomsk government. Within the last five years, the greater number of emigrants came from the governments of Kursk, those of Chernígov, Oriól, Poltáva and Khárkov having contributed to the movement in a somewhat less proportion

The following erections have been made at the cost of the fund of the Emperor Alexander III in the Tomsk government in order to satisfy the religious needs of the entire population dwelling within the range of the Great Siberian main line:

1) Three wooden churches at the Ob, Taigá and Bogotól stations.

2) Four wooden churches in the settlement of Alexándrovsk and in those of Oboyán, Bélgorod and Belovódsk (Maríinsk district).

3) The Nóvo-Rozhdéstvensk settlement (Tomsk district), and Sviatoslávsk (Maríinsk district), contain two wooden churches with schools.

4) A stone church is in process of construction iu the Novo-Nikoláevsk settlement on the Mid-Siberian Railway.

5) Eighteen churches (9 of wood and 9 of stone) are being erected in the following settlements: Constantínovo, Mokhovóe, Mikháilovo, Nikoláevo, Novoalexándrovka, Poltávka, Kulikóvo, Ivánovo, Mikháilovsk, Nóvo-Nikoláevo, of St. Alexandra, Mírgorod, Gromachévsk Mikháilovska (Semilúzhensk volost), Ulánovsk, Kazánskoe, Nekrásovo, Preobrazhénskoe.

6) Six schools have been built in the settlement of Oboyán, Belovódsk, Bélgorod, Oriól-Rozóvsk, Ivánovsk, Kursk (Maríinsk district), Novorozhdéstvensk, Mikháilovsk, Kazánskoe, Nekrásovo (Tomsk district).

7) Five schools in the settlement of St. Alexandra, Ulánovsk, Konstantínovo, Mokhovóe, Gromachévsk are in process of construction.

Agriculture, cattle-breeding, bee-keeping, hunting, forestry etc. are the, main sources of the prosperity of the inhabitants of the Tomsk government.

Agriculture is the predominant occupation of the inhabitants of the Tomsk government, exclusive of the swampy Narym region, the northern portion of the Maríinsk district and the hilly parts of the Bíisk and Kuznétsk districts. The Barnaúl, Bíisk and Zmeinogórsk districts present large areas of corn-land.

The system of husbandry adopted here is the same as in the Tobólsk government, characterised by the fallow land system; it can, however scarcely be considered as a settled one, as it depends upon the quantity of arable land, the condition of the soil and many factors, and above all upon the economic prosperity of each householder. The predominating type of „sokhá" or primitive plough is called „kolesiánka". The administration being chiefly occupied with the improvement of husbandry, is propagating more rational systems of agriculture and has established for this purpose agronomical schools with farms and apiaries, stores of agricultural machinery and various kinds of seeds.

The efforts of the West-Siberian Agricultural Society tend towards the improvement and progress of husbandry in the government.

The following statistics for the years 1894, 1895 and 1986, shew the quantity of grain sown and the total crops raised in the government during this period.

	1894.		1895.		1896.	
	Sown.	Raised.	Sown.	Raised.	Sown.	Raised.
Winter wheat.........	47,375	223,739	24,991	127,354	11,182	62,117
Winter rye...........	216,735	1,204,071	234,482	1,256,886	180,855	627,110
Spring wheat........	508,836	3,198,503	556,704	3,414,406	621,521	2,910,387
Spring oats..........	422,154	2,421,551	531,559	2,648,514	595,544	3,218,257
Spring barley........	74,702	455,931	78,291	434,347	72,014	411,786
Spring buckwheat....	21,313	109,724	12,973	74,605	12,988	61,280
Various corn crops...	159,382	796,726	145,125	457,085	170,110	890,466
Potatoes..............	98,409	676,936	135,908	868,384	242,159	880,234
TOTAL.....	1,545,906	9,086,781	1,730,033	9,281,781	1,905,373	9,061,637

The quantity of grain sown and the crops raised shewed no falling of during the following three years. As may be seen from the above figures, the quantity of grain sown in the government and especially in the districts of the Altái mining region, lying within the range of the Great Siberian Railway, not only suffices for the public supply, but also yields a surplus of grain, which can be exported into the interior of the Empire and abroad, to the amount of some millions of puds. According to the statistics of the Altái mining region, the grain surplus is 22,000 000 puds per annum, obtained in the region from the 1,000,000 desiatíns of land sown which is only 1/20 part of the total arable land.

Cattle-breeding in also an important element in the husbandry of the Tomsk government, constituting indeed the sole resource of the wandering Telengúts and Tatárs. The extensive pastures and abundant hay crops, which are frequent in this region, contribute in a great measure to the development of this feature, as is testified by the noteworthy increase in the number of cattle throughout the region. The following statistics from 1891 and 1896 illustrate the gradual progress of cattle-raising in the country.

	1891.	1896.
Horses	1,297,813	1,746,633
Cattle	867,330	1,627,848
Sheep	2,227,455	1,317,102

On the average, a peasant household owns: 6.1 horses, 4.1 head of cattle and 10 sheep.

With respect to the number of horses and other kinds of cattle, the Barnaúl district occupies the first and the Bíisk the second place.

For the improvement of horse-breeding, the administration of the State studs has organised stables in Tomsk, the stallions being sent in summer to different parts of the government.

The considerable quantity of meat required in Eastern Siberia for the mines and gold-works also serves as an inducement to extend cattle-breeding.

The rearing of the domesticated „marál“ or mountain deer (Cervus maral) is one of the local industries practised exclusively in the Bíisk district, which contains about 2,000 tame maráls. Their horns are particularly valuable. Taken from the male and sawn off at the root at the end of June, they are boiled in salt water in order to prevent decay, and are sold at the rate of R. 5 to 7 a pud. The wholesale merchants sell them in China for R. 20 to 25 a pud. The Chinese prepare a vivifying remedy from the extract of these horns.

The extensive development of beekeeping in the Tomsk government characterises this country among all others in Siberia, which in this respect surpasses all the governments of European Russia. This industry is practised in the Altái mining region, more especially in the Bíisk and Zmeinogórsk districts, which reckon 577,169 beehives and 14,163 apiaries, producing yearly over 3,000,000 pounds of honey and above 10,000 puds of wax.

Model apiaries with framed beehives belonging to new systems are already to be found in the Kuznétsk district. A beekeeper, living in the town of Barnaúl and editing the journal called „Northern Apiculture“, is appointed by the Government for the instruction of the population and the propagation of rational systems.

Fishing is the chief occupation of the Narym natives and of the inhabitants of the northern portions of the Tomsk and Maríinsk districts. It is of prime importance as a source of revenue in the central zone of the government only for the inhabitants along the river Ob. The fish taken in summer are salted and dried, while the winter catch is frozen. In summer, so called „pozióm“ is prepared from sterlet, syrók and muksún. The fish is split open, freed from bones, salted, dried in the air and slightly smoked.

Hunting and trapping are on the decrease every year in proportion to the increase of the population. This industry is still practised in the Narym country, in the taigá parts of the Kuznétsk and Maríinsk districts and in that of Bíisk. About 1,000 people are so occupied in the Narym country. Squirrel, kolónka, sable, fox, ermine, bear and otter, and wild duck, swan, geese, capercailzie and hazel-hen among birds, are the principal objects of the hunter. On an average, 100,000 squirrels are anually taken by Ostiák men and women. Next in importance come: 3,000 kolónkas, 1,500 sables, 1,000 foxes, 500 ermines, about 50 to 100 otters and about 30 bears Every year a great number of ducks are taken in this region; a hunter sometimes gets some 300 of them in one night. The Narym region abounds in lakes; in the autumn before their migration, the ducks gather in immense flocks and in the evening ly from one lake to another. The fowlers, availing themselves of this habit, select two lakes and, making a clearing between them, stretch a net across the opening. The ducks, frightened from one lake, fly by the clearing to the other and get entangled in the net. They are then removed one by one and killed by biting through the back of the head. Part of these ducks are sold and part salted, smoked or dried and stored for the coming year, About 300,000 squirrels, 100,000 striped squirrels, 15,000 hares, 10,000 „kolónka“, 3,000 skunks, 1,200 sables, 1,000 ermines, 350 foxes, 300 deer, 150 roebuck, 50 bears, 20 gluttons and as many otters are killed in the Kuznétsk district, where 2,000 people are engaged in this industry. The approximate number of birds taken in the same district are 50,000 hazel-hens, 1,000 capercailzie, 10,000 blackcock, 10,000 duck and 5,000 partridges. The Maríinsk district numbers only 300 trappers, the industry there being practised on a smaller scale. In the Bíisk district, there are at least 2,500 people engaged. Besides all the above mentioned animals, this southern and hilly district contains in addition various kinds of roebuck, mountain sheep, kabargá and marál. The average annual yield in this district is 20 maráls, 500 roebuck, 60 bears, 400 foxes, 100 badgers, 50 lynxes, 20 gluttons, 1,700 „kolónkas“, 100,000 squirrels, 200 sables, 400 ermines, 50 otters, 1,000 hares, 7,590 blackcock, 5,000 hazel-hens and 1,000 magpies, whose feathers are sent abroad to adorn ladies'hats. The law restricting hunting has not yet been introduced in the Tomsk government.

The cedar-nut trade is carried on in the Narym region in the northern parts of the Tomsk and Maríinsk districts and in the mountainous localities of the Kuznétsk and Bíisk districts. Tomsk is the chief market for the sale of these nuts. From 300,000 to 400,000 puds of nuts are gathered in a good year; they are sold at the rate of R. 1-50 k. to R 2-50 k. a pud. Nut gathering in the forests begins on the 10 August and ends on the 15 September. The cones are got by climbing or shaking the trees; in more remote spots, huge trees centuries old are ruthlessly felled with the same object.

The greater part of the nuts are sent by the rivers Chulym and Ob to Tiumén and thence to European Russia, while a part is conveyed by the Siberian Railway. In 1898, 132,306 puds of cedar-nuts were brought by the Midsiberian Railway to different places in the West.

The domestic industries carried on in the Tomsk government include the making of various articles of wood such as axles, wheels, „dugás" or yokes, sledges etc., the manufactory of felt boots, pottery, the dressing of skins, the tanning of hides and the smith's handicraft. These industries are not developed in the Barnaúl district, whose sheepskin shúbas dyed black are well known under the name of „barnaúlki".

Factories and works make but little progress in the Tomsk government, although agriculture, cattle-breeding, and the forest and mining industries yield abundance of raw materials. According to official information, there are 2,031 factories and works and 4,139 flour-mills in the government. In 1896, industry in towns and districts was represented as follows:

DISTRICTS.	Manufactories.	Workmen employed.	Output in rubls.
Tomsk	497	3,196	2,778,275
Káinsk	1,929	2,158	263,856
Maríinsk	231	469	218,953
Barnaúl	659	1,058	400,441
Bíisk	1,000	1,575	394,366
Kuznétsk	749	1,121	77,821
Zmeinogórsk	1,105	1,591	259,541
	6,170	11,168	4,393,253.

The chief industries represented are: 15 distilleries, with a revenue of R. 1,199,290; 12 breweries, yielding R. 558,045; 291 tanneries, yielding R. 427,833; 48 wheat-flour-mills, giving R. 401,630.

The following manufactories are particularly noteworthy on account of the technical processes employed: 1) 2 glass-works in the Barnaúl and Bíisk districts, producing glass and glass vessels, mainly for vódka. The material required is obtained within the government. The annual output amounts to R. 165,000. 2) The soda works of Mr. Prang, situated in the Barnaúl district, dates from 1864, and was the first of the kind to be established in Russia. The soda is obtained from the Glauber's salt of the Maríinsk Lake in the Barnaúl district. The annual production amounts to R. 40,000. 3) 51 wax bleach yards and taper manufactories sending most of their produce to Irbít. The value of their annual production exceeds R. 200,000.

Trade. A considerable quantity of raw products is sent from the Tomsk government to the home markets in the West of the Empire as also to Eastern Siberia. All colonial goods, groceries and drugs, almost all manufactured goods are imported. Buying and selling is carried on at the fairs, held in different districts, whose number exceeds 70 for the whole government. The most important among them are: the Suzúnskaya, Krutíkhinskaya, Bérdskaya, in the Barnaúl district; the Zmeinogórskaya, Antónievskaya in the Zmeinogórsk district; the Smolénskaya in the Bíisk district; the Briukhánovskaya in the Kuznétsk district and the Spas fair in the Káinsk district; the yearly business of the fairs amounts to about R. 6,000,000 to R. 7,000,000.

The Great Siberian main line, by bringing new life into the governments of Siberia, is already producing considerable changes in the trade, which is particularly noticeable by the towns and large villages situated along it.

The former dependence of the small trading firms on the town of Tomsk is little by little disappearing: in the shops of district towns and large settlements, are now to be found Vienna furniture, sewing machines, various instruments, and other goods obtained from the capitals, formerly—known only by hearsay to the country population, who had to be satisfied with the trash from the Irbít fair and the spoilt groceries of Tomsk. The foreign trade of the Tomsk government, which on the south is bordered by the frontier of the Chinese Empire, is carried on, in insignificant proportions, by the merchants of Bïisk by the highway for pack-animals through the Russian frontier settlement of Kosh-Agách, whence there is a carriage road to the Chinese town of Kobdó.

Altái. The river Chúya on the Kosh-Agách plateau (phot. by Sazónov).

The articles of export are manufactured and millinery goods, iron and copper wares, tanned leather and marál horns. In exchange, the Russian merchants get brick-tea, furs, silk stuffs and small wares of Chinese manufacture. This foreign trade, with a value of only a few hundred thousand rubls, has not yet attained its due development, on account of the difficulties of the communications with Kosh-Agách.

Little profit is yet got from the natural mineral wealth, hitherto scarcely explored, of the Tomsk government and the Altái mining district. New railway-lines however are projected to join the Grand Trunk, through the fertile lands lying at the foot of the Altái and Alatáu, with a view to promote the economical growth of the country. The most important direction of these contemplated lines will join one of the stations of the Mid-Siberian railway with Tashként, passing through the towns of Barnaúl, Semipalátinsk and Vérny.

BIBLIOGRAPHY.

1) List of inhabited localities in the Tomsk government. Publ. by the Central Statistical Committee, 1869.

2) Vólosts and inhabited places. 1893. Publ. by the Central Statistical Committee, 1894.

3) Materials for the study of the economic life of the peasants and natives of Western Siberia. Publ. by the Min. of State Domains. Pts. XIV—XIX

4) Notes of the West-Siberian branch of the Imperial Russian Geographical Society 1880—1899.

5) Appendix to the reports of the Governor of Tomsk presented to His Imperial Majesty.

6) Siberian trade and industry calendars. Publ. by Románov. 1897—1899. Tomsk.

7) Guide to the journey of His Imperial Highness the Tsesarévich. St. Ptg. 1891.

8) Report by State Secretary Kúlomzin on his journey to Siberia for the investigation of the emigration movement. St.-Petersbg. 1896.

9) Appendices to the reports of the Min. of Agriculture and State Domains presented to His Imperial Majesty, after his journey to Siberia in the autumn of 1895 and in the summer of 1898. St.-Petersburg. 1899.

10) Geological investigations and explorations along the line of the Siberian Raitway. Pts. I—XVI.

11) Scientific sketches of the Tomsk government. Edited by Professor Káshchenko. Tomsk. 1898.

12) In the Altái. Diary of the journey of Professor Sapózhnikov. Tomsk. 1897.

Eastern Siberia.

Eastern Siberia, in respect of its administration, is subjected to a Governor General, and comprises the Yeniséisk and Irkútsk governments and the territory of Yakútsk. It covers a superficial area of 132,600 square geographical miles, and contains a population of 1,328,150 as shewn by the census of 1897, principally concentrated within the range of the Great Siberian highway which, as the chief cemmercial artery of the country, ever attracted the economic life of Eastern Siberia. The Great Siberian mainline, running from the boundary of Eastern Siberia across the Tomsk government to Lake Baikál, has chosen its course through localities contiguous to the Siberian trade route, thus extending its mighty influence not only throughout the Yeniséisk and Irkútsk governments, but also over the more distant Yakútsk territory.

The Yeniséisk government, lying between 52°33′ and 77° N. lat. and between 47° and 80° E. long., comprises the western portion of Eastern Siberia. Having a greater extension from south to north (2,800 versts) than from west to east (1,300 versts), this government is only inferior in size to the Yakútsk territory, thus holding the second place in the Empire. It covers an area of 14,542 square miles and is for purposes of administration divided into 6 districts: Yeniséisk with the Turukhánsk region, Achinsk, Krasnoyársk, Kansk, Minusínsk und Usínsk situated on the border of the government.

The Irkútsk government, lying within 51° and 62°30′ N. lat., and within 66° and 86°30′ E. long., comprises the south-eastern part of Eastern Siberia, and has a superficial area of 14,542 square miles. It is divided into 5 districts: Nizhneúdinsk, Balangánsk, Kirénsk, Irkútsk and Verkholénsk.

With respect to its superficial configuration, the Yeniséisk government is very varied and may be divided into two sections: one lying to the north and containing the Turukhánsk region and the northern part of the Yeniséisk district characterised by a scarce population and stony and swampy districts unfit for cultivation; the other stretching southward and comprising the Achinsk, Krasnoyársk, Kansk, Minusínsk, Usínsk and part of the Yeniséisk, district with stretches of steppe land and mountain ranges fit for agriculture and cattle-breeding.

The Irkútsk government is essentially mountainous; plains and river valleys occupy only a small part of its area. Alpine mountains cover the south-western, the south and south-eastern part of the government and skirt the western and south-eastern shores of Baikál. The grand Sayán mountain-chain occupies the southern borders of both governments. A line of posts, representing the frontier dividing Russian territory from China, runs along the top of the mountains, following the direction of the Nérchinsk highway.

The Sayán chain stretches in a solid mass across the territory of Yeniséisk and through the western part of the Irkútsk government, putting out branches which run far into the interior of the territory. The Sayàn system is more intricate on the southeast of the Irkútsk government, where it separates into parallel ridges broken by perpendicular valleys, among which the numerous left tributaries of the Angará wind their course towards the plateau of Eastern Siberia. The Sayán chain, after joining the Altái mountains west of the river Yeniséi, bears the name Shabín-Olá or Belogórie, and is called Ergík-Targák-Taigá east of the Yeniséi. Towards the south, there is a wide plain within the limits of the Chinese Empire which, being surrounded by mountains, was the cradle of the Turkish tribes which thence spread all over Asia. The highest mountain group of the Sayán chain rises at the south-eastern corner of the Irkútsk government; its summits, covered with perpetual snow, reach an altitude of 11,430 feet at their most elevated point, Munkú-Sardyk or Silver Mountain which, feeding considerable glaciers, stands on the frontier of the Chinese Empire. Numerous ridges stretch north of these peaks, the Biriusínsk mountains rising to a height of 6,200 feet at the south-western corner of the Irkútsk government, being the most considerable among them. Further are the Idínsk mountains, the Kitói Alps and the Tunkínsk belkí following to the north the valley of the Irkút.

The Baikál mountains, the Khamár-Dabán, the Littoral and Okótsk ridges leaving the Sayán in detached parallel lines, skirt the wide valley, which yields shelter to the Baikál, one of the grandest fresh water lakes in the world.

The chief range of the Sayán and its branches consist mainly of crystalline rocks, such as granite, syenite, porphyry, diabase, diorite, gneiss and crystalline slate. Basalt and dolorite are to be found on the slopes of the Munkú-Sardyk at the Khangínsk Military Post and near the Túnka, along the river Irkút close to the south-western shore of the Baikál, und also between the rivers Sliudiánskaya and Tálaya, on the lower reaches of the Ilím, along the course of the Angará, while volcanic tufa, obsidian and pumice occur on the banks of ils affluents. The deep Túnka valley contains lava hills; the currents of lava on the Yełóvsky branch testify that this region in former times contained numerous volcanos, of which the earthquakes occurring somewhat frequently in Irkútsk bear evidence to the present day. The slopes of the Sayán mountains are covered with sedimentary rocks consisting of sandstone, slate and limestone of the silurian, devonian and carboniferous formations. At some distance from the Sayán ridges, sandstone predominates among the sedimentary rocks.

Eastern Siberia is endowed with very great mineral wealth; alluvial gold was first found in the year 1830, afterwards it was discovered throughout the vast territory of the government. Gold is mostly found in the sand of rivers and small streams.

The geological formation of the deposits is various, but shews a predominance of slate rocks. The thickness of the goldbearing strata varies from

2 to 3 sazhens, and their extent from 1 to 50 versts. The proportion of gold is also different according to the depth of the deposit. The gold strata are usually covered by a layer of alluvium, called the „turf".

The gold mining regions of the government are administered and managed by the two mining departments of Tomsk and Irkútsk. All the gold-mines of the Yeniséisk government pertain to the Tomsk departments, with the

Goldwashing machine in the South Yeniséisk district. Mine of Mr. Cheremnykh.

exception of those which, included in the Biriusínsk group are divided into three mining districts: Achinsk-Minusínsk, comprising the mines of the Achinsk, Minusínsk and Usínsk districts; South Yeniséisk, containing the southern part of the Yeniséisk district, the Krasnoyársk and Kansk districts; and the North Yeniséisk, with the northern part of the Yeniséisk district. The mining district of Biriusínsk is under the management of the mining department of Irkútsk.

In the Achinsk district, most of the gold mines occur in the valleys of rivers and small streams belonging to the basin of the Chulym, and along the unimportant rivers falling into the Yeniséi.

The mines wlth richest annual output belong to Ivanítsky (4—6 puds) and to Múkhin and Co. (3—4 puds). The Krasnoyársk district is not so rich in gold; it is found on the small rivers taking their rise in the Kemchúzhsk mountains, and in the mountains on both sides of the Yeniséi.

The gold mines of the Minusínsk and Usínsk districts form one system, comprising the tributaries of the rivers Yeniséi and Abakán, which do not contain any rich deposits. The gold-mining company of Usínsk, obtaining from 5 to 7 puds per annum, and the mines of Okúlov, which at the beginning of 1899 were purchased by a Belgian joint stock company, are the most important in this region.

In the Yeniséisk district, the gold mines are situated on the right side of the Yeniséi, between the rivers Angará and Podkámennaya Tungúska, and throughout the basin of numerous small rivers falling into the two above mentioned tributaries of the Yeniséi; gold is also to be found along the valleys of the affluents of the Pit, which crosses the gold-bearing region and divides it into the two almost equal, North and South Yeniséisk, mining districts. The gold mines situated in the Yeniséisk district on the rivers Uderéi and Mamóna have been worked since 1839, and soon became famous on account of their rich output. Within the period of the first ten years, the amount of the annual output was represented by 1,000 puds; since that time, the quantity of extracted gold has been decreasing from year to year, and now scarcely amounts to a few puds.

The total quantity of gold obtained up to the present time is 27,000 puds, with a value of R. 350,000,000. These mines, among all others in the Russian Empire, yield the greatest quantity of metal. Moreover, the following mines, situated in the South-Yeniséisk mining district, have some importance on account of their production: the mines of Perepléchikov, where 20 puds were obtained in each of the years 1894 and 1895; those of the Udréi gold mining company of Cheremnykh and Co., (from 10—14 puds per annum), Cheremnykh and Rátkov-Rozhnóv (5—8 puds per annum), Sharypov (4—5 puds annually). The mines of the Vostrótin Association (7 puds), of Kytmánov (9—10 puds) and of Khárchenko (3—4 puds). are the most important in the North-Yeniséisk

Getting gold from tailings (phot. by Arnold).

mining district. The richness of the mines and the inadequate methods applied in washing the gravel are well illustrated by the fact that mines long since abandoned which were considered already exhausted, are now being worked afresh by new owners.

The Biriúsinsk mining district, watered by the river Biriúsa, comprises the Kansk and Nizhneúdinsk districts of the Irkútsk government. In respect of its gold production, this group is now much inferior to others, whereas formerly it contained the richest mines of Eastern Siberia.

In 1842, the quantity of metal obtained during the summer was 204 puds; but, since that time, the annual output has diminished to a few puds. This fact is due not to the exhaustion of the mines, but to their inadequate prospecting. It may therefore be supposed that the Great Siberian Railway traversing this gold-bearing region will bring with it new and more rational systems of working, and thus secure the prosperity of the Biriúsinsk mining group.

Deposits of vein gold are worked in the Yeniséisk government only in the mines of Cheremnykh and Rátkov-Rozhnóv, and by Khilkóv in the Yeniséisk mining district. The metal is found in quartz rocks. The Irkútsk government is not so abundantly provided, and includes only a few mines distributed along the valleys of rivers falling into the Baikál, in the Nizhneúdinsk and Irkútsk districts, and also in the district of Verkholénsk and Kirénsk; the valley along the upper reaches of the Léna contains but poor gold gravels.

Church at the mines.

Silver and copper ores occur frequently in the valley of the Yeniséi river, and were known to the natives of the country, the ancient Chud. Silver ore is often found in connexion with copper pyrites. The first copper foundry of Lúgovsk, which has long since ceased to work, was established in Eastern Siberia in the Minusínsk district on the site of the old Chud mines, towards the end of the XVIII century.

Another foundry, which however soon stopped its operations, was established in 1874, in the Achinsk district; the copper produced, in respect of its quality, rivalled that of the Urál.

Eastern Siberia is especially well off for iron-ore; rich deposits of this metal occur in the Yeniséisk and Irkútsk governments and also throughout all the other districts. The Minusínsk district abounds, in particular, in rich beds of magnetic iron ore, and contains a foundry and iron-works, situated on the river Abakán, which belong to Rátkov-Rozhnóv and produce puddled, rolled, high-furnace and machinery iron.

The Irbínsk State lands, comprising an area of 124,000 desiatins, are situated within 100 versts to the north-east of the town of Minusínsk and 30 versts from the Túba, a tributary of the Yeniséi; this locality, watered by numerous rivers and provided with rich beds of iron, once contained an iron-foundry, which has however been idle for some 50 years. The estimated amount of ore in this region is 65,000,000 puds. Iron-ore has been found on the banks of the rivers Yeniséi, Kuskún and Buzyk, in the Krasnoyársk district, near the village Ozernáya, where it has been worked since the end of the XVIII century.

Rich deposits, which to the present time are worked in a most primitive way by the peasants, have been discovered in the Yeniséisk district at a short distance from the town of the same name, near the villages of Potápovo and Zaledéevo.

Although very abundant thoughout the Irkútsk government, iron is worked only on the lower reaches of the Oká, an affluent to the Angará, where stands the Nicholas cast-iron foundry, iron works and rail-rolling mill belonging to the company organised by Mr. Mámontov. Mining parties, which have been at work along the line of the Great Siberian Railway, have made remarkable discoveries of rich deposits of magnetic iron-ore on the rivers Kasiánka, Korshuníkha and Zhelézny Kliúch in the Irkútsk government. Numerous beds of iron are also situated round Lake Baikál. At the beginning of 1899, the Irkútsk merchant Glótov organised the Mining Company of Irkútsk, with a capital of R. 1,000,000 divided into 4,000 shares, to work these mines.

Green copperas occurs in the Irkútsk government, near the village of Zíminskoye, on the right bank of the Oká. The alum copperas soil contains green copperas in thin streaks of crystalline salt of a greenish colour, while at some points green copperas is represented by a yellow and reddish-brown sediment.

Deposits of the same formation are imbedded in the Shelun-Tong mountain above the source of the Tágna.

Coal deposits have been discovered throughout the vast territory of Eastern Siberia, and recently along the Great Siberian railroad, by geological parties specially despatched to explore this region.

The Nicholas foundry and iron-works.

The following deposits in the Yeniséisk government have a special importance:

1) in the Achinsk district, near the village of Antrópovo,

2) 30 versts from Krasnoyársk, near the village of Kubékovo,

3) along the river Kácha, near the village of Zaledéevo, and on the river Kemchúga, 100 versts from the town of Krasnoyársk,

4) in the Minusínsk district, along the righ bank of the river Abakán, within 55 versts of its junction with the Yeniséi at the mountain Izykh. A joint stock company has been organised by the Marquis de Vassall Montiel and Engineer Devi to work the coal deposits along the basin of the Yeniséi. Other coal regions with a kind of coal similar to anthracite, lie much further to the north, along the Nízhniaya Tungúska. Many coal seams have been discovered along the highway from the town of Kansk to Nizhneúdinsk, situated in the environs of the latter on the river Oká. Quite lately deposits of coal lying in the Balagánsk district, near the village of Cherenkóvo on the railway line, have been carefully explored. According to the analysis of Professor Alexéev, it belongs to the genuine coal formation.

Engineer Bogdanóvich classes this coal with the fatty dull kind found in the Lúnievsk pits. The basin of the river Great Bélaya and its tributaries also contain coal measures.

In connexion with the geological investigations conducted along the middle and lower reaches of the Angará, deposits of this mineral have been found along its banks, among which special attention is claimed by those near the vlllage of Selengínskaya. There are also deposits of coal in the region of the Angará and Léna, on the Irkút, southwest of Lake Baikál, and in the environs of Irkútsk.

Extensive beds of graphite, amounting to about 10,000,000 puds, are scattered over the Yeniséisk government, specially in the Turukhánsk district along the lower reaches of the Nízhniaya Tungúska and its tributaries. On being subjected to numerous tests, this graphite proved to be of excellent quality, comparable to that of Cumberland and Ceylon. The Irkútsk government also abounds in graphite deposits: within its confines, in the Tunkín mountains, graphite of excellent quality was found in 1842 by the merchant Aliber, and has been worked for a long time for Faber's pencil manufactory.

Naphtha has been discovered in small quantities within the range of the Irkútsk coal-bearing region called Idán, situated on the right bank of the Angará, 40 versts from Irkútsk. As stated by Engineer Bogdanóvich, coal containing such a large percentage of hydrogen points to the possibility of finding naphtha in connexion with it.

Salt beds are especially numerous in Eastern Siberia. In the Yeniséisk and Irkútsk governments, salt is obtained from brine. In the Yeniséisk government, it is produced in the Tumanshétsk works, situated in the Kansk district on the Biriúsa river, and in the Tróitsk works of the same district, on the river Usólka, tributary to the Taséeva. In the Irkútsk government, the valley of the Népa river, flowing on the left into the Nízhniaya Tungúska, abounds in saline springs; the brine flows from red sandstone, marl and clay, which evidently belong to the sub-devonian geological system. Salt is obtained at the Ust-Kutsk saltern, situated on tho river Kut, a tributary of the Léna. The famous salt spring Usólia is situated within a small distance of Irkútsk, 70 versts from the Angará and is worked by the Irkútsk works. Salt marshes, which represent a transition from the salt lakes, are to be found in various parts of the Yeniséisk government, along the course of the rivers Yus, Abakán and many others. Moreover, there are many brackish lakes in the Yeniséisk government, among which Lake Minusínsk, covering an area of 2½ square versts, is the most important.

Nephrite is found in large clusters at a distance of 50 versts from Irkútsk along the valleys of the rivers Bélaya, Kitói, Urík and Onóta.

Various coloured stones occur more plentifully in the southeastern part of the Irkútsk government.

Lapis lazuli is to be found on the Sliudiánka; garnet, on the Little Bystraya; serpentine, talc, chandrolite, lavrovite are scattered along the river Tálaya; while blue lime, spar, pink quartz, salite, bakalite, trenolite, aphanite and others are to be found on the Sliudiánka; and green apatite and black mica, near the Uluntái.

Fire-clay (kaolin) predominates on the banks of the Bélaya, close to the villages of Badáiskaya and Uzky Lug.

The Irkútsk government contains many mineral springs: the Turánsk springs having a temperature of about 30°R., situated near the Nílov hermitage on the river Ukhé-Ugún, at a distance of 250 versts from Irkútsk; Arshán-Su, a carbonic acid spring, situated within 40 versts from the Turánsk military post; the Okinsk springs on the Oká river, 500 versts from Irkútsk; the Barnaúl soda springs, near the village of Bólshe-Mamyrky, situated in the Nizhneúdinsk district.

Eastern Siberia is just as abundantly watered as its western part. The Yeniséisk government is watered by the great Yeniséi water system. Navigable throughout its entire course, the Yeniséi receives on the east its most important tributary the Tungúska or Angará which, affording a navigable way to Irkútsk, Lake Baikál and the Transbaikál, possesses a great importance for the trade of Eastern Siberia. The rivers Great Pit, Podkámennaya-Tungúzka are also important tributaries to the Yeniséi. Among the rivers flowing into the Arctic Ocean, the Abakán, bordering the Yakútsk territory, is deserving of notice; as yet scarcely explored, it flows through the government for a distance of 900 versts.

Numerous lakes occur in the government, but exclusively in its southern and most northern parts. The Ingól and particularly the Shiro lakes, containing mineral water, and situated in the Minusínsk district, are from year to year becoming better known. More lately, the department of State Domains has paid special attention to the properties of the lakes in the Yeniséisk governmeut and has undertaken the organisation of a health resort with a hospital for out-patients.

The Irkútsk government, which on the south-east is bordered by Lake Baikál for a distance of 600 versts, contains also numerous rivers and streams belonging to the basins of two large rivers, the Angará and Léna. The Angará represents the chief waterway of the government; along it is gathered the greater part of the population and it affords an easy communication by which the produce of the Irkútsk government is conveyed to the gold mines of the Yeniséisk government.

The Irkút, Kitói, Bélaya, Oká and Taséeva are the chief left tributaries of the Angará, which on the right receives the Kúda, Yánda, Ilím, Chadobéts and Irkátseva. The Léna, taking its rise on the northwestern slopes of the Baikál mountains, within 20 versts of Lake Baikál, waters the government for a length of 1,600 versts. Its slow current is raftable from the village of Kachúg, which is situated 200 versts from its estuary. This waterway is specially used for the transport of grain and manufactured articles to the Yakútsk territory. Its course is dotted by settlements belonging to the Verkholénsk and Kirénsk districts.

The climate of Eastern Siberia is raw and strictly continental. The influence of the sea is only felt on the extreme north of the Yeniséisk government, where it has little effect upon organic life. The average temperature at Krasnoyársk is +1.0, at Kansk —1.6, at Yeniséisk —2.4. at Minusínsk +0.,7.

The middle zone of the Yeniséisk government is open to all the western

The Khaitín china manufactory of Pereválov (Irkútsk gov.).

winds blowing from the plains and steppes of Western Siberia, while northern winds prevail iu the Minusínsk district, which to the south and west is sheltered by mountains.

The thickness of the snow cover, which has a great importance for agriculture, depends upon the wind. The unsheltered steppe lands are often subject to droughts; but little snow falls and it is easily blown away.

The climate of the Irkútsk government, which is more distant from the sea and has a high elevation, is still more continental than that of the Yeniséisk government and is characterised by a considerable annual range of temperature and continued cold. In the town of Irkútsk, the mean temperature during the year is —0.9, in the village of Kultúk on the Baikál,—1.5.

The minimum temperature in January is—45.6, the maximum rises to +34°6 in June shewing a range of 80°2. Summer is the dampest season; the small quantity of precipitation in winter is due to the scarceness of clouds caused by an almost total absence of wind and to the prevailing anticyclone.

The vegetation of Eastern Siberia is similar to that which covers the surface of its western part. Forests, containing the same tree species as in Western Siberia, are uninterrupted by any centres of population and stretch over immense areas representing an impenetrable virgin „taigá", in which firtrees predominate. Not with standing this extreme abundance of forests, the banks of the Yeniséi and other rivers which were once covered by a thick vegetation, are now quite bare. A regular system of forest management was only introduced into Siberia in the year 1895.

The fauna of Eastern Siberia is also the same as in its western part, represented by species of the túndra and of the Altái plateau. It may be mentioned as a remarkable phenomenon that the river Yeniséi forms the line on the east which is never passed by the beaver.

Population. The census of 1897 shewed a population of 1,066,419 (559,075 males, 507,344 females) in the Yeniséisk and Irkútsk governments. The former numbers a total of 559,902 (291,555 males, 268,347 females), while the latter contains a total of 506,517 (267,520 males, 238,997 females). In the Yeniséisk government the proportion is 92.0 women to 100 men, and in the Irkútsk government—85.6 women to 100 men. There are 0.24 inhabitant to every square verst in the Yeniséisk government.

The population is distributed according to districts in the following way:

Yeniséisk government.

DISTRICTS.	POPULATION.		
	males.	females.	total.
Achinsk	56,877	53,936	110,813
Krasnoyársk	49,409	44,904	94,313
Kansk	51,432	42,217	93,649
Minusínsk	92,558	90,091	182,649
Yeniséisk	34,245	30,969	65,214
Turukhánsk region	5,905	5,212	11,117
Usínsk region	1,129	1,018	2,147
Total	291,555	268,347	559,901

Irkútsk government.

DISTRICTS.	POPULATION.		
	males.	females.	total.
Nizhneúdinsk	49,916	33,687	80,603
Balagánsk	75,227	68,509	143,736
Irkútsk	81,155	77,582	158,737
Kirénsk	28,324	26,039	54,363
Verkholénsk	35,898	33,180	59,078
Total	267,520	238,997	506,517

The greater part of the population, represented by 865,600 inhabitants forming 81 per cent of the total number, is concentrated within the range of the Great Siberian Railway in the territories of the Achinsk, Krasnoyársk, Kansk, Minusínsk (Yeniséisk government), Nizhneúdinsk, Irkútsk (Irkútsk government) districts, comprising an area of 456,753 quare versts. The average proportion of the population in the region is 1.89 inhabitant to the square verst.

In the Yeniséisk government, the natives form almost 10 per cent of the total population; in the Irkútsk government, they are still more numerous, representing 21 per cent.

Upon settling in the Yeniséisk government, the Russians took possession of its best central portion driving one part of the natives towards the polar túndra in the Turukhánsk region and into the northern part of thé Yeniséisk district, and the other, towards the steppe lands of the districts of Minusínsk Achinsk and partially to the Kansk district. There is a well marked difference between these two native tribes evidenced by their type, life und pursuits.

Castrén includes the ancient and present population of the southern part of the Yeniséisk government in one Altái group, which he divides into five branches: Finns, Tungús, Mongols, Turks and Samoyéds.

The Finnish tribe was represented by the ancient, now extinct, Chud who have left some archaeological monuments at the foot of the Altái und Sayán mountains.

The Tungús people form the most numerous native tribe, throughout the territory of Eastern Siberia from the river Yeniséi to the Eastern Ocean and southwards to China. They are divided into settled, nomad and roaming or forest and reindeer Tungús.

They are mostly nominal Christians but, being ignorant of the Russian lauguage, and living at a great distance from Russian settlements, osit my profess Shamanism.

The Yeniséisk government contains a total of 3,500 Tungús.

The Mongolian stock is represented by the Kalmyks who, at a remote date, were a mighty race. Now they are entirely fused with the Turkish tribes.

Towards the end of the XVIII century, the Kalmyks emigrated in great numbers to the Chinese Empire; those remaining in Siberia are partly nomads, roaming over the highland bordered by the Sayán and northern Altái.

Museum of the Khaítin manufactory.

The Turkish tribes which are numerous fall into Tatar clans, known under the names of Méletsk, Kizylsk, Sagái, Káchinsk and Túbinsk Tatars.

The Melétsk Tatars dwelling in the Achinsk district along the river Chulym, are administered by a separate native local board. They ore quite russified, have adopted the Russian language and lead a settled life; their villages, called „ulús", with a population of 1,853 do not differ from true Russian villages.

The Kizylsk Tatars, numbering 5,825, occupy the south-western portion of the Achinsk and part of the Minusínsk districts; they are administered by their own local board; like the Melétsk Tatars they are russifled and belong to the orthodox religion.

The Sagáis, wandering along the river Abakán, are chiefly occupied with cattle breeding. They are all baptised but, as nomads, are still under the influence of their Shamans and retain a great attachment to heathen rites, which keep them in a condition of comparative savagery. They number 14,002 and are administred by the board of Askízsk.

The Káchinsk Tatars, (12,175) being nomadic cattlebreeders, dwell in the Káchinsk steppe bordered by the Abakán and Yus, and are under the management of the board of Abakán. A population of 12,175 Túbinsk Tatars, living on the Abakán and Uibát rivers, are reckoned to them.

Type of shamán of the polar túndra.

The Achinsk and Minusínsk districts contain about 33,855 natives; their number far from diminishing,has increased by 45 per ce nt dur ing tbe last 50 years.

The eventual passage from Shamanism to the Orthodox religion was effected gradually, together with the transition to more civilised conditions and the whole process of Russification; at the points where Russians entertained close relations with the Tatars and lived nearer to them, this transition was effected more quickly,while the same process was slow to penetrate to those tribes dwelling at a greater distance. A great number of natives openly professing the shamanistic faith are settled in the Minusínsk district, where various shamanistic figures, amulets or „toe" are to be found in the corner of each „yúrta" or tent.

The Samoyéd branch of the southern natives is far less numerous, being represented by only about 2,000 Koibáls and Matórs, wandering along the river Abakán; by 3,000 Bentírs settled on the middle reaches of the Abakán; by 400 Kamasíns, dwelling in camps in the Kansk district along the river Kan; and by 400 nomad Karagáses, dwelling in the Minusínsk district.

Besides the Tungús people, Ostiáks and Samoyéds, the Yuráks and Yakúts belong to the northern tribes of the Yeniséisk government, while the native population of the Irkútsk government is represented by Buriáts, Tungús, Tatárs, Ostiáks and Soyóts.

The class of exiles, playing an important part among the population of Ea stern Siberia, comprise the following divisions: 1) convicts, 2) exile-settlers deprived of all civil rights, 3) persons banished for a certain period, deprived of all personal and civil rights, 4) exiled by the administration without trial. From 950 to 1,000 convicts are annually forwarded by the Tiumén exile board to Eastern Siberia, to the penal settlements of the Irkútsk government, where they are kept in the Alexander Central Prison, in the Nicholas Iron Works and in the salterns of Irkútsk and Ust-Kútsk. The daily contingent of hard labour convicts varies from 1,400 to 2,000 in the Alexander Prison; from 50 to 200 in the Nicholas Works and from 45 to 50 in the Irkútsk State saltern.

The Irkútsk private saltern employs from 25 to 30 convicts and the Ust-Kútsk from 40 to 50.

In 1894, a considerable number of them were employed in the construction of the sixteenth section of the Midsiberian Railway, comprising a distance of 36 versts between the rivers Bélaya and Kitói. This experiment was attended by marked success.

The exile settlers who have passed the stage of hard labour, and those exiled by the administration retain their criminal propensities, and are a heavy burden upon the local population of Siberia, which they constantly demoralise.

According to the statistics of the Tiumén exile board, among the total number of 908,266 convicts exiled to Siberia from 1823 to 1898, 500,000 were forwarded during this period of 75 years to the government of Eastern Siberia and mainly to the Yeniséisk and Irkútsk governments.

Dress worn by shamán during the performance of religious rites.

Emigration. The Yeniséisk government, next to the favourite Tomsk region, is subject to the greatest pressure of emigration, The Russian peasants move especially to the Minusínsk district, where a great number of them have settled at their own risk, without any assistance from the Government,

From the year 1892, the Yeniséisk and Irkútsk governments have been occupied till quite lately with the choice of the localities to be colonised and with the regulation of the settlement system. Since the opening of traffic on the Great Siberian Railway, the pressure to the East has been gradually increasing; on this account, the Committee for the construction of the Siberian Railway, organised in the year 1896—1897, four medical and feeding stations within the confines of the Yeniséisk government: at the Achinsk station, for the assistance of the settlers tn the Achinsk district; at the station of Krasnoyársk, which is the meeting-point of emigrants bound for the Krasnoyársk and Minusínsk distrlcts; at the stations of Olgino and Kansk, for those bound for the Kansk district, where the greatest number of grants were made in 1895.

Before the opening of traffic on the Great Siberian Railway, cases of emigration to the Irkútsk government were quite a rarity, but now the organisation of medical and feeding stations has become most necessary. They are established at the station of Taishét for settlers moving to the western parts of the Nizhneúdinsk district; at the station of Tulún, for the colonisation of the Nizhneúdinsk district; and at the station of Irkútsk, which is a forwarding point whence the settlers move further east, towards the Transbaikál and Amúr.

Immense areas of untilled land suitable for colonisation, covering several millions of desiatins, are now being regulated with a view to future colonisation, which will bring new life into the region, and open wide prospects to the export of agricultural produce.

Idols of natives from the polar túndra.

The following buildings have been erected at the cost of the Emperor Alexander III fund, within the confines of the East-Siberian governments in order to meet the religious wants of the settlers and of the general population:

1) 3 wooden churches have been erected near the stations of Olginskaya, Petrúshkovo in the Yeniséisk government, and Zimá, in the Irkútsk government.

2) one wooden church in the village of Nóvo-Beriózovskoe, in the Minusínsk district.

3) 2 are in process of construction at the stations of Khánskaya and Polovína, in the Irkútsk government.

4) four are being built in the Achinsk district in the New-Alexander, Timónino, Yélnik and Gorby settlements.

5) two schools are being built in the New-Alexander and Iliá settlements in the Achinsk district.

Land tenure had never a regular character either in Eastern or in Western Siberia, a fact which has caused frequent abuses. Each peasant measured off for his use as much land as he wanted from the property of the community and, having cultivated it for some time, considered it as belonging to himself and his family.

According to the law regulating peasant land tenure, which since 1896 was put in force in the Tobólsk, Tomsk, Yeniséisk and Irkútsk governments, each peasant received a grant of 15 desiatins.

Beekeeping and cattle breeding are the chief sources of prosperity of the population in Eastern Siberia.

Agriculture in the Yeniséisk government reaches 59°30' N. lat. and even 61° N. lat. (for springcorn and barley). The entire Irkútsk government, exclusive of the Kirénsk district, is cultivable. Systems of husbandry vary in accordance with the locality and soil.

In the central zone of the Yeniséisk government, comprising the Krasnoyársk, Kansk, Yeniséisk and northern part of the Achinsk districts, the land is divided into two and even three parts, which are sown in rotation. However, the fallow land system also occurs.

In the forest regions, the trees are cut down, piled up into heaps and burnt on the spot. The land is then ploughed up (without the stumps being first drawn) and sown. After two or three rich crops have been raised, the land is allowed to lie waste for several years according to the nature of the soil, after which it is again brought under cultivation. In many places, springcorn is sown on winter-rye stubble fields without fresh ploughing. The two-field system is the predominating form of husbandry in the Irkútsk government, sometimes varied with the fallow land system practised in Nizhneúdinsk or with feeble attempts at the introduction of the more intensive threefield system, adopted in the Irkútsk district. The implements employed are of a primitive type: the „sokhá" (Russian plough) and, more to the south, the „sabán" (Little-Russian) and the „sokhá-kolesiánka". At the present time, new systems of husbandry are being introduced by the emigrants, and stores of agricultural machinery opened, chiefly from the Vótkinsk works.

Rye is mostly cultivated as a winter-corn; wheat, oats, „yáritsa", barley, buckwheat and millet are sown in spring, this season being preferred on account of the snowless winter, during which the corn is not sufficiently protected. The crops are very variable. The long continued early frosts in the autumn and the severe morning frosts are injurious to the spring corn.

Part of the working class being attracted to the gold mines and other profitable pursuits in the two old government of East Siberia, the quantity of grain sown and harvested scarcely suffices for future sowing and to supply the population for the year.

In 1896, which may be taken as an example for an average year, 1,992,461 chétverts of all kinds of grain were raised in the Yeniséisk, and 1,778,200 chétverts in the Irkútsk government, the population being 1,066,419. With such an insufficient extent of the cultivated area in Eastern Siberia, it is necessary to import grain and its products from the contiguous government of Western Siberia, especially for the maintenance of the local distilleries and to supply the people employed in the numerous gold-mines.

Besides agriculture, cattle-breeding is also a very important occupation of the population, representing the sole resource of the nomad natives of the Minusínsk and Achinsk districts, of the roaming population of the Turukhánsk region in the Yeniséisk government, and of the natives of Balagànsk and Verkholénsk in the Irkútsk government.

According to recent information, the Yeniséisk government possesses approximately 1,792,850 head of live stock, inclusive of 488,931 horses, 432,149 cattle, 714,570 sheep, 95,511 swine, 32,689 goats and 29,000 reindeer. At the same time, the Irkútsk government contains 1,000,464 head, represented by 264,856 horses, 335,549 cattle, 265,379 sheep, 85,862 swine, 48,045 goats and 773 reindeer.

The proportion of live stock to the total population of Eastern Siberia is very small and does not meet its wants, this important branch of husbandry being but very insufficiently developed throughout Eastern Siberia. Considerable droves of cattle are brought every year to the Yeniséisk and Irkútsk governments to supply the population, from the Tomsk government, the Semipalátinsk region and Mongolia.

The Soyót cattle, driven from China, are worthy of attention, being very fleshy and fine (about 2—2½ arshins high) with a weight of about 25 puds; but the cows do not gíve much milk. This cattle is brought from China by two different ways: one begins at the upper reaches of the river Kemchík and reaches the sources of the Kantegír and further the river Abakán; the other traverses the valley of the river Usa and comes to the upper reaches of the Oi. The Soyót cattle receive an admixture of the local stock and are forwarded by rafts along the Yeniséi to the north, mostly to the Krasnoyársk and Yeniséisk districts.

Beekeeping is much practised in the households of the Achinsk and Minusínsk districts, containing about 45 thousand bee-hives. Little Russian settlers, who are more experienced beekeepers, are introducing new and more rational systems.

Fishing The natives of the northern part of the Yeniséisk district and of the Turukhánsk region and those settled on the shore of the Baikál in the Irkútsk government are chiefly engaged in the fishing industry.

The peasants and native population dwelling on the Yeniséi and its well watered and abundant tributaries depend upon a few important fish-traders, who however do not at all contribute to the development of this profitable industry. The fish is salted in a most primitive way on the bank of

Town of Yeniséisk (phot. by Kytmánov).

the rivers, and although the Yeniséi basin is most abundantly provided with fish, which is not inferior to that of the Irtysh and Ob basin, it is not exported from Eastern Siberia, which is supplied from the adjacent Tomsk and Tobólsk governments with salted and dried fish.

Hunting is an important industry in both governments of Eastern Siberia practised on a considerable scale by the natives especially in the Kirénsk district of the Irkútsk government, in its southern part on the spurs of the Sayán, and in the Turukhánsk country, in the Yeniséisk government.

The birds and animals and the modes of hunting them are the same as in the the Tomsk government. The annual value of the industry is about R. 300,000.

Cedar-nut gathering, which is a great help for the natives and Russian peasants, is carried on thoughut Eastern Siberia in all the places touching the taigá, in the same manner as in the neighbouring Tomsk and Tobólsk governments.

In the southern part of the government, nut-traders also collect larch-tree „sulphur“, which is chewed by the natives and older inhabitants of Siberia.

Domestic industries have a second-rate importance in Eastern Siberia, being but imperfectly developed. Carpentry, coopering, the blacksmith's art, tarburning, earthenware and brick manfacture, knitting, thread spinning, weaving rough wool, cloth and worsted mittens and tanning sheep and other skins are the industries practised by 4 per cent of the total male population.

Although this region is richly endowed with natural wealth, the manufactures and industries do not meet the local demand, and are insufficiently developed, on account of the scarcity of the population, the high rate of wages and the attraction of capital to the goldmining industry. In 1896, the Yeniséisk government reckoned 485 factories and works with an output of R. 2,158,131, while the Irkútsk government contained 135, with R. 2,810,439.

There are 19 distilleries (R. 1,607,568), 168 tanneries (R. 576,832), 2 foundries and works (R. 508,000) and 5 salterns (R. 190,000).

Town of Yeniséisk. Nunnery of the Virgin of Iberia (phot. by Kytmánov).

The following manufactories are to be mentioned:

1) The first and only sugar refinery established in Siberia (in 1889) is situated in the Minusínsk district.

Experiments conducted over several years have shewn that the climate and soil are favourable for the cultivation of beetroot; hence the enterprise is being gradually extended. The refinery has an output of R. 85,000.

2) The china and earthenware manufactory, belonging to the Siberian China, Glass and Pottery Company of the Irkútsk merchant Pereválov, situated in the Irkútsk government.

3) The Abakán iron works and foundries of Rátkov-Rozhnóv in the Yeniséisk government, and the Nicholas works in the Irkútsk government, belonging to the joint stock company organised by Mámontov.

4) The cloth manufactory of Mr. Belogolóvy in the Irkútsk government.

Trade. Eastern Siberia consumes the manufactured articles brought from industrial centres, and raw agricultural produce imported from Western Siberia. The goods are sold at several permanent centres of commerce and at the numerous fairs held in the towns and villages.

Town of Minusínsk.

The export of raw materials from the East Siberian governments is very small, because most of the local agricultural products are sold within the limits of their own territory, and also because the working-class, neglecting agriculture, streams to the gold-mines, or is occupied with the carriage of goods by road along the highway of Siberia, which till lately was regarded as a most profitable employment. However, upon the opening of traffic on the Great Siberian Railway, the working-class will be obliged to return to agriculture and cattle-breding, thus giving both a further development. A like result will be obtained by the emigration movement and the colonisation of the governments of Eastern Siberia which, possessing such great natural wealth, will in the near future, like Western Siberia, become a granary of Europe, and supply its markets with animal produce.

The organisation of a regular Arctic Ocean route through the estuary of the Yeniséi, and the improvement of the navigation on the Léna and Angará will also contribute to the development of the commercial relations of Eastern Siberia and increase its productive capacity.

The Yakútsk territory, lying between 54° and 73° N. lat. and 73° and 141° E. long., is under the Governor-General of Irkútsk and administratively represents a separate territory, covering a superficial area of 3,452,655 square versts with a total population of 261,731 (136,061 males and 125,670 females), divided into 5 districts: Yakútsk (pop. 143,799), Verkholénsk (pop. 12,182), Viliúisk (pop. 67,418), Olékminsk (pop. 34,018), and Kolymsk (pop. 4,314).

The total absence of fertile land renders this region unfit for permanent Russian colonisation, nature itself predestined it for wandering tribes which, from a remote date, have been inhabitants of these polar regions, and fornomads who, having removed from the Central Asiatic steppes are now acclimatised and habituated to this polar forest zone.

Holy Trinity Monastery, Kirénsk (Irkútsk gov).

This far distant borderland can only be to Russia what North America, with the exception of Canada and Oregon is to Europe, offering a wide scope for the exploitation of the natural wealth contained in the immense area of this coldest country of the Old World.

Town of Yakútsk. Cathedral and remains of the ancient wooden fortification (phot. by Gavrílov).

Its wealth is chiefly represented by auriferous gravel. Mining, the only industry in this region, is widely developed, with an output of several million rubls.

Gold is obtained in two different ways: 1) either the deposits are worked after the removal of the covering of turf, or the gold is obtained from the auriferous gravel, found in the bottom of rivers which for the purpose are led into new beds by means of dams and other contrivances.

2) The metal is also obtained from underground galleries lying sometimes at a considerable depth; the gravel is brought to the snrface by vertical shafts by means of a horse-winch.

The work in the mines is carried on in a perpetually frozen soil, wood fuel being employed for melting it. In these mines the underground works are usually conducted by means of the pillar system, the worked spaces being faced with stone.

Town of Viliúisk.

The mines now being worked are situated at a distance of 1,700 versts north-east of Irkútsk, in the Olekmínsk district, and are divided into the Olekmínsk and Vitím groups under the management of the Irkútsk Mining Department. The working of the mines dates from 1851, the annual output of gold during 30 years varied from 419 to 939 puds. The maximum percentage of gold is 8 zolotniks 19 dólias to 100 puds of gravel, obtained by the Alexándrovsk mining company of the Vitím group.

The richest mines are: the Barabá mines of the goldmining company of the Olékminsk district, yielding from 72 to 85 puds per annum. Those of the gold mining company of the Olékminsk district yield from 84 to 129 puds per annum. From 160 to 180 puds are annually obtained in the mines belonging to the Lensk gold mining company of the Olékminsk district, and from 169 to 229 by the Vitím company in the same district.

BIBLIOGRAPHY:

1) Vólosts and settlements in the Yeniséisk government, pub. by the Stat. Commit. of the Minist. of the Int. St. Pbg. 1895. 2) Volosts and centres of population in the Irkútsk government, pub. by the Stat. Commit. of the Ministr. of the Int. St. Pbg. 1894. 3) Supplement to the reprts of the governors of the Yeniséisk, Irkútsk and Yakútsk governments presented to His Majesty. 4) Guide to the journey of His Imperial Highness the Tsesarévich. St. Pbg. 1891. 5) Siberia and the Great Siberian Railway, pub. by the Ministry of Finance. St. Pbg. 1896. 6) The Yeniséisk government, past and present, by Látkin, St. Pbg. 1892. 7) Siberian trade and industry calendars, by Románov, 1897—1899. Tomsk. 8) Geological explorations and prospectings on the Siberian Railway, pt. II, K. Bogdanóvich. Materials on the geology of the useful minerals of the Irkútsk government. St. Pbg. 1896, pt. III. Works of the Midsiberian Mining Party in 1894. St. Pbg. 1896. 9) Reports of State Secretary Kúlomzin after his journey to Siberia to investigate the emigration movement, presented to His Imperial Majesty. St. Pbg. 1896. 10) Appendices to the report of the Minister of Agriculture and State Domains, after his journey to Siberia in the autumn of 1895 and in the summer of 1898, presented to His Imperial Majesty. St. Pbg. 1899. 11) Natives of Minusínsk and Achinsk. Notes by Kuznetsóv and Mrs. Kulikóv. Publ. by the Stat. Commit. Krasnoyársk, 1898. 12) List of the most important gold mining companies and firms. Bisárnov, publ. by the St. Pbg. Mining Department, 1897. 13) Workmen employed at the gold-mines of Siberia, by V. I. Semévsky. St. Pbg. 1898.

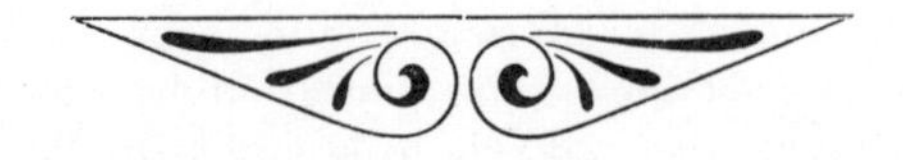

The Midsiberian Railway.

Direction of the line.—Character of the country.—Cost of construction.—Description of stations and localities traversed by the line.—Station of Ob.—Nóvo-Nikoláevsk settlement.—Sokúr.—Oyásh.—Bolótnoye.—Polomóshnaya.—Litvínovo.—Taigá.—Súdzhenka.—Izhmórskaya.—Berikúlskaya.—Town of Maríinsk.—Súslovo.—Tiázhin. — Itát. — Bogotól.—Krásnaya.—East-Siberian frontier.—Town of Achinsk. — Tarútino. — Chernoréchenskaya. — Kemchúg.—Kachá.—Mínino.—Town of Krasnoyársk.—Basin of the Yeniséi.— Station of Yeniséi.—Zykovo.—Sorókino.—Kamarchága.—Balái.-Olginskaya.—Tróitsko-Zaoziórnaya.—Tyrbyl.—Petrúshkovo.—Town of Kansk.—Ilánskaya.—Ingásh.—Tínskaya.—Kliuchínskaya.—Yúrty.—Taishét.—Bairónovka.—Razgón —Alzamai.—Zamzór.—Kamyshét.—Uk.—Town of Nizhneúdinsk.—Khingúi.—Khudoyelánskaya.—Kurzán.—Tulún. — Azéi. — Sheragúl.—Kuitún.—Kimeltéi.—Zimá.—Tyrét.—Zalarí.—Golovínskaya.—Kulutík. —Cheremkóvo. — Polovína. — Málta.— Télma.—Sukhóvskaya — Innokéntievskaya.—Town of Irkútsk.—Irkútsk-Baikál branch.—Tomsk branch.—Town of Tomsk.

THE Midsiberian railway commences at the right bank of the river Ob, at 55° N., and proceeds north-east to the town of Maríinsk and, running parallel to the 56° N, lat., reaches the town of Kansk (56° 13′ N. lat.); from this point, the line abruptly turns south-east, following this direction to the town of Irkútsk (52° 16′ N. lat.). From Irkútsk the line descends south-east to Lake Baikál and terminates somewhat south of the 52-nd parallel.

The line runs through the Tomsk and Maríinsk districts of the Tomsk government, through the districts of Achinsk, Krasnoyársk and Kansk in the Yeniséisk government, through those of Nizhneúdinsk, Balagánsk and Irkútsk, in the Irkútsk government and passes through the towns of Maríinsk Achinsk, Krasnoyársk, Kansk, Nizhneúdinsk, Irkútsk, and the town of Tomsk by the Tomsk branchline. The country traversed by the railway is essentially mountainous and woody, and is intersected by spurs of the Altái, Alatau and Sayan mountains. The mixed forest flora, alternating with meadows and at times cultivated fields, gradually passes into taigá and dense growths of fir. The mountain spurs offer a series of picturesque panoramas, but present great difficulties for the construction of the railway.

The country traversed by the railway may be divided into the following sections, according to the nature of the locality: the Ob-Achinsk section, 550 versts, is level land; Achinsk-Nizhneúdinsk, 698 versts, mountainous; Nizhneúdinsk to Zimá, 239 versts, hilly; from Zimá to Polovína, 138 versts, the country is mountainous; Polovína to Irkútsk, 90 versts, elevated land; from Irkútsk to the Baikál, 64 versts, also an elevated section; the Tomsk branch, 89 versts, mountainous.

From the town of Maríinsk, the line runs in proximity to the Siberian highway crossing several times its sinuous course.

The Krasnoyársk-Kansk section alone is more distant from the highway sometimes running at a distance of 30 versts from it, across a country offering easier technical conditions for the construction of the railway. The preliminary surveys for the construction of the Midsiberian railway were conducted in 1887—1888 by Engineer N. P. Mezhenínov, who was also entrusted with the construction of the line itself

The construction of the Irkútsk-Baikál branch was carried out under the direction of Engineer Púshechnikov, chief constructor of the Transbaikál railway.

The total length of the railway from the Ob station to Innokéntievskaya, near the town of Irkútsk, representing the main line, is 1,715 $1/2$ versts. With the Tomsk branch line, the total length of Midsiberian railway amounts to 1,868$1/2$ versts.

The estimated cost of the Ob-Krasnoyársk section, inclusive of rolling stock and rails was R. 36,257,171, or R. 50,994 per verst.

The cost of the construction of the Tomsk branch line was estimated at R. 2,494,198 or R. 27,917 per verst.

The estimated cost of the Krasnoyársk-Irkútsk section was, inclusive of rails and rolling stock, R. 71,779,464, or R. 71,493 per verst. The total cost of the whole Midsiberian railway from Ob to Irkútsk, inclusive of the Tomsk branch line, was R. 110,530,833.

The cost of the section from Innokéntievskaya to the Baikál 64 versts long was, without rolling stock, R. 3,626,336, or R. 56,660 per verst.

1) **Ob**, III class station. Buffet. (8 versts from Krivoshchékovo, 1,332 versts from Cheliábinsk.)

The station is situated on the lofty and picturesque right bank of the river Ob. Previous to the construction of the line, this hilly bank was covered with a dense virgin forest of fir, descending by abrupt cliffs to the edge of the broad waters of the river. The station buildings stand on a plot of land bordered by fir wood. As the starting point of the Midsiberian railway, the station is provided with a spacious brick enginehouse and workshops with fitting and waggon shops, a smithy and foundry, and locksmith and turner's shops, employing a total of 450 workmen.

A wooden church in honour of the Holy Prophet Daniel has been erected near the station at the cost of the Emperor Alexander III fund. A spacious wooden building containing a two class school for the children of railway employees stands on the other side of the station nearer to the Ob. This building contains a large room with a stage for amateur theatricals organised for charitable purposes by the railway employees; it is also used for Sunday lectures given to the workmen. Classes of sacred choral music are held in the school. With a view to encourage the singing and public lectures, the Managing Director of the Siberian Committee, State Secretary Kúlomzin presented the school with a harmonium and a magic-lantern. Close to it, stands a railway hospital with a reception room for the sick. From here a branch line runs to the river Ob, 3 versts in length and connected

Station of Ob.

with the saw-mill belonging to the Cabinet of His Majesty. This branch was constructed for the transport of goods brought by water to supply the demand of the Midsiberian and Transbaikál railways. In connexion with the increasing export of grain and animal products, from the Altái mining district, enlarging the operations of the Ob station, the branch line and the landing stage on the river will acquire great importance; the goods bound for Eastern Siberia and ofr the western markets of the Empire will be brought from the Barnaúl and Bíisk districts by river, the right bank of the river Ob being particularly well adapted for the anchorage and unloading of rafts, steamers and barges. These favourable conditions explain the preference shewn by senders of goods conveying them to the station of Ob instead of that of Krivoshchékovo, although it makes a difference, if they are sent west, of 1 R. 53 kop. per waggon loaded with grain. There are yet no arrangements at the landing-stage for storing and keeping grain and other water-carried goods; this is why the goods are kept on the barges or unloaded on the river's bank, the railway administration assuming no responsibility for possible damage.

Landing-stage on the Ob.

This unsatisfactory state of things greatly injures the interests of the owners and senders of goods and a better organisation of the landingplace is imperatively required, such as the construction of warehouses and elevators. The total quantity of grain conveyed from the station of Ob to Irkútsk, which receives the largest stream of grain from the fertile Altái, remains so far unascertained, on account of the recent opening of traffic on the main line, viz. in autumn of 1898. According to certain commercial data and information regarding the stock of grain within range of the station awaiting conveyance, the annual transport of goods from the Ob station may be estimated at 5,000,000 puds. Upon the opening of traffic to the east, towards the end of the year 1898, the amount of grain transported from the Ob station was 1,387,087 puds; half of this quantity was sent to Eastern Siberia: 369,562 puds to Krasnoyársk, 187,878 to Irkútsk, 41,288 to Tulún and 30,673 to Kansk.

View of the landing-place on the Ob.

One of the most important and best fitted medical and feeding stations for the benefit of the settlers bound for Tomsk, the Altái mining district and for the lands of the Cabinet

The settlement of Nóvo-Nikoláevsk.

of His Majesty is situated near the station, on the right bank of the Ob, and is the residence of an emigration official. Previous to the construction of the railway, a small peasant settlement Gúsevka, belonging to the volost of Krivoshchékovo in the Tomsk district with 24 houses and a population of 104 inhabitants, stood near the station. These peasants were furnished with land from His Majesty's Cabinet. From the year 1893, upon the construction of the Ob-Krasnoyársk section, the future commercial importance of the Ob station and its environs became apparent; peasants long settled in the Tobólsk, Tomsk and Yeniséisk governments, and a great nnmber of fresh emigrants from European Russia, streamed to this small settlement and even occupied without permission the adjacent Cabinet lands of His Majesty.

With a view to regulate the pressure and to meet the demands of the population, the Administration of the Cabinet lands allotted a piece of land watered by the small stream Kámenka, a tributary of the Ob, for permanent settlement by the emigrated households. It bears the name of Novo-Nikoláevsk settlement and contains a population of 15,000.

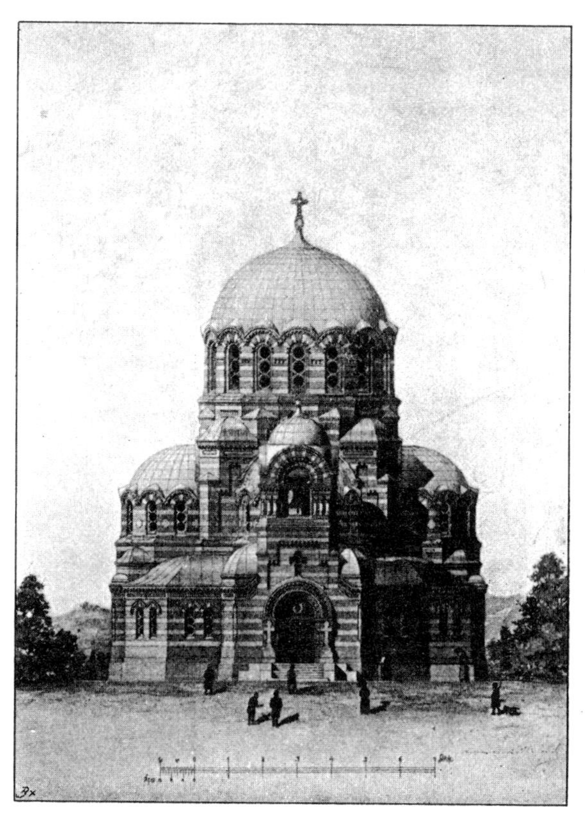

Church in the settlement of Nóvo-Nikoláevsk.

An area of 16,000 desiatins and 2,682 sites for building houses were granted to the population by the Administration of the Cabinet lands. Of these. 1,732 are already occupied and 1,130 are still free. They are leased for 30 years to all comers irrespective of class, for an annual rent of from R. 2. 50 kop. to R. 10, according to the situation of the spot chosen. The Administration reserves the right to raise the rent 10 per cent. after the lapse 6 years. Each building plot is 15 sazhens along the street and 17 on the yard side. The peasant population, having sreceived additions of burgesses and representative of the official class, has assumed the appearance of an industrial town.

In the centre of the settlement, stretching for ten versts along the banks of the Oká and its affluent the Kámenka, a fine brick church is being erected in honour of St. Alexander Névsky at the cost of His Imperial Majesty and some private individuals. This edifice will serve as a monument to the Tsar Pacificator, the initiator and founder of the Great Siberian Railway. Pending its completion, divine service is held in a prayer-house. So far the settlement possesses but two two-class schools, one a parish school, the other founded by the Administration of the Cabinet lands. There is no hospital, the sick being attended to as outpatients at the emigrant station.

All branches of industry are practised in the settlement. There are 113 shops and stores, a beer cellar, 4 beer shops, 2 wine cellars, 2 taverns, 7 bakeries, 1 confectionary shop, an hotel with coffee-rooms, furnished rooms and

50 inns. The bazaars do a brisk business in agricultural produce which, especially in winter, is brought a considerable distanceas much as 200 and 300 versts- from the Barnaúl and Bíisk districts. According to the cart-duty paid on the imports of local produce, the total business of the markets amounts to about R. 2,000,000 The settlement possesses a volunteer fire brigade. A hundred common hackney coaches without springs ply according to tariff: 20 kop. a drive, 30 kop. an hour, 50 kop. for passenger with luggage to the market place, and .70 kop. for a drive beyond the river Kámenka. There are several offices for the transport of goods, and an intelligence office giving information on the prices of goods etc.

Embankment at 28 verst.

After having crossed the river Ob, the railway line ascends to the watershed of the rivers Ob and Tom along the valley of the small river Yeltsóvka, and reaches the Sokúr ridge traversing a picturesque and woody country.

2) **Sokúr.** V class station (42 versts from Krivoshchékovo, 1374 from Cheliábinsk). The village of Sokúr (Barlákskoye) with a population of 700, in the Tomsk district, is situated within 12 versts of the station. A small quantity of rye and rye-meal is forwarded hence eastwards. From this point, the line descends to the valley of the river Oyásh, and after twice crossing the Bálta, its upper tributary, ascends through a mountainous country to the watershed of the rivers Oyásh and Inia falling into the Ob.

Bridge over the Krutáya Bálka.

3) **Oyásh.** V class station (84 v. from Krivoshchékovo, 1416 from Cheliábinsk). The village of Oyásh, with a population of 654, possesses a local village board, belongs to the Tomsk district, and is situated on the Siberian highway, within 10 versts of the station. The population forwards grain to the East. In the year 1898, about 63,188 puds of wheat-meal were conveyed from here to Achinsk, Krasnoyársk and Irkútsk. Leaving the station, the line descends to the rivers Sarbayázh and Oyàsh, spanning both by bridges 15 sazhens in length. Further on it passes through a swampy country.

4) **Bolótnoye.** III class station. Buffet. (126 v. from Krivoshchékovo, 1458 v. from Cheliábinsk).

The village of Bolótinskoye having a population of 590 belongs to the Tomsk district. It contains a wooden church to St. Nicholas and a parish school. Oats and wheat meal are forwarded east.

Station of Oyàsh.

Reaching the river Lebiázhia, the line crosses it at the 140 verst, by a wooden bridge of 20 sazhens. Ascending futher to the upper reaches of the river Yurgá, the line following the valley of that river crosses the Tom with its high banks at the 161 verst, near the village of Polomóshnoye by an iron bridge with 6 spans of 40 sazhens, and road-way upon the lower-chord girder of the semiparabolic system, supported on stone piers and abutments.

5) **Polomóshnaya.** IV class station (165 v. from Krivoshchékovo, 1497 v. from Cheliábinsk) is situated 4 versts from the bridge over the river Tom and near the trading village of Polomóshnoye belonging to the Tomsk district. It contains a population of about 500 and has 2 shops for manufactured articles, 4 other shops, 2 mercery shops and a wine-cellar.

Brídge at 98 verst.

The Engineer Knorre, owner of the vast railway workshops established for the construction of the bridge over the Tom, built at his own cost a church for the workmen which, now that the work is completed, will be removed to the station of Polomóshnaya.

A certain quantity of oats, rye and wheat-meal is forwarded from the environs of the station towards the east. From this point, the line ascends and crosses the small river Sosnóvka at the 185 verst over a culvert having a breadth of 3 sazhens laid under an embankment 8 sazhens high.

6) **Litvínovo.** V class station (191 v. from Krivoshchékovo, 1523 v. from Cheliábinsk). The line reaches the next station running through a level country and continuous taigá.

Bridge over the Lebiázhia.

7) **Taigá.** III class station. Buffet. (222 v. from Krivoshchékovo, 1554 v. from Cheliábinsk).

It received its name on account of its situation on a desert and desolate spot, amidst a virgin forest or taigá. From this point, a branch line runs to Tomsk. The station of Taigá, although surrounded by a desolate and inhospitable country poorly supplied with water, occupies an important place on the Great Siberian Railway as the junction of two branches. A numerous population, formed of settlers and the former inhabitants of the country, established a settlement on the line. At the present time, the number of inhabitants exceeds 2,000 exclusive of workmen employed on the line and in the workshops. A church in honour of St. Andrew of Crete was erected near the station, at the cost of the Emperor Alexander III fund, in commemoration of the 17-th October, 1888; there are also a house for the clergy and a school. The station has no importance as a centre of commerce; the inhabitants principally earn their living from the railway, which traverses a thinly populated country.

It must be said that thls point of junction was inconsiderately chosen. There are only a few small hollows in the vicinity, poorly provided with water; for this reason, to supply the engines and the numerous class of workmen and station employees, water is brought to the station in large reservoirs.

Bridge over the Tom.

Further east, the Great Siberian Railway runs through a level country covered with a dense and impenetrable virgin forest composed of pine, fir, aspen and birch.

8) **Súdzhenka.** V class station (259 v. from Krivoshchékovo, 1591 v. from Cheliábinsk). Stands at the head of the river Chendát, tributary of the Yáya and is better provided with water han the station of Taigá. Within a range of 20 versts, there are nine important settlements, some of them being recently established by the emigrants. The station is situated amidst rich coal deposits and is very important as a centre supplying the Midsiberian railway with fuel. Coal deposits, which are partly worked, have been discovered near the station close to the line and in its environs, in the settlement of Lebedínskoe and along the rivers Mazálovsky-Kitát and Achledát. At the 246 verst, a mine belonging to the Government lies within 600 sazhens of the main line; near by, two mines belong to private concerns, one to Mr. Michelson, the other to the Lebediánsk Company. The coal which is obtained from the Government mine is loaded at a terminus with 12 cars; from the mines belonging to Michelson, coal is conveyed by a branch line. According to investigations made in 1896 and 1897 by Engineer Krasnopólsky, all the carboniferous strata within the range of the Midsiberian railway, and those lying southwards along the river Borzás, form the continuation of deposits scattered throughout the neighbouring Kuznétsk district. Special attention must be paid to the Anzhér coalmine on the Anzhér river, tributary of the Alchedát. According to some existing data, a brilliant future lies in store for the mines of Súdzhenka. The coal occurs in thick seams and is considered fit to serve as fuel for engines; this is why the exploitation of the shafts laid by the Mining Department is left to the administration of the Midsiberian railway. Out of the fund for auxiliary undertakings connected with the construction of the Siberian railway, R. 82,000 have been appointed for this work, the additional outlay being provided by the capital assigned for the exploitation of the line.

Culvert on the river Sosnóvka.

The village of Súdzhenko with 794 inhabitants is situated within 9 versts of the station; it belongs to the Tomsk district and contains a village board.

Previous to the construction of the railway, the country within the range of the line lying east of Súdzhenka, was thinly populated; at present grants of wooded land in the taigá have been allotted to the emigrants on both sides of the line, some of which are already occupied while others are being settled. From the station of Súdzhenka, the line descends to the valley of the river Yáya and crosses it near the settlement of Shegárka by a bridge (at 279 v.) with an opening of 50 sazhens, having two spans supported by stone piers. At many places along the Yáya, outcrops of gabbro have been employed for engineering work on the line and for the casing of the bridge over the Kíya.

Porphyries occur on the right tributary of the Yáya, the Alchedát, beyond the Iversk settlement, and are used for the foundation of railway buildings. Gold mines are found southward of the line, throughout the basin of the Yáya and its tributaries the Golden Kitát, the Kelbés, the Borzás and others.

It may be stated as a fact that almost all the valleys which abut on the rivers contain a certain quantity of auriferous gravel occurring not only in valleys, but also on hills. The mines which are now worked on the tributaries of the Yáya yield about 5 puds of gold annually.

Station of Taigá.

9) **Izhmórskaya.** IV class station (293 v.) (from Krivoshchékovo, 1625 v. from Cheliábinsk).

The village of Izhmórskoe (pop. 650) is near the station, in the Maríinsk district. It contains a wooden church. A considerable quantity of grain is forwarded to the east from this region. In 1898, the export amounted to 22,778 puds of rye, 53,903 puds of oats, 5,013 puds of barley, 10,500 puds of rye flour.

From here, the line runs parallel to the Siberian highway, along the watershed of the rivers Yáya and Kíya, where a thin birch wood alternates with pastures and fields.

10) **Berikúlskaya.** V class station (329 v. from Krivoshchékovo, 1661 v. from Cheliábinsk). A village of the same name with a population of 949 is

situated within 12 versts, in the Maríinsk district. It possesses a stone church of St. Michael, the Archistrategus.

The fertile region surrounding the station yields annually a considerable quantity of grain and flour, exported to Eastern Siberia. In 1898, the total exports amounted to 13,615 puds of rye, 82,894 puds of oats, 1,528 puds of barley, 36,000 puds of rye flour and 2,275 puds of oil-seed.

Church at station of Taigá.

From the station, the line descends to the valley of the Kíya river and, at the 345 verst, spans the Antibés by a wooden bridge with an opening of 20 sazhens. Ascending further to the secondary watershed of the river Antibés at the 338 to 341 versts of the line, lies a large swamp having 2½ versts in length and an average depth of 1.20 sazhen.

11) **Maríinsk.** III class station. Buffet. (361 v. from Krivoshchékovo, 1693 v. from Cheliábinsk). The district town of Maríinsk is situated in proximity to the station (pop. 8,300; 4,323 males, 3,977 females), (56° 18′ N. lat., 57°25′ E. long.). It stands on the river Kíya, left tributary of the Chulym,

and on the great Siberian highway. Previously it was represented by the small village of Kíiskoe, which in 1856 was converted into a town. In 1857 it received the name of Mariínsk. The town contains 1,017 houses, mainly wooden, two orthodox churches, a stone cathedral of St. Nicholas, and a wooden church at the cemetery in honour of All Saints; a Jewish synagogue of stone

Schools: 2 urban elementary schools for boys and girls, 2 parish schools, a reading school. A poorhouse, a night shelter, an apothecary's shop. The factories are represented by 5 tanneries, 2 soap-boileries, 1 mead and beer brewery, 5 butter manufactories and two tallow-boileries. The output of the factories does not exceed a value of R. 50,000 to 70,000 per annum.

There are 32 commercial houses and manufactories, 37 shops, 6 inns, 2 taverns, 1 wine cellar, 10 wine-shops and no hotels.

Bridge over the Yáya.

Furnished rooms at R. 1 a day. The town revenue is estimated at R. 20,000 to 25,000 per annum. Upon the whole, the commercial operations transacted in the town are not considerable, in spite of the great percentage of Jews in its population and the proximity to the gold mines. This is explained by the fact that trade is concentrated in other localities lying near to the sources of industry, and the preference shewn by the Jews for a rapacious exploitation of the gold mines.

On the 3 and 4 July 1891, the town was honoured by the visit of His Imperial Majesty the present Emperor Nicholas II, then Heir Apparent to the throne, on his way from the Far East.

His Majesty was greeted by the representatives of the town, by school children and a crowd of people, and visited the cathedral of St. Nicholas the Miracle-worker. On the 4 July, His Majesty resumed his journey, and on his way to Tomsk was welcomed at every village by the people, who greeted the Imperial Traveller with holy images and bread and salt, thus manifesting their cordial hospitality. The river Kíya, on which the town stands, is about 328 versts long and from 10 to 50 sazhens wide. Navigation is carried on only with rafts; gold mines belonging to the Transaltái group occur on its upper reaches.

Town of Maríinsk.

The most important trading firms are represented by Akselrud (gold, grocery, trinkets, colonial goods), Gurévich (manufactured goods), Izikson (jewelry), Savéliev (manufactured and other articles; tannery, soap-boilery, brewery), Yudalévich (manufactured goods and a distillery).

A great quantity of grain products, mainly oats and rye flour, are forwarded to the east from the environs of the station.

Bridge over the Kíya.

In 1898, the export was 270,355 puds. Within two versts of the station, the line crosses the Kíya by a bridge of 100 sazhens (at 364 verst). It has four iron spans of 25 sazhens each, with roadway upon the lower chord, and stone piers.

From the Kíya, the line begins its ascent by level grades (0.008) to the high watershed of the latter and the river Tiázhin, the right affluent of the Kíya. The highest point of the watershed rises to an altitude of 64 sazhens above the station of Maríinsk.

12) **Súslovo.** V class station (384 v. from Krivoshchékovo, 1716 v. from Cheliábinsk). The village of the same name (pop. 1861) in the Maríinsk district is situated a verst and a half from the station. It contains a wooden church of St. Nicholas, a school and an elementary school for girls, 4 shops and 2 tanneries. Leaving the station, the line resumes its ascent to the

watershed and reaches its highest point at the 400 verst. Further on, the line descends to the river Kozyliúk, crossing a stone culvert with an opening of 2.50 sazhens under an embankment of 6 sazhens. A small quantity of rye is forwarded from here to the east. In 1898, the export amounted to 22,183 puds, mainly oats and rye flour.

13) **Tiázhin.** V class station. (418 v. from Krivoshchékovo, 1750 v. from Cheliábinsk). The village of the same name (pop. 1206) is situated at a distance of 4 versts, in the Maríinsk district.

The village possesses a church in honour of St Nicholas, a school, a parish school and 3 shops. This region supplies the East with grain. In 1898, as much as 43,394 puds, mainly oats and rye flour, were forwarded from this point.

From the station, the line continues its descent to the river Tiázhin, the right tributary of the Kíya and, within 3 versts of the station, crosses the latter at the 421 verst by an iron bridge of 20 sazhens.

Bridge over the Kosúl.

Hence the line ascends to the watershed of the rivers Tiázhin and Itát, for a considerable distance running by maximum level grades (0.008). Upon reaching its highest point, the line descends by lighter grades to the next station.

14) **Itát.** V class station (451 v. from Krivoschékovo, 1783 v. from Cheliábinsk). The village of Itát is situated at a distance of 4 versts on the Siberian highway in the Maríinsk district. It contains a wooden church of St Nicholas, a Jewish prayer-house, a school and an elementary school, 8 shops, a tannery, a soap-boilery and 6 flour-mills. Grain is forwarded from here to the East. In 1898, the export amounted to 51,397 puds, mainly oats. From the station, the line continues its descent to the river Itát, spanning it at the 403 verst by a wooden bridge of 15 sazhens. Further on, it crosses a low watershed and runs over the Kosúl by an iron bridge with an opening of 201 sazhens (469 v.). From the river, the line rises by maximum grades (0.008) to the plateau of the next station.

15) **Bogotól.** III class station. Buffet. (486 v. from Krivoshchékovo, 1818 v. from Cheliábinsk). A wooden church is erected near the station out of the Emperor Alexander III fund; it contains three aisles consecrated to St. Nicholas the Miracle-worker, the Yarosláv Saints Theodore, David and Constantine and the martyr St. Claudia. This was the hundredth church built at the expense of the same fund.

There is a medical and feeding station for the settlers bound for the forest localities in the Maríinsk district, which is also the residence of an official for the regulation of the emigration movement.

The trading village of Bogotól (pop. 4,673) is situated within 6 versts of the station on the left bank of the Chulym on the Siberian highway, included in the Maríinsk district. The settlement is provided with a stone church in honour of the Apparition of Our Lord, a Jewish prayer-house, 2 schools for boys and girls, a forestry school, and two poorhouses for exile settlers. There are 4 tanneries, 3 brick-kilns, 5 flour-mills, 25 shops, 3 wineshops, and a local village board. Oats, wheat and rye flour are conveyed from here to Eastern Siberia.

Bridge over the Kosúl.

From the station, the line proceeds along the high watershed of the rivers Kíya and Chulym, which has an elevation of 43 sazhens above the station of Achinsk.

16). **Krásnaya.** V class station. (517 v. from Krivoshchékovo, 1849 v. from Cheliábinsk). The trading village of Krasnoréchenskoe (pop. 3,167) is situated at a distance of 6 versts from the station on the left bank of the Chulym and the small river Krásnaya in the Maríinsk district. The village contains a stone church in the name of the Archistrategus Michael, a Jewish prayerhouse, 2 schools, a home preparator school, a poorhouse for settlers, 4 shops, a brick-kiln, 10 flour-mills. The goods traffic is yet insignificant.

Bridge over the Chulym.

Hence the line continues its descent to the valley of the Chulym and, at the 546 verst, passes the frontier of the Tomsk and Yeniséisk governments. At the 547 verst, it crosses the Chulym by a bridge of 130 sazhens, with one span of 50 sazhens and two of 40 sazhens, supported on stone piers.

17) **Achinsk.** III class station. Buffet. (550 v. from Krivoshchékovo, 1882 v. from Cheliábinsk). Is situated 2 versts from the town of Achinsk, connected by a roadway and within a verst from the Chulym A branch line of $1^{1/2}$ versts unites the station with the landing-place on the Chulym. A medical and feeding station is established within $2^{1/2}$ versts of the railway for settlers bound for the localities allotted for colonisation in the Achinsk and Minusínsk districts. It is the residence of an official entrusted with the regulation of the emigration movement.

Achinsk is a district town of the Yeniséisk government (pop. 6,714; 3,453 males, 3,261 females; 56° 16′ N. lat., 60° 13′ E. long.) situated on the Siberian highway, on the right elevated bank of the Chulym, within 13 versts of the boundary of the Tomsk government. The environs of the town are hilly and covered with copses of young birches, only the western part is level and contains a number of lakes provided with fish. Achinsk was founded in the XVII century. In 1642, the Tára voyevóda Tugachévski established the Achinsk stockaded post on the river Yus, tributary of the Chulym; in 1682 it was burnt down by the Kirgíz and built again on the site of the present town. In 1782, the town of Achinsk was ranked among the district towns of the Tomsk government, and in 1822 it was included in the Yeniséisk government.

Station of Achinsk.

Since the construction of the great Siberian main line, the town is much improved and enlarged, containing now 955 houses, four churches: a stone cathedral in honour of the Holy Trinity, a church in the name of Our Lady of Kazán, beyond the river, another in honour of the Elevation of the Holy Cross at the cemetery, and a prison church consecrated to the Archangel Michael. The educational institutions are: a preparatory gymnasium for girls,

Town of Achinsk.

a three-class urban school for boys and girls, and a parish school. There are also a public library and a small museum, a hospital of the Public Charitable Board, a poorhouse, an apothecary's shop, a private printing office. The town numbers 53 shops, 10 stores, 9 wine-cellars, 4 wine-stores, a public club, an hotel with rooms from R. 1 to R. 2 a day, 10 inns. The factories are represented by 3 tanneries, a candle and soap manufactory, 2 potteries and a fur manufactory. Their output does not exceed a value of R. 30,000 to 40,000 per annum. The fair held annually from the 15 November to the 15 December is insignificant, having a business of scarcely R. 40,000 to 50,000. No particular branch of industry is pursued in this town, where only a small quantity of manufactured and grocery goods are put on the market. The town revenue amounts to R. 40,000 per annum.

On the 2 July, 1891, Achinsk was visited by His Imperial Majesty the present Emperor Nicholas II, then Heir Apparent to the throne, on his way from the Far East. A triumphal arch, which exists to the present day, was erected for the reception of His Majesty on the eastern side of the town.

The Chulym, which is a tributary of the Ob, takes its rise in the Kuznétsk Alatáu and is composed of the Black and White Yus. Gold mines belonging to the mining district of Achinsk and Minusínsk are situated on its upper reaches. The course of this river is very sinuous and navigation only possible in spring during high water for a distance of 1000 versts, from the mouth of the river to the town of Achinsk.

Previous to the construction of the railway line, manufactured and iron goods to supply Eastern Siberia were mainly forwarded by the Chulym to Achinsk and conveyed further in carts to their destination. About 140,000 boxes of tea, sent overland from Kiákhta, were the chief article of transport conveyed by barges from Achinsk. The navigation on the Chulym was of great service during the construction of the Midsiberian railway line, for the conveyance of railway appliances and materials to Achinsk.

Station of Chernoréchenskaya.

From the 5—10 May to the 1 July, steamers with barges come to Achinsk from Tiumén, Barnaúl and Tomsk. The tariff for passengers and goods is appointed by the shipowners. These steamers perform the passage from Achinsk to Tomsk in 2½ to 3 days, and from Tomsk over 10 days. The wide and fertile region connected with the town of Achinsk and with the adjacent Minusínsk district is particularly favourable for agriculture, and will in the near future yield considerable quantities of grain for export to the East by the Midsiberian railway and by the Chulym for further conveyance by the Ob to Tiumén and the European markets.

In 1898, the quantity of rye, oats and wheat-flour was 81,807 puds. From the station of Achinsk to the east, the country becomes mountainous, the line ascends to the watershed of the rivers Chulym and Ulúi and spans the latter by a wooden bridge of 15 sazhens (566 v.).

18) **Tarútino.** V class station (570 v. from Krivoshchékovo, 1902 v. from Cheliábinsk). The village of Tarútino or Pokróvskoe is situated in the Achinsk district on the Siberian highway on both sides of the Ulúi, (pop. 1,726). It contains a village board and a wooden church in honour of the Intercession of the Holy Virgin.

The conveyance of goods from this station is insignificant. From here the line continues along the river Chórnaya and at the 583 verst crosses it by a bridge with an opening of 10 sazhens.

19) **Chernoréchenskaya.** IV class station (586 v. from Krivoshchékovo, 1918 v. from Cheliábinsk). The village of Chernoréchenskoe of the Achinsk district close by, on the small river Chórnaya, lies in a swampy and wooded country along the Siberian highway; it has a population of 1,406. This settlement was founded in the XVIII century and contains a church built in 1834 in honour of the Archangel Michael; some documents preserved in the church testify that previous to its construction, in the winter of 1833, a bell weighing 42 puds was brought in the night to the village and left there by an unknown individual. There is a parish school.

The conveyance of goods from the station is not considerable. From here the line ascends by maximum grades of 0.05 to the high watershed of the river Chórnaya and the tributaries of the Kemchúg, passes by the siding of Kozúlka (609 v.), descends to the river Sharováya and crosses the Great Kemchúg, left tributary of the Chulym, by an iron bridge of 15 sazhens. (623 v.). Throughout its course from the station to the 607 verst, the line runs through the taigá.

Bridge over the Great Kemchúg.

20) **Kemchúg.** IV class station (631 v. from Krivoshchékovo, 1963 v. from Cheliábinsk). The village Great Kemchúg of the Achinsk district is situated on the Kemchúg and on the Siberian highway (pop. 833); it has existed from 1787. There is a stone church in honour of St. Nicholas the Miracle-worker. The place is surrounded with taigá and swamps; this is why the inhabitants scarcely occupy themselves with agriculture, but mainly with overland transport, and partly with fishing and bee-keeping. The site of the station is picturesque and covered with a fir forest. The station has no importance as a centre of export. Hence the line ascends by light and further by maximum grades (0.15) to the watershed of the rivers Great Kemchúg, tributary of the Chulym, of the Ob system, and the Kácha falling into the Yeniséi. This watershed is the highest on the Ob-Krasnoyársk line. Passing here through a difficult country, the radius adopted for curves is 120 sazhens. After having crossed the Kácha by a stone bridge of 10 sazhens, thc line resumes it course along the valley of this river with maximum grades (0.15) and further mounts for 4 versts to the next station.

Station of Kemchúg.

21) **Kácha.** V class station (671 v. from Krivoshchékovo, 2002 v. from Cheliábinsk). Sukhóvskoe of the Krasnoyársk district is the nearest settlement with a population of 115; it stands on the Kácha and the Siberian highway.

22) **Mínino.** V class station (699 v. from Krivoshchékovo, 2,031 v. from Cheliábinsk). The settlement of Mínino is near by (pop. 590); the settlement of Aréiskoe is situated at a distance of 8 versts, in the Krasnoyársk district, on the great Siberian highway; it is also known under the name of Zaledéevo. The settlement of Aréiskoe is composed of three communes: Aréiskoe, Yemeliánovo, and Zaledéevo. These settlements stretch uninterruptedly along the highway for a distance of 10 versts, on the right bank of the Kácha, opposite its junction with the Aréi; there are many side streets, a large square and about 50 shops. The total population exceeds 4,000. In autumn and winter, the workmen are hired here for the Yeniséisk gold mines. The settlement of Aréiskoe contains a stone two-storeyed church, which was erected in the beginning of the past century: the upper story is consecrated to the Holy Trinity, the lower to the Intercession of the Blessed Virgin. The church possesses an image of the Holy Trinity which since the year 1799 is solemnly carried (a week after Easter) to the town of Krasnoyársk and to the villages of the Krasnoyársk and Yeniséisk districts, and is again brought back on the day of the Holy Trinity. There is a parish school for boys and girls.

View on the river Kemchúg.

From here the line descends (grade .15) along the valley of the Kácha to Krasnoyársk, standing on the Yeniséi.

23) **Krasnoyársk.** II class station. Buffet. (716 v. from Krivoshchékovo, 2,048 v. from Cheliábinsk). The station is situated near Krasnoyársk, a district town of the Yeniséisk government.

The passenger station is a large stone building; there are extensive workshops with 1,500 workmen employed in different kinds of work comprising waggon making, the fitting up of machinery, the black-smith's trade, electro-technical work, turnery and others. The machinery is provided with electric motors. A special workshop is attached to an engine-house holding 25 locomotives. A hospital with 30 beds contains a reception room and an ambulance for outpatients. An apothecary's shop. A store-house with materials required for the exploitation and construction of the line. In proximity to the station stands a wooden house, containing the first Siberian railway technical school in the name of the Emperor Nicholas II, and close by is a med-

Railway line at the 659 verst.

ical and feeding station for the registration and accomodation of emigrants bound for the Krasnoyársk and Minusínsk districts.

Several buildings stand along the railway line, accomodating railway employees and workmen. A branch line connects the station with a landing-place on the left bank of the Yeniséi. Previous to the construction of the Yeniséi bridge and before the opening of traffic on it, waggons, goods, passengers and emigrants were conveyed from the landing-place on the Yeniséi by barges and steamers of the Government. This landing-place is now used for the deposit of materials brought down by the Yeniséi for the needs of the railway, and for the embarcation of emigrants despatched up the Yeniséi to colonise the Minusínsk district.

Railway technical school in Krasnoyársk.

Krasnoyársk, the chief town of the Yeniséisk government, is situated on the left bank of the Yeniséi at its junction with the Kácha (56°N. lat., 43°4'E. long). According to the census of 1897, the population is given as 26,600 (14,573 males, 12,057 females) and as 27,299 (13,844 males and 13,455 females) by the statistical record of 1899. The town is picturesquely situated at an altitude of 913 feet above the level of the sea.

The Yeniséi, breaking through a mountain pass, has a rapid current and, in view of the town, is divided into two branches by pretty islands covered with birch trees. The right bank is fringed by the picturesque Kuisúm mountains composed of sharp, rocky and round cones, with slopes covered with dwarf trees. At the foot of these mountains, of which the Tokmáka is the highest, lie the former Cossack villages of Torgáshino and Bazaíkha, which now are inhabited by peasants. Lower down rises the cupola of the Batáiskaya mountain formed of round and fine porphyries. On the left bank, stands the Górnaya sopka, whose summit consists of horizontally lying rocks of dark jasper. The mountain Afóntova is nearer to the railway line; it is composed of red sandstone covered with a seam of red marl, from which the town received ist name. This mountain, falling to the Kácha, forms a steep and picturesque cape called Karaúlnaya Gorá, on the summit of which stands a chapel seen from a great distance, built in 1855 by the gold-miner Kuznetsóv.

The town was founded at the beginning ot the XVII century.

In order to oppose the invasions of the Tatar tribes, the Aríntsy and Káchintsy, the Yeniséisk voyevóda Dubénsky founded a fort named Kizil-

Yartúra by the Tatars which means town „of the Krasnoyársk bank". In 1882, when Siberia was divided for purposes of administration into Eastern and Western Siberia, upon the organisation of the Yeniséisk government, the town of Krasnoyársk ranked as a government town. A. P. Stepánov, a well known writer and author of the first description of the Yeniséisk government, was the first governor of the town (1822—31).

Krasnoyársk is regularly laid out; the large garden in the centre of the town is considered the finest in Siberia. The streets and squares are unpaved and have wooden side-walks.

The town contains 2,327 houses, of which only 98 are of stone.

The best street is the Bolsháya, where the trade is concentrated. There are II orthodox churches; 2 stone cathedrals, 5 parish churches, 4 house chapels (in the gymnasium for boys, the diocesan school for girls, the prison and the Archbishop's house).

The stone diocesan house which is in process of construction, will also contain a house-chapel. Among the churches, the cathedral of the Resurrection erected in 1759 is worthy of attention. It contains the following relics: a bell with a Slavonic inscription, a wooden chalice ornamented with a design dating from Borís Godunóv's reign (1598—1605). The new cathedral of the Nativity, built according to the plan of the famous architect Ton, is remarkable on account of its fine architecture and gilded cupolas. The construc-

Town of Krasnoyársk.

tion of this cathedral was commenced in 1843, on the birthday of the Tsesarévich Nicholas Alexándrovich, deceased in 1866. The gold miners of Krasnoyársk, wishing to commemorate this event by the foundation of a catheral, started its construction, but in 1849 the vaults fell down, and the cathedral was rebuilt and ornamented by the gold-miner Shchegolióv at a cost of R. 500,000. In 1858, the late Tsesarévich Nicholas Alexándrovich, wishing to participate in the adornment of the church, which was founded in commemoration of his birthday (8 September 1843), presented a silver-clad image of the Holy Virgin with the date of his birth inscribed in one corner. When the church was inaugurated (1866), the late Empress Mary Alexándrovna made a gift of all the sacerdotal vestments. This cathedral was visited twice by Imperial personages: on the 21 July, 1873, by the Grand Duke Alexis Alexándrovich on his way from the East, and on the 1 July 1891, by His Imperial Majesty, the present Emperor Nicholas II who, returning from his journey round the world, arrived at Krasnoyársk and visited the cathedral;

a short Te Deum was then celebrated in his presence and the Archbishop Tíkhon presented to His Majesty an image of the Nativity of the Holy Virgin with a few words of greeting.

The town of Krasnoyársk contains a Roman Catholic and a Lutheran chapel and a Jewish synagogue. The educational institutions are 26 in number: a gymnasium for boys, a gymnasium for girls, a seminary, a clergy school, a seminary for teachers, a public school, a town school with classes, a diocesan school for girls, the Shchegoliόv artisan's school with 2 classes, a railway technical school in the name of the Emperor Nicholas II, 9 parish schools, 4 church parish schools, 2 Sunday schools, a woman surgeon's assistants' school.

There are 10 charitable and medical establishments: the Vladímir orphanage under the patronage of the Empress Mary, with an elementary school, the poorhouse of the Public Charitable Board, a home for convicts' children, a poorhouse founded by the honorary citizen Mrs. Shchegoliόv and a feeding house for orphans with an elementary school organised by the same lady, a baby-home founded by the Sinélnikov Charitable Society, the night-shelter of the same Society, the hospital of the Public Charitable Board, a hospital for the poor founded by the Sinélnikov Charitable Society, the Olga Home for emigrants' children under the patronage of the Empress Alexándra Féodorovna, opened in 1899, the cost defrayed partly from a fund assigned by the Commitee for the construction of the Great Siberian Railway. There are also the following brotherhoods: that of the Nativity of the Blessed Virgin attached to the cathedral, the St. Alexander Névsky Relief Society for pupils of the Krasnoyársk ecclesiastic school, the Relief Society for school children in the Yeniséisk government, the Society for the promotion of elementary education in Krasnoyársk, the Sinélnikov Charitable Society, a branch of the Russian Red Cross Society, the Society of doctors of the Yeniséisk government, a branch of the Imperial Agricultural Society of Moscow, an amateur society of dramatic art, an amateur society of music and literature, a cooperative supply society.

The Christ's Nativity Cathedral in Krasnoyársk.

The most important and active society in Siberia is the Krasnoyársk branch of the Imperial Agricultural Society of Moscow, established in 1890. It has paid special attention to the improvement of seeds and to agriculture in general, that being the chief resource of the population. The Society exhibited its produce in Chicago in 1893, and in 1892 organised in Krasnoyársk the first agricultural and industrial exhibition.

The town possesses a small museum with a public library, a library for the lower class with the reading-room of the brotherhood of the Holy Virgin, the Skorniakόv private library, bookshops of the Society for the promotion of elementary education and of the Bible Society, 2 bookshops and 4 printing offices.

The periodicals are: „The Yeniséisk Government Gazette", „The Yeniséisk Diocesan Gazette", the private newspaper „Yeniséi" subject to the censorship, and the Transactions of the Doctors' Society of the Yeniséisk government. The town theatre was burnt down in 1898, and has not been yet rebuilt. There are a public and an industrial club. Hotels: Russia, with rooms from K. 2 to R. 5 a day. Gadálov's Hotel — R. I to R. 3. The Hermitage — R. 1 50 kop. to R. 3, Mrs. Kuzmín's, from K. 1 to R. 3. Central Hotel, 75 kop. to R. 1 50 kop. Siberia, R. 1 to R. 2. Furnished rooms charge from R. 1 25 kop. to R. 3 a day. The Hermitage Restaurant contains rooms at R. 1 to R. 2 a day. The Russia Hotel is considered the best. The town is furnished with a telephone which has over 100 subscribers paying R. 75 annually.

During the period from 1830 to 1850, when mining industry was carried on within the Yeniséisk government, the town of Krasnoyársk was characterised by a lively trade, but since the centre of this industry was removed to other points, the Krasnoyársk trade has diminished. At present, the town comprises 30 factories with an annual production of R. 582,000: a cast-iron foundry and machinery works, a bell foundry, two saw-mills, eight tanneries, three boileries, a wax candle manufactory, a distillery, two breweries a steam flour-mill, eight brick-kilns, two kvas-brewer ies. A fair is held in Krasnoyársk from the 20 December to the 26 January, with a turnover of R. 25,000 to R. 30,000. The town revenue during the last three years, from 1897 to 1899, on the average amounted to R. 115,000 annually. Financial institutions are represented by a branch of the State Bank, a town loan bank, and by a branch of the Siberian Trade Bank.

Important firms are:

I. G. Gadálov and N. G. Gadálov for manufactured goods, mercery, colonial wares, tea and sugar. N. N. Gadálov—shipowner. Smirnóv—manufactured articles. Zólotov—distillery. Komaróv—bookseller. Kuznetsóv — manufactured and other wares. Pareválov—pottery, china and glass of his own manufacture. Poliakóv—wine of his own manufacture. Razzorénov — ready-made clothes. Trífon Savéliev and Sons for manufactured goods and mercery. Shárykov—gold-miner and shipowner. Stebler—optician and gunsmith. Yúdin — wine of his own manufacture.

Transport offices: Russian Goods Transport Society, the Nadézhda Society, Kukhtérin, Chevelév, Poliakóv and Kuznetsóv.

The freights per pud are R. 2 60 kop. to St. Petersburg and R. 2 40 kop. to Moscow. For goods in transit there is a first-class custom-house in Krasnoyársk.

Agents of insurance societies: Dobzhínsky of the First Russian Fire Insurance Society; Zhílin—of the Russian Fire Insurance Society; Potékhin—of the Russia Fire Insurance Society, Smirnóv of the Northern Society.

Hackney coaches are represented by uncomfortable carts without springs, plying without a tariff.

Among the important events in the history of the town, may be mentioned the visit of His Imperial Majesty, the present Emperor Nicholas II, which took place on the 1 and 2 July, in 1891 on his way from the Far East. A triumphal arch, erected in honour of the Imperial guest near the landing-place on the bank of the Yeniséi, exists to the present day. After having surveyed the town relics, the educational and charitable institutions and the local troops, His Imperial Majesty examined with great interest some archaeological remains and shamanistic articles used by the natives, belonging mainly to the Káchintsy, exhibited in the Minusínsk museum.

There are two monasteries in the environs of Krasnoyársk: the monastery of the Ascension situated within 12 versts of the town higher up the Yeniséi on its elevated and picturesque bank; it is inhabited by a few monks; 2 wooden churches and a large stone building are attached to the monastery. The nunnery in honour of the Miraculous Apparition of the Holy Virgin is 30 versts from the town by the Siberian highway; it possesses 2 wooden churches and about 40 nuns, who teach reading, writing and handwork to the girls of the neighbouring villages.

Special mention is due to the library of the Krasnoyársk merchant Yúdin, at his pretty residence Tarakánovka situated at a distance of 4 versts from the town near the railway bridge over the Yenisséi. It is housed in a special two-storeyed building near the house inhabited by its owner. The library contains upwards of 150 cases with approximately 100,000 volumes. A sum of R. 126,957 K. 28 was expended on its maintenance till 1898. A catalogue, which is now being made, will in the future facilitate the arrangement of the books. Bibliography is very well represented. The library is also well furnished with works concerning Siberia. Almost all the periodicals which were issued from the beginnig of the XIX century are to be found there.

Mr. Yúdin's summer villa Tarakánovka, on the Yeniséi.

The quantity of goods conveyed from the Krasnoyársk station has not yet been ascertained, on account of the recent opening of the traffic to Irkútsk. In 1898, it amounted to 63,847 puds of grain, mainly wheat flour, forwarded east, and 65,494 puds of cedar-nuts sent west.

The Yeniséi, which is one of the largest rivers in Siberia, rises in Mongolia and is formed by the junction of the Khakém and Bikém. After entering the limits of Siberia, the river receives its name from the Tungus „Ioanesi", which means „wide water". Breaking through the Sayán ridge, the river forms a large bar over which it runs at the rate of 60 versts an hour. Further on, the river widens and slackens its course, but retains its mountainous character till the town of Minusínsk.

At a distance of 12 versts beyond Minusínsk, the Yeniséi receives the Abakán, which is navigable for a distance of 50 versts; its basin is provided with rich gold-mines, coal deposits and copper and iron ores. Twenty five versts further, the Yeniséi is joined by the navigable river Túba, flowing through a populous and fertile valley, where iron mines occur along its tributary the Irba. Entering the Achinsk district and flowing N. N. E. for a distance of 130 versts, the Yeniséi does not receive any important affluents. From the boundary of the Achinsk district to the town of Krasnoyársk, it traverses a mountainous country, receiving on the left the small river Biriúsa, remarkable on account of the numerous caves occurring in the limestone mountains, and the Mána on the right. The breadth of the Yeniséi, which above Krasnoyársk is confined between mountains, at some places narrows to 150 sazhens, whereas at others it expands to a verst and a half and sometimes more; the velocity of its current varies from 8 to 10 versts an hour. Down stream from Khasnoyársk, the river with its islands has a width of a verst. After its junction with the Kan, falling into it on the right, the Yeniséi turns north-west, and entering the Yeniséi district, runs northwards, where it receives the immense and full-flowing river Tungúska or Angará.

At this point, the river has a breadth of a verst and a half and more. Beyond the town of Yeniséisk, the Kas, belonging to the Ob-Yeniséi canal, and the Turukhán fall into it on the left; from the right it receives the Podkámennaya-Tungúska (rich gold mines occur along its tributaries), the Bákhta, the Lower Tungúska and the Koréika. In its lower course, the river

The Yeniséi near Krasnoyársk.

is from 3 to 5 versts wide and even more, including the islands. On reaching 70°51′ N. lat., the Yeniséi falls into Yeniséi Gulf.

Its total course is 3,100 versts. The Gulf of the Yeniséi comprises a distance of 250 versts, and a width of 20 to 50 versts. At Krasnoyársk, the ice on the river breaks between the 11 and 27 April and freezes again between the 27 September and the 11 November. In spring, the water rises 5 sazhens above its ordinary level. The Yeniséi abounds in fish, which however is of an inferior quality to that in the Ob. Although containing numerous bars and reefs, the Yeniséi is navigable nearly throughout its course, and is deep enough for moderate sized steamers, reaching the town of Yeniséisk.

During the navigation season, 26 steamers cruise in the Yeniséi basin:

1) The Krasnoyárets, a two-screwed iron steamer, 25 N. H. P., belonging to Cherepénnikov.

2) The St. Nicholas, double-wheeled iron steamer, 140 H. P., Sibiriakóv.

3) The Dédushka } two-wheeled iron steamers, 100 H. P., Gadálov.
4) The Rossía. }

5) The Moskvá, two-wheeled iron steamer, 60 H. P. Ivánov.

6) The Minusínsk, iron screw-steamer of the seagoing type, 25 H. P., belonging to the Popham Trading Company.

7) The Barnaúl, 40 H. P., François Labbon.

8) The Yeniséi, two-wheeled steamer with wooden hull, 60 H. P., Yeniséisk Co.

9) The Anna, wooden screw-steamer, 20 H. P., Budántsev.

10) The Ignatius, two-wheeled wooden steamer, 45 H. P., Kytmánov.

11) The Transport-boat N°I, iron screw-steamer, 6 H. P., Germánov.

12) The Abakánets, two-wheeled wooden steamer, 22 H. P., Poréchin.

13) The Gremiáshchy, two-screwed iron steamer.

14) The Khrábry, two-wheeled wooden steamer, Mechanical Engineer Knorre.

15) The Pioneer, two-wheeled iron-steamer.

The steamers Glenmore and Scotia were purchased by the Yeniséisk merchants Vostrótin, Kytmánov and Balandín from Popham's English Company.

Nine steamers belonging to the Government are at the disposal of the Engineers of Ways of Communication, to satisfy the needs of the railway, and serve for the clearing of the Angará.

Freight and passenger steamers ply regularly several times a week from Krasnoyársk to Yeniséisk. From Krasnoyársk to Minusínsk, navigation is only possible at high water; at other times, the steamers only reach the village of Sorókino. Between Yeniséisk and the mouth of the Yeniséi, navigation is carried on by tow-steamers. The opening of traffic on the Siberian main line, having already changed the former systems of trade in Siberia, will also contribute to the development of navigation on the Yeniséi, favourably situated as far as concerns the easy access to its mouth, offering every convenience for the establishment of a direct communication with Europe through the Arctic Ocean.

Inauguration of the future bridge over the Yeniséi.

The bridge over the Yeniséi (718—719 verst from Krivoshchékovo) has a total length of 434¼ sazhens and is composed of six principal spans, with metallic girders measuring 67.714 sazhens between the centres of bed-plates, and two small spans covering the space between the land piers and the abutments. The metallic superstructure of the principal spans carries the track on the lower chord and consists of two statically determined trusses with main struts of tubular section and ordinary flanged braces and intermediate struts.

The roadway has continuous longitudinal beams supported by tubular cross girders rivetted to the main frames. The breadth between the principal trusses is 19½ feet and their maximum height 71 feet. The trusses for the small spans are semiparabolic and carry the track on the upper chord. The bridgeflooring is suited for wheel traffic and is composed of timber baulks covered with planking fixed in longitudinals of trough section in the principal spans and to consols in the smaller ones.

The metallic superstructure is of cast-steel from the plans of Engineer L. D. Proskuriakóv, Professor of the Moscow Engineering school. The metal was delivered by the Nizhnetagíl Works belonging to the Successors of P. S. Demidov, Prince San-Donato.

The steel bearings were prepared at the Huta Bankowa works at Warsaw.

All the river piers are founded on iron pneumatic caissons and are constructed with starlings rising 1.25 sazhens above the highest water-mark. The western abutment is also founded on a metallic caisson, while the eastern stands on a timber one constructed according to the system of Engineer Knorre. The depth of foundation for the river piers is 8½ sazhens, for the

Construction of the Yeniséi bridge in winter.

western abutment, 5½ sazhens, and for the eastern (on rock) 2.59 sazhens, The whole masonry is of local granite, obtained from a village situated on the river 60 versts above the bridge. Most of the cement was furnished from the Glukhoozérsk works at St. Petersburg. The trusses are located 10 sazhens above low-water mark.

The whole construction of the bridge, including the pneumatic foundations, masonry, manipulation of iron work, erection and riveting was accomplished by Engineer Knorre.

The separate spans of the superstructure were framed on the embankment adjoining the abutments and by means of capstans were launched into position over rollers. The framing of the iron work was carried out with the help of a special rolling crane. This system of erection and launching, devised by the contractor himself, was applied here for the first time for the construction of a bridge of such magnitude and proved most successful, securing the rapid completion of the work.

Bridge over the Yeniséi.

24) **Yeniséi.** Buffet. (719 v. from Krivoshchékovo, 2051 v. from Cheliábinsk) is situated on the right bank of the Yeniséi. Considerable quantities of grain are conveyed from here to the East, carried to the station by the water-ways from the fertile districts on the upper Yeniséi. In 1898, the total export of grain amounted to 178,978 puds.

25) **Zykovo.** IV class station (744 v. from Krivoshchékovo, 2076 v. from Cheliábinsk) Near at hand is the settlement of Zykovo (pop. 170) and the trading village of Voznesénskoye (pop. 1069) on the Siberian highway, in the Krasnoyársk district. The village contains a wooden church in honour of the Resurrection of Christ, a school with one class and the local village board. Workmen for the Yeniséisk gold mines are hired here. On the 30 June, 1891, the present Emperor Nicholas II, on his way from the Far East, received here a deputation from the inhabitants of the Krasnoyársk district, who offered him bread and salt on a silver dish. His Majesty passed the night here and resumed his journey at 8 in the morning.

The station is not important as regards forwarding of goods.

The railway line continues its ascent elong the valley of the Berióżovka, flanked on both sides by high and steep, mostly rocky, banks and, following its bed to the 757 verst, spans the river by a bridge of 25 sazhens.

26) **Sorókino.** V class station (767 v. from Krivoshchékovo, 2039 v. from Cheliábinsk). From here the line mounts along the valley of the Sítik (ma-

ximum grade .01) and, after crossing this river by a bridge of 8 sazhens, ascends by a grade of 0.15 to a watershed, the highest point of which lies 126.8 sazhens above the roadway of the Yeniséi bridge. This ascent has three culverts made of stone passing under an embankment of 8 sazhens. Leaving the watershed, the line descends by an incline of .015 to the next station.

27) **Kamarchága.** V class station (791 v. from Krivoshchékovo, 2123 v. from Cheliábinsk).

The line again approaches the Siberian highway it had left before: the village of Tertézhkoye is situated within 8 versts, in the Krasnoyársk district (pop. 1250). It contains a wooden church and a reading school. From the station, the line descends by light grades and reaches the river Yesaúlovka, spanning it at the 799 v. by an iron bridge with an opening of 20 sazhens. Further on, the line ascends (maximum grades .015) to the watershed of the rivers Yesaúlovka and Balái having an altitude of 47 sazhens, and thence descends again.

28) **Balái.** V class station (813 v. from Krivoshchékovo, 2145 v. from Cheliábinsk).

The village of Baláiskoe (Nikólskoe) with a population of 836 is situated at a distance of 5 versts in the Kansk district, containing a church in honour of St. Nicholas the Miracle-worker, and a school.

Hence the line reaches the Balái river,—crossing it at the 821 verst by a wooden bridge of 25 sashens with a height of 4¼ sazhens, and further on, by a maximum grade of 0.15, mounts to the watershed of the rivers Balái and Rybnaya.

29) **Olginskaya.** III class station. Buffet. (837 v. from Krivoshchékovo, 2169 v. from Cheliábinsk).

This station and the settlement established by the emigrants in its vicinity, received their name in honour of the Grand Duchess Olga Nikoláievna. The settlement is inhabited by emigrants from the governments of Oriól, Tambóv, Poltáva and Khárkov. To meet the spiritual needs of the railway employees and of the inhabitants of the Olga settlement, a wooden church dedicated to St. Olga has been built at the cost of the Emperor Alexander III fund, in honour of the Grand Duchess Olga Nikoláievna. The first stone for the church was laid on the 11 July, 1897; it was inaugurated on the 27 March by Joachim, Archbishop of Yeniséisk and Krasnoyársk. His Imperial Majesty the Emperor favoured the church with the gracious gift of church utensils and a chime of bells.

There is a medical and feeding station for the registration and distribution of the settlers in the localities allotted to colonisation in the Kansk district. It is also the residence of an official entrusted with the regulation of the emigration movement.

The village of Uyár (Spasopreobrazhénskoye) is situated on the Siberian highway, in the Kansk district (pop. 1248). It possesses a wooden church in honour of the Transfiguration of Our Saviour and a parish school.

From the Olginskaya station, the line descends by maximum grades of 015 to the valley of the Rybnaya, crossing this river by an iron bridge with an opening of 60 sazhens.

30) **Tróitsko-Zaoziórnaya.** V class station (865 v. from Krivoshchékovo, 2197 v. from Cheliábinsk).

The settlement of the same name, with a population of 1,330, is close to the station; it belongs to the Kansk district and stands on the Bórcha, tributary of the Kan. There is a wooden church of John the Baptist and a school This village enjoys a certain reputation for its corn trade. At the end of the XVIII century, an iron mine situated at a distance of 7 versts was worked by the merchant Lobánov, a small iron works having been established for this purpose. At the present time, nothing is left of it. The estate of the nobleman Samóilov, the largest in Siberia, stretched along the Bórcha and covered an

Station of Olginskaya.

area of 25 versts in length and 15 versts in width. These lands have long since again become the property of the State.

Within 22 versts of the station, on the Siberian highway, is situated the village of Rybinskoye with a population of 4,461; it is one of the largest trading villages of the Kansk district.

The inhabitants are chiefly engaged in agriculture. The village contains a stone church of Peter and Paul, a Jewish prayerhouse, a model school with two classes, a parish school, a hospital and the village board. When His Imperial Majesty, the present Emperor Nicholas II, in 1891 halted at this village, the whole commune offered him three grey horses, which were graciously accepted by His Majesty and sent off to Tomsk. The Imperial traveller gave R. 500 for the local parish school.

Leaving the station, the line reaches the watershed of the rivers Bórcha and Kamála, and descends to the valley of the Kamála, crossing it at the 876 verst by a a wooden bridge with an opening of 20 sazhens.

31) **Tyrbyl.** V class station (885 v. from Krivoshchékovo, 2,217 v. from Cheliábinsk).

The settlement of Tyrbyl was established near the station by emigrants from the governments of Poltáva and Chernígov.

Hence the line descends to the river Tyrbyl, crossing the latter over a culvert with an opening of 2.75 sazhens, passing under an embankment of 2.5 sazhens. Further the line mounts to the watershed of the rivers Tyrbyl and the Little Uria and passes over its summit, which has an elevation of 100 sazhens, above the roadway of the Yeniséi bridge, following steep grades, which required a great quantity of earth and engineering work.

32) **Petrúshkovo.** V class station (908 v. from Krivoshchékovo, 2240 v. from Cheliábinsk).

Since the construction of the line, an emigrant settlement has been established near the station. A wooden church, inaugurated on the 21 March, 1899, in honour of the Moscow Saints Peter, Alexis, John and Philip, has been built at the cost of the Emperor Alexander III fund, in order to satisfy the spiritual needs of the settlers and railway employees. The church utensils are made of silver given by the Emperor. The bronze for the bells was also provided by His Majesty.

The trading village of Urínskoye of the Kansk district, with a population of 2,248, is situated within 20 versts of the station on the Siberian highway. It contains a local board, a one-class school, several shops and a stone church in honour of the Holy Trinity. His Imperial Majesty, the present Emperor Nicholas II, on his way from the Far East in 1891, visited this church and made a gift of R. 100. This donation was employed to purchase an altar cross on which the following inscription was engraved: „In remembrance of the visit of His Imperial Highness, the Tsesarévich.“

Hence the line resumes its descent to the Little Uriá, spanning it by an iron bridge with an opening of 20 sazhens; further on, it crosses the Great Uriá by an iron bridge of 25 sazhens and, entering the level valley of the Kan, follows this river to the station of Kansk.

The recent opening of traffic on the Midsiberain railway makes it impossible to ascertain the commercial importance of the stations between the Yeniséi and Kansk, lying at a distance of 200 versts. None of these stations was distinguished by an important export of local goods. However, it is evident that the agricultural district, which is now cultivated by the population formerly engaged in the conveyance of goods by road and in other industries and colonisation, will furnish a considerable quantity of goods for railway transport.

33) **Kansk.** III class station (941 v. from Krivoshchékovo, 2,273 v. from Cheliábinsk). It is situated near the district town of Kansk in the Yeniséisk government. There is a medical and feeding station, for the registration and accomodation of settlers bound for the Kansk district, where lands are allotted for a populatlon of 40,000. It is also the residence of an official entrusted with the regulation of the emigration movement.

The town of Kansk stands on the left bank of the river Kan, which is not navigable, and on the great Siberian highway, (56°10′ N. lat., 23°20′E. long.; pop. 7,504; 4,482 males, 3,022 females). In 1604, a stockaded post was founded on this site, which afterwards was transformed into a settlement. In 1823, it ranked among the towns of the Yeniséisk government. The town is situated on a level spot, which is often overflowed by the spring waters of the Kan. It contains 534 houses, of which only two are of stone, the others being of wood and of one storey.

There are two stone churches, one a cathedral in honour of Our Saviour, the other standing in the cemetery; a third, which was attached to the prison, was burnt down in 1898 and has not yet been rebuilt; and a Jewish synagogue. The schools are three in number: a school with two classes for boys, and two public schools with one class for boys and girls. In 1897, the Society for the Promotion of Elementary Education opened its operations and established a public library. The principal occupation of the inhabitants is agriculture, carried on over a vast area belonging to the citizens, comprising 21,809 desiatins. Manufactures and industry stand at a very low level; there are 2 tallow-boileries, 6 tanneries and a soap and 2 candle manufactories. No

View of the town of Kansk.

fairs are held in the town, but only markets twice a week. A town bank with a capital of R. 80,000 is located in the townhall. The annual town expenditure rises to R. 30,000. Since numerous lots of land have been settled in the district, the town has also improved, having become a centre whence grain and hay are exported by rail towards Irkútsk. There has recently arisen an export of pressed hay to the Irkútsk government.

The visit of the present Emperor Nicholas II to Kansk in 1891 was an auspicions event in the history of the town.

His Majesty arrived at Kansk at 8 o'clock in the evening on the 29 June, passing through a stone arch specially built for His reception. Two chapels stand at the two ends of the arch; one is consecrated to Saints Cosmo and Damian, the other to St. Nicholas the Miracle-worker. The arch is surmounted by two spires, adorned by Imperial Eagles. This handsome edifice is visible at a great distance from the railway line.

During the year 1898, the quantity of grain, exported to the East from the region surrounding the station, amounted to 227,684 puds, including 109,731 puds of oats, 79,920 puds of wheat flour and 25,736 puds of rye floure.

Within 2 versts of the station, the line crosses the river Kan by a bridge with an opening of 120 sazhens, consisting of three spans of 40 sazhens each.

From Kansk to Taishét, between the rivers Kan and Birúsa, the line runs for a distance of 158 verst through an immense coalfieed which is not yet worked.

34) **Ilanskáya.** IV class station (967 v. from Krivoshchékovo, 2,229 v. from Cheliábinsk). A church in honour of St. Alexander Névsky is in process of construction near the station, at the cost of the Emperor Alexander III fund.

The village of Ilánskoye, ot the Kansk district (pop. 874), is situated close by on the Great Siberian highway near the small river Ilánka. Agriculture is the chief pursuit of the inhabitants. A church of the Purification was erected in 1822 by Count Speránsky, Governor General of Siberia, at the cost of the Emperor Alexander I. There is a parish school.

Within 2 versts of the station, the line crosses the river Ilánka by a wooden bridge of 10 sazhens and passes over the watershed of the rivers Ilánka and Póima, tributaries of the Biriúsa.

35) **Ingásh.** V class station (994 v. from Krivoshchékovo, 2326 v. from Cheliábinsk). The settlement of the same name is situated at a distance of 2 versts on the great Siberian highway, in the Kansk district (pop. 674). The inhabitants occupy themselves mainly with agriculture. Within 6 versts of the station, the line spans the Póima by an iron bridge of 25 sazhens (at

Bridge over the Kan.

the 1000 v.) and further on, running along the watershed of the rivers Póima and Tína, crosses the latter near the station of Tínskaya by a wooden bridge of 24 sazhens.

36) **Tinskáya.** V class station (1,019 v. from Krivoshchékovo, 2,326 v. from Cheliábinsk). The village of Tíny stands 3 versts from the station, on the Great Siberian highway, in the Kansk district (pop. 804). It contains a church of the Presentation, a school with one class, and a village board, The inhabitants are principally engaged in agriculture. Here a deputation from the peasants offered a silver dish with bread and salt to the present Emperor Nicholas II when, as Heir Apparent to the throne, he traversed Siberia in 1891.

Further, the line runs across the watershed of the rivers Tína and Reshéta and, after having crossed the latter at the 1039 verst by a wooden bridge of 12 sazhens, ascends by maximum grades through a difficult section to the next watershed of the rivers Reshéty and Cheremshánka.

37) **Kliuchínskaya.** V class station. Buffet. (1049 v. from Krivoshchékovo, 2381 v. from Cheliábinsk). The settlement of Kliuchí of the Kansk district, with a population of 207 is situated 2 versts from the Siberian highway. Agriculture is the chief pursuit of the inhabitants.

In 1898, the quantity of grain conveyed from this station to the East, mainly to Tulún, was 169,495 puds, including 160,488 puds of wheat flour. Leaving the station of Kliuchínskaya situated at a high point of the watershed, the line, for a distance of 15 versts, runs along the broken summit of the watershed and crossing the river Cheremshánka at the 1,066 verst by a wooden bridge of 9 sazhens, passes over the steep watershed and descends by maximum grades to the river Cheremkóvka, spanning it near the station of Yúrta by a wooden bridge of 18 sazhens.

38) **Yúrty.** V class station (1071 v. from Krivoshchékovo, 2,403 v. from Cheliábinsk). The settlement Polovína-Cheremkóvskoe of the Kansk district lies in close proximity to the station, on the Great Siberian highway, (pop. 470). The inhabitants occupy themselves mainly with agriculture. Leaving the station, the line passes again over the Cheremkóvka by a wooden bridge of 17¼ sazhens, and continues along the valley of the Biriúsa, crossing the latter at 1,087 versts from Krivoshchékovo by an iron bridge with a opening of 160 sazhens, consisting of four spans of 40 sazhens. each. The river Biriúsa rises in the Sayán chain and has a total length of about 400 versts; it is celebrated for the richness of its gold mines occuring along its upper reaches.

The village of Kontórskoe of the Kansk district (pop. 913) is situated within 5 versts of the railway, on the Biriúsa and the Great Siberian highway on the frontier of the Irkútsk government. The village contains a church of St. Nicholas, a school and several shops. On the 29 June, 1891, His Imperial Majesty the present Emperor Nicholas II, halted here and visited the church and made a donation of R. 100. An inscription on a bronze plate fitted to the church wall remains as a memorial of this visit.

Passing the Biriúsa, the line runs over the small watershed of the rivers Biriúsa and Taishét, and spans the latter by a wooden bridge of 15 sazhens.

39) **Taishét.** III class station. Buffet. (1,099 v. from Krivoshchékovo, 2,431 v. from Cheliábinsk). There is a medical and feeding station close by, for the registration of the emigrants and their distribution in the lands allotted for colonisation in the western part of the Nizhneúdinsk district.

Within 10 versts of the station, the village of Biriúsa, of the Nizhneúdinsk district and Irkútsk government, with a population of 1,600, stands on the Siberian highway. The village possesses a wooden church of the Holy Trinity, and a two-class school. The population which, prior to the construction of the railway, occupied itself with the carriage of goods by road, is now engaged in agriculture. The whole distance from Taishét to Nizhneúdinsk, comprising the watershed of the Biriúsa and Udá, with a length of 150 versts, is covered with taigá. The population is principally collected in the lands bordering upon the highway; agriculture is yet undeveloped.

From here, the line resumes its course along the watershed, descending slightly to the river Okulshét and crossing it by a wooden bridge of 22 sazhens. Leaving the watershed, the line descends by maximum grades towards the Bairónovka and passes over it by a wooden bridge.

40) **Baironóvka.** V class station (1,119 v. from Krivoshchékovo, 2,451 v. from Cheliábinsk). Within 15 versts of the station, is the village of Bairónovskoe, in the Nizhneúdinsk district (pop. 900); it is situated on both sides of the Bairónovka near the Great Siberian highway. The village has a wooden church in honour of the Archangel Michael, and a parish school. The inhabitants are engaged iu agriculture and trapping.

41) **Razgón.** V class station (1.146 v. from Krivoshchékovo, 2,476 v. from Cheliábinsk). Is situated within 10 versts of the settlement of Razgónnoe with a population of 50.

Hence, the line proceeds by maximum grades towards the Mokhováya, spanning this river by a wooden bridge of 14 sazhens (1,157 v.). Further on, it crosses the Alzamái by a wooden bridge of 12 sazhens.

42) **Alzamái.** V class station (1,165 v. from Krivoshchékovo, 269 v. from Cheliábinsk). The village of Alzamái, in the Nizhneúdinsk district (pop. 840) stands in the vicinity, near the river of the same name, on the Siberian highway. The village contains a wooden church in honour of St Innocent of Irkutsk, a school with one class, a village board and a hospital with 5 beds, and is the residence of a doctor. The inhabitants occupy themselves with agriculture and also with hunting.

From the station of Alzamái to Zamzór, the line runs through a level country, traversing the rivers Kosói-Górod at the 1,176 verst, and Algashét at the 1,182 verst, by bridges of 20 and 10 sazhens.

43) **Zamzór.** V class station. Buffet. (1,184 v. from Krivoshchékovo, 2,516 v. from Cheliábinsk). The settlement of Zamzór in the Nizhneúdinsk district (pop. 225) stands next the station, situated in proximity to the district town of Nizhneúdinsk in the Irkútsk government (54°55' N. lat., 68°50'E. long.) standing on the right bank of the Udá and the Great Siberian highway. A stockaded post named Udínskaya was built in 1664 on the site of the present town. In 1783, it was converted into the town of Nizhneúdinsk. The town is picturesquely situated, surrounded by rocky mountains, forming the continuation of the Sayán ridge; the navigable river Udá, with a breadth of 200 sazhens, flows through the town. The census of 1897 shewed a population of 5,803 (3,355 males, 2,448 females). There are two stone churches: the cathedral of the Ascension and the church of the Resurrection, and a Jewish prayer-house. Schools: town school with two classes, the parish Michael school with one class, preparatory gymnasium for girls with three classes, parish school.

The town contains 570 houses; the buildings are mainly wooden. There are about 60 trading firms. The market held every day is supplied with agricultural produce. The town revenue amounts to R. 25,000—27,000 annually. Agriculture is the principal industry of the population. There are no factories and no important firms. Upon the whole, the town progresses very slowly; according to the latest statistics, its population fell to 4,500 since the opening of traffic on the Siberian Railway.

In 1891, the town was visited by His Imperial Majesty, the Emperor Nicholas II, then Heir Apparent to the throne. The inhabitants of the town erected a triumphal arch for the reception of the Imperial traveller, which exists to the present day. As a memorial of this historical event, prayers for the precious health of the Emperor are pronounced every year near the arch on the 27 July.

The river Udá, on which the town stands, takes its rise in the southwestern part of the Nizhneúdinsk district, on the ridge of Yerík-Targák-Taigá; it has a sandy and rocky bottom and a swift current. It is navigable from Nizhneúdinsk and its valley contains minerals. At distances of 18 and 100 versts above Nizhneúdinsk, its banks contain large caves. Ten versts beyond the town, the river flows through a narrow, gorge-like valley where it receives on the left the small river Uk, forming 12 cataracts from its headwaters to its mouth, where it falls into the Udá. The first two cascades fall from a height of 2 sazhens, near a small river of the same name, on the Siberian highway. There is a school with one class.

Further on, the line runs through a level country with a slight ascent. At the 1,188 verst, it passes over the Zamzór by a wooden bridge of 26 sazhens, at the 1,196 verst, it crosses the river Martynovka and, approaching the next station, spans the Kamyshét by a wooden bridge of 14 sazhens.

44) **Kamyshét.** IV class station. Buffet. (1205 v. from Krivoshchékovo, 2,537 v. from Cheliábinsk). Near the station, on the great Siberian highway, is the settlement of Kamyshétskoe, with a population of 200 and a cementworks, belonging to a Russo-Dutch joint stock company, built in 1895 and 1896.

Local lime, marl and clay, burned with charcoal are employed for the production of cement. The works is provided with a chemical and mechanical laboratory, four locomobiles of 160 H. P., a dynamo engine for electric lighting and a machinery and cooper's shop. The produce of two furnaces on the Liban system amounts to 45,000 barrels annually, and could be doubled.

Cliffs on the bank of the Udá.

The cement has been tested in the laboratory of the Institute for Railway Engineers and declared to be good.

Leaving the station of Kamyshét, the line crosses the rivers Beriózovaya and Kámennaya by bridges of 12 and 10 sazhens each and, by maximum grades of 0.15, reaches the watershed of the rivers Beriózovaya and Mára.

45) **Uk.** V class station. (1,222 v. from Krivoshchékovo, 2,554 v. from Cheliábinsk). The village of Uk, in the Nizhneúdinsk district (pop. 900) stands

on the Siberian highway, near the river Uk. There is a wooden church of St. George the Victorious, built in 1895, and a parish school. The population gets its livelihood by agriculture. Within a verst and a half of the station, the line traverses the Uk by a bridge of 10 sazhens. Further on, it ascends a low watershed and passing over its summit descends by maximum grades of 0.15 to the valley of the river Mára, crossing the latter by a stone bridge of 20 sazhens (1,236 v.) Spanning the river Kuriát at the 1,341 verst, by a wooden bridge of 8 sazhens, the line runs through a level country and reaches the station of Nizhneúdinskaya.

46) **Nizhneúdinskáya.** III class station. Buffet. (1248 v. from Krivoshchékovo, 2580 v. from Cheliábinsk). The total height of the wáterfall is 15 sazhens and its breadth 20 sazhens.

Waterfall on the river Uk.

The traffic to the East having been only recently opened, it is impossible to ascertain the commercial operations of the station, but it may be considered as certain that the progressive colonisation of the taigá and the influence of the railway will contribute to the development of agriculture in the Nizhneúdinsk district, although the conditions of the soil are less favourable than in that of Kansk.

From Nizhneúdinsk onwards, the country is more level, stretching to the station of Zimá for a distance of 240 versts. The grades occurring on this section of the railway are .009, and the curves have a radius of 250 sazhens.

Between the station of Nizhneúdinskaya and that of Khingúi, the line first crosses the small watershed of the rivers Kuriát and Udá and then rises to the station of Khingúi. In the valley of the Udá, there are three engineering works: a stone bridge of 12 sazhens, at the 1254 verst, spanning the river Rubákhina; an iron bridge over the Udá at the 1255 verst, having an opening of 180 sazhens with two spans of 40 sazhens and two of 50 sazhens; and a wooden bridge of 12 sazhens at the 1257 verst.

47, **Khingúi.** V class station (1270 v. from Krivoshchékovo, 2612 v. from Cheliábinsk). The village of Khingúi is 5 versts from the station and is situated on the Siberian highway, in the Nizhneúdinsk district (pop. 400). It contains a wooden church and a reading school.

48) **Khudoyelán.** V class station. Buffet. (1292 v. from Krivoshchékovo, 2658 from Cheliábinsk). The village of Khudoyelánskoe, in the Nizhneúdinsk district, stands close by on the Siberian highway, (pop. 500). It has a wooden church in honour of St. Nicholas the Miracle-worker, and a parish school.

49) **Kurzán.** V class station (1326 v. from Krivoshchékovo, 2658 v. from Cheliábinsk). At a distance of 8 versts, the village of Tráktovo-Kurzánskoe, in

the Nizhneúdinsk district (pop. 370) is situated on the Siberian highway. The village possesses a wooden church and a school with one class.

Hence the line descends to the river Saúr, spanning it at the 1335 verst by a wooden bridge of 18 sazhens and further, having passed over the summit of a low watershed, descends from the 1354 verst to the Kurzán, crossing this river by a wooden bridge with an opening of 30 sazhens. The station of Tulún stands within three versts of the bridge.

50) **Tulún.** III class station. Buffet. (1357 v. from Krivoshchékovo, 2688 v. from Cheliábinsk).

There is a medical and feeding station near the railway for the registration and distribution of the emigrants in the localities allotted for colonisation in the Nizhneúdinsk district. It is also the residence of an official entrusted with the regulation of the emigration movement.

The large trading village of Tulúnovskoe, in the Nizhneúdinsk district, is situated at a distance of four versts, on the Great Siberian highway, near the small stream Tulunchík and the river Uyá; it numbers 660 houses and a population exceeding 5,000. The village contains a wooden church in honour of the Intercession of the Holy Virgin, a school with two classes for boys and one with one class for girls; a poorhouse founded out of the fund of the church patronage, a reception room for outpatients, a chemist's shop, a fire brigade and a village board. The inhabitants occupy themselves with agriculture, carriage of goods by road and trade. There are over 70 trading firms in the willage with a yearly business exceeding R. 3,000,000. The opening of traffic on the Siberian main line has brought a great change in the modes of trade, as practised for some hundred years past, and delivered the small trading centres from their former dependence on the large towns and the leading firms, contributing also to the development of the commercial operations of this village. At present, the village of Tulúnovskoe constitutes an important centre of trade and export, whence various goods, avoiding Irkútsk, are despatched to the Angará and further to the landing-stages on the Léna, Ust-Kút or Zhigálov in order to supply the demand of the Léna gold-mining industry. This route is also taken by the workmen who, sometimes forming bodies of about 10,000 men, go to the gold mines. The fertile district within range of the railway supplies part of the grain exported to Irkútsk. In 1898, upwards of 18,000 puds of grain, mainly wheat, were forwarded from here to the East.

In June, 1891, the village of Tulúnovskoe was honoured by the visit of His Imperial Majesty, the present Emperor Nicholas II. A triumphal arch, which was erected for the reception of the Imperial traveller, remains as a memorial of this visit.

From the station of Tulún, standing on the watershed of the rivers Kurzán and Uyá, the line approaches the latter, crossing it by an iron bridge of 80 sazhens with two spans of 40 sazhens each. (1363 v.). The river Uya or Iyá, tributary of the Oká, falling into the Angará, has a total length of 600 versts; it is available for rafts and flows through a narrow and wooded valley; mineral springs occur along its upper waters on the northern slopes of the Sayán mountains.

51) **Azéi.** V class station. (1376 v. from Krivoshchékovo, 2708 v. from Cheliábinsk). Leaving this station, the line runs through a level country, traversing two small wooden bridges of 10 sazhens each (1382 v. and 1386 v.).

52) **Sheragúl.** V class station. (1396 v. from Krivoshchékovo, 2782 v.

from Cheliábinsk). The village of Sheragúl is situated in the Nizhneúdinsk district, within 6 versts of the station, on the Great Siberian highway. It numbers 320 houses and a population of 1,800. The village possesses a wooden church of the Archistrategus Michael, a school with one class and a parish school. Agriculture is the chief industry of the inhabitants. In June, 1891, His Imperial Majesty, the present Emperor Nicholas II, on His way from the Far East, passed the night in the house of the merchant Cheremnykh which, in commemoration of this visit, was given by its owner for the establishment of a parish school under the control of the Ministry of Public Education.

Hence the line rises to a low watershed, and then descends to the stream Ilí, crossing it at the 1407 verst by a wooden bridge with an opening of 6 sazhens and an altitude of 5 sazhens. After having reached the watershed, the line proceeds to the next station.

53) **Kuitún.** V class station. Buffet. (1431 v. from Krivoshchékovo, 2763 v. from Cheliábinsk).

The village of Kuitún, in the Nizhneúdinsk district, is at a distance of 3 versts, on the Great Siberian highway; it contains 320 houses and a population of 2,350. The village received its name from cold springs called „Kuitún", which in the Buriát language means „cold". It has a church in honour of the Prophet Elias, a parish school with two classes and a village board. Its inhabitants are engaged in agriculture. Hence the line proceeds along the summit of the watershed and, having traversed half of the distance to the next station, descends to the river Kimiltéi.

54) **Kimiltéi.** (1461 v. from Krivoshchékovo, 2793 v. from Cheliábinsk). The large trading village of Kimiltéi of the Nizhneúdinsk district, lies at a distance of 10 versts from the station (houses 455; pop. 3,300). It contains a large stone church of fine architecture in honour of St. Nicholas the Miracle-worker, a Jewish prayer-house, a school with two classes and parallel divisions, a parish school and village board. The population carries on trade and agriculture.

Within 2 versts of the station, the line crosses the Kimiltéi by a wooden bridge of 20 sazhens, and further ascends the watershed of the rivers Kimiltéi and Oká, having an altitude of 36 sazhens. Leaving the watershed, the line reaches the station of Zimá; whence it runs through mountainous districts.

55) **Zimá.** III class station. Buffet. (1487 v. from Krivoshchékovo, 2819 v. from Cheliábinsk). Near the station a wooden church was built at the cost of the Emperor Alexander III fund in honour of St. Theodor Tiron, and consecrated on the 14 May, 1898.

Within 5 versts of the station, is the large trading village of Zimínskoe situated at the junction of the rivers Zimá and Oká, on the great Siberian highway; it belongs to the Balagánsk district and has 464 houses and a population of 2,860. It contains a church, a parish school with one class, a reading school for girls, a poorhouse and village board. The inhabitants are mainly engaged in agriculture. Among them there are about 600 sectarians, the descendants of those who were exiled to this place on account of their religion at the beginning of the XIX century. On the 26 June, 1891, the village was honoured by the visit of the present Emperor Nicholas II, then Heir Apparent to the throne, on his way from the Far East. An exhibition of agricultural and other products of the Balagánsk district was organised for the arrival of His Majesty. A deputation from the local peasants offered His Majesty a folded image, representing the Holy Virgin and the Saints Innocent and Nicholas the Miracle-worker. Another deputation from the local Buriáts presented to the Emperor a model of a Buriat yúrta, cast in silver.

Within 3 versts of the station, the line crosses the river Oká by an iron bridge of 220 sazhens with two spans of 50 sazhens and three of 40 sazhens each.

The river Oká, which is a tributary of the Angará, has a total length of 750 versts; its current is very rapid, especially at its source. From its junction with the Zimá, the river is fit for rafting, becoming navigable only within 40 versts of its mouth. The basin of this river is richly provided with coal beds, which have been explored by the mining Engineers Obruchev and Bogdanóvich. The quality and the formation of the coal is the same as in the Moscow basin. According to the investigations of Bogdanóvich, the attention of promotors should be drawn to deposits of alum copperas. Iron copperas protrudes through seams of clay. The local inhabitants noticed long ago that the water possessed the property of blackening tanned skins. During the last epidemic of cholera, copperas earth was used for disinfecting. Many among the population living along this river suffer from goitre.

Down the river Oká, at the spot where it is crossed by the railway line, near the village of Burlúksk, are „painted stones" or cliffs standing on the bank adorned with numerous designs of riders, horses and cattle. Here are also situated famous grindstone quarries. From the river Oká onwards, the country assumes a more broken surface, retaining this character for a distance of 138 versts, to the station of Polovína. Here, the line is constructed according to specifications used in mountainous sections. Beginning its ascent from the valley of the Oká, the line passes over the high watershed of the rivers Oká and Tyrét and, after having crossed the latter by a wooden bridge of 10 sazhens (1515 v.), rises to the high watershed of the rivers Tyrét and Ungá.

56) **Tyrét.** V class station. Buffet. (1518 v. from Krivoshchékovo, 2840 v. from Cheliábinsk). The large village of Tyrét, in the Balagánsk district, is situated within 3 versts of the station, on the Siberian highway (houses 180, pop. 860).

Formerly this village belonged to the Buriát native board of the Balagánsk district, which consisted of 24 families, forming a population of 17,000 distributed in 150 villages throughout the territory between the rivers Oká and Zaláréya, covering a superficial area of 670,000 desiatins. Since 1898, the village of Tyrét, permanently settled by Christian Buriáts, has been subjected to the administrative rules generally adopted for peasants. There is a small wooden church and a parish school.

On the 26 June, 1891, the village was honoured by the visit of His Imperial Majesty, the present Emperor Nicholas II. His Majesty was greeted by the priest of the missionary church with images and holy banners; after having visited the church, where sang a chorus of pupils from the Tyrét native missionary school, His Majesty made a donation of R. 100 for the church and R. 200 for the teacher of the missionary school.

From the station of Tyrét, the line descends by a steep grade to the Ungá, spanning this river at the 1523 verst by a wooden bridge of 25 sazhens, and further on rises to the high watershed of the rivers Ungá and Sheragúl, which is intersected by ravines. Leaving its summit, the line crosses the Sheragúl (1536 v.) by a wooden bridge of 8 sazhens and, passing again over the low watershed of the rivers Sheragúl and Zalarí, on its way downwards reaches the station of Zalarí.

57) **Zalarí.** V class station. Buffet. (1540 v. from Krivoshchékovo, 2872 v.

from Cheliábinsk). The trading village of Zalarínskoe is near the station, on the river Zalarí and the great Siberian highway (houses 283, pop. 1650); it belongs to the Balagánsk district. The village contains a small but ancient church of St. Nicholas the Miracle-worker, parish schools with one class for boys and girls, a reading school built at the cost of the Irkútsk Diocesan Teaching Council, and a village board. On the 25 June, 1891, His Imperial Majesty, the present Emperor Nicholas II passed the night in this village. Within two versts of the station, the line runs over the river Zalarí by a wooden bridge of 30 sazhens, and ascends to the watershed of the rivers Zalarí and Kutulík.

58) **Golovínskaya.** V class station. (1560 v. from Krivoshchékovo, 2892 v. from Cheliábinsk). The village of Golovínskoe is situated within 3 versts of the station (houses 31; pop. 172), on the Great Siberian highway, in the Balagánsk district. The population consists of former Cossacks of the Balagánsk district. The village contains a chapel.

From here, the line gradually descends to the river Kutulík; coal beds occur throughout its entire course.

59) **Kutulík.** V class station. (1580 v. from Krivoshchékovo, 2912 v. from Cheliábinsk). The trading village of Kutulíkskoe in the Balagánsk district (houses 276, pop. 1996) lies within 6 versts of the station, on the great Siberian highway, near the river Kutulík. It possesses a wooden church of John the Baptist, three parish schools, a school for boys with one class, one for girls with one class, and a second class school for parish school teachers with one class. Carpentry and turnery workshops are attached to the schools. The chief industries of the population are agriculture and farming. Many of the inhabitants are afflicted with goitre.

Within 3 versts of the station, the line spans the Kutulík by a bridge of 10 sazhens and, further on, the Nóta by a short wooden bridge, on its way to the watershed of the rivers Nóta and Cheremkóvka.

60) **Cheremkóvo.** V class station. Buffet. (1601 v. from Krivoshchékovo, 2933 v. from Cheliábinsk). The large trading village of Cheremkóvo is situated in the Balagánsk district, in proximity to the station, on the great Siberian highway (houses 349, pop. 2,276). It contains a stone church of St. Nicholas the Miracle-worker, a parish school with two classes, a school for girls with one class, and a reading school attached to the church, a village board, dispensary for outpatients, poorhouse, several shops and stores. Markets are held every day; a lively trade is carried on in October before the feast of Our Lady of Kazán. The sphere of influence of the markets extends to a radius of about 100 versts.

As far as concerns agriculture and farming, this village and the whole volost of Cheremkóvo play an important part in the Irkútsk government.

The land bordering on the railway line, allotted for the use of the peasants and occupied by their dwellings, contains rich coal beds, which are very important on account of their position near the railway line and to the basin of the Angará, the latter being also plentifully provided with minerals.

The coal beds are worked partly by Engineer Markévich, who has attempted to supply the Midsiberian railway with mineral fuel. The chemical analysis of the coal shews the following results: volatile matters 44.17 (49.24), residue 55.49 (50.76), carbon 44.41 (47.72), ash 11.08 (3.04), sulphur 0.42 (0.60); carbon 65.09 (71.84), hydrogen 5.65 (6.05).

Within 2 versts of the station, the line crosses the Cheremkóvka by a wooden bridge of 6 sazhens and ascends to the watershed of the rivers

Angará and its tributary the Bélaya; on the watershed (1610 v.), the line traverses the frontier of the Balagánsk and Irkútsk district.

61) **Polovína.** III class station. Buffet. (1525 v. from Krivoshchékovo, 2945 v. from Cheliábinsk) A wooden church in honour of St. Basil the Great is being built at the station at the cost of the Emperor Alexander III fund.

The village of Polovínnaya, in the Irkútsk district, lies close by, on the Great Siberian highway (houses 300).

Hence the line descends to the Bélaya, left tributary of the Angará, and crosses it by an iron bridge with an opening of 100 sazhens, composed of four spans of 25 sazhens each.

The country here becomes level, and the specifications adopted for the construction of the railway from the station to Irkútsk are such as are generally used for foot-hill sections.

On the right bank of the Bélaya, opposite the village of Maltínskoe and near the villages of Uzky Lug and Badáiskaya, occur seams of fire-clay. The one found at a depth of 5 to 7 arshins is of a particularly good quality, being white and greasy like pure kaolin. The clay obtained from this deposit resembles the best kinds of Belgian clay from the environs of Anden near Nemours. As regards its quality, properties and chemical formation, the crystalline kaolin found at Usky Lug is very much like the well-known clay

Village of Télma.

in the Borovichí district of the Nóvgorod government. In 1869, the Irkútsk merchant Pereválov established a china and earthenware manufactory for the exploitation of these deposits. At the present time, the Khaitín manufactory situated at the mouth of the Khaitá, falling into the Bélaya, at a distance of 9 versts from the station, is under the management of the Siberian Company for the production of china, earthenware, glass and pottery.

The annual output of the manufactory amounts on an average to a value of R. 398,576.

62) **Málta.** V class station (1646 v. from Krivoshchékovo, 2975 v. from Cheliábinsk). Near the station stands, the large trading village of Maltínskoe in the Irkútsk district, on the great Siberian highway and on the river Bélaya. There are a stone church of the Ascension, parish school with one class, poorhouse and village board.

According to information supplied by Mining Engineer Bogdanóvich, former director of the works of the Midsiberian mining party, the country stretching from the river Bélaya towards Irkútsk along the upper reaches of

Village of Télma. Distillery and cloth manufactory.

the Khaitá, Télma and the tributaries of the Kitói, presents a vast swampy taigá, which has as yet been hardly explored; however, it may be supposed that it is plentifully provided with minerals and metals. The coal-field commences in the valley of the Maltínka and embraces an immense area on both sides of the Angará.

Within 2 versts of the station, the line spans the Maltínka by a wooden bridge of 6 sazhens and, passing over the watershed, crosses the swampy river Skipidárka or Usólka by a wooden bridge of 6 sazhens; further on, a bridge of 10 sazhens spans the Telmínka, from which the line rises to a low watershed.

63) **Telmá.** V class station. Buffet. (1667 v. from Krivoshchékovo, 2993 v. from Cheliábinsk). The trading village of Telmínskoe (pop. 3,000) is situated in proximity to the station, on the left bank of the Angará at its junction with the Telmínka, in the Irkútsk district. It contains a stone church in honour of Our Lady of Kazán, a village board, the Alexander school with two classes, a parish school for girls with one class, a poorhouse and a dispensary room for outpatients.

Here are the Télma cloth manufactory, glass-works and distilleries, belonging to Belogolóvy. The factory has existed since the beginning of the

XVIII century, and formed first the property of the State, then that of the Irkútsk comissariat and, only in 1862, became a private concern. The manufactory is supplied with wool from the Transbaikál region, with Glauber's salt from the Barguzínsk lakes, and with dyes from Russia. The annual production of cloth amounts to a value of R. 50,000 to 60,000.

A model school, with two classes for boys and girls, is attached to the factory. Glass of various sizes from 4×4 to 6×24 vershóks, and also other glass wares are made in the works.

The cloth manufactory and the glass works, having been in operation for a period of over 150 years, testify to the fact that manufacture and industry may be succesfully carried on in Siberia.

Within 7 versts of the village of Télma, down the Angará, at some distauce from the Siberian highway, lies the village of Usólie (pop. 5,000), with the famous State salterns, which give a commercial importance to this village. The brines worked by means of pit-holes are on the left bank of the Angará and on the island of Varníchnoe, where the buildings of the works are situated. The annual output of salt amounts to 300,000. The salt springs issue from deposits of lime, clay and calcareous slates.

Monastery of the Ascension (phot. by Gavrílov).

Throughout the Télma vólost on the Angará and especially in Usólie, goitre is of frequent occurrence.

From the Télma station, the line reaches the Kitói (left tributary of the Angará) by a light grade, crossing the river by an iron bridge with an opening of 70 sazhens, having a span of 40 sazhens, and two smaller ones of 15 sazhens each. Further on, the line ascends to the next station.

The Kitói rises on spurs of the Sayán ridge. The river is 240 versts long and 80 sazhens wide; the current is rapid, being navigable only in its lower reaches. Throughout its course, its banks are considered to be rich in gold.

64) **Sukhóvskaya.** V class station. (1691 v. from Krivoshchékovo, 3020 v. from Cheliábinsk). The village of Sukhóvskaya (pop. 300) is situated near the station on the Great Siberian highway and on the left bank of the Angará. There are a church, school and village board.

Naphtha has been found in the neighbourhood of the village, on the bank of the Angará, amidst carboniferous strata containing a large percentage of hydrogen.

Monastery of the Ascension. Relics of St. Innocent, first Bishop of Irkútsk (phot. by Shukachév).

From the station, the line runs along a slope on the left side of the Angará, crossing its small tributaries, the Yelóvka, by a wooden bridge of 7 sazhens and the Mechétly one of 10 sazhens.

65) **Innokéntievskaya.** III class station. Buffet. (1715 v. fròm Krivo-

shchékovo, 3044 v. from Cheliábinsk). The station received its name in honour of St. Innocent, Archbishop of Irkútsk, the first Miracle-worker of Siberia.

Near the station, on the left bank of the Angará, within 4 versts of Irkútsk is situated the St. Innocent firat-class monastery of the Ascension, created in 1672 by licence of Cornelius, Metropolitan of Tobólsk, by the monk Gerásim; the first wooden church was founded at the same time in honour of the Holy Image of Our Saviour.

The monastery played an active part in the civilising mission to the East. In 1726, a Russo-Mongolian school was added to it. The Irkútsk diocese was created in 1727, and St. Innocent appointed Archbishop.

St. Innocent (John Kulchítsky) was born in Little Russia in the government of Chernígov. Having been arch-monk in the fleet, and a student at the Slavo-Latin Academy of Moscow, he was appointed Bishop of Pereyáslavl and attached to the ecclesiastical mission to Pekin, in the presence of the Emperor Peter I, by the Metropolitan Stephen Yavórsky, the Archbishop Theodosius Yanóvsky aud Theophanes Prokópovich. He was named Archbishop of Irkútsk on the 15 January, 1727, and died on the 27 November, 1731. St. Innocent was buried under the altar of the Tíkhvin church, in the monastery of the Ascension. His remains were examined on the 29 January, 1801, by the Bishops Benjamin of Irkútsk and Justin of Sviázh, and according to an ukaz given by the Synod on the 1 December, 1804, they were declared to be holy; they

View of Irkútsk (phot. by Yastrémbsky).

were transported and exhibited for the veneration of the public on the 9 February, 1805. The rich monastery, which possesses six churches, including the cathedral of the Ascension and of the Assumption, contains a silver shrine with the relics of the first Miracle-worker of Siberia; it is surrounded by a stone wall with towers and is under the control of the Vicar of Irkútsk.

On the 17 June 1873, the monastery was visited by his Imperial Highness the Grand Duke Alexis Alexándrovich, and on the 24 June, 1891, by the present Emperor Nicholas II, then Heir Apparent to the throne. Attended by his suite and Bishop Benjamin, the Tsesarévich was greeted at the entrance gate by the superior of the monastery and the fraternity with ringing of bells and chanting of prayers in honour of St. Innocent.

After having listened to the singing, the Tsesarévich knelt at the shrine of the Siberian Saint, kissed the relics and received the image of St. Innocent, presented to him by Agathangelus, Vicar of Irkútsk. At the same time, a deputation from Shaman Buriáts expressed the desire of 250 men to adopt the orthodox religion and to receive the name of Nicholas in commemoration of the Tsesarévich's visit to Siberia, which was thus to be preserved in the memory of their descendants. The Imperial traveller gracioulу acceded to this request.

Running towards Irkútsk, the line at the 1720 verst crosses the Irkút, left tributary of the Angará, by a wooden bridge of 120 sazhens.

From the right bank of the Irkút, commences the Irkútsk-Baikál branch, which belongs to the Transbaikál railway line. Proceeding from the Irkút to the left bank of the Angará, the line reaches the suburb of Glázkovskoe, lying opposite Irkútsk.

66) **Irkútsk.** Buffet. (1722 v. from Krivoshchékovo, 3052 v. from Cheliábinsk). The station is situated within 2 versts of ths iron bridge over the Irkút, in Glázkovskoe, the suburb of Irkútsk, and is connected with the town by the pontoon bridge of the Tsesarévich Nicholas.

Irkútsk. is a government town and the administrative centre of the Irkútsk region which, under a Governor-General, comprises the Yeniséisk and Irkútsk governments and the Yakútsk territory.

Irkútsk. Cathedral of Our Lady of Kazán.

The town lies on the right bank of the Angará, opposite the mouth of the Irkút (52°17' N. lat., 124°51, E. long.) at an absolute height of 1,360 feet, in a dry and level country. Within the limits of the town, the Angará receives the river Ushakóvka, which separates the central part of the town from the suburb of Známenskoe and the suburb inhabited by the working class. The suburb of Glázkovskoe is on the left side of the Angará. The census of 1897 shewed a total population of 51,434 (26,517 males, 24,917 females). As regards its population, Irkútsk holds the second place throughout Siberia, yielding precedence only to the town of Tomsk. The town was founded in 1652, when the son of a noble, Iván Pakhóbov in order to collect the yassák, or tribute paid in furs among the Buriáts, established an entrenched post provided with towers, stockades, a ditch and barriers, which received the name of Irkútsk from its position on the Irkút. Afterwards it was transferred to the bank of the An-

ИРКУТСКЪ. IRKOUTSK.

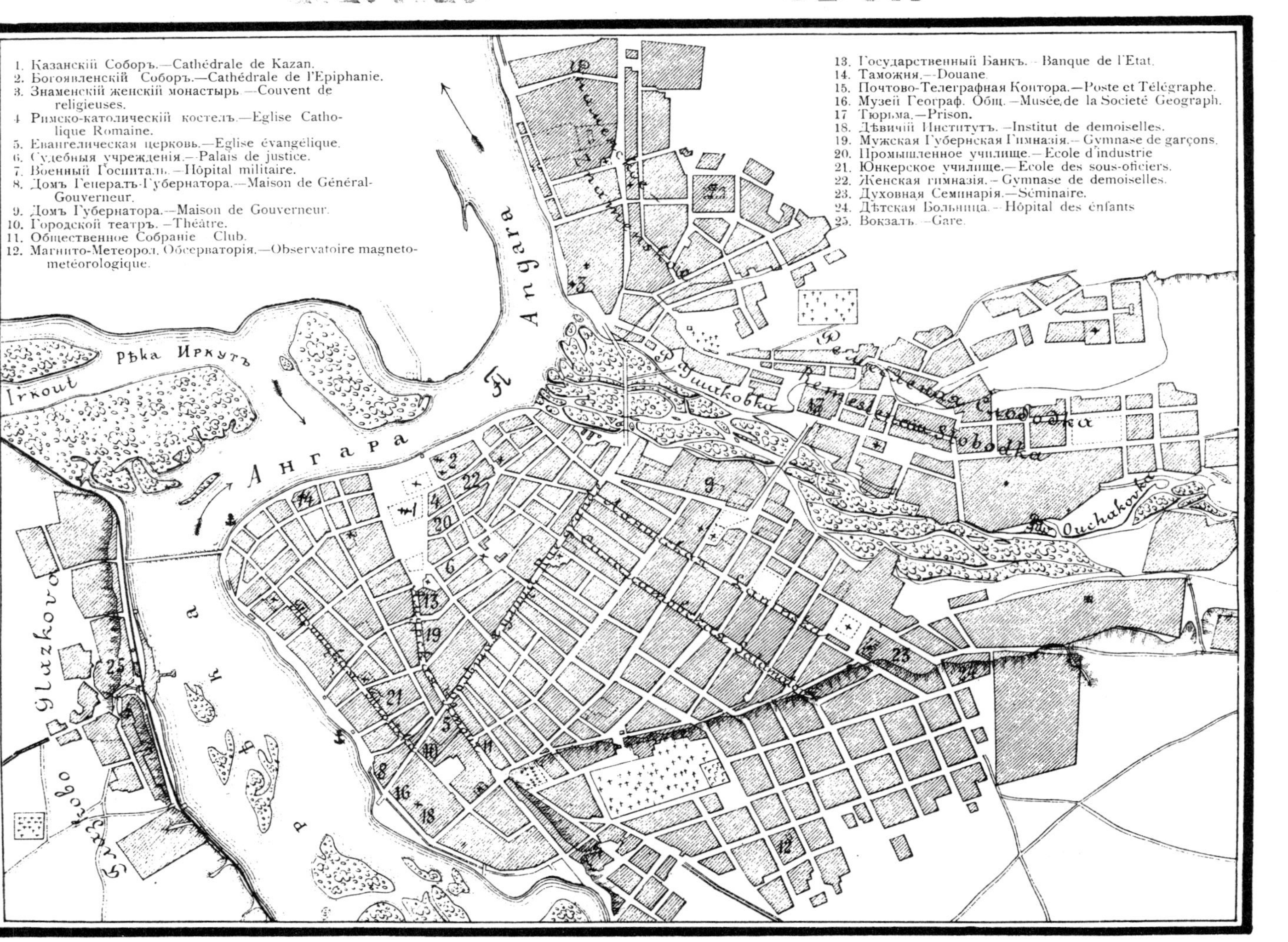

1. Казанскій Соборъ.—Cathédrale de Kazan.
2. Богоявленскій Соборъ.—Cathédrale de l'Epiphanie.
3. Знаменскій женскій монастырь.—Couvent de religieuses.
4. Римско-католическій костелъ.—Eglise Catholique Romaine.
5. Евангелическая церковь.—Eglise évangélique.
6. Судебныя учрежденія.—Palais de justice.
7. Военный Госпиталь.—Hôpital militaire.
8. Домъ Генералъ-Губернатора.—Maison de Général-Gouverneur.
9. Домъ Губернатора.—Maison de Gouverneur.
10. Городской театръ.—Théâtre.
11. Общественное Собраніе Club.
12. Магнито-Метеорол. Обсерваторія.—Observatoire magneto-metéorologique.
13. Государственный Банкъ.—Banque de l'Etat.
14. Таможня.—Douane.
15. Почтово-Телеграфная Контора.—Poste et Télégraphe.
16. Музей Географ. Общ.—Musée de la Societé Geograph.
17. Тюрьма.—Prison.
18. Дѣвичій Институтъ.—Institut de demoiselles.
19. Мужская Губернская Гимназія.—Gymnase de garçons.
20. Промышленное училище.—Ecole d'industrie.
21. Юнкерское училище.—Ecole des sous-officiers.
22. Женская гимназія.—Gymnase de demoiselles.
23. Духовная Семинарія.—Séminaire.
24. Дѣтская Больница.—Hôpital des enfants.
25. Вокзалъ.—Gare.
Angara
Рѣка Иркутъ
Irkout
Ангара
Ouchakovka
Glazkovo

Авто-литографія Т-ва Художественной Печати. Англійскій пр., 28

ВЛАДИВОСТОКЪ

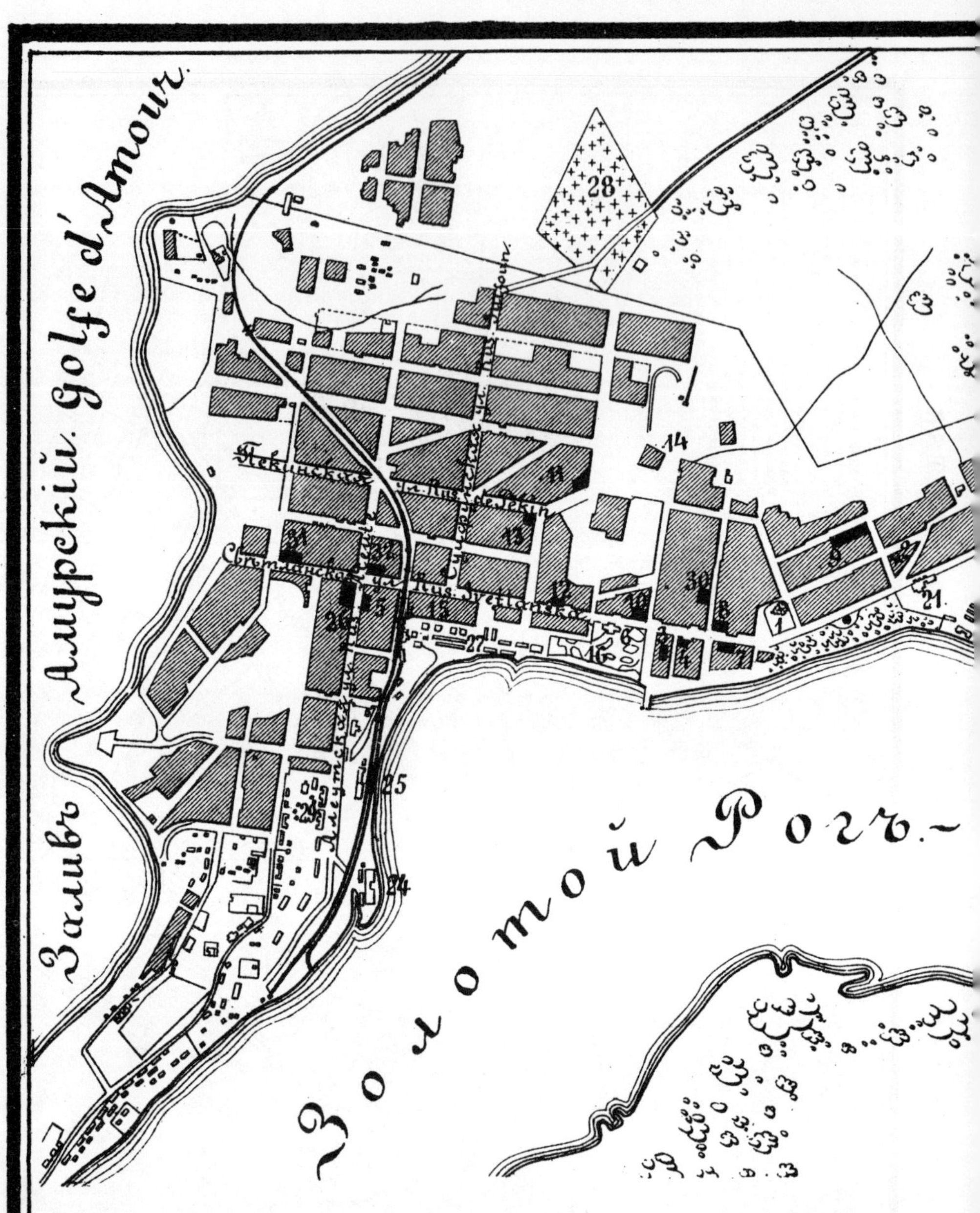

1. Соборъ во имя Пресвятой Богородицы.—Cathédrale de la Sainte Vierge.
2. Евангелическая церковь.—Eglise Evangélique.
3. Музей Географическаго Общества.—Musée de la Société Géographique.
4. Домъ Военнаго Губернатора.—Maison de Gouverneur.
5. Областное Правленіе.—Administration de la Region.
6. Домъ Командира Порта.—Maison du Commendant du port.
7. Штабъ Командира Порта.—Etat Major du Commendant.
8. Городская Дума и Училище.—Conseil Municipal et Ecole.
9. Мужская Гимназія.—Gymnase de garçons.
10. Женская Гимназія.—Gymnase de demoiselles.
11. Окружной Судъ.—Tribunal.
12. Почтово-Телегр. Конт
13. Полицейское управлен
   Corps de pompiers.
14. Больница.—Hôpital.
15. Городской садъ.—Jard
16. Адмиральскій садъ.—J
17. Морской Госпиталь.—
18. Экипажная казарма.—
19. Сухой докъ.—Dock.
20. Новое Адмиралтейств
21. Морское Собраніе и
   bliothèque.
22. Домъ Командира Экип

VLADIVOSTOK.

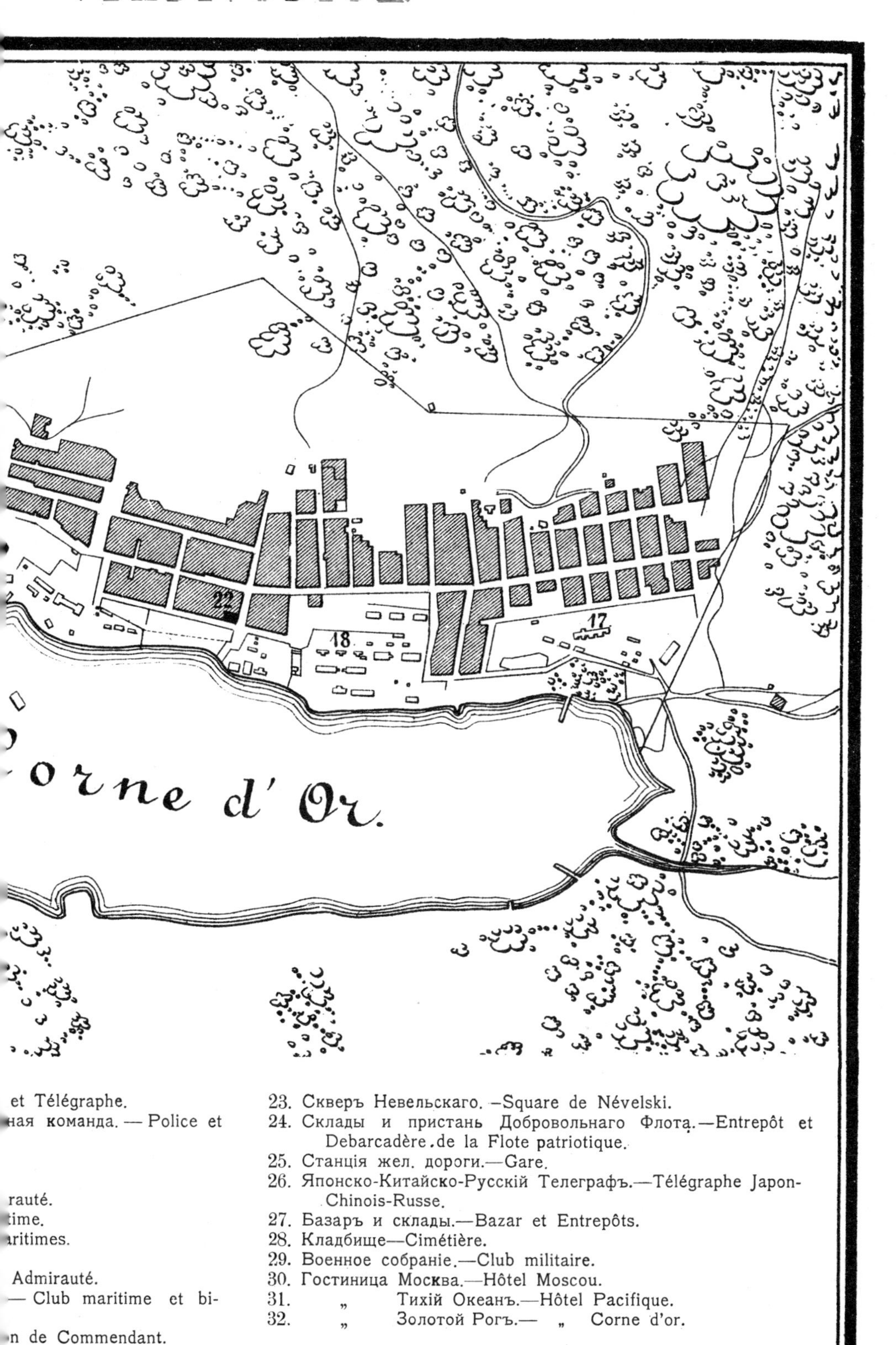

et Télégraphe.
ная команда. — Police et

rauté.
time.
ritimes.

Admirauté.
— Club maritime et bi-

n de Commendant.

23. Скверъ Невельскаго. —Square de Névelski.
24. Склады и пристань Добровольнаго Флота.—Entrepôt et Debarcadère de la Flote patriotique.
25. Станція жел. дороги.—Gare.
26. Японско-Китайско-Русскій Телеграфъ.—Télégraphe Japon-Chinois-Russe.
27. Базаръ и склады.—Bazar et Entrepôts.
28. Кладбище—Cimétière.
29. Военное собраніе.—Club militaire.
30. Гостиница Москва.—Hôtel Moscou.
31. „ Тихій Океанъ.—Hôtel Pacifique.
32. „ Золотой Рогъ.— „ Corne d'or.

ТОМСКЪ. TOMSK.

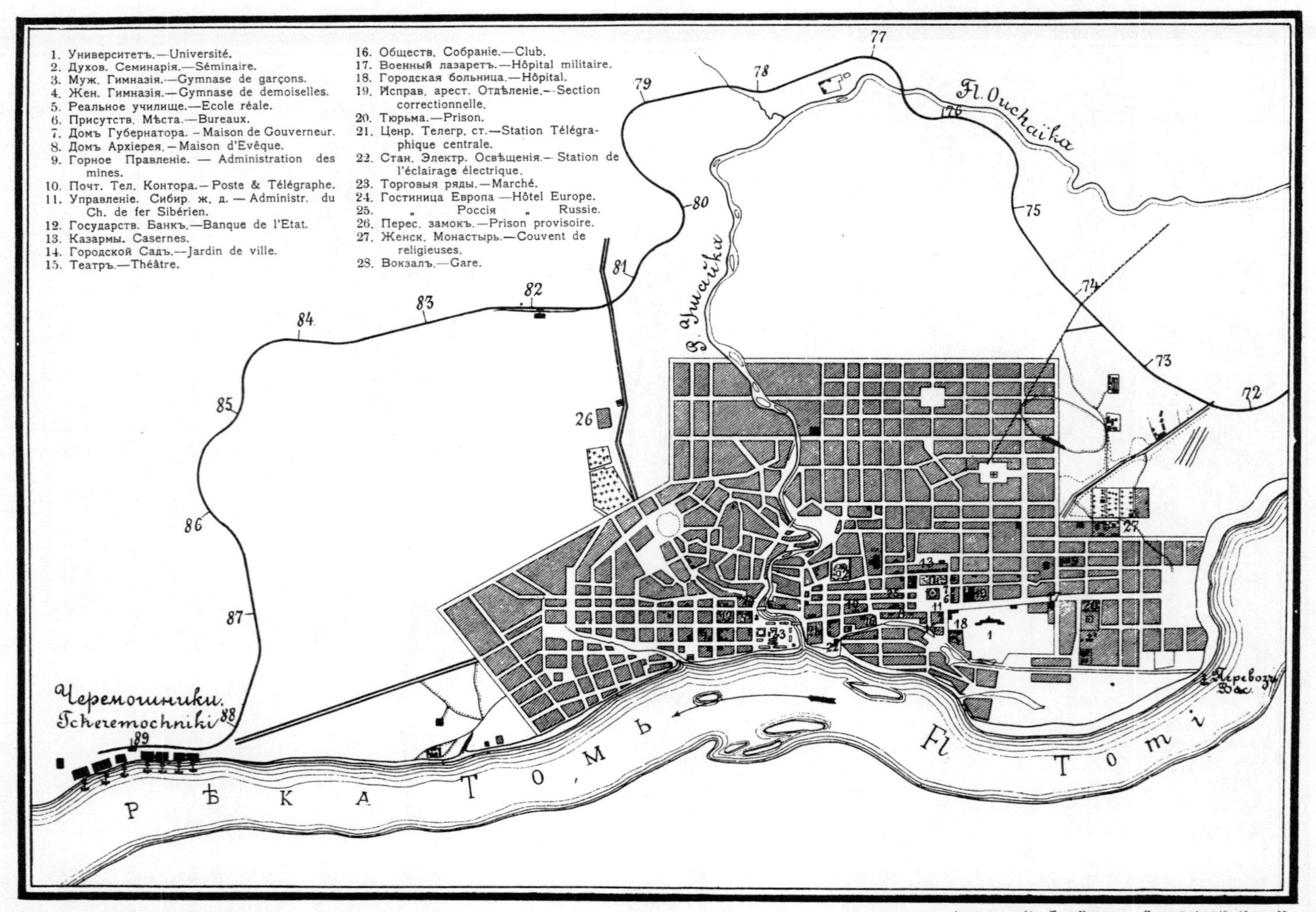

1. Университетъ.—Université.
2. Духов. Семинарія.—Séminaire.
3. Муж. Гимназія.—Gymnase de garçons.
4. Жен. Гимназія.—Gymnase de demoiselles.
5. Реальное училище.—Ecole réale.
6. Присутств. Мѣста.—Bureaux.
7. Домъ Губернатора.—Maison de Gouverneur.
8. Домъ Архіерея.—Maison d'Evêque.
9. Горное Правленіе. — Administration des mines.
10. Почт. Тел. Контора.—Poste & Télégraphe.
11. Управленіе. Сибир. ж. д. — Administr. du Ch. de fer Sibérien.
12. Государств. Банкъ.—Banque de l'Etat.
13. Казармы. Casernes.
14. Городской Садъ.—Jardin de ville.
15. Театръ.—Théâtre.
16. Обществ. Собраніе.—Club.
17. Военный лазаретъ.—Hôpital militaire.
18. Городская больница.—Hôpital.
19. Исправ. арест. Отдѣленіе.—Section correctionnelle.
20. Тюрьма.—Prison.
21. Ценр. Телегр. ст.—Station Télégraphique centrale.
22. Стан. Электр. Освѣщенія.—Station de l'éclairage électrique.
23. Торговыя ряды.—Marché.
24. Гостиница Европа —Hôtel Europe.
25. „ Россія „ Russie.
26. Перес. замокъ.—Prison provisoire.
27. Женск. Монастырь.—Couvent de religieuses.
28. Вокзалъ.—Gare.
Fl. Ouchaika
Р. Ушайка
Черемошники.
Tscheremochniki
Перевозъ
РѢКА ТОМЬ
Fl. Tomi

Авто-литографія „Т-ва Художеств. Печати“. Англійскій пр., 28.

gará, near the present cathedral and the Archbishop's house. In 1682, a special voyevódstvo under the command of a voyevóda or military chief, was established in Irkútsk and, in 1686, the stockaded post was transformed into a town. The ukáz, regarding the organisation of the Irkútsk government, was published on the 14 October, 1764 and, in 1783, the Irkútsk vicegerency was formed, comprising the Irkútsk, Nerchínsk, Transbaikál and Okhótsk territories.

In 1803, the whole of Siberia was subjected to the administration of a Governor-General, resident at Irkútsk. Among the holders of this office may be mentioned: Privy Councillor Selefóntov, Privy Councillor Péstel and M. M. Speránsky, who was appointed on the 22 March, 1819, and filled the post till 1822. During this period, Siberia for purposes of administration was divided into West and East Siberia. The first Governor-General of Eastern Siberia was Privy Councillor Lavínsky. The history of the town and of Eastern Siberia is closely connected with the names of such eminent administrators as Count M. N. Muraviόv-Amúrsky, under whose management the Amúr region was annexed to Russia, and Count A. P. Ignátiev, who contributed to accelerate the construction of the Siberian Railway, and applied himself to the study of the economic conditions of the country, which resulted in most valuable statistical works specially compiled on his initiative.

Irkútsk. Cathedral of the Epiphany.

Irkútsk. Governor-General's house.

In outward appearance, Irkútsk is one of the finest and best organised towns of Siberia It is supplied with telephones, but the streets are unpaved and badly lit. The town contains 124 streets, 15 lanes, 6 squares and 2 public gardens. The total number of buildings is 12,477, valued at R. 24,955,275; of them, 1,458 are of stone (value R. 17,651,750), 31 are made of mixed material (value R. 147,175), 10,988 of wood (value R. 7,156,350). A second class nunnery of the Miraculous Apparition of the Holy Virgin was founded in

1693. There are two cathedrals, one of Our Lady of Kazán, the other of the Epihhany; 29 orthodox churches: 14 parish churches of stone, 13 house-chapels, one at the cemetery, one stone church out of town, near the Archbishop's summer villa; a Catholic and a Lutheran chapel. two Jewish synagogues and a Mohammedan mosque. The best buildings of tbe town are the theatre, museum, the Governor-General's house, the Girls' Institute of the Emperor Nicholas I, Mrs. Medvédnikov's orphanage, an industrial school, a public club, and Sukachév's house, containing the court of justice and the district tribunal.

The educational institutions are 45 in number: a church seminary, a church school for boys, commercial, mechanical and technical school, seminary for teachers, elementary school attached to the seminary, mining school, town school with classes, commercial aud educational school of N. P. Trapéznikov, the institute for girls of the Emperor Nicholas I, Kháminov's gymnasium, for girls Mrs. Beliáev's preparatory gymnasium for girls, central schools for women surgeons' assistants, Mrs. Medvédnikov's orphanage, orphans' commercial school, military school, military surgeons' assistants school, preparatory school for the Siberian Cadet Corps, 5 parish schools, one infant school, 15 parish schools for boys and girls and 2 Sunday schools.

Irkútsk. Sukachév's house, containing judicial institutions.

There are 14 charitable institutions: the Alexander children's home, the chidren's home bearing the name of the Empress Maria Feodorovna, the home of the Charitable Society, a home for convict children, a correctional and educational home for boys and girls, Sibiriakóv's poorhouse, Bazánov's foundling home, the poorhouse attached to the Kuznetsóv Hospital, the poorhouse attached to the Relief Society of the Mater Dolorosa, Mrs. Sukachév's poorhouse, the Mary Sisters of Mercy Society, the Jacob Alexander Sisters of Mercy Society, and a night shelter.

There are the following missionary, charitable, scientific and other societies operating in accordance with their charters: Diocesan committee of the orthodox missionary society, local department of the Russian Red Cross Society, Relief Society of the Mater Dolorosa, Irkútsk Roman Catholic Relief Society, Relief Society for Poor Emigrants, Relief Society for destitute schoolchildren in Eastern Siberia, a clerks' mutual aid society, a branch of the Relief Society for the Blind under the patronage of the Empress Mary Alexándrovna, a mutual aid society for scholars and teachers of the Irkútsk government, the East Siberian branch of the Imperial Russian Geographical Society opened in 1851, Society of Doctors of Eastern Siberia, a volunteer fire brigade, a society of amateur cyclists, the Society of Siberian Sportsmen, an amateur's society of music and literature, a cooperative supply society, the Irkútsk public club, a military club, and a clerks' mutual aid society club. Musical classes were established in 1899, the only organisation of this kind throughout Siberia.

The town theatre, which is one of finest provincial theatres was built according to the plan of the architect Schröter at a cost of R. 294,473, including a donation of R. 198,159. The construction of this building is entirely due to the Governor-General A. D. Goremykin, who collected private donations and superintended the work.

Theatre in Irkútsk.

Among scientific societies, may be mentioned the East Siberian branch of the Imperial Russian Geographical Society, which was the first scientific society in Siberia established in 1851, in the time of Count Muraviòv - Amúrsky. It occupies a fine buliding on the bank of the Angará, and possesses an extensive museum with rich ethnographical and archaeological collections.

The objects composing the Buddhist collection are particularly worthy of attention, being very well selected.

The museum library contains 4,225 works and 508 maps; the Siberian division is especially complete and interesting. The publication of the „Memoirs" of the Siberian Geographical Society began in 1854; the first numbers were printed in St. Petersburg, and the next following in Irkútsk. Since 1870, the Society has published its „News" containing short reviews and articles, aiming at the rapid communication of information offering any particular interest. For some years past, the „Memoirs" have ceased to be published by the Society. The „News" comprises XXIII volumes from 1898.

Museum of the East Siberian branch of the Imperial Geographical Society.

Since 1897, the Society has published periodical „Transactions", of which two editions have been issued. The scientific activity of the Society is closely connected with the names of Maak, Chekanóvsky, Dybóvsky, Godlévsky, Chérsky, Miliútin, Potánin, Pozdnéev, Yádrintsev, Przewálski, Poliakóv, Adriánov, Máikov, Jochelsohn, Klemenz, Obruchev and others.

Libraries: public town library with fixed entrance fee, containing over 27,000 volumes, a free public reading-room, the East Siberian Imperial Russian Geographical Society's library free; that of the ecclesiastical seminary, which is one of the best, possessing 20,000 volumes and including rare and valuable editions. Makúshin's bookshop, Mrs. Vitkóvski's printing offices, and those of the Government Board, Kokóvin, Leibóvich, Makúshin and Sízykh.

Irkútsk. Catholic church.

Photographic studios: Arnold, Hofmann, Degtiarióv, Mamónov, and Milévsky.

Periodicals published in Irkútsk: The Irkútsk Government Gazette (weekly), Irkútsk Diocesan Gazette (twice a month), Circulars for the East Siberian schools under the control of the Ministry of Education (twice a month). The Irkútsk Municipality News (issued twice a month), the East Siberian Imperial Geographical Society's News (irregularly issued five times a year), Transactions of the same Society (irregular publications), Transactions of the Society of Doctors of Eastern Siberia. The Eastern Review (literature and politics, daily) R. 9 a year; the Siberian Magazine is published as supplement to the Gazette, subscription R. 2 a year.

Irkútsk. Lutheran church.

Hospitals and sanitary institutions; Kuznetsóv, Soldátov, for citizens of the lower class, the Iván and Matrióna children's hospital, the Mikhéev dispensary, a military hospital, and a sanatorium for animals.

There are 4 chemist's shops, a druggist's and the chemical store of the military department.

Being the centre of the administrative and judicial institutions, Irkútsk contains also other establishments meeting the requirements of the country:

the Irkútsk customhouse, the magnetic and meteorological observatory and the mining department with goldmelting laboratory.

Works und factories of Irkútsk, comprising 88 various concerns, have a total production exceeding a million rubls (R. 1,060,451); there are 15 tanneries (R. 249,700), 6 fur manufactories (R. 64,100), 4 soap and tallow boileries (R. 82,000), 5 distilleries and rectifying works (R. 170,277), 5 breweries (R. 71,777), 3 saw-mills (R. 66,599), and 6 rope-yards (R. 20,560). According to data obtained from the revenue deparment, the annual turnover of the commercial enterprises paying duty amounts to R. 19,604,500.

In this respect, the first place belongs to drapery and manufactured wares—R. 3,850,000, grocery — R. 3,046,000, haberdashery and iron wares—R. 1,466,000, tea and Chinese goods,—R. 1,210,000, furs—R. 684,000, shoes—R. 630,000, wine cellars—R. 589,600, mining goods—R. 535,000, shipping enterprises—R 400,000, fish industry—R. 235,000, iron and pig-iron—R. 175,000 etc.

Irkútsk. Commercial school.

The duties, levied (mainly on tea) at the Irkútsk customhouse, amounted in 1897 to R. 9,434,231. 23 k. gold.

The annual turnover of the commercial enterprises shews Irkútsk to be an important trading centre. The following financial institutions meet the requirements of local trade and industry: a branch of the State Bank, branch of the Siberian Trade Bank, branch of the Russo-Chinese Bank, Mrs. Medvédnikov's Bank, an agency of the Nízhni-Nóvgorod-Samára and Yarosláv-Kostromá Land Bank, a town loan-bank. The capital and savings deposited at the local branch of the State Bank of Irkútsk amount to a sum of R. 22,000,000.

According to the local data of 1899, the town revenue amounted to R. 681,529, including R. 275,476 interest on private capital presented to the town.

The property of the town, besides real estate, consists of a capital amounting to R. 4,946,419 at the disposal of the town board; the interest is employed for the maintenance of educational and charitable institutions. The largest capital (R. 2,456,493) belongs to Trapéznikov.

The most important firms are Belogolóvy—distillery, cloth and glass wares; Vtórov—manufactured articles; Glótov, shipping on the Léna and Angará; Zhárnikov—Mining goods; Kalmeer, manufactured and mercery goods; Sibiriakóv, mining, navigation on the Amúr; Telnykh—haberdashery and iron wares; Korolióv—tea and sugar; Molchánov—tea; Nemchínov—tea, navigation on the Baikál; Stakhéev—manufactured wares; Kuznetsóv—grocery, and the Léna—Vitím Company, belonging to Nemchínov, Bazánov and Sibiriakóv,

Transport offices: Andréev, Bliakher, Brothers Kuznetsóv, Kukhtérin and Sons, Poliakóv, Púshnikov and Shádrin.

Hotels and furnished rooms: „Decot" (hotel and restaurant) is the best, with rooms from R. 2 a day. „Europe", „Siberia" (hotel and restaurant), the „Amúr Inn" (furnished rooms), „Jung", with good restaurant and excellent dinners.

Hackney-coach tariff: drive in the town 30 k. in the day, 40 k. at night. To the Jerusalem mountain, to the Upper-Amúr barrier and the Bazánov children's hospital, 30 k. in the day, and 50 k. at night. To the suburbs of Glázkovo, Znaménie and to the Trading Settlement 40 k. in the day, 60 k. at night. The toll for the passage of the bridge of the Tsesarévich Nicholas and over the Angará is paid by the passenger. An hour's drive costs 50 k. in the day, and 60 k. at night. The day lasts from 7 o'clock in the morning to 10 in the evening, the night commences at 10 in the evening and ends at 7 in the morning.

Among the historical events in the life of the town, may be mentioned: the visit of the Grand Duke Alexis Alexándrovich in 1873, on his way round the world, and in 1891, that of the Tsesarévich, the present Emperor Nicholas II. His Imperial Majesty arrived in Irkútsk, the 23 June, in the steamer „Speránsky" by the Angará; the landing-place was adorned with a triumphal arch, which remains to the present day. During his stay in the town from the 23 to the 24 June, His Imperial Majesty visited many educational establishments, the museum of the Eastern Branch of the Imperial Russian Geographical Society, the gold-melting laboratory, the Monastery of the Ascension, and the camp of the reserve battalion. He also attended the consecration and opening of the pontoon bridge over the Angará, which was built at the cost of the town in commemoration of the Imperial visit. On the 24 June, after having been present at a ball in the public club, His Imperial Majesty left Irkútsk on the steamer „Speránsky" and, steaming down the Angará, reached the settlement of Bárkhotovo, whence accompanied by A. D. Gorémykin, Governor-General of Irkútsk, he proceeded in an open carriage to Tomsk. Within the last years of the century, the history of the town and of the whole of Siberia has been marked by events important for civilisation: the introduction of new laws in 1896, and the opening of traffic on the Great Siberian Railway in 1898, connecting Irkútsk and Europe by an uninterrupted railway line.

Bridge over the Angará in the town of Irkútsk.

Leaving the station of Irkútsk, the line runs along the left bank of the Angará.

67) **Mikhálevo** (1748 v. from Krivoshchékovo, 5076 v. from Cheliábinsk) is situated near the village of Mikhálevo (pop. 352). Continuing its course along the left bank of the Angará, the line, within 3 versts of the station crosses the Kurmá, left tributary of the Angará, by a wooden bridge of 10

sazhens. Further, at the 50 verst, it runs over the Lánka by a wooden bridge of 15 sazhens. From this station to the Baikál, there are 44 small wooden bridges.

68) **Baikál.** (1786 v. from Krivoshchékovo, 3116 v. from Cheliábinsk). From this station, the line runs for a distance of about 400 sazhens and, reaching the Baikál, terminates at the landing - place, whence the trains are transported by an icebreaking ferry.

Arrival of the first train at Irkútsk on the 16 August, 1898.

The ruling grade throughout the Irkútsk-Baikál line is of .093

The Tomsk branch line.

The branch line leaves the main Siberian track at the station of Taigá, (222 v. from Krivoshchékovo and 1554 v. from Cheliábinsk). Running to the north-east towards the town of Tomsk, the line has a total length of 89,345 versts. For a distance of 20 versts, the line proceeds along the watershed of the rivers Katát and Kuyerbák, falling into the Yáya, Tuguyánovka and Basandáika, tributaries of the Tom. The country is monotonous and covered with continuous and mostly swampy taigá.

1) **Basandáika.** V class station (45 v. from Taigá, 1599 v. from Cheliábinsk). From here the line proceeds along the watershed of the river Basandáika and Usháika. The country becomes more hospitable and even picturesque.

2) **Mezhenínovka.** IV class station (73 v. from Taigá, 1627 v. from Cheliábinsk). Leaving the station, the line crosses the Usháika (77 v.) by an iron bridge, with an opening of 20 sazhens, and gradually ascending the Voskresénskaya mountain reaches the town of Tomsk. A considerable quantity of goods, mainly wheat-flour, are conveyed from this station to Eastern Siberia: in 1898, the export of wheat-flour amounted to 214,340 puds.

View of the Tomsk branch.

3) **Tomsk.** III class station. Buffet. (82 v. from Taigá, 1636 v. from Cheliábinsk). Is situated within 2 versts of the town of Tomsk, being connected

with it by a macadam road. The country is level, dry and covered with young birch wood. The goods traffic is considerable, and increases in connexion with the expansion of commercial relations evoked by the railway.

Bridge over the Usháika.

During the year 1898, the goods imported from the station amounted to 3,000,000 puds. About 284,989 puds of wheat-flour were conveyed from the station to Eastern Siberia in 1898. Hence the line descends with maximum grades of .015 towards the river Tom.

4) **Cheremoshnikí.** V class station (89 v. from Taigá, 1643 v. from Cheliábinsk) is situated on the bank of the Tom near the landing-place, where commences the steamship communication by the rivers of the Ob basin. Large buildings stand close at hand for the accomodation of goods entrusted to the shipowners for further conveyance to Tiumén, Barnaúl and other centres, and for the storage of goods coming by water, mainly from European Russia through Tiumén, to be forwarded to the East by the Great Siberian Railway.

Quay of the Usháika in Tomsk.

A medical and feeding station has been established iu proximity to the landing-places for the use of emigrants, arriving by steamers from Tiumén and proceeding to the localities allotted for colonisation. It is the residence of an official entrusted with the regulation of the emigration movement.

The Tomsk branch line throughout its course has many curves, the profile of the roadway shews grades of .015, with curves having a radius of 150 sazhens. The construction of the branch line was commenced during the summer of 1895, and completed in the autumn of 1896.

The Alexis Monastery in Tomsk.

Tomsk is a government town, standing on the right bank of the Tom at its junction with the river Usháika (56° 29′ N. lat. 54° 37½′ E. long). The locality occupied by the town is formed partly by the low branches of the Kuznétsk Alatáu (343 feet), and partly by lowland lying at the foot of these branches. The river Tom skirts the town, forming an almost regular semicircle from the south-west and western side. The population of the town was given at 52,430 by the census of 1897, (27,140 males, 25,290 females). In this respect, Tomsk holds the first place among the towns of Siberia.

The town was founded at the beginning of the XVII century. By command of the Tsar Borís Godunóv, the Cossack Major Písarev and the noble's son Tyrkov, established the Tomsk stockaded post, which received its name from the river Tom and stood in a locality resorted to by the wandering Tatar tribe of Yeushtíntsy ruled by the Prince Tayán. The entrenched post soon became of great importance for the subjection of the native tribes. In 1629, the Tomsk post was transformed into a town; in 1708, after the organisation of a Siberian government with the chief town of Tobólsk, it ranked as a district town; in 1719, Tomsk was included in the Yeniséisk province, in 1726, in the Tobólsk government; in 1782, after the establishment of the Tobólsk vicegerency, it ranked again as a district town; in 1797, it was transformed into a district town of the Tobólsk government, and in 1804, after the organisation of a special Tomsk government, it became its capital.

Cathedral of the Annunciation in Tomsk.

The climate of Tomsk is rather severe. The mean annual temperature is 0.7. The ice on the river Tom near the town breaks on the 30 April, and sets again on the 2 November; thus the river remains free of ice for 186 days in the year. Southern winds prevail. At the present date, Tomsk is a well built town containing many fine edifices of stone, fitted with electric light and telephones; some of the streets are paved. The total number of buildings in the town exceeds 13,000, there are over 3,200 estates. Tomsk possesses 2 orthodox monasteries and 23 churches, including 8 parish churches.

The Alexis monastery was founded in 1605; it contains a church with an aisle in honour of Our Lady of Kazán, of Alexis the Servant of God and of the Saints Frol and Lavr. There are only four monks, the Superior is endowed with the rank of Archimandrite. Among the ancient relics kept in the monastery, a large wooden cross and a local image of the Holy Virgin, painted in 1661, are particularly noteworthy. The first Tomsk school was created in the monastery in 1746. The enclosure of the monastery contains the grave of the monk Theodore Kuzmích, who died in 1861 and was particularly venerated on account of his ascetic life. Many legends are attached to this personage, which have even been spread by the press! (Russian Antiquity, 1880, 1887, 1894, pamphlet published in 1895 and 1896).

The nunnery of John the Baptist was founded in 1864 at the cost of the Tomsk merchant's widow Mikhéev, who was the first Lady Superior of the

The Trinity Cathedral in Tomsk.

nunnery. It contains the Cathedral of the Assumption, with aisles in honour of the Assumption of the Holy Virgin, of Alexis, the Metropolitan of Moscow and John, the Metropolitan of Nóvgorod: and the church of St. Innocent, consecrated to the first archbishop of Irkútsk. A workhouse is attached to the monastery. The following orthodox churches are connected with historical events: the Nativify or Nicholas church, formerly belonging to the nunnery founded in 1671, which has long ceased to exist. From 1740 to 1742, the walls of this nunnery held the unhappy bride of the Emperor Peter II, the Princess Catherine Dolgorúky, who was set free by the Empress Elizabeth Petróvna, upon her ascending to the throne.

The church of the Miraculous Apparition of the Holy Virgin, built in the middle of the XVIII century by the noble Kalachóv, contains several ancient images. Cathedrals: of the Annunciation, erected in 1804 in the name of the image of the Annunciation and of the Presentation; of the Holy Trinity, founded in 1845, and now finished with aisles consecrated to the Holy Trinity, Saint Nicholas and St. Alexander Névsky. The Cathedral of the Holy Trinity was erected according to the plans of the architect Ton, and is in the same style as the church of the Presentation belonging to the Semiónov regiment in St.-Petersburg. In 1855, the cupola which had just been finished fell in, and the work was abandoned for some time. It was resumed only in 1885, thanks to the efforts of the former Archbishop of Tomsk and Semipalátinsk, Vladímir, and of the honorary citizen Mikháilov, who both collected private donations for the construction of the cathedral. The largest sum was given by Mrs. Zibúlskaya.

Chapel of the Iberian Mother of God in Tomsk.

Besides these churches, the town possesses 4 chapels. The chapel of Our Lady of Iberia, erected in 1854 at the cost of Mr. Petróv, enjoys special veneration; it is built on the model of the Iberian chapel in Moscow and the image of Our Lady of Iberia is an exact copy of the Moscow painting.

Foreign churches: Lutheran church of St. Mary; Catholic church in honour of the Intercession of the Holy Virgin; 3 Jewish synagogues and a Mohammedan mosque.

On account of the number of its schools and the general level of education, Tomsk holds an important place among the government-towns of the Empire. It contains: one first class school, 5 second class, 7 lower and 43 elementary schools, forming a total of 56 educational institutions.

Tomsk University.

The Tomsk Imperial University with two faculties (medicine, 232 students and law, 159 students), a government gymnasium (418 pupils), the Alexis modern school, founded in memory of the Grand Duke Alexis Alexándrovich's visit to the town (179 scholars), the Mary gymnasium for girls

(698 pupils) an ecclesiastic seminary (237 students), a diocesan school for girls (239 pupils) a clergy school for boys (163 scholarsp), a district school (218 pop.), 28 parish schools (11 for boys with 1086 pupils, 9 for girls with 927 pupils), 11 parish schools (216 boys, 219 girls), a church parish school with two classes for training peasant boys as teachers for village reading schools (78 pup.), a commercial school (93 pup.) the Brothers' Koroliòv commercial school (67 pup.), a veterinary and surgeon's school (43 pup.), a school for midwives (82 pup.), 3 Sunday schools (90 boys, 402 girls), 4 private mixed schools (145 boys, 111 girls), 4 home schools (81 boys, 100 girls), a Tatar school of the Ministry of the Interior (37 pup.). The total number of pupils in all the educational establishments of Tomsk, with the exception of the university, on the 1 January was 5,989, forming a proportion of one pupil to 9 inhabitants of the town, or one elementary school pupil to 15 inhabitants.

Archaeological Museum of Tomsk University.

The first place among the numerous educational institutions belongs to the Tomsk Imperial University, which is the only one in Siberia and in the whole of the Asiatic dominions; it was founded on the 26 August, 1880, and, inaugurated on the 22 July, 1888, on the name day of the Empress Mary Feódorovna.

Possessing only a faculty of medicine, the university, during a period of ten years, had over a thousand students, of whom 239 took degrees as doctors of medicine up to the year 1898.

Although it had only a medical faculty, the university exerted a most civilising effect upon Siberia, providing with young physicians some of the distant and desert districts of the country, and also furnishing a series of scientific expeditions to the North-Asiatic continent.

The opening of a faculty of law in the Tomsk University, which took place in 1898, will in the near future introduce a new element of civilisation in the life of Siberia, and furnish fresh pioneers for the promotion of public justice in far off regions, lying aloof from the centres of civilisation.

The university possesses a zoological and botanical museum with beautiful collections from polar countries, made by the Vega expedition under the command of the celebrated Nordenskjöld.

It further contains a herbarium gathered by Potánin on the Tarbagatái and near the Zaisán, collections made by professors of the Tomsk university: Korzhínsky, Káshchenko and others.

The mineralogical and geological museum is enriched by valuable specimens given by Maximilian Duke of Leuchtenberg, viz. a palaeontological collection made in the years 1840—1850, (3,565 species). The archaeological and ethnographical museum is due to the efforts of Florínsky, the former curator of the West Siberian district and founder of the university. A description of the museum, with detailed catalogues and explanations regarding archaeological excavations made in Siberia, is to be found in the works of Florínsky.

The most important and interesting collections are contained in the Sídorov cases; viz. a collection of Tobólsk antiquities found by Známensky, that of Dmítriev-Mamónov containing objects excavated from kurgans and found during explorations conducted near Tobólsk; this collection is composed of objects dating from prehistoric times, which have been presented to the museum by the explorer. Besides these, there are articles collected by Florínsky (Semiréchensk antiquities), by Nekrásov (Tomsk antiquities), by Kuznetsóv (antiquities of the Minusínsk district) etc.

Anatomical Museum of Tomsk University.

The anatomical and physical cabinets and a chemical laboratory have been organised with the aid of liberal donations made by Sibiriakóv.

The library of the museum is its chief ornament, numbering over 100,000 volumes. The first gift to the library was made by Count Stróganov, who presented a valuable collection of books, engravings, original designs and sketches referring to various sciences. The books are beautifully bound and some of them belong to the earliest editions; others are unica and add an inestimable value to this enlightened gift. A valuable donation of 5000 volumes was made by Prince Golítsyn, and the successors of Count Litke presented his library to the museum.

Library of Count Stróganov in the Tomsk University.

In course of time, other books were added to the university library, by private donations; such are the books which belonged to the poet Zhukóvsky, tutor of the Emperor Alexander II (4674 vol.), to the Academician

Nikítenko (2000 titles); to Count Valúev, former Minister of the Interior; to Manaséin, former Professor of the Military Academy of Medicine (9000 vol.); to Professor Pfeifer in Weimar (2014 titles); to Nekliùdov, former Assistant Minister of the Interior, to Professor Gneist in Berlin (about 10,000 books and pamphlets).

The physical cabinet of the Tomsk University.

The following clinics are attached to the university: therapeutic, lying-in, surgical, dermatological, for children and lunatics. The clinics are open from the 1 September to the 1 May, with a fee of R. 7 a month. The rate for a separate room is R. 50 a month.

Near the university, stands a three-storeyed building inhabited by 80 students, which was erected by private subscription. As it does not suffice for the increased number of students, since the addition of a new faculty to the university, subscriptions for the construction of a new building are now being solicited and a special committee of the Tomsk municipality has been organised for this purpose. A substantial aid to the students is furnished by scholarships, 58 of which are at the disposal of the university, 20 of them being provided by the Government with a value of R. 300 each, the others derived from the interest on the money given at different times and by different persons to the university. The capital employed for scholarships, composed af private donations, at the present time amounts to R. 4,000,000; the largest sums were given by Solomónov (R. 59,000), Portnóv

(R. 70,000), Zybúlsky (R. 33,000), Kuznetsóv (R. 43,000), Count Ignátiev (R. 28,000), Sivers (R. 24,000) and the Kiákhta merchants (R. 17,000).

The erection of a Technological Institute, which will be the first in Siberia, promises to create a centre for the diffusion of the practical sciences in Siberia.

Students' College at Tomsk.

Charitable institutions: a charity board, hospital, poorhouse, a lunatic asylum (founded 1805) maintained at the cost of the board and from sums obtained by taxation. The hospital of the board, being situated close to the clinic of the University, serves the same purpose. The Mary children's home under the patronage of the Empress Mary, founded in 1844 at the cost of Commercial Councillor Popóv. This establishment owns a capital of R. 140,000, given by the goldminer Astashóv and Mrs. Zybúlsky; the Mary orphanage, founded by the honorary citizen Púshnikov and his wife, in commemoration of the miraculous escape of the

Clinics of the Tomsk University.

Imperial family from the railway accident which happened on the 17 October, 1888. The orphanage is provided with a capital of R. 60,000; foundlings and orphans are admitted to it. The Vladímir Home, founded in 1869 in commemoration of the Grand Duke Vladímir Alexándrovich's visit to Tomsk, is under the control of the Empress Mary Department. The building of the home was constructed at the cost of the merchants Petróv and Mikháilov. This institution possesses a capital of R. 80,000. There are further a poorhouse for the lower class citizens; the Pokróv poorhouse; the poorhouse of the Jewish Society; a night-shelter near the landing-place of Cheremoshnikí; a home for emigrants' children, founded in 1898 on the initiative of Mrs. Lomachévsky, wife of the Tomsk governor, by voluntary donations.

Missionary and charitable societies operating in accordance with their charters: The Committee of the Orthodox Missionary Society, a branch of the antisectarian brotherhood of Saint Demetrius, relief societies attached to a great number of parish churches throughout the town. These societies were organised and developed by the Archbishop Macarius of the Tomsk diocese. The Society of the Exaltation of the Cross maintains a baby-home, offering a day-shelter to children whose parents are away at work. The activity of the societies consists in relieving the poor, orphans and persons incapable of working, and in affording pecuniary relief in cases of extreme necessity.

The parish societies established a workhouse, which in 1898 passed under the control of the general workhouse ward, enjoying the patronage of Her Imperial Majesty the Empress Alexándra Feódorovna. The charitable society organised in 1886, with a far-reaching philanthropic activity directed by its president Giliárov, maintains the Pokróv poorhouse and a night-shelter, as well as providing cheap dinners and a home for children and old people. The Scholars' Relief Society, founded in 1873, has for its object the assistance of students of the Tomsk University and of other higher educational establishments. There are also an institution for destitute pupils of the Tomsk ecclesiastical seminary, a relief society for destitute pupils of the Alexis modern school, and a society for the promotion of elementary education, organised on the initiative of Makúshin, which has been operating since 1882. The successful development of elementary education to be noticed in Tomsk is largely due to the valuable activity of this last society.

It organises sunday lectures, maintains a needlework school, a culinary school for girls, and technical and commercial Sunday classes for boys. The public library, opened by the society, is deposited in a beautiful building given by Valgúzov, with a hall holding about 400 people. There is also a small museum for practical science. The local department of the Red Cross Society, existing since 1874, possesses a capital of R. 50,000; it maintains a society of sisters of mercy, with a hospital for children and a dispensary. Other organisations are the General Board of the Imperial Russian Humane Society, the

Governor's House at Tomsk.

Roman Catholic Charitable Society, attached to the Tomsk church of the Intercession of the Holy Virgin, and a relief society for workmen and miners in the Tomsk mining district, founded in 1894.

The last Society aims at the assistance of workmen and mine employees, incapable of further work, disabled by accident or other casuality. The Agricultural Colonies and Commercial School Society was founded in 1896, with a view to improve the condition of boys and girls confined in penitentiaries; among smaller organisations are the Clerks' Mutual Aid Society, the Mutual Aid Society for Women employed at Tomsk, and the „Ant-hill" workmen's club.

Scientific societies: The Naturalists' and Doctors' Society, attached to the Tomsk university, contributing to the progress of all branches of natural history and medicine, occupied with the study of Siberia and the contiguous countries in connexion with natural history and medicine, their population (mainly the natives) from an anthropological standpoint, and with the mode of life of the prehistoric inhabitants of Siberia according to the data of archaeology. This society organises excursions or facilitates them, arranges public lectures and publishes a journal: „Transactions of the Tomsk Natural-

Archibishop's House in Tomsk.

ists' and Doctors' Society". The West-Siberian Agricultural Society has existed from 1895; it studies the requirements of local agriculture and organises public lectures, which are published under the title of „Scientific Review of the Tomsk Region". Among the societies following a certain speciality, the most active are: the Tomsk branch of the Imperial Russian Musical Society, organised in 1879 by Mrs. Dmítriev-Mamónov, the first president of the society, and a musical school, the first in Siberia, attached to it, a volunteer fire-brigade; a racing society, with a course of its own; the Legitimate Sport Society; the Sportsmen's Society; the Horticultural Society; the Tomsk Cooperative Supply Society; the Railway Cooperative Supply Society; the Society for the Promotion of Physical Development, founded in 1896—it arranges games, has built public baths etc. and has created summer colonies for weak children. In 1897, an extensive space of wooded land belonging to the State was granted for the temporary use of the Society for the arrangement of summer colonies.

The stone theatre built by Koroliòv is now leased by its owner to strolling players; it contains 2 rows of boxes, a gallery, 11 rows of fauteuils and chairs, and a pit with 780 places. Public and Commercial clubs.

Libraries: Besides the libraries of the university and of other establishments, Tomsk is provided with two public libraries founded by Makúshin and a free reading room for the lower classes maintained by the Society for the Promotion of Elementary Education.

The local press: the „Tomsk Government Gazette", since 1857; the non-official part has been published since 1858, serving to unite the local intellectual powers in their efforts to study the country; the „Tomsk Diocesan Gazette"; the „Siberian Life" (non-official), editor Makúshin; the „Siberian Messenger" (non-official), editor Preismann; „Circulars for the West-Siberian Educational District"; „Memoirs of the Tomsk Imperial University"; „Gold-Mining and Mining Messenger", edited by Mining Engineer Reutóvsky.

Printing offices: the Government Administration, Beliáev, Kónonov, Makúshin, S. P. Yákovlev and Co., the Diocesan.

The mineral wealth of the government and the contiguous regions and the conditions of trade and industry have transformed the town into an administrative and judicial centre, containing some other special establishments serving local requirements, such as the mining department with gold-melting laboratory, the department of the Midsiberian railway, and the commercial department of the Siberian Railway.

The town of Tomsk presented long ago an important commercial centre of Siberia, on account of its favourable position and as the eastern terminus of the navigable route of the Ob basin. Having been avoided by the railway, it was apprehended that the further progress of the town would be stopped and that it would become exclusively a centre of administration; these surmises however have proved untrue, and the town continues to grow and extend its commercial operations. Having lost part of the goods in transit by the railway, Tomsk in return has widened its local operations, the railway enlarging more and more the local demand. The navigation commencing at town of Tomsk receives as well a further development thanks to the progress of the productive capacity of the country caused by the railway. The establishment of an exchange for ascertaining the general commercial conditions of Siberian trade

Theatre in Tomsk.

will greatly influence the growth of the town and exert its effect upon trade and industry.

Manufactures and industry more extensively developed in Tomsk than in the other towns of Siberia, are gradually increasing. The following official data shew the number and production of the factories situated within the town-line:

FACTORIES.	Number.	Production in rubls.
Distilleries	33	520,000
Beer and mead breweries	4	513,000
Vodka distillery	1	10,000
Yeast manufactories	4	20,700
Potteries	4	18,000
Rope-yards	20	21,000
Brick-kilns	48	156,620
Tanneries	7	234,000
Butter manufactories	5	8,500
Saw-mill	1	20,000
Soap boileries	7	81,000
Wax candle' man'ies	3	35,000
Tallow candle man'ies	5	46,000
Tallow boileries	2	18,000
Match man'ies	3	140,000
Fur man'ies	3	13,000
Carriage man'ies	3	160,000
Machinery works	2	5,450
Cast-iron and iron works	1	6,000
Joinery works	24	54,285
Harness man'ies	10	19,550
Locksmiths	7	21,300
Forges	39	49,500
Total	211	2,149,405

Four banks testify to the extensive commercial operations of the town: Branch of the State Bank, the Siberian Trade Bank, the Russian Bank for Foreign Trade, and the Siberian Public Bank.

Agencies: The Yarosláv-Kostromá and Nízhni-Nóvgorod-Samára Land Banks.

The town revenue for 1898 was estimated at R. 396,811. 39 k., the expenditure at R. 374,918. 83 k. In 1889, the revenue amounted to R. 176,717, the expenditure to R. 168,205. During a period of ten years, the town revenue more than doubled.

Important trading firms are represented by Kukhtérin and Sons, Mikháilov—draper's goods, tea and sugar, Nekrásov—iron wares, Pastukhóv—wine-cellar. Korolióv—tea and sugar. Reutóvsky—technical and trading office; Tomsk Electric Lighting. Stakhéev—draper's goods. Serebriakóv—tobacco shop. Shvetsóv—tea and sugar. The Alexander Sugar Refineries Company (Bródsky's refined sugar), Bogomólov—ironware. Golovánov—readymade shoes.

Agencies of Insurance Societies and Transport Offices: Beláev, of the Russian Fire Insurance Society of 1827. Ginsberg, of the Commercial Insurrance Society. Dmítriev, of the St.-Petersburg Insurance Society. Kótov, of the Nadézhda Society. Korolénko, of the Northern Insurance Society. Vladislávlev, Russian Insurance and Goods Transport Society. Leshévits, the Salamander Society. Románov, Russian Society for Insurance of Capital and Income of 1835. Tetskóv, the Anchor Insurance Society. Kháov, Second Russian Insurance Society. Shmurúgin, the Russian Fire Insurance Society. Liúlin, Kaménsky's Goods' Transport Office.

Hotels: „Russia", „Europe", „Siberian Hotel". The first and second are the best. Rates, from R. 1 a day. Dinner with two dishes, 50 k., with four dishes R. 1. The hotels are fitted with telephones. The best furnished rooms belong to Baránov and Khvórov. Hackney-coach tariff: twelve hours in the day or night, R. 2, an hour 30 k., a drive 20 k. To the railway station or back 75 k. To the landing-place of Cheremoshnikí or back R. 1.

River Tom, near town of Tomsk.

Among the historical events may be mentioned the visits of Imperial personages. The first visit took place in 1868, and was paid by the Grand Duke Vladímir Alexándrovich. In 1873, the town was visited by the Grand Duke Alexis Alexándrovich.

In 1891, the inhabitants of Tomsk had the honour of receiving an Imperial traveller, the present Emperor Nicholas II, then Heir Apparent to the throne. The Tsesarévich arrived from Irkútsk by the Siberian post-road and continued his journey from Tomsk by the rivers Tom, Ob and Irtysh, passing through the towns of Tobólsk and Omsk.

Grand Chemin de fer Transsibéren CHELABINSK–BAÏKAL.

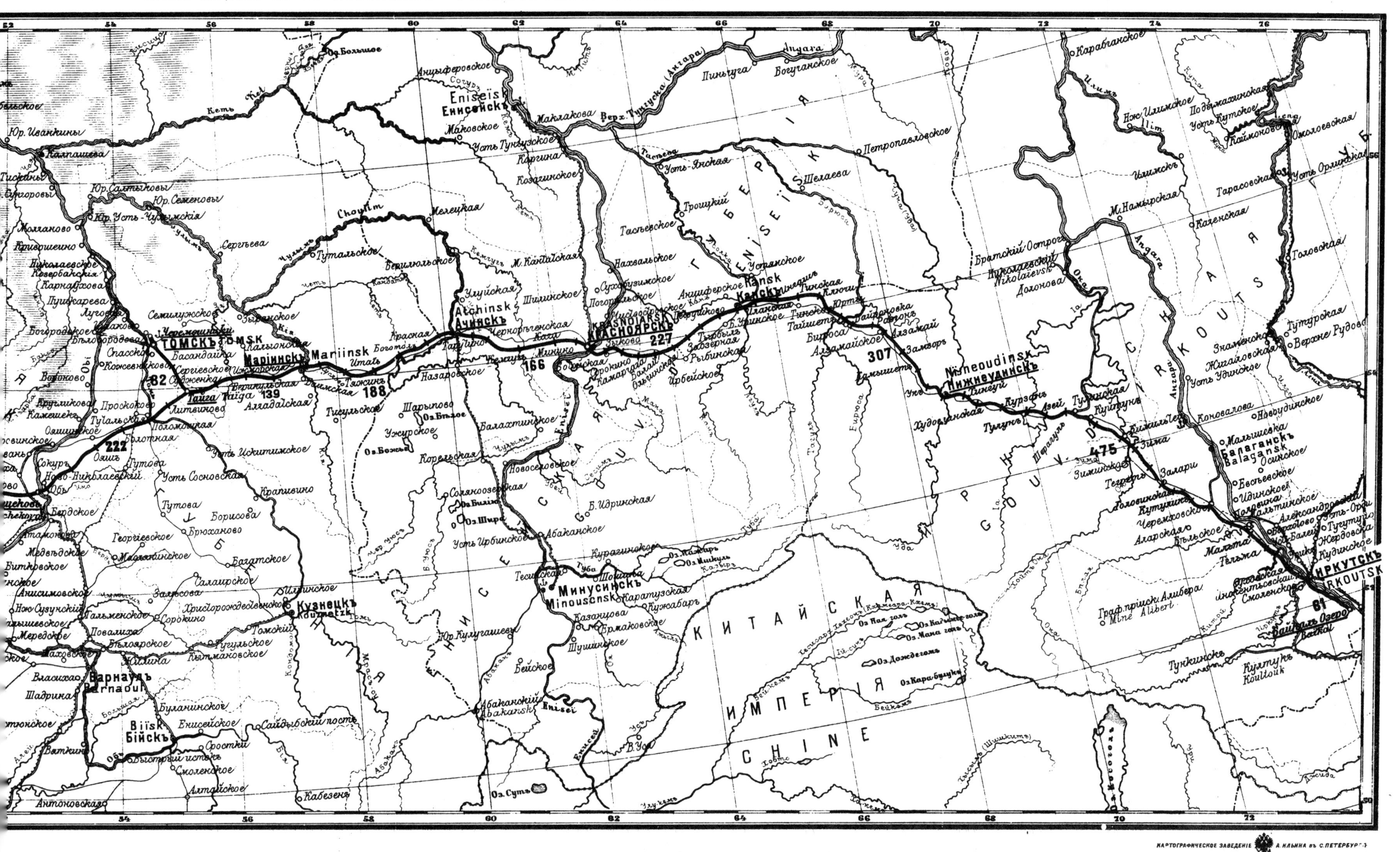

Великая Сибирская ж. д. ЧЕЛЯБИНСКЪ-БАЙКА.

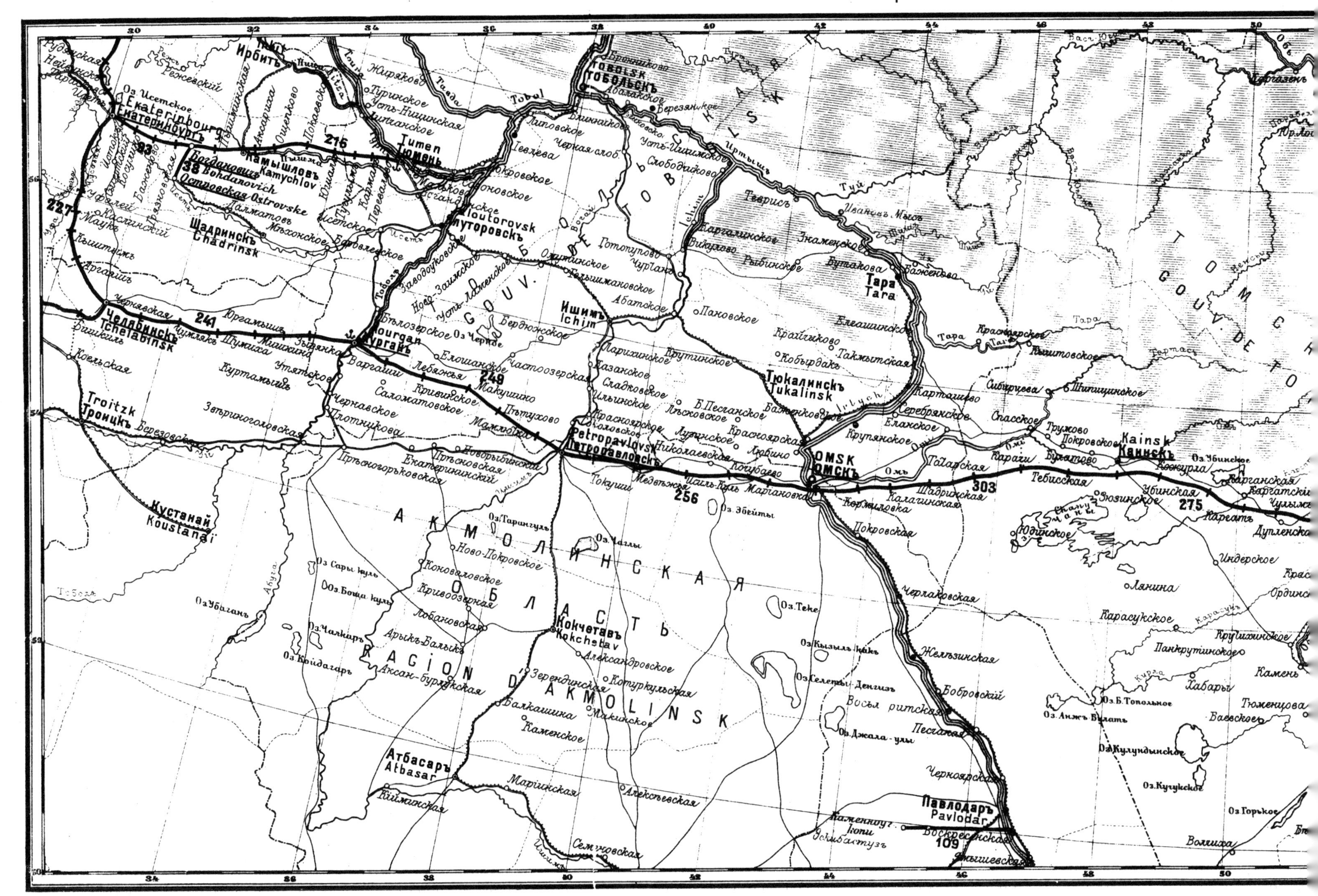

Lake Baikál.

Position and extent of the lake.—Surrounding mountains, their geological formation.—Capes, superstitions and legends.—Earthquakes.—Tributaries and sources.—The water and its temperature.—Winds.—Ice-cover.—Flora and Fauna.—Commercial importance of the Baikál aquatic fauna.—Navigation and steamship communication on the Baikál and its river basins.—Surveys for the Circumbaikál R[illegible] Ice-breaker.—Bibliography.

THE BAIKAL, one of the largest alpine lakes in the world, is called the Holy Sea by the local Russian population. It is the largest fresh-water lake in the old world, and lies between 50°28' and 55°50' N. lat. and 73°25' and 80° E. long. The Chinese call it Pe-Khoi, which means Northern Sea, the Mongols, Dalai-Nor, Holy Sea or Bai-kul, Rich Sea. The north American Lakes, Superior, Michigan, Huron and the African Nyanza alone surpass it in size. The extent of its clear surface and its configuration recall Lake Tanganáika situated in Central Africa in proximity to the Nyanza.

The superficial area of the Baikál is 30,034 square versts (34,179 square kilom.), its length, 600 versts. It bends slightly from south-west to north-east; its breadth is not so considerable and varies from 27 to 85 versts. The depth of the lake in its southern part, sounded by Engineer Bogoslóvsky, is 791 sea sazhens or 3,185 feet. Situated 1,561 feet above the level of the sea, the bottom of the lake at its deepest parts is much lower than the level of the ocean. According to the soundings, which give but a slight idea of the relief of the bottom, it may be said that the bottom of the lake presents an immense basin, with deep cavities which, at some places, begin at the shore and run almost through its whole extent.

This basin, at one-third of its entire length from the south-west, is divided into two unequal parts by a submerged ridge, according to Drizhénko, who has investigated the lake, composed of alluvium brought down by the river Selengá and partly by the Great Buguldéika, above which the water is not more than 234 sazhens deep. The soundings made near the shore shew that, although the cavities at some places begin close to the shore, there are considerable areas where the water has a depth of only 30 sazhens. The largest of these areas lying under water occur along the mouth of the Selengá, the Chivirkúlskaya Bay, the delta of the Upper Angará and the Little Sea. It may be supposed that the bottom near the shore represents

The Baikál, Little Baranchúk, source of the Angara (phot. by Drizhénko).

the continuation of the surrounding relief, which retains its various forms under the surface of the water.

The mountains bordering the valley of the Baikál rise in several elevated ridges, which give a peculiarly picturesque and imposing beauty to this region. The mountains on the western side of the lake are called Baikál Mountains and consist of two parallel ridges, the Littoral and Onótsk chains The mountains on the shore are known under the name of Transbaikál Mountains, dividing the rivers Selengá and Barguzín into three parts: on the south-west stands the Khamár Dabán, in the centre, the Selengá Barguzín Mountains, on the north-east, those of Barguzín-Angará. The absolute height of the mountain summits does not exceed 6,000 feet, or 4,500 above the level of the lake.

Almost all the elevations surrounding the Baikál consist of granite blocks and gravel; syenite, gneiss, crystalline slates and porphyry alternating with old limestone, sandstone and seams of breccia. The investigations made by Chérsky shewed tbat the mountains standing near and on the shore of lake Baikàl contain seven geological systems: archaean constitues the leading system; silurian, bordering on the northern slope, contain the first system; devonian, abounding in red sandstone occurs on the Angará; jurassic, composed of clayey limestone; tertiary system of sandstone, soft clay and limestone of aqueous formation: post tertiary and recent formations. Volcanic eruptions were found on the south-western side of the lake, N.—W. of Khamár Dabán.

The surrounding mountains assume peculiar shapes and, protruding into the water, form numerous capes of which 80, more characteristic than the others, have received names according to their shape or colour, or after some plant, animal or fish occurring there. The native tribes attached different superstitious legends to many of the cliffs and capes; this explains why many

The Baikál. Place of the building of the dock for icebreaker near of Lístvennichnaya (phot. by Drizhénko).

points on the shore of the stormy Baikál and its islands enjoy a special veneration to the present day. The Buriát shamans and the lama priests consid-

The Baikál. Lístvennichnaya (phot. by Drizhénko).

er the island of Olkhón as the dwelling place of the evil spirit Begdozí, and offer him frequent sacrifices. The Academician Georgi, who visited the island in 1772, stated that the number of sacrifices made there was quite astonishing. Mongolian folklore connects the island with tales of their oldest hero Chingiz-Khan, saying that his camp lay there.

The cape at the upper end of the island, as stated by Drizhénko, presents a strange phenomenon: a peculiarly shaped and immense cliff rises from the water's edge forming a narrow but long wall which, from a certain point, presents a perfectly regular profile several sazhens in height. Opposite to the island of Olkhón, a large peninsula, called the Holy Cape, protrudes from the eastern shore, having on both sides the deep bays of Chivirkúl and Barguzín. This peninsula has the form of a regular triangle, in the middle of which a mountain ridge stretches for a distance of 30 versts. The extreme northern end of the peninsula presents a high wooded almost vertical ridge with a craggy summit, from which flows a liquid called „Imushá" by the Tungús. According to Georgi, it is a kind of mineral oil (vitroleum unctuosum); others believe it to be produced by the decomposition of the guano of cormorants, herons, seagulls and other birds, which come to the island in infinite numbers, mainly during their migration. The rocky Cape Shamán is situated on the eastern shore, north of the Holy Cape (55° N. lat). Among its numerous cliffs, three are very high, rising in a vertical line to a height of 200 feet above the level of the lake. One of them has the form of an immense head with a huge nose and big holes instead of eyes; the crevice which represents the mouth affords shelter to flocks of sea cormorants (Phalocrocorax carbo). The other cliffs consist of dark quartz of horny formation. The Tungús give the name of Khamanríl to this cape, and consider the first cliff to be the sea god Diánda, while the other two represent inferior deities. The shamans render worship to Diánda, in order that he may forbid the waves to drown the Tungús falling into the sea, order them to drive shoals of fish to the shore etc. On the western side, to the south of Olkhón, the Kolokólnaya (Bell-tower) Bay is very picturesque; it is so called on account of two cliffs standing on both sides of it and looking at a distance like two belltowers. At the western edge of the Baikál, the Shamán Cliff, venerated by the Buriáts, stands near the Kultúksk bay. At the outflow of the Angará, there is a submerged granite cliff, called Shamánka, with a circumference of 7 sazhens, which rises for only one sazhen above the level of the Baikál and is considered by the Shamáns and Lamas to be the dwelling place of the invincible White God, to whom they offer sacrifices on this cliff. The lake is surrounded by places which are held in veneration, accounting for the name of Holy Sea given to the lake.

The Baikál. The upper end of the Island of Olkhón.

The numerous rocky fragments torn from the main-land found all around the lake, the islands lying in close proximity to the shore and retaining traces of their former identity with the surrounding mountains, and the unfathomable depth of the water near the cliffs, rising above its surface, testify to the violent origin of the lake. Georgi believes that the area occupied by it is the continuation of the valley of the Angará, and that the basin of the lake was formed by a sinking produced by a violent earthquake, which to the present day is followed by slight but annual tremors of the surface. According to observations, it is evident that earthquakes occur more frequently in the environs of the lake lying to the south-west near Túnka, bearing traces of former volcanic eruptions.

The ridges surrounding the Baikál give rise to numerous streams. Chérsky reckons 336 tributaries to the lake, among which the most important are the Upper Angará, falling into the lake on the north-eastern side; the Barguzín, almost at the middle of the eastern shore; the Selengá, on the south-eastern shore. The only outflow of the lake is through the Lower Angará, on the south-western shore.

The water of the Baikál is clear and trasparent. Its temperature has as yet been very insufficiently investigated, and is only now being examined by the expedition under Drizhénko. The investigations of Dydóvsky and Godlévsky, made in 1869—1876, shewed an invariable temperature at deep

The Baikál. The Posólsk Monastery of the Transfiguration (phot. by Drizhénko).

places and a slight fluctuation at the surface near the shore; this is in their opinion, the characteristic property of the water in the Baikál. The temperature at the surface of the lake varies and does not exceed 10° C., at a greater depth, the fluctuation is less, and 48 sazhens deep, the difference between the lowest and highest temperature during the year is 2°. 5,70 sazhens deep, it is 1° C. still deeper, the temperature does not vary during the year and is +3°. 5 C. On the surface of the lake, mostly on its eastern part, between the Holy Cape and the mouth of the Túrka, there frequently occurs floating wax or „bikerít“, which is used by the inhabitants as a medicine for rheumatism and scurvy. It burns very quickly with a bright flame and leaves much soot. This substance was subjected, by Shamárin in Irkútsk, to analysis by dry distillation: (volatilisation 140° C.) 8.44 per cent of liquid distillate—burning oil, 61.17 per cent of solids—parafin of the best quality. In connexion with sea-wax, springs containing an oily liquid very much like naphtha have been discovered at the bottom of the Baikál, opposite to the Túrka.

The climate of the Baikál is very severe, the summer being short and the nights cold. The meteorological observations of the Drizhénko expedition are not yet properly elaborated, but former explorations shew that N. E. and S. W. winds prevail.

From the end of May to the beginning of July, a N. E. wind with the local name of „Barguzín", blows on the southern part of the lake; from August, there is the „Kultúk" coming from the N. E. The strongest winds are called „Sormá" and blow from the N. W. They produce short but high waves, which sometimes rise to a height of a sazhen; at the same time, the waves are so rough that small vessels guided by unskilled hands are easily lost. During a storm, the waves of the Baikál rise to 6 or 7 feet. According to Georgi, the equilibrium of the water and air is very easily disturbed on account of the extraordinary unsteadiness of the Baikál, which is explained by the peculiar lightness and the great depth of the water. Storms occur frequently but are of no long duration, breaking against the surrounding cliffs. Thunderstorms gather from all sides in summer, but never pass over the lake. In June and July, the Baikál is almost calm. During this lull, numerous aquatic plants float on the surface of the water; the local inhabitants call this time the „blossoming" of the Baikál. The lake begins to freeze in November, but it is never frost-bound before the middle of December or the beginning of January; this fact cannot be explained by the absence of cold, but only by the unsteadiness and agitation of the water-surface. Being frost-bound for a period of 4 to 4½ months, the lake has an ice-cover sometimes 9½ feet deep. Sledge traffic lasts for three months; at the end of April, the ice melts near the shores and softens. During the winter time, although the ice-cover is very thick, wide cracks break its surface; when it meets again, the ice piles up in heaps called „tóros". These crevasses, which have a breadth of 3 to 6 feet and more, are sometimes a verst long and form a serious impediment to communication on the ice. Their origin remains as yet unexplained; some believe that the ice breaks under the force of the wind and air pressure, others suppose that it is produced by the ebb and flow, but this is still insufficiently proved by science. The breaking of the ice surface, as in the alpine glaciers, is accompanied by a loud crash, recalling an explosion, followed by a long rolling noise. The crevice is instantly filled with water to the level of the ice, forming a kind of river. In 8—14 days it freezes again, and a new crevice appears at another place. The ice melts slowly and this process lasts nearly two months.

The Baikál flora is of the same nature as the alpine or sub-alpine flora. The craggy mountain slopes are mostly covered by juniper, service trees, meadow-sweet, wild rose and other bushes. The wood bordering the Baikál contains some foliage trees, but mainly consists of conifera such as fir, pine, Siberian „cedar" and others.

The fauna of the Baikál is very varied and numbers many species; it plays an important part in the industry of the country. The Baikál is most plentifully provided with fish and supplies the surrounding district. In the fish industry, the omúl (Salmo or Coregonus omul), the Baikál gwiniad (Coregonus baicalensis), the char (Salmo thymallus) and the Salmo fluviatilis occupy the first place. A most interesting and little known fish, characteristic of the Baikál, is the dracunculus (Comephorus baicalensis). It is 6 vershóks long, the head occupying a third of its entire length; the eyes are uncommonly large and protruding; from the gills to the tail, fins are attached on each side. This fish occurs in the deepest places of the lake (over 300 sazhens) and lives under the pressure of an immense body of water; when brought to the surface, the fish is torn to pieces and melts in the sun. This is the reason why nobody ever saw a living specimen. Some of the zoologists reckon the dracunculus to the species of fish developing their ova inside the fish, and some of the fish traders say that it produces two little fish alive. According to the investigations of Dýbóvsky, the Baikál also abounds in crustaceans (Gamarus) and gasteropods. In these waters, there are four kinds of sponges (Spongia baicalensis, S. bacillifera, S. intermedia, S. papiracea) of a dark emerald colour, containing much chlorophyl. The inhabitants use a fresh sponge for polishing copper (tea-urns etc.), and a dried sponge is employed to polish metals by the silversmiths of Irkútsk; the lower classes attribute to it medicinal properties.

The Baikál. Nemchínov's landing-place Mysováya.

Among the most characteristic inhabitants of the Baikál waters is the seal (Phoca baicalensts) called „nerpa" by the local inhabitants and khansaganún by the Buriáts. This form is exclusively proper to the Baikál and recalls the European Phoca annelata. The local population kill the nérpa during the whole summer, from the end of June, and employ the skins of the young animals in making valuable over-coats called „dokhá".

The inhospitable Baikál is designed by nature herself to be the chief way of communication with the contiguous country, which is covered by mountain ridges and has no other overland communications beyond a few impracticable paths. Already at the end of the XVII century, the Baikál possessed a navy which served for postal communications.

At the present time, the navigation of the Baikál, connected with that of the rivers Selengá and Angará, reaching to the bars, is in the hands of the Nemchínov Company, owning 10 steamers and 18 barges. Besides these, there are only a few sailing craft on the Baikál, belonging to fish traders.

Nemchínov and Co. make the following trips on the Baikál: from the landing-place of Lístvennichnaya to the Upper Angará, calling at the Túrka mineral springs; between Lístvennichnaya and Mysováya, from one side of the Baikál to the other; from Lístvennichnaya to the mouth of the Selengá and further towards the towns of Verkhneúdinsk and Selengínsk, to the landing-place of Biliúta in the direction of Kiákhta.

On the 23 June 1891, the present Emperor Nicholas II, on his way from the Far East crossed Lake Baikál an the steamer „Speránsky" from the landing-place Boyárskaya to the source of the Angará and further to Irkútsk.

With a view to comply with the Imperial command, relative to the establishment of uninterrupted railway communication from the Urál to the Pacific Littoral, surveys were conducted with a view to surmount the difficulties connected with the construction of a railway line round the Baikál, skirting the lake from the south. The preliminary surveys, made by Engineer Viázemsky in 1888--1890, shewed the possibility of establishing a railway route from Irkútsk up the valley of the Irkút which, approaching the lake near the settlement of Kultúk, should proceed further along its shore to the landing-place of Mysováya and join the Transbaikál line. In order to straighten the line and to avoid the construction of elevated viaducts in the pass of Zyriánskaya Luká, formed by the Irkút breaking through the Zyrkuzún Chain, the construction of a tunnel of 1700 sazhens was projected. The total length of the line comprised 282 versts, at a cost of R. 25,000,000, or R. 80,000 per verst. In 1894, the expedition of Engineer Adriánov tried to take the line from the summit of the neighbouring mountains towards the headwaters of the rivers Olkhá, tributary of the Irkút, and the Krutáya Gubá, falling into Lake Baikál. From 1895 to 1896, the expedition of Engineer Doks repeated the surveys of Engineer Viázemsky, and made explorations in fresh directions, with a view to cross the Baikál Mountains and to approach the

The Baikál. Mole at the landing-place of Mysováya.

Baikál along the rivers Polovínnaya and Angasólka. All the surveys which have been made shew that the construction of this line offers great technical difficulties. The project of Engineer Doks included a tunnel of 3½ versts, with an estimated cost of R. 80,000 per verst, and a total length of 291 versts. In 1898, the expedition of Engineer Savremóvich again conducted surveys for the line round lhe Baikál in other directions.

The explorations made in the environs of the Baikál, within range of the projected Circumbaikál line, shewed the different nature of the country from Irkútsk to the settlement of Kultúk, and from the settlement to the station of Mysováya.

The first western section contains several valleys, which are favourably situated for the gradual ascent to the watershed of the rivers Irkút and of the rivers falling into the Baikál, allowing of the line being taken in different directions, whereas in the eastern section only one direction can be adopted, running along the shore and the valley of the Baikál.

With a view to establish the most advantageous route in the westere section, four directions were surveyed in 1898 by the expedition under Engineer Savremóvich from the Midsiberian line to the settlement of Kultúk:

1) From the station of Innokéntievskaya along the left bank of the Irkút

across the Zyrkuzún ridge to the settlement of Kultúk, or along the right bank of the Irkút approaching the station of Irkútsk.

2) From the station of Innokéntievskaya by the valleys of the Great Olkhá and the Krutáya Gubá, and further along the shore of the Baikál to the settlement of Kultúk.

3) From the settlement of Belekutói situated at the 960 verst of the 11

The Baikál settlement of Kultúk.

section of the Midsiberian railway line, across the Tunkín ridge, to the settlement of Kultúk.

4) From the station of Baikál a branch line to the Baikál, along the shore of the lake to the settlement of Kultúk.

Among these routes, the first, running from Innokéntievskaya to the station of Mysováya for a distance of 288 versts, and the last, along the Baikál to the station of Mysováya 243 versts in length, are considered the most suitable,

Final surveys of these two routes in connexion with geological explorations are being made, and the results obtained will serve to fix the precise direction ef the Circumbaikál railway line. In the eastern section, admitting only one route, the line will run along the shore of the Baikál. Starting at the station of Kultúk, the line of the eastern section runs first through a swampy meadow, crosses the Kultúchnaya by a bridge and, traversing at the 3 verst the Shamán Cape, proceeds by a sandy valley separating Shamán from the Baikál, At the 9 verst, spurs of the Khamár Dabán, pressing closely to the Baikál, prevent the line belng taken along the shore; its course passes through cliffs stretching for a distance of a verst.

At the 11 and 12 verst, the line runs through the abrupt and steep Cape Kerkidái, protruding far into the lake and presenting a heap of fragments from the cliff. At this place, the Baikál is very deep near the shore, there is no strip of land near the water, and the Cape has to be traversed by a cutting at its narrowest point. Between the 31 and the 47 verst, the

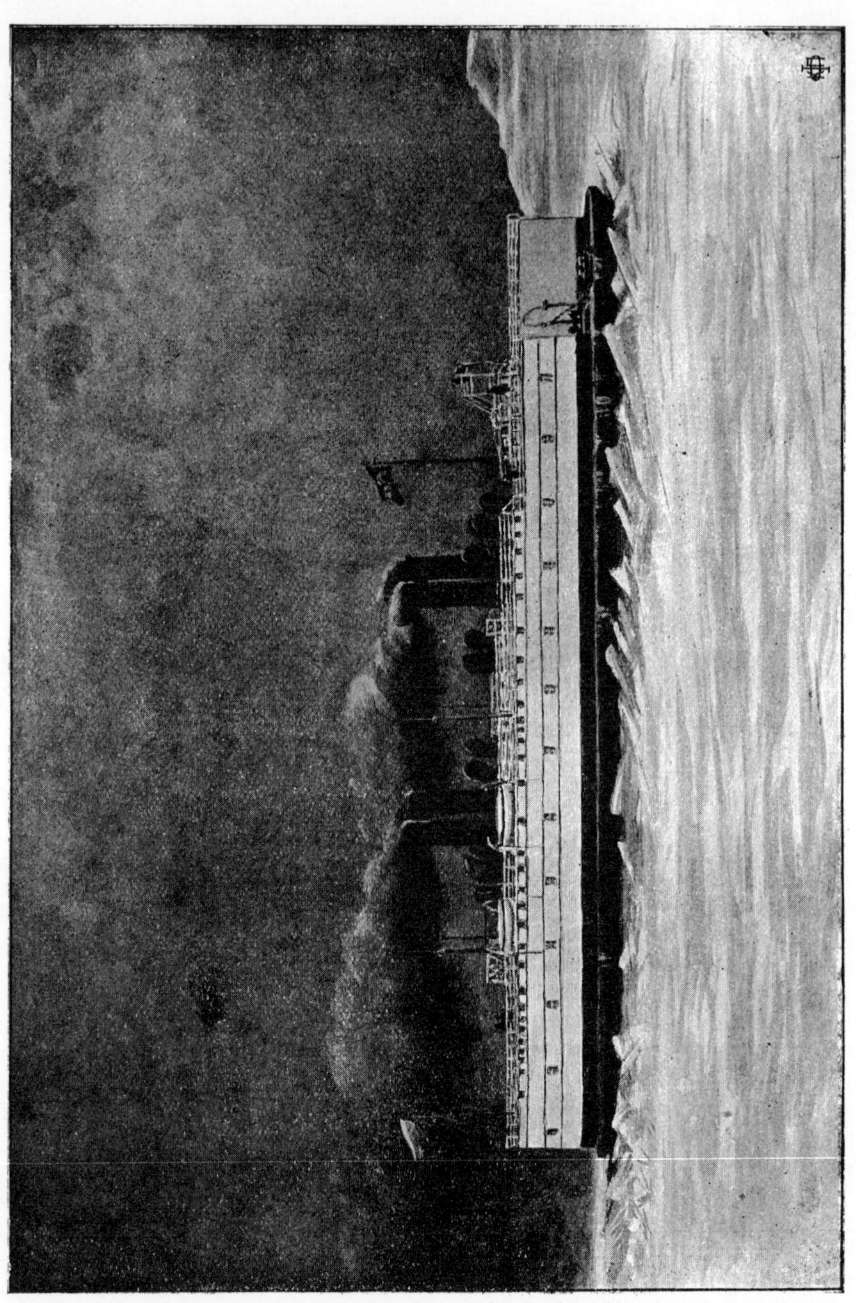

Icebreaker on the Baikál.

mountain spurs retreat from the Baikál, forming an undulating plateau; here the line leaves the lake, skirts the settlement of Utulík and at the 47 verst again approaches the Baikál. From the 47 to the 55 verst, the line runs by a steep slope intersected by streams and springs and crosses the Snézhnaya, the largest river in the Kultúk-Mysováya section. At the 113 verst, the line traverses the Pereyémnaya within a verst of its mouth, through a locality contained between high capes, jntting into the lake. At the 118 verst, the line enters a level plateau and follows the shore; at the 139 and 140 verst, it runs through the valley of the Míshikha, avoiding Cape Kliúev, and, at the 158 verst after having passed over the river Mysováya, turns abruptly and joins the Transbaikál line at the station of Mysováya. The total length of the eastern section is 162.04 versts: it is projected according to specifications adopted in level sections, but admits 4.1 per cent of curves with a radius of 150 sazhens and grades of .006. Part of the line in the eastern section has been in process of construction since 1899, for a distance of 40 versts from Mysováya to Pereyémnaya. The construction of fhis part of the line to the station of Pereyémnaya, standing on the other side of the lake opposite to the station of Baikál, will offer a much shorter way for passengers and goods than the stormy lake.

The exploration of the mountainous country contiguous to the southern part of the Baikál basin, in connexion with the difficult technical conditions attached to the construction of an uninterrupted Great Siberian main line, evoked the scheme for building a special steam-ferry for the transport of trains over the Baikál, which was to be supplied with icebreaking appliances and should establish continuous steam communication between the terminus of the Midsiberian railway line on the Baikál and the starting point of the Transbaikál line.

The application in the old world of these means of transport for trains, as in the United States effected with the help of icebreakers, is entirely due to the initiative of Prince Khilkóv, Minister of Ways of Communication, who first saw the advantage of applying icebreakers to Russian marine and river navigation.

The icebreaker „Baikál" was constructed at the works of Armstrong in England for the transport of trains over the Baikál. It was forwarded in separate pieces, which were put together on the shore of the lake. The fittings and the engines, boilers, water-pumping machinery etc. were made here. For the launching of the ship, stocks were built under and above the water; their construction offered great difficulties on account of the rocky shores and the frequent storms on the Baikál.

The icebreaker was put together by Russian workmen, who were partly brought from St. Petersburg. The general supervision of the construction of the icebreaker and of the docks was entrusted to the ship engineer Zablótsky.

The icebreaker is made of solid Siemens and Marten steel. Entire length 290 feet, beam 57 feet, draught 18 feet fore and 20 feet aft, speed 20½ versts. Displacement with full cargo 4,200 tons. The icebreaker is provided with three triple-expansion engines with a total of 3,750 H. P. Two engines are placed in the stern and are separated by a longitudinal water-tight partition; they work the propellers of the icebreaker. An engine in the fore part of the vessel serves to work the forescrew breaking the ice. The screws are provided with four paddles. There are 15 cylindrical boilers enclosed in two compartments divided by transverse water-tight partitions.

The icebreaker contains ballast distributed in different tanks between the double bottom of the ship and also fore and aft, holding 580 tons of water.

The belt, on the water line, consists of steel plates an inch thick, the sheathing is even and with inner layers. With a view to stop the blows of the ice a gainst the hull of the ship and to render more solid its inner side, throughout its length at the level of the ice it is provided with wooden wedgeshaped chocks covered with longitudinal beams; thus the timber belt has a thickness of about 2 feet.

This icebreaker is somewhat like Nansen's famous „Fram", with stem and stern adapted for icebreaking, capable of forward and backward motion. It carries 25 loaded waggons placed on the maindeck on three pairs of rails laid along the axis of the ship; the cabins on the upper deck accomodate about 150 passengers. The ship breaks the ice to a depth of 4 feet. In addition to this icebreaker, which is the second in the world in size, another has been constructed at the station of Lístvennichnaya. It has received the name of „Angará", and is smaller than the first. Length 195 feet, beam 34, draught 15 feet, speed $12^{1}/_{2}$ knots. The engine is triple-expansion with 1,250 H. P.; there are four boilers on the locomotive type. The engine and boilers are also separated by a transverse watertight partition. The construction of this icebreaker will be completed in the autumn of 1900 It well serve mainly for the transport of passengers.

For the repair of this vessel, wooden docks have been built on the Baikál. The landing-places, Baranchúk on the western side and Mysováya on the eastern, are provided with protecting moles and dams.

The cost of the whole steam communication, including landing-places, amounts to R. 5,621,000.

After the completion of the Circumbaikál line, which will connect the Midsiberian and the Transbaikál railways, the icebreaker might be employed with some success for purposes of navigation on the Baikál, and serve to develop trade and industry in the Transbaikál region, plentifully supplied with mineral wealth.

The measures due to the hydrographic expedition of Drizhénko have already much contributed to the progress of navigation on the Baikál. It established two beacons on the lake, which project their light for a great distance over the stormy and unfriendly waters. One of the beacons stands on the Olkhón Strait, on the cliff called Mare's Head, at a height of 45 feet above the level of the Baikál. The other is placed at the mouth of the Selengá, rising 48 feet above the level of the lake. Both beacons burn with a white and constant light, reaching for a distance of 18—20 versts. They are lit every day, and burn from sunset to sunrise.

BIBLIOGRAPHY:

Land administration in Asia. Eastern Siberia. St. Pbg. 1879. Ritter. Record of the geological explorations of the Baikál shore. Memoirs of the Siberian branch of the Imperial Geographical Society, vol. XI, 1874, XII, 1886, by Chérsky. Exploration of the Baikál. News of the Imperial Russian Geographical Society, by Dubóvsky and Godlévsky. The Baikál Review. Works of the East Siberian Branch of the Imperial Geographical Society. Irkútsk. 1897. Exploration of Lake Baikál in 1896. Memoirs of the Imperial Russian Geographical Society. St. Pbg. 1897. Drizhénko.

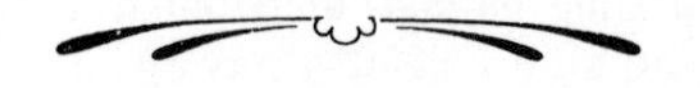

The Transbaikál Territory.

Its geographical position and extent. — Configuration of the territory. — Hydrography and the progress of navigation. — Geological structure and mineral wealth. — Iron mines. — Coal mines. — Silver lead mines. — Copper and tin mines. — Mercury. — Precious stones. — Salts. — Mineral springs. — Climate. — Flora and fauna. — Historical review of the Transbaikál. — Population. — Peasants. — The Transbaikál Cossack troops and their organisation. - Natives: Tungús and Buriàts. — Town population. — Emigrants. — The Nerchínsk penal settlement.—Exile settlers.—Land tenure and exploitation.—Industries.— Agriculture and cattle-breeding. — Fishing. — Hunting. — Forestry. —Carriage by road. — Mining industry. — Domestic industry. — Manufactories and works. — Trade. — The orthodox church. — Lamaism — Public education. — Influence of the Siberian Railway upon the economic growth of the region. — Bibliography.

THE Transbaikál territory, forming part of the Amúr territory under the administration of a Governor-General, lies between 49° 54' and 57°N. lat., and 72°18' and 91°7' [illegible] long. and comprises an area of about 56,152,260 desiatins or 547,965 square versts; it surpasses in size Austria-Hungary, Germany and many other European countries.

For purposes of internal administration, the territory is divided into the following 8 very irregular districts:

1) Barguzínsk, 2) Verkhneúdinsk, 3) Selengínsk, 4 Tróitsko-Sávsk, 5) Chitá, 6) Akchínsk, 7) Nerchínsk, 8) Nerchínsk Works.

On the west, this region is bounded by the government of Irkútsk, on the north by the Yakútsk territory, on the east by the Amúr territory coming up on the south-east to the boundaries of the Chinese Empire.

The whole surface of this territory is essentially mountainous, with the exception of the narrow steppe stretching between the rivers Onón and Argún. The Yáblonovy Chain, running through the territory from south-west to north-east, divides it into two almost equal plateaus; tho north-western part of it bears the name of Baikál-Daùria, while on the south-east it is called Nerchínsk-Daúria after the „Daúrs", who were the former inhabitants of this country.

The Yáblonovy Chain commences in the Chinese territory at the mountain masses of Kentéi. Upon entering the Transbaikál territory, it sends out the mountain-chain of Chokondó, rising to an elevation of 8,000 feet above the level of the sea. The Baikál-Daúria presents a country which consists of narrow and level valleys, separated from each other by mountain ridges with uplands lying between. Many of these ridges rise to a considerable height above sea-level and some of their peaks, called „goltsy", reach the line of perpetual snow. Leaving these mountains, the Ulán Burgási stretches to the north and the Khamár Dabán to the south, bordering the southern bank of the Baikál, with its desert and steep cliffs. The Nerchínsk-Daúria has a more level surface. The Nerchínsk ridge, running in a long line from south to north with an altitude of from about 3,050 to 4,150 feet, forms the watershed of the river systems of the Argún and Shílka. The mountains of this plateau covered with thick woods, assume softer outlines, and are considerably lower than those of the western part of the territory. As they approach the Chinese frontier, the mountains become lower and the plains widen, especially along the rivers Argún, Onón and Agá beyond the limits of Mongolia, gradually passing into the desert steppe Góbi.

The water systems which enliven this region belong to the Baikál, Léna and Amúr basins.

The Selengá is the most important river in the Baikál basin; taking its rise in Mongolia, it crosses its boundary near Kiákhta and, entering the western part of the Transbaikál territory, waters its most fertile districts: Tróitsko-Sávsk, Selengínsk and Verkhneúdinsk. The total length of the Selengá is about 1,250 versts; it is navigable within Russian territory for a distance of 350 versts. Separating into several branches, it falls into the Baikál by a delta. At present the commercial traffic by the Selengá mainly consists of tea transport, amounting from 500,000 to 800,000 puds during the navigation season. Thousands of puds of grain, barrels of spirit, wool and other produce are annually forwarded by the waterways. Upon the opening of traffic on the Great Siberian Railway, the Selengá will undoubtedly acquire a still greater importance as a trade waterway from China and Mongolia to Russia, although the greater part of the tea transport will be transferred to the railway. The Selengá is frost-bound from the end of October to the middle of April, the water level varying within the limit of a sazhen.

The bar at the mouth of the river is one of the chief impediments lying in the way of regular navigation. Small river steamboats and flat-bottomed barges of unsolid construction do not venture to cross the stormy Baikál whereas the vessels plying on the lake, having a deep draught, cannot enter the branches of the Selengá; for this reason, the goods are transferred from the river barges to the lake barges and back again at the junction of the river with the Baikál.

In 1894, navigation on the Selengá and on Lake Baikál was maintained by the Kiákhta Steamboat Company; at present, the company has stopped its operations and the whole fleet and the landing-places belong to the General Angará, Baikál and Selengá Navigation Co, belonging to the merchant Nemchínov. Four iron passenger tow-steamers with 20 to 80 H. P. and 18 wooden barges with a tonnage of 3,000 to 22,000 puds are kept by Nemchínov for navigation on the Selengá. The absence of competition leaves Mr. Nemchínov free to fix rates, which considerably exceed the real cost of transport by this waterway.

Within the confines of Mongolia, the Selengá receives two important tributaries: the Edingól on the left, and the Orkhón on the right. Entering into Russian territory, it is joined on the left by the rivers Dzhída, Temník, aud Oronchái, taking their rise on the southern slope of Khamár-Dábán. The basin of these rivers has an essentially mountainous character with the exception of their lower reaches, which are suitable for agriculture and cattle-breeding. From the right, three large rivers: the Chikói, Khilók and Udá taking their rise in the western slope of the Yáblonovy chain, fall into the Selengá.

The Chikói, although having a rapid current, is navigable its lower reaches for a distance of about 250 versts. The valley of this river is most fertile, and has an exclusively Russian population. It also abounds in fish of various kinds.

Valley of the Khilók.

To the north of the Selengá, the rivers Túrka, Barguzín and the Upper or Great Angará, taking their rise in the snow-covered peaks of the surrounding mountain ranges, discharge the mass of their waters into Lake Baikál.

The river Vitím, of the Léna basin, flowing for a distance of about 800 versts within the limits of the Transbaikál territory, receives many short and rapid streams from the mountains of the Yáblonovy chain.

The river systems of the Shílka and Argún, uniting their waters beyond the limits of the Transbaikál, belong to the Amúr basin.

The joint streams of the Onón and the Ingodá form the Shílka.

The former, taking its rise in the Kentéi mountains, flows along the high and steppe-like plateaus of northern Mongolia.

Entering the confines of the Transbaikál territory, it continues its course amidst treeless steppes and mountains. The latter, having a smaller basin, flows from the Chokondó mountain group, retaining throughout its entire course a thoroughly mountainous character.

The water of the Ingodá is extraordinarly clear and, for many versts after its junction with the Onón, the turbid waves of the Mongolian river do not mingle with the pure current of the Ingodá. The combined waters of the two rivers form the Shílka and continue their course along a narrow valley bordered by hills. The mountainous character of the Ingodá is retained by the Shílka throughout its entire course. With its steep and wooded banks and rapid current, the Shílka is one of the most picturesque rivers of the Transbaikál, the steep and lofty right bank being particularly beautiful. The total length of this river, from the junction of the Onón with the Ingodá to the mouth of the Argún, with which it forms the beginning of the Amúr, is over 500 versts, whereas the distance from Srétensk to the Amúr is 359 versts. The breadth of its bed varies but slightly and is on an average 150 to 200 sazhens. The current flows at the rate of 6 to 7 versts an hour. At the bars, which occur frequently and are 143 in number, it increases to 9 versts and more. On account of the stony and rocky bed, the bars never shift, and are not influenced by the tide.

The basin of the Shílka may be considered as navigable in its whole extent, but regular navigation is maintained only from Srétensk to the mouth of the river, a distance of 350 versts. From Srétensk to the village of Mitrofánovo, a distance of 150 versts, steamers ply and tow barges at intervals, this section not being included in the number of the obligatory trips, made by the Ship and Trade Amúr Company, subsidised by the Government. This inadequate development of the navigation is due to the lack of energy on the part of the Amúr Steamship Companies. Although forming part of the waterway of the extensive Amúr basin, the Shílka is not provided with a special fleet and the service is performed by the Amúr steamers.

The navigation on the Shílka lasts a little over 5 months, from the end of April to the beginning of October. The frequent fogs, which cover the river and hinder the passage of the steamers till 8 and sometimes 10 o'clock in the morning, are a great impediment to navigation. These fogs begin in July and last till the navigation closes. Under the influence of melting snows and abundant rainfall, the water rises sometimes 4 sazhens above its ordinary level; it however rapidly falls again aud the river gradually becomes shallow, so that, almost every year the water communication is interrupted for about 20 days, during the navigation season.

Mouth of the Nércha.

About 20 versts from the head of its basin, near the town of Nerchínsk, the Shílka receives on the left the Nércha, falling from the high Váblonovy ridge. The Nércha has a considerable fall and a great number of rapids, which render the river unfit for navigation. The Kuengá is another important tributary, flowing in on the same side. Among the right tributaries, the most important is the Kurengá. At its junction with the Shílka, near Srétensk, are the docks of the Amúr Steamship Company.

The other river forming the Amúr is the Argún, rising beyond the limits of this territory. Its head-waters are formed by the Kailár river, falling down the slopes of the Great Khingán, and connected with the lake Dalái-Nor. The Argún valley, in its upper part, presents a level surface. The bottom of the river consists of clay and mud, its depth is not considerable, and the current very slow. Along its middle course, the valleys pass into mountains mainly clothed with larch. Here the river bottom becomes hard, being composed of stone and sand. Within its lower reaches, where the depth is sufficient for navigation, stone ridges hinder the passage of steamers, which ply only for a distance of 50 versts above its junction with the Shílka.

Rafts, carrying mainly grain, move along the Argún, from the Cossack village of Argún. The most important tributary of the Argún is the Gazimúr rising amidst the heights of the Nerchínsk Mountains. Among the lake basins, besides the Baikál, are remarkable the mountain lakes Baúntskoe, Gusínoe, Sosnóvoe, Zun-Khargá and the steppe lakes Barún and Zun-Taréi.

The geological structure of the Transbaikál territory, which was carefully examined from a scientific point of view in connexion with the surveys conducted for the construction of the Great Siberian Railway, offers great variety. The geological expeditions of V. Obruchev, A. Gerásimov and A. Hedróitz, discovered the following geological formations in the Transbaikál: 1) post-tertiary alluvial, 2) carboniferous, tertiary and jurassic formations, 3) metamorphic slates, 4) lamellated crystalline rocks, 5) massive crystalline rocks.

The mineral wealth of the Transbaikál, including varied geognostic formations, is very considerable. This territory contains innumerable mineral treasures, of which only a few are raised and partly exploited.

Iron ores are found at many places in the Transbaikál terrifory. The richest bed of magnetic iron ore is that of Balegínsk situated on the Zagán Dabán ridge, lying within 35 versts of the Petróvsk iron-works, on the left bank of the Baléga river. This mine has been worked for more than a hundred years, 8,000,000 puds of iron having been obtained during this period. Recent explorations shewed that the actual supply of ore amounts to 2,000,000 puds. It however may be supposed that it contains a still greater quantity. Another bed of magnetic iron ore is to be found along the river Bélaya, 4 versts from the Pétrovsk works, in the Zmeínaya Gorá or Snake Mountain.

Further, iron deposits occur: 1) in the valley of the rivers Udá and Kirengá; 2) on the northern slopes of Khamár Dabán, near the landing-place of Mysováya, on the right bank of the river Mysováya; 3) on the Zagán-Khuntéi ridge, near the crossing of the post-road; 4) near the station of Makavéyevskaya; 5) at four points in the Nerchínsk Works district.

Coal deposits were discovered in the Transbaikál in the middle of the XVIII century. More careful explorations have been made of late years with a view to meet the additional demand for coal occasioned by the construction of the Siberian Railway. According to recent data, coal-measures occur in the following districts:

1) Along the shore of the Baikál, at more than 20 points, with outcrops near the Baikál and in the valleys of the mountain streams falling into the lake.

The analysis of the coal, near the river Míshikha, shewed the following results: specific gravity 1.36, coke 40 per cent, volatile matter 50 per cent, ash 10 per cent.

2) At 9 points in the valley of the Ingodá. One of the beds situated on the left bank, near the village of Nóvaya Kúka, at a distance of 4 versts from the Siberian line, claims special attention, on account of the many practical advantages offered by its future exploitation.

The analysis of the coal in this district gave: specific gravity 1.38, coke 43 per cent, volatile matter 53 per cent, ash 4 per cent.

3) At 7 points in the valley of the Khílók.

4) At two points in the environs of Lake Gusínoe.

5) At 5 points in the valley of the Shílka.

6) At two points in the valley of the Argún.

7) In the valley of the Udá.

8) In the valley of the Chikói.

9) In the valley of the Onón.

10) Near Lake Khára Nor, within the confines of the Nerchínsk district.

The auriferous gravel of the Transbaikál territory has been worked from the year 1777, and the quantity of metal obtained increases every year. At present, part of the gold-mines belong to the Cabinet of His Imperial Majesty; the other part is worked by private persons and numbers about 185 mines. The total output of gold on the average amounts to about 228 puds annually; the half of this quantity being obtained from the mines of the Cabinet.

In the western part of the Transbaikál, the greatest number of gold mines are centred in the Barguzínsk district (81). In the eastern portion, the Nerchínsk district is the richest and contains 32 gold mines: 21 private mines, 11 belonging to the Imperial Cabinet. The western part of the region is far superior to the eastern in respect to the quantity of metal raised, and the abundance of the auriferous gravel.

Besides the gold mines of the Imperial Cabinet, the eastern mining district of the Transbaikál contains important private mines, belonging to the Daúria Gold Mining Company, to the Transbaikál Society of Vtórov and Co. and the Onón Company of Sabáchnikov Brothers.

Silver and lead mines occur at many places in the Nerchínsk Works district and belong to the Cabinet of His Imperial Majesty. They were discovered near the remains of Chud mines in 1689, and were chiefly worked from 1763 to 1768. Afterwards, the works were considerably reduced, on account of the inundation of the mines and economic considerations.

Among the 90 vein and nidus mines, only four are worked at present, yielding about 60 puds annually.

Copper deposits exist at several points throughout the Argún and Onón basins, but they have not been worked up to the present time.

Tin ores were discovered in 1811. They occur in the valley of the Little Kulindá, tributary of the Onón; near the village of Nízhni-Sharanéi; near the settlement of Zavitínsk, to the left of the Onón and on the right side of the Ingodá. The Onón mine was worked during 30 years; by order of the Government, small quantities of metal were obtained from it at various times. This locality is the only one throughout the Russian territory which affords „tinstone“ or cassiterite, found in quartz veins, in grains or imperfectly formed crystals of a deep red-brown colour. In consequence of the bad organisation of the mining industry, the working of the copper mines stopped long ago. At present, thanks to their proximity to the Siberian main line, it may be hoped that the exploitation of the mines will be resnmed and attended with success, and that the Onón tin, on account of its superior uqality, will enjoy the same renown in the world's market as the tin of the Malay and Sunda Islands.

Mercury was discovered in 1759, in the Ildikánsk mine of the Nerchínsk dictrict; however as no success attended the working of the limestone veined with cinnabar, the exploitation oi the mine was soon abandoned.

Precious stones occur frequently in the Transbaikál. Most remarkable is the granite mountain Adún-Chillón, rising between the rivers Onón and Onón-Borsiá, where topaz, beryl, aquamarine, Siberian topaz and other stones are plentiful. Garnets in small crystals are also found on the Onón, 85 versts from Nerchínsk; blocks of nephrite occur on the Onón and its tributaries.

Salt is obtained at the following works: of Selengínsk in the district of the same name, and in Tiránsk, Tróitsko-Sávsk district, where brine is obtained from salt lakes. Among salt lakes, there is only Lake Bórzinsk in the

Nerchínsk Works district; the salt does not settle every year. Glauber's salt, employed in glass works, is got from the Dorínsk lakes in the Barguzínsk district. The total output of salt in the Transbaikál amounts on the average to 40,000 puds annually.

There are a great number of mineral springs in the Transbaikál but they are as yet insufficiently explored. The most important are:

List of springs, t° Cels.	SITUATION.
	Chemically inert.
Turkínsk, 56,75°	In the Barguzínsk district on the south-eastern shore of the Baikál, near the village of Goriáchinskoe. A hospital under the direction of the Transbaikál board, doctor and assistant. The hospital contains 9 rooms and baths. The season lasts from April to September. This spring is considered as of some importance.
	Chalybeate springs.
Gazimúrsk	190 versts from Nerchínsk. The Gazimúrsk works, situated at a distance of only $1^1/_2$ versts, receives visitors. These springs are under the management of the Mining Department of the Nerchínsk district. Baths and bathing houses. Season from the 1 May to September.
Stáro-Darasúnsk	140 versts from Chitá, on the post-road. The season is from the 15 May to the 1 September. A doctor is appointed every year for sanitary inspection and attendance. The neighbouring village of Darasúnskoe contains suitable buildings for visitors and baths.
Mólokovsk	12 versts from Chitá, has only houses and barracks for the visitors, without any bathing accomodation or any other resources.
	Alkaline and chalybeate springs.
Uliatúevsk	347 versts from Chitá, has two wooden houses for the accomodation of visitors and baths. The season is from the 15 May to the 1 September.
	Chalybeate and calcareous springs.
Yamórovsk 1,5°	In the Verkhneúdinsk district. Were opened to the public by an ukaz of 1896. A two-storeyed building is attached to the springs with a dining-room for 40 persons; there are a building for baths, and a bathing-house. Houses have been purchased with lodgings for the patients. Doctor and assistant.
Kúkinsk	45 versts from Chitá, near the village Nizhnekúkinskoe. Has 7 barracks. The season is from the 15 May to the 15 August.

List of springs, t° Cels.	SITUATION.
	Calcareous springs.
Makavéevsk	50 versts from Chitá, within 12 versts of the Makavéevo station on the Transbaikál railway, and 10 versts from the Cossack village of the same name. Houses and barracks for the accomodation of visitors, and hot and cold baths. The season is from the 1 May to the 1 September. The mineral water of this spring is sold in Chitá at the rate of 8 to 10 kop. a bottle.

Besides the above mentioned mineral springs, the following springs have been discovered during the latest explorations made along the Great Siberian line.

1) On the right bank of the Khilá, near the station of Mogzón, containing iron, various salts and natural carbonic acid.

2) In the Arshán valley, within 4 versts of the railway.

3) In the valley of the Brián, 1 verst from the railway.

The climate of the Transbaikál territory is characterised by the same properties as that of the central and northern part of the Asiatic continent. It serves as a transition from the more typically continental conditions of the Irkútsk territory to that of the Amúr and Littoral regions.

The mean annual temperature, registered at the observation points throughout the region, is below—0° Cels. (In Tróitsko-Sávsk — 0.8, in Selengínsk — 0°.6, in Verkhneúdinsk—2°.3. In Chitá—2°.7, at the Nerchínsk-Works—3°.7, at the Petróvsk-Works — 4°.6). The climate may be noted as very severe, especially when compared with the temperature of the corresponding latitudes in the same zone of European Russia.

This great difference between the above stated average temperatures and that of the Transbaikál, is explained by the elevated position of the greater portion of the region above the level of the sea, and by the very low temperature of the winter months. The annual range of temperature, that is to say the difference between the average temperature of the hottest month and that of the coldest, is far greater in the Transbaikál, than in any other country lying within the same latitude in European Russia, and is as follows:

	In January.	In July.	Difference.
Tróitsko-Sávsk...	25°.1	+18°.7	43°.8
Selengínsk	26°.0	21°.8	47°.8
Verkhneúdinsk ..	27°.8	19°.1	46°.9
Petróvsk Works.	28°.1	16°.1	44°.2
Chitá............	27°.1	18°.6	45°.7
Nerchínsk Works	29°.5	18°.5	48°.0
Corresponding latitudes in European Russia:			
Warsaw.........	— 4°.3	+18°.5	22°.8
Chernígov.......	6°.9	20°.3	27°.2
Urálsk	14°.2	23°.2	37°.4

The essentially continental climate characteristic of the Transbaikál is only surpassed in the Yakútsk territory, where the annual range of temperature exceeds 60° Cels.

The temperature in the Transbaikál varies greatly during the space of a month. In summer, when the thermometer rises to a maximum of over 30° Cels, the air sometimes suddenly cools to a temperature below 0° Cels. There is no frost in July only.

In winter, the cold is often below 40° Cels. without interruption; the population of the Transbaikál is not howerer too severely affected by this excessive cold, thanks to the absence of wind in the winter and to the clear atmosphere. The rapid and sudden changes of temperature occurring during the space of 24 hours are much more unhealthy; they depend entirely upon the condensation of the clouds and on the rainfall.

The low mean temperature produces a phenomenon characteristic of the Transbaikál, consisting in a perpetually frozen soil.

According to observations made by Yachévsky, there are districts containing zones of frozen soil alternating with areas of unfrozen ground, as for example on the headwaters of the Chikói, containing warm springs with a temperature of + 28° C.

As stated by Yachévsky, the area of frozen subsoil gradually descends towards the south-east from the town of Turukhánsk to the headwaters of the Léna, and turning south, embraces the mountain range stretching along the western shores of the Baikál; moreover, the frozen surface extends over the whole of the Transbaikál, from the estuary of the Selengá on the west, to the junction of the Argún with the Shílka on the east, and the Kulusutáevsk military post on the south. The depth of the frozen soil and the melting of its upper layers during the summer depend upon how much heat penetrates through the upper strata.

Another phenomenon characteristic of the Transbaikál climate consists in rivers and lakes freezing to the very bottom, observed during a snowless winter. The rivers freeze first at the banks, then at the bottom and in shallow places. As stated by Kriúkov, who studied the climate of the Transbaikál territory, the rivers in freezing form a belt of ice stopping the flow of the water and presenting a kind of bulwark across the river.

The amount of the rainfall, at different parts of the territory, varies from 20 to 30 centimetres, which is somewhat less than the amount of rainfall in European Russia. With respect to the quantity of precipitation, January and February are the driest months of the year, being generally snowless. The rainfall during the summer months, upon the whole, corresponds to that of European Russia. The abundance of rainfall during the period of vegetation, the cloudless and clear atmosphere, aud the beneficial effect of the sun's rays contribute to the development of agricultural industries, in spite of the perpetually frozen soil.

The flora of the Transbaikál territory presents two different types under the influence of soil and climate.

In the part of the Transbaikál, situated between the northern slope of the Yáblonovy ridge and the Baikál, the vegetation has the character of the mountain flora found at the eastern extremity of the Altái Sayán mountains.

On the south-eastern side of the Yáblonovy chain, the flora changes and includes species proper to the extreme east of the temperate zone of the Asiatic continent.

The monotonous fir forests, covering vast areas in the western part of the Transbaikál, are mingled, in the east, with foliage trees partly belonging to the species which cease to occur in Siberia beyond the Urál: oak (Quercus mongolica), elm, (Ulmus campestris), hazel (Coryllus heterophyla) and wild apple (Pyrus baccata). Characteristic specimens of the Mongolian and Amúr flora occurring in the eastern part of the Transbaikál, together with some forms from the Asiatic continent represent the vegetation of Trans-yàbloniya or Daúria, and compose the Daúrian flora. Many species of bushes found also in Mongolia are particularly characteristic, such as Daúrian sallow-thorn (Rhamnus dahurica), a variety of the same, (Rhamnus erythroxylon), wild almond, (Amygdalus pedunculata), wild apricot, (Prunus sibirica), a kind of wild rose (Rosa alpina) a kind of tamarisk (Myricaria longifolia) and others. Yáritsa or spring corn, which covers the greater portion of the tilled land, and represents the principal food of the population, is the cereal mostly cultivated in the Transbaikál. This corn is of the best quality, its full and large grains in size and weight are not inferior to wheat. The latter is also extensively cultivated and occupies about 14 per cent of the total cultivated area; the quality of the wheat is very good, yielding sometimes very abundant crops of about 270 puds to a desiatin, with a thirtyfold increase. The oats sown in the Transbaikál are also of superior quality, and of the same kind as that cultivated in the central European zone. Oats cover from 10 to 15 per cent of the total cultivated area, while barley is sown on 4 to 7 per cent, of the total area. In the western part of the Transbaikál, buckwheat and millet occupy a comparatively small portion of the land; but in the east buckwheat holds an equal place with wheat. The cultivation of winter-rye is insignificant, on account of the insufficient snow-cover.

All rhizocarpic plants and vegetables of various kinds shew a luxuriant growth in this region.

The fauna of the Transbaikál territory assumes many various forms and contains, besides the species characteristic of the whole of Siberia, the steppe animals of Mongolia and some forms found in the Amúr and in the Littoral countries of the Asiatic continent. The Siberian fauna, occurring almost throughout the whole country, keeps preferably to the west and northern parts of the territory, while the steppe animals are to be found in the south-eastern part, between the rivers Argún and Onón.

Among the mammals (Mammalia) the most common are:

Carnivora—wild cat (Felis manul), lynx (Felis lynx) rare in the territory, tiger (Felis tigris), at times wanders from China without staying in this region; wolf (Canis lupus), polecat (Foetorius altaicus sibiricus), ermine (Foetorius altaicus), weasel (Foetorius vulgaris) and sable (Mustella zibellina).

White sable occurs in the Barguzínsk district; it is very rare and precious. Steppe fox (Canis corsac), bear (Ursus arctus), and badger (Meles taxus) met with mostly along the banks of the Selengá, glutton (Gulo borealis), otter (Lutra vulgaris).

Pinnipeds: seal (Phoca baicalensis) which, sometimes leaving Lake Baikál goes up the Selengá to the town of Selengínsk. They are killed by the local inhabitants during the summer from the end of June, their skins being used for making very expensive seal overcoats called „dokhá“.

Rodents (Glires): „letiága“ (Pteromys volans), squirrel (Sciurus vulgaris). The Nerchínsk, Zakaménsk and Barguzínsk squirrels are considered the best, and above half a million are taken every year; striped squirrel (Tamias striatus).

Siberian marmot (Spermophilus Eversmanni), rat (Mus documanus), mouse (Mus musculus, silvaticus, agrarius, minutus), water-rat (Arvicola amphibius), harvest-mouse (Arvicola ratticeps, obscurus, rutilus, rufocanus) occur principally in the countries contiguous to Mongolia, hare (Lepus jaculus sive mongolicus. Springhaase Brehm), (Lepus variabilis), (Lepus totai), hamster (Cricetus furunculus), creeper (Lagomys hyperboreas).

Pachyderms—(Pachydermata): wild boar (Sus scrofa) found in the valleys of the Khilók and Chikói and close to the Baikál. Ruminant animals—(Ruminantia): elk (Cervus alces) plentifully represented throughout the region, the roedeer (Cervus elephas) occurs all over the country, the horns are sold in China where they are employed as medicine; the deer (Cervus tarandus), the roe-buck (Capreolus pygargus), the musk-deer (Moschus moschiferus), inhabits preferably the south-western part of the region; the wild goat (Aegocerus sibiricus) is only found in the most desert forests.

The two-humped camel (Camelus bactrianus), domesticated by the natives is employed for the cultivation of the land and for carrying burdens: the horse (Equus), the wild horse (Equus tarpan) or „dzhigitái" principally dwelling in the northern part of the Góbi and Tibet deserts; within the limits of the Transbaikál region, it occurs only in its southern part along the rivers Gazimúr and Onón Borziá. These horses live quite like wild animals and are the object of a peculiar and very interesting mode of hunting carried on by the natives. They kill only the stallions, using their flesh as food, and consider the tail to be an infallible remedy against sickness in animals. For this hunt, the native chooses an isabel or light-bay mare and, riding in the middle of the steppe, fastens his horse and lies down in the grass. Perceiving the mare, the fiery dzhigitái rushes at her, believing her to be a mare of his own species but, remarking his mistake, stops short and at this moment is killed by the hunter.

The bird species are particularly numerous, reckoning about 328 varieties; 240 of them are common to Europe, 43 to Japan, India, the Sunda Islands and Australia, and 45 belong strictly to Eastern Siberia. This great number of birds is plentifully represented only in summer, in winter the ornithological fauna consists barely of 50 species of European and Siberian birds, all the rest flying southwards across the Mongolian steppe. The arrival of the birds from their warmer sojourn commences at the beginning of March. Choosing their way along river valleys and lakes, avoiding mountain ranges, they fly across a country situated between the Angará, the Baikál and the Toréi-Nor; this locality is separated by the chain of the Kentéi mountains, which divides the flight of the birds into a north-western and north-eastern stream. The passage across the desert of the Mongolian steppe is very trying to the birds. Upon reaching Daúria, they take a rest and regaining strength resume their flight to the north. The animation of the bird fauna reigning in summer declines at the beginning of August, when part of the birds are ready to migrate. The cranes (Grus virgo) open the migration, forming regular triangles and, steering with harsh screams towards the lonely Mongolian steppe. The backward migration of the birds is not of long duration and closes at the beginning of October.

As far as concerns snakes and reptiles, not frequent in Northern Siberia, they are rather abundant in the Transbaikál. Besides the harmless snake (Coluber rufodorsatus) and the common viper (Vipera berus) there are venomous snakes, belonging to the family of rattle-snakes (Crotalida) and two forms of trigonocephals (Trigonocephalus intermedius Strauch and Tr. Blomhomffii Boje).

The ichthyological fauna is particularly abundant and various. The division of the fauna which is observed throughout the country is still more evident among the fish species. The Northern fauna and the fauna of the Amúr present a marked difference, having only seven species in common: Lote (Lota vulgaris), salmon (Salmo fluviatilis), umber (Salmo caregonoides), salmon trout (Phoxinus revularis), char (Phoxinus perenurus), „pitálka" (Cobitis toni), and „pishchúkha" (Cobitis tacnina). All the other forms belong either to the northern species, exclusively dwelling in the Baikál water system or to the species of the southern Amúr region, found in the Onón, Ingodá, Shílka and Argún rivers.

Among the domestic animals, may be mentioned the Transbaikál horse; it is small, very hardy and not particular in its food.

The historical past of the Transbaikál territory points to the fact that the Tungús or Daúrs and the Mongols were its original inhabitants. It is here, on the banks of the Onón, that was born their famous chief Chingiz-Khan, whose name, to the present day, is held in great veneration, and to whom are attached many legends handed down from one generation to another. The Russians discovered Daúria on their way to the East in search of furanimals. In 1644, sixty-three years after Yermák had taken the capital of Kuchúm lying on the banks of the Irtysh, the Russian militia entered the Transbaikál under the command of their leader Skorokhódov. This was the first time the Russians penetrated into the region and beyond Lake Baikál. In 1647, a detachment of Yeniséi Cossacks, under the command of Kolésnikov, founded the first Upper Angará stockaded post in the Transbaikál. In the following year, a nobleman's son Gálkin established the Barguzínsk post in order to oblige the Buriáts and the other natives to pay a tribute in fur called „yasák". From this time began the gradual and parmanent colonisation of the country. The Udínsk stockaded post was established in 1649. In 1658, the first voyevóda Páshkov founded the town of Nerchínsk and in 1666, the Selengínsk post was established by order of the voyevóda Tolbúzin, with a view to protect the Russian settlements from the invasions of the Mongols. The first settlers of the Transbaikál belonged to the military class and were sent there in order to promote the Russian dominion, and were voluntary settlers as at the present time. In 1681, the Trinity and the Posólsk monasteries were built in Selengínsk and on the shore of the Baikál with a view to satisfy the religious requirements of the Christian population and to promote the orthodox missionary movement in the East. In the same year, the first ecclesiastical mission was established in the Transbaikál for the conversion of the natives. Very soon, this region was chosen as a place of exile for criminals, particularly with a view to colonise this distant country.

The famous dissenter, the protopóp Avakúm, was the first exile to Daúria; later on, the Cossack Hetman Demián Mnogogréshny was sent there; his life in Daùria was usefully employed for the benefit of the country. The regular exile system was established on the 12 March, 1722, by an Imperial ukaz stipulating that the convicts, reprieved from the death penalty by manifesto and condemned to distant exile with their wives and children, were to be sent to the silver mines of Daúria.

From the time the Russians took possession of the Transbaikál, this region became the centre of a lively intercourse with China, affording the shortest way for all commercial relations with the adjacent countries. The embassy of the Illyrian Count Sáwa Wladisláwowicz Raguzínski, which began in 1726 and terminated in 1727 by the treaty of the 20 August, fixed definite boundaries between the two countries and established trading laws for China, which were very important for the Kiákhta market; at the same time, Count Raguzínski founded the Nóvo-Tróitskaya fortress on the river Kiákhta which is now the town of Tróitsko-Sàvsk, and established a trading village on the frontier line.

The Transbaikál territory, which formerly was included in the government of Irkútsk, has existed as a separate province with an internal administration of its own since the. 16 August, 1851. The visit of His Imperial Majesty, the present Emperor Nicholas II who, during his journey to the Far East, in 1890—1891, stayed in this country from June 10 to 22, is an important historical event reverently remembered by the entire population.

Upon entering this territory on the 10 June, His Imperial Majesty arrived, by the Shílka at the station of Srétenskaya on the steamer „Véstnik"; on the 14, he arrived with His suite at Nerchínsk, one of the most ancient towns of the territory, and on the 22 traversed the country to the Mysováya station

Buriát types (phot. by Máslov).

whence, taking the steamer „Speránsky", His Imperial Majesty continued his journey by the Baikál and the Angará to Irkútsk. The population of the region may be said to comprise the following three classes: the peasants, the Cossacks and the natives. Citizens, military, convicts and exiles form the smallest portion of the population.

The peasants are principally settled in the Selengínsk, Verkhneúdinsk and Chitá districts. Part of them belong to the orthodox church and part to the sect of the Old Believers; the latter are called „seméisky". Both draw their origin from the voluntary settlers; the greater number however are descended from exiles from European Russia: the orthodox exiles were principally banished for different crimes, while the „seméisky" suffered for their religious belief, and received this characteristic popular name, because, unlike other exiles, they went into banishment accompanied by their families.

The Cossacks principally occupy the land lying along the frontier; at many places however, their settlements alternate with peasant villages. The Cossacks inhabit the valleys of the river Dzhidá, the lower reaches of the Chikói, the Onón, the Ingodá, the Shílka and all the eastern portion of the territory.

The natives are represented by the Tungús and Buriáts. The former occur only in three districts: Chitá, Selengínsk and Barguzínsk, the latter are irregularly distributed all over the country but mostly in the districts of Selengínsk, Verkhneúdinsk, Chitá and Barguzínsk.

The first census of 1897 shewed a total population of 664,071, settled in the following districts:

DISTRICTS.	Square versts.	Population by the census of 1897.					Density of population per squ. verst.
		Village.	Town.	Total population.			
				Males.	Females.	Total.	
1) Barguzínsk	144,401	22,263	1,432	11.904	11,791	23,695	0.17
2) Verkhneúdinsk	112,514	159,773	5,881	82,448	83,206	165,654	1.59
3) Selengínsk	30,305	101,214	1,093	51,002	51,035	102,307	3.37
4) Tróitsko-Sávsk	19,175	23,263	9,213	16,009	16,467	32,476	1.69
5) Chitá	112,746	130,048	11,106	75,502	65,562	141,154	1.39
6) Akshínsk	32,373	30,664	1,679	15,750	16.593	32,243	0.99
7) Nerchínsk	38,193	84,393	6,419	47,090	43,727	90,817	2.37
8) Nerchínsk Works	58,258	75,625	—	39,017	36,608	75,625	1.29
Total	547.965	627,248	36,823	338,722	325,349	664,071	1.27

In proportion to the whole area of land, the most thickly populated is the district of Selengínsk; then come the Nerchìnsk, Tróitsko-Sávsk, Verkhneúdinsk, Chitá, the Nerchìnsk Works, Akshínsk and Barguzínsk districts. However, the density of the population is inferior to all northern governments of European Russia, with the exception of the Archangel government which has a population of 0.5 to the square verst. The Russians predominate amont the population, forming 64.7 per cent of the total, then come the Buriáts representing 30.4 per cent, the Tungús 4.5 per cent, Tatars and Jews 0.4 per cent.

Buriát village.

The Cossacks, forming over 30 per cent of the total population, constitute the military class gradually formed by representatives of the native and Russian population. In the middle of the XVIII century, when the colonisation of the Transbaikál was enlarged by a contingent of exiles and the Siberian Cossacks were entrusted with the protection of the frontiers, a Tungús regiment of 500 men was formed from the local Tungús and Buriáts and added to the Siberian Cossacks with a view to strengthen the military force. In 1764, 4 regiments of 600 men each were composed of the Selengínsk Buriáts. All these regiments were stationed on the frontier. According to a statute issued on the 17 March, 1851, relative to ths organisation of the Transbaikál Cossack troops, the frontier and the stanítsa (village) Cossack troops, descendants of the Siberian Cossacks and the new-comers from Russia, as well as the Tungús and Buriát regiments, were included in the contingent of the Transbaikál Cossack troops. In 1854 part of the Cossack regiments, representing a male population of about 50,000, was transferred to the Amúr region in order to increase its population; thus the Cossacks of the Transbaikál troops formed the foundation of the Amúr and Ussúri Cossack troops. At the present time, the military class comprises a total of 200,000 dissenters and sectarians and over 28,000 Lamaists.

Buriát winter dwelling.

With respect to their total number, the Transbaikál troops hold the fourth place among the II regiments, which may be classed in the following order: the Don, Kubán, Orenbúrg, Transbaikál, Terék, Siberian, Urál, Astrakhan Semiréchensk, Amúr and Ussúri regiments. In wartime, the Transbaikál Cossacks are under the obligation to furnish 3 horse regiments of 600 men each, 6 battalions of foot of 500 men, 3 horse-artillery batteries, with six guns, a total of 234 officers, 9,319 privates and 4.050 horses. In time of peace, half of this contingent is discharged

Buriát summer camp.

All the land allotted to the use of the army, comprising a total of about 3,000,000 desiatins, is under the management of the community, represented by the population of the Cossack village or stanítsa and by every sótnia or hundred soldiers. The number of sectarians known under the name of „seméisky“ amounts to 27,990 among the peasant and Cossack population. Among the native tribes of the Transbaikál, the Tungús mostly profess Shamanism; the number of Christians is very small. The former occupy themselves with breeding reindeer and with hunting and pay their tribute or yasák in furs.

The Buriáts, whose local Russian name is „Brátskie“ (fraternal), are either Buddhists or Lamaists; they speak the Mongolian language but formerly, having no alphabet, possessed no literature, which has existed only from the time they embraced Buddhism. It consists mainly of spiritual books translated from the Tibetan language. The Bandido-Khambá or Khambá-Láma is the religious chief and first representative of the clergy; the Lamas repre-

The datsán (monastery) of Lake Gusínoe.

sent the common priesthood. The dwelling-place of the Khambá-Láma, who is officially confirmed by the Russian Government, is the „datsán“ or monastery situated within 25 versts of the town of Selengínsk, near Lake Gusínoe, which the Mongols call Gelung-nor or Lake of the Priests. The datsán resembles a small town, containing a three-storeyed temple of Chinese architecture, near to which are 17 small wooden one-storeyed temples with Buddhist cupolas, called „sumé“; each sumé is consecrated to a special „burkhán“ representing the object of worship. A whole set of neat little houses clusters around the datsán; they are inhabited by some hundreds of lamas and by over a hundred „khuvárka“, Buddhist seminarists educated in the school of the datsán. In this school, which has a course of study of ten years, they learn the prayers, the Tibetan theology, the literature of Tibet and Mongolia, Tibetan medicine, astronomy, astrology and Buddhist philosophy.

Interior of a datsán (phot. by Máslov).

The Buriáts are mainly engaged in cattle-breeding and for this purpose mostly dwell on steppe lands. They are under the management of a special native hereditary administration.

The comparative scantiness of the town population (36,823 in seven towns) points to the still insufficient development of trade, industry and manufacture. As to the peasant emigration from Russia, it hardly contributes to the increase of the population in this territory; the emigrants generally pass through the country on their way to the Amúr, and only a small number of those eastward bound stay in the Transbaikál territory.

The class of convicts and exile-settlers plays a particularly important part among the population. Prisons and exile exert a pernicious influence upon the local life of the Siberian governments and have a most evil influence upon the inhabitants of the country. The exile convicts and the exile settlers form 3 per cent of the total population. Special prisons are designed for the accomodation of the exiled convicts, concentrated in the Nerchínsk Works district and in the regions of Zerentúi and Algachí.

Lama at the entrance of the prayer-house in a datsán (phot. by Máslov).

The first district contains 4 prisons: the Zerentúi, Máltsev, Kadaínsk and Kutomár prisons.

The second division comprises the prisons of Algachí, of Pokróvsk and the Alexander poorhouse for old exile settlers. The Akatúi prisons for political prisoners is under the management of the Nerchìnsk Penal Board.

The population of all these prisons varies from 2,200 to 2,700. The convicts are employed in work entrusted to them by the Mining Department and receive one tenth of the value of their work; moreover they discharge all ordinary household and other duties.

After the completion of the hard-labour sentence, the convicts pass to the stage of exile-settlers, and present an improvident, dangerous and thriftless element which lies as a heavy burden upon the whole of the population.

The total number of exile-settlers throughout the territory is 17,000; the dwelling places of one-third of them is unknown. The tenure and exploitation of the land is not regulated in the Transbaikál, as no proper boundaries have yet been traced. This however constitutes one of the chief anxieties of the Government, occupied with the welfare of the country.

According to the calculations of Strelbítsky, the territory covers a total area of 56,152,260 desiatins of land, excluding 54,410,323 desiatins of water The area of settled land is 14,826,925 desiatins.

Thus only 27 per cent of the total area of land in the Transbaikál is cultivated, while 40,000,000 desiatins are lying vaste. This immense area of unoccupied land is hardly explored to the present day; it is mostly covered with dense forests and rocky mountain ranges, but undoubtedly contains localities which are fit for colonisation.

The greater portion of the settled land, 45 per cent, belongs to the natives; the Cossacks own 35 per cent, the peasants 12 per cent. The rest forms the property of His Imperial Majesty's Cabinet, of towns, of monasteries and of the former peasants of the metallurgical works.

The division of the land, not being regulated, is very unequal among the various groups of the population; many possess an excess of land, whilst others have too little. This irregular distribution occurs more frequently among peasants and natives; the first possess from 8 to 32 desiatins to every male member, the second even much more.

The chief industries and occupations of the population are represented by agriculture and cattle-breeding. The considerable elevation of the country above the level of the sea, its mountainous surface, the gravel soil and severe climate have a most unfavourable influence upon the general development of agriculture in the country.

Under these conditions, agriculture requires much practical experience and labour. The Russian colonist settled in an unknown land, with peculiar conditions of soil and climate, has to adapt his husbandry to them, and to abandon many of his original customs, changing his mode of life and in many things imitating the half savage native nomad.

Interior of the school in a datsán.

The fallow land system, varying in accordance with the climate and soil, predominates throughout the territory. There is no improved agricultural machinery and the land is mostly tilled with the help of ordinary two-wheeled ploughs and harrows of very primitive construction. The most abundant crops of yáritsa, wheat, oats, buckwheat and barley are raised in the Nerchínsk and Akshínsk districts; the average crops for yáritsa are 4.7-fold, for wheat 4.6 fold, for oats 5.1-fold, for buckwheat 7.3-fold, and for barley 4.7-fold. With the gradual development of agriculture in the Transbaikál, the the area sown with spring-wheat and oats widens from year to year.

Masks of lama images used in mysteries.

For some time past, the public commissariat was an object of solicitude for the Government, but now the conditions are so far changed that the

Transbaikál may serve as a granary for the gold-mines of the adjacent Amúr territory.

After the completion of the Great Siberian main line and with the general rise of the economic life in the region, agriculture will make still greater progress as regards the expansion of its area, and the technical improvement of the modes of cultivation and the systems of husbandry.

Being provided with vast pastures, the Transbaikál offers particularly favourable conditions for cattle-breeding, which has a very important economic significance as the principal feature of industry, upon which depends the welfare of the natives.

Horses, cattle, camels, sheep, goats and swine are the domestic animals reared by the inhabitants. The horses of the Transbaikál belong to the local stock and only very few are obtained by crossing with stallions brought from Western Siberia or, as within the last 4—5 years, from the stables of the Imperial studs in Russia. The cattle is also home-bred, and the camels yaks buffalos, sheep, goats and swine come exclusively of the local stock.

The number of cattle belonging to the inhabitants is distributed in the following proportion:

DISTRICTS.	Horses.	Cattle.	Sheep.	Goats.	Swine.	Totals.
Barguzínsk	16,396	78,213	58,271	1,701	705	155,286
Verkhneúdinsk	144,839	338,054	280,596	29,362	48,664	841,515
Selengínsk	79,120	196,936	191,138	44,641	15,485	527,320
Tróitsko-Sávsk	16,492	27,487	42,287	9,618	9,878	99,762
Chitá	161,419	371,928	331,140	51,679	19,860	916,026
Akshínsk	76,661	111,857	174,717	22,041	9,787	395,063
Nerchínsk	79,817	109,678	74,927	11,077	24,651	300,150
Nerchínsk Works.	53,554	70,960	48,266	7,591	15,726	226,057
TOTALS	628,288	1,305,115	1,201,342	178,090	138,756	3,451,691

The number of camels in the territory is about 9,650; most of them belong to the wandering natives of the Chitá district.

The inhabitants possess a total of 3,550,519 head of cattle, including camels.

The cattle are kept in herds. They a: not looked after and, feeding all the year round on the pastures, are exposed to bad weather, to the danger of epizootic diseases, to wild beasts and other dangers.

The animal produce not only serves as a help to the population but often represents the sole source of their welfare.

Meat is exported from the Transbaikál to the government of Irkútsk, to the Amúr territory and the gold-mines; the hides are forwarded to the government of Irkútsk and part of them is employed for packing tea boxes. Wool and fat are also articles of export.

Fishing is chiefly practised on the shores of the Baikál and in the estuaries of the rivers Selengá, Barguzín, and the Upper Angará. The omul, predominating in this industry, is salted without delay immediately after being caught, and sold by the fishmongers in the government of Irkútsk. The temporary rules for fishing, which as an experiment were introduced by the Amúr Governor-General in 1895, somewhat diminished the shameless extermination of the fish, by regulating its capture and submitting it to control.

Hunting is a profitable occupation of the local wandering and nomad natives, principally carried on in the desert and wooded mountain ridges to the north of the Transbaikál. This industry is also pursued in the upper parts of the rivers Dzhidá and Témnik, south of Lake Baikál, on the mountain masses of Kentéi and on the southern chain of the Yáblonovy mountains near the sources of the Chikói, Ingodá and Onón. The squirrel is the most important animal hunted. The sable is hunted with dogs, which are trained to follow its traces. The best sable are to be found on the highest mountain summits; their capture offers many difficulties. The maral is also much hunted at the end of May and the beginning of June, on account of its horns called „pánty“ which are sold in China at a considerable price.

Transport of tea.

Average horns weigh from 10 to 12 pounds, but they sometimes attain a weight of 30 pounds; they are sold on the spot for R. 3 to R. 5 a pound. All th produce of the chase is generally sold at the local fairs, or bought up by traders, traversing the countries where the industry is most extensively developed.

Forestry is carried on almost throughout the Transbaikál, and consists in cutting down and floating the timber. The gathering of „cedar“ nuts is closely connected with this industry, and is pursued in the south-eastern and southern parts of the region. The Yáblonovy mountain ridge, specially at the head-waters of the Ingodá and Chikói are the centres of it.

Transport of tea.

Carriage by road, constituting an important source of income to the population from the landing-place of Mysováya to the station of Srétensk, and along the highway from Kiákhta to Mysováya and Irkútsk, must necessarily be reduced by the construction of the Siberian Railway, which will carry the greater portion of the goods in transit through the region from the confines of the Amúr basin and Manchuria.

The inhabitants have another source of profit in the gold-mines, which are situated within the territory and in the adjacent Amúr country. This branch of industry will surely receive a further development in the near future under the influence of the railway. Till the present time, the expensiveness of the necessary machinery and technical appliances and the high prices of all commodities beginning with food products have stood in the way of the proper development of this branch of industry; the establishment of easy and cheap transport and the flow of fresh capital will contribute to

View of the town of Tróitsko-Sávsk.

the working of auriferous areas which formerly were considered as unfit for exploitation.

The opening of the great steam communication will also exert its influence upon other enterprises and increase the demand for workmen. According to statistical data, about 15,761 households are not occupied with agriculture but earn their living by different other pursuits. This number forms 16.8 per cent of the total of the households in the Transbaikál, obtaining an annual income of R. 1,500,000.

Domestic industry is hardly developed and meets only local requirements; it is chiefly exercised by the natives, producing small articles of wrought-iron such as stirrups, horseshoes, knives etc., and articles of cast copper: bells, idols etc.

The natives prepare coarse cloth and felt from wool.

Manufacturing industry is at a very low stage of development in the Transbaikál. Excluding the mining and gold-mining industries, its annual business hardly exceeds R. 1,500,000.

The demand for manufactured articles is supplied by produce imported from European Russia, which is also required in Mongolia and China.

Distilleries yield the greaterst annual output.

The greater number of factories and works is centred in the Nerchínsk, Tróitsko-Sávsk and Chitá districts, mainly in the towns. Among them, the most important are: the stearine manufactory of Osókin and Co., who also possess a soap-boilery in Kiákhta, and the cement manufactories, principally of the Amúr Cement Company, built in 1865 on the Shílka, near the settlement of Kokertói and near the railway station of Bayán.

A chemical industry for obtaining salt from „guzhír", which is a mixture of different kinds of salts containing mostly sulphide of soda, is being established in the district of Barguzínsk.

Trade iu the Transbaikál is characteristic of all Siberian governments and territories. Exporting exclusively raw produce, the territory receives in return different manufactured articles from European Russia and from abroad.

Commercial transactions are carried on at the fairs. The Verkhneúdinsk fair is held from the 18 January to the 1 February, the Spáso-Preobrazhénie fair, in the village of Chertokvínskoe, near the mouth of the Selengá (from the 1 August to the 20 September), the Argínskaya. in the Chitá district (from the 1 to 6 December), and many others of inferior importance, which take place in some nomad villages and other places with a view to exchange animal and hunting produce for articles essentially needful in agricultural and nomadic households. The total turn-over of these fairs amounts to R. 7,000,000. The most important is the Verkhneúdinsk fair, with a business exceeding R. 4,000,000.

The special importance of the Transbaikál consists in the share it takes in the foreign transit trade with China and Mongolia, due to the communi-

View of Kiákhta.

cation through Irkútsk and Kiákhta, and in the barter of produce at the places situated along the frontier of the Akshínsk district, suchas Zurukhaitúi, Abagatúi, Zagan-Alúi etc.

Out of the total imports of tea into the Russian Empire, amounting to 2,500,000 puds annually, 1,720,000 puds come from the Asiatic frontier and are mostly carried through Kiákhta. This great movement of goods in transit, after the completion of the Great Siberian main line, will mostly be transferred to the railway. At the same time, the barter trade will be enlivened throughout the Asiatic frontier by the opening of fresh markets and the production of new articles for export to China and Mongolia.

There are four monasteries in the territory, in order to meet the spiritual requirements of the orthodox population: the Bogoródsk nunnery in Chitá, the Chikói monastery of John the Baptist, in the Verkhneúdinsk district, the Selengá monastery of the Holy Trinity, with an antisectarian mission, in the village of Ilínskoe of the Selengínsk district, and the Posólsk monastery of the Transfiguration of Our Lord, in the village of Posólskoe of the Selengínsk district. The territory contain 268, parish and registered churches; 242 of them are distributed all over the vast country. The insufficient quantity of orthodox churches, and their distance from centres of population is particularly evident, when their number is compared with that of the settled localities which are about 1435 in number, and with the total orthodox population forming about 60 per cent of the whole population, viz. 40,0000.

The brotherhood of the Saints Cyril and Methodius and St. Innocent, the Miracle-worker of Irkútsk, has started its operations within the confines of the territory.

Upon the construction of the Great Siberian Railway, part of the Emperor Alexander III fund has been employed to satisfy the spiritual needs of the population: in the Chitá district, a church will soon be finished in the settlement of Shundúi, and another is being built in honour of St. Nicholas the Miracle-worker in the settlement of Karkasár, lying in proximity to the rich Buriát datsán of Zangól; in the Nerchínsk district, a church is in course of construction in the settlement of Bókhtin; in the Nerchínsk Works district, the construction of a church was begun on the 28 September, 1898, in the village of Zolotonósha in honour of the image of Our Lady of Smolénsk; new churches are either built or in process of construction at the stations of Mysováya, Khilók, Magzón and Chitá.

For the spiritual needs of the Lamaists, 32 datsáns were established by the law of the 15 May, 1853, containing a fixed contingent of priests.

The public instruction is still at a very primitive stage, but its progress is evident and very remarkable when the present number of schools and

Bazar. Tea-store in Kiákhta (phot. by Mrs. Petróv).

pupils is compared with the data for the preceding years. The territory contains a total of 375 schools with 12,761 boys and girls. This includes 4 middle schools classical gymnasiums, two schools for girls and a modern school. There are 15 third-class schools and 356 lower institutions. Ten years ago, the territory possessed only 151 schools with 5,925 school children.

Among the scientific societies there are: the Chitá and Tróitsko-Sávsk-Kiákhta branch of the Imperial Russian Geographical Society of the Amúr division. The Transbaikál branch of the Imperial Society for the Preservation of Animals useful to the Hunter and Trader and the encouragement of legitimate sport. The Transbaikál Doctors' Society in Chitá.

Entrance gate of Maimachin.

The railway constructed within the confines of the territory, constituting a link in the Great Siberian main line, will in the near future completely change all the economic and other conditions of this country, and by giving a wide scope to the development of productive industry and enlarging the sphere of export for local produce, will also raise the level of public education and intelligence.

BIBLIOGRAPHY:

1) From Vladivostók to Urálsk. Guide to the Journey of His Imperial Highness the Tsesarévich, by the Centr. Stat. Comm. of the Ministry of the Interior, 1891. 2) Journey of His Imperial Majesty Nicholas II to the Far East in 1890—1891, by Prince E. E. Ukhtomsky. III vol. St. Petersburg, 1897. 3) Statistics of the Russian Empire XXVIII. Vólosts and centres of population, 1893. Transbaikál territory. Publ. by the Central Stat. Comm. of the Ministry of the Interior. St. Pbg. 1894. 4) Siberian trade and industry calendar for 1896—1897, publ. in Tomsk by Románov. 5) Selengínsk Daúria. Review of the Transbaikál region by Ptítsyn. St. Pbg. 1896. 6) Western Transbaikál as regards Agriculture. Publ. by the Ministry of Agriculture and State Domains by Kriúkov, St. Pbg. 1896. 7) Eastern Transbaikál as regards agriculture. Publ. by the Min. of Agr. and State Dom. Kriúkov, St. Pbg. 1895. 8) Siberia and the Great Siberian Railway. Publ. by the Ministry of Finance, St. Pbg., 1896. 9) Memorandum for the Transbaikál territory for 1898. Publ. by the Transbaikál Stat. Comm. Chitá, 1898. 10) Materials for the Imperially sanctioned Commission presided over by State Secretary Kúlomzin, for the investigation of land tenure and agriculture in the Transbaikál territory. St. Pbg. 1898. 11) Geological investigations and explorations on the Siberian railway, pt. 1—VI, St. Pbg. 1896—1897. 12) The Amúr country at the Russian Exhibition in Nízhni Novgorod, by Kriúkov. Moscow, 1896. 13) Review of the chief waterways of the Amúr country by V. E. Tímonov. St. Pbg. 1897. 14) Appendix to the Report of the Minister of Agriculture and State Domains, presented to His Imperial Majesty, after his journey to Siberia in the autumn of 1895. Publ. by the Ministry of Agr. and State Dom. St. Pbg. 1896.

The Transbaikál Railway.

Direction of the line. — Cost of construction. — Description of the stations and localities traversed by the railway. — Mysováya. - Posólskaya. — Selengá. — Tataúrovo. — Town of Verkhneúdinsk. — Onokhói. — Zaigráevo. — Ilka. — Mkhe-Gorkhón. — Kuzhí. — Petróvsk Works. — Tarbagatái. — Talbóga. — Báda. — Khilók. — Khushengá. — Taidún. — Magzón. — Sakhandó. — Yáblonovaya. — Ingodá. — Town of Chitá. — Kruchína. — Makavéevo. — Karymskaya. — Kaidalóvo. — Branch line to the East - Chinese railway. — Urulgá. — Zubarévo. — Onón. — Shílka. — Town of Nérchinsk. — Biánkina. — Bayán. — Srétensk.

The Transbaikál railway begins at the landing-place of Mysováya, on the eastern shore of Lake Baikál and, proceeding by way of Verkhneúdinsk and the Petróvsk Works across the Yáblonovy chain to the towns of Chitá and Nérchinsk, terminates at the station of Srétensk, where commences the steamboat communication by the rivers Shílka and Amúr. The total length of the line is 1033.5 versts. The cost of its construction amounts to R. 59,250,381, inclusive of rails and rolling-stock.

The preliminary surveys were conducted by Engineer Viázemsky.

The construction of the line was commenced on the 11 April 1895 under the direction of Engineer Púshechnikov. The Transbaikál railway numbers 34 stations.

1) **Mysováya**, IV class station, it is situated on Lake Baikál, near the landing-place of the same name. Near the station a church is being built in honour of the Martyr St. Platón, at the cost of the Emperor Alexander III fund. Upon the opening of traffic, a halting-place and a medical and feeding

station was established near the landing-place of Mysováya for the use of the emigrants bound for the Transbaikál and Amúr regions.

The settlement of Mysovóe of the Selengínsk district, situated near the landing-place, previous to the construction of the railway, contained only 72 houses and a population of 298; at present it is much extended and the population has increased to such a degree that the local administration contemplates the creation of a town on the shore of the Baikál.

The locality surrounding the settlement and adjoining the railway is divided into regular sections, which are temporarily leased. The settlement of Mysovóe is the residence of a police officer and contains a post and telegraph office with a savings bank. Fifteen versts to the south of the village of Mysovóe, on the northern slope of Khamár Dabán, occur beds of magnetic iron ore. On the 22 June, 1891, His Imperial Majesty, the present Emperor Nicholas II, then Heir Apparent to the throne, arrived at the station of Mysováya on his way from the Far East. A spacious and elegant pavilion was erected by the merchants of Kiákhta for the reception of the Imperial visitor and his suite. Having been received here by General of Infantry Goremykin, Governor-General of Irkútsk, His Imperial Majesty took leave of Baron Korf, Governor-General of the Amúr territory, and of the persons belonging to the local administration who had accompanied him on his journey through the Amúr region.

From the station of Mysováya, the railway runs along the shore of Lake Baikál, skirting the branches of the Khamár Dabán mountain ridge, which at many places falls to the lake in an almost perpendicular line. The line crosses many mountain streams and brooks flowing from the Khamár Dabán The most important among them are the Mantúrikha and the Bolsháya spanned by stone bridges with iron girders. Throughout its course to the station of Posólskaya, the line runs through a desert, swampy and thinly settled forest region or taigá, unfit for cultivation.

2) **Posólskaya.** Is a V class station (45 v.) situated near the village of Posólskaya on Lake Baikál, iu the Selengínsk district (houses 141 pop. 751: 379 males, 378 females). In the vicinity is situated the second-class monastery of the Transfiguration of Our Lord, built in 1681 by command of the Tsar Theodore Alexéevich by the ecclesiastical mission sent to Western Daúria consisting of the abbot Theodosius and the monk Macarius. The monastery stands on the spot where Yeroféi Zabolótsky, the son of a nobleman of Tobólsk, was treacherously murdered by the Buriáts in 1650, together with his son and his companions on his way to the land of Mungánsk as ambassador to the Khan sysán. At first a prayer-house was erected there to serve for missionary purposes the first orthodox preachers in the Transbaikál; later on, in 1771, a wooden church with a bell-tower was erected in honour of the Transfiguration of Our Lord, and cells for the brotherhood and their superior were built at the cost of the merchant Oskólkov, of Kiákhta. At the present time, the monastery possesses two stone churches: one of these is a cathedral, having two storeys, erected in place of the former wooden church; the upper church is consecrated to the Transfiguration of Our Lord, the lower in memory of the Miraculous Apparition of the Virgin Mary. The second church is built on the northern side of the monastery ,in honour of St. Nicholas the Miracle-worker. The monastery is surrounded by a stone wall; to the left, on the western side, there is a stone chapel over the grave of the ambassador

Zabolótsky. The enclosure of the monastery contains two stone and 6 wooden detached buildings: one of them is inhabited by the vicar of Irkútsk, the others are occupied by the brotherhood, the missionary school, the dining hall and the poor-house.

The ground on which the monastery and the surrounding villages are situated is composed of alluvium brought down by the Selengá river.

Many thickly populated settlements are situated in the neighbourhood; in that of Chertóvkinskoe, an annual fair is held in the beginning of August, with a turn-over of a thousand rubls. The landing-place of Boyárskaya, on the Lake Baikál, lies near the station of Posólskaya. Here is the post station of the Verkhneúdinsk highway, the halting-place or étape for convicts and a convoy commando, whose duty it is to escort parties to the next étape.

At the 50 th verst, the railway line issues into the valley of the river Selengá, and follows its left bank up the river. The valley of the Selengá between the 50 and 125 verst is rather wide. The bordering mountains, which are branches of the Khamár Dabán, only at a few places come down to the river. Throughout this part, the Selengá widens and is dotted with many islands.

3) **Selengá.** IV class station (80 verst). The village of Ilínskoe is situated near the station, on the river Selengá, in the Selengínsk district (100 houses, pop. 476; 221 males, 255 females). It was built at the end of the XVII century and known under the name of the stockaded post till the beginning of the XIX century. The village contains the Selengínsk monastery of the Holy Trinity with an antisectarian mission. This monastery was founded in the XVI century for missionary purposes. It possesses a stone cathedral and, as memorials of the past, two wooden churches. One of these was built at the end of the XVII century, the other at the beginning of the XVIII. The holy images and the ikonostasis have still the same appearance as at the time of its construction. A stone church was erected in 1806 above the Holy Gate.

The monastery was visited in 1891 by His Imperial Majesty, the Emperor Nicholas II; special attention was paid to the antiquities of the monastery dating from the time of the Tsar Alexis Mikháilovich. In remembrance of his visit, His Imperial Majesty presented an enamelled altar-cross to the monastery.

4) **Tataúrovo.** IV class station (119 v.) situated near a village of the same name on the river Selengá (31 houses, pop. 156; 84 males, 72 females). From the 125 verst, the valley of the river Selengá narrows to a mere pass between the mountains, along the steep slopes of which the line runs as far as the 130 verst, where it passes to the right bank by an iron bridge with roadway upon the lower chord and six spans of 40 sazhens each, and two on each side of 8 sazhens supported by stone piers laid on caissons. Along the right bank of the Selengá, the line follows steep slopes as far as the town of Verkhneúdinsk. Reddish and grey granite protrudes at some places on the banks.

5) **Verkhneúdinsk.** IV class station (154 v.) Lies close to the district town of Verkhneúdinsk (51° 49′ N. lat. and 77° 14′ E. long.) and is picturesquely situated in a deep vale between the spurs of the Yáblonovy chain, and at the junction of the rivers Uda and Selengá (pop. 8.002; 4964 males, 3038 females). The town is regularly planned and has wide streets; it contains 901 houses (about 40 of stone), 4 churches (3 of stone) among which may be mentioned on account of their ancient architecture the Odigídri cathedral,

founded in 1745, and the church of Our Saviour, dating from the year 1796. There are 5 chapels (3 of stone), a Jewish synagogue, 6 schools, a preparatory gymnasium with four classes for girls, a district school for boys, 3 urban parish schools, a church parish school, a town public library.

Here we find the office of the manager of the IV division of the Transbaikál line; the first battery of the Transbaikál Cossacks; the local body-guard; post and telegraph office with a savings-bank; the department of the Western Transbaikal Mining district and an agency of the Russo-Chinese Bank.

The military post of Udínsk, to which were banished the Streltsy in the year 1668, stood on the site of the present town. In 1775, Udínsk was transformed into a town.

Its favourable position on the navigable river Selengá and the vicinity of the fertile regions of the Transbaikál have made it the chief centre of trade in the western part of the country. Every year, in January, a fair is held in the town with a business of about R. 3,000,000. The following industrial concerns are situated near the town: a distillery, a brewery, a butter manufactory, four tallow-boileries and candle manufactories, 17 tanneries, 3 soap boileries. The butter manufactory was established by Fédchenko in 1894

View of the town of Verkhneúdinsk.

with steam motors. Cedar-nut oil is produced by means of the nut-shelling apparatus of Griadásov. Within 45 versts of the town, is situated the steam flour-mill of the merchant Goldóbin, grinding about 125,000 puds of wheat annually.

There are two hotels under the management of Jews, with rooms from R. 1. 50 k. to R. 2 a day; the rate is higher during the fair. Hackney coaches according to tariff: a drive 20 k. the hour 40—50 k.

On the 22 June, 1891, His Imperial Majesty, the present Emperor Nicholas II on his way from the Far East arrived at Verkhneúdinsk and, on the 21 June, anniversary day of the confirmation of the statute for the organisation of the infantry battalions of the Transbaikál Cossack troops, assembled the „voiskovoi krug“ or general meeting of the Cossack troops, and held a review of them.

The more important firms are: Vtórov—manufactured goods; Nemchínov—navigation; Sobenikóv and Molchánov brothers—tea and sugar; Fainberg—hard-ware; Buivid—wine-cellar, vegetable oil, etc. Kravétsky—brewery; Manzúrov—soap-boilery; Goldóbin — wheat flour-mill; Trunév — hard ware; Fédchenko—butter and grocery.

Agents: Stasiván—of the Rossía Company; Mashánov—of the St. Petersburg Insurance Society.

Skirting Verkhneúdinsk on the north, the line crosses the river Udá at the 162 verst by a bridge of 50 sazhens, with iron girders, roadway upon the lower chord, and stone piers on caisson foundations.

6) **Onokhói.** IV class station. (187 v.). Is situated next to the village of the same name on the river Udá (houses 97, pop. 486; 233 males, 253 females) and is inhabited by Mongols and Buriáts, placed under the council of the Khorínsk steppe, in the Verkhneúdinsk district. The village contains a post station. Hence the line, having previously followed the main post-road of Moscow, leaves it, and proceeds along the valley of the river Brián.

7) **Zaigráevo.** V class station (207 v.). A cement works established near the station on the river Brián, belongs to the merchant Tetiukóv and has a yearly output of 20,000 barrels. Passing by the station, the line crosses the river Brián at the 215 verst by an iron bridge of 20 sazhens and continuing along the valley of the Ará Kizhí, a tributary to the Brián, ascends to the Station of Ilka and further on to Mkhe-Gorkhón with spêcifications as usually applied on level sections.

8) **Ilka.** IV class station (229 v.) received its name from the river Ilka, which is a right tributary of the Ará Kizhí.

9) **Mkhe-Gorkhón.** V class station (256 v.). From the station, the line ascends to the mountain range of Zagón Dá, forming the watershed of the tributaries to the rivers Udá and Khilók. The specifications generally used for mountainous sections are adopted on this ascent (grade .0175). The station of Kizhí is situated at the highest point of the mountain ridge, at an elevation of about 200 sazhens above the level of Lake Baikál.

10) **Kizhí.** V class station (270 v.). Hence the line descends to the valley of the Baliága, falling into the Khilók, and reaches the Petróvsk Works, belonging to His Imperial Majesty's Cabinet. The country traversed by the main line, between the town of Verkhneúdinsk and the Petróvsk Works, is settled only for a distance of 50 versts, and that by emigrants long since arrived from European Russia, mainly engaged in agriculture and cattle-breeding. Further on, in the direction of the Petróvsk Works, the country presents a thick taigá inhabited only by half-nomad Buriáts. Between Mysováya and the Petróvsk Works, the road considerably deviates from the straight line, connecting these two points. From Mysováya it runs north-east, then along the valley of the Selengá, south-east to the town of Verkhneúdinsk, further along the valley of the Udá, north-east again and finally, on leaving this valley, it takes a south-eastern direction towards the Petróvsk Works. All the attempts made to find a shorter cut across the mountain range of Khamár Dabán, for the location of the main line from Mysováya to the Petróvsk Works, proved unsuccessful and shewed the necessity of avoiding the mountains following the valleys of the rivers Selengá, Udá and Brián.

11) The **Petróvsk Works.** IV class station (288 v.) situated close to the Petróvsk Ironworks, belonging to the Cabinet of His Imperial Majesty, on the river Baliága, tributary of the Khilók, in the Verkhneúdinsk district (houses 681, pop. 3,673; 1,864 males, 1,809 females).

This works was established in 1790, principally with the view to supply iron to the Nérchinsk mines and the gold mines belonging to the Government. A considerable quantity of iron and cast-iron are sold in the country. An area of 104,637 desiatins, including 94,550 desiatins of forest land, pertains to the works. At the present time, only the Baliága mine is being worked; it lies on the Zagán Dabán ridge 25 versts from the works, on the river Baliága, and supplies them with magnetic iron-ore. The works contain: 1 blast furnace, 2 puddling furnaces, 1 reverbatory furnace, 3 welding and other furnaces, 1 cupola furnace, 1 blasting engine, 11 pig-iron furnaces, 7 forges, 1 steam hammer, 17 hydraulic hammers, 14 water-wheels of 204 H. P.; 3 steam engines of 130 H. P. and give employment to 250 men.

The average quantity of iron produced is 50,000 puds; the quantity of puddled and pig-iron amounts to 20,000—30,000 puds.

The settlements round the works compose a separate Petróvsk vólost containing a church to St. Peter and St. Paul erected in 1837, a school and a hospital. Here are the offices of the V division for the construction of the Transbaikál railway line and of the local department for the ironworks.

The Petróvsk Works was a place of exile for many of thode who were condemned for participation in the conspiracy of the 14 December 1825, known under the name of the Dekabrísts. They were confined in a prison specially constructed in a locality chosen by Lepársky, the director of the prison, and were brought over from the prison of Chitá in the year 1830. This prison, standing apart from that of the convicts condemned to hard labour in the mines for non-political offences, was a low and dark building with an inner court. By Imperial permission, the wives of the Dekabrists were allowed to follow their husbands from Chitá to the Petróvsk Works; they were the Princesses Trubetskói and Volkónsky, and Mesdames Annenkov, Muravióv, Naryshkin and Davydov. Later on, the Dekabrists were transported from here to different parts of Siberia, and also as soldiers to the Caucasus. About the year 1840, the political prison of Petróvsk became vacant. Only Gorbachévsky, who died 1870, lived to the end of his days in the Petróvsk Works, first as an exile-settler, then as a nobleman, and died there in the office of arbitrator on the lands of His Imperial Majesty's Cabinet.

Leaving the Petróvsk Works, the line follows the valley of the Baliága, crossing it twice at the 293 and 299 verst, over iron bridges of 15 and 20 sazhens, and then turns north-east into the valley of the Khilók, ascending along the right bank of this river to the summit of the Yáblonovy mountain range.

12) **Tarbagatái,** V class station (319 v.), is situated near the village of the same name on the Khilók, and belongs to the Verkhneúdinsk district, (houses 51, pop. 258; 138 males, 120 females).

The village of Tarbagatái has a wooden missionary church to the Holy Trinity erected in 1872, and a school.

At the 324 verst, the line crosses the river Tígni by an iron bridge of 15 sazhens and, continuing its course through the valley of the Khilók along the right bank of this river, ascends the Yáblonovy ridge. On the right side of the Khilók, below the mouth of the Tígni, occurs an outcrop of brown coal, embedded in soft clayey sandstone and clay slates. This bed was explored in 1889 by the administration of the Petróvsk Works, but its productive capacity was imperfectly ascertained. This coal, tested in 1892 in the gold-smelting laboratory of Irkútsk, was pronounced to be chinky, efflorescent and with uncaked coke.

13) **Talbóga,** IV class station (337 v.). Office of the VI division for the construction of the Transbaikál railway. The valley of the Khilók traversed by the main line is quite destitute of permanent population, being only visited by wandering Buriáts with their herds. This valley for a considerable distance is bordered by mountains; at some places, their spurs approach the river and fall to the water in a steep and almost perpendicular line. At such points, the location of the line was attended with great difficulties.

14) **Báda,** IV class station (381 v.) is situated amidst the wide spreading Báda steppe, near a village of the same name, inhabited by Buriáts belonging to the Khórinsk department of the Verkhneúdinsk district (houses 253, pop. 1,230; 600 males, 630 females.) From this station, the line runs east, gradually ascending, along the right bank of the Khilók.

15) **Khilók,** IV class station (427 v.). A church was erected near the station in honour of St. Nicholas the Miracle-worker and the Martyr Saint Queen Alexándra in commemoration of their Imperial Majesties' coronation, at the cost of the wife of Major General E. I. Kúkel. The first stone for the construction of this church, which was the first on the Transbaikál line, was laid on the 1 August 1897, in the presence of State Secretary Kúlomzin. Following the right bank of the Khilók, the line turns north-east, having on the other side the Khogói and Shentói mountains forming branches of the Tsagán Khuntéi ridge.

16) **Khushengá,** V class station (462 v.).

17) **Taidún,** V class station (502 v.).

18) **Ragzón,** IV class station (541 v.). Office of the VII section for the construction of the Transbaikál railway. Next to the station, a church consecrated to the Apostles Peter and Paul is being built from the Emperor Alexander III fund. Close by are several mineral springs containing iron, different kinds of salts and natural carbonic acid.

19) **Sakhandó,** V class station (580 v.) The line leaves the Khilók valley between the stations of Sakhandó and Yáblonovaya and at the 590 verst passes over a depression in the Yáblonovy ridge, with an elevation of 250 sazhens above the level of Lake Baikál, and with 487 sazhens absolute height at the head-waters of the river Kúka, a tributary to the Khilók and Kúka, falling into the Ingodá. The descent along the eastern slope of the mountains, from the summit to the station of Yáblonovaya, is so steep that the specifications used in mountain districts were here adopted for a distance of 12 versts (grade .017, radius 150 sazhens).

20) **Yáblonovaya,** IV class station (603 v.). From this station, the line descends along the valley of the river Kúka, tributary to the Ingodá, and further winds its course along the narrow and sinuous valley of the Ingodá, belonging to the Amúr basin, taking a general north-eastern direction till the station of Chitá.

21) **Ingodá,** V class station (638 v.). At the bottom of the left bank of the Ingodá, named Krutói Yar, situated 2 versts beyond the village of Nóvaya Kúka, were found two seams of brown coal. Engineer Obruchev considers that these beds are worth working on account of their proximity to the railway station (3—4 versts) and their favourable position on the banks of the raftable river, at a height of 7—8 sazhens above the level ot the water.

22) **Chitá,** III class station (674 v.) is situated at a distance of 2 versts from the town of Chitá, separated from it by the river of the same name.

A church in honour of St. John is being erected near the station at the cost of E. I. Kúkel and the Emperor Alexander III fund. Chitá is the chief town of the Transbaikál territory. It is the residence of a military governor, and the centre of the local administration (51° 1' N. lat. and 83° 10′ E. long.). The town is situated on the left bank of the river Chitá, near its junction with the Ingodá. The small river Kaidalóvka, a tributary of the Chitá, flows through the town. The Chitá is not navigable; rafts are floated on the Ingodá. In the middle of the XVIII century, a Cossack stockaded post stood on the site of the present town. This unknown place, which formerly was a poor village consisting of 26 peasants huts with 300 inhabitants, became in 1827 from administrative considerations the place of banishment for those who were condemned for participation in the conspiracy of the 14 December, 1825. Buildings, narrow, low and dark, surrounded by a high wall of pointed stakes, were allotted for the accomodation of the exiles, and received then the name

View of the town of Chitá.

of the Casemates, each being marked with its №. The unsatisfactory conditions of the building required the construction of a new prison, which was begun in the spring of the year 1827. All the prisoners of the casemates were obliged to take part in the work, and thus the new building was ready by the autumn of the same year. Most of those condemned for the conspiracy of the 14 December lived three years and seven months in this prison built by their own hands.

During this period, the poor village of Chitá, which formerly, on account of its situation on the low bank at the junction of the rivers Chitá and Ingodá, was used as a suitable spot for the construction of rafts floated along the rivers Ingodá and Shílka, became a considerable settlement. It owed its outwardly prosperous appearance to the Dekabrists, who drained the place, filled up ditches etc., while the actual prosperity of the inhabitants was due to the money expended by the prisoners in the satisfaction of their daily requirements. One of the streets of the town up to this day is called the Dámskaya or Ladies' street in memory of the ladies Trubetskói, Volkónsky, Muravióv, Annenkov, Naryshkin and Davydov, wives of the Dekabrists, who accompanied their banished husbands and had their own houses in it. Having developed into a commercial centre under the influence of the exiles, Chitá very soon acquired the foremost position in the country. On the organisation of the Transbaikál territory in 1851, it became the centre of the local administration. From that time, the newly founded town has developed rapidly.

The last census shewed a population of 11,480 (6,877 males, 4,603 females). The town is very well laid out, but the streets are unpaved and very badly lighted. On the 1 July, 1899, the town was supplied with a telephone at Government cost for the use of the public. The total number of the mostly wooden houses is 1,412. There are 9 churches and a nunnery of the Holy Virgin; a vast stone cathedral, founded on the 12 August, 1899, in commemoration of His Imperial Majesty's visit to Chitá in 1891, and of the Sacred Coronation in Moscow in 1896; a Roman catholic chapel and a Jewish synagogue. There are 13 schools: gymnasium for boys and girls, diocesan school for girls, central missionary school attached to the Archbishop's house, artisans' school, urban three-class school, and two parish schools; one of them was founded in memory of His Imperial Majesty, the Emperor Nicholas II's visit to Chitá on the 17—18 June in 1891; the other was established in commemoration of the marriage of Their Imperial Majesties, the Emperor Nicholas II and the Empress Alexándra Feódorovna; a Sunday-school and three parish schools attached to the convict children's home, to the central missionary school, and to the nunnery; a military school for surgeons' assistants and a school for midwives. The children's home is under the management of the Transbaikál Relief Society.

Charitable and scientific societies:

The Chitá Brotherhood of the Apostolic Saints Cyril and Methodius and St. Innocent the Miracle-worker of Irkútsk. The Transbaikál branch of the Relief Society for the families of exile convicts, under the patronage of Her Majesty the Empress Mary Feódorovna. The Transbaikál Committee for the assistance of emigrants. The Chitá branch of the Imperial Russian Geographical Society of the Amúr region, with museum and library. The Doctors' Society in Chitá. The Transbaikál branch of the Imperial Society for the Preservation of Animals and for Legitimate Sport. Local committee of the Red Cross Society. An amateur society for singing, music, literature and dramatic art. A pupils' aid society.

There is an official daily paper „The Transbaikál district Gazette" published in Chitá. In 1897, a newspaper entitled: „Life in the Eastern Borderland" was published in Siberia without censorship, in Russian and Mongolian, edited and published by Mr. Badmáev.

The town contains the following military institutions: headquarters of the Transbaikál territory; department of the Transbaikál military commander; local commissariat administration, artillery stores; artillery park; military medical department; military economic department of the Transbaikál Cossack troops; the reserve battalion of Chitá; 1 Transbaikál Cossack regiment of Chitá; 1 Transbaikál Cossack regiment of Nérchinsk; 2 Transbaikál battery; local brigade.

Medical establishments: military hospital of Chitá; military hospital for the Transbaikál Cossacks; branch lunatic asylum; and town hospital. A station for experimental medicine, for the study of the plague and inoculation of anti-plague serum was established in 1899.

The hotels are: „Tokio" and Bianchínsky with rooms at R. 2 a day. The rooms are very bad.

Chitá has a general club and that of the Clerks' Mutual Aid Society. The town of Chitá, being the commercial centre of the greater portion of the

Transbaikál, is rapidly developing its trade and industry; the annual income of the town amounts to R. 100,000 and the transactions to R. 3,000,000. There are a branch of the State Bank and an agency of the Russo-Chinese Bank. The town line includes Kolesh's fur manufactory and tannery, with a turnover of R. 150,000, soap boileries and candle manufactories.

The first agricultural and industrial exhibition in Chitá took place in 1899, from the 15 August to the 10 September. Its chief objects were to give a complete idea of the agricultural condition of the Transbaikál and to acquaint the population with better methods of agriculture. The exhibition committee organised a sale of agricultural machinery which was tested in an experimental field. The exhibition contained an orchard, a nursery garden, an apiary etc. During the exhibition, teachers and gold-miners held meetings and conferences with a view to establish agricultural schools in this country. The most important firms are: Kolesh—drapery and haberdashery; a wholesale in tea; tannery, soap boilery etc.; office for the transport of goods. Schlesinger—manufactured and drapery goods, Ignátiev—manufactured articles, iron goods, wine-cellar. Kóstin — grocery goods, wine-cellar for Russian and foreign wines. Bútin—hardware. Badmáev and Co.—manufactured goods and wine-cellar. Goldóbin – wheat flour-mill, glass wares. Vtórov—manufactured articles. Stakhéev—manufactured articles. Pereválov—china and earthenware.

Near the town and the station, there is a medical and feeding station for the emigrants, which is the residence of an official entrusted with the regulation of the emigration movement. Leaving the station, the line crosses the river Chitá by an iron bridge having a total length of 75 sazhens with three spans of 25 sazhens each, and track on the bottom. It will be adapted for wheel traffic, in order to facilitate the communication between the station and the town. Further on, the line runs along the left bank of the Ingodá, and at 692 verst crosses the Nikítikha tributary of the Ingodá, by an iron bridge of 20 sazhens and, at the 708 verst, the Kruchína, also a tributary of the Ingodá, by an iron bridge of 25 sazhens.

23) **Kruchína.** IV class station (708 v.). Situated near the Cossack settlement of Kruchína, in the Chitá district, on the Ingodá and the great post-road to Moscow (houses 22, pop. 128,61 males, 67 females). The whole settlement was detroyed by an inundation in 1897.

24) **Makavéevo.** IV class station (729 v.) situated near the Cossack village of the same name in the Chitá district, on the Ingodá and the great Moscow post-road (houses 115, pop. 655; 305 males, 350 females). The stanítsa or village has a wooden church consecrated to the Saints Peter and Paul, a village board, a school and a post office with a savings-bank. The mineral (calcareous) springs of Makavéevo lie within 12 versts of the village. Near the station there are iron-ores, which remain yet unexploited.

From Makavéevo to Karymskaya, the line following the left bank of the Ingodá runs to the south-east, and further on turns north-east.

25) **Karymskaya.** V class station (767 v.) near the village of Karymskoe belonging to the native Buriat board of Urulchánsk, is situated on the river Ingodá and on the great Moscow post-road (houses 21, pop. 106; 51 males, 55 females). Deposits of iron have been found at the junction of the Ingodá with the Budungúi.

26) **Kaidalóvo.** (783 v.). Is situated near the Cossack village of the same name in the Chitá district, on the Ingodá and the great Moscow post-road (houses 149, pop. 849; 432 males, 418 females). The village possesses a

stone church of the Holy Trinity, and a wooden one at the cemetery. Local board, military medical station, post and telegraph office with savings-bank.

Within 4 versts of Kaidalóvo, a branch line which is still in construction leaves the Transbaikál line and runs to the frontier of China towards the Manchurian town of Khailár and joins the East-Chinese railway. At its very commencement, the branch line crosses the Ingodá by an iron bridge having a length of 80 sazhens with two spans of 40 sazhens each, and traverses a mountain ridge forming the watershed of the rivers Ingodá and Agá, which on the left falls into the Onón. At the 26 verst, the line passes over the summit at a low point of the ridge at the headwaters of the river Míra, belonging to the basin of the Ingodá and Míra, tributary of the Mogoitúi of the Onón basin. At the 75 verst, the line crosses the river Aga by an iron bridge of 30 sazhens and further on, at the 85 verst, the river Khilá by an iron bridge 15 sazhens long; at the 127 verst close to a tin mine, the line passes across the Onón spanned by an iron bridge of 180 sazhens consisting of two spans of 50 sazhens and two of 40 sazhens each and proceeds along the river Turgá, joining the Onón from the east. Further on, the branch line crosses the Turgá at the 161 verst by an iron bridge 25 sazhens long, and following the Tsungurúk depression passes over the Adún Chelón mountain ridge. Leaving the latter, the line at the 217 verst near the military post of Chindán crosses the river Borziá by an iron bridge of 50 sazhens and reaches the stations of Sibír and Nagadán at the frontier of the Chinese Empire.

The country traversed by the branch line has the character of a steppe, with the exception of the passages over the watershed of the Ingodá and Agá and though the Nérchinsk mountains. The population of this locality partly consists of wandering Buriáts, and partly of Cossacks mainly engaged in cattle-breeding.

The length of the line within the boundary of the Transbaikál territory to the frontier of Manchuria from the station of Kaidalóvo to Sibír is estimated at 324$^{1}/_{3}$ versts. The specifications for the projected line are those used on level sections, excepting a distance of 29 versts of mountain section with grades of .015. The estimated cost of this branch line is R. 28,323,158, inclusive of rails and rolling-stock.

27) **Urulgá,** IV class station (807 v.) is situated near the small village of Urulgínsk in the Chitá district (houses 44, pop. 239; 126 males, 113 females). The village contains a wooden church in honour of Our Lady of Kazán, a school and the office of the X division for the construction of the Transbaikál line.

In the neighbourhood, there is a spring of mineral (chalybeate) water and a stone quarry. Near the station, at the 807 verst, the line crosses the river Urulgá, tributary of the Ingodá, by a bridge with iron girders supported on stone piers; its total length is 60 sazhens, and it consists of spans of 20 sazhens each.

Further on, to the station of Zubarévo, the line follows a north-eastern direction guided by the course of the Ingodá. At the 821 verst, it traveress the river Tológa by an iron bridge with an opening of 40 sazhens and two spans of 20 sazhens each.

28) **Zubarévo.** IV class station (804 v.). Close to the station on the river Ingodá and on the great Moscow highway, is situated the small Cossack village of Zubarévo, in the district of Chitá (houses 20, pop. 138; 63 males,

75 females). Hence the Ingodá and the railway line turn east and retain this direction to the station of Onón.

29) **Onón.** IV class station (883 v.) is situated at the junction of the rivers Onón and Ingodá, forming the Shílka. Here the line turns again to the north-east, and running in this direction, follows to the end the banks of the Shílka.

30) **Shílka.** IV class station (907 v.). Proceeding along the bank of the Shílka, the line passes at the 908 verst over the river Kíya by a bridge having iron girders supported on stone piers and an opening of 25 sazhens. Before reaching the station of Nérchinsk, the line crosses the river Nércha at the 921 verst by an iron bridge of 150 sazhens with 5 spans of 30 sazhens each.

31) **Nérchinsk.** IV class station (950 v.), is situated near the town of Nérchinsk, which is a district town of the Transbaikál territory (51°58' N. lat., 86°14' E. long.). The town was founded in 1654, on the river Nércha, 5 versts from its junction with the Shílka (pop. 6,713; 3,886 males, 2,827 females). It is chiefly built of wood, having only a few stone buildings and churches; it contains 727 houses. There are 3 stone churches, one of them the cathedral of the Resurrection erected in 1825, and a Jewish synagogue. The number of schools is 8: ecclesiastical and district school, preparatory gymnasium for girls, 4 parish schools ond a church parish school. Town museum.

Department of the third division of the Transbaikál Cossack troops; the Transbaikál artillery division, containing two batteries; convoy command. town bank. Administration of the East-Transbaikál mining district, and office for the construction of the XI division of the Transbaikál railway. The annual revenue of the town amounts to R. 50,000. Nérchinsk carries on trade with the population of the district, and having a limited working capital cannot be considered as an important commercial centre. The fair, although officially established, does not exist in reality. The town contains the Hotel Daúria with rooms from 50 k. to R. 2 a day. Hackney coach tariff: a drive 20 k., per hour 40 k. Within the town line are only two tanneries and two candle and soap manufactories. On the 14 June, 1891, Nérchinsk was honoured by the visit of the present Emperor Nicholas II; His Majesty entered the town through a triumphal arch specially erected for this occasion.

The important firms are: Bútin, distillery and manufactured goods. Nizhegoródtsev, haberdashery. Riff, manufactured articles. Búivid, wine of home manufacture. Golumb, tannery. From Nérchinsk, the line follows the left bank of the Shílka along steep and rocky slopes intersected by deep ravines.

32) **Biánkina.** IV class station (974 v.). The small Cossack village of Biánkina is close to the station, belongs to the Nérchinsk district and is situated on the Shílka (houses 66, pop. 352; 183 males, 169 females), Between the stations of Biánkina and Bayán, the line proceeding along the rocky slope of the Shílka, at the 884 verst, crosses the river Kuengá by an iron bridge with an opening of 70 sazhens having two spans of 35 sazhens each.

33) **Bayán.** IV class station (1002 v.). Near by is situated the Kokertói Portland cement manufactory of the Amúr Cement Company established in 1895, on the left bank of the Shílka, four versts from the small village of Kokertói, in the Nérchinsk district. The machinery and tools are made in Germany at the works of Nagel and Kampe in Hamburg. The production of cement is effected by the so-called dry system, the cement being burnt in Dietsch's patent furnaces heated with charcoal. The annual output is 40,000

barrels, containing each 10 puds of pure cement. The materials employed are limestone found within 12 versts of the manufactory, clay within 25 versts, and gypsum conveyed from the environs of Irkútsk. This is the first manufactory in the Amúr region, its establishment being entirely due to the gracious attention and approval evinced for this enterprise by the Imperial President of the Siberian Railroad Committee at the sitting of the 12 April, 1895.

On its course between the stations Bayán and Srétensk, the line crosses the river Manatán by an iron buidge with an opening of 15 sazhens.

34) **Srétensk.** IV class station (1,035 v.). The Cossack settlement of Srétensk (1,450 feet above sea level) is situated near the station at the junction of the Kurengá with the Shílka.

According to the census of 1897, this village consisting of 349 houses contained 1,710 inhabitants (889 males, 821 females). The last statistical record shewed that the village grew considerably under the influence of the Great Siberian mainline; the number of houses is now doubled and the population increased to 8,000. Previously this village was a convict prison, which in 1783 was transformed into a district town of the Irkútsk vicegerency. In 1789, the town of Srétensk was superseded. At the present time,

View of Srétensk.

the Cossack village of Srétensk is included in the Nérchinsk district. It is the residence of a police officer, judge, lawyer, tax inspector and contains a village board. Military hospital. Military medical station. Headquarters of the Srétensk reserve battalion. Convoy command. Supply stores and commissariat depot. Crown saltern. Post and telegraph office with savings bank. Manager's assistant's office for the 1 section of the Amúr Steamship and Trade Company.

There are two churches: of the Purification erected in 1739, and of St. George built in 1890. A school with two classes with a division for artisans and a parish school. A branch of the Siberian Trade bank opened its operations in April 1899.

Near the landing-place of the Amúr Steamship and Trade Company is an hotel kept by Mikúlich.

For the assistance of the emigrants, a medical and feeding station was established in proximity to the Cossack village; it is also the residence of an official entrusted with the regulation of the emigration movement.

Representing now an important and populous centre of trade and industry, the population of Srétensk contains only 15 per cent of Cossacks, the remaining 85 per cent consist of different classes (40 per cent) and peasants

(45 per cent). The village is particularly enlivened during the season of navigation, when the total population increases to 10,000, by an addition of foreign workmen. Here are found representatives of almost all the firms of Kiákhta and Chitá. Tea traders: Kokóvin, Básov, Lúshnikov, Sobénnikov and Molchánov, the successors of Gúbkin have their own stores. Among the local firms the most important are: Lukín, Shustóv and Andovérov. The trading firm of Kunst and Albers, which is well known throughout the Amúr region, has a branch in Srétensk. Within recent time, representatives of the Irkútsk firms are also met with here. In consequence of the great number of trading offices and of the quantity of strangers of the trading class, a clerks, mutual aid soctety has been established here.

Srétensk presents now the most lively centre of the Transbaikál, not excepting even Chitá. The commercial transactions accomplished in 1897 amounted to R. 6,769,600. The Cossack administration somewhat hinders the commercial progress of Srétensk, and stands in the way of a regular organisation, considering itself as the owner of the estates and lands adjoining the settled centre. The establishment of a public municipal administration will be the only means to secure the development of Srétensk.

Manufactories and works are represented in Srétensk by the steam flour-mill of Lukín, opened in 1895; the central body is of wood and has three storeys. The steam engine is of 120 H. P. It is lighted by electricity. The mill is provided with a drying apparatus on the Sivers system. About 400 puds of grain are ground every day. Fur manufactory of Serédkin. Sheep-skins are bought in the Transbaikál; the manufactory turns ont 12,000 sheepskins. Tanning materials are brought from Hamburg; flour and salt are obtained in the same locality. The soap-boilery of Weinerman, with an annual produce amounting to 5,000 puds; soap is sold at an average rate of R. 4 60 k. per pud in the Transbaikál and in the Amúr region.

On the 13 June, 1891, Srétensk was honoured by the visit of His Imperial Majesty, the present Emperor Nicholas II, then Heir Apparent to the throne, coming from the Far East on the steamer „Véstnik". The village was handsomely decorated for this occasion. All the Cossacks and their children from the neighbouring villages assembled there to meet their Imperial Commander or Atamán. At 7 o'clock in the evening of the same day, after having held a review of the assembled troops, the Imperial Guest resumed his journey on the same steamer, ascending the Shílka to Nérchinsk.

At a distance of 25 versts from Srétensk, the steamer stopped at the right bank of the river, and His Imperial Majesty proceeded to a neighbouring mountain, where he took part in the lighting of a bonfire. A beautiful view offered itself from the summit of the mountain with the Shílka winding its course below and gradually disappearing amidst the surrounding hills. His Imperial Majesty and his suite stayed long in contemplation of the beautifu. scenery and only at 12 o'clock in the night returned to the steamer.

Throughout the distance from Chitá to Srétensk (360 v.), the line runs along the steep and mostly rocky side of the river valleys of the Ingodá and Shílka. These valleys further on narrow to passes bounded by lofty and steep elevations. At this place, the construction of the line required a great amount of blasting work.

From Srétensk, the Shílka-Amúr waterway runs east, connecting the Transbaikál railway with the Ussúri line terminating at Vladivostók.

Amúr Territory.

Geographical position and extent of the territory.—Configuration of the surface. — General characteristics of the Amúr river. — Hydrographical data.—Duration of navigation aud importance of the lower Amúr.—Tributaries: the Zéya, Buréya, Sungarí.—Geological structure and mineral wealth (iron-ores, coal deposits, auriferous gravel and gold mining industry, silver-lead and copper ores, grey antimony ore, mineral springs.). Climate.—Perpetually frozen soil. - Flora.—Fauna.—Historical review of the Amúr country and its colonisation.—Population. (Amúr Cossack troops. Peasants. Population of the mines. Nomad natives. Settled natives). Land tenure and land exploitation.—Industries (Agriculture. Cattle-breeding. Post traffic. Carriage of goods by road. Fishing. Hunting. Forestry. Household industries).—Works and manufactories.—Trade.—Ways of communication.—Results of surveys for the Amúr railway.--Necessity of Railway communications. — Bibliography.

THE AMUR territory, composed of the lands stretching along the left bank of the Amúr between the junction of the Shílka with the Argún and the river Ussúri, is situated between 47° and 56° N. lat., 91° and 104° E. long. Lying within the temperate zone, it belongs to one of the most southern countries of Eastern Siberia. Its frontiers are: the river Amúr on the south and on the south-west, from the junction of the rivers Shílka and Argún to the river Ussúri; a conventional boundary line on the west, from the mouth of the Argún to the Yáblonovy ridge; the Stanovói or Yáblonovy ridge on the north, and a straight line on the east, running from the mouth of the Ussúri to the source of the Buréya, and further the watershed parting the rivers Zéya and Buréya, and the tributaries of the Amgúna, the rivers Tugára and Uda. It is bounded on the south by two Manchurian provinces: Khei-lun-tsian-shen and Tsin-lin-shen, on the west by the Transbaikál territory, on the north by the Yakútsk territory and on the east by the Littoral territory. Holding the last place among the Siberian governments and territories as to its extent, it covers a superficial area of 393.366,6 square versts, corresponding to the territory of Sweden without Norway.

As regards the configuration of its surface, the Amúr territory belongs to the category of mountainous countries.

The Stanovói or Yáblonovy ridge, which forms the watershed of the Amúr and Léna basin and divides the Yakútsk and Amúr territories, within the limits ot the Amúr region, rises to an altitude of 7,000 feet above sea-level, with some places and passes falling to 2,000 feet. The main range has no ridge, and presents a vast and flat elevation with immense blocks of grey granite irregularly scattered over it. The bare summits or goltsy are only at some places covered with lichens of various colours or with creeping cedars, whereas the lower gradients of the mountains are clothed with dense forests of fir trees. These mountains bear a gloomy character, their spurs, stretching into the Amúr territory between the tributaries of the Amúr, give the same lugubrious appearance to the banks of these rivers which, especially on their upper reaches, are hardly accessible.

Among the branches sent out by the mountains, the Tukaríngra is the most important as to its extent and dimensions; it is situated at the upper part of the watershed of the Zéya, in the northwestern portion of the territory. Further south, the low and wooded ridge Niúkzha is the most extensive, running in close proximity to the Amúr Basin.

The Great Khingán, widely stretching its spurs over northern Manchuria, crosses the Amúr in its upper course and, covering a small part of this territory, occupies the watersheds of the rivers Amazár and Oldói. In the northwestern corner of Manchuria, the low mountain ridge Ilkhurí Alín branches off from the Great Khingán and, running perpendicularly to its chief axis, forms a slight curve following the right bank of the Amúr from the river Albázikha to the ridges of the Little Khingán, mingling with the branches of the latter. All these chains of mountains, which at some points rise to a height of 5,000 to 6,000 feet above the sea-level, are characterised by a severe climate.

The Little Khingán or the Buréi ridge crosses the Amúr in its middle reaches and, following the meridian line, with its branches pushes the Amúr towards the south, compelling the river to describe a wide bend. The average height of these mountains does not exceed 2,500 feet above the level of the sea, but in their northern part, near the source of the Buréya, many of them rise vertically out of the swampy taigá and attain an elevation of 6,000 feet. The main ridge of this chain is mostly endowed with bare summits studded with fallen stones. As they approach the Amúr, these mountains become lower and gradually pass into hills rising to a height of only 1,000 feet above the level of the river; they are covered with a thick vegetation and cut by deep valleys.

The connecting link between the Little Khingán and the Stanovói mountains is the Dzhugdyr ridge, forming the watershed of the rivers Amúr and Udá, falling into the Okhotsk Sea.

The Buréi ridge sends out to the west the mountain-chain of Turán, constituting the watershed of the middle tributaries of the rivers Zéya and Buréya. Further south runs the Vandá chain, forming a passage for the bed of the Amúr between the villages of Radde and of Yekateríno-Nikólsk.

All the watersheds throughout the territory are occupied by elevated plateaus, which together present an area falling to the Pacific Ocean; at some places near river basins, these plateaus pass into plains, which are sometimes of wide extent. The most important pasture plains are those of the

Zéya and Buréya and of the Middle Amúr. The first occupies the whole of the left bank of the Zéya, from the point where the river issues from the pass, and stretches to the Amúr till the Little Khingán. The other comprises the left bank of the Amúr, from the Little Khingán to the mouth of the river Dondón, having a breadth of 50 to 100 versts. The Zéya and Buréya plain is particularly well adapted for colonisation and agriculture, covering an area of about 20,000 square versts. It contains most fertile lands. The territory is watered by a network of rivers and streams, forming one water-basin.

The Amúr, which is one of the largest rivers of Asiatic Russia, is called Khei-lun-tsian by the Chinese, Sakhalín-ulá by the Manchúrs, Khará-murén by the Mongols, Shilkár by the Tungús, Mangú or Mamú by the Gold Olchis, and Lia or Lia-erri by the Giliáks. The origin of the Russian name is not ascertained; it is most probable that it comes from the Gold word Mamu; others believe that it is derived from the Tungús word „amúr" meaning „good peace", by which the natives greeted the first Russian emigrants in this distant region of the Far East.

From its very beginning, viz. from the junction of the Shílka with the Argún, to the Cossack village of Albazín, the Amúr flows in an eastern direction, rolling its waters amidst rocky banks, intersected with rare valleys, covered mainly with firtrees. It receives on the left the rivers Amazár and Oldói, and on the right the Sapozhkí and Albázikha. Near the village of Albazín, the mountains fringing the Amúr leave its banks and form velleys which are suitable for colonisation. The river separates into several branches. Beyond Albazín, the Amúr issues from the mountain mass of the Great Khingán and flows towards the south-east, but the country retains its previous character, the river holding its course along the branches of the Niúkzha and other ridges. At some places the bed of the river widens, forming numerous islands, at others it is confined between high cliffs. Here the vegetation changes perceptibly and foliage trees predominate in the valleys, in which occur black birch and poplar. The Amúr retains the same character till the river Kumará, its important right tributary; as it approaches this point, the Amúr widens and more and more frequently divides its course into numerous branches.

Mail and passenger steamer „John Cockerill" of the Amúr Steam ship and Trade Company.

Near the village of Kumará, the mountain ridges from both sides again press closer to the river, hindering its expansion, but further on, towards the town of Blagovéshchensk, the mountains become lower and gradually retire into the interior of the country.

The town of Blagovéshchensk stands at the mouth of the Zéya, which is the most important left tributary of the Amúr and represents the extreme point of the mountainous country on the upper course of the Amúr. Here the vegetation is mainly composed of foliage trees: dwarf oak, hazel, black and white birch, Siberian apple-tree, hawthorn, linden and acacia.

Between the rivers Zéya and Buréya. which are other two important tributaries, a level steppe borders upon the Amúr for a distance of about 300 versts, stretching to the north. Beyond the village of Innokéntievskaya, below the mouth of the Buréya, the conntry gradually changes, assuming a more broken surface, mountains appear again which, at the village of Radde approach the river and run parallel to its bed for a distance of 100 versts, forming a steep and high ridge known under the name of the Buréi or Little Khingán.

The steamer „Ingoda" of the Amúr Steamship Company.

The flora, which further off from Blagovéshchensk assumes more and more varied forms, here becomes luxuriant. Issuing from the Buréi ridge, near the village of Yekateríno-Nikólsk, the Amúr once more widens, forming a great number of islands. Its shores are generally low and sloping, with a steppe vegetation growing on a swampy soil. Among the affluents falling into the Amúr within this district, the most remarkable are, on the right: the Ui, Sungarí and the Ussúri; on the left: the Khóra, the Great Bíra and the Tungúska. From the mouth of the Sungarí, falling into the Amúr 150 versts below the Little Khingán, under 47° 42′ N. lat. and 102° E. long, the Amúr flows N. E. A plain follows its course from the Sungarí to the Ussúri and stretches further for a distance of 150 versts. The yellowish and turbid waves of the Sungarí, upon falling into the Amúr, do not mingle with its waters, but form two distinct white and black currents. Further on the waters mix together, and assume a yellowish tint. Upon its junction with the Ussúri, the Amúr flows within the confines of the Littoral territory. From the mouth of the Ussúri to the Lake Kizí, the river runs northwards for a distance of 800 versts. The islands become larger and are covered with a scanty vegetation. The mountains first follow the right bank, which is intersected by the narrow valleys of its tributaries, among which the most important is the Dondón. At a distance of 150 versts below the mouth of the Ussúri, the mountains pass to the left side and at some places between the Sungarí and Gorín come up close to the river. Below the mouth of the Sungarí, the vegetation becomes more scanty, assuming gradually the character of the flora proper to the upper parts of the Amúr. From the mouth of the Corín commences a plain dotted with lakes which stretches along the left bank of the Amúr. The opposite side is covered with the spurs of the Sikhoté Alín. At the mouth of the Amgún, flowing in on the left under 53° N. lat., the left bank of the Amúr becomes also mountainous, the Amgún mountains come up close to the river. After having received this important tributary, the Amúr skirts the northern extremity of the Sikhoté Alín, which hinders its junction with the ocean, and pours its waters into the Tatar Strait, forming a wide liman called the Amúr liman. The breadth of the Amúr at its mouth between Capes Tebákh and Pongé is 14 versts. Here the banks of the river are fringed with wooded mountain ridges which at some places fall to the water's edge forming steep and rocky cliffs. The basin of the Amúr comprises about 37,000 square geographical miles, its approximate length is 4,500 versts, if the river Argún is taken as the source of the Amúr basin. From the junction of the Shílka with the Argún to the town of Nikoláevsk, the Amúr has a length of 2,600 versts. No general levelling has yet been made, and its level and velocity can only be determined from some occasional observations; on the

Passenger steamer „Amúr" of the Ministry of Ways of Communication.

average it may be supposed that between Ust Strélka and Blagovéshchensk the water level falls I foot per verst, whereas further on to Nikoláevsk it only falls one-quarter of a foot per verst. The depth of the water is very various, from 2 and 3 feet to several sazhens.

The Amúr is navigable throughout its entire course, although the existing bars, mainly consisting of large boulders, present a serious impediment. The number of bars, from the junction of the Shílka with the Argún to the mouth of the river is 121, the depth of the water covering them varying from 2¼ to 13½ feet. The water level is very inconstant. The river overflows its banks in July and August, when the water rises sometimes 7 sazhens above its ordinary level and causes great damage. The water freezes gradually. The navigation season between Srétensk and Nikoláevsk on the average comprises 140 days. The river is navigable in May, June, July and August between Nikoláevsk and Blagovéshchensk on vessels with a draught of 5 feet, above Blagovéshchensk to Srétensk with a draught of 3½ feet. In September, vessels drawing over 4 feet bound for Blagovéshchensk and 3 feet for Srétensk, run serious risks. The lower reaches of the Amúr, between the town of Sofíisk and its mouth, for a distance of about 400 versts, having a breadth of 2—3 versts and more, and a very deep channel of several scores of sazhens may be designated as the maritime part of the Amúr, suitable for the navigation of large sea-going vessels. This characteristic of the lower Amúr, with speculations concerning the establishment, of a sea-port at Sofíisk in the interior of the continent, is to be found in the work of Professor Tímonov, the eminent explorer of the water-ways of the Amúr country.

Among the numerous tributaries of the Amúr, watering the territory and representing the most important waterways, may be mentioned the Zéya and Buréya falling in on the left, and the Sungarí, on the right.

The Zéya is the most extensive left tributary of the Amúr; it rises in the southern slope of the Stanovói ridge and flows towards the Amúr from north to south along a picturesque and hilly valley, passing further on into a plateau.

At the present time. the basin of the Zéya has a special significance in the country, its lower valley and that of its tributaries representing the part of the Zéya and Buréya plain most fit for colonisation. The upper and middle tributaries abound in rich gold mines. The total length of the Zéya is not exactly ascertained, its upper reaches being hardly explored; it is approximately estimated at 1,000 versts. Its breadth varies from 100 sazhens to 3½ versts at the mouth of the Little Bélaya. The depth is from a few feet to 10 sazhens, the water level being very uncertain varies in a proportion of 5 to 6 sazhens. The water surface rises several times during the summer in a very short time, considerably damaging the banks; the river periodically overflows the pasture valleys which then present an immense body of water. The navigation on the Zéya, like on the Amúr, lasts for more than 5 months, from the 1 May to the 1—10 October. The Zéya affords a very important and busy waterway, being practicable for large vessels for a distance of 657 versts from the mouth, and generally navigable for a distance of 1000 versts; the bars offer the sole impediment to navigation. Chief among its tributaries is the Selímdzha with a total length of 700 versts. and navigable for 250 versts from its estuary.

The Buréya or Niumán Bíra rises in the Buréya or Little Khingán ridge and has two sources, which have the character of mountain streams. Uniting their course into one bed with a breadth of 50—60 sazhens, the river enters a wide valley. After its junction with the Nimán, falling from the right, the mountains again press the valley on both sides forming granite cliffs with

Tow-steamer Khabaróvka of the Ministry of Ways of Communication.

a height of 800 feet above the level of the river. Within 200 versts of its mouth, the high rocks vanish and the river flows along a level plain endowed with an abundant vegetation. The Buréya has a length of about 900 versts and a breadth varying from 40 to 350 sazhens, it is pretty deep, but its bed is rocky and full of bars, and characterised by a swift tide. The change of the surface depends mainly on the rainfall and is very rapid; sometimes the water rises 3 sazhens above its ordinary level in the space of a day, and as quickly falls again. For a distance of 200 versts, from the mouth to the Paikónsk stores, the river is navigable for steamers, thence to the Chekundín stores situated within 400 versts of the mouth, navigation is possible, although offering some difficulties on account of the rapid current The country, within range of the Buréya, is scantily settled, although its headwaters and those of the Níman are the centre of the richest gold mines, and are undoubtedly provided wich other mineral treasures.

The Sungarí, flowing beyond the confines of Russian territory and belongling to Manchuria is specially important in the Amúr region, affording a natural connexion with China. This river takes its rise in the Chan-bo-shan mountains near Korea and winds its course as a narrow mountain stream, but near the town of Girín, within 150 versts of its source, it widens to a breadth of 100 sazhens and attains a depth of 12 feet.

Near the town of Boduné, the Sungarí receives the Nonni, whence it takes the name of Gu-án-dun, and changes into a sluggishly flowing stream studded with islands, with a breadth of 2¼ versts and a depth of 3—4 feet. Upon receiving the tributaries Mudán-tsián, Khilán-khé, Taún-khé and others, the Sungarí deepens and, separating into several branches, falls on the right into the Amúr, 35 versts above the Cossack village of Mikhaíl-Simiónovsky forming a whole archipelago of islands. The course of the Sungarí extends to 2,000 versts. Its water is of a dirty brown colour and so turbid in its lower part as to be unfit for drinking without being previously strained.

The dredger „Amúr".

From the town of Girín, the river valley is thickly settled, containing a population of several millions. Its lower reaches, at about 200 versts from the mouth, remain almost deserted, the right bank alone affording shelter to rare settlements of Golds. In the XVII century, this river was known to the Cossacks under the name of Shungalá, and one of the pioneers of this epoch, the Cossack Stepánov, twice went up the river in search of provisions. Since the conclusion of the Aigún treaty, the Russians have possessed the right of free navigation on the Sungarí.

The geological structure of the Amúr basin and of the Amúr territory, as yet insufficiently explored, offers the same formations throughout the regions investigated, permitting a rough determination of its general character. The Stanovói ridge, bounding the northern part of the territory, as well as its branches, consists mainly of crystalline rocks. On the southern slope, there is a streak of limestone, extending from the source of the Zéya through the headwaters of the Oldói to the Shílka. Then comes a marked and broad strip of lamellated clay slates and conglomerates with considerable seams of coal. Judging by the rich collection of impressions of plants found by Schmidt in the clay slates, these strata belong to the jurassic formations and, in their organic remains, present a great likeness to the carboniferous strata of jurassic formation, occurring in other more completely explored countries. White sandstone and clay with seams of coal of inferior quality extend to the south. These are the geological systems characterising the middle Amúr besin. The frequent remains of foliage trees and the quantity of timber are evidence of the tertiary formation in this basin. The high cliffs of white clay and sandstone, occurring in this district, are known under the name of Tsagayán. Appearing on the Amúr above the civer Kumará, they are remarkable on account of the smoke emitted by their summits on a windless and clear day. Glenn has proved that it comes from a seam of self-burning brown coal embedded in the heart of the mountain. On the whole expanse, consisting of tertiary systems, occur also crystalline rocks with various transitions to sedimentary formations. The crystalline rocks include sometimes seams of coal transformed into graphite. Outcrops of volcanic rocks have been discovered near the Cossack village of Bíbikovo and in some other localities, mainly at the junction of the Amúr with the Ussúri. Within 20 versts of the junction with the Tungúska, Batsévich discovered the solitary mountain Alé, which proved to be an ancient volcano, consisting of dark basalt. The geological map of the Amúr territory and the great extent of the various formations require much scientific amplification and explanation, offering a wide scope for further scientific researches The mineral wealth of the Amúr basin is represented by an inexhaustible supply of various ores.

Iron-ores occur so plentifully that they may be said to form the subsoil of the Amúr basin. Great masses and layers of these ores are found amidst limestone, diorite and melaphire. The abundance of iron lying close to the surface, according to Bogoliúbsky, explains the strong magnetic action observed in some places of the Amúr region, as for example in the depression bounded by the Daurian plateau, the Stanovói ridge and the Buréya mountains. In spite of this almost incredible abundance of iron, this metal remains unexploited.

Coal-measures heve been found at many places. Numerous outcrops of black slate of jurassic formation have been discovered in the upper part of the Amúr, near the river Oldói and the village of Cherniáev. Lower down the Amúr, near the settlement of Anósov, brown coal or lignite has been found in cuttings of the Zagayán mountain, near the mouth of the Kumará. Between the settlements of Korsákov and Kazakévich, occur sandstone and clay slates with seams of brown coal; 30 versts above Blagovéshchensk, there are outcrops of foliated brown coal of tertiary formation; 9 versts above the station of Inokéntievskaya, deposits of the same mineral have been found along the right bank of the Amúr, which also occur further on; on the Zéya, coal has been discovered within range of its upper reaches; on the Buréya it was found in 1844, by the Academician Middendorf and was qualified as good; according to its composition, this coal is of jurassic formation. The Buréya coal has since been more fully tested and, from its quality and the physical conditions attending its exploitation, has been declared to be the best mineral fuel hitherto found in the upper and middle parts of the Amúr basin.

The gold mines of the Amúr basin, on account of their abundance and extent, render the gold-mining industry the chief economicial feature of the country. Among the gold-mining districts of the Russian Empire, the Amúr territory ranks third, yielding precedence to the Urál and the Yakútsk territory, as far as concerns the quantity of gold gotten. As regards the proportion of gold found in the mines of the Amúr, it is only inferior to that of the Yakútsk mines.

Geographically, the gold mines comprise the following systems:

1) System of the rivers Dzhalínda and Oldói.

These mines were discovered in 1866 by engineer Anósov for the part of the Upper-Amúr Company. Assiduously working the mines, the company obtained from them, during a space of twenty years, 2,500 puds of gold. In 1886 these mines, containing still a considerable supply of gold, were leased to employees of the company, who even now, by careful and economic digging, obtain about 60 puds of gold annually. Out of the 58 areas named, 15 are worked by small miners and the owners of the Upper Amúr Company. Situated on the upper waters of the Dzhalínda and Oldói, the mines are within 100 versts of the Amúr. Communication with them is maintained by wheel traffic, from the Dzhalínda landing-place on the Amúr to the central Vasíliev mine. All the other mines are situated at a distance of 5—7 versts from each other. The workmen, employed in the mines by contract, are mainly Siberian peasants, and voluntary gold-diggers who, having received the permission to rework the auriferous area, are under the obligation to deliver the gold obtained to the owner of the mine at a previously fixed and generally very low rate; they go by the name of „starátel“ and are mainly Chinese. The maintenance of a workman varies from R. 600 to R. 1000 a year.

2) System of the Zéya.

a) Mines of the Upper Amúr Company.

This company, which is the oldest throughout the Amúr region, was founded by Bernardáki in 1863. It owns a total of about 50 auriferous sections, in which only 10 mines are worked every year. The exploitation is carried on in an economical fashion by means of open cuttings, the gold gravel is conveyed to the washing apparatus on trucks set on rails or with the help of cranes; the gold gravel is washed mainly in a one-barrel machine, worked by steam. The annual amount of gold received by the company varies from 120 to 150 puds. The contingent of miners mostly consists of peasants; the annual pay due to a workman employed by contract amounts to R. 1,260. The population attached to the mines amounts to 2,500. The headquarters of the company is situated on the Zéya, 657 versts above Blagovéshchensk. It is connected with the Amúr water system by a navigable route by means of steamers belonging to the company; the numerous mines are reached by carriage roads. All the mines worked are connected with each other and with the landing-place on the Zéya by telephone, itself connected with the whole network of telegraphs of the Empire. The mines are provided with several churches and hospitals and with two schools for the elementary education of the employees' and workmen's children.

b) The mines of the Zéya, Upper Zéya, Dzhalón, United, of the Ilikan and Magot Company, were formed in 1894 into a joint stock company under the name of the United Gold Mining Company. All these mines are united under a common administration. The Leónov mine is the richest; it belongs to the Dzhalónsk Co. and, worked continuously from 1883 to 1885, has yielded 738 puds of gold. The contingent of workmen is mainly composed of peasants, among them the Chinese forming 15 per cent. The annual pay due to a workman varies from R. 1,480 to R. 1,650. The company possesses two steamers in the Amúr basin for the conveyance of supplies and men. Among the 250 gold sections allotted for exploitation, only about 30 or 40 are under work. The system of exploitation and the conditions of the miners are the same as in the mines of the Upper Amúr Company.

3) System of the Buréya.

The mines belonging to this system are situated along the Níman, the right tributary of the Buréya, within 700 versts of Blagovéshchensk. These mines were discovered in 1874 and the gerater part of them belong to the Níman Gold Mining Company and to the brothers Bútin. Conveyance from the mines to the town of Blagovéshchensk offers great difficulties; in summer it is effected partly by steamers on the Amúr and Buréya, partly by boats tugged up the Buréya by men or horses, and also on horseback in the rocky and mountainous districts. Among the 65 auriferous sections, not more than 8 or 10 are worked at a time. The work is done by means of open cuttings and shafts The gold gravel is conveyed to the machine by trucks on rails drawn by a steam engine, the washing apparatus is also worked by steam. The quantity of gravel washed annually in the mines amounts to 15,000,000—19,000,000 puds, the output of gold is 70 puds with an average proportion of 1½ to 4½ zolotníks to a pud of gravel.

The workmen hired by contract for a year are mainly peasants; the Tungús (60 per cent), Chinese and Koreans (30 per cent) predominate among the free gold-diggers. The Chinese are also employed for domestic work, fulfilling the office of servant and cook in the houses of mine employees. The maintenance of one workman varies from R. 1,500 to R. 1,800 per annum. A church is attached to the mines and there are several hospitals with rooms for outpatients and dispensaries; a meteorological station has been established at the Sofía mine, supplied with implements by the Chief Physical Observatory.

4) System of the Khingán.

This system is situated on the headwaters of the rivers Sutarí and Bidzhán, which are small tributaries of the Amúr. The exploitation of these mines was started in 1886 and, on account of their easy access and their situation within 60 versts of the Amúr, they attracted a great number of miners, but no important discoveries having been made, they soon fell off, and the mines were contracted to Russian and Chinese free golddiggers at the rate of R. 2.50 k. per zolotník.

With respect to exploitation, the auriferous strata in the Amúr mines are favourably conditioned, lying on an average about a sazhen deep. The auriferous seam attains a thickness of about half a sazhen, and the mines are generally worked by open cast, shafts being laid only in the Níman system. In spite of the distance which lies between the gold mines and water communication, the difficult transportation, the expensive maintenance of the workmen, together with many other unfavourable economic conditions, the production and the number of worked mines gradually increases in the Amúr territory. It has been noticed that till the year 1892, large gold-mining enterprises predominated over small gold industry and free gold-digging, which hardly existed before but, within the last ten years, have received a considerable development.

To the present time, all the gold-mining companies have carried on a rapacious exploitation of the gold gravel, working only the strata with a proportion of over 1½ zolotník to 100 puds of gravel, abandoning or entirely neglecting places where the gravel contained a proportion of even one zolotník. Upon the opening of traffic on the Great Siberian Railway, reducing the rate of transport for all gold-mining goods and appliances, the working of the gravel, hitherto considered insufficiently rich, will undoubtebly be resumed and prove profitable. Besides auriferous gravel, rock gold has been found in the systems of Dzálta and Dzhalón.

Silver and lead ores have been discovered on the slopes of the Stanovói ridge, near the headwaters of the Kupúri, tributary to the Zéya.

Copper-ore occurs on many, ridges running along the Amúr, the Zéya and Buréya, and also on the Khingán mountains.

Antimony has been recently discovered by the mining engineer Batsévich on the Bikuchán mountain, situated near the Sagíbovsk settlement, 332 versts beyond Blagovéshchensk. It occurs in solid masses or forms pointed crystals of lead-grey colour. From a practical standpoint, this discovery is very important, mainly because till lately no antimony fit for exploitation has ever benn found in the Russian Empire, whereas its import has been increasing every year.

Mineral springs. On the left bank of the Amúr, within 3 versts of the settlement of Ignáshina and 740 versts above Blagovéshchensk, is the Ignáshensk mineral spring containing alkaline and chalybeate water, characterised by a very low temperature (+0.5° C.). There is no accomodation for patients and the springs are rarely visited.

As regards other minerals, the Amúr territory still remains quite a terra incognita. The climate of the Amúr territory is continental, and in spite of its southern position is unfavourable. Professor Voéikov includes this country among those constituting the northern border of the vast monsoon region extending over Korea, Manchuria, the whole of China to Khuán-khé, and the eastern part of Indo-China. The winter throughout this territory is very long and cold, the summer, which lasts only for three months, being very hot. The spring begins after the 20 March, the summer in the beginning of May, the autumn in the first days of September and the winter in the beginning of October. The mean annual temperature fluctuates between —4.3° in Albazín, —0.7° in the town of Blagovéshchensk, +0.7° in Yekateríno-Nikólsk and +0.6° in Khabaróvsk, thus the average temperature throughout the territory is below zero. The difference between the mean temperatures of the coldest and hottest months is very great:

Albazín .... $\frac{-28.4° \text{ C.}}{+18.8° \text{ C.}} = 47.2°.$

Blagovéshchensk ...... $\frac{-25.5° \text{ C.}}{+21.4° \text{ C.}} = 45.90°.$

Yekateríno-Nikólsk ..... $\frac{-21.8° \text{ C.}}{+21.1° \text{ C.}} = 42.9°.$

Khabaróvsk .... $\frac{-22.4° \text{ C.}}{+21.1° \text{ C.}} = 43.5°.$

The irregular distribution of the rainfall, which depends on the direction of the monsoon, exerts a marked influence on the temperature. During the five months corresponding with the period of vegetation, from May to September, the rainfall amounts to 271.7 mm. in Albazín, and 493.3 mm. in Khabaróvsk; during the other seven months, the rainfall attains only from 62.3 mm. to 109.4 mm. This abundance of the rainfall in summer combined with snowless and cold winters is very unfavourable to vegetation, particularly to corn, producing an unnatural growth which diminishes its nutritiousness. The dew has very little effect on the vegetation, thanks to the abundance of the rainfall and the clouds during the warm season. The total quantity of dew falling in the region has never been ascertained. Clouds and rainfall occur more frequently in summer than in winter. The rainy and damp season commences at the end of June or in the middle of July, and reaches its maximum in August, lasting throughout this month and very often to the middle of September. This abundance of rains, produced by the winds blowing from the east, turns the soil into mud, rendering it for a space of several weeks and generally throughout the month of August unfit for cultivation. Already at the end of September, the temperature falls so low that the stagnant waters and small streams freeze. Near Albazín, the Amúr is covered by a thin cover of ice about the 3 September, and at Blagovéshchensk about the 8 th. The Amúr freezes fast in its upper reaches between the 15 and 25 October, and at Blagovéshchensk between the 22 October and the 5 November. The frost is so extreme and so continuous that the thickness of the ice covering the Amúr is from 1³/₄ to 2¹/₄ arshins; the lakes and the small rivers freeze to the bottom. The greatest cold experienced in the environs of Blagovéshchensk is—32° R. and at the mines of the Nimán Company—40° R. The very low mean annual temperature, the snowless winter and the swampy and uneven soil covered with a thick vegetation, not being sufficiently warmed through during the summer, account for the formation and the preservation of a perpetually frozen stratum. Their extent remains as yet unknown, it is certain that thick layers of pure ice occur at the Nimán mines and in some other northern districts.

The vegetation of the Amúr territory has been explored by many naturalists, among them may be mentioned such eminent men as Middendorf, Maksimóvich, Maak, Radde, Schmidt and Korzínski. In spite of the severe climate, which greatly affects the development of the vegetation, the flora of the Amúr territory and of the entire Amúr region is characterised by a great variety of forms and by the luxuriance of some particular species. Along the course of the Amúr, we see peculiar and new plants which, being unusual in the interior of continental Asia, testify to the proximity of the Ocean and form a transition to the vegetation of North America. In the northern parts of the territory, adjoining the Stanovói ridge, fir-trees predominate, represented among others by larch (Larix dahurica), spruce (Picea obovata), (Picea ajonensis), Siberian fir (Abies sibirica), pine (Pinus silvestris) and „cedar" trees growing on the tops of the mountains. Approaching the Amúr basin, the fir forests gradually lose their gloomy character, being enlivened by an admixture of foliage trees.

The vegetation of the Amúr basin may be divided into four natural regions: from the Ust-Strélochny military post to Albazín, from Albazín to the mouth of the Zéya, from the Zéya to the Buréya mountains and from these mountains to the Ussúri.

1) From the Ust-Strélochny military post to Albazín, the forests consist mostly of larch and common birch mingled with solitary pine, aspen and alder. Spruce and fir occur very rarely. Throughout this locality the trees are small, not exceeding a foot in thickness, the wood is not dense and has no undergrowth. Among the shrubs are: the alpine rose (Rosa cinnamomea and R. acicularis), the spiraea and the cornel (Cornus alba), Rhododendron dahuricum, growing upon cliffs and damp slopes. This region contains but few meadows which, with the exception of those occupying low islands, are covered with scanty grass. Their situation amidst cliffs and the abundance of bitter and aromatic plants recalls the neighbouring steppes of Daúria. In

low-lying places, the meadows assume a richer colour, being covered with thicker and higher grass, which however consists of a less variety of species.

2) Beyond Albazín, the country becomes more level, fir forests occur at greater intervals, being replaced by foliage trees which, at the border, receive an admixture of ash (Fraxinus mandshurica) and oak (Quercus mongolica) growing on dry hillocks. It is only beyond the Kumará that the vegetation becomes different; here the woods, clustering amidst mountains, give shelter to linden and to solitary elm and ash trees. The meadows characterising this locality retain the typical forms of the Daurian flora.

3) After the junction with the Zéya, the vegetation considerably changes. Steppe-like meadows, which at a few points are covered with forests where oak and black birch predominate, extend from the mouth of the Zéya to the Buréya ridge. Drier and steppe-like localities are charactericed by an abundance of leguminous and umbelliferous plants and by lilies and orchids of a great variety of colours. The level and damp places are covered with various grasses and meadow plants with peculiarly luxuriant leaves. Under this cover of thick grass, the aldine rose (Rosa cinnamomea) presenting a little twiggy bush, finds shelter and, together with vetches and other climbing plants, hinders the advance.

Beyond the mouth of the Buréya, recommences a stretch of forest composed of lofty oaks and black birches; at more elevated points, they receive an admixture of common birch and Salix caprea. The valleys contain aspen, birch, elm, alder, cork-tree (Phellodendron), poplar (Populus suaveolens, dogberry (Prunus padus) and dwarf maple (Acer ginnala). Nearer to the Little Khingán, the southern tree-species occur more and more frequently. Near the water, the vegetation becomes so thick as to be almost impenetrable, the bushes being enveloped by climbing plants such as Maximoviczia amurensis and wild vine, which frequently rises to a height of 15 feet and in autumn is adorned with clusters of dark blue berries. Among the trees and bushes the most characteristic in this locality are: the dwarf maple (Acer ginnala), about 10 feet high and the Panax sessiliflorum, remarkable on account of its leaves resembling five fingers, and also of its black fruit attached close to the stem. Retiring from the banks of the Amúr into the interior of the territory, the vegetation becomes still more luxuriant; here the Daúrian birch and the Mongolian oak, with their wide spreading branches, attain a height of 60 to 70 feet.

4) From the Little Khingán down the Amúr to the junction with the Ussúri, the steppe-like meadows are dotted with solitary and lofty trees. At some points, the hills on the right bank are embellished by fine foliage woods consisting of oak and black birch mingled with elm, linden, maple and cork-tree. In the halfdarkness prevailing under the trees, which sometimes stand a sazhen apart, the ground is covered by Sespedeza bicolor, full of red blossoms. Among these flowering bushes, stand out the blue flowers of the Vicia pseudorobus, and Metalepsis Stauntoni, and the white blossoms of the Beotia discolor and Sanguisorba tenuifolia.

According to an approximate estimate, forests occupy about two-thirds of the total area of the Amúr territory, but the greater portion of this immense surface is totally inaccessible to exploitation. As regards trade, special importance is now attached to the fir groves, stretching along the middle waters of the Zéya and westwards along the upper course of the Amúr to the station of Pokróvskaya, as well as to larch and „cedar“ occurring on the Little

Khingán. Among the foliage trees, only oak and black birch are available as timber.

Injurious insects are almost unknown in the Amúr territory; the forests are however considerably damaged by the strong winds prevailing during the summer monsoon, and by fires lit by Russians and natives.

The luxuriant herbaceous vegetation, abounding in motley-coloured flowers, is considered by the inhabitants themselves to be a bad fodder for domestic animals.

The fauna of the Amúr region is just as peculiar as its flora, being characterised by the mixture of northern animals with representatives from the south, and of the western with the eastern species, but till now it is very insufficiently explored. Best known are the warm-blooded vertebrates. There are 53 kinds of mammals in the Amúr territory, represented by 20 carnivora, 4 insectivora, 4 cheiroptera, 18 rodents (Glires), 1 pachyderm and 6 ruminants.

The following animals are important to industry; the bear (Ursus arctos, U. tibetanus), sable (Mustela zibellina), „kolónok" (Mustela sibirica), otter (Lutra vulgaris), lynx (Felis lynx), fox (Canis vulpes), squirrel (Sciurus vulgaris), the reindeer and stag (Cervus tarandus, C. elaphus), muskdeer (Moschus moschiferus), rock deer (Cervus capreolus), elk (Cervus alces), and in a lesser degree, the glutton (Gulo borealis), tiger (Felis tigris), panther (Felis irbis), wolf (Canis lupus) and wild boar (Sus scrofa).

The tiger is met with only in the south-eastern part of this region, from the Buréya. The natives are so much in awe of the tiger that they will not hunt him. The size of a big tiger is about 3½ arshins; they have a thicker and longer fell than the southern representatives.

The bird fauna is also very various although little explored. Up to the present time, 244 species have been ascertained, distributed as follows: Rapaces 31, Passeres 8, Scansores 10, Columbinae 4, Gallinacei 8, Grallatores 42, Natatores 34. The birds are particularly varied and abundant where the Amúr, making its last bend to the south, breaks through the chain of the Little Khingán and joins the immense basins of the Sungarí and Ussúri.

Special attention is due to the ichthyological fauna of the Amúr basin, on account of its peculiar character and the commercial importance it is sure to acquire by its extraordinary abundance. This basin numbers a total of 63 species, of which 31 are local. The characteristic feature of this fauna is the great number of carp (Cyprinidae) and salmonoid species (Salmonoidei). The great wealth of the Amúr basin is constituted by fish of passage, which appear during the spawning season. The „gorbúsha" (Salmo proteus) sometimes appears in such large shoals that about 3,000 of them are taken in one net. In Nikoláevsk about 193,000 puds of Kéta (Salmo lagocephalus) are salted to supply the local demand, the fish industry not having yet spread beyond the confines of this region; about 4,000,000 of the same species are dried, and 540,000 of them are prepared as food for dogs. Besides the ketá, about 600,000 gorbúshas, 10,000 kalúga (Huso orientalis) and sturgeon are preserved annually. The following species may be of industrial importance: lote (Lota vulgaris), silurus (Silurus asotus), tolpyga (Hipophthalmychthys Dybówski), cerambix (Macrones fulvi-draco), carp (Cyprinus carpio), crucian (Carassius vulgaris), bream (Parabramis bramula), roach (Pseudaspius leptocephalus), rud (Pseudorasbora parva), tench (Sarcochilichtys lacustris), gwiniad (Coregonus chadary), khairús (Thymallus Grubii), salmon grayling (Salmo coregonoides), taimén

(Salmo fluviatilis), khunchá (Salmo leucamaenis), sea trout (Salmo cellaris), pike (Esox Richentii) and others.

At the end of the XVIII century, pearls were still found in the upper rivers of the Amúr basin. Recently some have again been found in the river Selímdzha, falling into the Zéya.

Historical review, and colonisation of the Amúr region.

The territory of the Amúr was discovered by the Russians about the middle of the XVII century. In 1643, the Yakútsk voyevóda despatched thither the elder Vasíli Poyárkov with 130 Cossacks. After having crossed the Stanovói ridge, he went down the Zéya and its tributaries to the Amúr and, following its course to the mouth, returned across the sea and by the Léna to Yakútsk.

This expedition left no traces of its visit on the Amúr. The honour of the occupation of the Amúr in the XVII century is due to Yerofféi Khabaróv, who with his party reached the Amúr in 1649—50, and began the conquest of this ceuntry by destroying the small Daúrian towns, occurring on his way below Albazín. The vanquished natives applied for help to the Chinese of Manchuria, and since that time began the constant strugle for the possession of the Amúr. In 1689, the Nérchinsk treaty for a long time put a stop to the further colonisation of the Amúr region by the Russians; after its conclusion, all the lands occupied by the Russians had to be evacuated, and the Amúr during about two centuries was lost to Russia; the river Górbitsa, tributary of the Shílka and Argún, constituted the frontier of Russia and China. The discovery of the Amúr delta by the Russian transport Baikál under the command of Captain Nevelskói in 1849, and of its mouth by a sloop of the same transport under the command of Lieutenant Kazakévich induced the Russian Government to explore more fully the mouth of the Amúr, the Tatar Strait and the Island of Sakhalín. The Amúr expedition was organised in 1851 and, in August of the same year, Nevelskói hoisted the Russian military flag on the banks of the Amúr, and founded within 25 versts of its mouth the military post of Nikoláevsk. The order to navigate the Amúr was given by the Emperor in 1854 and carried out by Count Muraviów, Governor-General of Eastern Siberia, who started Russian navigation between Ust-Strélki and the mouth of the Amúr.

The Russian colonisation of the country dates from this time. Finally, the Aigún treaty concluded in 1857, admitted the Russian supremacy on the left bank of the Amúr. The misunderstandings caused by the Chinese, evoked the treaty of Pekin in 1857, by which the Chinese Government allotted to Russia the exclusive right to the Amúr river and the whole of the Ussúri country.

The first settlers of the Amúr territory were Cossacks. From 1856, the left bank of the Amúr, from the junction of the Shílka with the Argún to the Tungúska, comprising a distance of 1630 versts, was settled by Cossacks from the Transbaikál with a view to form a cordon, for guarding the frontier and for the defence of the country from hostile invasions. The Cossack settlements established at a certain distance from one another served to maintain communications along this line, constituting the only link uniting Nikoláevsk and Vladivostók with Russia. The Amúr Cossacks heroically achieved their task, submitting to the semi-compulsory settling of an immense area. During the first years passed in the new country, they endured severe trials, in an utterly unknown land, with rivers bordered by dense, uninterrupted forests and impenetrable taigá hindering all advance. Men and cattle perished from all kinds of diseases, and the mortality was extreme among the children. All this was aggravated by dreadful and unexpected overflowing of rivers, destroying the work but just commenced, and by clouds of mosquitoes which particularly worried the cattle. If the Amúr was annexed to Russia without bloodshed, it was however, at the cost of many victims. Their number was so great that, according to Kriúkov who studied the colonisation of the Amúr by the Cossacks, it was equivalent to a war. But the sacrifices were not evident and were neither described in history nor sung by poets.

The Amúr Cossacks with their sweat and blood opened the way for subsequent colonisation, they perished with resignation under the pressure of all kinds of misfortunes and bravely bore the consequences of the first mistakes and reverses; this was the great service they rendered to Russia.

The Transbaikál Cossacks, who were compelled to emigrate by the Government, in a short time, from 1856 to 1860, established throughout the Amúr basin above 60 villages and settlements with a population of 11,850.

Voluntary peasant colonisation soon followed that of the Cossacks; the first party of emigrants numbering 240 arrived on the Amúr in 1869 from the Tauric and Samára governments and consisted of adherents of the Molokán and Jumper sects.

From the year 1861, when the regulations for settlement in the Amúr and Littoral territories were made known, an uninterrupted stream of voluntary emigrants took its course towards the Far East. The emigrants went there and are now going to the Amúr territory of their own accord, without any encouragement from the Government. They obtain the means necessary for the journey by realising their household goods and selling their land. The registration of the emigrants is only effected when they arrive at the localities allotted to them. Whole families are added to communes already organised, which still have free land at their disposal; they are then admitted without previous agreement, in the contrary case, the new-comers are received only upon having obtained the permission of the commune. Emigrants forming 15 or more families from the same locality, and wishing to establish a new settlement organise a commune which receives its name according to the desire of the settlers and is established in an appropriate locality. The maximum quantity of land allotted to the use of communes and separate families for a space of 20 years is 100 desiatins, free of taxes and with the right of redeeming the grants and buying new ones at the rate of R 3. After a period of 20 years, all the settlers are obliged to pay a land tax, and those who have not obtained full proprietorship are subjected to an additional rent. After a three years' use of the land, all the settlers are freed from duty in money and kind.

The population of the Amúr territory, gradually increased by colonisation and natural growth, according to the census of 1897 amounted to a total of 118,570 (66,595 males, 51,975 females), in the proportion 0.3 to the square verst. It is concentrated mainly throughout the Amúr basin and partly on the lower reaches of the rivers Zéya, Buréya, Tom, Tíma and Bélaya, whereas the interior of the territory still remains unoccupied.

The whole of the population may be divided into the following groups: Cossacks, 23,000, peasants, 35,000, town inhabitants (Blagovéshchensk) 31,515; workmen employed in the mines, from 7,000 to 9,000; nomad natives, 6,000, Manchu-Chinese, 14,000, Koreans, 1,000.

The Amúr Cossack troops are under the command of the Nakaznói Atamán, with rights equal to those of the commander of a division, and are composed of a Cossack regiment which, in time of peace, consists of three sótnias, and in war, of 6 sótnias, and of a Cossask division of 300 men. The territory occupied by the Cossack troops forms a district divided into 3 sections; the police and administration are under control of the commander of the regiment, endowed with the title of chief ot the Amúr Cossack troops district, and of three section managers, who are selected from among the active officers of the same regiment. The whole of the Cossack male population, between the ages of 17 and 56, is liable to military service.

The chief occupations of the Cossack population, forming the sources of its material prosperity, are agriculture, fishing, trapping, management of post stations and forestry. The whole of the Cossack population belong to the Orthodox faith with the exception of 5 Catholics, 6 Jews and about 18 adherents of the Old Belief. Reading and writing are gradually spreading among the Cossacks with the help of schools opened in the villages.

The peasant population is concentrated in 6 vólosts, subjected to the authority of the chief of the district and to three police officers.

The contingent of the peasant population of the Amúr territory is characterised by a great number of dissenters (over 7,000) represented by Molokáns, Bezpopóvtsy, only admitting priests conse crated by Austrian Archbishops, and the Seméisky sects. Within recent times, the beneficent influence of the Emperor Alexander III fund and the donations of Father John Sérgeev have reached the distant Amúr country, whose population particularly stands in need of spiritual support. The first church built at the cost of the fund, in honour of the Orthodox Saint Princess Olga was consecrated on the 20 September, 1898, in the village of Great Sazónka, situated on the Zéya, within 160 versts of Blagovéshchensk, having been erected during the years 1883—1890 by the exertions of emigrants from the government of Poltáva and from the lands of the Don Cossacks.

The population of the mines is distributed in three mining-districts: the Upper Amúr, Buréya, Khingán, of which two are under the authority of a police officer attached to the mines, whereas the last is subject to the director of the 3-d division of the Amúr Cossack troops district. The nomad population consists of Tungús, Orochén, Manégr, Birár and Gold tribes.

The Tungús are exclusively engaged in hunting, and roam at large in the desert taigá; as regards ethnographical conditions, they do not differ at all from their East Siberian brethren. They all belong to the Orthodox faith and, although fairly ignorant of religious rites, the spirit of the Christian faith being in accordance with their natural disposition soon became familiar to them; such at any rate is the statement of those who have studied the character of this nation.

The Orochéns form a branch of the wandering Tungús, dwelling on the upper waters of the Amúr; they received their name from the Tungús „oro" which means „deer", and differ from their brethern mainly by their slim build. They have a tawny complexion, a flat face with prominent cheek bones, a protruding and wedgeshaped chin, and black, thick, coarse hair; their eyes are small and raised at the outer corners, their lips thick. The men generally have no beard or a very thin one. They have comparatively large heads and long arms. The smallness of their extremities is particularly striking. Their main occupation is trapping and breeding reindeer; they profess the Orthodox faith but often, when roaming in the taigá, perform their own shamanistic rites.

The Manégrs (Manchur „avanki", Chinese Geography „E-Lun-Chun") calling themselves Maniakhyr, belong to the Tungús stock, and inhabit the right bank of the Zéya, along the Amúr from the settlement of Permykino to the river Kumará, wandering sometimes along the right bank of the Amúr to the town of Blagovéshchensk. Their language is similar to that of the Orochéns, including many Manchúr words. In their outward appearance, they present two different types: the one characterised by a broad purely Mongolian face, with a small nose and prominent cheek bones; the other by an oval face and fine features, well proportioned cheek bones, a long straight and slightly hooked nose. They are generally of a hardy complexion and a tall stature. The men usually shave their heads, with the exception of a long pig-tail; the women wear two tresses. They are all nomads, dwelling in summer on river banks, and retiring for the winter to the forests and mountains. Their dwellings are represented by hive-shaped yúrtas, made of stakes covered with birch-bark and elk skins. The Manégrs are all Shamanists.

The Birárs, belonging to the Tungús race, wander along the Buréya and the Amúr near the village of Radde. With respect to shape of figure and face, to customs and dress, they possess some likeness to the Manchurians, but their language has more resemblance to that of the Manégrs, containing many Manchurian and Chinese words. Some of them occupy themselves with agriculture, using their hive-shaped reed yúrtas as permanent dwellings, forming a settlement surrounded with orchards. They are Shamanists.

The Golds are a branch of the Tungús stock. They are now split into three tribes: the Kiléns, dwelling on the Sungarí and the Amúr, above Khabaróvsk, the Khodz, found on the Amúr, below Khabaróvsk, and the Mangús living on the Ussúri. There is but a slight difference between these three tribes as regards customs and dress, but a very marked one in language. With respect to their mode of life, the Golds may be reckoned among the settled population; they generally live in buildings made of beaten clay, recalling in miniature a Chinese hut. They are below the average stature, and have a broad and flat face with a snub nose, thick lips, eyes shaped after the Mongolian fashion and prominent cheek-bones; the hair of the head is coarse and black, on the face sometimes brown, but very thin. They are all bony and muscular. Wrist and ankles are small. The men wear a pig-tail, the women two plaits and the girls often let their hair hang about the shoulders. Both men and women wear silver and bone rings on the fingers, and silver and iron bracelets. Besides this, the women adorn themselves with earrings with pendants. Some of them, as a mark of particular elegance, introduce one or several small rings into the partition of the nose. The people of this tribe are characterised by great honesty, frankness and good will. Their religion is Shamanism. Their costume is very various and of all colours; they may at different times be seen wearing a Russian overcoat, a fish-skin suit or the Chinese dress.

The total number of natives belonging to the Tungús stock at present amounts to from 5,000 to 6,000.

Settled natives. The Chinese and the Daúrs, now quite assimilated to them, form the autochthonous population of the territory. According to the Aigún treaty, the population on the left bank of the Amúr consisting of Chinese subjects was to remain in its former dwelling-place, which had been annexed to the Russian territory, retaining the right to the use of the land which prior to the conclusion of the treaty belonged to them.

The Manchú-Daúrian and Chinese population occupies an area which, along the Amúr, stretches east of Blagovéshchensk for a distance of 66 versts and, settled on scattered plots of land, extends for 20 versts into the interior of the country. Leading a settled life devoted to agriculture, the entire population numbering 14,000 lives in 65 villages composed of Chinese huts. According to an ancient custom, the settlements and even each separate dwelling are surrounded with groves of poplar, elm and willow, which give them a pleasant appearance.

The Koreans, whose number is about 1,000, live in the settlement of Blagoslovénnoe, situated at the junction of the Samára with the Amúr. Having retained the language, the customs, the modes of cultivation and all the peculiarities of their former life in their native land, this population assumed the Orthodox faith upon having settled on the Amúr within the confines of Russian territory in 1872.

Land tenure and exploitation. The law of the 25 March, 1861, which authorised private land tenure in the Amúr region, on lots of Crown lands remaining free, was somewhat restricted by the regulations of 1892 and 1895 and although in force for 30 years, never found an extensive application. Private land tenure in this distant country is quite exceptional. The total area of private lands comprised only 40,868 desiatins in 1895, when the allotment of Crown lands to private individuals was forbidden within a range 100 versts wide on either side of the Ussúri railway and along the projected Amúr line.

The conditions of the land tenure of the Cossack population, consisting of 22,000 distributed in 67 villages and settlements, occupying immense areas along the Amúr, are still unknown on account of the peculiar conditions of the Amúr country.

In 1869, it was decided to grant land to all the Amúr Cossacks, to be used in common in the proportion of 30 desiatins to every man. The boundaries were not yet entirely fixed, when in 1877 the greater portion of the fields under cultivation stretching along the Amúr were overflowed and covered with sand and pebbles and the lands which had already been allotted to the Cossacks were declared unfit for cultivation. The project of Baron Fredricks, former Governor-General of Eastern Siberia, granting to the use of each village, irrespective of the number of houses, all the lands stretching for a distance of 8 versts into the interior of the country from the Amúr, comprising about 12,800 desiatins, did not meet the requirements of the population on account of local physical conditions. This system applied to whole villages was unjust to those containing a great number of houses and did not satisfy the Cossacks who still claimed additional grants. The administration of the Cossack troops aimed at acquiring a territorial right over the lands, as given to other Cossack troops in European Russia and Siberia; thus, the Cossack troops fund made the acquisition of numerous lots of land which should in the future serve as a source of revenue.

Baron Korff, the Governor-General of the Amúr region, assigned to the troops a territory extending 25 versts into the interior of the land, from the Amúr throughout the course of this river from Pokróvskoe to Khabaróvsk, constituting about 50,000 square versts or approximately 5,000,000 desiatins. This regulation of Baron Korff, to the present time, is not sanctioned by law and the Cossacks of the Amúr region still do not possess a territory of their own, the land being only allotted to them for temporary use.

The insufficient quantity of land fit for colonisation on the Amúr, and the establishment of settlements requiring a certain area available for cultivation is evidenced by the fact that the more completely explored regions betweeh Pokróvskoe and Blagovéshchensk, with a breadth of 10 to 25 and even 45 versts, does not contain, besides the lands already allotted to the peasants aud Cossacks, enough for a settlement, but only a few lots sufficient for the establishment of farms with a grant of 3 to 5 desiatins to every man. The whole of the remaining area is covered with wood or bush growing on swamps.

As regards the question of the subsequent colonisation of the Amur territory and the development of agriculture closely connected with the emigration movement, being without any precise information, we can only state the following approximate results. The authors of the well known work „Description of the Amúr territory", P. P. Semiónov and Grum-Grzhimáilo, considering that only one-third of the territorial area is as regards the climate fit for agriculture, state that the government has at its disposal 12,000,000 desiatins which can be colonised; if, however, one takes into consideration that, in order to secure the future prosperity of the country, at least the half of the wooded area must be preserved by a forestry law, only 6,000,000 desiatins are left for colonisation. If the grants are made in the same proportions (36 desiatins to every man), the Amúr territory might still afford shelter to 300,000 settlers, but if the latter be added to the existing population with a grant of 18 desiatins, their number could be raised to 600,000.

The investigations made for agricultural purposes along the projected railway lines across the Amúr territory, in directions most in accordance with economic considerations, shewed only a total of a million desiatins suitable for colonisation. The above mentioned results are very uncertain, as only detailed surveys and agronomic investigations can afford more precise data.

The chief industry of the population and source of its welfare is agriculture. Generally, the cultivated lands belong to the commune: the roads destined for the passage of cattle are common property, the arable land is allotted in such proportions as can be cultivated by every man, the strips of meadows are divided every year between the owners; the lots occupied by the houses and household buildings pass strictly to the descendants. Of the vast area belonging to the communes, only 60,000 desiatins are under cultivation, on which above 500,000 puds of various grain are sown annually.

The whole of the Russian population has adopted a most wasteful system of husbandry, by which a certain lot of land is sown every year, without interruption and without any manure, until it becomes entirely exhausted. From 6 to 8 crops are raised from the fields, and then fresh land is sown. The exhausted land is abandoned for about 10 years, after which space of time it yields again several crops. The fields which have already been once cultivated are not willingly worked again; the peasants generally look out for fresh expanses, thus enlarging the cultivated area. This fact has increased the demand for agricultural implements and machinery, mainly mowing machines, which does not prove that husbandry has become subjected to a more rational organisation or progressed in any way. The owners of new implements and machines, represented mainly by Molokáns, Dukhobórtsy and other sectarians, neither improve nor change their mode of cultivation, which does not differ from that of those who are only supplied with primitive implements. All this new machinery only serves to extend the wasteful exploitation of the land. No winter corn is sown throughout the territory. The emigrants have often attempted to sow winter rye, but have not met with any success. The principal reason of it is to be found in the utterly snowless winters and the extreme cold. In the localities more protected by snow, winter rye cannot ripen and be raised on account of the heavy July rains.

The kinds of grain mainly sown are: spring wheat, spring rye (yáritsa), oats and buckwheat. The yield of other kinds forms about 10 per cent of the total, consisting of barley, hemp, flax, maize and millet.

The grain of the Amúr yáritsa is finer and lighter than that of winter rye, the husk is thicker. The emigrants affirm that the bread made of local yáritsa is far less nutritious than Russian rye-bread. There are two kinds of wheat: red wheat, imported from Russia, and white wheat, from Manchuria; the latter is better adapted to the conditions of the climate, but falls out more easily if not cut in time. The oats were imported from different places: from Central Russia, the Transbaikál, and Manchuria. The emigrants also pretend that the oats are not as nutritious as in Russia. The millet sown here is of two kinds: the fine and grey so-called „budá“ (Setaria italica) growing in spikes, and „yar-budá“ having larger seeds forming a brush, which is the real millet. This kind of grain is particularly abundant in the fields lying between the Zéya and Buréya. In spite of the immense quantity of land, there is no regular system in the succession of crops. The work in the fields lasts from the middle of April to the 20 of September. Sowing begins in April and continues to the middle of June. The first grain sown is yáritsa, followed by wheat, barley, oats, flax, millet (in the beginning of June) and last of all buckwheat. Injurious insects and mildew are of rare occurrence. Harvest begins in August and ends in September. On an average, the crops of spring corn are 4-7-fold.

The husbandry of Koreans and Manchurians is characterised by great intensiveness; the cultivated area is not extensive, but carefully tilled. The Koreans use special Chinese ploughs drawn by a pair of oxen. The corn is sown in rows, and the fields are ploughed several times during the summer. Besides cereals, they cultivate all sorts of vegetables.

The Manchurians have the same systems of husbandry as the Koreans; they cultivate the so-called buda and employ a considerable part of the cultivated area for sowing leguminous plants (Phaseolus, Joja etc.) Among the plants exclusively cultivated by the Manchurians should be mentioned the „sutsá“ (Sesamum orientale), whose seeds are employed for the production of vegetable oil, used in the preparation of food. The Chinese also occupy themselves with the cultivation of poppies for opium. With this object, they make a circular cut in the unripe head of the flower and gather the thick juice coming out of it. Among the vegetables of the Amúr territory, the first place is occupied by potatoes, followed by cabbage, cucumber, onions etc. Having no markets for the sale of fruit, the cultivation of orchards does not constitute a special feature of industry.

Horticulture is still at a very low stage of development. The gradual widening of the cultivated area and the fertility of the soil accounts for the sufficient quantity of grain supplying the Amúr territory, and for the possibility of exporting it. If at present the local commissariat sometimes purchases grain on the Sungarí and abroad, this is to be explained by the low price of the Manchurian corn, and partly by the conditions of the market and the lack of ways of communication in the territory. The Transbaikál grain competes with that of the Amúr only in the mining regions of the Upper Amúr, whence it can be transported at a lower rate from Srétensk, down the river, than from Blagovéshchensk.

Cattle-raising does not present a special feature of husbandry for want of good pasture lands.

The horses in the territory belong to two different stocks: the Transbaikál and Tomsk. In summer, they are kept in droves, and in winter, they are fed with hay or bran wetted in salt water. The chief enemy of cattle-raising is the Siberian plague which rages there almost every year. The cattle is derived from a mixture of the Transbaikál with the Manchurian stocks. The local cow is characterised by an udder covered with hair, with undeveloped nipples, which accounts for the extraordinarily small quantity of milk. The crossing with the Manchurian stock had a bad effect, caused by the fact that the Manchurians do not milk their cows. During five months, the cattle are left grazing and for seven they are fed with dry fodder. The working cattle was brought to this territory by Little Russians after the year 1875. The principal impediment in the way of cattle-breeding is the Manchurian plague which gives rise to disastrous epidemics. The cattle is also attacked by innumerable clouds of mosquitoes.

Camels appeared in the Amúr territory only recently; they belong mainly to the Molokáns, who purchase them in the Transbaikál.

Sheep-breeding is not extensively developed for want of suitable elevated pasture land; the sheep come from the Transbaikál stock.

The breeding of swine is very considerable throughout the territory; almost every peasant owns from one to three head. They are of a small kind with inferior meat.

According to statistical data, of late years the livestock throughout the territory amounted to 115,000 head: 49,200 horses, 45,000 cattle, 14,000 swine, 6,000 sheep, and 600 camels.

Among other industries, which have some significance in the economic life of the population, may be mentioned post-driving, in which are engaged the ten Amúr Cossack districts. Many post-stations are under the management of Cossacks, yielding a profit of R. 135,000 to 160,000 annually.

Carriage of goods by road. This industry is supported by the gold mining companies on the upper waters of the Amúr, whence goods are conveyed by horses, mainly in winter.

Fishing is very important for the native and specially for the Cossack population. The fish is mainly taken in autumn, when the „ketá" migrates from the sea towards the Nikoláevsk liman. On the Amúr, these fish reach a distance of about 200 versts above Blagovéshchensk, when they are tired out and assume another form and name: they get teeth like the pike and are hence known under the name of „zubátka".

The ketá is salted whole in tubs, while the back and belly also are prepared by being dried and smoked. The salt is obtained from the Transbaikál. The systems adopted for the storing of fish are mostly very primitive. In spite of its great abundance in the Amúr, containing mainly ketá (in taste recalling the salmon of the White Sea), there are no established markets for the sale of this rich natural product. The first attempts at the sale of ketá were made only in 1898 and 1899, at the markets of Irkútsk and Tomsk.

At some Cossack villages, a good pressed caviar obtained from sturgeon and white fish is offered for sale. The smoked Amúr gwiniad is not inferior to that of the Nevá.

The profit obtained from this industry is as yet very insignificant, not exceeding some ten thousand rubls.

Hunting is the chief occupation of the natives wandering in the Amúr territory, and is also the source of a certain proflt to the Cossack population. The season for hunting is restricted: for some animals it is forbidden from the 15 March to the 1 May, for sable — to the 15 October,

The animals hunted are: sable, squirrel, fox, elk, roedeer, roebuck and musk deer. For the natives, the most profitable industry is that of the sable, whereas the Russians obtain more profit by shooting roebuck, which pass in immense herds. In these localities, the flesh of the roebuck is stored for winter and the skin used for the, preparation of a superior shamoy leather. Fowling is only practised by the Russian population.

The furs are sold at Blagovéshchensk, Albazín and at fairs held by the natives. The total value of the furs amounts annually to from R. 120,000 to R. 150,000.

Forestry plays an important part in the economy of many localities in the territory. The approximate supply of timber, with the exception of the sections which in summer and winter remain inaccessible, according to the estimates made in connexion with the surveys for the Amúr railway, does not exceed 5,000,000 desiatins, viz. one-eighth of the total area of the forests in the territory. The chief rivers used for floating timber are the Tungúska, Khára, Buréya, Zéya, Selímdzha, Bírma, the Tom and all the important tributaries of the upper Amúr. The inhabitants of the villages which are situated on the banks of the large rivers furnish great quantities of wood for the steamers. Others supply Blagovéshchensk with building material. The profits obtained by the population from this industry exceed R. 300,000 annually. The want of a regular and more extensive exploitation of the forests with export abroad, namely to China and Japan which stand in need of timber, is explained by the absence of the spirit of enterprise.

Household industry is still at a very primitive stage of development; the local population pursuing more profitable occupations, prefers to supply itself with articles imported from European Russia and Western Siberia. Only at Blagovéshchensk, which is the chief centre of the territory, domestic industries such as soap-boiling, tanning, fur-dressing, rope and carriage manufacturing have a greater development.

Manufactures are but just beginning in the territory and are at present to be found only in Blagovéshchensk. Together with the gold-mining industry, which is ever on the increase, the annual production exceeds R. 10,000,000 of which 8,000,000 are obtained from the gold mines, Trade in the Amúr territory becomes more animated every year. The export is still confined to the sale of agricultural products to the Lıttoral territory, of furs to Europe and Russia and Manchuria, and keeps within moderate proportions, but the local trade progresses considerably, and the articles imported from European Russia and abroad find a ready sale. The value of the imported goods exceeds R. 7,000,000, including Russian goods for over R. 4,500,000 and foreign articles R. 2,500,000. The chief commercial centres of the territory are the town of Blagovéshchensk and the Cossack villages of Albazín, Cherniáevskaya, Yekateríno-Nikólsk and Mikháilo-Semiónovsk.

Ways of communication. The most important overland communication of the territory is afforded by the post road, running along the Amúr for a distance of 1,664 versts, from the station of Pokróvsk to the town of Khabaróvsk. It serves for carriage and pack-animal traffic. According to official data, the first mode of transportation is carried on for a distance of 899 and the second for 765 versts. From the station of Pokróvsk to the station of Bussé, the road can only be used by pack-animals and further east the wheel-traffic at some points must give place to them. The absence of a continuous carriage road, ferries and bridges does not make a great difference between the two modes of conveyance. In summer, the post-road crosses 117 rivers and streams, of which only the Zéya is provided with a convenient passage. Consequently, in spring and at the time of the ice-drift, all communication is practically impossible. During the winter, mails, passengers and goods are conveyed by the ice on the Amúr. All the other overland roads in the territory are no more than paths.

The want of roads for wheel-traffic and especially the position of the great highroad along the Amúr attracted the special attention of the Committee for the construction of the Siberian railway. In the spring of 1899, the Committee undertook the construction of a road leading from Srétensk to the town of Blagovéshchensk and from Khabaróvsk to the village of Mikháilo-Semiónovsk. For want of voluntary workmen, the exile convicts and other prisoners confined in the prisons of the Amúr region were admitted to work on the overland route.

The absence of convenient communications is compensated by the abundance of waterways in the Amúr territory. Besides the Amúr, which presents the chief artery of the region, there are the navigable rivers Zéya and Buréya, the most important tributaries of the Amúr.

Navigation on the Amúr has been only recently started. In 1844, by order of the Emperor, a tender was offered to a Russo-American company to equip a vessel at the cost of the Government in order to explore the mouth of the Amúr. On the 5 May, 1846, the vessel „Konstantín" under the command of Gavrílov entered the Amúr, being the first ship which ever navigated its waters. In 1857, five steamers belonging to the Government were plying on the Amúr. At the same time, private individuals and various Government institutions provided themselves with steamers. The first private steamers appeared on the Amúr in 1859; the Telegraph Department possessed five steamers in 1868, the Engineering Department owned three; thus, in 1870, the total number of steamers on the Amúr was 25.

According to the stipulation of the Committee of Ministers sanctioned in 1871, the maintenance of permanent steam navigation on the rivers of the Amúr basin was entrusted to the „Company for the Establishment of Regular Navigation on the Rivers of the Amúr Basin", under the engagement to maintain navigation by mail and passenger steamers at fixed dates, from Srétensk to Nikoláevsk and back, starting at an interval of 15 days; by mail steamers, without fixed times, from Khabaróvsk to Lake Khánka and back, starting every seventh day, and from Lake Khánka to Kámen Rybalóv and back, twice a week; and irregularly by steamers from Srétensk to Nikoláevsk, as required.

This company, subsidised by the Government, managed its business so badly that in 1891 further assistance was refused to it. In May of 1892, the Department of Trade and Manufactures concluded a 15 years' contract with

Sibiriakóv and Shevelióv, commencing from 1894, for the establishment of regular navigation on the rivers of the Amúr basin, engaging them to make regular passages for mails and passengers from Srétensk to Nikoláevsk and back at least once in ten days, and once a week by the Ussúri and Lake Khánka from Khabaróvsk to Kamén Rybalóv and back.

The contractors, by mutual agreement with Makéev, organised a company under the name of the Amúr Steamship and Trade Company.

At present, according to the list of the commercial and Government fleets plying on the rivers of the Amúr basin, they consist of the following craft:

Steamers.		Tonnage.		Freights tugged.		Barges.		Tonnage.	
wooden	steel and iron	wooden	steel and iron	wooden	steel and iron	wooden	steel and iron	wooden	steel and iron
35	59	310,900	73,700	950	119,500	36	87	455,800	1.553,900
94		384,600		1,204,500		123		2,009,700	

Of the whole commercial fleet, the Amúr Steamship and Trade Company owns 21 steel steamers and 45 barges of. The Amúr Navigation Company possesses 18 steel steamers and 55 barges of various construction.

All the other vessels of the Commercial fleet are distributed among the Government and 35 owners.

All the vessels navigating in the Amúr basin are of two kinds: mail (passenger) and tugs. The greater number of engines, the hulls of steamers and the iron barges are made abroad, mostly in Belgium at the works of Cockerill and Co., in England by Armstrong and Co., at Glasgow, by Alley and Maclelland.

There are no special steamers on the Amúr for the conveyance of passengers; freight and tug-steamers are used for this purpose. They are lacking in comfort and do not in any way meet the requirements of the public, as might be expected from a link in the universal transit route. The food served on the steamers is far from being good, the purchase of provisions on shore is very difficult, as most of the Cossack villages along the Amúr are far from prospering.

In spite of the inadequacy of the Amúr navigation, characterising all the river basins of Siberia, a considerable increase of the Amúr commercial fleet has been provoked by the local demand, clearly testifying to the commercial and economical importance of the country.

The development of traffic on the waterways in the Amúr territory will however not be sufficient to enliven the country, on account of its physical conditions. The construction of a railway connecting it with the outer world will alone increase its importance as one of the areas in Asiatic Russia best adapted for colonisation and plentifully provided with mineral wealth.

Among the three routes projected in the Amúr territory from the station of Pokróvsk to the town of Khabaróvsk, the one passing along the northern border lands is considered the more favourable, as traversing a country available for colonisation and running almost throughout its entire course at a distance from the Amúr basin. Its total length is estimated at 1304½ versts.

The Amúr railway, planned to skirt the country occupied by Russian colonisation, will remain for coming generations a valuable monument recalling a memorable event in the history of the Far East, namely the visit to this region of the Heir Apparent to the Russian throne, the present Emperor Nicholas II.

BIBLIOGRAPHY.

1) From Vladivostók to Urálsk. Guide to the Journey of His Imperial Highness the Tsesarévich. Publ. by the Central Statistical Committee of the Min. of the Int. St. Pbg. 1891. 2) The ourney of the Emperor Nicholas II to the East (in 1890—1891) by Pr. Ukhtomsky, vol. III St. Petersburg. 1897. 3) Statistics of the Russian Empire XXVII. The vólosts and inhabited localities in 1863. The Amúr Territory. Publ. by the Cent. Statist. Comm. of the Min. of the Int. St. Pbg. 1893. 4) The Siberian Trade and Industry Calendar by Románov. Tomsk. 1896—1899. 5) The Geographical and Statistical Dictionary of the Amúr and Littoral Territories, by Kirílov. Blagovéshchensk. 1894. 6) Description of gold and mining industries in the Amúr and Littoral territories. Record of the manager of the Irkútsk Mining Department. Mining Engineer Bogoliúbsky. St. Pbg. 1897. 7) Siberia and the Great Siberian Railway. Publ. by the Min. of Finance. Trade and Industry Department St. Pbg. 1896. 8) Description of the Amúr territory by Grum-Grzhimáilo, revised by Semiónov. St. Pbg. 1894. 9) Surveys for the Amúr railway of 1894 and 1896; Min. of Ways of Com. Blagovéshchensk. 1896. 10) Review of the most important waterways of the Amúr region by Tímonov. St. Pbg. 1897. 11) Works of the III congress in Khabaróvsk by Kriúkov. Khabaróvka. 1893.

The Shílka-Amúr waterway.

Names of settlements and stations.	Distance from Srétensk.	Description of the settlements, stations and route.
		By the Shílka.
Srétensk.		Cossack village in the Nérchinsk district of the Transbaikal Cossack troops.
Set. of Mangidáisk...	61	Cossack settlement of Lómovsk.
Village of Shílkino... Houses 191. Pop. 490 m. 467 f. 957	$88^1/_4$	In the Nérchinsk Works district, at the junction of the Chalbúga with the Shílka. Village board. Two wooden churches of the Transfiguration, built in 1827, and of St. Innocent in 1884. School with one class. Post and telegraph office. Post station. Medical station of the Nérchinsk Works district. A silver works, formerly existing here has been abolished on account of the scarcity of the silver ore and of the difficulty of transport, and also because gold-mining is the chief industry. Close by is the Yekaterína mine, situated on the left bank of the mountain-stream Matikán, falling into the Shílka, opened in 1775, plentifully supplied with iron-ore running in veins amidst clayey slate and containing white lead-ore.
Village of Ust-Kára .. Houses 124. Pop. 306 m. 300 f. 606	106	In the Shílka vólost, belonging to the Nérchinsk Works district, at the junction of the Káma with the Shílka. Two wooden churches of St. Nicholas the Miracle-worker of Mirlicia, built in 1877, and of St. Elias erected in 1893. Telegraph office. Post station. The former Kára penal prison was situated at a distance of a verst and a half. The following gold mines, belonging to the Cabinet of His Majesty, are situated within 10 versts down the Kára, on its right bank: 1) The Upper Kára mine discovered in 1838; 2) the Yekateríno-Nikoláevsk or Middle Kára mine, within $3^1/_2$ versts from the first, found in 1852; 3) the Lower Kára mine, 4 versts from the latter, discovered in 1839; 4) The Luzhánka, falling into the Shílka, 8 versts from the Lower Kára. Bar 3 versts below Ust-Kára. Lowest water level $2^1/_4$ feet.
Sett. of Górbitsa..... Houses 99. Pop, 245 m. 260 f. 505	$160^3/_4$	Cossack settlement of the village of Górbitsa on the left bank of the Shílka, near the mouth of the Little Górbitsa (1220 feet above sea level). The river Górbitsa formerly represented the frontier of China and Russia; the settlement established was the boundary post, which received the name of village upon the organisation of the Transbaikál troops. Wooden church of St. Procopius, built in 1886. School. Post station. Beyond Górbitsa, in the rocks, on the banks of the Shílka occur granite and syenite with large crystals of spar, syenitic porphyry and clusters of diabase. Marble of good quality is found on the Gazimúr ridge in the environs of the Górbitsa.

Names of settlements and stations.	Distance from Srétensk.	Description of the settlements, stations and route.
Stat. of Sobolínaya...	209 1/2	Post station. Bar near Berióżov with lowest water level of 2 3/4 feet.
Sett. of Ust-Serebriánsk	260 1/2	Cossack settlement from the Olochínsk village, belonging to the Nérchinsk Works district. Post station. Bar called „Anikínsk reach" with lowest water mark of 2 feet.
Stat. of Povorótnaya..	309	Post station. Slate and roof slate are found beyond the station.

By the Amúr.

Names of settlements and stations.	Distance from Srétensk.	Description of the settlements, stations and route.
Settl. of Pokróvsk ... Houses 69. Pop. 189 m. 187 f. 376	358 3/4	Cossack village founded in 1858. The first settlement established in the Amúr territory along the Amúr. It is situated 4 versts below the junction of the Shílka with the Argún. There is a wooden church in honour of the Intercession of the Holy Virgin. A chapel built in commemoration of the miraculous escape of the Imperial Family from the accident of the 17 October 1888. A school and post and telegraph office. Grain store, five shops; wholesale wine-cellar. Residence of the director of the I section of the 2 department of the waterways of the Amúr basin. Eastern longitude from the observatory of Púlkovo, 6 hours 4 m. 50 sec. On the way from Pokróvsk along the left bank of the Amúr, stands out the steep cliff of Byrkinsk deriving its name from the Tungús word „Berke", which means „bold"; the Amúr rushes past this cliff with an extraordinary velocity. Within 12 versts of Pokróvsk occurs the Mangaléisk Bar, very dangerous on account of the stones lying at the bottom of the river.
Vil. of Ignáshinskaya. Houses 38. Pop. 119 m. 105 f. 224	412 1/2	Cossack village founded in 1858 at the junction with the Ignáshina. Church in honour of the Holy Prophet Elias, school, village board, post and telegraph office, 4 shops, wine stores, amunition store, grain store. Within 8 versts of the village, there are alkaline-chalybeate springs. On the right bank of the Amúr, opposite the village, is situated the centre of the Chinese gold mining industry „Mokho", with a military camp of 500 soldiers. At a distance of 35 versts in the interior of Manchuria, on the Zheltúga, tributary of the Albázikha, are situated the Zheltúga gold mines discovered in 1883, which attracted in 1884 and 1885 a population of over 10,000. These mines were known under the name of the Zheltúga Republic. In 1886, the Manchurian troops dispersed the plunderers and burnt all the buildings.

Names of settlements and stations.	Distance from Srétensk.	Description of the settlements, stations and route.
Sett. of Dzhalinda ... (Reínovo). Houses 100. Pop, 266 m. 262 f. 528	537 1/2	Cossack settlement established in 1858, named in honour of engineer Reine who took part in the Amúr expedition. Church of the Archangel Michael, 3 shops, carrying on trade with the owners and workmen of the neighbouring mines. The annual business amounts to several hundred thousands of rubls. Grain store. Post and telegraph office. Here are the office and warehouses of the Upper-Amúr gold mining Company. Beyond Reínovo, the Amúr enters a wide valley, where the islands increase in number.
Vil. of Albazín ...... Houses 150 Pop. 407 m. 379 f. 786	552 3/4	Cossack village founded in 1858, opposite the Albázikha, important tributary of the Amúr. Two churches of the Holy Trinity and of St. Nicholas the Miracle-worker stand in the cemetery; school with two classes, post and telegraph office, grain store, shops. The village was built on the ruins of the old town of Albazín, founded in 1651 by the Cossack chief Khabaróv on the site of a town which formerly belonged to the Daurian prince Albazá, from whom the town derived its name. In 1685, Albazín was attacked by a Chinese army of 15,000 men. After a short siege, the Russians surrendered the town, having obtained the right to return to the Transbaikál. Albazín was destroyed by the Chinese. When their army retired, the Cossacks returned, In 1686, Albazín was again besieged being defended by 737 Cossacks under the command of Tolbúzin and, after his death, under that of Beiton. The siege lasted a whole year, till the Chinese army left the place. In 1689, by the Nérchinsk treaty, Albazín was evacuated by the Russians and again destroyed by the Chinese. Among the curiosities of Albazín, there is an old image of the Holy Virgin, kept now in the cathedral at Blagovéshchensk, and the grave of the hero of Albazín, Alexis Tolbúzin On the initiative of the Amúr Governor-General, by order of the Emperor issued in 1898, voluntary donations were collected throughout the Russian Empire for the erection of a monument in the village of Albazín to Alexis Tolbúzin, Lieutenant Colonel Beiton and other heroes, who 200 years ago defended the town of Albazín against the attack of the Chinese and Manchurians.
Sett. of Bekétovsk... Houses 27. Pop. 83 m. 78 f. 161	646 3/4	Cossack settlement established in 1859. It received its name in honour of the sótnik Peter Bekétov, founder of the Nérchinsk penal prison in 1654, The settlement contains a chapel, a post and telegraph office, grain stores. From here the course of the Amúr widens, islands occur more frequently, the river flows first eastwards and then southeast. The Bekétov Bar is within 6 versts of the settlement, being practicable when the water is 4 feet deep.

Names of settlements and stations.	Distance from Srétensk.	Description of the settlements stations and route.
Vil. of Cherniáevo ... Houses 54. Pop. 184 m. 160 f. 344	746	Cossack village founded in 1858. It received its name in honour of Colonel Cherniáev, first commander of the Cossack brigade. Church of St. Innocent of Irkútsk, village board, school, post station, grain stores. Residence of the manger of the 2 section for the 2 department of the waterways of the Amúr basin. From the station, the postroad leads to the mines situated on the Zéya. Telegraph. A Chinese picket is posted on the right bank. From Cherniáyevo, the Amúr flows to the S. E.

Station of Cherniáyevo.

Names of settlements and stations.	Distance from Srétensk.	Description of the settlements stations and route.
Stat. of Tsagayán....	843½	Post station. Here the bank rises like a wall from the water's edge to an altitude of 250 feet The smooth summit of this wall is covered with moss and, as recalling the closely shorn head of a Lamá the Manégrs call it Lamá-Khadár or Lamá cliff. The locality designated by the name of Tsagayán (Tsag-Yan or white mountains) is held in veneration by the Amúr tribes and the Chinese. It stretches from the Lamá-Khadár for a distance of 1½ versts and is characterised by steep slopes. The whole of the Tsagayán consists of yellow sandstone in horizontal strata with streaks of brown-coal, which is perpetually smouldering. Thus the Tsagayán mountains, being constantly lit up, offer a beautiful sight to the traveller passing along the Amúr in the night. Upon reaching the Tsagayán, the Amùr makes a wide bend, its course turning from east to south and further on west.
Vill. of Nóvo-Voskresénskoe........ Houses 48. Pop. 193 m. 157 f. 350	875¼	Peasant settlement created, in 1870, at the junction of the Innokán, by emigrants from the Astrakhan, Vorónezh, Tomsk and Irkútsk governments and from the Transbaikál territory. Chapel of Christ's Resurrection, school, grain stores, telegraph station. From the mouth of the Innokán, the Amúr turns south-west and, for a distance of 12 versts rolls its waves through a wide and open valley furrowing it with its branches. The breadth of the river here

Names of settlements and stations.	Distance from Srétensk.	Description of the settlements, stations and route.
		reaches $3^1/_2$ versts. Further on, the Amúr turns west and its left bank, consisting of red sandstone rises to a height of about 300 feet above the level of the water, forming a cape named Kazakévich (Ilikán by the natives). Seen from the south-west, the cape represents a human figure of immense size with a helmet on its head.
Sett. of Koltsóvsk.... Houses 12. Pop. 22 m. 18 f. 40	$894^3/_4$	Cossack settlement established in 1859. It received its name in honour of the Cossack ataman Iván Koltsó, a companion of Yermák's. Post station. Near this station, the right bank forms the so-called Korsákov Cape or the Oil Mountain with an altitude of 300 feet above the water-level. This mountain consists of blocks of amygdaloid melaphire projecting in regular semicircles towards the river and rent by deep crevasses. The naphtha flowing from this mountain accounts for the name of Oil Mountain given it by the Cossacks; by the natives it is known under that of Vangán.
Stat. of Alaxándrovka	$929^1/_2$	Post station. Within 3 versts of the village of Kumará, opposite the mouth of the Kumará, rises a fine vertical cliff with a flat summit. This cliff is known under the name of Cape Korsákov or Langoper by the natives, Dashikhada by the Manchus. By desire of Baron Korff, first Governor-General of the Amúr territory, an immense iron-covered cross was placed on the upper plateau of the cliff; the cross is painted white and has a brass plate attached to it on which are traced the words spoken by the Baron at the opening of the meeting of „competent men", which took place at Khabaróvsk with a view to ascertain the requirements of the country: „Power lies not in force, but in love". This cross surrounded by a rail fence of castiron is visible at a distance of 50 versts from the Ushakóv settlement.
Vil. of Stáro-Kumará Houses 30. Pop. 128 m. 152 f. 280	$974^1/_4$	Cossack village founded in 1858. Church of the Nativity of John the Baptist, school, post and telegraph office, village board, grain stores. After the inundation of 1872, part of the inhabitants settled on the Buréya and established, 9 versts lower, the settlement of Nóvo-Kumará.
Stat. of Samadón....	$991^1/_4$	Before reaching the settlement of Korsákov, the Amúr describes several sharp bends. This remarkable winding bears the name of the Uluso-Modónsk Bend. The curve is double and represents the figure 8. The Amúr, keeping in a bed from 250 to 400 sazhens wide skirts two peninsulas, of which the left belongs to the Russian dominions, and the right to the Chinese. The peninsulas have a circumference of 30 to 35 versts, and are connected with the continent by narrow strips of land one verst and a half,

Names of settlements and stations.	Distance from Srétensk.	Description of the settlements, stations and route.
		and a verst wide. On the isthmus of the Russian peninsula of a verst broad is situated the settlement of Korsakóv, and opposite to the other, belonging to the Chinese, stands the settlement of Bussé. Both peninsulas have an elevated surface, covered with various trees, which descending to the river in a steep line, falls abrnptly to the isthmus. The banks at the bend are rocky and consist of granite, syenite, porphyry and clayey slates, among which occur seams of coal and graphite. In former times a Chinese post and a temple in honour of Confucius stood on the bend of the river.
Sett. of Bussé ...... Houses 45. Pop. 192 m. 187 f. 379	$1035\frac{1}{4}$	Cossack settlement established in 1857. It received its name in honour of Major Bussé, member of the expedition who occupied the mouth of the Amúr in 1849 to 1853, later on Governor of the Amúr territory. Chapel of the Intercession of the Holy Virgin, school, grain stores, post and telegraph office. A Chinese picket is posted on the right bank Below the settlement of Bussé, the Amúr assumes a S. S. W. direction, keeping in one bed of 300 to 400 sazhens wide amidst rocky banks.

Town of Blagovéshchensk.

Names of settlements and stations.	Distance from Srétensk.	Description of the settlements, stations and route.
Town of *Blagovéshchensk*........ Houses 3500. Pop. 19665 m. 12941 f. 32606	$1160\frac{1}{2}$	Capital of the territory and the only town in the Amúr region; residence of the Governor-General, centre of the military, civil and judicial administration. The town lies under 50° 15'N. lat. and 97° 15'E. long. (from the observatory of Púlkovo near St. Petersburg), at the junction of the Amúr and the Zéya, and stands on the left abrupt but level bank, bounded by hills on the west and north west. The eastern longitude from Púlkovo in hours is 6 h. 28 m. 44.7 s. The town was founded in 1856, and existed as a military post under the name of Ust-Zéisk. In 1857, it was reduced to the rank of

Names of settlements and stations.	Distance from Srétensk.	Description of the settlements, stations and route.
		a village and in 1858 was transformed into a township, which became a centre of administration in the Amúr territory. On the 21 May, 1858, Count Muraviòv-Amúrsky upon his arrival at the Ust-Zéisk post, reported to the Emperor the conclusion of the Aigún treaty with the Chinese; on the same day, the Archbishop Innocent laid the first stone for the construction of a church in honour of the Annunciation to the Holy Virgin; at the same time, the Ust-Zéisk post received the name of the town of Blagovéshchensk in commemoration of the fact that the good news of the annexation of the Amúr territory to the Russian dominions first reached this point. During the church parade, which took place upon this occasion, Count Muraviόv issued the following prikáz (order of the day) to the Ust Zéisk troops: „Comrades! I congratulate you! Our efforts were not in vain, the Amúr has become the property of Russia. The holy orthodox church prays for you! Russia is grateful. Long live the Emperor Alexander II! May the newly acquired country prosper under his mighty protection! Hurrah!“. The new town, on account of its favourable position on two navigable rivers and the proximity to the settled portion of Manchuria, has gradually expanded. Its growth has been particularly noticeable from the year 1880, caused by the development of the gold mining industry and by the extraordinary stream of emigration to the Zéya ând Buréya plains. The town is regularly laid out and the streets are wide and straight. Four streets stretch along the Amúr divided into regular quarters; they are unpaved. The quay of tho Amúr is embellished by a pretty boulevard. The best gardens in the town are those of the cyclists, and of the public club, near the military governor's house. Many private houses have little gardens, especially in the new portion of the town nearest to the Zéya. Vegetation is scanty in the environs of the town, where occur only small groves of trees. The number of inhabitants according to the last census, is given at 32,606 (19,665 males, 12,941 females), the number of houses exceeds 3,500, they are mainly of wood with the exception of 50 to 60 stone buildings erected in recent times, among which the most important are seminary, poorhouse for the clergy, the houses belonging to Chúrin and Co., Kunst and Albers, the goldminer Lárin. Henrichsen, containing the Survey Departament for the Amúr railway. Amur Steamship Company. There are 8 churches and 4 house chapels. The first stone church of St. Nicholas the Miracle-worker was completed and inaugurated on the 15 May, 1883, on the day of the holy coronation of the Emperor Alexander III. Educational institutions: classical gymnasium, gymnasium for girls, ecclesiastical seminary opened in

Names of settlements and stations.	Distance from Srétensk.	Description of the settlements, stations and route.
		1871, clergy school and model school attached to the seminary, three town schools for boys, school for girls, artisans' school and four church parish schools for boys and girls. The establishment of two new institutions is contemplate din the near future: a seminary for teachers and a diocesan school for girls. The brotherhood of the Holy Virgin started its activity in 1887; besides religious and missionary purposes, it aims at the conversion of the local sectarians to Orthodoxy. The town has no charitable institutions and the medical and charitable society founded in 1866 is most valuable in its help to the poor population. It maintains a hospital for the poor, two dispensary rooms for the sick, a home for the aged, cripples and orphans, and also assists the poor with grants of money. The only good dispensary throughout the Amúr territory exists in Blagovéshchensk at the cost of this society. It operates according to a charter confirmed by the Ministry of the Interior and is under the direction of a patronage council. The annual revenue and expenditure of the Society amount respectively to R. 30,000 and R. 40,000. The Kamchátka diocesan Relief Society for the poor belonging to thec lergy is remarkable for its extensive activity; in 1889, it instituted a poorhouse and a home for widows and orphans of the clergy. The majority of persons belonging to the civil administration obtain medical assistance in the military hospital containing 100 beds. A doctors' society exists from the year 1899. A public library with about 10,000 volumes and a little museum are attached to the town board. Two unofficial newspapers are published in Blagovéshchensk: „The Amúr Region“ and „The Amúr Gazette“. Official organ: „The Kamchátka Diocesan Gazette“, twice a month. The first printing office in the Amúr region was opened in Blagovéshchensk in 1862 and was provided with two kind of type containing Russian and Manchurian letters, which were to be used for the publication of the „Friend of the Manchus“ in both languages. At the present time, there are 3 printing offices in Blagovéshchensk, two of them belong to private individuals, and the other to the chancery of the military governor. Manufactures are concentrated in Blagovéshchensk, but are not extensively developed for want of persons with a technical education and on account of the attraction exercised upon looal capital by the goldmining industry. The town line includes the following works: two machinery works and castiron foundries. (The cast iron aud copper foundries and the machinery shops of Mrs. Lvov founded in 1887, producing from 6,000 to 7,000 puds of various goods, have considerable business; the other works belong to Pérshin). Seven tanneries (among them the most impotant belong to Chúrin and C°., Lukín and Lonvín.

Names of settlements and stations.	Distance from Srétensk.	Description of the settlements, stations and route.
		Two soap boileries (Strugálin and Cherkáshin), Three beer-breweries. Three steam flour-mills (Tiutekóv, Alekséev are the most important); each grinds annually above 100,000 puds of various grain. Three saw-mills. Two rope-yards (owned by the Amúr Trade and Industry C°, and Chúrin). Trade is carried on by 20 important firms and in 150 shops with a turnover of R. 4,000,000 to R. 6,000,000 annually. Together with the trade of which Blagovéshchensk is the centre, trade with Manchuria is gradually developing. The following four banks operating in the town meet the requirements of the manufacturers: State Bank, Public Bank, Siberian Trade Bank and Russo-Chinese Bank. The town revenue and expenditure amount to R. 200,000 annually. The military staff and two sòtnias of the Amúr Cossack regiment, the 2-d and 4-th active battalions and the 2-d batteries of the East Siberian artillery brigade are located in the town, which also contains the Department for the Waterways of the Amúr basin, the office of the director of the II division and the residence of the manager of the 3-d section in the II division. Public club, housed in a stone building opened in the year 1889 and containing a hall adapted for theatricals, and rooms for the accomodation of travellers. Among the hotels, the best is the „Russia“ with rooms from 50 k. to R. 3 a day. The hackney coaches ply according to tariff: 50 k. an hour in the day time, and 75 k. from 10 in the evening. Upon the whole, life in Blagovéshchensk is expensive, the cost of all necessary articles being very high. For the assistance of emigrants and pioneers, a station with barracks and hospital has been organised in Blagovéshchensk; supplies are offered for sale under the control of the official entrusted with the regulation of the emigration movement, residing there. Among the historical monuments concerning important events which took place in the region, there is one situated $2^1/2$ versts above the town in a garden on the bank of the Amúr, in the form of a kind of small obelisk, erected in 1858 on the spot where the tent of Count Muraviòv-Amúrsky was pitched during the expedition of 1854, and later on during the negotiations with the Chinese preceding the conclusion of the Aigún treaty. The chief ornament of the town consists in a triumphal arch commemorating an important historical event, and erected in 1891 on the occasion of the visit of His Imperial Majesty, the present Emperor Nicholas II. This arch stands on the banks of the Amúr. His Imperial Majesty stayed two days in Blagovéshchensk and visited the Public Club, where the boy and girl pupils of the gymnasinms gave a concert. On the following day, His Majesty was present at the parade of the Blagovéshchensk garrison and at the races of the first division of the Amúr regiment, inspected the camp pitched on the banks

Names of settlements and stations.	Distance from Srétensk.	Description of the settlements, stations and route.
		of the Amúr, and honoured with his visit the officers' barracks of the Amúr cavalry regiment. Then His Majesty left Blagovéshchensk in order to proceed further up the Amúr in the steamer „Véstnik". The most important firms are: Kunst and Albers. Wholesale and retail trade of foreign and Russian goods, Chúrin and C°., silver and gold articles, trinkets, grocery and iron wares. Cellar for Russian and foreign wine. Yeltsóv, N. V. representative of the Company Yéltsov and Levashóv, gold mining and navigation. Kokóvin, M. A. firm of Kokóvin and Básov, tea and sugar. Lukín V. M. various goods, factories: distillery, brewery, saw-mill, flour-mill, navigation (Chief office in Srétensk), Pérshin, gold mining industry, machinery works. Tetiukòv, gold mining industry, wheat flour-mill. Emeri, various Russian and foreign goods, agricultural implements. Borovkóv, agent of Gúbkin and A. Kuznetsóv. Brodovikóv, mine manager of the Amúr C°. Ballod, general manager of the Níman gold mining industry. Brothers Gúrikov, copper goods, navigation in the Amúr basin. Kotélnikov, trade in various goods, navigation. Lárin, gold mining industry and navigation. Opárin, trade in various goods, gold industry, navigation Li-Va-Chan, Yun-Kho-Zan, Chinese and Japanese goods. Agents of Fire Insurance Society, 1827. Petróv of the Russian Society, Yefímov of the Rossia Society. Kloss of the Anchor Society. Ruzhítsky of the Nadézhda Society. Mámontov of the St. Petersburg Society. Brothers Piánkov of the Russian Goods Transport Society. Bank agents: Filátov, Khlusévich, agents of the Yarosláv-Kostromá-Bank.
		After its junction with the Zéya, the Amúr assumes a southern direction. The breadth of the river, from Blagovéshchensk to the town of Aigún and even to the settlement of Nízmennoe, varies from 1 1/2 to 2 versts, widening at some places to 3 and 5 versts. Upon its junction with the Zéya, the left bank of the Amúr assumes the character of a treeless plain. This plain abounds in pasture wastes and hollows intersected by branches of the river and valleys extending in all directions. Copses standing out in marked lines on the horizon are met with in this plain, near Manchurian villages always shaded by trees, Masses of foliage trees cover the slopes of the banks and the islands, presenting a mixture of willow, blackberry, wîld apple, birch, wild rose, currant, at some places, cork tree (Phellodendron amurensis), wild vine (Vitis amurensis), and nut bushes. The mountains on the right bank of the Amúr, retiring from the rivor 1 1/2 verst above Blagovéshchensk, extend down the Amúr for a distance of 75 versts, and then somewhat above the settlement of Nízmennoe touch the water's edge, forming a high and rocky wall which is a spur of the Ilkhuri-Alin ridge. This elevation seems to be cut in the shape

Names of settlements and stations.	Distance from Srétensk.	Description of the settlements, stations and route.
		of a compressed cone. Its summit commands the level plain of the Amúr spreading below like an open map. The road leading to the town of Aigún runs for a distance of 40 versts above the valley from the Manchu village of Sakhalín, standing opposite Blagovéshchensk. Beyond Aigún the road leaves the Amúr, retiring into the interior of Manchuria towards Mergén and Tsitsikár. From the mouth of the Zéya to the settlement of Nízmennoe, there are reckoned to be about 30 islands. At low water, there are many shoals near them.

Winter anchorage of steamers at the landing-place in Blagovéshchensk.

Names of settlements and stations.	Distance from Srétensk.	Description of the settlements, stations and route.
Town of *Aigún*....	1196	Aigún, town of Manchuria in the Khei-Lun-Tsian province (Manchu, Sakhalinula-khotón) is situated on the right bank of the Amúr. Citadel, residence of the Chinese governor, admiralty department of the Chinese fleet. Houses (fanzas) are small, one-storeyed and built of bricks and clay, with straw roofs. The number of inhabitants is 15,000, including a few hundred Mohammedans, who have their own mosque and school. The chief articles of sale are: grain, mustard, tobacco and oil. The Aigún treaty was concluded in this town on the 6 May 1858, according to which tbe left bank of the upper and middle Amúr, and lower down-both banks of the river, became the property of Russia.
Village of Poyárkovo. Houses 105. Pop. 404 m. 433 f. 837	1321	Large Cossack village founded in 1858. Named in honour of the head-clerk Vasíli Poyárkov, chief of the first expedition despatched from Yakútsk the Amúr in 1643. Church, village board, post and telegraph office, school with two teachers, grain stores, 3 shops with an annual business amounting

Names of settlements and stations.	Distance from Strétensk.	Description of the settlements, stations and route.
		to about R. 150,000, salt depot, military ammunition stores, residence of the manager of the 4 section in the II division of the Amúr basin waterways. This village may be ranked among the most thriving of the Cossack settlements. In its course to the village of Poyárkovo, the Amúr, retaining its north-eastern direction, forms islands on both sides of the river, and opposite the mouth of the Górnaya falling in on the right, 12 versts above the village, there is a whole group of islands. After having received on the left the river Zavitáya, 4 versts above the village, the Amúr separates into two currents, having each a breadth of 400 sazhens. The left current further on is divided into two beds, thus forming an island $2^1/_2$ versts long and $1^3/_4$ versts wide. The island formed by the two chief branches, 10 versts in length and $4^1/_2$ versts in breadth is known by the name of Polúdenny. Having again collected its waters ínto one channel $1^3/_4$ versts wide, the Amúr flows east and then S. S. W. and E. S. E.
Village of Innokéntievskaya .... Houses 51. Pop. 164 m. 140 f. 304	1435	Large Cossack village established in 1858. It received its name in honour of the Archbishop of the Kamchátka diocese, later on the Metropolitan of Moscow. Church of Christ's Resurrection, ammunition stores, post and telegraph office, vlllage board, salt depot. Here the Amúr has one bed $1^1/_2$ versts in breadth. Throughout its course, between the mouths of the Buréya and the Bir-Ara or Khára, the right bank of the river is mountainous, the left presents a pasture land with beautiful meadows endowed with a luxuriant vegetation; at some distance from the river, the banks are enlivened by groves of trees.
Settl. of Páshkovsk .. Houses 23. Pop. 86 m. 112 f. 198	$1536^1/_2$	Cossack settlement established in 1857. It received its name in honour of the Nérchinsk voyevóda Athanasius Páshkov, who ruled the Russian dominions on the Amúr from 1665. Chapel, school, grain stores, post-station. Leaving the settlement, the Amúr abrnptly turns southwards entering the Kaminfyn pass and making its way through the valleys and gorges of the Little Khingán ridge. At a distance of $2^1/_2$ versts below the mouth of the Khingán and beyond the Páshkov settlement, the spurs of the mountains come up close to the Amúr which, abruptly turning to the south and even to the S. S. W., directs its current between the so called „shchéki" or cheeks represented by the rocky and mountainous banks. The mountains are clothed with forests which, contain conifera such as fir, spruce aud larch. Here the river perceptibly narrows, to a breadth of 250—300 sazhens. Following a S. S. W. direction, the Amúr reaches its right tributary the Uya. Half way of this distance, the steep and rocky right bank contains outcrops of spar and porphyry. The left bank is wooded.

Names of settlements and stations.	Distance from Srétensk.	Description of the settlements, stations and route.
Settl. of Storozhévsky (Guard post). Houses 63. Pop. 152 m. 117 f. 269	1500	Cossack settlement established in 1859. It derives its name from its situation near the former Khingán military post, which served as a guard post. Chapel, grain stores, post station. Beyond the mouth of tho Uyá, the Amúr pressing close to the Shakhtá-Khadá mountain, standing on the right bank, turns suddenly to the E. S. E. and enters the Khingán pass. The Amúr breaks through these mountains, making abrupt bends and sudden changes in the direction of its course. The water, striking violently agains the banks, transforms them into steep and almost vertical walls. As an effect of its frequent bends, the body of water seems to be enclosed in a stone through with walls formed by the rocky slopes of the banks. Bare and craggy cliffs, called Siksiakháda by the natives, rise on the right. Opposite them is the mouth of the Lagár, which is an important tributary of the Amúr. Prior to reaching the Lagár, the Amúr meets a steep mountain spur covered with scattered stones, separating the Iláchka spring from the Lagár. From the mouth of the Lagár, the Amúr turns abruptly to the south and keeps this direction for a distance of 11 versts. On the left, the river is bounded by vertical cliffs. At the seventh verst from the mouth of the Lagár. this chain of cliffs is interrupted by a plateau 2 to 2¹/2 versts wide, bordered by mountain spurs known by the name of Khóchio.
Vil. of Radde .... Houses 109. Pop. 272 m. 257 f. 529	1575¹/4	Large Cossack village founded in 1858. Named in honour of the naturalist Radde who, during the year 1857, was occupied in scientific investigations near this place. Church in honour of the Holy Trinity, school, ammunition stores, post and telegraph office, village board, grain stores, salt depot, 4 shops. On the slope of the mountain, behind the village, a chapel has been erected in commemoration of the Emperor Alexander II's miraculous escape from death on the 4 April, 1866. Beyond this village situated on a plateau, the mountains rise again like a wall on the left bank; the Amúr here flows with an extraordinary velocity.
Pompéevka	1615³/4	Post and telegraph office. Cossack settlement now abandoned.
Village of Yekateríno-Nikólsk .... Houses 206. Pop. 605 m. 590 f. 1195	1692¹/2	Large Cossack village founded in 1858, designated by the name and patronymic of Countess Catherine Nikoláevna Muraviόv-Amúrsky. Church of the Martyr Saint Catherine, 2 schools, post and telegraph office. Meteorological station. Village board. Ammunition stores, grain stores, salt depot, 3 shops. Residence of the manager of the I section in the III division of the Amúr basin waterways. Headquarters of the Amúr Cossack division staff. The village extending along the Amúr in three parallel streets in the most populous and prosperous

Names of settlements and stations.	Distance from Srétensk.	Description of the settlements, stations and route.
		among the villages of the Amúr Cossack troops, as may bee seen by its outward appearancc and the material welfare of the inhabiiants. During the establishment of the village were found remains of ancient fortifications and bulwarks. A Chinese picket is posted opposite to the village on the right bank. Here the Amúr reaches its southern limit, 47° 42′ 18 N. lat., and changes its former general southern and S. E. direction, turning eastwards to the mouth of the Sungarí. Upon leaving the mountains, the Amúr is bordered on both sides by a vast and level plain, resembling a steppe, at some points dotted with copses, consisting of oak and elm.

Village of Radde.

		Part of the pasture steppe forms an immense plain, most suitable for agriculture, covered with thick grass. The surface of the river is dotted by many islands. Further off from the Khingán, frequently occur strips of alluvial soil brought down from the banks of the river, rising to a height of several sazhens and composed of soft yellow sand with layers of blue and yellow clay. Somewhat below the village, the Amúr forms 2 islands a verst in length, and flows to the east.
Settl. of Blagoslovénnoe Houses 158. Pop. 615 m. 579 f. 1194	1732	Village at the mouth of the Samára, founded in 1871 by Koreans emigrated from the South-Ussúri region. Having adopted the orthodox faith, the Koreans have retained their own language, their typical customs and their systems of agriculture. There is an orthodox church of St. Alexander Névsky,

Names of settlements and stations.	Distance from Srétensk	Description of the settlements, stations and route.
		school, grain stores, post station. In its outward appearance, this village differs from the Russian settlements: it consists of little houses (fanzas) separated by tracts of tilled fields, intersectəd by streets and lanes. The fanzas are made of wattle thickly plastered with clay within and without. The sloping roofs made of straw or twigs, also coated with clay, at the same time serve as ceilings. Every fanza stands in the middle of a little yard, containing tiny buidings kept in good order and cleanliness The fields are as carfully cnltivated as gardens. Among the plants, attention is mainly directed to the cultivation of buda, (in Chinese, chumidza, Korean millet), then wheat, oats, and maize. A total of 1300 desiatins is allotted to the use of the settlement, constituting only $2^3/_4$ desiatins to every man. In spite of these comparatively insignificant allotments, the Korean population enjoys a considerable prosperity thanks to the rational cultivation of the land.
Mouth of the Sungarí.	1826	
Settl. of Mokhankó...	1830	Settlement by Golds on tle right bank of the Amúr. The branches meet again much below the junction with the Sungarí, and flowing in an easterly direction form a wide expanse of about 12 versts opposite the mouth of the Sungarí, occupied by islands, consisting of alluvium brought down by the joint efforts of the two rivers. These islands are partly bare, and partly clothed with vegetation, they have their own axes, which do not follow the current of the Amúr, but lie almost across the river bed. This phenomenon is explained by the more violent tide of the Sungarí, which the Chinese and Manchus consider to be the main branch of the Amúr. In any case, the right branch, to wit the Sungarí, is more abundant in water and brings down more alluvium, whereas the left branch has a swifter and longer course. The water of the Sungarí is of a dirty and turbid colour produced by very fine particles of clay. For a long time, the waters of both rivers flow together marked by a great difference in colour and clearness, till the Amúr gradually overwhelmed by the force of the turbid current loses its original transparency. After having received the Sungarí, the main current of the Amúr holds its course to the N. E. and flows thus to the village of Mikháilovo-Semiónovsk. The total breadth of the Amúr with the islands and, the numerous branches, at some places comes up to 12 versts.
Village of Mikháilovo-Semiónovsk..... Houses 92. Pop. 331 m. 324 f. 655	1855	Large Cossack village created in 1858 and named in honour of Michael Semiónovich Korsákov, then manager of the floatage and founder of the village, later on Governor-General of Eastern Siberia. The village contains a church of the Archangel Michael, a school with two teachers, a village board, grain stores, post and telegraph office, salt depot,

Names of settlements and stations.	Distance from Srétensk.	Description of the settlements, stations and route.
		3 shops. Being situated iu proximity to the mouth of the Sungarí, it serves as a trading centre for the Chinese who forward grain to this point. The breadth of the Amúr opposite to the village is $10^1/_2$ versts. From here the main current turns to the east and further to the north-east, receiving on the right the tribute of the Baidzín. On the right bank of this river are steep cliffs forming two sloping shelves descending to the main branch of the Amúr. The lower shelf is covered with thick grass, climbing plants aud shrubs, the upper with a dense forest of foliage and fir trees. The summit of this elevation commands a beautiful and far reaching view. From the mouth of the Baidzhín, the Amúr turns more and more to the N. N. E. The right edge of the valley rises here straight from the water, forming either slopes clad with oak, or inaccessible almost vertical rocks. The first are called Mangatí, the latter Kenú.
Settl. of Lugovói .... Houses 9. Pop. 42 m. 40 f. 82	1984	Cossack settlement established in 1858. Grain stores, landing-place for timber, post station.
Settl. of Upper Spassk Houses 2. Pop. 5 m. 6 f. 11	2010	Cossack hamlet created in 1858. Abandoned by the inhabitants after repeated inundations. Steep cliffs rise opposite to the Upper Spassk settlement on the right bank of the Amúr known under the name of Khorrokhó; they are intersected by passes and little streams hurrying to join the Amúr. Maak was astonished by the luxuriant vegetation found in the damp passes. Lower down, Cape Kyrmá projects into the river bed. From here the chief current finds its way amidst an archipelago of islands.
Lower Spassk .... Houses 3. Pop. 5 m. 8 f. 13	2022	Cossack hamlet founded in 1858. Landing-place for timber. Here the Amúr separates into two branches, of which the right receives the Ussúri. On the left bank of the Ussúri, at its junction with the Amúr, stands a post, marking the frontier of Russia and China and the extreme N. E. limit of the Chinese Empire.
Town of Khabaróvsk	2066	Littoral Territory.

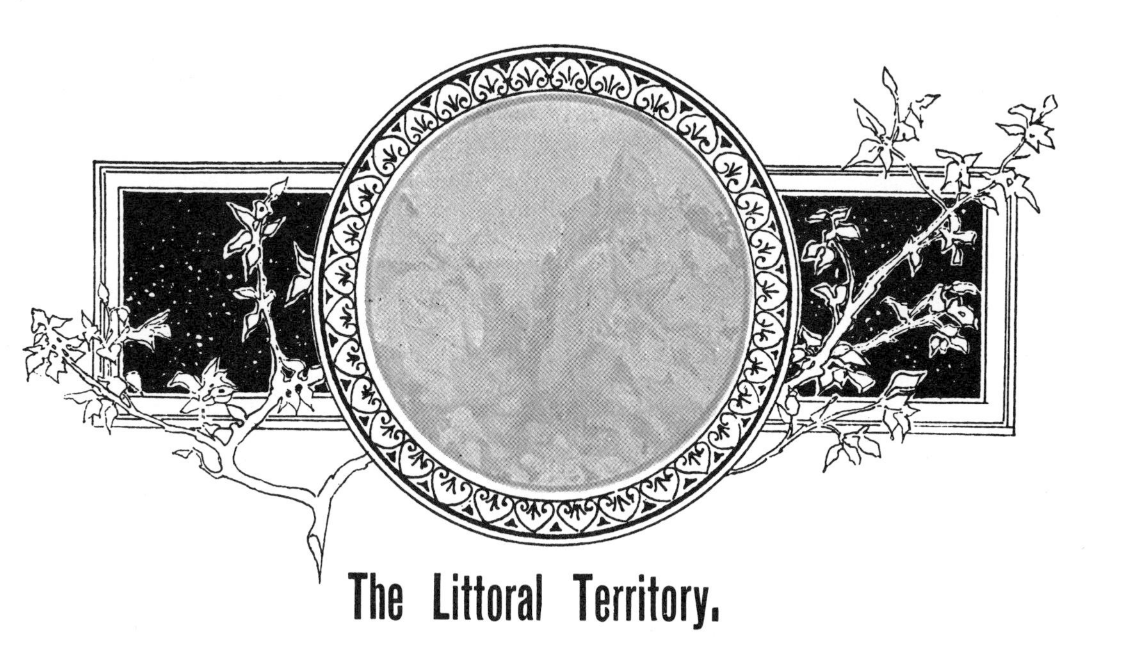

The Littoral Territory.

Geographical position and area of the territory.—Okhótsk and Kamchátka region. — Peninsula of Kamchátka.—Discoveries of the Okhótsk-Kamchátka expedition.—Gold mines on the Okhótsk coast.—Chukch land and its exploration. — Komandór Islands. — Hydrography.—Climate.—Flora.—Fauna.—Whale and seal industry.—Population (Chukch, Koriák, Lamút, Kamchadál, Aleút tribes). — Ussuri and Littoral region.—Configuration of the surface.—Geological structure and mineral wealth.—Hydrography.—Gulf of Peter the Great.—Navigation on the Ussúri and its basin.—Climate.—Flora.—Fauna.—Colonisation and settlement.—The Ussúri ossack troops, peasant population, natives: Koreans, Chinese, Golds, Olchís, Orochís).Industries.—(Agriculture.—Stock raising.—Forestry.—Trapping.—Hunting.—Fishing.—Sea-cabbage industry.—Crayfish, prawn and trepang fishing).—Works and manufactories.—Trade by land and sea.—Future importance of the port of Vladivostók as terminus of the Great Siberian transit way.—Bibliography.

THE LITTORAL territory presents the farthest eastern border of the Russian dominions in Asia. It occupies the eastern coastland of Siberia between 42° — 70° N. lat. and 100° — 160° E. long. The northern limit bordering upon the Arctic Ocean lies within the northern zone, whereas the southern part belongs to the temperate zone, corresponding to the northern portion of the Caucasus. Its superficial area is approximately estimated at 33,504 square geographical miles. Its length from south to north is 4,000 versts. By its dimensions, it holds the third place among the Siberian governments, being surpassed only by the Yakútsk territory and the Yeniséisk government, and is equal in extent to Austria, Germany, Denmark and France taken together. According to its configuration, climate and general nature, this territory is divided into two well-marked portions: North and South, viz. Okhótsk-Kamchátka and Ussúri-Littoral region. The Okhótsk-Kamchátka region covers an area of over 20,000 square miles and geographically consists of the narrow north-western coast of the Okhótsk Sea (districts: Udsk, Okhótsk, Gizhigínsk), of the peninsula of Kamchátka (Peter aud Paul district), the Chukótsk (or Chukch) land and the islands of the Okhótsk and Bering Seas (districts: Anadyr and of the Komandór Islands). The Stanovói ridge, with an average height of 3,000 feet, separates the Okhótsk-Kamchátka region from the Yakútsk territory, sending out, all over the coast of the Okhótsk Sea, spurs which abruptly fall in steep cliffs to the water.

The geological formations of the Okhótsk coast are very varied, containing crystalline rocks such as granite, diorite, porphyry, syenite and labrador, and volcanic rocks represented by trachyte, basalt and dolerite.

The Stanovói ridge in its southern part is in particular endowed with a great variety of rocks.

The peninsula of Kamchátka covers an area of 237,266 square versts, and offers considerably elevated points; it is traversed from N. to S. by the Central Kamchátka ridge, whose northern portion consists of tertiary sandstone and volcanic rocks, whereas the southern part is formed of crystalline slate, granite, syenite and porphyry. A series of active and extinct volcanoes occur along the eastern coast of the peninsula, stretching parallel to the Central ridge. This ring of fire includes 12 active and about 30 extinct volcanoes. Among the active volcanoes, the Kliuchévskaya Sópka is the highest, rising to an altitude of 16,000 feet above sea-level. This giant, which is the highest active volcano of the Old World, is surrounded by several rows of terraces and lower summits which seem to serve as a pedestal to the gigantic mountain, which at its base has a circumference of about 300 versts. The summit of the sópka, cracked on all sides, is always smoking and throws out stone fragments and ashes twice or thrice a year, spreading volcanic dust for a great distance round. The next in size among the active volcanoes are the Krestóvsky and Siveliúch, rising to an altitude of 11,000 feet. Among the extinct volcanoes, the highest is the Ichínsk sópka, 16,900 feet high, constituting the culminating point of the peninsula.

According to the data collected by Ditmar and Erman in 1829, the geological structure of Kamchátka at the places of juxtaposition of the old crystalline rocks with the sedimentary formations, point to the auriferous nature of the peninsula. Later on, in 1894, the Transbaikál expedition, which explored the coast of the Okhótsk Sea and the Shantár Islands, ascertained the presence of gold throughout the Udsk region, from the river Togúr to port Ayán and the Shantár Islands.

These data served as an inducement to organise a special Okhótsk-Kamchátka expedition, despatched in 1895 for three years in order to conduct surveys and prospectings for gold and other minerals along the coast of the Okhótsk Sea, on the Shantár mountains and Kamchátka.

The work done by the expedition demonstrated the presence of gold at many places on the coast of the Okhótsk Sea, containing a proportion of 3 to 10 zolotníks of gold to 100 puds of gravel. Rich deposits of coal of good quality have been found near Gizhigín Bay. The exploration of Kamchátka was connected with the observation of the volcanoes, and the discovery of glaciers, and led to the ascertainment of coal-fields and gold on the upper waters of the Oglukámennaya.

According to the data obtained in 1898, the Ministry of Agriculture and State Domains admitted the private exploitation of the following districts according to the authorised rules: 1) part of the Okhótsk coast and the adjoining localities comprising the left tributaries of the Udá, with the exception of the Yána or Dzhána system, and all the rivers flowing into the Okhótsk Sea, commencing with the river Ulkán, on the northeast to the river Siglín, south of the Olá, together with the Shantár Islands; 2) the area bounded by the river system of Maimasyn and Alá and by the coast of the Okhótsk Sea, stretching between the mouths of both rivers.

Among other minerals found in Kamchátka, there are native copper, magnetic iron-ore, native sulphur and amber. Some peculiar properties of the geological structure account for the number of hot springs, occurring throughout the peninsula, mainly in connexion with volcanic rocks.

The Chukótsk or Dénezhnev Peninsula, mainly occupied by the basin of the river Anadyr, constitutes the extreme northern limit of Asia, parted from America by Bering Strait. It is much indented with fiords.

The Anadyr country, within recent years, has been carefully explored by N. L. Gondatti, well known by his scientific expeditions. Presenting in its northern part a continuous tundra intersected by numerous rivers, only the region in the south up the Anadyr is covered with dwarf trees.

The Komandór Islands lie, in the neighbourhood of Kamchátka, in the Bering Sea; they rise to a considerable altitude, consisting of volcanic rocks, and comprise two large islands called Bering and Médny, and two smaller ones Ari-Kámen and Toporkóv. These islands, inhabited by Aleúts, are universally known for their seal and other fisheries. The whole of the eastern coast of the territory bounded, north of the Amúr basin, by the Okhótsk, Kamchátka and Bering Seas and by Bering Strait, has a great number of gulfs and bays of various forms of which the most important are: the Ulbán, Tugúrsk and Udá gulfs, the Penzhínsk, Gizhigín and Taússa bays in the Okhótsk Sea, the gulfs of Anadyr and of the Holy Cross in the Bering Sea, and the Avachín Bay in the Kamchátka Sea, with a beautiful harbour, where the Peter and Paul port is situated.

Almost all the rivers in this region drain into the basin of the Pacific Ocean. The Udá, having a total length of over 700 versts and a breadth varying from 1½ to 2 versts, flows into the southern part of the Okhótsk Sea. The bed of the river is rocky and contains a great number of sandbanks. Further the principal rivers are: the Okhóta (400 versts), the Kóva (500 versts), the Penzhína (300 versts). Among the rivers, the most extensive is the Anadyr, falling into the Anadyr Gulf and having a length of 1,080 versts. Its bed is very tortuous, being contained by high mountains and cliffs; it abounds in fish. The only important river on the peninsula of Kamchátka is the Kamchátka, 470 versts long. It is navigable throughout its course, excepting the head waters, and flows through a plain which, on account of its fertility, has attracts a considerable part of the population, settled along the river. This region abounds in lakes, situated mainly in its southern plains, in the Amúr basin.

The climatic conditions of the greater portion of the Okhótsk-Kamchátka region are very unfavourable. The Okhótsk Sea, although not reaching as far north as the Baltic, has the nature of an arctic sea. At the most southern ports of Udsk and Ayán (under 54° 31′ and 56° 27′ N. lat.) the mean annual temperature is —4°; in Okhótsk, situated under 59° 20′ N. lat., the mean annual temperature is still lower (—5°). This severe climate, with a mean temperature which during the period of vegetation lasting 5 months is +8° to +12° in Okhótsk and Ayán, renders the development of agriculture utterly impossible. The extreme austerity of the climate is due to the northern ocean currents and to the accumulation of great masses of ice, gathering mainly in the southern part of the Okhótsk Sea, near the Shantár Islands and in the Amúr liman. The prevailing fogs and monsoons have also a marked effect upon the cooling of the atmosphere. Only on the eastern coast of Kamchátka, bounded by the waters of the more open Bering Sea, and in the river valleys of the peninsula protected by mountains, the mean annual temperature rises to +2.4°. In the Peter and Paul port, where the mean annual temperature is +2.2°, in the winter the temperature is—8.2°, in spring—0.4°, in summer +10° and in autumn.—4.6°.

The flora of the Okhótsk-Kamchátka region is poorly provided with species. The southern forms of the leafy forests, abounding in the valley of the Amúr, give place to fir-trees; as the mountains approach the coast of the Okhótsk Sea, the limits of the forest zone retire lower down, and the side of the mountains turned towards the sea and their summits are almost utterly devoid of vegetation. In close proximity to the arctic Okhótsk Sea, the forests assume the character of the dwarf polar vegetation. The tree species are represented here chiefly by larch, Siberian „cedar" or pine, birch, poplar and ash with an addition of shrubs such as clematis, wild-rose and honeysuckle. The herbaceous vegetation, although containing a small number of species, is very luxuriant, thanks to the abundant moisture; the grass grows sometimes higher than a man and consists mainly of species of umbellifers, lilies and iris. At some places, it attains a height of over 2 arshins and sometimes yields three crops of hay during the summer.

The fauna of the whole of the north-western coast of the Okhótsk Sea in no way differs from that of Siberia, but in Kamchátka it partly assumes the character of the island fauna, which manifests itself by the absence of several animals such as squirrel, elk and others, characteristic of the adjoining part of the Siberian continent. The aquatic fauna is far more important. especially because the fauna of the arctic seas was never met with so far south as in the Bering and Okhótsk Seas, where animals and fish are brought down from the Arctic Ocean by the sea-current and the ice.

The extent of the coast of the Okhótsk-Kamchátka region, bounded by the Okhótsk-Kamchátka and Bering Seas and by the Bering Strait, is 11,000 versts The Okhótsk Sea, locked in between the coast of the Asiatic continent and the peninsula of Kamchátka, is characterised by quite peculiar climatic conditions. In spite of its geographical position within the moderate zone (between 44° and 62° N. lat.), it possesses the typical properties of a polar sea like Hudson's Bay, under the effect of sea-currents filling its waters, mainly the southern portion, with drifting ice, which partly obstructs the entrance from the Pacific Ocean. Moreover, this sea is characterised by the abundance of its flora and fauna. A great number of aquatic plants, mollusks and fish, and in particular shoals of ketá (Salmo logocephalus) and málma (Salmo callaris) serve to attract the large mammals from the Arctic Ocean. These polar mammals are represented by six forms of seal (Phoca), two dolphins (Phocaena orca, Delphinapteros leucas), and three species of whale (Balaenoptera rostrata, borealis, longimana).

On this eastern borderland, which as yet is not sufficiently protected by the Government, whale-fishing has been carried on for a long time in a rapacious fashion mainly by American smugglers, who demoralise the natives of the coast and islands, the Chúkches and Aleúts, by furnishing them with brandy. The whale-fishing carried on by American schooners has been particularly extensive from 1847. Whole fleets of schooners leave New Bedford and, according to the testimony of the American ship-owners, the blubber and whale bone exported by them during a period of 14 years (from 1847 to 1861) amounted in value to 130,000,000 dollars. This robbery much reduced the number of whales in the Okhótsk Sea and partly dispersed them. At the time the Americans started their operations on the Okhótsk Sea, a Russo-Finnish whale company was organised in Finland; it did well at the beginning, but the further development of this industry was hindered by the Anglo-French war. Having for a time dropped whale-fishing, the Americans in 1888 took it up again in the Bering and Okhótsk Seas. According to information annually published in the Whaler's Shipping List, New Bedford, and in other publications devoted to the same subject, it may be supposed that the foreign whalers export annually, from the Pacific coast of Siberia, from 100,000 to 150,000 pounds of whalebone, about 100,000 puds of blubber, 100,000 pounds of walrus teeth and other products of this kind. This industry, with a value of R. 1,500,000 annually, escapes regular control being constantly carried on by smuggling,

As stated by doctor Sliúnin, who studied on the spot the conditions of this industry in the Far East, the success of whale-fishing depends on the exact knowledge of the time of the migration of the whales and their appearance on the coasts, always connected with the movements of the fish and of the small sea-animals. It has been observed that this industry is pursued mainly from the Bay of St. Olga throughout the coast to southern Korea. April and May are the best season for whalefishing on the south of Sakhalín, June and July are preferable in the Okhótsk Sea, near the Shantár Islands as far as Okhótsk; this time is also chosen for the same purpose on the eastern coast of Kamchátka. From the middle of June, the whalers pass to Penzhín Bay. As rightly remarked by Dr. Sliúnin, the organisation of a regular fishery and whale industry must be preceded by the establishment of zoological stations in the waters of the Far East.

Russian whale-fishing restarted in 1877 by retired Captain Dydymov, with the material assistance of the Government and the support of the Grand Duke Alexander Mikháilovich, came to an end in 1892 when Dydymow perished with all his crew.

In 1894, whale-fishing was again started by Midshipman Count Keiserling, who received a subsidy from the Government and the right of free fishery near the Siberian coast. Having purchased in Norway a steamer and two sailing schooners specially adapted for whale-fishing, Count Keiserling established a factory in East Bay for boiling blubber and cleaning the whalebone. This industry is also carried on in Pacific waters by the Russian firm of O. V. Lindholm.

Lying within more northern latitudes (between 52° and 64° N. lat.) the Bering Sea, separated from the Pacific Ocean only by a series of islands, presents the type of an open oceanic sea, with a more maritime climate than the Okhótsk Sea. The northern side of this sea, traversed by the polar circle, lies in winter under a cover of ice, whereas in the southern part, with a mean annual temperature of + 3, that of the coldest month is somewhat below zero and that of the hottest month + 7°. These climatic conditions account for the total absence of arboreal vegetation on the islands of the Bering Sea, and for the impossibility of carrying on agriculture not only on the islands, but throughout the coast.

This sea being abundantly provided with flora, mollusks, crustaceans and fish was always in great favour with the sea-animals which still resort there in shoals.

The Bering Sea abounds principally in seals (Ottaria ursina), which are the object of an extensive industry.

After the discovery of the Pribylov and Komandór Islands, sea fishing was not subjected to any control, and the animals were killed irrespective of sex and age.

A regular organisation of the seal industry was introduced in 1798 by a Russo-American company, sanctioned by the Government. The privilege given to this company lasted to the year 1868; during the time it was in force, upwards of 2,500,000 seals were killed. In 1871, the seal fishing was again leased for a space of 20 years to the Alaska trading Company of Hutchinson, Cool, Philippeus and C⁰. During a period of 20 years, the company obtained on the Russian islands of the Bering Sea over 760,000 seals. By an order, confirmed by the Committee of Ministers on the 21 December, 1890, the seal fishing in the Far East was again leased for ten years to the Russian Seal Fishing Company organised by Grünwald, Lepéshkin, Prózorov and Sávich. The rapacious extermination of seals in the Russian waters, by the Anglo-American schooners pursuing them on the sealing ground, served as an inducement to the promulgation of a law in 1893, forbidding the killing and taking of seals on the water, and allowing it only on land and that with the permission of the Government according to a special regulation. The infringement of the rules is punished by imprisonment lasting from 2 months to a year and 5 months; at the same time, the fishing tackle, the catch and the vessels used for it with freight and all are confiscated. Cruisers now guard the seals from the rapacity of foreign schooners.

Within the last few years, about 30,000 seals have been taken annually.

Another animal which is valuable to industry is the sea-otter (Enhydris lutris). Some years ago, a great number of them were taken in Kamchátka, but again the rapacious mode of fishery has frightened off these timid animals. Now they have only two refuges: one between the capes of Kamchátka and Stolbovói, the other at the Yellow Cape. The other mammals occurring in the Bering Sea are the same as in that of Okhótsk.

Some fish species, such as herring, cod, and gwiniad, appear periodically in innumerable shoals near the islands and coasts of the Bering Sea.

With a view to exploit the ichthyological wealth of the waters bounding Kamchátka, the Russian Seal Company at the beginning of the year 1899 applied for the permission to erect a tinning establishment in the town o Petropávlovsk in Tária Bay.

As a consequence of the unfavourable climate, the Okhótsk-Kamchátka region possesses a scanty population which, by the census of 1897, was given at 51,556 (28,845 males, 22,711 females); this country, not being fit for agriculture and colonisation, is mainly inhabited by native tribes (36,984) representing its aborigenal population and comprising wandering Chúkches, Koriáks, Lamúts, Kamchadáls, Aleúts and Yakúts, getting their livelihood by fishing, trapping and partly by rearing reindeer. The number of Russians, including mainly peasants, citizens of the lower class and Cossacks, is 14,572.

The Ussúri-Littoral region comprises the whole south of the Amúr territory, extending on both sides of the lower Amúr, bounded on the north by the basin of the Udá, on the west by the basin of the Ussúri and on the south-east by the Sea of Japan.

Within these limits, the region occupies upwards of 12,000 geographical miles (districts: of Khabaróvsk, Ussúri-Kazáchi, South-Ussúri and part of the

Udsk district). The northern part of this country, lying north of the Amúr, is covered with mountain ranges, branching off from the Stanovói ridge under the name of Dzhugdyr. These mountains, rising to an average height of 2,000 feet, send out spurs all over the basin of the Udá, giving it a hilly and swampy character. The mountain range leaving the southern Dzhugdyr group, known under the name of Makhtél, stretches eastwards to the Okhótsk Sea, falling in a steep line to the coast, whereas its sloping branches enter into the river valleys of the Amúr tributaries. This mountain range is designated by different names, according to the locality it covers with its spurs. The branch extending from the eastern slopes of the Little Khingán, forming the watershed of the rivers Goryn and Amgún, is the Vánda ridge, running east and gradually passing into the Chaltyn ridge, which covers the country lying on the lower waters of these rivers. The Dayán range stretches between the rivers Kur and Goryn.

The southern part of the region, throughout its entire extent, is traversed by the low and thickly wooded ridge of Sikhoté Alín, running nearly parallel to the coast of the Sea of Japan and separating the narrow sea-coast from the Ussúri basin. The height of the Sikhoté Alín is not great; in some passes, it varies from 1,270 to 2,370 feet, whereas its culminating point, the Camel or Khuntámi, rises to an elevation of 3,600 feet.

The geological structure and mineral wealth of the Ussúri-Littoral region are not as yet sufficiently explored. In the locality lying to the left of the Amúr basin in the so called Udsk district, which is covered by the spurs of the Stanovói ridge, the rocks characterising the geological formation of the southern part of this ridge predominate. The mineral wealth of the Udsk region is illustrated by the auriferous land on the Amgún system, exploited a long time since as the most important. Gold-mining industry was started there in 1872.

The principal way connecting the mines with centres of population is the Amgún, by which all supplies and articles are forwarded from Nikoláevsk by means of steamers to the mining stores situated at a distance of 450 versts along the river. In winter the communication of the mines with the town of Nikoláevsk is exclusively maintained by means of sledges drawn by dogs, in consequence of the great masses of snow attaining a depth of over a sazhen. As regards gold-mining operations and the organisation of the mines, the principal companies are: the Amgún Company, obtaining from 30 to 60 puds annually and the Yeltsóv and Levashóv Company, having from 30 to 40 puds per annum. The gravel is conveyed to the washing apparatus and brought away by means of mechanical appliances. The gold-washing machines are made on the barrel-system, worked by an engine which also serves to propel the dynamos producing electric lighting for the buildings belonging to the mines.

The mines of the Amgún Company are provided with a church, hospital, library containing the works of Russian authors and new magazines, billiard room and a magic lantern for the workmen. There is not one school in this group of mines. The workmen are mainly represented by peasants hired at Blagovéshchensk. The annual wages of a workman amounts to R. 1,700. In 1898, the Amgún mines were worked by 14 gold-mining companies. The total number of employees and workmen at the mines was 4,063 (Chinese 318, Koreans 498, Yakúts 78). For the conveyance of goods and workmen, the companies disposed of 6 steamers and 10 barges. Gold mines have also been discovered in tha basin of the Udá, along the coast opposite the Shantár Islands, close to the sea-coast and north of the town of Nikoláevsk; they occur on the rivers rising on the Mevachán ridge, all the beds being characterised by a considerable extent and richness.

The north Ussúri region, which had been explored by private geological expeditions conducted by Maak (1858), by Basnín (1860) and Engineer Ivánov (1893), only recently, upon the construction of the railway, became the object of a more careful investigation. The works of the mining engineers Batsévich and Ivánov illustrate the geological structure of the greater portion of the country.

The following rocks occur in the upper basin of the Ussúri: granite, syenite, gneiss and granite, slate, diabase, quartz and quartzless porphyry and breccia, marble-like limestone and basalt. This section does not contain any valuable rocks. Practical use is found for limestone, employed for revetting, and for kaolin clay, used to coat walls and ceilings. Considerable areas, with symptoms indicating the presence of iron-ores, have been found in the basins of the rivers Imán and Bikín, right tributaries of the Ussúri; well ascertained is the presence of gold in the Arúm, Tinzá-khé („tinzá", gold), and Alchán valleys, where the local Orochéns and Manzas have long since obtained gold in a wasteful manner. The mineral wealth of the South-Ussúri region is much better explored. The first find worked was the coal-pit in Possiét Bay which, between 1859 and 1878, supplied the warships with coal. The coal-seam lies here close to the sea and, falling abruptly, continues at the bottom of Expedition Bay; when the coal was worked to the level of the sea, the shafts filled with water and exploitation thus came to an end. Other coal deposits have been discovered on the rivers Seúanka, Mongúgaya and Ambabír, but they are particularly numerous on the coast of the Amúr Gulf, in its northern portion, viz, from the Peschánaya Bay, on both sides of the Suifún and throughout the coast of the Gulf to Uglováya Bay. All these deposits contain brown coal. The best coal-bed, St. Macarius, of importance for the railway, was discovered in 1894 by Engineer Górlov; it lies in proximity to the railway line, 22 versts from the town of Vladivostók. This coal, worked by a Dutch joint stock company, occurs in small pieces, containing an admixture of earth. The South-Ussúri mining expedition, under the direction of the geologist Ivánov, ascertained that the field of brown-coal comprised not only the Amúr Gulf, but also the Russian Island, the peninsula of Muraviόv-Amúrsky and the whole of the eastern coast of the Ussúri Gulf. Smithy coal was found by the expedition on the right bank of the Suifún, opposite Nikoláevsk; more extensive beds were discovered on the Suchán, falling into America Gulf. The expedition ascertained three coal-seams with a depth of 1/2 to 1 sazhen and a considerable extent. According to the analysis, this coal presents a kind of semi-anthracite ressembling Welsh coal. In this locality, the supply of coal capable of exploitation is estimated at 500,000,000 puds. A more careful investigation of the seams will certainly raise this figure. The mining expedition only hurriedly examined the eastern portion of the South Ussúri region, and it may be that rich deposits of mineral fuel will be discovered in the valleys of the rivers falling into Lake Khánka, the Ussúri and the sea. A railway has been constructed to Nakhódka Bay, for the exploitation of the Suchán coal, and a landingplace serves for the direct transport of coal from the waggons to the ships.

Iron-ores occur along the sea-coast in the Olga district, and although, up to the present time, but a relatively small number of beds have been indicated, the abundance of them is evidenced by a fact, which has been observed by all ship-captains navigating near the coast from Cape Povorótny northwards to Plastún Gulf and further on, which consists in the irregular deviation of the compass, explained by the attraction exercised by the great mass of iron embedded in the Sikhoté Alín mountains. This mineral wealth promises a profitable export to Japan, which stands in need of iron, and to China, also offering a good market

Silver and lead mines exist at many places on the coast: near Transfiguration Bay, where ore is raised by Mr. Traubenberg; on the bank of the Vaizín; within 80 versts from St. Olga Bay, where the ore is worked by Messrs Cooper and Galétsky.

Beds of copper-ore were discovered near the station of Konstantínovskaya in the valley of the Suifún.

Auriferous areas were found on Askold Island, lying in St. Peter Bay, within 50 versts to the south-east of Vladivostók and 6 versts from the coast of the continent.

All the data obtained point to the future development of mining industry in this rich country.

The eastern and south-eastern border of the region throughout its extent is bounded by the Sea of Japan and by Tartary or Nevelskói Strait, forming numerous harbours and bays available for the anchorage of ships. The most convenient are: the Gulfs of Peter the Great, St. Olga, St. Vladímir, Plastún and the Imperial and de Castri Bays.

The Gulf of Peter the Great, having a length of 175 versts from Cape Povorótny to the mouth of the Tumén Ulá and a breadth of 80 versts, is provided with a number of small gulfs, bays and harbours and contains an archipelago of islands abounding in monoliths, rocks and stones. Among the gulfs, the principal in respect to their size are: America Gulf with Nakhódka Bay at the eastern side near Povorótny, Eastern, Strelók, Ussúri aud Amúr Gulfs. The latter are both formed by the peninsula of Muravióv-Amúrsky and Russian and Rynda Islands, projecting from north to south. Russian Island is separated from the continent by Eastern Bosphorus Strait, having a breadth of 1 to 1½ versts and a depth of 17 to 20 sazhens. Among the bays formed by the strait, the best lies on the west, extending far into the peninsula of Muravióv-Amúrsky, and bearing the name of the Golden Horn. This bay is about 2 sea-miles long, from 1 to 1½ miles wide and from 5 to 10 sazhens deep. Its northern side forms the extensive and sheltered basin of Port Vladivostók. Among islands, the most important are: Putiátin opposite to Strelók Strait, and Askold, lying south-west of Putiátin.

The Gulf of Peter the Great was discovered in 1852 by the French corvet „Capricieuse" under the command of Captain Rocmorel, who named it Golfe d'Anville; in 1855, English warships, having reached the central part of the gulf near Askold Island, gave it the name of Victoria Bay. Only one vessel of the English squadron, the „Winchester", penetrated as far as the Bay of Vladivostók, and inserted it for the first time on the map under the name of Port May; the peninsula on which the town now stands was named in honour of Prince Albert. More carefull explorations of the Gulf were made in 1859 by the corvet „America" and the clipper „Strelók", when it received its name in honour of Peter the Great.

Among the smaller bays of this immense sea depression, the most important is Possiét Bay lying south. This bay consists of three parts: Palláda roads, representing its outward side, Nóvgorod and Expedition Bay. Expedition Bay has a length of 16 versts; at some places, it widens to a breadth of 10 versts and has a depth of 5 sazhens; Nóvgorod Bay extends for a distance of 11 versts, with a breadth of 1 to 4½ versts and a depth of about 6 sazhens, and is more convenient for the anchorage of ships. This bay was discovered in 1854 by Vice-Amiral Prince Putiátin, and explored in 1859 by the squadron of Count Muraviόv-Amúrsky, Governor-General of Siberia.

The Gulf of Peter the Great remains free of ice all the year round at some distance from the shore, but the small bays on the coast, from the beginning of December, are covered with an ice-crust, which lasts to the end of March.

The Ussúri-Littoral region is plentifully provided with rivers belonging to the Amúr basin and to the basins of the Sea of Japan and the Tartary Strait.

The Amúr, from its junction with the Ussúri to the sea, flows through the territory from south-west to north-east for a distance of 900 versts. It receives here the rivers Kur, Dondón, Mylka, Goryn, Amgún and others. The unfavourable climate prevailing at the mouth of the Amúr, which during 6 months, from the beginning of November to the beginning of May, keeps the river frost-bound near the Port of Nikoláevsk, is the principal reason which hinders the establishment of a port at the mouth of one of the most extensive rivers of Asiatic Russia. The chief water-way in this region is the Ussúri, a right affluent of the Amúr; the Chinese, Manchus and natives call it Uzúli, Vusulikhé, Imá-khuzé and Utsykayán. It is formed by the junction of the Daubí-khé and Ulá-khé, rising in the branches of the Sikhoté Alín. The general direction of the Ussúri is almost that of the meridian from south to north, along the western frontier of the Littoral territory; only the right bank lies within the confines of the territory, while the left is under Chinese dominion. The total length of the river is about 850 versts, with a breadth of 50 sazhens to 2 versts.

On the left, the Ussúri receives the Sungách (outflow of Lake Khánka), Imán, Bikín, and Khor; on the right: the Murén, Sikhulín and Nor. On its upper waters predominate plains with wide meadows and swampy lowlands; the locality generally abounds in mountains, which occur mostly between the mouth of the Murén and upwards of Bikín and approach the river, falling sometimes in steep cliffs to the water's edge. On its lower reaches, there are again plains, although the Khekhtsyr ridge rises on the right bank, at a distance of about 50 versts. On account of its natural wealth and relatively good climate, the Ussúri plain is well adapted for colonisation. However, these favourable conditions are reduced to nil by the periodical floods, during which the water rises 5 sazhens above its ordinary level. The Ussúri is navigable for a distance of 700 versts, the only impediment consisting in bars, which however appear only during low-water in summer.

The river freezes at the beginning of November and breaks up in the middle of April. Previous to the opening of traffic on the Ussúri railway, the river Ussúri with the Sungách and Lake Khánka afforded the only means of communication between Khabaróvsk and Vladivostók. This route consisted of the following stages: steamer from, Khabaróvsk to the Kámen Rybalóv on Lake Khánka; post-road between Kámen Rybalóv and the village of Razdélnoe on the Suifún; steamer along the river and sea-going steamers anchoring beyond the bar; steamers from the bars of Suifún to Vladivostók. Thus, the journey from Khabaróvsk to Vladivostók was accomplished in 7 to 10 days.

The steamers now plying on the Ussúri belong to the Amúr Ship and Trade Company and to the Amúr Steamship Company. The first carries on regular mail and passenger traffic between Imán and Khabaróvsk (once in 3 days) and to Kámen Rybalóv (once a month). The second conveys passengers and goods without any fixed dates of departure and arrival. Besides the Crown vessels of the Amúr fleet, belonging to the Ministry of Ways of Communication, others belonging to the Amúr and Ussúri Cossack fleet navigate on the waters of the Ussúri (3 steamers and 2 barges).

As regards the rivers flowing into the Eastern Ocean, they all take their rise in the eastern slopes of the Sikhoté Alín; they are not large and upon the whole are not suitable for navigation, having mostly a steep fall and containing rocks and bars. Among all these rivers, some attention is due to the Suifún, flowing along the south-eastern corner of the South-Ussúri region. This river rises in Manchuria and, holding its course first to the east and further to the south-east, falls into the Amúr Gulf. It is practicable for small steamers for a distance of 60 versts from its mouth. The valley of the river

Valley of the Suifún (phot. by Matskévich).

widens only at its lower part, offering an expanse suitable for colonisation; many Russian and Korean settlements are established there. At the lower part of the valley, mainly on the left bank, occur remains of old entrenchments with bulwarks and ditches.

Among the lakes, the Kízí and Khánka are remarkable on account of their dimensions. The first lies in the north-eastern portion of the country, in proximity to the Amúr, being united with it by a branch. The superficial area of this lake is 390 square versts. The other lake is situated on the south-west at the Chinese frontier; it is 80 versts long and 60 versts wide with an area of 3,330 square versts. The Sungách serves as an outflow to the lake and falls into the Ussúri.

The climate of the Ussúri-Littoral region is far from being as mild as is generally the case in a littoral country. The mean annual temperature at Nikoláevsk is — 2.7° C., at Khabaróvsk + 0.6° C. at St. Olga Bay + 4.2° C. and at Vladivostók + 4.5° C. being much inferior to the mean temperature of the parts lying within corresponding latitudes on the continent of European Russia. Upon the whole, the annual temperature of this region is 4° to 7° lower than that of corresponding zones in Europe.

This low annual temperature is the result of the chilly summer but mainly of the great cold in winter. The mean annual temperatures of the seasons are as follows:

	Nikoláevsk.	Khabaróvsk.	St. Olga Bay.	Vladivostók.
Winter	— 19.0	— 21.9	— 10.6	— 12.0
Spring	— 4.2	— 1.4	+ 3.5	+ 3.7
Summer	+ 15.3	+ 20.1	+ 17.2	+ 18.2
Autumn	— 0.7	+ 2.8	+ 6.6	+ 7.9

The severity of the climate is due to the effect of the northern current, flowing past the coast in the northern part of the Sea of Japan, to the sea winds prevailing in spring and summer bringing much moisture, to the properties of the virgin soil and to the immense areas of taigá. However, the mean annual temperature during the 5 months'period of vegetation, which from Khabaróvsk to Vladivostók is + 16°, may be considered as favourable enough for agriculture and for the growth of a luxuriant flora. The S. E. winds prevailing in spring and summer bring to the region abundant evaporations from the sea, accounting for the moisture in the atmosphere, which is mostly felt on the coastland of Sikhoté Alín, where dense fogs occurring sometimes from March to the end of July, greatly retard the growth of corn. The N. W. winds blowing in winter produce on the contrary a dry air. In connexion with the prevailing winds, a great mass of moisture falls in July and August, the winter is generally snowless and severe, almost without intervals of thaws. Spring comes late. The first snow generally falls in the middle of October, somewhat earlier in the mountains.

The water freezes and is free of ice at the following dates: At Vladivostók, the Bay of the Golden Horn freezes on the 2 or 3 December and breaks up on the 25 or 26 March; St. Olga Bay is frost-bound at the beginning of November and becomes free of ice at the beginning of April. The Ussúri, in its upper waters, freezes at the end of November and breaks up at the beginning of April; in its lower part, at the Cossack village of Kazakévich, it sets on the 8 or 9 November and thaws on the 8 April. The Amúr at Khabaróvsk is frost-bound from the 10—11 November to the 11—12 April.

The flora of the Ussúri-Littoral region is very varied in its forms, including the greater part of the characteristic and peculiar plants of the Amúr territory.

The vegetation is strong and luxuriant.

The forest jungle, herbs and shrubs, at some places, attain an extraordinary height and density, containing forms, proper to the Amúr, north-eastern Asia, Kamchátka, North America and to the warmer climes of Japan and China. Species peculiar to the north and the south are here found mingled;

thus, fir trees hung with wild vine with small sour berries (Cissus humilifolia) and elm; cork-tree and walnut occur side by side with pine and cedar. Among the herbs, 80 species have been found in this region which do not occur in the Amúr territory; many of them are common to northern China, Japan and America.

Strictly local plants found in the Ussúri region form 17 species with an essentially southern character. They include leguminous plants, such as the climbing Glycine ussuriensis; of the exotic forms: the Pontederaiceae, a fine marsh plant, the Monochoria Korsakowii, the Eriocaulacea—the Ericaulon ussuriense; among the ferns, the subtropical Pleopeltis ussuriensis, and the famous zhen-shen or chinzeng (Japanese Nin-sí) Panax gienzeng, having an amber-coloured root containing starch and resembling a kind of carrot; it is considered by the Chinese as a panacea, capable of restoring lost strength and even of prolonging life.

On the northern side of the country, the flora changes; the luxuriant vegetation of the southern zone vanishes little by little, giving place to the local flora which is much poorer in species. Beyond the junction of the Goryn with the Amúr, northwards the scantiness of the northern flora becomes more and more apparent.

The fauna like the flora contains forms, which occur both in the north of Asia and in the southern countries of the continent. The following animals occur here on the same territory: sable (Mustella zibellina), elk (Cervus alces), tiger (Felis tigris), antilope (Antilopa crispa), Neral or Himalaya marten (Mustella flavigula) and ibis (Ibis nipon). With the exception of the spotted deer (Cervus axis), plentifully represented on the coast of the Sea of Japan and near the source of the Ussúri, a few rodents and the fish of the Japan Sea, the fauna of the Ussúri-Littoral country is similar to that of the Amúr country. But, upon comparing the two faunas, it becomes evident that the southern animals, inhabiting in great number the Ussúri basin, are met with more rarely within range of the Amúr, whereas some of the northern species decrease visibly within the Ussúri region, and some of them, as for instance the elk (Cervus alces), do not occur further south. As in the northern taigá, clouds of all kinds of insects—gnats, thrips, gadflies etc., mainly on the Ussúri and the Sungách, are a real plague to the country and present a serious impediment to colonisation.

The population of the Littoral territory is given by the census of 1897 as 223,336 (152,061 males, 71,275 females) including 50,722 town inhabitants (41,142 males, 9,580 females).

The number of inhabitants in the proper Ussúri-Littoral region (districts of Khabaróvsk, South-Ussúri and Ussúri) is estimated at 171,780 (123,216 males, 48,564 females). Thus, the territory appears to be very thinly settled, and in this respect holds one of the last places among the Siberian governments and territories; only the southern portion of the Ussúri-Littoral territory is better provided, surpassing the adjoining Amúr territory in the number of its inhabitants. The predominance of males over females affects unfavourably the economic life of the population, as also does the comparatively great percentage of the consuming town population. The ethnographical division of the Ussúri-Littoral region is very varied. Besides Russians, forming here 72 per cent of the total population, the country contains Koreans, Chinese, Japanese, Europeans, Americans and finally 10 per cent of natives, the wandering aborigenes of the region, belonging to the Tungús and Giliák tribes.

Prior to the annexation of the Amúr region to Russia, the Far East and its coast represented a desert, where one met wandering and half-wild natives and Chinese fugitives, pao-tui-tzy or manzas, who had fled from the severity of Chinese justice, and occupied themselves mainly with the rapacious exploitation of the natural treasures of the country and of its native inhabitants. The settlement of the Ussúri-Littoral region was started in 1855, when the first party of settlers was forwarded to the lower Amúr under the supervision of Prince M. S. Volkónsky.

In 1858, began the settlement of the lower part of the Ussúri. However, the colonisation of the Littoral territory progressed very slowly, chiefly on account of the difficulties attending the long journey from Russia. In 1882, the Council of the Empire resolved, with the authorisation of the Emperor,

Manzas hewing stones (phot. by Matskévich).

to make a trial during three years, and transport every year from Odéssa about 250 families at the cost of the Government, having assigned R. 315,000 per annum for this purpose. The emigration movement became more rapid and, during a period of three years, 37 settlements were established in the South-Ussúri region.

After this temporary trial, the emigration movement continued its progress, according to the rules of the 26 March, 1861, established for emigration to the Amúr and Littoral territories.

With a view to assist the settlers and to establish them without delay in the new localities, the Committee for the Construction of the Siberian Railway appointed R. 95,000 for the construction of warm barracks for the emigrants and despatched survey parties, putting them at the disposal of the South-Ussúri Emigration Board. For the assigned money, eleven warm barracks have been built at Vladivostók, two of which are provided with accomodation for the sick emigrants. Barracks were also established in Nikólsk, on the Suchán and in the settlement of Vladímir-Alexándrovsk. The survey parties, working within range of the railway, explored many sections of land from an agricultural standpoint in order to form new settlements and farms. The Ussúri valley, occupied by Cossack settlements, was also subjected to investigation in 1898, with a view to ascertain the possibility of

Korean workmen employed on the railway (phot. by Matskévich).

further colonisation. How far the emigration movement to the South-Ussúri region has increased within the last few years, is evidenced by the statistics for the emigrated families.

In 1895, 255 families (1,703 members) arrived by sea; in 1898, the steamers of the Volunteer Fleet transported 578 families (3,520 members) In 1898, the Committee for the Construction of the Siberian Railway conferred the right of emigration to the Amúr region on Ugro-Russians and Galicians living in America, providing them with land on the same terms as Russian settlers.

In order to satisfy the spiritual needs of the Russian population, 6 churches have been built in the South-Ussúri region from money given by the Ministry of the Interior, and tho following erections have been undertaken at the cost of the Emperor Alexander III fund: church schools in honour of Our Lady of Kazán in the settlement of Komaróvka, in commemoration of the happy deliverance of the Grand Duchess Xenia Aleksándrovna; in the settlement of Gráfskoe, a church of St. Theodor Tiron; in the settlement of Khvalynka, church of St. Andrew Pervozvánny; in the settlements of Kropovéts, Gródekovka and Aleksándrovsk, churches are in course of construction; in the first, it is consecrated to St. Nicholas the Miracle-worker, und in the second to the Assumption of the Holy Virgin.

The Russian population in the South-Ussúri region settled mainly in the valleys of the rivers Suifún, Lefú, Suchán and of Lake Khánka, along the right banks of the Ussúri, Sungách and near St. Olga's Bay.

Out of the whole contingent of the population, upwards of 11,000 belong to the Ussúri Cossack troops. All the troops, as regards administration, form a special Ussúri district divided into 3 sections; for civil administration, it is divided into stanítsas or villages. The extent of the territory occupied by the troops is not yet fixed: part of the Cossacks enjoy a temporary grant of 40 desiatins to each man, others possess teritorial rights over 8 versts from the settlements up and down the river, and 10 versts into the interior of the country. In time of war, the troops furnish a cavalry division, in time of peace a cavalry sótnia.

The tenure of the land and its exploitation by the peasants and other classes are subjected in the Littoral territory to the rules established on the 26 March, 1861, which are the same as those for the Amúr territory. Throughout this immense extent, private land tenure exists only in 70 households, belonging to individuals who availed themselves of the right to purchase their own lands.

The Koreans occupy the south-western part of the Ussúri region, adjoining Possiét Bay and the Manchurian frontier. The emigration of the Koreans began in 1863. They are all Russian subjects.

Chinese workmen on the railway (phot. by Matskévich).

The Chinese, so-called „manzas", live in desert and scarcely explored valleys, in the neighbourhood of the natives whom they exploit. Part of the manzas found a shelter in Vladivostók and Nikólsk, where they occupy themselves with petty market trade. This population lives apart from the Russians and remains subject to China.

The Golds live near the mouth of the Ussúri, part of them being scattered about the tributaries of the Goryn, Imán, Bikín and Daubí-khé.

The Olchís or Mangúns occupy the locality stretching down the Amúr to the town of Sofíisk.

The Giliáks inhabit the lower reaches of the Amúr and along the coast of the Okhótsk Sea, constituting the most numerous native tribe.

The Orochís are met with along the coast of the Strait of Tartary and on the upper waters of the right affluents of the Ussúri. All the wandering natives profess Shamanism.

The industries and occupations of the inhabitants in the Littoral territory and in the Ussúri-Líttoral region are as varied as the country itself, its climate and population.

Convicts at work on the Ussúri railway (phot. by Matskévich).

Agriculture is mainly carried on in the southern portion of the Littoral territory, where the fertile steppe plains offer a wide scope for the development of agriculture. As a consequence of the abundance of free land, the fallow system is adapted.

The following plants are cultivated: oats, (31.6 per cent), wheat, (28 per cent) yáritsa, (22.6 per cent) buckwheat, (8.4 per cent), millet (3.8 per cent), barley (3.2 per cent), winter rye (2.4 per cent). The heavy and chiefly clayey soil is tilled by ploughs; there are here many ploughs on the Sakk and Dir systems (with a seat) and American ploughs with one share; the fallow land is ploughed by a team of 3 to 4 pairs of oxen.

The firm of Kunst and Albers supplies the village population with agricultural implements and machinery; it operates in Vladivostók and sends fitters to the villages who shew how the machines are to be managed. There is no regular alternation of crops, and the land is sown with various grain as long as it has not lost its productive capacity. Yáritsa and wheat sown on fallow land yield, under favourable conditions, about 120 and more puds to the desiatin; on land previously used, the output of the same grain is 50 to 70 puds after a space of 4 or 5 years. After the land has been under cultivation for 7 to 10 years, it is abandoned for an indefinite time. The area cultivated in the Ussúri-Littoral region widens from year to year and now comprises upwards of 60,000 desiatins but as, besides the agricultural population, the region has to supply the commisseriat, the distilleries, the gold mines, the railway employees and workmen, the deficiency is imported from Manchuria, China, Japan, Odéssa and America. The quality of grain in the Ussúri region is not good The corn fields, especially yáritsa, are affected by the abundance of moisture and invaded by weeds. The grain contains too little starch. In general, the leguminous plants and millet thrive well in the Ussúri region.

Stock-raising has received a considerable development in this country. On the average, every peasant and Cossack household possesses 8 or 9 head of cattle and 2 or 3 sheep or other stock. Among the latter, are mostly swine, the raising of sheep meeting with but little success on account of the dampness of the swampy pastures. The quality of the cattle is still very inferior, the cattle is small and unproductive; the horse comes of the Transbaikál stock and is also not large. The demand for stronger and larger horses is satisfied by a supply of some thousand horses, which are annually driven from the Tomsk government. The territory is often ravaged by the Siberian pest and the plague brought from Manchuria, which naturally exert a bad effect on the economic condition of the population and impede the improvement of cattle by means of proper selection. Deer are reared mostly in the northern part of the territory.

The wandering natives tend immense herds of deer and dogs.

According to the statistics for the last few years, the territory numbered 190,618 deer and 33,300 dogs employed for driving.

Forestry in the South-Ussúri region, plentifully provided with land, increases every year. All the forests in this country are divided info three categories according to their importance:

1) forests situated on inaccessible ridges, apart from raftable rivers,

2) forests supplying the population with building materials for the purposes of their households,

3) forests exploited for sale.

The area occupied by the latter amounts approximately to 5,000,000 desiatins. In connexion with the increase of the population and the lowering of wages for the workmen, export of wood abroad might be expected in the future, In spite of great variety, the trees growing here are not of a good quality. Only the larch possesses solid timber, all the other species are easily attacked by decay, even the oak. The best material for joiner work is offered by cork or velvet tree.

Trapping and hunting play an important part in the Littoral territory. Besides whale, seal, and beaver fisheries which are leased by the Government (described in the review of the Okhótsk, Kamchátka and Bering Seas), a considerable part of the permanent, native and wandering population is devoted to trapping and hunting.

The animals hunted are:

The roebuck, (Cervus capreolus) migrating in spring in immense herds from Manchuria to the Amúr and Ussúri, and returning when the rivers cover with ice. The inhabitants profit by this movement and kill a great number of roebuck, supplying themselves with meat for the whole year. The skins are employed for overcoats called dokhá,costing from R. 10 to R 20. The tiger (Felis tigris). About 120 to 150 tigers are shot or poisoned annually in the Ussúri region. The skin of this animal is valued at R. 100 to R. 200. The bones, bile, heart, claws and other parts of the tiger are bought by the Chinese, who grind them into powder and administer them especially to the soldiers in order to keep up their pluck. The maral (Cervus elaphus). The young horns of this animal called „pánty" are purchased by the Chinese at a high rate. They are used by them for the preparation of various medicines, and are most valuable when developing a second branch. The price of the panty fluctuates between R. 100 and R. 600. The maral is hunted in the middle of May. The great value attached to the horns, and the possibility of getting them every spring from the same deer, suggested the idea of capturing living deer and keeping them in special fenced areas. The deer get accustomed to their confinement and even breed. Maral studs are met with in St. Olga's Bay and on the Suchán.

The white bear (Ursus arctos) and black bear (Ursus tibetanus), elk (Cervus alces), spotted deer (Cervus apis), boar (Sus scrofa ferus), antilope (Antilope crispa), muskdeer (Moschus moschiferous). The sable (Mustella zibellina) with the increase of the population, retires more and more from the inhabited centres. The cost of a sable fell varies from R. 5 to R. 20, according to the quality of the fur.

Fox (Canis vulpes). The dark-brown fox occurs very rarely and its skin is sold at the rate of R. 100 to R. 250 each. Squirrel (Sciurus vulgaris). The skin of the squirrel is of a superior quality and is sold at the local markets for 20 k. or 30 k. a piece.

The remaining fur animals are of less importance. Among the birds, geese, various forms of duck, pheasant, wood-cock, hazel-hen, and quail are important from an industrial point of view. The quantity of animals taken and their value cannot be stated, but it may be said that trapping yields approximately a profit of R. 200,000 to the population of the territory, exclusive of what is leased by the Government. With a view to maintain trapping, rules have been published, which fix the dates for hunting while prohibiting many ways of conducting it. Hunting has been forbidden in Crown forests for 12 years in order to increase the quantity of useful game.

Fishing which, in the northern portions of the territory, principally supplies both men and domestic animals with food, is here considerably developed. Among the various fish species occurring in the rivers and along the sea-coast, the foremost industrial importance belongs to the keta (Trutto lagocephalus). It is preserved according to various methods, being salted, dried and hung. The skin of this fish is used by the natives for sails, dress and boots. The flesh is extensively consumed by the population, and is even used as food for dogs aud sometimes for swine and cattle. The quantity of keta caught amounts to several million puds, which are consumed within the confines of the region. The want of knowledge on the preservation of fish and the scarceness of salt account for the small export of fish products abroad.

The fish taken for local use is not subject to any state duty, whereas for the fish exported abroad Russian subjects have to pay 5 k. per pud and foreigners 7 k. Foreign export is carried on in moderate proportions on the southern coast of the territory.

The sea-cabbage industry has been a long time pursued and is still, by the Chinese along the coast of the Sea of Japan and of the Strait of Tartary.

A considerable quantity of cabbage is forwarded to China. The conditions for the gathering of sea-cabbage by Russians and foreigners are the same as in the case of fishing.

Crayfish, crab and trepang are taken on the coast of the South Ussúri region mainly by the Chinese, who pay a certain duty to the Government for every sloop and boat. At present, trepang is caught with the help of divers.

Works and manufactories are still at a very low stage of development, employing not more than 2,000 workmen, with an annual production of only about R. 1,500,000. The most important factories are:

Piánkov's distillery; 7 steam flour-mills belonging to the military department and private persons; Buring's cast-iron and copper foundry with machinery workshop; Suvórov's Swedish matches manufactory.

The internal trade of the territory, with the exception of Vladivostok, consists mainly of the sale of imported goods; together with the increase of the population by way of colonisation, it develops from year to year, amounting to an annual turnover of R. 4,000,000 to R. 5,000,000. The trade carried on with the natives cannot be determined by figures, being subject to quite peculiar conditions: nearly all the natives are dependent on traders of some other nationality. The Golds and Orochís are entirely under the influence of the Chinese, who deliver them goods on trust, being guaranteed by the furs collected by the natives, which they take for half the price. The Tungús are in a like manner dependent on Yakút merchants.

The external trade is carried on by land with the adjoining countries of Manchuria and Korea, and by sea is gradually extending to all other countries.

The statistics for the barter between the Ussúri region, Manchuria and Korea, thanks te the immense extent of the boundary line and the insufficient number of barriers, give no idea of these operations but only on illustration of the trade by land. The total imports from Manchuria barely amount to R. 1,000,000 per annum, the chief article, forming upwards of 50 per cent, being cattle and horses; the remaining sum is obtained from raw animal products and partly from flour and grain. The imports from Korea are quite inconsiderable and at present scarcely exceed a value of R. 100,000 per annum, 70 per cent of this sum being yielded by cattle. The export of goods to Manchuria, mostly in transit through the Ussúri region, does not exceed the item of import; the greater part of the exported articles are made abroad and consist of various cotton goods of inferior quality. The export of goods to Korea by land is identical with the export to Manchuria and within recent years amounted on an average to R. 150,000 annually.

Sea trade, placed in close connexion with the development of commercial navigation, increases every year. The number of ships arriving at Vladivostók and Nikoláevsk is increasing from year to year and, upon the completion of the Great Siberian Railway, this increase will go on still more rapidly.

In proportion to the growing number of ships, the imports and exports undergo the same process. In 1891, the goods imported to the port of Vladivostók by 153 steamers amounted to 7,062,944 puds; in 1896,—12,155,753 puds were carried by 267 steamers. In 1894, a total of 2,165,183 puds were exported from the same port; in 1896, the total was 3,172,204 puds. The proportion of imported and exported goods according to nationalities was illustrated in 1896 by the following figures:

Russia	31.5	America	2.9
Germany	28.9	Denmark	1.0
Norway	17.0	Austria	0.9
England	10.6	Korea	0.2
Japan	6.6		

The goods brought to Vladivostók during the navigation of 1898 may be distributed in the following fashion with reference to countries: 46.3 per cent from Russian ports, 19.5 per cent from Chinese ports, 11.6 per cent from Japanese ports, 9.2 per cent from the ports of the Littoral territory and the Island of Sakhalin; 8.2 per cent came from English, 3.3 per cent from German, 1.4 per cent from American and 0.5 per cent from Korean ports.

The goods exported from Vladivostók during the season of navigation in 1896, mostly forwarded to Sakhalin, Nikoláevsk, Kamchátka and other ports of the Littoral region, formed 86.9 per cent, to the Chinese ports 11.4 per cent, to the Japanese ports, 2.0 per cent and 0.06 per cent to European Russia.

Among the goods imported to Vladivostók, the first place is taken by manufactures, forming 25 per cent, about 15 per cent are represented by grain and flour, and 10 per cent by other foods. Next come metal wares, sugar, spirit, metals etc. Foreign, principally German, goods hold an important place, although Russian articles acquire every year a greater predominance among the imported goods.

The part played in trade by the Russian ports and goods is demonstrated by the following figures drawn from the transactions of the Russian Trade and Industry Congress.

YEARS.	Russian goods imported into Vladivostók and Nikoláevsk.		Foreign goods imported to Vladivostók and Nikoláevsk.		TOTAL.	
	Puds.	Rubls.	Puds.	Rubls.	Puds.	Rubls.
1888	684,000	4,900,000	2,503,000	7,900,000	3,187,000	12,800,000
1889	881,000	5,040,000	2,125,000	5,350,000	3,046,000	12,800,000
1890	2,042,000	6,910,000	1,457,000	4,330,000	3,499,000	11,240,000
1891	3,623,000	11,770,000	1,348,000	3,960,000	4,971,000	15,730,000
1892	4,125,000	11,910,000	1,350,000	4,490,000	5,475,000	16,400,000
1893	3,786,000	11,200,000	2,253,000	7,700,000	6,139,000	18,900,000
1894	4,105,000	11,875,000	3,425,000	10,210,000	7,580,000	22,085,000

The comparison of the imports of Russian and foreign goods during a period of 7 years yields the following results:

	GOODS.	
	Russian.	Foreign.
Imports increased, in weight	6 fold	1.4 fold.
„ „ „ value	2.4 „	1.4 „
In 1888 goods, according to weight	21 per cent	79 p. c.
„ 1894 „ „ „ „	54 „ „	46 „ „
„ 1888 „ „ „ value	29 „ „	61 „ „
„ 1894 „ „ „ „	54 „ „	46 „ „

Among the articles which shew an increasing export, the chief place is taken by the produce of the whale and seal fisheries, and by various furs; next come sea-cabbage, trepang, maral horns or panty and timber.

The trade at Nikoláevsk consists mainly of goods in transit which, not being consumed on the spot, are forwarded up the Amúr; of these, tea forms about 35 per cent, sugar 11 per cent, metal wares and locomotives 10 per cent, manufactured articles 9 per cent, groceries etc. 8 per cent.

The opening of continuous steam communication by the Great Siberian Railway, in connexion with the construction of a commercial port in Vladivostók, meeting all the future requirements of commercial intercourse at the terminus of the great transit route, will serve to promote the progress of trade in this port, giving it a universal and powerful significance in the history of civilisation.

BIBLIOGRAPHY.

1) From Vladivostók to Urálsk, Guide to the Journey of His Imperial Highness the Tsesarévich. Publ. by the Centr. Stat. Commit. of the Minist. of the Int. St. Pbg. 1891. 2) The Emperor Nicholas II's Journey to the East in 1890 and 1891, by Prince Ukhtomsky, vol. III St. Pbg. 1897. 3) Siberian trade and industry calendars, edit. by Románov, in Tomsk, for 1896—1899. 4) Siberia and the Great Siberian Railway, publ. by the Min. of Fin. Board of Trade and Manufactures St. Pbg. 1896. 5) Geological explorations and investigations along the Siberian railway, pts. I—VI. St. Pbg. 1896—1897. Publ. by the Geological Committee. 6) Appendix to the Report of the Minister of Agriculture and State Domains presented to His Imperial Majesty, after his journey to Siberia in the autumn of 1895 St. Pbg. 1896. 7) The Littoral region at the Russian exhibition in Nízhni Nóvgorod, by Kriúkov. Moscow. 1896. 8) Geographical and Statistical Dictionary of the Amúr and Littoral territories, by Kiríllov, Blagovéshchensk. 1894. 9) Sketch of the chief waterways in the Amúr region, by Tímonov. St. Pbg. 1897. 10) Description of the gold and mining industries of the Amúr Littoral regions, by Bogoliúbsky. St. Pbg. 1895. 11) Industrial wealth of Kamchátka, Sakhalín and the Komandór Islands, by Sliúnin. St. Pbg. 1895. 12) The Far East, by Schreider. St. Pbg. 1897. 13) Works of the eastern sub-commission relative to the construction of the Ussúri and Amúr railways. 14) Review of the activity of the Ministry of Agriculture and State Domains for a period of 4 years. St. Pbg. 1898.

First class saloon.

The Ussuri Railway.

Construction of the line. — Its cost. — Description of the stations and localities traverse by the railway: town of Khabaróvsk. — Stations: Kórfovskaya. — Dukhovskáya. — Dormidóntova. — Viázemskaya. — Ilováiskaya. — Rozengártovka. — Bikín. — Bochárova. — Kurdiúmovka. — Imán. — Muraviów. — Amúrskaya. — Prokhásko. — Ussúri. — Shmákovka. — Sviágino. — Spásskaya. — Chernígovka. — Nevelskáya. — Nikólskoe. — Town of Nikólsk — Ussúrisk. — Stations: Razdólnoe. — Nadézhdinskaya. — Vladivostók. — Description of the town of Vladivostók. — Sea port.

THE plan to construct a railway line within the confines of the Ussúr region dates from the year 1875, when the local administration urged teh establishment of steam communication from the town of Vladivostók to Lake Khànka. The necessity of this route was pointed out by the Committee presided over by the Grand Duke Alexis Alexándrovich; however, the execution of this railway was postponed, from economic considerations. It was only in 1887 that the question of the surveys for the Ussúri railway was definitely settled, and an expedition under the direction of Engineer Ursáti despatched for conducting the surveys, which were made during 1887 and 1888.

The projected route of the South Ussúri section, from Vladivostók to the station of Gráfskaya, was approved of, and the execution of the line authorised, with the sanction of the Emperor, by the Committee of Ministers on the 15 February, 1891. The director of the survey expedition, Engineer Ursáti was appointed manager of the works, which were started without delay; when on the 19 May, 1891, the work and the construction of the station of Vladivostók was solemnly inaugurated by His Imperial Majesty, the present Emperor Nicholas II, then Heir Apparent to the throne, the earthworks and the permanent way were completed for a distance of $2^1/_2$ versts, which were then traversed by the first train.

From the beginning of 1893, the construction of the line was entrusted to Engineer Viázemsky, who completed the work. On the 3 February, the Committee of Ministers fixed the direction of the North-Ussúri line, and its construction was commenced On the 6 December, 1894, temporary traffic was opened from Vladivostók to Gràfskaya; on the 3 September, 1897, the first train arrived at Vladivostok from Khabaróvsk, having left it on the 1 September.

The South-Ussúri line (382 versts) was completed and open for regular traffic on the 1 February, 1896; the North Ussúri line (339 versts), on the 1 November. 1897.

The cost of construction of the North Ussúri line, inclusive of rolling stock, amounted to R. 22,458,879 and that of the South Ussúri section to R. 20,583,509, forming a total of R. 43,042,388, for a length of 721 versts. The number of stations and sidings along the line is 39.

1) Town of Khabaróvsk of the Littoral territory, centre of administration of the Amúr province under a Governor-General. (8,944 versts from St. Petersburg) (48° 28′ N. lat. 152° 47′ E. long.).

View of the town of Khabaróvsk.

In 1858, Count Muraviόv-Amúrsky, Governor-General of Eastern Siberia, founded a military settlement for the 13-th active battalion on the right elevated bank of the Amúr at its junction with the Ussúri, which received the name of Khabaróvka in honour of the gallant Cossack ataman Yerofei Khabaróv, who was one of the conquerors of the Amúr region in the XVII century.

Enjoying a favourable position at the junction of three important waterways, formed by the middle and lower Amúr and its tributary the Ussúri, the settlement grew rapidly. In 1880, it was transformed into a town and became the centre of administration in the Littoral territory, transferred from the town of Nikoláevsk on the Amúr; in 1884, when the Amúr region was detached from Eastern Siberia and subjected to a Governor-General, Khabaróvka became the residence of the latter. In 1883 Khabaróvka received the name of the town of Khabaróvsk.

It is picturesquely situated on two terraces and three elevations, approaching the banks of the Amúr and abruptly falling to the water's edge. These elevations are intersected by the unimportant rivers Pliúsninka and Cherdymovka falling into the Amúr and dividing the town into three parts or hills: the Artillery, Central and Military hills. The highest is the first, rising to an elevation of 20 sazhens above the level of the Amúr, next come the Central hill 17 sazhens high and the Military hill of 13 sazhens. The entire elevation, on which Khabaróvsk stands, consists of clayey slate and clay which, at some places, is covered with a grey argillaceous soil and with a slight layer of fertile blackearth. The nature of the soil accounts for the difficulties attending communication over the steep hills and explains the presence of wooden stairs connecting at certain points the upper and lower parts of the town. The town is planned so as to have a principal street at the middle of each part, stretching along the top of the hill and crossed by transverse streets running through two or three hills and connected by means of bridges spanning the streams Pliúsninka and Cherdymovka.

The principal street, following the Central hill, has received the name of Muravióv-Amúrsky, in honour of Count Muravióv-Amúrsky.

The breadth of the streets is about 15 sazhens; they are unpaved and only at a few places have wooden side-paths. The town consists mainly of small wooden houses over 1,000 in number; some of the buildings are of Chinese architecture. There are only about 40 stone buildings, which mostly belong to Crown institutions, and 3 churches of which 2 are of wood and one is a stone cathedral in honour of the Assumption of the Holy Virgin. Many of the houses are completely hidden by trees which, together with the picturesque situation of the town, gives it a pleasant appearance. The traveller, approaching the town by steamer, obtains an exceptionally fine view from the deck.

Special attention is claimed by the stone cathedral. On the left, are the Governor-General's house, the military club, the museum of the geographical society, the town garden; on the right rise various Government buildings

Monument to Count Muravióv-Amúrsky (phot. by Matskévich).

surrounded by groves of trees and a pavillion with stairs descending to the waters of the Amúr. There is also the market place and the Chinese town with its temple.

The town garden, situated on an elevated promontory commanding a wide view over the Amúr and the environs, contains a monument to Count Muravióv-Amúrsky, founder of the town.

The inauguration of the monument coincided with the memorable visit to Khabaróvsk of His Imperial Majesty, the present Emperor Nicholas II.

It was erected after the design of the Academician Opekúshin and inaugurated in the presence of His Imperial Majesty on the 30 May 1891.

A high stone pedestal (5 sazhens 1 arshin) hewn in syenite and sandstone, representing a truncated pyramid, supports the artistically worked bronze figure of the famous conqueror of the Amúr. On each side of the base are attached bronze plates, on which are engraved the dates of important events, and the names of Count Muraviów-Amúrsky's associates in the annexation of the country and those of the members of the Amúr expedition. Close to the monument, was erected out of the remainder of the memorial fund, a home for veteran Cossacks, who supply the guard.

The number of inhabitants is 14,971 (11,730 males, 3,241 females). The Korean and Chinese population amount to about 4,024 (3,854 males, 170 females).

Triumphal arch in Khabaróvsk in commemoration of the journey of His Imperial Majesty in 1891.

The characteristic feature of the population is the considerable predominance of males over females (27.9 women to 100 men) explained by the quartering of troops and the influx of a purely male Chinese population.

Representing the chief centre of administration in the Amur region, the town of Khabaróvsk contains the civil establishments of various departments, and all the central institutions belonging to the military district.

With the gradual development of commercial business, now amounting to about R. 2,000,000 per annum, the town revenue has also increased and fluctuates between R. 70,000 and R. 80,000 annually. The town bank has been open since the year 1899.

The local works and manufacturing industry have not as yet received any expansion: the town line includes only the following factories: a beer-brewery, a pig-iron foundry, a steam-mill, a tannery, a fur dressing manufactory, an establishment for the preparation of mineral water, and 15 brick-kilns. Moreover, red wine manufactured by Khlébnikov is for sale. The wine is obtained from the wild vine growing in abundance in the valley of the Ussúri; it is of inferior quality, without any flavour and costs from 70 k. to R. 1 a bottle. At the present time, the Japanese are serious competitors in the preparation of mineral waters, furnishing also natural Japanese water of a very superior quality.

The conditions of life in Khabaróvsk are not attractive, on account of the absence of comfortable dwellings, and the expensiveness of some products and of the most necessary articles. Lodgings with 4 or 5 rooms are charged R. 300 to R. 700 per annum; imported colonial goods are also sold at a high rate and only fish is very cheap.

Educational institutions: Preparatory School of the Siberian Cadet Corps. Technical railway school. Gymnasium for girls with 4 classes and a boarding school. Town school for boys with 2 classes. The Alexis school for girls. with 2 classes, created in commemoration of the Grand Duke Alexis Alexandrovich's visit to Khabaróvsk. Town parish school. Church parish school. Private work and trade school and children's home.

Being the centre af all the administrative institutions answering the requirements of so vast a country, the town of Khabaróvsk also represents the centre of the intellectual forces, contributing to develop spiritual and intellectual life in the Eastern borderland.

At present, the following societies are located in Khabaróvsk.

Town of Khabaróvsk. Governor-General's house.

The Amúr branch of the Imperial Russian Geographical Society. Committee for public reading. Ladies' Relief Society. Red Cross Society, with sisters of mercy. Volunteer fire brigade. Amateur Photography Society Amateur Art Society. Relief Society for emigrants.

The Amúr branch of the Imperial Russian Geographical Society was instituted in 1894, its activity being chiefly marked by the organisation of a museum for natural science and history, and of the Nicholas public library. The museum was founded by the late Baron Korff, Governor-General of the Amúr region, and supplied by him with the first ethnographical collections. The museum building is three-storeyed and was erected in 1897 out of R. 100,000 given by the Government and in voluntary donations. The ethnographical and zoological collections comprise 20,000 articles. The library of this division is mainly composed of presentation books, of which many are the liberal gift of His Imperial Majesty, the present Emperor Nicholas II. The library was opened on the 6 December, 1894, and received the name of the Nicholas library in honour of His Majesty. Recently it was enriched by a valuable donation from the Grand Duchess Alexandra Iósifovna, who presented it with the books of the late Grand Duke Constantine Nikoláevich. Thus, the total number of books included in the library amounts to 40,000 volumes, of which a catalogue is now being made. The duplicate copies are sent to the branches of the Amúr section and partly to Seúl, where a Russian library has been opened.

The reports of the members are published in „Memoirs" periodically issued.

The committee for public readings, which started its activity in 1894 on the initiative of S. M. Dukhovskói, former Governor-General of the Amúr region, has also founded school libraries in the distant centres of population in the Ussúri region.

In the autumn of 1899, the first exhibition of agriculture and industry was organised at Khabaróvsk. At its close, on the 16 September, the Amúr Governor-General distributed the following prizes: 4 gold medals, 53 of silver, 71 of bronze and 514 testimonials.

There is a military and public club for the benefit of the inhabitants. An official weekly journal „The Amúr gazette", strictly devoted to local interests, is published in Khabaróvsk.

The town contains 2 hotels, with rooms from R. 1 to R. 2 a day. The hackney-coach tariff is R. 1 an hour, 50 k. the drive. The local firms:

Bogdánov-manufactured, colonial, haberdashery, grocery and other goods. Bayankévich, wine stores. Ikner-iron foundry. Liubben-brewery. Lucht-chemicals and mineral water. Kunst and Albers-wholesale colonial, iron and other wares. M. Piánkov-grocery and wine-cellar. Pliúsnin-manufactured, colonial, haberdashery, grocery and other goods. Tifontái-fur, Chinese, Japanese and other goods. Khlébnikov Brothers-grocery, wine - cellar containing wine of their own manufacture. Chúrin and Co manufactures, haberdashery, drugs, iron and grocery goods. Emeri-wholesale and retail trade in various goods, depot of agricultural implements. Electrotechnical department.

Town of Khabaróvsk. House of Department of the Ussúri railway.

Khabaróvsk. II class station. Buffet (716 v. from Vladivostók). Is situated near the town, the number of buildings increasing in the direction of the station. The passenger station commands a beautiful view of the town set off by the background of the Amúr and the Khekhtsírsk ridge. At the station, all the buildings are of wood: passenger station, II houses for the accomodation of employees, engine-house, hospital, goods platform and storehouse. Moreover, a special group of buildings is formed by the erections meeting the needs of the military department: barracks for a company of the Ussúri railway battalion employed in the exploitation of the Ussúri line, and a feeding station for the troops forwarded from the railway along the Amúr and back again. The buildings used by the battalion comprise barracks for 100 active soldiers, exempted from service on the railway, a dining room, bakeries, a small house for the officers, baths and other buildings. The feeding station consists of a dining room accomodating 500 people, a kitchen and the commandant's house with adjoining buildings. Gardens have been planted in front of the station and near the houses. A church in honour of Christ's Nativity has been erected at the station out of the Emperor Alexander III fund. Within a distance of about a verst from the station, a fine two-storeyed building containing a technical railway school has been built in one

Landing place on the Amúr (phot. by Matskévich).

of the new quarters of the town, according to the same plan as that of Krasnoyársk. A wooden house for the inspector and other officials is attached to the school.

The plateau on which the station stands is 30 sazhens above the low-water mark on the Amúr. A branch line, 5 versts in length, runs from the station to the landing place on the Amúr. This branch skirts the town on the north, winding its course along a slope, and approaches the river at a place where it is protected from the pressure of the tide by the cliff, on which stands the monument to Count Muraviόv-Amúrsky.

The landing place presents a wide embankment, rising to a height of 0.60 sazhens above the high water mark and of 4 sazhens above low-water. It is connected with the town by a carriage road made at the same time as the railway.

At a short distance, is the old port serving in winter for the anchorage of steamers plying on the Amúr and belonging to a steamship company.

Someway up the river stands a water-tank with a reservoir, supplying the station with water. The aqueduct is 2½ versts long and traversing the town reaches the Military Hill.

From the station of Khabaróvsk, the line runs southwards at a distance of 2 to 4 versts from the bank of the Ussúri.

2) Siding of **Krásnaya Réchka** (Red River 697 v.). From here a branch-line, 6½ versts in length, reaches the landing place on the Ussúri, both having been established by the East Chinese Railway.

Leaving the siding, the line retires from the Ussúri, and running through a continuous taigá composed mainly of cedar trees, with some specimens attaining 2 arshins diameter at the root, proceeds to the south, winding its course amidst a series of elevations. On its way to the Kórfovskaya station, the line crosses the Khekzir ridge, which is a spur of the main mountain ridge, the Sikhoté Alín. This rídge is of a volcanic nature and consists of separate conical elevations. Skirting one of them, the line passes along the valleys of the Krásnaya and Chírka, tributaries of the Ussúri.

3) **Kórfovskaya,** V class station (680 v.). The Cossack settlement of Korsákov lies on the Ussúri within 18 versts of the station, and was founded in 1858 (pop. 180).

Between this station and the siding of Krúglikov, the line continues through the taigá, which here receives an admixture of larch; at the 671 verst, it crosses the Chírka by a bridge of 20 sazhens.

4) Siding of **Krúglikov** (668 v.). The village of Kazakévich lies 34 versts hence, founded in 1858 and named in honour of Kazakévich, member of the Amúr expedition (pop. 300). The village contains two wooden churches consecrated to our Lady of Kazán and St. Nicholas the Miracle-Worker, school, post and telegraph office, and village board.

From here, the line runs across a swampy country intersected by many rivers.

5) **Dukhovskáya.** V class station (653 v.). From this station to the siding of Khor, the line assumes a south-western direction, approaching the Ussúri and within 3 versts of the station crosses the river Kiyá by a wooden bridge with a span of 120 sazhens.

Bridge over the Kiyá (phot. by Matskévich).

The river Kiyá, Chinese Tsinián-khé, right affluent of the Ussúri, rises in the branches of the Sikhoté Alín. It has a total course of 150 versts and a breadth varying from 15 to 25 sazhens; the river is scantly provided with water, but is practicable for rafts. Since the construction of the railway, numerous settlements have been established along its banks among which the Sérgievo-Mikháilovsk possesses already a church and is thriving well, thanks to the good contingent of settlers and the high qualities of the soil.

The settlement of Pereyaslávl, extending down the Kiyá, looks forward to future prosperity. The locality adjoining the right bank of the Kiyá, is most favourable for cultivation. The vegetation is represented by oak groves scattered along the high bank, alternating with open spaces, affording beautiful hay employed to supply Khabaróvsk, also fit for cultivation.

Within 27 v. of Dukhovskáya, the Cossack settlement of Cherniáevsk is situated on the left bank of the Kiyá; it was founded in 1870 (pop. 50).

6) Siding of **Khor** (645 v.). Between Khor and the station of Dormidóntovka, the line still runs southwest approaching the Ussúri. At the 638 verst, it crosses the river Khor by an iron bridge measuring 160 sazhens, and further the Podkhoriónok by a wooden bridge of 80 sazhens.

The river Khor is one of the largest and full flowing right tributaries of the Ussúri, rising in the slopes of the Sikhoté Alín. The length of its course

Briage over the Khor (phot. by Matskévich).

is about 350 versts, its breadth from 50 to 60 sazhens; it has a depth of $1\frac{1}{2}$ to 13 feet and falls into the Ussúri by three branches. The bridge over the Khor, with 4 spans of 40 sazhens each, is the most important construction on the Ussúri railway, which was attended with many difficulties presented by the turbulent stream, subjected to frequent and unexpected overflows. An inscription is engraved on one of the piers shewing that the construction of the bridge extended over the period between the 10 January and the 14 May in 1897, exclusive of the preliminary work. During the construction of the bridge, a considerable settlement was temporarily established there, part of which became permanent.

The contractor Krylóv, who was entrusted with the masonry work, erected a church, thus creating a new village. The remaining part of the Khor valley is inhabited by Chinese living in a few huts, and by about 100 Orochén families.

The Cossack settlement of the Three Saints is situated at a distance of 23 versts on the Ussúri and was founded at the beginning of the sixties (pop. 30). The valleys of the rivers Kiyá, Khor and Podkhoriónok are parted by low and sloping watersheds. During high-water time, part of the water of the Khor flows over into the Kiyá at the point called Tabón.

7) **Dormidóntovka.** V class station (627 v.). Is situated within 10 versts of the Ussúri and 11 versts from the Cossack settlement of Kúkelev, named in honour of B. K. Kúkel, one of Count Muravióv-Amúrsky's fellow workers, who later on was chief of the staff in the East Siberian military district. The settlement was founded in 1859, and stands on the Ussúri (pop. 250). There is a chapel in honour of the Martyr Saint Catherine.

From the station of Dormidóntovka to the siding of Krásitsk, the line follows a south-western direction, and after having crossed the Podkhoriónok by a wooden bridge, enters into a more broken country covered with woods alternating with meadows.

8) Siding of **Krásitsk** (614). The post station and the former Cossack village of Budogósskaya lie at a distance of 13 versts; the latter wes founded in 1859 and named in honour of Budogósski, Colonel of the General Staff and member of the Amúr expedition.

Between this siding and the station of Viázemskaya, the line proceeds through a country of a like character, but marked by a more frequent admixture of foliage trees, such as aspen, birch and others; it continues in the same south-western direction, approaching closer to the Ussúri.

9) **Viázemskaya.** III class. Buffet (596 v.). Is the most important station on 'the North-Ussúri section; it is provided with a depot for locomotives and small workshops. Here also are situated barracks for a company of the railway battalion of the same dimensions as at Khabaróvsk. A wooden church in honour of St. Nicholas the Miracle-Worker and of the Holy Virgin Mary is in process of construction at the station, at the cost of the Emperor Alexander III fund. A new settlement has arisen on the extensive and open plain lying close to the station. Within 14 versts of the station, the Cossack village of Veniukóvo is situated on the right bank of the Ussúri; it was founded in 1859 and named in honour of Second Captain Veniukóv, who was

Station of Viázemskaya (phot. by Matskévich).

then exploring the Ussúri (pop. 352, 193 males, 159 females). The village possesses a wooden church of Christ's Nativity, a school and a post and telegraph office. Frøm the station of Viázemskaya, the line continues to the south-west gradually approaching the Ussúri; near the station of Ilováiskaya, it runs through its valley at a distance of only 3 versts from the river.

10) **Ilováiskaya.** V class station (575 v.). This station received its name in honour of one of the victims of the hard life led by the surveyors and constructors of the railway, the young and energetic Engineer Ilováisky, who having been obliged to live in a damp earthen hut, fell ill of fever and died. His grave is in the churchyard of Veniukóvo.

The landing place of Shchebenchíkha is situated on the Ussúri, 3 versts from the station.

From this point, the country changes suddenly. An impenetrable taiga, formed by all the representatives of the varied arboreal flora, covers the hilly surface cut by deep ravines. Side by side with the „cedar“ occur larch, alder, maple, willow, elm, cork-tree, acacia, walnut and other species, thickly covered with wild vine and surrounded by shrubs of wild-rose, jasmine etc.

11) Siding of **Gédike** (568 v.). The Cossack settlement of Kedróvsky founded in 1859 is situated on the Ussúri at a distance of 10 versts (pop. 180).

Cutting at the 562 verst (phot. by Matskévich).

Between the sidings of Gédike and Snárski, the line passes through a more broken and hilly locality, requiring many bridges and culverts and crosses its highest point, the watershed of the rivers Shchebenchíkha and Kamenúkha, lying 63.65 sazhens above sea-level. The line, always running south-west, winds its course along the mountain slope. At the summit of the second important spur of the Sikhoté Alín, numerous cuttings had to be made in the rocks; the location of the roadway at their bottom and at the top of embankments was attended with the greatest difficulties ever encountered on the North-Ussúri line. A picturesque panorama of distant mountain ranges appears over the thick vegetation bordering the railway track.

12) Siding of **Snársky** (547 v.). Within a few versts of the siding, the line leaves the intricacies of the mountainous locality and runs through a more level district amidst aspen and birch groves, which by its character recalls the central zone of European Russia. Upon approaching the station of Rosengártovka, the line crosses the marshy valley of the river Tópkaya and the border of the Ussúri valley.

The Cossack settlements of Sheremétev and Vídny (pop. 200 and 80) established in 1858, are situated on the right bank of the Ussúri at a distance of 15 versts. The former contains a chapel of St. Innocent of Irkútsk.

13) **Rozengártovka.** V class station (537 v.). The Cossack settlement of Lonchakóvsk lies within 9 versts on the right lofty bank of the Ussúri; it was founded in 1859 (pop. 476; 236 males, 240 females). There are two chapels, one of the Archangel Michael in the village, and the other of the Holy Prophet Elias, standing on a cone 4 versts above this place. The occupations of

the inhabitants besides agriculture consist in the supplying of steamers with timber and in fishing.

Within two versts of the station, the line crosses the river Birá by an iron bridge with an opening of 25 sazhens, and retiring from the Ussúri ascends to the third summit which has nearly the same height as the Khekhtsírsk ridge. This summit is not cut by so many ravines and is less thickly clothed with taiga.

14) Siding of **Beitsúkha** (516 v.). Hence the line continues through the swampy valley of the Beitsúkha running along its left bank to the station of Bikín.

The village of Kozlóvskaya is within 16 versts, established on the right bank of the Ussúri in 1859 (pop. 589). It possesses a wooden church of St. Nicholas the Miracle-Worker, a school, village board, grain stores and a post and telegraph office. The inhabitants are engaged in agriculture, trapping, fishing and supplying the steamers with timber.

Station of Bikín (phot. by Matskévich).

15) **Bikín.** IV class station. Buffet (498 v.). Near the station, which during the construction of the railway presented one of the most lively centres of activity, arose a temporary settlement, part of which became permanent. On the opposite side of the Bikín, freshly emigrated Orenbúrg Cossacks established a village, and now most successfully occupy themselves with the cultivation of the land. The banks of the Bikín present a locality, which within the confines of the Ussúri region is particularly favourable for colonisation as possessing a raftable and even navigable river (the steamers plied for a distance of 40 versts upwards from the mouth during the construction of the railway), without having the inconveniences of the other large affluents of the Ussúri, which several times during the summer overflow the valleys to a considerable extent. The Bikín rolls its waves between terraces inaccessible to the water, lying at the foot of steep mountains surrounding the valley.

Leaving the station, the line crosses the Bikín at the 495 verst by an iron bridge with two spans and a total length of 80 sazhens.

The river Bikín, right tributary to the Ussúri, rises in the main range of the Sikhoté Alín, in proximity to the Sea of Japan. The length of its course is 450 versts, its breadth varies from 60 to 80 sazhens, the average depth from 5 to 9 feet. The mountains bordering the upper waters of the river are clothed with luxuriant forests of foliage trees and conifera, offering shelter to sable, which attract the natives of the Ussúri and the Amúr. Deposits of coal occur along the left bank.

The settlement of Vasílievsk is situated 15 versts from the station on the right bank of the Bikín at its junction with the Ussúri; it was founded in 1862 (pop. 180). The Pokróvsk settlement stands on the other side of the Bikín (pop. 70).

Bridge over the Bikín (phot. by Matskévich).

After having crossed this river, the line runs along the left bank, following a southern direction to the 467 verst. This is one of the most picturesque parts of the line, offering an alpine scenery. At times rocky cliffs come up close to the river and the line creeps along a cornice cut in the mountain. The cuttings made in basalt rocks seem to be protected by columns of cyclopean construction. Wide expanses lying amidst the cliffs are covered with a most various vegetation, shading numerous Chinese huts. The river is enlivened by the small boats of the Golds and other natives, moving swiftly on the water's surface.

The saw-mill of the merchant Briner is situated here. Amid the wild and beautiful scenery, it presents comparatively a certain animation.

16) Siding of **Alchán** (477 v.). Hence to the station of Bochárova, the line runs in nearly a straight line south-west along the bank of the Bikín and continuing by the swampy valley of the Khemkhéz.

17) **Bochárova.** V class station (464 v.). The Cossack settlement of Zarúbinsk is situated at a distance of 20 versts, on the river Ussúri; it was founded in 1862.

The line proceeds in the same south-western direction, leaving on the right the Zarúbinsk mountain group, and crosses the swampy valleys of the affluents of the Ussúri.

18) Siding of **Chórny** (436 v.). The Nizhnemikháilovsk settlement is within 14 versts, on the bank of the Ussúri (pop. 70). The line keeps to the former direction approaching the Ussúri through the valley of this river.

19) **Kurdiúmovka.** V class station (420 v.). A fresh settlement has been established near the station by the Orenbúrg Cossacks. The post station of Krutobérezhnaya is situated 12 versts hence, on the low bank of the Ussúri, where a village was founded in 1859, but after an inundation its inhabitants passed over to the adjoining villages.

The line proceeds south-west along the Ussúri valley, first retiring from the river and then approaching it again; at the siding of Eberhardt the distance between the line and the river is reduced to somewhat over a verst.

20) Siding of **Eberhardt** (399 v.). The settlement of Kniázhevsk lies at a distance of 6 versts on the Ussúri and was founded in 1862 (pop. 90). Within 2 versts of the railway, emigrated Don Cossacks established the hamlet of Sálsky. The line continues along the valley of the Ussúri, running almost at the same distance from the latter, and at the 389 verst crosses its tributary the Imán by an iron bridge of 120 sazhens. At the time of high water, the Imán submerges an extent of over 5 versts, its current being very unsteady on account of the soft bottom. The construction of the railway through this valley was attended with the greatest technical difficulties, and required solid strengthening and water-averting erections, particularly on the left part of the river.

Bridge over the Imán (phot. by Matskévich).

The river Imán or Imá, Chinesé Imá-khé, which is a right tributary of the Ussúri, rises in the Sikhoté Alín and joins the Ussúri 4 versts below the settlement of Gráfsky. Its total length is about 375 versts, with a breadth of 60 to 70 sazhens, which at the mouth widens to 120 sazhens. The average depth is 6 feet. The upper waters of this river flow along a narrow valley fringed by mountains, whereas the central and lower reaches pass through an open plain endowed with a good soil fit for cultivation. The valley and the surrounding mountains contain many superior and varied tree species. Here also occur remains of former settlements, which were little Korean fortified towns. The station of Imán is situated 3 versts from the bridge.

21) **Imán.** V class station (387 v.). Close by is the Gráfsky or Count's settlement, standing on the left bank of the Imán. It was founded in 1858 and received its name in honour of Count Muraviów-Amúrsky. In 1895 to 1897, previous to the opening of traffic on the North-Ussúri line, the station of Imán was the terminus of the South Ussúri line, which here joined the Ussúri and Amúr water systems.

A branch, 1½ versts in length, connects the station with the landing stage on the Imán. This stage served as a príncipal base during the construction of the North-Ussúri section, whence materials and produce were forwarded to Khabaróvsk and deposited at the landing-places along the Ussúri for further conveyance along the line. Rails, rolling stock and other railway appliances are loaded here and forwarded by sea through Vladivostók to supply the demand of the Transbaikál railway.

Landing stage on the Imán (phot. by Matskévich).

This little known place, which prior to 1894 was quite uninhabited, became at once the centre of great animation. Within the space of a few months, arose a settlement with hotels and shops, inns and a row of houses, to which a Chinese village forms a suburb bearing the name of Chifú from that of the town whence come the greater number of Chinese workmen.

This point was selected for a dockyard for the construction of steamers, barges and dredgers, which are erected by the Ministry of Ways of Communication as well as by private concerns and individuals; it is at present occupied with building steamers for the East Chinese Railway. If the rail communication somewhat diminished the importance of Imán as a transferring point, the new settlement, owing to its favourable situation, may still look forward to develop into a town, partly on account of the troops located in the neighbouring settlement of Gráfsky, wbich is extending in the direction of Imán. At the station of Imán are situated the 3-d company's yard of the Ussúri railway battalion, and a feeding station for passing troops.

22) **Muravióv-Amúrsky.** V class station. Buffet (377 v.).

A settlement arose gradually near the station during the construction of the railway. In 1896, fresh emigrants represented by Orenbúrg Cossacks were added to it. A wooden church of John the Baptist is being built here out of the Emperor Alexander III fund.

Within 6 versts, the settlement of Krasnoyársk stands on the Ussúri, containing a church, a post and telegraph office and school (pop. 100).

Between the station of Muraviόv-Amúrsky and that of Prokhásko, the line runs south along the valley of the Ussúri through a locality covered with scanty woods of foliage trees, and at the 362 verst passes by the siding of Bussé.

23) **Prokhásko.** V class station (350 v.). Proceeding in the same direction along the lofty plateau of the Ussúri valley, the line crosses this river at the 328 verst by an iron bridge 120 sazhens long and reaches the left

low bank of the river. At a distance of a verst from the bridge, is the Ussúri station.

General view of the Muraviów-Amúrsky station (phot. by Matskévich).

24) **Ussúri.** IV class station, buffet (327 ver.). In 1895 — 1897, emigrants established fresh settlements near the station on both sides of the Ussúri.

From the Ussúri station, the line assumes a south-western course, retaining the same direction to the station of Nikólskaya, and enters the vast steppe plain constituting the so-called Prikhankóisk depression.

It is supposed that, at a remote date, the level of Lake Khanká was much higher than at present, and that consequently this depressiòn formed the

Bridge over the Ussúri.

bottom of the lake. At times during a rainy year, the whole locality gets transformed into an immense water-basin, as the rain-water retires but slowly from the surface of the slightly inclined slopes, being retained by the clayey subsoil. This fact was observed in 1895. On account of the frequent stagnation of the water, the whole surface of the plain is dotted with hillocks, thus recalling a swamp in spring and autumn, which only in the summer is clothed by a luxuriant herbaceous vegetation. The blooming meadows look very enticing but, on attempting to pass them, one is utterly exhausted after a space of a few sazhens by jumping from one hillock to the other. It is proposed to drain this plain, which will then be converted into a cultivable area, being endowed with a most fertile soil.

25) **Shmákovka.** V class station (293 v.). On the hilly elevation bordering the Ussúri valley, the first monastery of the region, consecrated to the Holy Trinity, was founded in 1895. It now attracts a great number of pilgrims. New buildings arise around and the lands allotted to its use are being cultivated. In the vicinity, carbonic and chalybeate springs have been discovered at the foot of the Medvézhia Sópka, which are to be exploited in the future. At a distance of 25 versts from the station, the village of Uspénskoe is situated on the Ussúri (pop. 688, 366 males and 322 females). From the station of Shmákovka to that of Sviágino, the line follows the swampy plain.

26) **Sviágino.** V class station (256 v.). The large village of Zénkovka lies close to the station (pop. 890; 484 males and 406 females).

From Sviágino the line winds its course along the broken branches of the elevations separating the valley of Lake Khanká from that of the Daubikhé river.

27) **Spásskaya.** IV class station, buffet (224 v.). The village of the same name, founded in 1886, stands near, on the left bank of the Santá-Khezá (pop. 1086, 599 males and 487 females). All the inhabitants are exclusively engaged in agriculture. The village contains a wooden church, a church parish school and 6 trading establishments.

From the Spásskaya station, the general character of the locality adjoining the railway changes visibly. Cultivated fields are scarcely seen throughout the section lying between Khabaróvsk and Spásskaya. The villages occuring are still in process of organisation and present rare oases in the neighbourhood of stations.

Leaving the station of Spásskaya, the line enters a thickly settled country with wide cultivated areas, meadows and roads running in every

Bridge over the Lefú.

direction, the horizon dotted with villages built after the Little Russian style, characterised by white-washed huts.

The South Ussúri region, from Vladivostók to Spásskaya, was considerably settled before the construction of the railway, but within recent years the population has increased and the cultivated areas have widened.

From the station of Spásskaya to that of Chernígovka, the line runs along the slopes surrounding Lake Khanká and further on continues through the valley of the Lefú, which falls into the lake.

28) **Chernígovka.** V class station (185 v.). The village of the same name is situated near the station, on the upper waters of the Chernígovka. It was created in 1884, (pop. 1299, 694 males and 605 females). The village contains a wooden church of the Holy Virgin's Nativity, a public school, the residence of the police officer, the local board and 10 shops. Close to the station stands a large steam-mill of the Commissariat, supplying flour to the Amúr military district.

Hence the line proceeds by the valley of the Lefú, and at the 156 verst passes over this river by an iron bridge measuring 38 sazhens.

29) **Nevelskáya.** V class station (147 v.) The line rises here to the watershed of Lake Khanká basin and the Pacific Ocean (Amúr Gulf), and reaching the highest point of the South Ussúri section (63 sazhens above sea

Station of Nevelskáya.

level) descends to the valley of the Suifún and through the siding of Dubíninsk, reaches the Nikólsk station, situated in the valley of the Suifún.

Descending the watershed, the line assumes a tortuous course and forms a zigzag on which the rails are seen at two and three places at the same time.

30) Siding of **Dubíninsk.** (120 v.) Possesses a certain importance as a point connected by the post-road with Anúchino and with settlements scattered in the valley of Daubi-khé, where several regiments are quartered.

31) **Nikólskoe.** III class station. Buffet. (102 v.) Situated in a steppe-like plain, within a verst of the town, the principal station of the Ussúri railway presents a separate town, which will grow still further when the adjoining plots of land are leased by the officials.

A wooden church of St. Nicholas the Miracle-Worker is attached to the station, it was erected by voluntary donations and out of R. 4,000 from the Emperor Alexander III fund. Among the station buildings, special attention is due to those containing large workshops, standing to the left of the entrance to the station. The main building contains the machinery and fitting shops, a forge and iron and copper foundries with all requisite appliances. A stone building standing apart contain a shop for the preparation of timber. The waggon framing shop is housed in a wooden building. The total area occupied by the interior of the workshops covers 1100 square sazhens. On account of the great distance at which this region lies, and the importance

General view of the station of Nikólskoe.

attached to Nikólsk as the junction of the East Chinese Railway, an extensive activity lies in store for these workshops, which may possibly develop into machinery works. Hard by stands a stone warehouse in which is stored the material for the Ussúri Railway. On the opposite end of the plateau

Station of Nikólskoe.

occupied by the station, to the right, stands a stone engine-house containing 6 locomotives, and the wooden building of the hospital; on the left rises an edifice containing the company's yard for the Ussúri railway batalion, built according to the same style as that of Khabaróvsk and at the stations of Viázemskaya and Imán. In the centre of the station, stands a stone water-tank; the houses of the railway men, surrounded by little gardens, are situated on both sides of the line. The station has a small platform for goods with a warehouse and a weigh-bridge. The railway department maintains a school with two classes for the employees' children; the number of pupils exceeds 60, and the opening of a boarding school is projected. Town of Nikólsk—Ussúrisk. The site of the town, which to the year 1898 was a village bearing the same name, presents a vast grassy plain watered by tho Suifún; in time long past it offered shelter to various nations. This vast plain witnessed the peaceful prosperity of its inhabitants as well as the conflicts which occurred between the warring tribes of the East.

A legend says that here was formerly situated the kingdom of Bokhái, to which testify a few ruins preserved to the present day. After a period of several centuries, the rule of the Manchús took the place of the vanished kingdom, but was in turn destroyed by the hordes of Chingiz-Khan. At present this plain offers a centre attracting the stream of Russian emigration.

In 1866, emigrants from the Astrakhan and Vorónezh governments, forming 19 families, established the Nikólsk settlement within 2 versts of the mouth of the Supútenka at its junction with the Rákovka. In 1868, when the Khunkhús were driven from the Askóld Island situated in proximity to Vladivostók, where they were engaged in the rapacious exploitation of gold, they took vengeance by burning the Nikólsk settlement. When order was restored, the inhabitants of Nikólskoe returned again to their former dwellings, and from that time the settlement has received every year a contingent of fresh emigrants.

After a space of two years, in 1870, the church of St. Nicholas the Miracle-Worker was built and inaugurated in the new settlement. Abundantly provided with land adapted for agriculture, allotted for use in the proportion of

Bridge over the Supútenka at the 99 verst.

27,999 desiatins of arable and 3,586 desiatins waste land, and being situated at the junction of the principal roads of the South-Ussúri region, the settlement of Nikólsk soon acquired a foremost importance in the country. In the eighties, it became an important military centre, which greatly affected the course of village life; a soldier's village was added to the settlement, besides a great number of military buildings and houses for married officers and officials.

The importance of Nikólskoe increased still more upon the construction of the Ussúri railway, and particularly of the East Chinese line, which branching off from the station of Nikólskoe runs for a distance of 108½ versts towards the Chinese frontier, reaching it at the station of Pogranichnaya.

Counting the numerous foreign element formed by the working class attracted to Nikólsk by employment on the railway, the number of its inhabitants amounted to 8,982 (7,007 males and 1,975 females) according to the census of 1897. Since the village has been transformed into a town, its population has risen to 15,000. The town line includes three churches and a stone cathedral in course of construction. A wooden church was erected near the station out of the Emperor Alexander III fund and inaugurated on the 10 April, 1899, in honour of St. Nicholas the Miracle-Worker. The town contains

Suifún Cliffs.

a school and a library attached to the police office, founded at the cost of His Imperial Highness, the Grand Duke Alexis Alexándrovich, who visited Nikólskoe in 1873 on his way from Vladivostók. The first printing office belonging to Mrs. Missiuroi was opened in 1899. The publication of a newspaper containing advertisements and town gossip is contemplated.

Representing the centre of administration of the entire South-Ussúri district, Nikólsk is the residence of numerous military organs; there are the residence of the commandant of the troops of the South-Ussúri military division, the staff of the military division, 1 East-Siberian rifle brigade, 3, 4 and 5 rifle batalions, 2 batteries of the East-Siberian rifle brigade, 1 mortar battery of the East-Siberian artillery brigade, Ussúri cavalry brigade, and first Transbaikál Cossack regiment. The troops dispose of a library and a military club.

Manufactures and industry in Nikólsk grow rapidly, being represented by some important firms from Vladivostók such as: Chúrin, Kunst and Albers and Langelitier. The Chinese own upwards of 120 little shops. The annual commercial operations amount to a total of R. 3,000,000. Trade in grain is particularly lively, cattle and agricultural produce being also offered for sale at the daily markets. Among the industrial establishments, special attention is due to the steam flour-mill of Lindholm situated near the town, to the soap-boilery of Monákhov, and the distillery of Piánkov. The town has two hotels, 18 inns, 4 hot-bath houses and 7 bakeries.

On the 22 May, 1891, His Imperial Majesty the present Emperor Nicholas II, on his way from the Far East, arrived at the village of Nikólskoe, having been conveyed with horses from Vladivostók for a distance of 100 versts. Here His Imperial Majesty held a review of the troops assembled at the place of muster, among which the 1 East Siberian rifle battalion was included. From here His Majesty continued his journey with horses to Kámen-Rybolóv, a landing stage for steamers on Lake Khanká, and on tho 24 May went down the tortuous course of the Sungách on the Amúr Company's steamer „Ingodá“, proceeding further by the Ussúri to the Amúr.

From the station of Nikólskoe and further through the siding of Baránovsk to the Razdólnaya station and to the siding of Kiparísovo, the line follows the valley of the Suifún, running southwards. Upon reaching the 83 and 84 verst, the line, for a distance of a verst, passes along the abrupt and rocky bank of the Suifún through a locality bearing the name of Suifún or Bear (Medvézhie) Cliffs. This is one of the most picturesque places on the South-Ussúri railway.

32) Siding of **Baránovsk.** (81 v.). The village of Trékhovka is situated in the vicinity on the bank of the Suifún (pop. 125).

33) **Razdólnoe.** V class station (66 v.) The village of the same name (pop. 355, 182 males and 173 females) lies near the station on the left bank of the Suifún, which from here is navigable to where it falls into the sea. This village was founded as a military post in 1865; later on, peasants emigrated from various governments of European Russia settled there. It contains a church of Our Lady of Kazán and a church parish school. The

Station of Razdólnoe.

inhabitants are engaged in agriculture. There are also barracks of the 1 East-Siberian rifle batalion, residence of the police officer, post station, landing place, post and telegraph office, and several shops. The barracks of the Ussúri dragoon regiment are situated in the environs. From this village a post-road leads to Possiét Bay.

34) **Siding of Kiparísovo** (54 v.). From here the line turns east, leaving the valley of the Suifún and rising to the elevation separating the Suifún from the Uglovói Bay. This altitude is thickly clothed with wood, consisting mainly of oak-trees. This is one of the principal points whence the railway is supplied with timber. The coast land with its rocky cliffs offers but few expanses fit for cultivation, and beyond the station of Razdólnoe, the country assumes again a more desert and inhospitable character.

35) **Nadézhdinskaya.** V class station. Buffet (42 v.). Following a south-eastern direction, the line reaches Uglovói Bay, and turning to the south continues along the coast of the sea, skirting Uglovói and further on the Amúr Gulf.

36) **Khilkóvo** (19 v.). This station, situated on the peninsula of Muravióv—Amúrsky, received its name in honour of Prince M. I. Khilkóv, Minister of Ways of Communication. The post station lying in the vicinity, the first from Vladivostók, was the point to which on the 22 May, 1891, military and naval officers, as well as representatives of the town of Vladivostók accompanied the Imperial Traveller, the present Emperor Nicholas II, wishing Him a happy journey across Great Siberia.

In the locality adjoining the railway, deposits of coal have been discovered, which have been exploited by Engineer Górlov and also by order of the railway administration, the coal being employed as fuel for the engines.

37) **Sedánka** (16 v.). The picturesque valley of the Sedánka is the summer resort of the inhabitants of Vladivostók. Here is situated the match manufactory of Suvórov.

38) **Siding of Pérvaya Réchka** (5 v.). According to the previous plan, a large station was to have been built at this point, serving as terminus to the Ussúri railway, with a branch connecting it with the town and the landing stage. Later on, the branch line was changed into a main track, and the terminus station built in the town itself; a steep grade of.015 was adopted throughout this section, over which the train is hauled by an additional engine, awaiting its arrival on a side-track. A water-tank, wanting in Vladivostók, supplies the locomotives with water, thus forming in a certain sense part of the Vladivostók station.

The siding is connected with the seashore by means of a suspension railway supported on piles, serving for small trucks conveying naphtha to Lindholm's reservoirs.

In the vicinity are disposed the camp of the Vladivostók garrison (1 battalion and sapper company) and a small settlement called Convicts' Hamlet, inhabited by exile settlers who here obtained their freedom after the completion of their term of punishment.

From here the line, running along the seashore, crosses the principal street of Vladivostók, the Svetlánskaya and reaches the western bank of the Bay of the Golden Horn, on which stands the station of Vladivostók at an elevation of 1½ sazhen above sea-level.

39) **Vladivostók.** II class station. Buffet. The construction of the passenger station built of local grey sandstone, was inaugurated on the 19 May, 1891, in the presence of His Imperial Majesty, the present Emperor Nicholas II, then Heir Apparent to the throne. On a high natural terrace rising above the road-way, stands a stone two-storeyed building housing the Railway Department. Houses for the employees, for the accomodation of workmen and soldiers of the railway battalion, are situated next to the passenger station.

Opposite the station is a stone quay, 220 sazhens in length, for the use of sea-going ships. At the south-western end of the quay is the landing—stage of the Volunteer Fleet, on the station platform continuing towards Cape Egersheld to the west, a landing-place and a quay is being built for the use of the East-Chinese Railway.

Town of Vladivostók (43° 6′ N. lat., 101° 35′ E. long., 9,922 versts from Petersburg) Chinese, Khai-Shen-Véi which means „Trepang Bay". Being situated in the same latitude as Vladikavkáz, more southerly than Sevastópol and

Venice and only 1/4° farther north than Florence and Nice, Vladivostók by its climate recalls the localities of Pskov and Révél, having an annual mean temperature of 4°.6 C. The mean maximum is 30°.6, the minimum – 25.6° C.

The town is situated on the southern side of the Peninsula of Muraviόv-Amúrsky, at an elevation of 487 feet above sea-level, extending along the sinuous and steep mountain-sides, bounding the northern and western coast of the Bay of the Golden Horn and the eastern coast of the Amúr Gulf. The Bay of the Golden Horn follows a western direction from the East Bosphorus Strait, parting Russian Island from the continent, but within 2 versts of its entrance it describes a curve and turns south-east. From the side of the Amúr Gulf, the bay is sheltered from the straits and from Russian Island by the Shkott Peninsula and by that of Goldόbin. These peninsulas seem to form a kind of gate. The length of the bay from Cape Goldóbin to its extremity is 6 versts, the greatest breadth is about a verst and the depth from 4 to 15 sazhens. Considering its extent, suitable bottom, sufficient depth and convenient outlet, this bay forms a harbour skilfully created by nature. Throughout the area occupied by the anchored ships, the harbour is frostbound from the 15 December to the 4 April, viz. for 110 days. The plan to employ an icebreaker for the maintenance of an ice-free channel for the ships entering the port was first executed in the winter of 1893 and 1894 and virtually proved that navigation could be kept up in Vladivostók during the whole winter.

View of Vladivostók.

Stretching along the bay shore for a distance of over 7 versts, Vladivostók, seen from the sea-side, looks like a large port-town. The topography of the town is very peculiar, the streets provided with side-walks made of planks run in every direction; there are 6 open places and 45 streets, the number of buildings exceeds 2,000 among which 1,269 of wood and 251 of stone belong to private individuals; the engineering and naval departments own 505 wooden, 52 stone and 20 iron buildings. The real estate of the town amounts to a value of R. 9,485,100. There are two Orthodox churches; a stone cathedral of fine architecture of the Assumption and a church of the Siberian Ship Company. The orthodox churches not being sufficiently spacious and the town not disposing of the capital needed for the construction of another cathedral in Vladivostók, capable of meeting the requirements of the orthodox faith in this distant borderland of the Empire, His Imperial Majesty authoris-

Passenger station in Vladivostók. Its construction was inaugurated in the presence of H. I. M., the present Emperor Nicholas II, on the 19 May, 1891.

ed the collection of money on the 15 August for this purpose in all the churches of the Empire, during 3 years commencing from 1900. The first assistance to this great Christian work was given by the Emperor himself, who made a donation of R. 5,000.

There are Catholic and Lutheran churches and Chinese, Japanese and Korean temples.

Several beacons are situated near the town: that of Lariónov, on the north-western extremity of Russian Island; of Skryplévsky, on the island of the same name, at the entrance of the Eastern Bosphorus from Ussúri Bay; and of Askóld standing on the southern cape of Askóld Island in Ussúri Bay, at the entrance of the river Suifún.

The coast of Peter the Great Gulf was known to Europeans from 1852, when the French Government sent out the corvet „Capricieuse" to explore the coast of the Sea of Japan. In 1854, the frigate „Pallada", whose voyage was described by Goncharóv, explored the shores of Korea to Cape Gámov under the command of Admiral Putiátin. In 1856, one of the ships of the Anglo-French squadron, the „Winchester" during her search for the Russian fleet which had left Petropávlovsk, discovered the Bay of the Golden Horn and gave it the name of Port May.

The actual occupation of the Bay of Vladivostók by the Russians was effected on the 20 May, 1860, when on the war-sloop „Manchúr", commanded by Captain Schefner, arrived a crew of 40 soldiers and 3 companies of the 4 battalion of the line under the command of Ensign Komaróv. These first emigrants erected a barrack and houses for the officers and thus founded the military post of Vladivostók.

The first church, that of the Assumption of the Holy Virgin, was founded here in June, 1861, and consecrated on the 1 April, 1862. In 1865, Vladivostók ranked as port and was made a porto-franco.

In 1864, it was appointed as residence for the direction of the southern harbours of the coast of Peter the Great's Gulf; the port workshops were then established, serving as a basis for the creation of the machinery works and of the premises used for the mounting of the ships belonging to the Siberian fleet. Within the same year, 157 voluntary settlers arrived from Nikoláevsk. In 1868, Vladivostók was connected by telegraph with Khabaróvsk, and in 1871 with Nagasaki and Shanghai by the international sub marine cable of the Danish Company.

From the year 1872, when the chief port of the Pacific Ocean was transferred from Nikoláevsk on the Amúr to Vladivostók, the population of the new port increased rapidly, extending at the same time its commercial operations. In 1873, His Imperial Highness, the Grand Duke Alexis Alexándrovich visited Vladivostók on the frigate „Svetlána" which, together with the corvets „Vítiaz" and „Bogatyr", was included in the expedition of Adjutant-General Possiét. In commemoration of this event, the principal street of the town received the name of Svetlánskaya.

In 1876, the port was subjected to the general municipal law of 1870, and in 1880 Vladivostók was elevated to the rank of a town; from this year direct communication with Odessa was established by means of the steamers of the Volunteer Fleet. Within the period from 1882 to 1887, a floating dock, transported in pieces, was erected here. In 1887, the Grand Duke Alexander Mikháilovich visited Vladivostók on one of the vessels of the Pacific Fleet, the corvet „Rynda", on which he sailed during two years under the command of the present Admiral Avelán, then post captain. From the year 1888, Vladivostók was included in the Littoral territory, becoming the centre of the local administration; the post of commandant of the port was created at the same time. A third-class fortress, defending the town from the land side and from the sea, was consecrated on the 30 August, 1889.

The events which took place in 1891 essentially raised the importance of Vladivostók, contributed to the development of its trade and enlarged the operations of the port. On the morning of the 11 May, His Imperial Highness the Grand Duke Tsesarévich, the present Emperor Nicholas II, arrived at Vladivostók on the frigate „Pámiat Azóva".

Opposite the landing—stage of the Admiralty, on the spot where His Imperial Majesty first trod his native soil after his long voyage, a triumphal arch was erected, which received the name of Nicholas Gate. The image of St. Nicholas the Miracle-worker of Mirlicia, with the memorable date of the 11 May, 1891, traced underneath, was placed in the large semiarch turned towards the road-stead.

During the sojourn of His Imperial Highness the Tsesarévich, was laid the first stone of the monument to Admiral Gennádi Ivánovich Nevelskói, the first promoter of Russian dominion in the Far East. On one of the sides of the pyramid are engraved the memorable words of the Emperor Nicholas I referring to the exploit of Novelskói: „Where the Russian flag is once hoisted it never must be lowered". The monument was inaugurated in September of 1897.

On the 18 May 1891, His Imperial Highness the Tsesarévich solemnly inaugurated the construction of a dry-dock named Tsesarévitch Nicholas dock, completed in 1897.

Site of the inauguration of the Ussúri railway by His Imperial Majesty in May, 1891.

Two floating docks (one on the Clark system), accomodating 2-d class cruisers, have been ready for use from 1889.

The rescript given to the Tsesarévich on the 17 March, 1891, by the Emperor, with reference to the execution of a railway on the Russian coast of the Pacific was an universally important event which like a ray of light reached the Far East. On the 19 May, 1891, divine service was held within 2½ versts of the town, on account of the inauguration of the railway's construction, in the presence of the Emperor. After divine service, the Tsesarévich himself filled with earth a wheelbarrow prepared for this purpose and emptied it on the embankment of the future Ussúri railway.

Further, His Imperial Highness played an active part in the inauguration of the passenger station, laying the first stone for this building. In commemoration of this fact, an image of St. Nicholas the Miracle-Worker of Mirlicia was placed on the spot where His Highness laid the first stone.

On the day on which was inaugurated in Vladivostók the construction of the Siberian railway, the 19 May, the Imperial rescript given to the Tsesarévich was published in St. Petersburg in order that all the true subjects of the Tsar might join in their hearts in the memorable and historical solemnity performed by the wish of the Emperor in the distant borderland of the Empire.

On the 21 May, His Imperial Highness the Tsesarévich quitted Vladivostók, proceeding further across Siberia.

The population of Vladivostók is ever on the increase and within the last ten years it has doubled.

According to the data of 1890, the number of inhabitants was 14,466, including 9,365 Russians and 4,193 Chinese; by the census of 1897, it increased to 28,933 (24,433 males; 4,500 females). The predominating element is the military class, numbering about 12,000, next come foreign subjects, the Chinese, Koreans and Japanese forming 12,577 (11,621 males, 956 females).

During the summer, when the navigation season is at its highest, the town population is further increased, mainly by the stream of foreign Chinese workmen from Chifú and of Japanese traders and artisans.

The town owns 6,407 desiatins of arable land and 207 desiatins waste. The annual revenue exceeds R. 300,000. The municipality has raised the question of supplying the town with electric lighting, and conducting water-pipes from the valley of the Pérvaya Réchka. Certain houses, as for example the firms of Kunst and Albers and Chúrin, are already provided with electric light.

.Educational institutions: the Eastern Institute, opened on the 21 October, 1899, ranks among the first-class establishments aiming at providing its pupils with special education, training them for employment in the administrative and commercial institutions of East-Asiatic Russia.

The chief purpose is the practical knowledge of the Chinese, Japanese, Korean, Mongolian and Manchu languages. A college for 30 bursars is to be attached to the institute. Classical Gymnasium for boys with a course of Chinese language. Gymnasium for girls. Town 3 class school for boys. Port-trading school. Alexander navigation classes. Two elementary schools of the local charitable society. Sunday school of the local Society for public reading. Private school kept by Mrs. Kuster.

Moreover, in commemoration of their Imperial Majesties' Coronation, the town council assigned R. 10,000 for the establishment of a trades school, under the engagement to pay a certain sum annually for the maintenance of this school. The merchant Shevelióv gave R. 2,000 for the same object.

In commemoration of the above mentioned event, the local Chinese gave R. 10,000 for the establishment of a Russo-Chinese school.

Scientific and charitable institutions: Society for the Investigation of the Amúr Region. Doctor's Society of the South Ussúri region. Branch of the Imperial Russian Technical Society. Public Reading Society. Vladivostók Relief Society. Branch of the Red Cross Society. Shooting Society. Society for the assistance of Vladivostók gymnasium pupils sent up to the higher educational institutions of European Russia and Siberia.

The Society for the study of the Amúr region, under the patronage of His Imperial Higness the Grand Duke Alexander Mikháilovich, started its operations in 1884, and erected a stone museum including mainly ethnographical collections referring to the natives of the Far East. A library, containing valuable gifts from Veniukóv and Bussè is attached to the museum. The first plantations in the botanic garden kept by the Society were made in 1896.

The works of the local members are printed in the periodically published Memoirs of the Society. This Society disposes of a prize of R. 3,000 given by the late F. F. Bussè's sister in memory of her brother, for the best work regarding the country.

A Pasteur station was attached in 1899 to the Doctor's Society of the South Ussúri region.

There is no proper theatre in Vladivostók, and strolling actors play in merchant Galétski's private hall at the Hotel of tbe Golden Horn, and at times in the Naval or Clerks' Club. In 1900, a theatre hall with a stage will be arranged in the Pacific Ocean Hotel. An amateur singing, musical and even gymnastic society sometimes manifests its activity; the German colony under the leadership of the trading firm of Kunst and Albers organised a special choral society known under the name of the „Lyre". This society is not accessible to the public; it disposes of rooms lighted by electricity.

The town is provided with three clubs. Military Club in the building of the Engineering Department; Naval Club, more accessible to the public, where evening parties, concerts and theatricals take place; and a clerks' club with evening parties, concerts etc.

Three periodicals are published in Vladivostók: the „Vladivostók" founded in 1883, organ of the naval department (weekly): The orders of the commandant of the port, articles and notes relative to naval questions are inserted in the naval part of the gazette. The subscription is R. 11.50 k. annually. „The Far East" founded in 1892, thrice a week. Subscription R. 10 per annum. The „Advertiser" issued from 1899.

There are three hotels; the best is the „Pacific Ocean", then comes the „Golden Horn" and the „European Hotel"; furnished rooms are kept by Gamartelli. The hackney coach tariff is 80 k. an hour, and 20 k. the drive within the limits of one part of the town, and 40 k. beyond it. In the night the tariff is doubled.

Trade and manufactures grow rapidly; at present, the following factories are at work in the town of Vladivostók and its environs:

	Number of factories.	Output in rubls.
Brick-kilns	8	250,000
Beton manufactory	1	20,000
Machinery works (Buring)	1	50,000
Tannery	1	40,000
Butter	1	40,000
Rope-yard	1	5,000
Match manufactory (Suvórov)	1	120,000
Saw-mills	3	30,000
Beer-brewery	1	10,000
Establishment for the preparation of mineral water	2	10,000
Machinery works	3	40,000
Breweries (manza beer)	4	80,000
	27	695,000

The Chineese beer tastes of corn and is very sweet; it is drunk hot or cold and costs 15 k. a bottle.

Printing offices of Remézov, Panov and Sushchínski.

Photographic (studios) the best belongs to Matskévich, next comes that of Múkhin and of the Japanese Koïto.

According to its position, Vladivostók presents the best and most important centre of trade throughout the Russian coast in the Far East. With the construction of the railway, its importance as regards commerce is ever on the increase. With the exception of a few important Russian and foreign European firms, almost the whole trade was in the hands of the Chinese; but, since the completion of steam communication, the number of Russian firms has augmented considerably.

The progress of the commercial relations of Vladivostók with the other ports may be illustrated by comparing the figures drawn from the data concerning the arrival of steamers in the Vladivostók roadstead.

Number of steamers arrived during the navigation season of 1894:

Russian steamers, 53 with a tonnage of 56,919
Foreign „ 93 „ „ 90,463

During the navigation of 1896:

Russian steamers, 72 with a tonnage of 76,854
Foreign „ 181 „ „ 118,874

In conjunction with the rising figures of arriving vessels, the number of ports with which Vladivostók entered into commercial relations also increased considerably. Besides the ports of European Russia, China, Japan and Korea, goods are now transported by Russian steamers from such distant points as Glasgow, Colombo, Port-Said, Singapur and Hongkong.

A greater animation also is noticed in the intercourse of Vladivostók with the seabords of China and Korea, carried on by means of Chinese junks and barges, their number amounting to 1,500.

The chief articles of import are: rice, flour, wheaten flour, butter, salt, cloth, cotton and silk stuffs, boots, china, vegetables, fresh and preserved ruit, as well as coal, agricultural implements and cartridges.

The principal articles of export to foreign countries are sea-cabbage, zhen-shen root, mushrooms found on oak stumps, lichens growing on corn, trepang etc., forwarded to China, and quite useless to the Russian population.

For the promotion of industrial activity, a branch of the State Bank was established in Vladivostók in 1894; from 1898 there is also a branch of the Russo-Chinese Bank. The Town Bank and the Yarosláv-Kostromá Land Bank operate likewise in the town.

In 1899, the Emperor authorised throughout the Empire a subscription for the erection of a monument to the late Admiral Vasili Stepánovich Zävóiko, the eminent administrator of the Amúr region and hero of the defence of the Peter and Paul Port, attacked in 1854 by the Anglo-French fleet.

The principal firms of Vladivostók are:

Briner, firm of S. S. Briner, Kuznetsóv and Company, unloading of ships, freight transport, with an association of Korean workmen for the discharge of cargoes, possesses boats and a steam cutter. Important timber trade. Saw mills in the Littoral territory and Korea.

Languelitier, wholesale in various goods. Wine and spirit stores. Lindholm, firm of Lindholm and Co. wholesale and retail trade in flour goods and petroleum. Brick and cement manufactory.

Commercial house of Kunst and Albers, wholesale and retail trade in various Russian and foreign goods. Spirit and wine stores. Petroleum, flour and butter. Banker's office.

Semiónov and Co., obtaining sea-cabbage and fish in the Sea of Japan. Commercial house of Chúrin and Co., wholesale and retail trade in manufactures, drugs, iron, copper, perfumery, tobacco, grocery and other goods.

Banker's office: Sheveliöv and Co., navigation with regular postal and freight service between China, Japan, Korea, the Island of Sakhalín and the posts of the Tartary Strait. Stores and sale of gunpowder. Commission agent. Commercial house of Brothers Borodín, sale of various goods.

Zhunlévich, „Littoral tannery of Zhunlévich and Co.“ Piánkov, commercial house, firm of M. Piánkov and Brothers. Wholesale and retail trade in wine and spirit, distillery. Shulyngin, wholesale and retail trade in tea, sugar and flour. Cable and rope-yard.

Aurenhammer, company under the name of Hautmann and Aurenhammer, trade in metal wares and American goods.

Bürgen, machinery works. Zenzinov, bookseller. Suvórov, match manufactory of Suvórov, Sushínsky and Co., printers & lithographers and publishers. Agents of Russian insurance societies and transport offices: Andresi, of the Russian Fire Insurance Society, Datton, of the Anchor Insurance Society. Romérsky, of the St. Petersburg Insurance Society. Languelitier, of the Russia Insurance Society. Merkúlov of the Northern Insurance Society. Skóblin of the Russian Freight Transport and Insurance Society.

Sheveliόv, of the Nadézhda Society. Spengler of the First Russian Insurance Society.

Steamship agents: Teréntiev, of the Volunteer Fleet. Terami, of the „Nipon-Iuzen-Kaisha". Vasíliev of the Amúr Steamship Company. Sigiur, of the Japanese Steamship Company „O'une".

From Vladivostók, the sea-route by the waters of the Pacific Ocean lies open to the steamers of the Volunteer Fleet and to those belonging to the East Chinese railway, and likewise to steamers of foreign countries, which from year to year enlarge their commercial relations with the ports of the Far East.

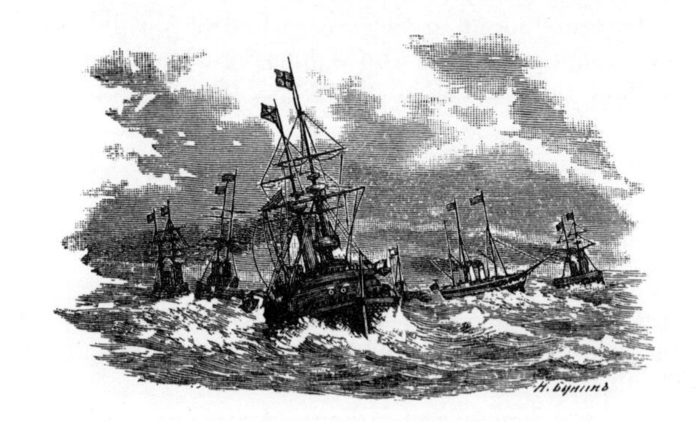

Великая Сибирская ж. д. БАЙКАЛЪ-ВЛАДИВОСТОКЪ.

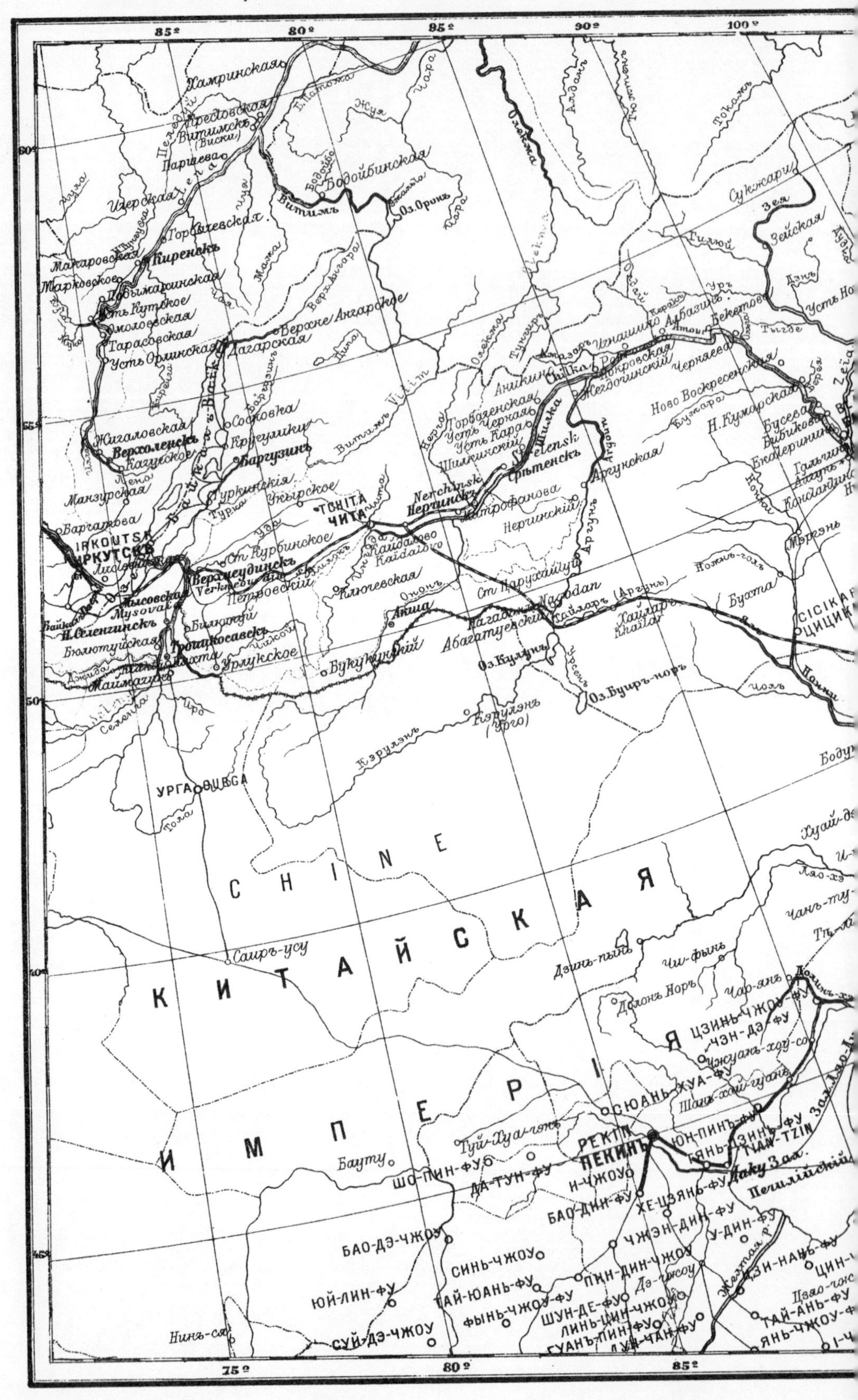

Grand Chemin de fer Transsibérien BAÏKAL-VLADIVOSTOK.

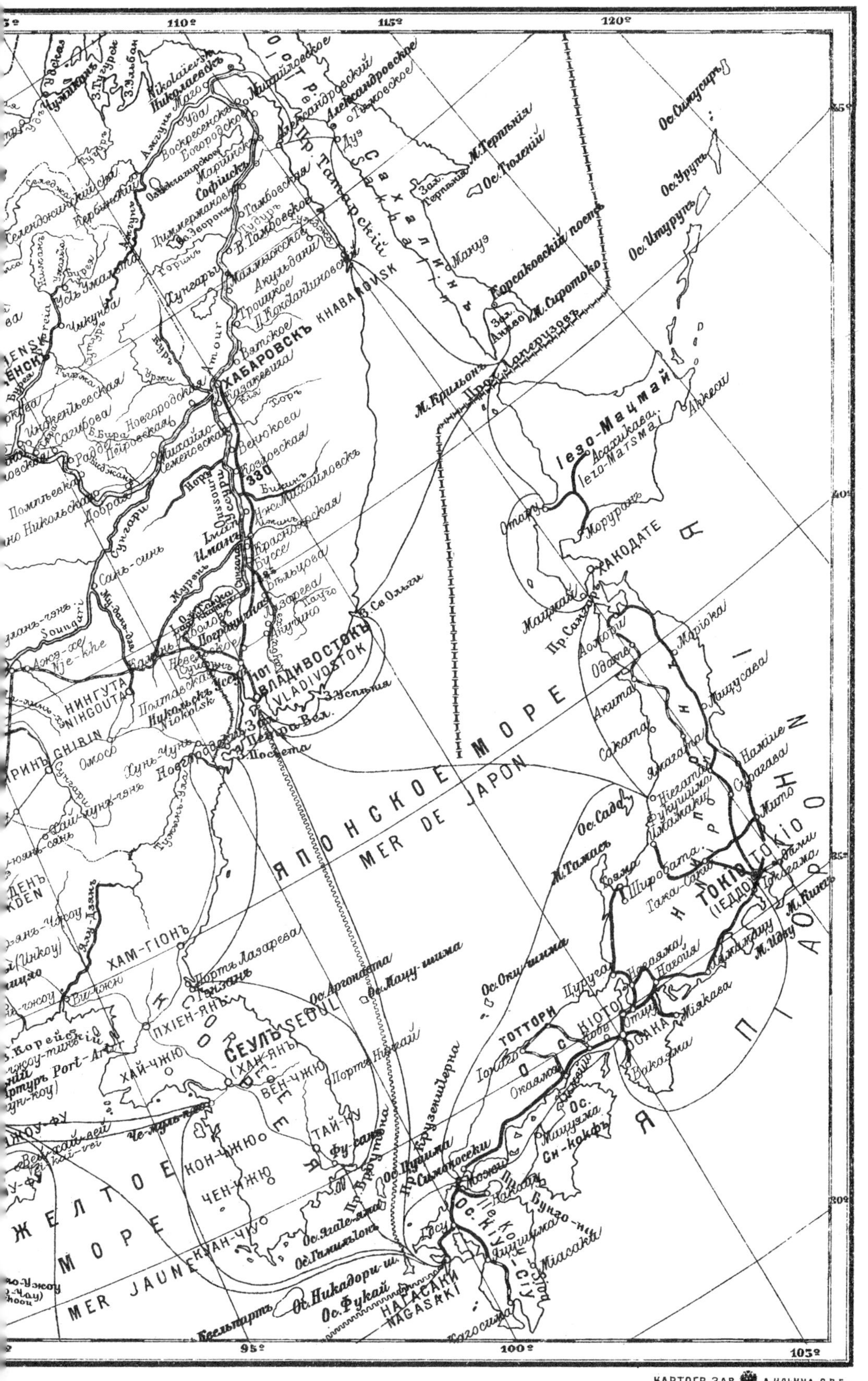

КАРТОГР. ЗАВ. А. ИЛЬИНА, С.П.Б

The Island of Sakhalín.

The economic and commercial relations of the Island of Sakhalín with the Ussúri region. — Geographical position and superficial configuration of the island.—Geological structure and mineral wealth. Coal pits, naphtha springs, auriferous areas, amber. — Hydrography. — Climate.— Flora.— Fauna. — Historical past.—Administration. — Population. — Convict prisons and penitential colonies. — Industry. — Agriculture. — Cattle-raising. —Trapping.—Fishing.—Sea-cabbage industry.— Fishing for crayfish, crabs and trepang. — Prison workshops. — Handicraft productions. — Trade. — Ways of communication. — Future importance of the island — **Bibliography.**

THE Littoral territory and particularly the Ussúri region are in close economic and commercial connexion with the Island of Sakhalín, lying off the continent. Upon the opening of direct steam traffic on the Great Siberian main line, the economic interests of both territories will be still more closely united, both tending towards the further development of trade and industrial exchange at the terminus of the great transit road.

The Island of Sakhalín stretches in a long and narrow line along the eastern shore of the Littoral territory (between 45° 54′ and 54° 24′ N. lat. and III° 21′ and 118° 29′ E. long. from St. Petersburg), separated from it by the northern part of the Sea of Japan (Tartary or Nevelskói Strait). Its southern portion, assuming the shape of a horseshoe and forming Aníva Bay, extends towards Japan, divided from it by La Perouse Strait. The extent of the island from north to south is about 900 versts, its narrowest point is 25 versts, at the military post of Kusunnái, the widest near Sertunái being 150 versts. The island has a superficial area of 1379 square geographical miles, approximately corresponding to Greece or to the Moscow and Riazán governments taken together.

The surface of the island is hilly; the mountains form long meridional chains, among which isolated summits of bare rocks rise to an altitude of about 2,008 to 5,000 feet above sea-level, without however attaining the line of perpetual snow. The principal plain stretches on the northern side of the island, on the western shore from 50° 20′ N. lat., and on the eastern from 51° 40′ to 53° 50′ N. lat., being partly covered with a scanty vegetation characteristic of the northern seabord. Another wide plain lies between the western and eastern coast ridges, in the interior of the island, and reaches the northern shore of Patience Gulf.

This plain, falling to the south, widens more and more, being crossed by two large rivers the Tymi, draining into Nyisk Gulf, and the Poronái, falling into Patience Gulf. Here the vegetation is far more abundant and diversified, especially in the meadows. Besides these plains, there are a few smaller ones in the southern part of the island. The richest vegetation is found in the plains occurring on the western coast of the southern side of the island.

The geological structure of Sakhalín is yet insufficiently investigated but, according to the explorations already effected, it mainly consists of clayey sandstone and limestone slates of tertiary formation. In conjunction with these predominant rocks, the mountain ridges contain crystalline and volcanic rocks, diorites and basalts. In the environs of Dué are found seams of grey marl with huge ammonites and a great number of various fossils: in the southern part of the island occur strata of green sandstone and cretaceous formation.

The mineral wealth is chiefly constituted by coalbeds occurring plentifully throughout the island. This coal has been known to Russian sailors since 1859, when they began its exploitation. Since that time, the coal deposits situated in the environs of Port Dué have been constantly worked, being from 1875 in the hands of the private joint stock company „Sakhalín" which has of late obtained an annual output of 1,000,000 puds of coal. The coal is found in a series of seams with a thickness of two to five feet; it is of superior quality, equal to the best Welsh coal; it contains from 74 to 84 per cent of carbon, a small quantity of ash and 60 per cent of coke. This coal is mainly used to supply Russian vessels navigating near the shores of the Ussúri region, and is also employed by foreign ships running into the Russian ports of the Pacific Ocean. The loading of the ships being attended with great difficulties, many of the foreign vessels prefer to supply themselves with coal from Japan; in order to overcome these inconveniences, a special expedition was organised in 1898 and despatched to the Island of Sakhalín for the purpose of finding a convenient route for the transport of coal. The expedition was commissioned, 1) to find a harbour within range of the collieries of Dué and Vladímir suitable for the arrangement of a port; 2) to make surveys. It projected a railway of 40 versts with 4 tunnels, one of 60 sazhens long, in the direction of Dué, and three towards the Vladímir mine of 100, 200 and 400 sazhens. The entrance to the mole will be from the south at a distance of 800 sazhens from the shore of the harbour selected by the expedition. Throughout the western coast, north and south of the post of Dué, have been found numerous coal-beds, which in respect of their quality and abundance are not inferior to the beds of Dué. There are also deposits in the interior of the island along the river Kummunái and on the eastern shore, on the rivers Otsobóuka and Ayá. Among the beds worked besides the Dué mines, the most important are: the Mgachínsk mines belonging to the gold-mining concern of Makóvski and Co., obtaining annually upwards of 500,000 puds of coal; and the Alexándrov and Vladímir mines of the Prison Department, with an annual output of 600,000 to 800,000 puds.

Naphtha has been discovered at many places on Sakhalín, principally in its northern extremity. Special attention is due to the springs found on the eastern coast of the island, in its northern part, near the Nabílsk Gulf, accessible to deep draught sea-going vessels.

According to the explorations made by Engineer Batsévich, deposits of naphtha extend along the meridian, having their centre near the Okhótsk Sea and at a distance of 5 to 25 versts from it. The specific gravity of the naphtha obtained from the upper layer or turf, measuring about 3 sazhens in depth and situated in different parts, varies from 0.890 to 0.895; the daily output amounts to several puds. According to the specific gravity and the results obtained from distillation, the Sakhalín naphtha has properties analogous to that of the Caucasian naphtha. Another important bed was discovered by Engineer Kleie in 1898, on the same eastern coast near the river Nútov. The analysis of the naphtha drawn from the upper layers of the soil shewed the following results: specific gravity 0.905; heated to 150° C., contains a very small percentage of benzin; heated to 300°, yields 27 per cent of pure petroleum; heated upwards of 500°, produces a very good oil for greasing machinery. The naphtha springs throughout a considerable extent of the island territory, their abundance, the richness of the superficial and subterranean deposits of kir or asphalt of recent formation and the daily flow of the oil point to the existence of considerable supplies of naphtha at a certain depth.

In 1898, gold mines were found in the central part of Sakhalín by Dr. Cherdyntsev and the nobleman Kirchner, who ascertained the proportion as 1 to 2 zolotniks of gold to 100 puds of gravel. According to certain indications, the auriferous area which has been discovered offers a wide scope for the development of gold-mining industry. The Sakhalín Goldmining Company has been organised in order to work the mines.

Amber occurs on the eastern coast from Patience Gulf to Lake Tunáicha, and likewise near Cape Kryllión, where it is cast up by the sea.

The coast of Sakhalín is intersected with gulfs and bays, among which the most important is Aníva Gulf, on the eastern side, in the central part of the island. The numerous gulfs and bays do not however afford the conditions for convenient harbours, partly because they are too wide and unprotected, and partly because they remain frost-bound for a long time.

The island is abundantly watered: numerous fresh-water lakes richly provided with fish are scattered all over its territory, many rivers and streams falling from the mountains run in every direction. These water systems, although of inconsiderable extent, play no important part in the economic life of the island, as they offer no convenient means of transportation. Only the large river Poronái, falling into Patience Gulf, being 300 versts long, is navigable for a distance of 40 to 50 versts from its mouth, and that for small vessels only. The other rivers are narrow and shallow and of a mountainous character.

The climate of Sakhalín is very severe, which is largely due to the northern sea-current flowing round the island. It brings down masses of ice, which remain unmelted as late as June. These unfavourable conditions are still further aggravated by the humidity of the air, and the constant fog, rain and snow. According to meteorological observations, there are only from 39 to 63 clear days yearly. The mean annual temperature at Dué (50° 49′ N. lat.) is —0°.59, at Kusunnái (47° 59′ N. lat.) — 1°.79, and at Aníva (46° 2′ N. lat.) — 3°.1.

The flora of the Okhótsk coast-land. The vegetation found in the south-western portion of the island is almost the same as on the Amúr and in Northern Japan. The tree species occurring here are: larch, pine, fir, cedar, birch, poplar, blackberry; yew and cedar grow on the mountains. In the southern localities protected from cold winds, are maple, oak, ash, several varieties of wild cherry, apple and cork-tree. Among the shrubs are found honey-suckle, elder, prick-wood, white hazel and wild vine.

The flora is also represented by some plants proper to the coast of north America, such as: Epilobium affine Boug. Ribes affine Boug. Vaccinium ovolifolium Sm. and others, and a special kind of bamboo, attaining a man's height and covering the mountains together with the Kamchátka dwarf birch. Upon the whole, three quarters of the territory of Sakhalín, viz. about 4,600,000 desiatins, are occupied by forests. Fires, occasioned by the carelessness of the settlers, destroy wide areas; the inhabitants, being deprived of their freedom, care but little for the future prosperity of the island.

The fauna of Sakhalín contains the same species as are found on the adjoining mainland and in the surrounding waters.

The earliest historical information about Sakhalín dates barely from the XVII century. In the forties of this century, Russian Cossacks in search of distant lands reached the mouth of the Amúr, and one of them named Poyárkov discovered the existence of an island opposite the mouth of the Amúr. Almost at the time of Poyárkov's campaign in 1643, a Dutch expedition under the leadership of Martin Herriz de Vries discovered Patience Gulf (Bot van Patientie) without suspecting that Sakhalín was a separate island. The first fairly exact chart of Sakhalín was made by the Japanese travellers Mohama—Tonkai and Mamio—Rinzo at the beginning of the XIX century, but, as it only later on became known to Europeans, Sakhalín was considered to be a peninsula up to the middle of the XIX century.

The geographical explorations effected by the expedition under Nevelskói during the occupation of the mouth of the Amúr (1849—1852) ascertained that Sakhalín was an island and that the Strait of Tartary was fit for navigation. From this time, Sakhalín was explored with a view to study its relief, climate, natural wealth etc. To the end of the XVIII century, Sakhalín was under Chinese dominion, having received its name from the Manchur „Saghalian anga hata" which means cliffs at the mouth of the Black river, and is explained by the position of the hilly part of the island covered by the Engyspál ridge, situated opposite the mouth of the Amúr. From the XVIII century the Japanese found their way to Sakhalín, and having occupied its southern extremity gave it the name of Krafto. It is only since the lower reaches of the Amúr were occupied that the Russians could firmly establish their posts on Sakhalín; thus, according to the treaty with Japan concluded on the 26 January, 1855, the northern part of the island was recognised to belong to Russia. Military posts were established in 1857 at Dué and Sartunái and in 1858, at Kusunnái. The attempts made by the Government to utilise convict labour at the coal-mines near the port of Dué refer to the same time. At first, small bodies of exile settlers were forwarded to the Island of Sakhalín and it is only in 1869 that a large party of 800 convicts was sent there. The experiments made in the establishment of a great number of criminals on the island proved successful, and it was resolved to employ convict labour for the cultivation of the island and for the working of coal in the mines belonging to the joint stock company „Sakhalín", to which the Government ceded its rights of exploitation, concluding a contract containing the condition to utilise convict labour. After the conclusion of the treaty with Japan in 1875, according to which the island passed entirely under the dominion of Russia, the first prison settlement Korsákov Post, now the centre of a district, was founded in southern Sakhalín. Such settlements were also established in other parts of the island, receiving a contingent of convicts discharged from hard labour as exile settlers.

All exile settlers receive grants of land and a loan from the Government for the organisation of the household; they are under the inspection of the administration and, on obtaining a good character, are allowed to settle in the Littoral and Amúr territories. The organisation of the Sakhalín convict stations and of the exile settlers' life are due to the activity of the former director of the Chief Prison Department, M. N. Gálkin Vráski, now member of the State Council, who repeatedly visited the eastern borderland of Siberia.

With a view to secure the family principle, required for colonisation since 1883, all women condemned to hard labour are forwarded to this island from European Russia. Since 1884, convicts are transported from Odessa on the steamers of the Volunteer Fleet.

The administration of the island is in the hands of the Military Governor under the control of the Governor-General of the Amúr territory. Alexándrovsk Post is the residence of the Military Governor.

For purposes of administration, the island is divided into three districts. Alexándrovsk, on the western coast reaching to the river Nayás. Tymóvsk: occupying the valleys of the rivers Tym and Poronái; and Korsákov in the southern part of the island, extending along the western coast to the river Nayás and along the eastern side to Cape Patience. According to the census of 1897, the population shewed the following figures:

	Males.	Females.	Total.
Alexándrovsk district	8,518	2,634	11,152
Tymóvsk	5,833	2,628	8,461
Korsákov	6,167	2,386	8,553
	20,518	7,648	28,166

The population is composed of Russians and four native tribes: the Giliák, Tungús, Orochén and Aino. The number of natives is about 4,000.

Tribes allied to the Giliáks, Tungús and Orochéns inhabit the lower streams of the Amúr: and the aborigenes of the island do not in any way differ from those of the mainland.

The Ainos are allied to the inhabitants of the island of Yezo, who belong to the European race.

The Russian population of the island comprises the following categories: 1) Officials of the civil and military class (about 2,500), 2) Free peasants (5,000), 3) Exile peasants (3,000), 4) Exile settlers (7,500) and 5) Exile convicts (7,000).

The permanent population is concentrated in 98 settlements, of which 36 are in the Alexándrovsk, 21 in the Tymóvsk, and 42 in the Korsákov districts. There are only 8 churches in all the districts; however, the organisation of fresh parishes is projected. The number of schools is 28, among which 5 have two classes, whereas the others have only one class with a total of 720 pupils. The question regarding the establishment of an agricultural school is now being started.

Industry in Sakhalín is still in the bud. Having undertaken the colonisation of Sakhalín and wishing to give to its population a permanent character, the Government applies the greatest care to the development of agriculture, which is carried on at the seven existing convict prisons by the exile convicts themselves. The extent of the prison husbandry is not considerable, with the exception of potatoes and hay, which are obtained in the proportions required by the prisons.

Agriculture increases from year to year among the peasants and settlers, in spite of the small quantity of land suited for cultivation; in order to obviate this defect, fresh lands are cleared every year, although this labour is attended with great difficulties. At present, the cultivated area represents only a desiatin to every peasant's and settler's household. The corn mainly sown is wheat, next come barley, oats, yáritsa and a smaller quantity of winter rye. Potatoes are mostly cultivated. Owing to the good quality of the soil not yet exhausted by tillage, fourfold and in favourable years upwards of sixfold crops are obtained. The slow progress in the extension of the cultivated area depends not alone on the amount of labour needed for the clearing of the forest land, but principally on the want of steadiness of the compulsory colonists, who are deprived of the possibility of having their own homes and families. The absence of women or, more exactly, their limited number is one of the chief impediments hindering the development of agriculture and of industry in general on Sakhalín. The proportion of housewives to housemasters is 40 per cent, i. e. among 100 homesteads, 60 lack the presence of a woman. How much their absence is felt may be seen by the fact that, as soon as a party of women settlers or prisoners is brought from Odessa, they are immediately taken up by the settlers without any reference to age, merely as women, wives and housekeepers.

Cattle-raising, like agriculture, is still at a primitive stage of development. The cattle belong to the Transbaikál stock. The horses come from the Tomsk and Transbaikál races. Sheep-breeding is carried on in very small proportions. On the average, every household owns about $1^{1}/_{2}$ ox and $^{1}/_{2}$ horse.

Trapping being the constant occupation and the chief resource of the natives is extensively practised in the northern part of the island, where sable and deer are hunted with success.

The fisheries form the greatest wealth of Sakhalín. Innumerable shoals of various fish approach the desert coasts of Sakhalín, as stated by Doctor Sliúnin in his report regarding the industrial wealth of the Far East.

Certain species of fish keep to the shore, and very often the stormy sea casts them up on the sloping beach, thus forming a bulwark of dead fish, 5 to 6 feet in height: a cruel irony for those who do not know how to avail themselves of nature's gifts. Other fish move in shoals to the rivers, blocking their streams, even hindering the passage of boats, only to perish there and fill the air with contagion. This aquatic wealth constitutes an abundant source of welfare and prosperity for this distant region. The time is near when these treasures will take an important place and the inhospitable and desert shores acquire a more lively character.

Sakhalín will become a more valuable fishing station than Heligoland and Newfoundland taken together. At present, the chief objects of fishing are the ketá and gorbúsha, which generally are exported after having been first dried.

The Japanese every year develop and extend the fisheries along the shores of Sakhalín; they dry the fish and prepare a kind of manure from herrings. In 1896, the export of this manure amounted to 269,247 puds. The fish which is taken for local use is tax-free, whereas on the fish exported abroad a duty of 5 k. per pud is levied from Russian and 7 k. from foreign subjects. The Japanese traders are also subject to pay duty for every steamer going out to fish, according to the ship's papers and to the new registered tonnages.

The sea-cabbage industry is very important at Sakhalín, where for a long time it has been extensively carried on by Chinese and Japanese. The sea-cabbage is also gathered by the Semionóv and Démbi Co. of Vladivostók, exporting from 170,000 to 200,000 puds of this produce to China and Japan annually.

The rules applied to sea-cabbage gathering are included in the fishery regulations, and the rate of duty on this article is fixed in accordance with the duty levied on fish.

The taking of crayfish, crabs and mainly trepang presents also a profitable industry. On the island of Sahkalín, the rate of the duty for a pud of dried trepang is 60 k. for Russian and R. 1 for foreign subjects.

Oysters, occurring of the southern and central part of the island, are not exported.

The prison workshops, subjected to the management of the prison department, contain foundry, locksmith, joinery, saw mill, brick-kiln shops etc., producing various articles for the use of the department, only part of them being made for sale. At times, private orders are received, such as for the construction of barges for the Amúr Steamship and Trade Company. The population numbers many skilful artisans; the joinery goods are particularly famous, but do not find a ready sale.

The external commercial relations of Sakhalin are maintained by means of Russian and foreign steamship companies, their number increasing from year to year. Navigation opens at the end of April when, in spite of floating ice, private steamers venture to approach the island. Regular navigation commences in the middle of May, when the mail service is performed by the steamers of Sheveliόv and Company subsidised by the Government, and subject to the obligation to pass once in two weeks along the Strait of Tartary. The mail steamers run into port Korsákov not more than once a month.

From the end of October to the end of December, when the Amúr liman is completely frost-bound, and from the middle of March to the end of April, the island is completely deprived of communication with the mainland, except by telegraph. During the remaining winter months, the post is carried by dogs from Nikoláevsk to the Amúr on the 1-st and 15-th of each month. Passenger traffic is also performed with sledges drawn by dogs.

The natural wealth of Sakhalín, consisting in numerous coal deposits, gold mines, naphtha springs, virgin forests of fir and foliage trees, in the abundance of marine animals and fish, sea-cabbage and trepang, gives great importance to this island, promising its future development into a vast trading and industrial colony.

BIBLIOGRAPHY:

Voyage to the Island of Sakhalín in 1880—1882, by Poliakóv. St. Pbg. 1883. The Island of Sakhalín and its fauna (vertebrate animals), by A. Nikólsky. St. Pbg., 1889. Sketch of the Amúr region, the southern part of the Littoral territory and of the Island of Sakhalín from a geological and mining standpoint, by Bogoliúbsky, St. Pbg. 1876. Visit to Sakhalín and Seal Island, by Bosset. Memoirs of the Company for the exploration of the Amúr region, vol. I. 1895.

Industrial wealth of Kamchtátka, Sakhalín and the Komandór Islands, by Sliúnin, 1895. The Amúr region at the Nízhni Nóvgorod exhibition by Kriúkov, 1896. The Sakhalín calendars for 1896 and 1897. Siberian trade and industry calendars for 1895 to 1899, edited by Románov. Tomsk.

Manchuria and the East-Chinese railway.

Geographical sketch of Manchuria.—Configuration of the surface.—Hydrography.—Climate.—Flora.—Fauna.—Population.—Industry and Trade.—Administration.—Organisation of the Kwantún territory.—The East Chinese railway and the South Manchurian line.—Bibliography.

Manchuria covers the north-eastern part of the Chinese Empire, lying approximately between 53° and 38° N. lat, 86.5 and 104.5° E. long. from St. Petersburg. On the north-west, north and west it is bounded by the Russian Empire, on the west and south-west by Mongolia and China proper, and on the south and south-east by the Yellow Sea (the Gulfs or Korea and Liao-dún) and Korea.

This country derives its name from the tribe of Manchú, its predominant inhabitants. In China it is known under the name of Dun-san-shen, which literally means „Three eastern provinces“ (Khei-lun-tsian-shen or Amúr province, Tsin-lun-shen or Girin, and Shen-tsin-shen or Mukden province).

The superficial area of Manchuria somprises about 600,000 square versts, nearly equal to that of the Transbaikál territory and twice as large as Japan. The northern and greater portion is occupied by the Amúr and Suifún basins, and contains the two provinces of Khe-ilun-shen and Tsin-lun-shen traversed by the future East Chinese Railway; the southern and smaller part, watered by the basins of the rivers Liso-Khe and Yalun-tsiau and the Yellow Sea, consists of the Shen-tsin-shen province and is traversed by the future South Manchurian line.

In respect of the character of the surface, that of northern Manchuria is mainly mountainous. On the west, running along the meridian, stretches the Great Khingán, forming a far-spreading mountain range extending from the frontier of China proper along the Amúr, for a distance of 1000 versts, with an average breadth of 300 versts.

Valley of the river Dzhad-unúr-gol.

On the north, the Great Khingán borders on the Il-Khurí-Alín mountain system, further east it joins the spurs of the Little Khingán. The area eastwards of the Sungarí and a great portion on the south are covered by the mountain system of Chan-bo-shán and its numerous branches. The highest point of this mountain system is the summit of the Baitón-shán (1800 feet above sea-level) presenting a gigantic column standing on the frontier of Manchuria and Korea, in the vicinity of which rise the three chief water arteries of the country: the Sungarí, the Tumyn-ulá and the Yabí-tsin. The population of Manchuria and Korea particularly venerates this locality, consecrated to the forefathers of the Manchurian dynasty reigning in China. The Bai-tou-shan is an extinct volcano, whose crater is converted into a deep lake with a circumference of 9 to 10 versts, fringed with sharp-pointed peaks rising 500 feet above sea-level. The top of the mountain is covered with fragments of pumice and is of a white colour, which accounts for its name of White-headed Mountain. The local inhabitants designate the mountain lake by the name of Lun-van-tán or Lake of the Dragon King.

The western spur ot the Chan-bo-shan system bears the name of Ku-le; between the Sungarí and its tributary, the Mudán-tsián, stretches another far and wide spreading branch of the Chzhan-guan-tsan-lín. The eastern spurs occupy an extensive area between the rivers Tumán-ulá, Suifún and Ussúri. They all have here different names (Kharbilín, Sao-e-lin, Chan-lin-tsa, Kentei-Alín, Van-lun-hóu, Mukhdekhén etc.) and are cut at several points by the future railway line.

The character of the surface in southern Manchuria is like that of the northern part; it is mainly covered with low ridges divided into two groups by the broad valley of the Liao-khé, falling into the Liao-dún Gulf. All these mountain ridges, with the exception of those coming up to the western border of the Liao-khé valley, form part of the Chan-bo-shán system.

Southern Manchuria, known under the name of the Liao-dún Peninsula, having the form of a triangle, projects into the Yellow Sea. It is also covered with low mountains, whose summits do not exceed a height of 3,000 to 5,000 feet above sea-level.

In spite of the inconsiderable elevation of the mountain masses, the area occupied by the Liao-dun Peninsula, endowed with but a scanty vegetation and owing to the rugged outlines of the mountains, has a very dreary character. The southern extremity of Liao-dún or the so called Guandún or Kwangtúng Peninsula is also mountainous, although possessing softer outlines. A range of rocky hills here runs from N. E. to S. W. The valleys interspersed between these ranges are mostly endowed with clayey soils.

The coast of the Guan-dún at some places falls abruptly to the sea, but all the elevations assume a softer and rounder outline.

The expedition of Engineer Sviágin in a gorge of the Wan-lun-hóu ridge.

The mineral wealth of Manchuria is not yet fully explored but, according to certain data, it may be regarded as very considerable. Coal-beds occur at many places along the line of the future railway, and principally on the Liao-dún Peninsula and throughout the coast of the Yellow Sea. Iron, silver, tin and gold are to be found on the Khingán and also in the spurs of the Chan-bo-shan ridge. The recent explorations of the Guan-dun peninsula ascertained the extraordinary auriferous nature of the whole territory. Gold has been found here in gravel and veins. In this respect, special attention is due to the environs of Bitsy-vo-Tsin-chzhóu and Port-Arthúr.

The hydrography of Northern Manchuria is the same in character as that of the neighbouring sections of the Siberian territory, viz. in the Amúr and Littoral regions.

The rain brought by the monsoons accounts for the numerous streams and swamps. In connexion with the distribution of the rainfall, the rivers of

Manchuria overflow twice a year, in spring, from the effect of the melting snow and in summer, in consequence of the abundant rainfall.

The greater number of rivers in Northern Manchuria belong to the Amúr system; however the chief artery of the country is not the Amúr, representing over a great extent the frontier of Russia and China, but its affluent the Sungarí, flowing across the centre of the country.

Among the streams forming the Amúr and its right tributaries flowing within the limits of Manchuria, the principal are: the Khailár, composing the upper part of the Argún with its affluent the Ibén-hól; the Albozíkha receiving the Zheltúga, known for its rich gold mines, and the Kumará, Chem, Khurpí, Ui-khé, the Sungarí or Sún-khuá-tsián having a length of about 2,000 versts.

Types of Chinese.

The whole course of the Sungarí, according to its conditions, may be divided inio three parts: the upper part to the town of Girin which is not navigable, the central part from Girin to the town of Bodune, navigable only during high water, and the lower part which is navigable throughout its course. The most important left affluents of the Sungari are: the I-tún-khé, the partly navigable Nonni, the Khilún-khé, the Taún-birá; on the right, it receives the Solín-khé and the Mudán-tsián or Khurkhá.

Among the tributaries of the Ussúri watering Manchuria, the most important is the Sungách, taking its source from Lake Khanká, the Murén and Nor.

Among the rivers of northern Manchuria, belonging to the basin of the Yellow Sea, the principal are: the Tumén-ulá, navigable in its lower reaches, and the Suifún navigable within the limits of Russian territory.

Southern Manchuria, subject to the influence of the Yellow Sea and to an abundant rainfall, is irrigated by numerous running waters. The largest of its rivers is the Lia-khé falling into the Liao-dún Gulf and having a length of 800 versts; another important river bordering on Korea is the Yalü-tsián.

The mountainous character of the Liao-dún Peninsula, devoid of forests which could serve to direct the course of the running waters, prevents the formation of considerable water basins. All the rivers traversing the pennsula have a very inconsiderable length and an inconstant level, possessing the character of mountain streams.

As regards the Guan-dún or Kwan-túng Peninsula, the running water assumes there the form of mountain streams, which are irrepressible and full-flowing during the period of snow and rainfall, and dry up utterly during the other seasons. Upon the whole, the peninsula suffers from an absence of water, in spite of the abundance of rainfall. There are only a few wells, containing water of a bad quality, which can be employed for drink only after having been boiled or filtered.

Among the lake basins, the most important in northern Manchuria are the Dalái-nór or Kulún with an extent of about 1000 square versts, the Buír-nór, somewhat inferior in size, and the Khanká occupying about 4,000 square versts.

Chinese woman.

The coast-line bounded by the Yellow Sea, flowing round the Liao-dun Peninsula, is comparatively even in outline containing only on the south several deep bays on the eastern and western coasts.

The eastern shore comprises the bays of Liui-shun-kóu (Port Arthur), Da-lian ván (Talienván) and others of lesser importance. Sini-shun-kou Bay is over 2 versts long and about 11½ versts broad, being connected with the open sea by a long and narrow passage, of about a verst in length, with a breadth of 150 to 200 sazhens. At the entrance of this bay, lies a wide roadstead suitable for the manoeuvering of a great number of vessels, being well protected by the surrounding elevations from northerly and westerly winds, but very dangerous during southerly and easterly winds, making the water very rough.

This roadstead is free of ice all the year round. Situated 45 versts north east of Sini-shun-kou (Port Arthur) Da-lian-ván Bay (Talienván) is better protected from winds and from the violence of the waves, by elevated capes projecting into the sea, and for this reason has a great advantage over the southern bay. Dalian-van presenting a wide gulf, about 12 versts long and 10 versts broad, with several bays, which never freeze, offers every convenience for the arrangement of a commercial port.

On the western shore of the Liao-dún Peninsula at its southern extremity, are two bays Pigeon and Louisa, with an anchorage for ships.

Further north on the Liao-dun coast, Company Bay is provided with a convenient anchorage for ships, sheltered as it is by numerous island groups.

The climate of Northern Manchuria is particularly severe and much colder than in other parts of the world lying within the same latitudes. In proximity to the northern part of the Sungarí, the cold attains a maximum of—45° R., whereas west of the Khingán it is often—50° R.

Navigation on the Sungarí is practicable only from the middle of April to the end of October. Winter lasts here for 5 months. The ice covering the Sungari attains a thickness of 3 feet. Further west, near the source of the Argun, the duration of the winter is about 6 months. The spring is short, the greater part of the corn is already sown in April. The change from cold to warm weather is very sudden, accompanied by an extraordinarily rapid growth of the vegetation. The summer is very warm. The autumn commences early, the leaves fall at the beginning of September, and morning frosts begin at the end of this month.

The southerly and south-easterly winds, prevailing during the summer, bring a great amount of moisture turning into rain. In the valley of the Sungarí and throughout the central part of Manchuria, the rain, season commences in the middle of June, and in the north-western portion in July. As a consequence of the northerly and north-westerly dry winds blowing in winter, the quantity of snow falling in Manchuria is not considerable, with the exception of the high ridges of the Great Khingán.

Temple.

The climate of the southern part of Manchuria, and especialy of the Liao-dún Peninsula, whose south-eastern coast is bounded by the warm Korean current, is considerably-warmer. The extreme northern port which does not freeze is the Bi-tsy-vo. The average winter temperature at Port-Arthúr is 6°—7° 5 C. below zero. In the middle of March, the temperature rises considerably, a short spring precedes a warm summer, characterised by rain and thunderstorms. The best time of the year at Liao-dún is the autumn, which like the spring is very short.

The flora and fauna of Northern Manchuria, upon the whole, are like those of the Amúr territory and the Ussúri region. The vegetation of Southern Manchuria, as well as its animal life, offers a mixture of North Chinese and Amúr representatives, with species from south-eastern Mongolia, Korea and Japan.

Together with forms common to the extreme north, such as the sable, the Bengal tiger, the most dangerous carnivore of Asia, occurs in Manchuria.

The population of Manchuria, according to approximate calculations, for want of any official data, may be estimated at about 15,000,000 (the Kheilun-tsian-shén province about 2,000,000, Tsian-lun-shén 7,000,000 and Shentsin-shén 6,000,000).

Among the most populous localities are the valley of the river Liao-khé, the Peninsula of Liao-dún and the central part of the Sungarí basin.

The population consists of Chinese, Manchus, Koreans, Daúrs, Orochéns, Birárs, Manégrs, Golds, Solóns, Buriáts, Chipchíns and Olóts. The most numerous are the Chinese, who a long time since gradually colonised the country and founded the first towns in Southern Manchuria. The stream of Chinese emigrants was greatly increased from the middle of the past century by the addition of peasants and runaway criminals, gold-hunters and gatherers of the zhen-shen root. Part of these outlanders became brigands called khunkhúz, who hold the peaceful inhabitants in awe. By this time, the Chinese occupy the whole of the Shen-tsun-shén province, they are scattered all over that of Tsin-lin-shén, and form a considerable percentage in the Khei-lun-tsian-shén province. Owing to the energy and industry of the Chinese population, the southern and part of the central portion of Manchuria, now but slightly differ as regards culture from the adjoining Chinese countries.

Group of Chinese officials, Buriáts and Solóns.

The number of Manchús is given at 600,000 to 700,000, mainly settled in towns, where they enjoy a privileged position, being enrolled in the Manchú troops or serving as officials in various administrative institutions. The Manchús form part of the country population only in the two northern provinces, whereas they are totally absent therefrom in the southern, Shen-tsian-shén province.

Among the other tribes, the most numerous are the Koreans, represented by 50,000.

The prevailing religion is Buddhism in its various forms.

The chief occupation of the permanent population of Manchuria is agriculture. Latterly, the Chinese Government paid special care to its development, taking measures for the settlement of the free lands and for the expansion of the cultivated tracts. The cereals cultivated are: wheat, oats, barley, various kinds of millet and buckwheat, maize and rice in the southern districts. Among the forms of barley, the first place is occupied by Indian barley and Chinese gao-lin, which is used in making vodka.

Among the numerous leguminous plants, the da-dou, yielding oil, is extensively cultivated. Poppies are also sown in great quantity for the preparation of opium. Considerable tracts are occupied by plantations of tobacco, smoked by old and young, including the women. In the south of the Shen-tsian-shén province, cotton is cultivated. The orchards are a great help to the population. Every Chinese hut is provided with a carefully kept kitchen garden, provided with the vegetables usually cultivated in the central zone of the European continent, with a profusion of onions, garlic and pepper,

Carriage of Chinese official.

pointing to the preference of the Chinese for vegetable food seasoned with strong spices.

In the southern portion of Manchuria, mainly in the Liao-dún Peninsula, the inhabitants occupy themselves with silk cultivation, the following towns being the chief centres of this industry: Siu-yan-chzhou, Tsin-chzhou-fu, Fu-chzhou. The silk is obtained from the cocoon of the Bombyx Pernyi, feeding on oak-leaves (Quercus Mongolica, Sinensis and dentata).

Fruit-trees such as apple, pear, peach, plum etc. occur throughout Manchuria, with the exception of the northern parts, but it is only in the south that these trees attain a fair growth. Vineyards are met with in the south of the country.

Among profitable industries may be mentioned the gathering of the zhen-shén root (zhinzéng or Panax gyezeng), which the Chinese consider as a panacea and a restorer of lost vigour.

Cattle-raising is extensively practised in Manchuria. A great quantity of cattle is bred in the Kheilún-tsian-shén province, exclusively for agricultural purposes and for transport; the Chinese scarcely ever eat meat, and very rarely kill their cattle. Milk products likewise are not used by them for food.

The horses of northern Manchuria are famous. The camels are employed as pack-animals in this country. In the southern portion of the Liao-dún Penin-

Solón tent in the steppe.

sula, poorly provided with pastures, cattle breeding is less developed. The north of Manchuria exports droves of cattle for slaughter to the Amúr region,

Chipchíns in the Sigeldzhí steppe.

sending them from the town of Khailár to Blagovéshchensk for further conveyance by the Amúr.

Fishing is carried on in the localities watered by the Amúr and the Sungarí, but mostly along the sea-coast where fish, besides representing the chief food of the population, are also an article of export to other countries, after having been dried in the open air. Very good oysters are to be had in Dalian-ván and Bi-tsy-vó.

Manufactures, on account of the small development of mining industry and the low stage of prosperity of the population, is exclusively represented by handicraft production, calculated to meet the daily needs of a hardly civilised population. The chief forms of industry are oil-pressing and brandy distilling. Oil is obtained trom beans and peas by means of very primitive presses.

Chinese vodka is prepared mainly from millet (gaolin).

Local cotton and silk are used in weaving stuffs.

Daúrs with their waggons.

Trade in Manchuria is mainly concentrated in its southern ports and in the towns of the Shen-tsian-shén province. The larger part of European and American goods are imported through the ports of In-tsy, Port Arthúr, Bi-tsy-vó and Da-gu-shán. A lively trade is also carried on through the frontier with the Amúr province. Among European and American goods, the first place belongs to cotton stuffs, metals, woollen produce and opium. Along the frontier line bordering the Amúr territories, trade assumes a local character and consists in the barter of mainly animal products.

For purposes of administration, Manchuria is divided into three provinces each being subject to a special Tsian-Tsiun or Governor-General; thanks to the many peculiar customs always characterising a diversified population, the forms of administration are very complicated. The ancient Manchús with remains of their former military organisation, foreign Chinese having imported forms of administration from the central provinces of the Empire, wandering Mongols, Tungús trappers and other nomad tribes with their primitive customs found a shelter in Manchuria and influenced its administrative organisation. As stated by travellers, in Manchuria no living bond exists be-

Divine service on the 16 August, 1897, held at the inauguration of the works on the East Chinese railway.

tween the population and the administration, and their mutual intercourse is very often based on hatred of each other. Espionage and denunciation hold their sway everywhere, the raising of taxes is accomplished without any control and justice is very irregularly administered. Complaints against the inertness of the police are heard on all sides, and thefts and robbery go unpunished. The workmen, as well as the Russian agents and engineers employed in the construction of the railway, are constantly attacked by bands of armed khunkhús.

Being leased to the Russian Government by a special agreement, concluded on the 15 March, 1898, part of Liao-dún, the so called Guan-dún Peninsula, received a separate administration by the statute of the 16 August, 1899, sanctioned by the Emperor. The whole of the said territory inclusive of the islands, forms the Kvantún province, whose administration being entrusted to the Commander of the Territorial Troops and of the Pacific Fleet, is subject to the Ministry of War. The centre of administration is Port Arthur. The following places are raised to the rank of towns in the territory: Port Arthúr, Bi-tsy-vó, Tsin-chzhóu and Dálni (Talienván), constituting a separate governorship under the Ministry of Finance. The organisation of the new town of Dálni is left to the East Chinese Railway Company, under the chief direction of the Minister of Finance.

The unfavourable conditions and technical difficulties attending the projected construction of a railway line on the northern side of the Amúr, uniting the Transbaikál Railway with the Ussúri line, evoked the project of a railway from the Transbaikál to Vladivostók by a more southern and direct route across Manchuria.

The choice of this route was in so far desirable as thus the railway passed through a more populous and fertile country, with a better climate than the Amúr region. Including in the sphere of Russian influence a rich and thickly-settled country, the projected line moreover reduces the length of the Siberian main line and the distance run by transit goods, this also being a very important fact in connexion with the future competition between the Siberian Railway and the sea-routes to the Far East. The negotiations with the Chinese Government regarding the construction of the Siberian main line across Manchuria terminated in a concession for the construction and exploitation of the Manchurian railway granted to the Russo-Chinese Bank.

According to the contract, concluded on the 27 August, 1896, between the Chinese Government and the Russo-Chinese Bank, the East Chinese Railway joint stock Company was organised within the confines of Manchuria for the construction and exploitation of the line.

The statutes of the East Chinese Railway Company, sanctioned on the 4 December, 1896, stipulated that the construction of the line was to be started not later than the 16 August, 1897, with a gauge corresponding to that of the Russian railways, viz. 5 feet.

On the expiration of 36 years after the completion of the whole line and the opening of traffic, the Chinese Government possesses the right of redemption, repaying to the Company the capital and the debts contracted for the needs of the railway, with interest. After a period of 80 years, during which the line is to be exploited by the Company, the Chinese Government takes gratuitous possession of the railway and its plant.

The management of the affairs of the Company is entrusted to a board composed of a president and 9 members. The president, acting as intermediary between the Company and the Chinese Government, is appointed by the latter, whereas the members are elected by all the shareholders.

The immediate management of affairs devolves on the vice-president chosen from among the members of the Company. The chief office is in St. Petersburg, with a branch in Pekin.

Solemn inauguration of the East Chinese Railway on the 16 August, 1897.

The following elections took place in December of 1896, when the Company started its activity. Railway engineer S. I. Kerbédz — vice-president, D. D.

Pokotílov — member of the board in Pekin, privy councilor P. M. Románov, A. Y. Rotstein, prince E. E. Ukhtomsky, the railway engineers Alexéev and Kovánko — members of the board in St. Petersburg and engineer Zigler von Schafhausen — managing director. The latter having been appointed in the autumn of 1899 as director of the Railway Department in the Ministry of Finance, railway engineer A. N. Wentzel was elected to the post. Engineer A. I. Yugóvich, former constructor of the lines of the Riazán-Urál railway Company, was engaged as chief constructor of the Manchurian line, engineer S. V. Ignátius being his assistant and substitute.

In January of 1897, by a decree of the Chinese Emperor, the Chinese statesman Sui-tsin-chén, former ambassador in St. Petersburg and Berlin, at present member of the Tsun-li-yamén, was named president of the board.

In the beginning of April, 1897, the first body of engineers and agents set forth for the Far East and, upon arriving at Vladivostók, under the immediate direction of the chief engineer began the surveys for the future railway and the preliminary works required for its construction. On the 16 August of the same year, in presence of the Tsian-Tsiun of Girin, the military governor of the Littoral territory and of the local Russian and Chinese officials, the works commenced near the Cossack village of Poltávskaya, situated in proximity to the boundary of the South-Ussúri region. On undertaking the execution of the East Chinese railway, the Company had in view the construction of a railway crossing Manchuria from west to east, viz. from the boundary of the Transbaikál to that of the South-Ussúri region. After the convention between Russia and China regarding the cession of Port Arthúr and Da-lian-ván to Russia for a 25 years' lease was signed in Pekin on the 15 March, 1898, and a supplementary protocol in St. Petersburg on the 15 April of the same year, the Imperial Chinese Government granted the Company permission to continue the construction of the railway from one of the stations of the Manchurian main line to Da-lian-ván and Port Arthur, with the right of exploitation of the branch, which received the name of South-Manchurian branch of the East Chinese railway.

Upon the conclusion of this treaty, the Company began directly to make surveys and commenced the construction of the South-Manchurian line. As a result of repeated surveys, the following directions were adopted for the main route and its branches.

Crossing the Transbaikal frontier at the station of Sibír on the Transbaikál railway and entering into the confines of the Chinese Empire at the village of Nagadán near Lake Dalái-Nór, the main line reaches the town of Khailár (pop. 3,000). Further on, it runs a distance of 300 versts along an elevated plateau and ascends to the Great Khingán ridge and then descends again to the valley of the river Nónni, crossing it within 15 versts to the south of the town of Tsitsikár (pop. 70,000). Within 30 versts of the town of Khulinchén (pop. 70,000), the line crosses the river Sungarí near the settlement of Kharbín, which is the headquarters of the central department for the construction of the East-Chinese railway, and proceeds towards the town of Azhekhé (pop. 40,000). At the 340 verst, south-east of the Sungarí, after having crossed the river Mudan-tsián, the line enters a mountainous country and follows it to the frontier of the Ussúri region.

On the west, the East Chinese and the Russian railways are connected by the branch of the Transbaikál line, serving as link between the East Chinese Railway and the Siberian line, the station Kaidálovo being the point of junction. On the east, the East Chinese railway joins the Nikólsk branch of the Ussúri line.

Group of representatives and visitors at the inauguration of the East Chinese Railway, on the 16 August, 1897.

The South-Manchurian branch, leaving the main track after crossing the Sungarí at the settlement of Kharbín, runs to the south through the towns of Kuan-chen-tsy, Chan-tu-fú, Mukdén (pop. 20,000), In-kóu (pop. 70,000) to

Port Arthúr (pop. 20,000) connected by a short branch line (16 v.) with Dalian-ván, which has received the name of Dálni.

Street in Khailár.

Following this direction, the main line and the southern branch of the East-Chinese railway run through the whole of Manchuria from the Trans-

Temple in Khailár.

baikál boundary to the Ussúri region and southwards to the extremity of the Liao-dún Peninsula, passing on the way through most populous localities suitable for agriculture. The length of the main line is estimated at 1,440 versts, the South-Manchurian line — 980 versts and the total length of the whole East-Chinese railway — 2,420 versts.

The materials required for the main line upon reaching Vladivostók are forwarded by the Ussúri railway to the station of Khabaróvsk whence, by means of steamers belonging to the Company (which has organised navigation on the river for want of any other convenient means of communication in Manchuria) they are taken up the Sungarí to Kharbín for further distribu-

Temple in Tsitsikár.

tion along the line. The materials which are destined for the South-Manchurian line are transported to Port Arthúr in sea-going steamers. Part of the railway material is carried by shallow-draught vessels to Port In-kóu, whence it is forwarded by a temporary branch line to its further destination.

For purposes of administration, the East-Chinese Railway is divided into three: the Eastern, Western and Southern divisions, comprising 22 sections.

The managers of these divisions are: Engineer Sviágin, of the Eastern, Engineer Bochárov, of the western and Engineer Hirschmann of the southern division, under the immediate control of the head engineer. The central department for the construction of the line, including the chancery, the book-keeping, technical and machinery departments, is situated in Kharbín. The department for steamship navigation on the rivers has its headquarters in Vladivostók.

Besides the above mentioned persons, upwards of 150 railway and technical engineers are employed on the construction of the East Chinese railway.

With a view to preserve the health of all those who are employed on the works throughout the line, a medical inspection, consisting of 24 physicians and 75 assistant surgeons, has been organised and entrusted to the direction of the head doctor Polétika.

Not only the higher employees, but also the lower agents, surveyors, blacksmiths and locksmiths and other artisans come from Russia and are carried to their point of destination by the steamers of the Volunteer Fleet, taking regularly every voyage an average of 40 agents of the company.

The contingent of common workmen consists mainly of Chinese. By this time, about 100,000 Chinese workmen are employed on the construction of the line.

With a view to supply the employees with provisions and articles indispensable to Europeans, the Company established in Kharbín special stores for this purpose.

Taking into consideration the great importance which the commercial port Dálni will acquire for the East-Chinese railway as its terminus, the company is also entrusted with the construction and exploitation of this post.

Foreseeing that after the construction of the commercial port Dálni, an industrial population consisting of different nations will be attracted to it and give it the character of a town, and with a view to preserve the unity of the technical administration regarding the construction of both port and

The Tsian-Tsiún of Tsitsikár and his staff.

town, the Company was also entrusted with the organisation of the town in Dálni under the chief direction of the Minister of Finance.

The chief constructor of the port and town is railway engineer Sakharov who, accompanied by his assistants, is already at his post.

In order to secure the regular transport of freights, materials and workmen required for the construction of the East-Chinese Railway, and to establish in the future a regular and quick transport for passengers and goods carried from Russia and Western Europe to the Far East and back, the Company of the East-Chinese Railway obtained the right to establish a special ocean steamship navigation in the Far East. The increase of the quantity of goods conveyed by the railway being in accordance with the interests of the Ocean S. S. Company, the latter will as soon as its fleet is sufficiently developed, contribute also to the export of Russian goods from the Littoral territory to China, Japan and Korea. Captain A. N. Bostelman, residing in Port Arthúr, is director of the Ocean Steamship Navigation Co.: its board is also located there.

Street in the Town of Ningút.

In 1899, voyages were accomplished by 6 steamers belonging to the Company, 3 freight steamers, 2 goods and passenger and 1 passenger steamer.

Temple in San-cha-kóu.

The Company arranges landing-stages and stores at the places visited by the steamers. By this time, it owns wharves at Vladivostók, Port-Arthúr,

Dálni, Chifú, Inkóu, and in the near future contemplates to have them at Possiét, Kástri, Petropávlovsk and Shanghai; coal-stores exist at Port Arthúr, Chifú and Nagasaki. Agencies have been opened at Vladivostók, Nikoláevsk (on the Amúr), Dué (in Sakhalín), Nagasaki, Chifú, Niuchwán, Shanghai and Chemúlpo; very soon their number will be increased by the opening of fresh agencies in Petropávlovsk, Possiét, Tiantsín, Hongkong, Futsán and Khakodate. The agents in nearly all the ports are Russians.

In 1900, the commercial fleet belonging to the Company will be enlarged by the addition of two steamers (200 feet in length) constructed in Shanghai and destined to cruise on the Sea of Okhótsk; high speed steamers built in England and Germany for cruises from Port Arthúr and Dálni on the waters of the Pacific Ocean are to be completed by the same time.

Upon the conpletion of the East-Chinese Railway, with its branches to the Transbaikál and Ussúri lines, and the continuation of the South Manchurian Railway to Port Arthúr and the town of Dálni, the Imperial Will proclaimed by the rescript of the 17 March, 1891, commanding the construction of a continuous railway line through Siberia to the coast of the Pacific Ocean, will be so far fulfilled.

BIBLIOGRAPHY.

Description of Manchuria, publ. by the Minist. of Fin. St. Petersburg 1895—1896, by Pozdnéev. Manchuria and the East-Chinese Railway by Digamma. Siberian trade and industry calendars, publ. by Románov. Tomsk, 1897—1899. Liao-dún and its ports: Port-Arthúr and Da-lian-ván, by V. Kótvich and Borodóvsky. St. Pbg. 1898. Historical sketch of the development of railways in Russia, publ. by the Ministry of Ways of Communication. St. Pbg. 1899.

APPENDIX OF

FARES AND TIME TABLES.

The information as to railway communications in this Appendix is taken from the Official Guidebook for railway, steamer and other passenger communications published by the Ministry of Ways of Communication, preserving the NN of the routes therein contained.

FARES

between St.-Petersburg, Moscow, Warsaw and the chief stations of the Siberian Railway.

	STATIONS.	Distance, versts.	Fast train.		Passenger train.			10 lbs. lugg.	Days available.
			I cl.	II cl.	I cl.	II cl.	III cl.		
			r. k.	r. k.	r. k.	r. k.	r. k.		
FROM St.-PETERSBURG.	Moscow	604	19 50	11 70	15 00	9 00	6 00	33¾	3
	Samára	1728	38 40	23 05	29 50	17 70	11 80	77¼	6
	Ufá	2219	44 60	26 75	34 50	20 70	13 80	92¼	7
	Cheliábinsk	2669	50 00	30 00	39 00	23 40	15 60	105¾	8
	Kurgán	2910	52 50	31 50	41 00	24 60	16 40	111¾	9
	Petropávlovsk	3159	55 50	33 30	43 50	26 10	17 40	119¼	10
	Omsk	3415	59 00	35 40	46 50	27 90	18 60	128¼	10
	Ob	4001	65 70	39 40	52 00	31 20	20 80	144¾	12
	Taigá	4216	68 60	41 15	54 50	32 70	21 80	152¼	12
	Maríinsk	4354	69 90	41 95	55 50	33 30	22 20	155¼	13
	Achinsk	4543	71 30	42 80	56 50	33 90	22 60	158¼	13
	Krasnoyarsk	4712	74 60	44 75	59 50	35 70	23 60	167¼	13
	Kansk	4939	77 10	46 25	61 50	36 90	24 50	173¼	14
	Nizhneúdinsk	5246	80 70	48 40	64 50	38 70	25 80	182¼	15
	Tulún	5355	82 90	49 15	65 90	39 30	26 20	185¼	15
	Irkútsk	5718	86 60	51 95	69 50	41 70	27 80	197¼	16

	STATIONS.	Distance, versts.	Fast train.		Passenger train.			10 lbs. lugg.	Days available.
			I cl.	II cl.	I cl.	II cl.	III cl.		
FROM MOSCOW			r. k.	r. k.	r. k.	r. k.	r. k.		
	Samára	1118	26 90	16 15	22 50	13 50	9 00	56¼	4
	Ufá	1609	33 60	20 15	28 00	16 80	11 20	72¾	6
	Cheliábinsk	2059	39 —	23 40	32 50	19 50	13 00	86¼	7
	Kurgán	2300	42 —	25 20	35 00	21 00	14 00	93¾	7
	Petropávlovsk	2349	43 —	25 70	35 50	21 30	14 20	95¼	8
	Omsk	2805	48 —	28 80	40 00	24 00	16 00	108¾	9
	Ob	3391	55 20	33 10	46 00	27 60	18 40	126¾	10
	Taigá	3606	57 60	34 55	48 00	28 80	19 20	132¾	11
	Maríinsk	3744	58 40	35 65	49 50	29 70	19 80	137¼	11
	Achinsk	3933	61 80	37 10	51 50	30 90	20 60	143¼	12
	Krasnoyársk	4192	63 60	38 11	53 00	31 80	21 20	147¾	12
	Kansk	4329	66 60	39 95	55 50	33 30	22 20	155¼	13
	Nizhneúdinsk	4636	70 20	42 10	58 50	35 10	23 40	164¼	13
	Tulún	4745	71 40	42 85	59 50	35 70	23 80	167¼	14
	Irkútsk	5108	75 60	45 35	63 00	37 80	25 20	177¾	14
FROM WARSAW.			r. k.	r. k.	r. k.	r. k.	r. k.	r. k.	
	Moscow	1239	30 20	22 12	24 00	14 40	9 60	60¾	5
	Samára	2357	36 10	27 67	35 50	21 30	14 20	95¼	8
	Ufá	3848	42 30	31 37	40 50	24 30	16 20	110¼	9
	Cheliábinsk	3298	47 70	34 62	45 00	27 00	18 00	123¾	10
	Kurgán	3539	50 70	36 62	47 50	38 50	19 00	131¼	11
	Petropávlovsk	3788	63 70	38 22	50 00	30 00	20 00	138¾	11
	Omsk	4044	66 70	40 02	52 50	31 50	21 00	146¼	12
	Ob	4630	73 90	44 32	58 50	35 10	23 40	164¼	13
	Taigá	4845	76 30	45 77	60 50	36 30	24 20	170¼	14
	Maríinsk	4983	78 10	47 12	62 00	37 20	24 80	175¾	14
	Achinsk	5172	80 50	48 32	64 00	38 40	25 60	180¾	15
	Krasnoyársk	5341	82 30	49 37	65 50	39 30	26 20	185¼	15
	Kansk	5568	85 30	51 17	68 00	40 80	27 20	192¾	16
	Nizhneúdinsk	5875	87 90	52 72	70 00	42 00	28 00	198¾	16
	Tulún	5984	90 10	54 07	72 00	43 20	28 80	204¾	17
	Irkútsk	6347	94 30	57 57	75 50	45 20	30 28	215¼	18

FARES

between Cheliábinsk and the chief stations of the Siberian Railway.

STATIONS.	Distance, versts.	Fast train.		Passenger train.			10 lbs. lugg.	Days avail.
		I cl.	II cl.	I cl.	II cl.	III cl.		
		r. k.	r. k.	r. k.	r. k.	r. k.	r. k.	
Cheliábinsk	—	—	—	—	—	—	—	—
Kurgán	241	—	—	7 58	4 55	3 03	13 86	2
Petropávlovsk	490	—	—	13 00	7 80	5 20	27¾	3
Omsk	746	—	—	17 50	10 50	7 00	41¼	3
Ob	1332	30 00	18 00	25 00	15 00	10 00	63¾	5
Taigá	1547	32 00	19 20	26 50	15 90	10 60	68¼	6
Maríinsk	1685	30 80	20 90	29 00	17 49	11 60	75¾	6
Achinsk	1874	37 20	22 30	31 00	18 60	12 40	81¾	6
Krasnoyársk	2040	39 70	23 40	32 50	19 50	13 00	86¼	7
Kansk	2267	42 00	25 20	35 00	21 00	14 00	93¾	7
Nizhneúdinsk	2574	45 70	27 35	39 00	22 80	15 20	102¾	8
Tulún	2683	46 80	28 10	39 00	23 40	15 60	105¾	8
Irkútsk	3049	51 00	30 60	42 50	25 50	17 00	116¼	9

Note. I. Each passenger has the right to take one child under five years of age free. For other children and children aged from 5 to 10 years, a fare is charged at the rate of 1/4 of that for adult passengers.

II. Each passenger ticket gives the right to the conveyance of one pud of luggage and each child's ticket—20 lbs.; for the conveyance of luggage in excess of this, a charge is made for every 10 lbs. according to the luggage tariff.

III. In the fast train, all places are numbered and the passengers must, moreover, take place-cards at the rate of R. 1 50 k. for each line separately and pay for bed-linen R. 1 a change, serving not more than three days.

Samára-Zlatoúst Railway.

(Office in Samára).

Syzrán-Cheliábinsk . . . . № 170.
Samára-Orenbúrg . . . . № 171.
Krótovka-Sérgievsk . . . . № 171a.

170. Syzrán—Cheliábinsk and back.

Ft. 2 I—II	Pr. 6 I—III	Ml. 4 I—III	Versts.		*Samára-Zlatoúst r. w.*		Versts.	Pr. 5 I—III	Ft. 1 I—II	Ml. 4 I—III
2 52	**9 34**	11 47	—	Dep.	**Syzrán** bf.	Arr.	—	7 23	1 0	4 5
3 10	**9 55**	12 10	—	Arr.	**Batrakì** Syzr. V. bf. . .	Dep.	1057	7 0	12 40	3 40
3 20	**10 5**	12 28		Dep.		Arr.		6 50	12 25	3 30
—	—	—	—	„	Batr. S.-Zl.	„	—	—	—	—
—	—	—	—	„	Prav. Volga (sid.)	„	—	—	—	—
—	**10 45**	1 8	17	„	Obshárovka	„	1041	6 17	—	2 57
—	—	—	—	„	Sam. Luká s.	„	—	—	—	—
—	**11 17**	1 40	33	„	Mylnaya	„	1025	**5 41**	—	2 19
—	—	1 54	—	„	Bashkìr. sid.	„	—	—	—	2 0
4 55	**11 57**	2 21	—	„	Maitúga	„	—	**5 5**	11 10	1 34
—	**12 19**	2 44	56	„	Bezenchùk	„	1002	**4 40**	—	1 6
—	—	—	—	„	Yerikì sid.	„	—	—	—	—
—	**1 9**	3 34	80	„	Tomylovo	„	978	**3 52**	—	12 18
—	—	—	—	„	Zhigulì (sid.)	„	—	—	—	—
—	**1 49**	4 15	101	„	Lipiági	„	957	**3 4**	—	11 30
—	**2 7**	4 35	109	„	Kriázh	„	948	**2 42**	—	11 8
6 34	**2 22**	4 50	116	Arr.	**Samàra** bf.	Dep.	942	**2 25**	9 20	10 48
7 10	**4 0**	**6 20**	116	Dep.	**Samára**	Arr.	942	**1 15**	8 44	8 8
—	—	—	—	„	Bezimiánka	„	—	—	—	—
—	**4 40**	**7 0**	136	„	Smyshliàevka	„	922	**12 41**	—	7 34
8 14	**5 22**	**7 42**	155	Arr.	**Kinél** bf.	Dep.	902	**11 50**	7 33	6 45
8 29	**5 37**	**8 0**		Dep.		Arr.		**11 35**	7 22	6 30
8 59	6 13	**8 34**	169	„	Turgénevka	„	889	**11 13**	7 3	6 8
—	6 37	—	—	„	Rab. Sarbài	„	—	—	6 36	—
9 30	6 56	**9 10**	190	Arr.	**Kròtovka**	Dep.	867	**10 25**	6 19	**5 17**
9 33	7 6	**9 20**	190	Dep.	**Kròtovka**	Arr.	867	**10 12**	6 17	**5 2**
	7 34	**9 48**	204	„	Mukhànovo	„	853	**9 50**	—	**4 40**
10 12	7 59	**10 13**	220	Arr.	Cherkàsskaya	Dep.	837	**9 20**	**5 36**	**4 10**
10 27	8 10	**10 25**		Dep.		Arr.		**9 5**	**5 24**	**3 54**
—	—	—	—	„	Tungùz (sid.)	„	—	—	**5 8**	—
—	8 59	**11 15**	244	„	Kliuchì	„	814	**8 26**	—	**3 15**
—	—	—	—	„	Avérkino (sid.)	„	—	—	—	—
11 36	9 42	**11 58**	266	Arr.	**Pòkhvistnevo** bf.	Dep.	791	**7 37**	**4 15**	**2 27**
11 50	10 0	**12 23**		Dep.		Arr.		**7 22**	**3 57**	**2 2**
—	—	—	—	„	Savrùkha (sid.)	„	—	—	—	—
12 18	10 32	**12 55**	285	Arr.	Buguruslàn	Dep.	773	**6 50**	**3 20**	**1 30**
12 21	10 42	**1 20**		Dep.		Arr.		**6 35**	**3 28**	**1 11**

*) The fast trains 2 and 1 are without changing for comm. Moscow-Irkútsk. These trains leave: Moscow (№ 17) on Sat. (№ 2) Batrakí on Mond. (№ 1) Irkútsk on Frid., Cheliábinsk on Thurs.

**) Without changing: Moscow—Irkútsk I—II cl. trains 2 and 1. Moscow—Túla—Cheliábinsk I—III cl. trains 4 and 3.

Night time from **6.0** P. M. to **5.59** A. M. indicated by heavy type.

Ft. 2 I–II	Pr. 6 I–II	Ml. 4 I–III	Versts.	*Samára-Zlatoúst r. w.*	Versts.	Ft. 1 I–III	Pr 5. I–II	Ml. 3 I–III
—	—	—	—	Dep. Zaviálovo (sid.) . . . . Arr.	—	—	—	—
—	11 24	**2 4**	306	„ Zagliádino . . . . . . „	751	—	—	**12 35**
1 19	11 50	**2 35**	316	„ Asekéevo . . . . . . „	742	5 43	**2 43**	**12 14**
—	—	—	—	„ Kísla (sid.) . . . . . „	—	—	—	—
—	12 42	**3 30**	335	„ Filíppovka . . . . . . „	723	5 1	—	**11 32**
—	—	—	—	„ Mochegái . . . . . . „	—	—	—	—
—	1 24	**4 14**	353	„ Sarái-Gír . . . . . . „	705	4 21	—	**10 52**
—	—	**4 85**	—	„ Yakúpovo (sid.) . . . . „	—	—	—	—
2 56	1 57	**4 49**	374	Arr. **Abdúlino** . . . . . . Dep.	684	3 31	**1 1**	**10 0**
3 21	2 27	**5 15**		Dep. Arr.		3 1	**12 41**	**9 30**
—	2 46	—	—	„ Ik (sid.). . . . . . . „	—	2 45	—	—
—	3 10	**5 58**	392	„ Taldy Bulák . . . . . . „	665	2 25	—	**8 59**
—	—	—	—	„ Turáevo (sid.) . . . . . „	—	—	—	—
4 31	3 51	6 40	408	„ Priyútovo . . . . . . „	649	1 48	—	**8 25**
—	—	—	—	„ Riabásh (sid.) . . . . . „	—	—	—	—
5 5	4 29	7 18	427	Arr. Beleb. Aksákovo . . . . Dep.	630	1 8	**11 20**	**7 47**
5 8	4 35	7 30		Dep. Arr.		1 0	**11 10**	**7 37**
—	—	—	—	„ Maksiútovo. . . . . . . „	—	—	—	—
5 44	5 13	8 8	444	„ Glukhovskáya. . . . . . „	613	12 30	—	**7 7**
—	—	—	—	„ Gáina . . . . „	—	—	—	—
6 19	5 52	8 52	464	„ Aksiónovo . . . . „	593	11 46	**10 10**	**6 23**
—	**6 4**	—	—	„ Aldárovo (sid.) . . . . . „	—	—	—	**6 3**
6 47	**6 26**	9 28	479	„ Shafránovo. . . . . . „	578	11 0	—	5 38
—	—	—	—	„ Slak (sid.). . . . . . . „	—	—	—	—
7 16	**6 59**	10 1	499	Arr. **Ráevka** bf. . . . . . . Dep.	558	10 10	**8 50**	4 48
7 30	**7 52**	10 21		Dep. Arr.		9 50	**8 82**	4 26
—	**8 18**	—	—	„ Tiulián (sid.). . . . . . „	—	—	**8 17**	—
8 3	**8 36**	10 59	517	„ Davlekánovo . . . . . . „	540	9 15	**8 2**	3 51
—	—	—	—	„ Kazangúl . . . . . „	—	—	—	—
8 36	**9 10**	11 33	539	Arr. Shingák Kúl . . . . . . Dep.	518	8 30	—	3 4
8 46	**9 20**	11 43		Dep. Arr.		8 21	—	2 54
—	—	—	—	„ Udriák . . . . „	—	—	—	—
9 34	**10 10**	12 35	563	„ Chishmy. . . . . „	494	7 40	**6 53**	2 13
—	—	—	—	„ Alkino . . . . „	—	—	—	—
—	**10 53**	1 16	586	„ Yumátovo . . . . . . „	472	6 49	—	1 24
—	—	1 37	—	„ Dióma (sid.) . . . . . . „	—	—	—	—
10 40	**11 31**	1 55	607	Arr. **Ufá** bf. . . . . Dep.	450	6 0	5 36	12 35
11 10	**12 1**	2 30		Dep. Arr.		**5 20**	5 16	12 0
—	—	—	—	„ Cherníkovka (sid.) . . . „	—	—	—	—
12 15	**1 9**	3 38	628	„ Urákovo. . . . . „	430	**4 24**	—	11 4
—	**1 38**	4 7	640	„ Iglino. . . . . „	417	**3 53**	4 4	10 36
—	—	—	—	„ Chuvashí (sid.) . . . . . „	—	—	—	—
—	**2 20**	4 49	658	„ Tavtimánovo . . . . . . „	399	**3 10**	—	9 57
—	**2 44**	—	—	„ Kudéevka (sid.). . . . . „	—	**2 43**	—	—
1 50	**3 10**	5 37	683	„ Ulú Teliák. . . . . . „	374	**2 4**	2 37	9 4
—	—	—	—	„ Kazayák (sid.) . . . . . „	—	—	—	—
2 24	**3 50**	**6 17**	704	Arr. Ashá Balashóvskaya bf. . Dep.	353	**1 11**	1 53	8 20
2 30	**3 58**	**6 26**		Dep. Arr.		**1 5**	1 43	8 10
—	—	—	—	„ Gremúchi Kliúch (sid.) . . „	—	—	—	—
—	**4 37**	**7 8**	723	„ Miniár . . . . „	334	**12 29**	—	7 34
3 36	**5 10**	**7 41**	736	„ Símskaya . . . . „	321	**11 58**	12 47	7 3
—	—	—	—	„ Yerál (sid.) . . . . . . „	—	—	—	—
4 38	6 26	**8 52**	758	„ Kropachóvo. . . . . . „	299	**11 10**	12 0	6 15
—	—	—	—	„ Yákhino 590 ver. . . . „	—	—	—	—
5 15	7 4	**9 30**	77	„ Ust Katáv . . . . . . „	284	**10 17**	—	**5 13**
—	—	**9 50**	—	„ Yurezán . . . . „	—	**9 52**	—	—
5 46	7 40	**10 8**	791	Arr. Viazováya bf. . . . . . Dep.	266	**9 25**	10 38	**4 28**
6 1	7 55	**10 23**		Dep. Arr.		**9 7**	10 23	**4 7**

For trains №№ 1 and 2, tickets of reduced tariff are not available.
Night time from **6.0** P. M. to **5.59** A. M. is indicated by heavy type.

Ff. 2 I—II	Pr. 6 I—II	Ml. 4 I—III	Versts.	*Samára-Zlatoúst r. w.*	Versts.	Ft. 1 I—III	Pr. 5 I—II⁰	Ml. 3 I—III
—	—	—	—	Dep. Tiubialiás (sid.) . . . . . Arr.	—	—	—	—
—	8 50	**11 21**	813	„ Mursalímkino . . . . . . „	245	**8 19**	—	**3 19**
—	9 21	—	—	„ Kúkshik (sid.) . . . . . . „	—	—	9 20	-
—	9 51	**12 18**	837	„ Suleyá . . . . „	221	**7 14**	—	**2 22**
—	—	—	—	„ Yedinovér (sid.) . . . . . „	—	—	—	—
8 21	10 50	**1 17**	859	„ Berdiaúsh . . . . „	199	**6 20**	8 12	**1 27**
—	—	—	—	„ Salgán (sid.) . . . . „	—	—	—	—
—	11 42	**2 9**	878	„ Tundúsh. . . . . „	179	5 23	7 14	**12 25**
—	12 5	**2 32**	—	„ Kusínskaya platf. . . . . . „	—	4 56	—	**11 49**
—	—	—	—	„ Ai (sid.) . . . . „	—	—	—	—
9 50	12 39	**3 6**	—	„ Zavódskaya pl. . . . . . . „	—	4 25	6 22	**11 15**
10 1	12 52	**3 19**	907	Arr. **Zlatoúst** bf . . . . Dep.	151	4 10	6 10	**11 0**
10 21	1 7	**3 36**		Dep. . . . . Arr.		3 41	**5 54**	**10 31**
—	—	—	—	„ Taganái (sid.) . . . . . . „	—	—	—	—
—	2 3	**4 32**	925	„ Urzhúmka . . . . „	132	3 3		**6 53**
—	2 24	**4 53**	—	„ Khrebiót . . . . „	—	2 25	**4 54**	—
—	2 52	**5 21**	947	„ Syrostán . . . . „	111	1 46	—	**8 45**
—	—	—	—	„ Turgoyák s. . . . . „	—	—	—	—
12 35	3 49	6 18	967	„ Miáss bf. . . . . „	90	12 50	**3 39**	**7 45**
—	—	—	—	„ Kisegách . . . . „	—	—	—	—
—	4 40	7 10	990	„ Chebarkúl . . . . „	68	11 47	—	**6 40**
—	—	—	—	„ Shakhmátovo . . . . „	—	—	—	—
2 6	5 35	8 5	1009	„ Bishkíl . . . . „	48	10 59	**1 58**	5 46
—	—	—	—	„ Birgíl. (sid.) . . . . . . „	—	—	—	—
—	**6 27**	9 0	1033	„ Poletáevo . . . . . . „	24	9 53	—	4 40
—	—	9 25	—	„ Smólino (sid.) . . . . . . „	—	9 24	—	—
3 30	**7 15**	9 50	1057	Arr. **Cheliàbinsk** bf. . . . . . . Dep.	—	8 50	**12 15**	3 45
5 0	**9 15**	12 20	—	Dep. *Cheliábinsk* . . Arr.	3049	**5 12**	**11 0**	1 0
9 25	2 31	**7 22**	746	„ *Omsk* . . 172 „	2303	11 33	**6 37**	7 28
7 15	5 0	5 40	3049	Arr. *Irkútsk* . Dep.	—	**1 20**	9 45	**4 0**
—	—	10 48	—	Dep. *Cheliábinsk.* . . Arr.	698	—	—	2 44
—	—	**8 42**	231	„ *Yekater. I* . 175 „	467	—	—	**5 26**
—	—	12 13	698	Arr. *Perm* . . . . . Dep.	—	—	—	1 16

Night time from **6.0** P. M. to **5.59** A. M. is indicated by heavy type.

Steam navigation on the rivers Vólga, Káma and Bélaya.

Steamers leave Samára daily up and down the Vólga. They belong to the following companies: 1) „The Vólga S. S. Company founded in 1843", 2) „The Vólga Trading and Passenger S. S. Company", 3) „The Nadézhda", 4) „The Caucasus and Mercury" and 5) „The Samoliót".

(Information on sailings and fares is contained in the Official Guide of the Ministry of Ways of Communication, №№ 365—368).

Between Ufá and Nízhni Nóvgorod, on the rivers Bélaya, Káma and Vólga, ply the steamers belonging to „Yakímov and Sons" and „Burlychóv".

(Sailings from Ufá four times a week).

(Information on sailings and fares is to be found in the Official Guide of the Ministry of Ways of Communication, № 363).

Perm Railway.

(Office in Perm).

175. Yekaterinbúrg-Cheliábinsk and back.

Mixed 26 II-IV	Mail 4 I-III	Versts.	*Perm railway.*	Versts.	Mail 3 I-III	Mixed 25 II-IV
12 37	**5 26**	467	Dep. **Yekaterinbúrg** bf. . . . . . . Arr.	231	**8 8**	**1 10**
12 58	**5 37**	471	„ Yekaterinbúrg II . . . . „	227	**7 59**	**1 1**
1 23	**5 57**	477	„ Uktús . . . . „	221	**7 42**	**12 36**
2 46	7 14	507	„ Mrámornaya . . . . „	191	**6 38**	**11 23**
3 50	8 15	536	„ Poldnióvnaya . . . . „	162	5 50	**9 54**
4 58	9 23	565	Arr. **Ufaléi** bf. . . . . Dep.	133	4 18	**8 36**
5 13	9 37		Dep. Arr.		4 4	**8 16**
6 19	10 40	592	„ Maúk . . . . „	106	3 1	**7 13**
7 8	11 27	613	Arr. **Kyshtym** . . . . Dep.	84	2 6	**6 14**
7 29	11 38		Dep. Arr.		1 56	**6 2**
8 42	12 54	646	„ Argayásh . . . . „	52	12 49	4 55
9 29	1 53	675	„ Yesaúlskaya . . . . „	24	11 43	3 54
10 40	2 44	698	Arr. **Cheliábinsk** bf. . . . . Dep.	—	10 48	2 55
12 20	5 0	—	Dep. ***Cheliábinsk*** . } 172 Arr.	3049	**5 12**	1 0
7 22	**9 25**	746	„ ***Omsk*** . . . . } 172 „	2303	11 33	7 28
5 40	7 15	3049	„ ***Irkútsk*** . . . } 172 Dep.	—	**1 20**	**4 0**
—	3 45	—	Dep. ***Cheliábinsk*** . . } 170 Arr.	2060	9 50	—
--	10 48	942	„ ***Samára*** . . . } 170, 169 „	1118	**6 20**	—
—	**9 30**	1681	„ *Riázhsk* . . . } 169, 163 „	379	10 10	—
—	6 43	1877	„ ***Túla*** . . . . } 108, 163 „	183	**11 25**	—
—	2 20	2060	„ ***Moscow*** . . } 108, 163 Dep.	—	2 30	—

Night time from **6.0** P. M. to **5.59** A. M. indicated by heavy type.

176. Yekaterinbúrg—Tiumén and back.

Mixed 26 II-IV	Mail 4 I—III	Versts.	Perm railway.	Versts.	Mixed 25 II—IV	Mail 3 I—III
2 55	10 48		— Dep. *Cheliábinsk* } 175 Arr. 231		10 40	2 44
1 10	8 8		231 Arr. *Yekaterinbúrg* } 175 Dep. —		12 37	5 26
2 56	10 0	—	Dep. **Yekaterinbúrg** bf. . . . . Arr.	304	11 19	4 20
3 8	10 12	4	„ Yekaterinbúrg II . . . . „	300	11 9	4 10
3 46	10 39	15	„ Istók . . . . „	289	10 40	3 44
4 43	11 27	33	„ Kosúlino . . . . „	271	9 44	3 0
5 47	12 13	53	„ **Bazhénovo** bf. . . . . „	251	8 46	2 6
6 40	1 2	75	„ Griaznóvskaya . . . . „	229	7 36	1 5
7 20	1 38	94	Arr. **Bogdanòvich** bf. . . . . Dep.	210	6 42	12 10
—	2 20		— Dep. *Bogdanóvich* } 179 Arr. 38		—	11 13
—	3 43		38 Arr. *Ostróvskaya* } 179 Dep. —		—	9 50
7 50	2 03	94	Dep. **Bogdanòvich** bf.	210	6 22	11 51
8 34	2 42	113	„ Pyshminskaya	191	5 35	11 9
9 18	3 23	134	Arr. **Kamyshlòv** bf. . . . . Dep.	170	4 39	10 13
9 48	3 43		Dep. **Kamyshlòv** bf. Arr.		4 13	9 14
10 43	4 31	151	„ Aksárikha . . . . „	153	3 38	9 12
11 36	5 18	171	„ Oshchépkovo . . . . „	133	2 49	8 14
12 33	6 15	201	Arr. **Poklévskaya** bf. . . . . Dep.	103	1 34	7 10
1 20	6 35		Dep. **Poklévskaya** bf. Arr.		1 9	6 54
2 45	7 43	232	„ Yushalà . . . . „	72	12 6	5 52
3 30	8 25	248	„ Tugulym . . . . „	56	11 24	5 14
4 31	9 06	266	„ Karmàk . . . . „	38	10 32	4 29
5 21	9 51	285	„ Perevàlovo . . . . „	19	9 48	3 47
5 58	10 24	304	Arr. **Tiumén** bf. . . . . Dep.	—	8 53	2 56

Siberian Railway

(Office in Tomsk).

Cheliábinsk—Irkútsk—№ 173.
Taigá—Tomsk—Cheremóshniki—№ 173.
Omsk (station)—Omsk (town)—№ 173a.

172. Cheliábinsk—Irkútsk and back.

Without changing Moscow—Irkútsk I—II cl. in trains 2 and 1.

12 5	**8 35**	2 30	—	Dep. *Moscow* . .	108	Arr.	2058	6 43	**7 0**	6 35
12 15	**2 30**	**11 35**	182	„ *Túla* . . .	108 / 163	„	1876	2 0	2 20	**11 20**
9 40	8 37	10 10	379	„ *Riázhsk* .	163	„	679	**9 30**	7 34	9 10
4 0	7 10	**6 20**	1117	„ *Samára* . .	169 170	„	942	10 48	9 20	**2 25**
7 15	3 30	9 50	2058	Arr. *Cheliábinsk*		Dep.	—	3 45	**12 15**	8 50
—	1 16	**7 40**	—	Dep. *Perm* . . .	175	Arr.	698	**3 50**	—	12 13
—	2 44	10 40	698	Arr. *Cheliábinsk*		Dep.	—	2 55	—	10 48

Gp. 12 II—IV	Fst. 2 I—II	Mail 4 I—III	Versts.	*Siberian railway.*	Versts.	Mail 3 I—III	Fst. 1 I—II	Gp. II II—IV
9 15	5 0	12 20	—	Dep. **Cheliàbinsk** bf. . . . . Arr.	3049	1 0	**11 0**	**5 12**
9 39	—	12 43	—	„ Siding . . . . „	—	12 41	—	**4 44**
10 17	—	1 5	—	„ Siding . . . . „	—	12 18	—	**4 6**
11 18	**6 27**	1 53	41	„ Cherniávskaya . . . . . „	3008	11 37	**9 29**	**3 14**
12 10	—	2 31	—	„ Siding . . . . „	—	10 45	—	**2 17**
1 13	**7 52**	3 25	83	„ Chumliák bf. . . . . . . „	2966	9 58	**7 58**	**1 21**
2 9	—	4 4	—	„ Siding . . . . „	—	9 3	—	**12 22**
2 46	**8 56**	4 35	117	Arr. **Shumìkha** bf. . . . . Dep.	2932	8 28	**6 39**	**11 38**
3 36	**9 11**	4 55		Dep. . . . . Arr.		8 13	**6 20**	**10 38**
4 31	—	5 41	—	„ Siding . . . . „	—	7 33	—	**9 51**
5 38	**10 29**	**6 27**	156	„ Míshkino bf. . . . . . . „	2893	6 53	5 2	**9 4**
6 25	—	**6 50**	—	„ Siding . . . . „	—	6 18	—	**8 27**
7 18	**11 37**	**7 45**	188	„ Yurgamysh . . . . . . „	2861	**5 35**	3 43	**7 36**
8 16	**12 16**	**8 32**	206	„ Zyriánka . . . . „	2843	**4 51**	2 59	**6 38**
8 50	—	**8 56**	—	„ Siding . . . . „	—	**4 17**	—	5 58
9 20	—	**9 2**	—	„ Siding . . . . „	—	**3 49**	—	5 14
9 52	**1 21**	**9 47**	241	Arr. **Kurgàn** bf. . . . . Dep	2808	**3 20**	1 29	4 30
11 27	**1 41**	**10 42**		Dep. . . . . App.		**2 56**	12 57	3 8
12 22	—	**11 20**	—	„ Siding . . . . „	—	**2 21**	—	2 24
1 24	**3 9**	**12 9**	276	„ Vargashí . . . . „	2765	**1 41**	11 41	1 37
2 20	—	**12 55**	—	„ Siding . . . . „	—	**12 53**	—	12 33
3 26	**4 40**	**1 49**	318	„ Lebiázhia . . . . „	2731	**11 59**	10 11	11 31
4 3	—	**2 17**	—	„ Siding . . . . „	—	**11 17**	—	10 41
4 41	—	**2 51**	—	„ Siding . . . . „	—	**10 53**	—	10 10
5 21	6 8	**3 23**	363	Arr. **Makùshino** bf. . . . . . Dep.	2686	**10 22**	8 33	9 29
6 20	6 39	**3 35**		Dep. . . . . Arr.		**10 7**	8 13	9 14
7 22	—	**4 23**	—	„ Siding . . . . „	—	**9 18**	—	8 15
8 28	8 23	**5 16**	407	„ Petukhóvo . . . . „	2642	**8 36**	6 47	**5 50**
9 15	—	6 2	—	„ Siding . . . . „	—	**7 48**	—	**4 20**
10 16	9 55	6 56	449	„ Mamliútka . . . . „	2601	**7 4**	**5 20**	**3 24**
10 58	—	7 29	—	„ Siding . . . . „	—	**6 22**	—	**2 34**
11 30	—	8 2	—	„ Siding . . . . „	—	5 57	—	**2 4**
12 3	11 18	8 29	490	Arr. **Petropàvlovsk** bf. . . . Dep.	2559	5 32	**3 36**	**1 29**
12 43	11 40	8 54		Dep. . . . . App.		5 12	**3 18**	**12 39**
1 25	—	9 27	—	„ Siding . . . . „	—	5 40	—	**12 0**
2 19	12 50	10 10	523	„ Tokushí . . . . „	2526	4 8	**2 17**	**11 19**
3 26	—	11 4	—	„ Siding . . . . „	—	3 9	—	**10 9**

*) Fast passenger trains 2 and 1 are without changing for communication Moscow—Irkútsk. These trains leave: № 17 Moscow, on Saturdays; № 2 Cheliábinsk on Thursdays, arriving at Irkútsk on Mondays; № 1 Irkútsk, on Fridays; № 18 arrives at Moscow on Saturdays.

Night time from **6.0** P. M. to **5.59** A. M. indicated by heavy type.

Gp. 12 II—IV	Fst. 2 I—II	Mail 4 I—III	Versts.		*Siberian railway.*		Versts.	Meil 3 I—III	Fst. 1 I—II	Gp. 11 II—IV
4 32	2 21	11 56	567	Dep.	Medvézhia	Arr.	2482	2 29	**12 48**	**9 16**
5 30	—	12 40	590	„	Kára-Gugá (sid.)	„	2479	1 39	—	**8 9**
6 1	—	1 11	—	„	Siding	„	—	1 14	—	**7 32**
6 36	3 52	1 38	617	Arr.	**Isíl-Kúl** bf.	Dep.	2432	12 40	**11 7**	**6 55**
7 11	4 5	1 58		Dep.		Arr.		12 20	**10 55**	5 38
8 1	—	2 38	—	„	Siding.	„	—	11 40	—	4 48
9 7	5 23	3 25	657	„	Kochubáevo	„	3392	11 3	**9 42**	3 47
10 10	—	4 8	—	„	Siding	„	—	10 7	—	2 27
11 30	**6 46**	4 58	700	„	Mariánovka	„	2349	9 25	**8 21**	1 38
12 35	—	5 44	—	„	Siding	„	—	8 20	—	12 33
1 21	—	**6 18**	—	„	Omsk (post)	„	—	7 42	—	11 48
1 35	**8 15**	**6 32**	746	Arr.	**Omsk** bf.	Dep.	2303	7 28	**6 37**	11 33
2 31	**9 25**	**7 22**		Dep.		App.		6 25	**6 7**	11 1
3 16	—	**8 0**	—	„	Siding	„	—	**5 50**	—	10 17
3 49	—	**8 27**	—	„	Siding	„	—	**5 23**	—	9 43
4 35	**11 4**	**9 6**	790	„	Kormílovka.	„	2259	**4 57**	4 37	9 11
5 24	—	**9 40**	—	„	Siding	„	—	**4 14**	—	8 23
6 11	**12 12**	**10 13**	820	„	Kaláchinskaya	„	2229	**3 47**	3 33	7 52
7 8	—	**10 53**	—	„	Siding	„	—	**3 0**	—	7 0
8 27	**1 51**	**12 0**	859	„	Shádrinskaya.	„	2195	**1 58**	1 56	**5 55**
9 37	—	**12 59**	—	„	Siding	„	—	**12 58**	—	**4 40**
10 37	**3 38**	**1 49**	904	Arr.	**Tatárskaya** bf.	Dep.	2140	**12 2**	12 8	**3 41**
11 50	**3 58**	**2 4**	904	Dep.	**Tatárskaya** bf.	Arr.	2140	**11 47**	11 53	**2 1**
12 54	—	**2 59**	—	„	Siding	„	—	**10 48**	—	**12 56**
2 16	6 10	**4 9**	953	„	Karachí	„	2096	**9 45**	9 57	**11 41**
3 26	—	**5 7**	—	„	Siding	„	—	**8 35**	—	**10 29**
4 35	8 3	6 3	996	„	Tebísskaya.	„	2053	**7 45**	8 9	**9 33**
5 17	—	6 36	—	„	Siding	„	—	**6 55**	—	**8 40**
7 52	—	**7 4**	—	„	Siding	„	—	**6 25**	—	**8 11**
8 52	9 46	7 55	1049	Arr.	**Káinsk** bf.	Dep.	2000	5 30	6 15	**7 10**
10 48	10 1	8 15		Dep.		Arr.		5 10	**5 55**	**6 38**
11 48	—	9 6	—	„	Siding.	„	—	4 18	—	5 39
12 38	11 29	9 50	1090	„	Kozhurlá	„	1959	3 42	**4 36**	4 58
1 21	—	10 28	—	„	Siding	„	—	2 53	—	4 2
3 5	12 49	11 20	1128	„	Ubínskaya	„	1921	2 13	**3 11**	3 12
3 58	—	12 4	—	„	Siding	„	—	1 28	—	2 10
5 1	2 15	12 47	1166	„	Karg t	„	1883	12 44	**1 50**	11 12
5 58	—	1 27	—	„	Siding	„	—	11 53	—	10 8
6 50	3 33	2 9	1209	Arr.	**Chulym** bf.	Dep.	1840	11 15	**12 27**	9 17
7 40	3 48	2 24		Dep.		Arr.		11 0	**12 14**	8 59
8 32	—	3 5	—	„	Siding	„	—	10 22	—	8 10
9 32	5 17	3 59	1249	„	Dupliónskaya	„	1800	9 46	**11 7**	7 20
10 27	—	4 39	—	„	Siding	„	—	9 0	—	6 21
11 22	**6 41**	5 28	1285	„	Kóchenovo	„	1764	8 27	**9 53**	**5 35**
12 7	—	**6 7**	1299	„	Chik (sid.)	„	1750	7 49	—	**4 34**
12 40	—	**6 32**	—	„	Siding	„	—	7 15	—	**3 52**
1 10	**8 5**	**6 58**	1324	Arr.	**Krivoshchékovo** bf.	Dep.	1725	6 50	**8 13**	**3 18**
1 30	**8 21**	**7 8**		Dep.		Arr.		6 40	**8 0**	**2 58**
2 0	**8 46**	**7 33**	1335	Arr.	**Ob** bf.	Dep.	1714	6 15	**7 35**	**2 28**
5 20	**9 30**	**8 23**		Dep.		Arr.		**4 40**	**7 10**	**12 30**
6 21	**10 20**	**9 12**	—	„	Kámenka (sid.)	„	—	**3 52**	**6 22**	**11 42**
7 17	**11 3**	**9 51**	1366	„	Sókur.	„	1683	**3 8**	5 48	**10 58**
8 15	**11 34**	**10 40**	—	„	Anísimovka (sid.)	„	—	**2 8**	4 56	**8 52**

*) All I, II and III class carriages sleeping.

*) Fast trains 2 and 1 without changing for communication Moscow -- Irkútsk. These trains leave: № 17 Moscow. on Saturdays; № 2 Ob, on Thursdays, arriving at Irkútsk on Mondays; № 1 Irkútsk, on Fridays, arriving at Moscow on Saturdays.

Night time from **6.0** P. M. to **5.59** A. M. indicated by heavy type.

Gp. 12 II—IV	Fet. 2 I—II	Mail 4 I—III	Versts.		*Siberian railway.*		Versts.	Mail 3 I—III	Fst. 1 I—II	Gp. 11 I—IV
9 50	**1 6**	**11 54**	1408	Dep.	Oyásh	Arr.	1641	**1 2**	3 53	**7 34**
10 58	**2 2**	**12 50**	—	„	Chebulá (sid.)	„	—	**10 55**	2 56	5 50
—	—	—	1450	Arr.	**Bolótnoe** bf.	Dep.	1559	**9 52**	1 54	4 35
12 27	**3 31**	**2 4**		Dep.		Arr.		—	—	—
1 15	**4 10**	**2 47**	—	„	Barnaúlsky (sid.)	„	—	**8 58**	1 10	3 47
2 39	**5 14**	**3 53**	1490	„	Polomóshnaya	„	1560	**7 56**	12 9	2 43
4 4	**6 20**	**5 0**	1515	„	Litvínovo	„	1534	**6 48**	11 3	1 32
5 20	7 32	6 15	1547	Arr.	Taigá bf.	Dep.	1502	**5 25**	9 48	12 10
6 0	—	8 30	—	Dep.	*Taigá* . . } **172a** .	Arr.	82	4 35	—	7 25
9 30	—	12 0	82	Arr.	***Tomsk*** . .	Dep.	—	1 10	—	**3 50**
6 20	7 57	9 29	1547	Dep.	**Taigá** bf.	Arr.	1502	4 10	9 21	11 9
7 0	8 40	10 23	—	„	Lebediánka (sid.)	„	—	3 31	8 42	10 30
7 57	9 34	11 19	1584	„	Sùdzhenka	„	1466	2 34	7 50	9 30
8 50	10 25	12 11	—	„	Yáya (sid.)	„	—	1 27	7 1	8 38
9 42	11 4	12 59	1617	„	Izhmórskaya	„	1432	12 50	6 25	8 2
0 22	11 43	1 38	—	„	Voskresénski (sid.) . . .	„	—	11 47	**5 44**	7 12
11 44	12 38	2 36	1654	„	Birikúlskaya	„	1396	10 42	**4 49**	6 8
11 0	1 53	3 50	1686	Arr.	**Marìinsk** bf.	Dep.	1364	9 20	**3 38**	**4 50**
1 36	1 58	4 4		Dep.		Arr.		8 50	**3 28**	**1 10**
2 46	2 51	4 59	1708	„	Súslovo	„	1341	7 56	**2 36**	**12 16**
4 16	3 41	5 52	—	„	Kliuchevskói (sid.) . . .	„	—	7 3	**1 46**	**11 15**
6 6	4 42	**6 57**	1742	„	Tiázhin	„	1307	6 2	**12 47**	**10 4**
7 30	**6 4**	**8 21**	1775	„	Itát	„	1274	**4 38**	**11 28**	**8 23**
8 53	**7 25**	**9 45**	1810	Arr.	**Bogotól** bf.	Dep.	1239	**3 10**	**10 0**	4 32
9 17	**7 30**	**9 57**		Dep.		Arr.		**3 2**	**9 53**	3 33
10 28	**8 47**	**11 11**	1841	„	Krásnaya	„	1208	**1 50**	**8 43**	2 20
11 56	**10 5**	**12 26**	1874	Arr.	**Achinsk** bf.	Dep.	1176	**12 81**	**7 25**	12 53
12 49	**10 25**	**12 50**		Dep.		Arr.		**12 20**	**7 15**	12 3
2 4	**11 26**	**1 40**	1894	„	Tarútino.	„	1155	**11 82**	**6 26**	11 14
—	—	—	1910	Arr.	**Chernoréchenskaya** bf.	Dep	1139	**10 39**	**5 41**	10 20
3 9	**12 15**	**2 32**	1910	Dep.	**Chernoréchenskaya** bf. .	Arr.	1139	—	—	—
4 34	**1 21**	**3 39**	—	„	Kozúlka (sid.)	„	—	**9 28**	4 30	8 45
5 50	**2 28**	**4 52**	1955	„	Kemchúg	„	1094	**8 21**	3 25	7 31
7 10	**3 33**	**5 58**	—	„	Zhúkovka (sid.)	„	—	**7 2**	2 19	6 1
8 55	**4 14**	6 39	1996	„	Kácha.	„	1054	**6 18**	1 42	**4 40**
9 36	**4 46**	7 11	—	„	Yelóvka (sid.)	„	—	5 25	1 7	**3 27**
10 9	**5 11**	7 36	2023	„	Mínino	„	1026	4 56	12 42	**2 50**
10 50	**5 45**	8 10	2040	Arr.	**Krasnoyársk** bf.	Dep.	1009	4 15	12 7	**2 0**
12 20	**6 15**	9 0		Dep.		Arr.		3 0	11 40	**1 10**
—	—	—	2045	Arr.	**Yeniséi** bf.	Dep.	–	2 40	11 25	**12 50**
12 55	6 35	9 20		Dep.		Arr.		—	—	—
2 6	7 40	10 30	2070	„	Zykovo	„	979	1 34	10 23	**11 47**
4 12	9 11	12 10	2093	„	Sorókino	„	957	12 0	9 1	**10 15**
5 32	10 27	1 34	2116	„	Kamarchága	„	934	10 30	7 40	**8 40**
6 43	11 32	2 43	2140	„	Balái	„	910	9 14	6 38	**7 35**
7 40	12 28	3 40	2164	Arr.	**Olginskaya** bf.	Dep.	886	8 10	**5 35**	**6 33**
9 10	12 33	3 55		Dep.		Arr.		7 55	**5 25**	**6 13**
10 28	1 40	5 12	2191	„	Tróitsko-Zaoziórnaya . . .	„	858	6 50	**4 19**	5 6
11 55	2 36	**6 21**	2211	„	Tyrbyl	„	838	**5 46**	**3 20**	3 10
1 24	3 33	**7 30**	2235	„	Petrushkóvo	„	815	**4 30**	**2 15**	1 28
2 41	4 27	**8 25**	—	„	Filimónovo (sid.)	„	—	**3 27**	**1 20**	12 4
3 15	5 0	**8 58**	2267	Arr.	**Kansk** bf.	Dep.	782	**2 52**	**12 45**	11 20
3 45	5 5	**9 87**		Dep.		Arr.		**2 35**	**12 30**	10 40
4 48	**6 8**	**10 40**	2293	Arr.	**Ilánskaya** bf.	Dep.	756	**1 32**	**11 27**	9 37
4 56	**6 13**	**11 2**		Dep.		Arr.		**1 27**	**10 38**	9 17
9 53	**7 24**	**12 24**	2320	„	Ingásh	„	729	**12 17**	**9 48**	8 5
11 8	**8 37**	**1 46**	2346	„	Tínskaya	„	704	**11 2**	**8 42**	6 50
—	—	—	—	„	Reshety (sid.)	„	—	—	—	—
—	—	—	2375	Arr.	**Klúichinskaya** bf.	Dep.	675	**9 50**	**7 24**	**5 30**

Gp. 12 II—IV	Fst. 2 I—II	Mail 4 I—III	Versts.	Siberian railway.	Versts.	Mail 3 I—III	Fst. 1 I—II	Gp. II I—IV
12 44	9 53	3 0	2375	Dep. **Kliùchinskaya** bf. . . . Arr.	675	—	—	—
2 12	10 52	4 10	2397	„ Yurty. . . . . „	653	8 30	6 17	4 7
3 0	11 28	4 44	—	„ Biriusà (sid.) . . . . . . „	—	7 47	5 41	3 5
3 58	12 13	5 40	2425	Arr. **Taishét** bf. . . . . . . Dep.	624	6 50	4 55	1 57
6 57	12 18	5 55		Dep. Arr.		6 35	4 50	12 0
8 30	1 12	6 58	2445	„ Bairónovka. . . . . „	604	5 35	3 57	11 0
—	—	—	—	„ Gar (sid.) . . . . „	—	—	—	—
10 10	2 26	8 22	2472	„ Razgón . . . . „	577	4 4	2 45	9 30
11 35	3 17	9 31	2490	„ Alzamài . . . . „	559	3 6	1 55	8 24
2 2	4 15	10 37	2510	„ Zamzór . . . . „	539	2 0	12 55	7 4
3 20	5 12	11 55	2532	„ Kamyshét . . . . „	518	12 54	11 53	5 51
4 16	5 59	12 49	2548	„ Uk . . . . „	501	9 50	11 5	4 30
5 43	7 16	2 17	2574	Arr. **Nizhneùdinsk** bf. . . . Dep.	476	8 10	9 50	2 45
6 45	7 32	2 37		Dep. Arr.		7 23	9 35	2 10
8 26	8 41	3 46	2597	„ Khingùi . . . . „	453	6 15	8 34	12 45
9 38	9 15	4 54	2618	„ Khudoyelànskaya . . . . . „	431	5 6	7 30	11 37
10 27	10 30	5 43	—	„ Siding № 2 . . . . „	—	4 12	6 41	10 34
11 45	11 25	6 50	2652	„ Kurzàn . . . . „	397	3 17	5 51	9 34
1 20	12 54	8 22	2683	Arr. **Tulùn** . . . . Dep.	366	1 25	4 20	7 58
2 10	1 10	8 34		Dep. Arr.		12 54	4 10	7 32
3 24	2 6	9 31	2703	„ Azéi . . . . „	347	11 56	3 17	6 40
5 30	3 10	10 50	2722	„ Sheragùl . . . . „	327	10 40	2 15	5 38
7 30	4 55	12 34	2757	„ Kuitùn . . . . „	292	8 30	12 31	3 52
9 16	6 33	2 18	2787	„ Kimeltéi . . . . „	262	6 40	10 56	2 11
10 50	7 45	3 52	2814	Arr. **Zimà** bf. . . . . Dep.	236	5 10	9 32	12 25
11 18	7 53	4 20		Dep. Arr.		4 55	9 17	10 3
12 1	8 36	5 2	—	„ Shchétik (sid.) . . . . . . „	—	4 15	8 40	9 22
12 57	9 28	5 55	2844	„ Tyrét . . . . „	206	3 25	7 49	6 51
2 18	10 26	7 2	2867	„ Zalarí. . . . . „	183	2 14	6 43	5 23
3 40	11 23	8 21	2886	„ Golovínskaya . . . . „	163	1 11	5 50	4 4
4 52	12 20	9 33	2906	„ Kutulík . . . . „	144	11 50	4 48	2 34
7 55	1 20	10 14	2927	„ Cheremkóvo . . . . „	123	10 42	3 50	1 10
9 28	2 25	11 56	2952	Arr. **Polovìna** bf. . . . . . . Dep.	97	9 30	2 40	12 0
11 17	2 30	12 16		Dep. Arr.		9 10	2 30	8 8
12 43	3 29	1 27	2973	„ Maltà. . . . . „	76	8 6	1 32	6 36
1 55	4 37	2 45	2995	„ Telmà. . . . . „	55	6 57	12 19	4 35
3 12	5 41	3 53	3018	„ Sukhovskàya . . . . „	32	5 43	11 11	3 15
—	—	—	3042	Arr. **Inokéntievskaya** bf.. . . Dep.	7	4 28	10 3	1 55
4 32	6 49	5 14		Dep. Arr.		—	—	—
5 0	7 15	5 40	3049	Arr. **Irkùtsk** bf. . . . . . . Dep.	—	4 0	9 35	1 20

173. Taigá—Tomsk—Cheremoshniki and back.

Gp. 12 II—IV	Mail 4 I—III	Versts.	Siberian railway.	Versts.	Gp. II II—IV	Mail 3 I—III
9 15	12 20	—	Dep. *Cheliábinsk* . } 172 . Arr.	1547	5 12	1 0
5 20	6 15	1547	Arr. *Taigá* . . } 172 . Dep.	—	12 10	5 25
4 0	—	—	Dep. *Irkùtsk* . . } 172 . Dep.	1502	5 40	5 0
4 10	—	1502	Arr. *Taigá* . . . } 172 . Arr.	—	9 29	6 20
6 0	8 30	—	Dep. **Taigà** bf. . . . . Arr.	89	7 25	4 35
6 46	9 16	—	„ Siding № 1 . . . . „	—	6 1	3 50
7 58	10 23	45	„ Basandáika . . . . „	45	5 38	2 47
9 10	11 40	74	„ Mezhèninovka . . . . „	16	4 23	1 33
9 30	12 0	82	„ **Tomsk** bf. . . . . „	8	3 50	1 10
—	—	89	Arr. Cheremóshniki . . . . Dep.	—	—	—

Night time from 6.0 P. M. to 5.59 A. M. indicated by heavy type.

173a. **Omsk** (station)—**Omsk** (town) and back.

P. 230 II-III	P. 228 II-III	P. 222 II-III	P. 218 II-III	P. 212 II-III	Versts.	*Siberian railway.*	Versts.	P. 211 II-III	P. 217 II-III	P. 221 II-III	P. 227 II-III	P. 229 II-III
9 40	**7 35**	2 45	11 40	7 35	—	Arr. **Omsk** (stat.) Dep.	3	6 45	10 45	2 0	**6 10**	**8 20**
9 55	**7 50**	3 0	11 55	7 50	3	Dep. **Omsk** (town) Arr.	—	6 30	10 30	1 45	**5 55**	**8 5**

Steam navigation of Western Siberia.

The steamers of the West Siberian Steam Navigation and Trade Company ply once a week on the rivers Irtysh, Toból and Turá between the towns of Omsk, Tobólsk and Tiumén on the one hand and Semipalátinsk on the other. The Company notifies arrivals and sailings on each occasion by special advertisements.

197. **Tiumén—Semipalátinsk** and back.

Once a week.

Versts.	West Siberian Steam Navigation and Trade Company.			Versts.
—	Dep.	**Tiumén**	Arr.	2583
256	„	Iyevlevo	„	2328
412	„	**Tobôlsk**	„	2171
547	„	Bereziànskoe	„	2036
763	„	Ust-Ishím	„	1820
897	„	Tevríz	„	1686
992	„	Ivànov Mys	„	1591
1160	„	Tàra	„	1423
1257	„	Iziùk	„	1326
1331	„	Karatyshóv	„	1252
1428	„	Krupiànka	„	1155
1555	„	**Omsk**	„	1028
1732	„	Cherlàk	„	851
1845	„	Zheleziònka	„	738
1937	„	Vosmerítskoe	„	646
2141	„	Pavlodàr	„	442
2166	„	Voskresénskaya wharf	„	417
2394	„	Semiyàrskoe	„	189
2583	Arr.	**Semipalàtinsk**	Dep.	—

Passenger and luggage tariffs of the West Siberian Steam Navigation and Trade Company.

To or from stations:	Tiumén.				Tobólsk.				Omsk.				Semipalátinsk.			
From or to stations:	I	II	III	1pud lug.	I	II	III	1pud lug.	I	II	III	1pud lug.	I	II	III	1pud lug.
	r. k.	r. k.	r. k.	k.	r. k.	r. k.	r. k.	k.	r. k.	r. k.	r. k.	k.	r. k.	r. k.	r. k.	k.
Tiumén	—	—	—	—	4.00	3.00	2.00	20	10.00	8.00	4.00	45	20.00	15.00	8.00	70
Iyevlevo	3.00	2.00	1.20	15	2.00	1.50	1.00	15	9.00	7.00	3.75	40	19.00	14.00	7.50	65
Tobólsk	4.00	3.00	2.00	20	—	—	—	—	8.00	6.00	3.50	35	17.00	13.00	7.00	60
Bereziánskoe	4.50	3.50	2.20	25	2.00	1.00	0.60	15	7.50	5.00	3.00	35	16.50	12.50	6.50	60
Ust-Ishím	6.00	4.50	2.50	25	3.00	2.00	1.20	20	6.00	4.50	2.75	30	15.00	12.00	6.00	55
Tevríz	6.00	4.50	2.50	30	4.00	2.50	1.80	20	6.00	4.00	2.50	30	15.00	11.50	5.75	50
Ivánov Mys	6.50	5.00	3.00	30	5.00	3.00	2.00	25	5.50	3.50	2.25	30	14.50	11.00	5.50	50
Tára	8.00	6.00	3.00	35	5.50	4.00	2.25	25	4.00	3.00	2.00	25	13.00	10.00	5.50	45
Yevgáshchinskoe	8.25	6.50	3.25	35	6.00	4.50	2.25	30	3.50	2.50	1.50	25	12.50	9.50	5.00	45
Kartashóvo	8.50	6.50	3.50	40	6.50	5.00	2.75	30	3.00	2.00	1.00	20	12.50	9.00	4.80	40
Krupiánka	9 00	7.00	3.75	40	7.00	5.50	3.00	35	2.00	1.50	0.60	15	12.00	8.50	4.50	35
Omsk	10.00	8.00	4.00	45	8.00	6.00	3.50	35	—	—	—	—	11.00	8.00	4.20	35
Cherlák	12.00	9.00	4.50	50	11.00	7.00	4.00	40	2.50	1.50	0.70	15	9.00	7.00	4.00	30
Zheleziónka	13.00	10.00	5.00	55	11.00	8.00	4.00	45	4.00	2.50	1.20	20	8.00	6.00	3.50	30
Vosmerítskoe	14.00	11.00	5.50	55	11.00	9.50	4.50	50	5.00	3.50	1.80	25	6.00	5.50	3.00	25
Pavlodár	15.50	12.00	6.00	60	13.00	10.50	5.00	50	7.50	5.00	2.50	25	5.00	5.50	2.00	25
Voskresénskoe	17.00	13.00	6.50	60	14.00	11.50	5.50	50	8.00	6.00	3.00	25	3.00	2.00	1.50	20
Semiyárskoe	19.00	14.00	7.00	65	16.00	13.00	6.00	55	10.00	7.00	3.40	30	2.00	1.50	1.00	15
Semipalátinsk	20.00	15.00	8.00	70	17.00	13.00	7.00	60	11.00	8.00	4.20	35	—	—	—	—

Children from 2 to 10 yrs. old half-price, under 2—free.

There further ply between Semipalátinsk and Tiumén, at irregular intervals, steamers belonging to: 1) The „Yermák" Company, 2) M. Plótnikov, 3) The Bogoslóvsk mining District and 4) Korníloy.

No fixed rates for freights.

Between the towns of Tomsk and Tiumén, ply steamers belonging to the following companies: 1) The West Siberian Steam Navigation and Trade Company, 2) The „Yermák" Company, 3) Plótnikov, 4) The Bogoslóvsk Mining District and 5) Korníloy.

On the rivers Tom, Ob, Irtysh, Toból and Turá.

396. Tiumén—Tomsk and back.

Once a week (from 18 May).

Versts.	West Siberian Steam Navigation and Trade Company.			Versts.
—	Sails	**Tiumén**	Arr.	2219
256	„	Iyevlevo	„	1964
412	„	**Tobólsk**	„	1807
595	„	Uvát	„	1624
673	„	Demiánskoe	„	1546
951	„	Samárov	„	1268
1216	„	Surgút	„	1003
1720	„	Tymskoe	„	499
1839	„	Narym	„	380
1959	„	Kolpashóva	„	260
2219	Arr.	**Tomsk**	Sails	—

Passenger and luggage tariffs of the West Siberian Steam Navigation and Trade Co.

To or from landing-stages of.	From or to Tiumén.				From or to Tobólsk.				From or to Tomsk.			
	I	II	III	lug.	I	II	III	lug.	I	II	III	lug.
	r. k.	r. k.	r. k.	k.	r. k.	r. k.	r. k.	k.	r. k.	r. k.	r. k.	k.
Tiumén	—	—	—	—	4 00	3 00	2 20	20	15 00	10 00	5 00	60
Iyevlevo	3 00	2 00	1 20	15	2 00	1 50	1 00	15	13 00	9 00	4 80	55
Tobólsk	4 00	3 00	2 00	20	—	—	—	—	11 50	8 50	4 50	50
Uvát	5 00	4 00	2 25	25	1 50	1 00	0 70	15	10 50	8 00	4 00	45
Demiánskoe	6 00	4 50	2 50	30	2 50	1 50	1 00	20	10 00	7 00	3 50	40
Samárovskoe	7 00	5 50	3 00	35	3 50	2 50	1 50	25	9 00	6 00	3 00	35
Surgút	8 50	7 00	3 50	40	6 00	4 00	2 00	30	7 50	5 00	2 50	30
Tymskoe	10 00	8 00	4 00	45	6 50	5 50	3 00	35	5 00	4 00	2 00	25
Narym	11 00	8 50	4 50	50	7 50	6 50	3 50	40	4 00	3 00	1 50	20
Kolpashóvo	12 50	9 00	4 80	55	9 50	7 00	4 00	45	3 00	2 00	1 00	15
Tomsk	15 00	10 00	5 00	60	11 50	8 50	4 50	50	—	—	—	—

Children from 2 to 10 yrs old half-price, below 2 yrs—free.

Between Tomsk, Barnaúl and Bíisk, ply twice a week steamers belonging to E. I. Mélnikov and V. E. Eldstein.

On the rivers Tom and Ob.

From town of Tomsk.	I cl.		II cl.		III cl.		One pud luggage.	
	r.	k.	r.	k.	r.	k.	r.	k.
to Ust-Chaús (Kolyván)	5		4		1	90		25
„ Nóvo-Nikólsk	6		5		2			30
„ Bersk	6	30	5	20	2	50		30
„ Kámen	8		7		3	40		40
„ Barnaúl	10		8		4			50
„ Bíisk	14		11		6			80

Steam Navígation

of Eastern Siberia.

From the town of Irkútsk up the river Angará to the vill. of Konoválovo and down stream to the vill. of Lístvennichnoe, ply the tug steamers of A. Y. Nemchinov.

I cl.		II cl.		III cl.		One p. lug.	Down the Angará.	I cl.		II cl.		III cl.		One p. lug.
r.	k.	r.	k.	r.	k.	k.		r.	k.	r.	k.	r.	k.	k.
9	90	6	80	4	60	55	from vill. Konoválovo.	—	—	—	—	—	—	—
8	90	6	10	4	10	45	to t. Balagànk. . .	1	—	—	70	—	50	10
5	—	3	50	2	50	35	„ v. Barkhátovo .	4	90	3	30	2	10	20
4	30	3	—	2	20	30	„ „ Usólie	5	60	3	80	2	40	25
2	—	1	50	1	—	20	„ t. Irkútsk . . .	7	90	5	30	3	60	45
—	—	—	—	—	—	—	„ s. Lístvennichn .	9	90	6	80	4	60	55

From the settlement of Lístvennichnoe, on Lake Baikál and the river Selengá, ply the tug steamers of A. Y. Nemchinov.

From Lístvennichnoe to Boliutáya and back.

I cl.		II cl.		III cl.		One p. lug.	Up the Angará.	I cl.		II cl.		III cl.		One p. lug.
r.	k.	r.	k.	r.	k.	k.		r.	k.	r.	k.	r.	k.	k.
17	80	14	10	8	40	86	from s. Lístvennichn.	—	—	—	—	—	—	—
10	80	8	10	5	40	56	to Ust-Selengínsk .	7	—	6	—	3	—	30
9	80	7	35	4	90	51	„ Chertóvkin . . .	8	—	6	75	3	50	35
5	20	3	90	2	60	26	„ Verkhneúdinsk .	12	60	10	20	5	80	60
1	20	—	90	—	60	6	„ „ Selengínsk . . .	16	60	13	20	7	80	80
—	—	—	—	—	—	—	„ Boliutàya . . .	17	80	14	10	8	40	86

TARIFF for conveyance of passengers, luggage, freights, carriages and animals by regular mail and passenger steamers of **A. Y. Nemchinov** on Lake Baikál.

	Versts.	Passengers.						Luggage per pud.		Freights.		Carriages.						Animals.			
		I cl.		II cl.		III cl.				1	2	3		2		Carts.		Large.		Small.	
Between Lístvennichnoe and Upper Angará.		r.	k.	r.	k.	r.	k.	r.	k.	r.	k.	r.	k.	r.	k.	r.	k.	r.	k.	r.	k.
From Upper Angára to Sosnóvka . . .	190	7	60	5	98	3	26	—	27	19	14	5	43	3	80	2	72	2	18	1	09
„ „ „ „ Kruguli̇́k . . .	220	8	80	6	92	3	77	—	31	22	16	6	29	4	40	3	15	2	52	1	26
„ „ „ „ Ust-Bargúz. . .	365	14	60	11	48	6	26	—	52	36½	26	10	43	7	30	5	22	4	18	2	09
„ „ „ „ Tur. min. wat.	440	17	60	13	82	7	55	—	63	44	31	12	57	8	80	6	29	5	04	2	52
„ „ „ „ Pesóchnoe . . .	620	24	80	19	48	10	63	—	89	62	14	17	71	12	40	8	86	7	09	3	55
„ „ „ „ Lístvennichn. .	700	28	22	22	—	12	—	—	—	70	50	20	—	14	—	10	—	8	—	4	—
Between Krestóvskaya landing.st. (in Lístv.) and **Mysováya**	—	5	60	4	80	2	40	1	24	16	11	8	—	6	—	4	—	4	—	2	—
From Lístv. to Pesóchnoe	80	3	20	2	52	1	37	—	11	8	6	2	29	1	60	1	14	—	91	—	45
„ „ „ Tur. min. wat.	260	10	40	8	18	4	45	—	37	26	19	7	43	5	20	3	71	2	96	1	48
„ „ „ Ust.-Bargúz.	335	13	40	10	52	5	74	—	48	33½	24	9	57	6	70	4	78	3	82	1	91
„ „ „ Kruguli̇́k	480	19	20	15	08	8	23	—	69	48	34	13	71	9	60	6	85	5	48	2	74
„ „ „ Sosnóvka	510	20	40	16	12	8	74	—	73	51	36	14	57	10	20	7	28	5	82	2	91
„ „ „ Upper Angará	700	28	—	22	—	12	—	1	—	70	50	20	—	14	—	10	—	8	—	4	—

Note: 1) Emigrants, their luggage, horses and carts are charged half the ordinary tariff.
2) First-class freights include: tea, furs, manufactured and fancy goods etc.; second-class—corn, meat, iron, building materials etc.

Transbaikál Railway.

(Office in Irkútsk).

Passenger trains daily leave Irkútsk by Baikál branch line to Baikál and thence by Transbaikál railway from the Mysováya st. to Srétensk (1,034 versts).

The time-table for this line is not yet published.

Steam Navigation

on the rivers of the Amúr system.

398.

Amúr Steam Navigation Co.

Amúr line:

Passengers and goods taken at and for towns of *Nikoláevsk, Khabaróvsk, Blagovéshchensk, Srétensk* and landing-stages on way.

Ussúri line:

Passengers and goods taken at and for towns of *Nikoláevsk, Khabaróvsk, Blagovéshchensk, Srétensk* and other points to the Imán st. of Ussúri railway and back.

Zéya line:

Passengers and goods taken at and for towns of *Nikoláevsk, Khabaróvsk, Blagovéshchensk, Srétensk* and other points to Zéisk Warehouse and back.

Amgún line:

Passengers and goods taken at and for towns of *Nikoláevsk, Khabaróvsk, Blagovéshchensk, Srétensk* and other points to Kerbínsk Warehouse and back.

I and II class passengers are accomodated with cabins, and III class are placed on the decks of steamers and barges under awnings.

The sailings of steamers from: *Nikoláevsk, Khabaróvsk, Blagovéshchensk* and *Srétensk* are each time specially advertised.

Passenger and luggage tariff of Amúr Steam Navigation Co.

Length of voyage.	Versts.	I	II	III	1/10 kop. per pud (lugg.) and verst.
		r. k.	r. k.	r. k.	r. k.
From Srétensk to Blagovéshchensk	1279	25.58	19.19	6.40	1.27
„ Blagovéshchensk to Khabaróvsk	855½	17 11	12.84	4.28	0.85
„ Blagovéshchensk to Zéisk wh.	657	—	10.—	5.—	0.65
„ Khabaróvsk to Nikoláevsk . .	939¾	18.80	9.40	4.70	0.94
„ Khabaróvsk to Imán st. . . .	390	7.80	5.85	1.95	0.30
„ Nikoláevsk to Undínsk wh. .	200	—	5.—	3.—	0.00
„ Nikoláevsk to Kerbínsk wh. .	450	—	10.—	5.—	0.00

Each passenger has the right to take one pud of luggage free.

Ussúri railway.

(Office in Khabaróvsk).

174. Vladivostók—Khabaróvsk and back.

From 1 April, 1900 (Vladivostók time).

*) G. P. 6 II—IV	M. P. 4 I—III	Versts.	*Ussúri railway.*	Versts.	*) G. P. 5 II—IV	M. P 3 I—III
3 25	9 25	—	Dep. **Vladivostòk** buf. . . . Arr.	721	10 10	1 25
3 57	9 46	—	„ Pérvaya Rèchka (sid.) „	--	9 50	1 9
4 32	10 16	—	„ Sedánka (sid.) . . . „	—	9 2	12 34
5 0	10 33	—	„ Khilkóvo buf. . . . „	—	8 44	12 19
6 12	11 28	42	„ Nadèzhdinskaya buf. „	680	7 35	11 30
7 3	12 6	—	„ Kiparísov (sid.) . . „	—	6 25	10 38
7 46	12 38	66	„ Razdólnoe buf. . „	655	**5 49**	10 10
8 20	1 10	—	„ Baranóvski (sid.) . „	—	**5 7**	9 37
9 10	1 51	102	Arr. **Nikòlskoe** buf. . . . Dep.	620	**4 17**	8 55
9 42	2 5		Dep. Arr.		**3 40**	8 40
10 28	2 47	—	„ Dubíninski (sid) . . „	—	**3 2**	8 8
12 5	3 58	147	„ Nevelskáya . . . „	575	**1 52**	7 4
12 54	4 36	—	„ Monastyrishche . . „	—	**12 50**	6 12
2 5	5 18	185	„ Chernígovka . . . „	537	**11 50**	**5 32**
2 50	5 56	—	„ Knorring (sid.) . . „	—	**10 50**	**4 47**
3 40	**6 37**	224	Arr. **Spásskaya** buf. . . Dep.	498	**10 0**	**4 6**
4 22	**6 47**		Dep. Arr.		**9 30**	**3 56**
5 10	**7 28**	--	„ Drozdóv (sid.) . . . „	—	**8 45**	**3 20**
5 58	**8 6**	256	„ Sviágino . . . . . „	466	**8 10**	**2 48**
6 40	**8 43**	—	„ Kraèvski (sid.) . . „	—	**7 10**	**2 7**
7 31	**9 25**	293	„ Shmakóvka . . . „	429	**6 30**	**1 33**
8 12	**10 4**	—	„ Ryzhóv (sid.) . . „	—	5 37	**12 40**
8 41	**10 30**	327	Arr. **Ussúri** buf. . . . . . Dep.	394	5 6	**12 12**
8 56	**10 35**		Dep. Arr.		4 51	**12 2**
10 10	**11 22**	350	„ Prokhásko . . . . „	372	4 2	**11 20**
—	—	—	„ Bussè (sid.) . . . . „	—	—	—
11 15	**12 14**	377	Arr. **Muraviòv-Amúrski** buf. „	344	2 42	**10 20**
11 54	**12 14**		Dep. „		2 18	**10 10**
1 5	**12 55**	387	„ Imán . . . . „	335	1 50	**9 46**
—	—	—	„ Eberhardt (sid.) . . „	—	—	—

*) Daily between Vladivostók and Nikólsk, and as announced between Nikólsk and Khabaróvsk.

*) G. P. 6 II—IV	M. P. 4 I—III	Versts.	*Ussúri railway.*	Versts.	*) G. P. 5 II—IV	P. M. 3 I—III
2 35	**2 5**	420	Dep. Kurdiúmovka . . . Arr.	302	11 45	**8 36**
—	—	—	„ Chórny (sid.) . . . „	—	—	—
4 30	**3 36**	464	„ Bochárovo . . . . „	258	9 50	**7 0**
—	—	—	„ Alchán (sid.) . . . „	—	—	—
5 10	**4 38**	498	Arr. **Bikin** buf. . . . . . Dep.	224	8 30	5 46
6 10	**4 48**		Dep. Arr.		8 10	5 20
—	—	—	„ Beitsúkha (sid.) . . „	—	—	—
8 10	6 15	537	„ Rosengártovka . . „	185	6 25	4 10
—	—	—	„ Snárski (sid.) . . . „	—	—	—
9 45	7 31	—	„ Gèdike (sid.) . . . „	—	**4 45**	2 54
10 20	7 56	575	„ Ilováiskaya . . . . „	146	**4 16**	2 23
—	—	—	„ Yevgènievka . . . „	—	—	—
11 13	8 38	596	Arr. **Viázemskaya** buf. . . Dep.	125	**3 10**	1 30
11 40	8 48		Dep. Arr.		**2 40**	1 15
1 22	9 57	627	„ Dormidóntovka . . „	95	**1 10**	12 15
1 55	10 23	—	„ Khor . . . . „	—	**12 20**	11 40
2 52	11 1	653	„ Dukhovskáya . . . „	69	**11 50**	11 13
—	—	—	„ Krúglikov (sid.) . . „	—	—	—
4 18	12 3	680	„ Kórfovskaya . . . . „	41	**10 10**	10 7
5 8	12 41	—	„ Krásnaya Rèchka (sed.) „	—	**9 10**	9 16
6 0	1 20	716	Arr. **Khabaròvsk** buf. . . Dep.	6	**8 10**	8 35
6 25	1 50		Dep. Arr.		**7 35**	8 5
6 40	2 5	721	Arr **Khabaròvsk** landing-stage . . . . Dep.	—	**7 20**	7 50

Marine Steam Navigation.

Between Vladivostók, Nagasaki, Port-Artúr, Singapur, Colombo, Perim or Aden, Port-Said, Constantinople, Odessa and S. Petersburg, ply the steamers of the Volunteer Fleet and of the Russian East Asiatic S. S. Co.

(Official Guide of M. W. C., № 395).

JOINT STOCK COMPANY
YEAST, SPIRIT-RECTIFICATION AND BRANDY DISTILLERY
A. Wolfschmidt
in RIGA.
Established in 1847.
4 honorary diplomas,
14 gold medals,
4 silver medals,
4 bronze medals.
1847
Office: № 32, Plavúchaya street.
I Distillery: № 25, Vygonnaya Dámba.
II Distillery: № 4—5, Málaya Sbórnaya str.
Branches: in St. Petersburg, № 34, Gorókhovaya str. in Hamburg: № 18, Catherine str.
OFFERS FOR SALE:
RECTIFIED SPIRIT OF HIGHEST QUALITY, CLARIFIED AND TABLE WINE.
Genuine Riga Kuntsen Herboreal Balsam.
BRANDIES OF ALL KINDS:
Benedictine, Abricotine, Chartreuse, Quirasso, Cacao, Mocca, Marasquino, fruit infusion and liquor, Kiev liquors, Kümmel, Orange and other liquors, Sorb-apple № 00, Nézhin Sorb-apple, English Double-corn, Livonian bitter, Redlóvka, Ziklitóvka, Little-Russian spiced brandy, Livonian cranberry infusion, Red-pilberry infusion, English bitter and Quinine brandy.
RUM, COGNAC AND ARAC
with ticketed tax;
Fresh compressed yeast.
Brandies of our own manufacture are sold by all important wine-merchants.
Catalogues post-free on application.

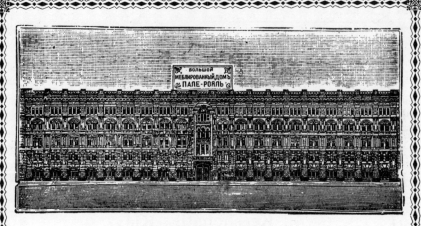

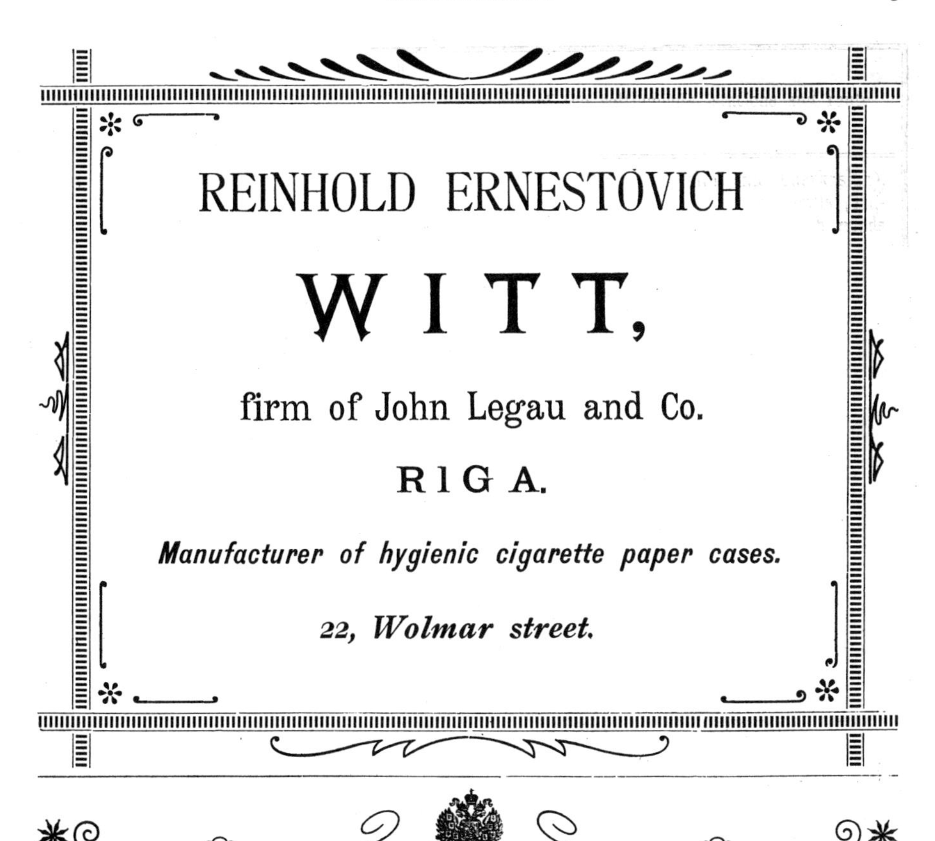

THE VOTKINSK
STATE WORKS
ON THE KÁMA RIVER

22 prizes at exhibitions, including first prizes at the Chicago and Nízhni-Nóvgorod exhibitions.

GOODS:

1) *Passenger and goods steamers, marine schoonrs, iron barges.*
2) *Locomotives.*
3) *Puddled, welded, assorted, sheet marine iron, boiler plate, and rivetting iron.*
4) *Marten and iron welding steel.*
5) *Bridges and bridge appliances.*
6) *Railway fastenings.*
7) *Naphtha reservoirs and spirit tanks.*
8) *Steam boilers.*
9) *Engnes.*
10) *Chains and anchors.*
11) *Agricultural implements.*

And other articles according to desire.

The goods are forwarded from the Galév landing-stage on the Káma.

Telegrams: Vótkinsk, District Department.
Letters: Vótkinsk Works, Viátka government, Káma, Vótkinsk Mining District Department.

V. R. BORMÓTKIN.

St. Petersburg.

Stock of Steam Engines, Boilers, Locomobiles etc.

Steam, tubular and other boilers, reservoirs and cisterns for petroleum and mineral oils and other boiler-smith's work.

Representatives of the HARTLEY and SUGDEN Works in Halifax — Boilers for water and steam heating.

Warehouses: 78, Obvódny canal, own house (near the Gas Works).

Office: 1, Chernyshóv str. (near the arch).

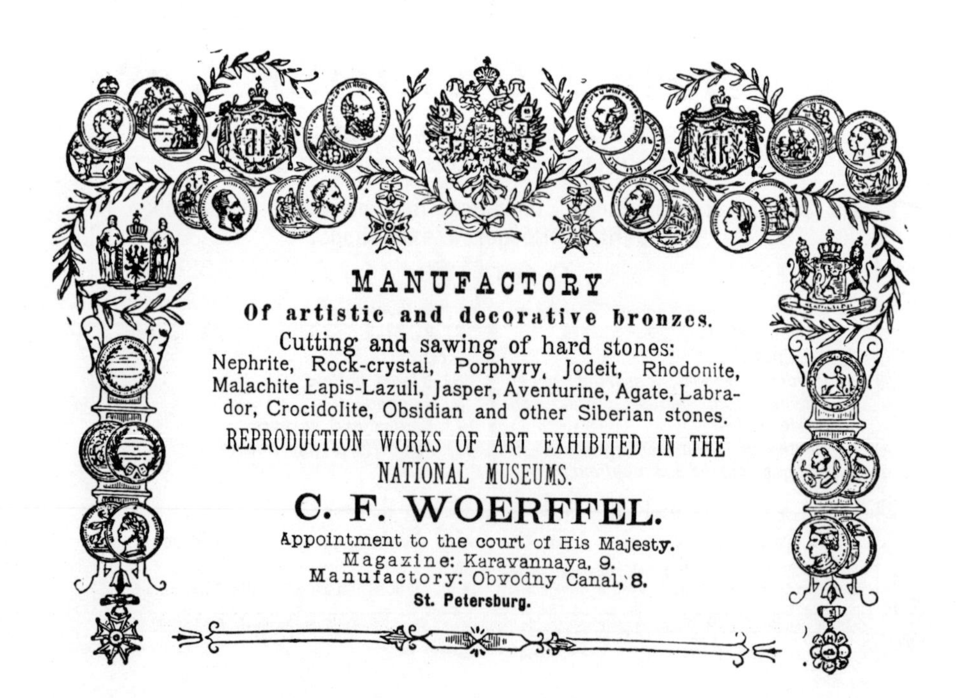

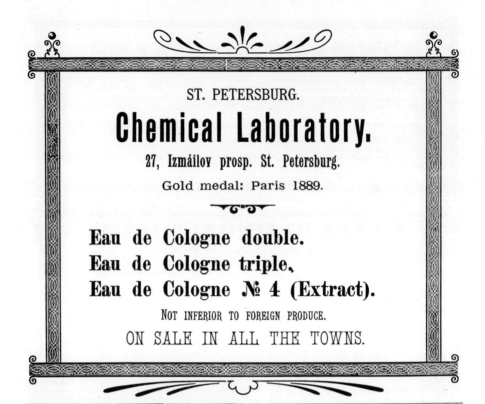

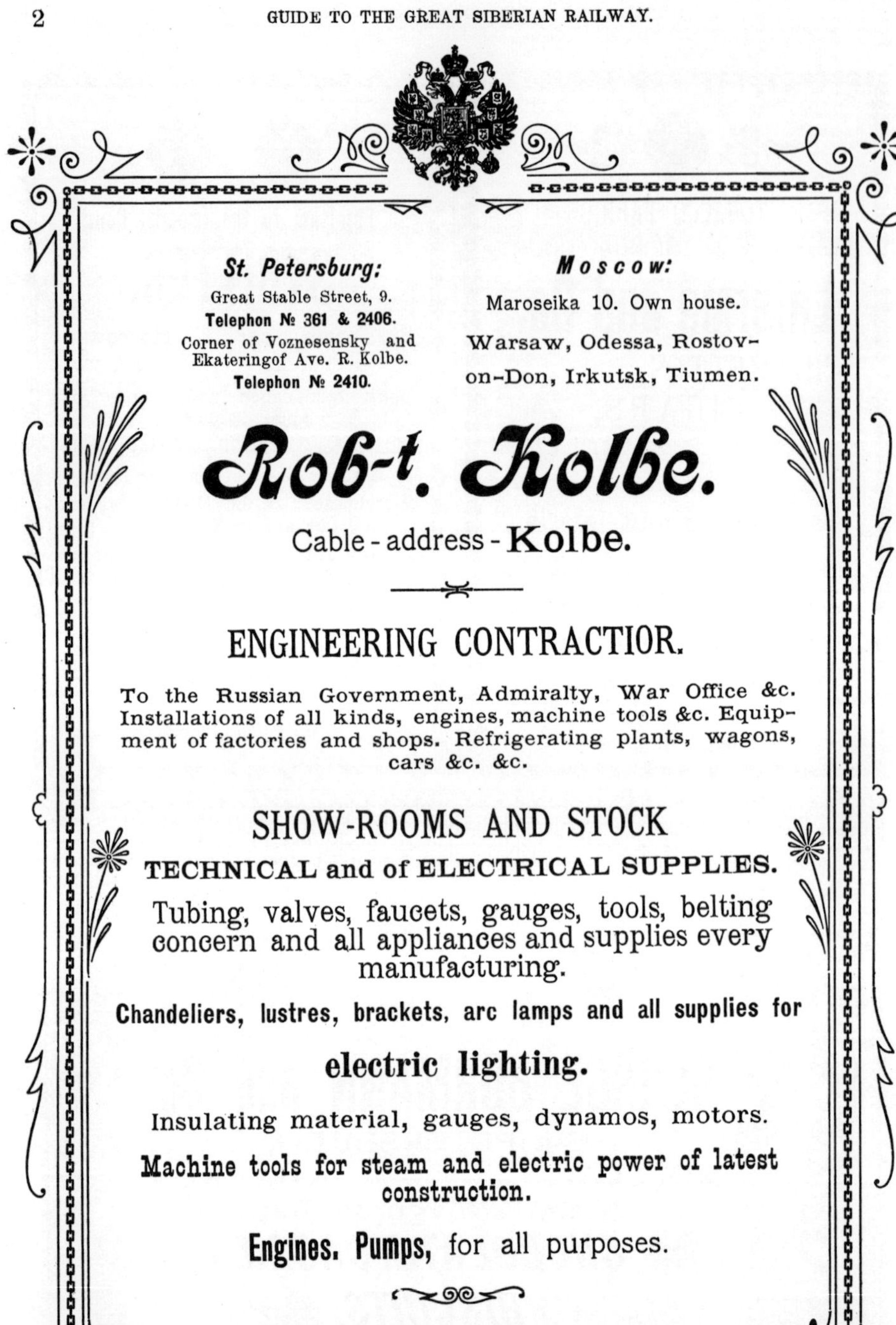
St. Petersburg:
Great Stable Street, 9.
Telephon № 361 & 2406.
Corner of Voznesensky and Ekateringof Ave. R. Kolbe.
Telephon № 2410.
Moscow:
Maroseika 10. Own house.
Warsaw, Odessa, Rostov-on-Don, Irkutsk, Tiumen.
Rob-t. Kolbe.
Cable-address-Kolbe.
ENGINEERING CONTRACTIOR.
To the Russian Government, Admiralty, War Office &c. Installations of all kinds, engines, machine tools &c. Equipment of factories and shops. Refrigerating plants, wagons, cars &c. &c.
SHOW-ROOMS AND STOCK
TECHNICAL and of ELECTRICAL SUPPLIES.
Tubing, valves, faucets, gauges, tools, belting concern and all appliances and supplies every manufacturing.
Chandeliers, lustres, brackets, arc lamps and all supplies for
electric lighting.
Insulating material, gauges, dynamos, motors.
Machine tools for steam and electric power of latest construction.
Engines. Pumps, for all purposes.

Catalogues estimates, projects on application.

Exhibition 1896.

A. B. Bary, Engineer, Constructor.

Main office — Moscow, Miasnitskaya Street, House of the Industrial Museum.

Branch offices — in St. Petersburg (Nevsky, 68), Saratov, Tula & Lipetsk.

Improved horizontal and vertical water tube, steam boilers,

Engineer **V. G. SCHUKHOV'S** Patent,

manufactured at the Boiler Works of A. B. BARY, engineer.

Heaters for feed water (economisers) and superheaters.

THE OFFICE CONSTRUCTS:

Steel barges to carry naphtha products.

Steel Tanks to store naphha products and spirits of wine.

The metallic construction of **Nich furnaces.**

Iron buildings of different systems for various factory purposes.

THE OFFICE UNDERTAKES:

The complete outfitting of Naphtha Refineries aud Pipe—lines;

The complete mechanical outfitting of grain elevators.

The office Keeps constantly on Stock and imports from America:

American steam pumps, manufactured by the Blake Mfg. Co in Boston;

American scales of the renowned **Nowe Scale** Co. in Rutland.

Thelegraphic addresses:—Moscow, Bary.—Petersburg, — Ingebary.— Saratov, Bary.

Over 1900 boilers sold, whose total heating surface exceeds 975.000 square feet.

Over 1900 boilers sold, whose total heating surface exceeds 975.000 square feet.

OTTO SCHWADE and Co.
Steam Pumps „Automaton".
Number of
workmen employed
1000
BRANCH in MOSCOW:
35, Lubiánka prospect.
Best References.
Warehouses
in Moscow.
Automat
Speciality:
Fourfold acting horizontal and vertical pumps for all purposes.
„Automaton", Compound and Triple
expansion steam pumps with small consumption of steam. Electric motor. Patent
umps. Mining pumps. Uuderground
and waterraising engines.

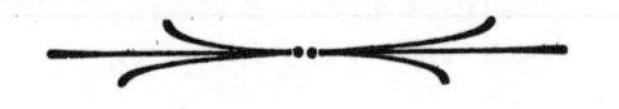

T. Denker and Co.

from 1815.

St. Petersburg.

Foreign and Russian wines, Champagne, Cognac, Rum and Liquors.

Red and White Claret, Burgundy and Rhine wines of superior quality. Very old Sherry (Amontillado), Madeira, Portwine, sweet and dry dessert wines.

Own 12 wine cellars in St. Petersburg.

Office: 6, Vólkhov str. Vasílievsky Ostrov.

Catalogues post-free on application.

M. KONRADI.

ST. PETERSBURG.

20, Stáro-Peterhof prospect, own house.

SHOPS:

1) 20, Névsky prospect.
2) 36, Névsky prospect.
3) 106, Névsky prospect.
4) 25—1, Vasílievsky Ostrov, opposite the Nicholas bridge.
5) 109, Sadóvaya square (in the Apráxin yard).